3/28

MYCENAEAN PICTORIAL
VASE PAINTING

MYCENAEAN PICTORIAL VASE PAINTING

Emily Vermeule   Vassos Karageorghis

HARVARD UNIVERSITY PRESS   1982   Cambridge, Massachusetts, and London, England

Publication of this volume has been aided by a grant from the
Loeb Classical Library Foundation

LIBRARY OF CONGRESS CATALOGING IN PUBLICATION DATA

Vermeule, Emily.
    Mycenaean pictorial vase painting.

    Bibliography: p.
    Includes index.
    1. Vase painting, Mycenaean.   I. Karageorghis, Vassos,
joint author.   II. Title.
NK4646.V47 1981   738.3'7   80-18787
ISBN 0-674-59650-1

To the memory of Adolf Furtwängler and Georg Loeschcke

PREFACE

This book has grown by fits and starts over a number of years and owes great debts to a number of colleagues who have offered encouragement and advice in the many spheres which Mycenaean pictorial vase painting touches. From the beginning we relied upon the pioneering collections by Adolf Furtwängler and Georg Loeschcke, the analyses by Arne Furumark, and the basic articles by Sara Immerwahr, J. L. Benson, Hector Catling, and Frank Stubbings. Martin Robertson encouraged Karageorghis with his dissertation on pictorial material found in Cyprus (London University, 1957), the first step in a long series of articles about the field. Museums with large collections of Mycenaean pictorial vases and fragments were generous in opening their storage rooms; the British Museum, the Musée du Louvre, the Medelhavsmuseet in Stockholm, and the National Museum in Athens have, over the years, made particular efforts to encourage the study of their holdings. We also thank the private collectors who made their vases available to us.

We are deeply indebted to our colleagues Mary Littauer and Joost Crouwel for undertaking the Appendix on Mycenaean chariots and for bringing professional precision to the observation of chariots on vases; to Professor Åke Åkerström for his work on the chariot and his generosity in showing the material from Berbati; to J. K. Anderson for enlightenment on horses and harnessing; to the American School of Classical Studies in Athens, and particularly to E. Smithson, O. Broneer, H. Thompson, and E. Vanderpool for the Agora, North Slope, and Mycenaean Fountain material; to the British Museum and Bernard Ashmole, Denys Haynes, Reynold Higgins, and Peter Corbett; to the British School at Athens and H. Cat-

ling, E. French, S. Hood, A. Megaw, M. Popham, H. Sackett, and Lord William Taylour; to the German Archaeological Insitute in Athens for access to the Mycenae and Tiryns photographic archives, and for discussions with E. Slenczka of his Tiryns material; to the National Museum in Athens for access to fragments on and off display, and especially to A. Sakellariou, B. Philippaki, and N. Yalouris; to many colleagues working in Cyprus, including P. Åström, H.-G. Buchholz, J.-C. Courtois, F. Maier, and C. F. A. Schaeffer; to the Cyprus Museum for many drawings by E. Markou, and to the photographic laboratory and the Director's office; to Bryn Mawr College and M. L. Lang for discussions of the connections between pictorial painting and the Pylos frescoes; to the University of Cincinnati and J. and M. Caskey for the Kea material; and to the Guggenheim Foundation for support in 1964.

At the Museum of Fine Arts, Boston, space was provided and a great deal of help was given over the years by Kristin Anderson, Edward Brovarski, Timothy Kendall, and Cornelius Vermeule. We owe a very special debt of gratitude to Suzanne E. Chapman, who replaced many unsatisfactory photographs by drawings, often under circumstances of haste and inconvenience to her; and above all to Mary Comstock and Florence Wolsky who checked the references for the entire manuscript and read the proof with awe-inspiring accuracy, correcting errors with wonderful tact and scholarship; Florence Wolsky also made maps and drawings. Within the Museum Pictorial Compound others labored heroically to bring the chaotic material into order, particularly Mary Hollinshead and successive clear-headed, meticulous Shelmerdines: Juliet, Cynthia, and Susan, who made the indexes. At Harvard

University Louise DeGiacomo typed long stretches of illegible manuscript, some of them twice; Professor Hugh Hencken took a special interest in advising on helmet forms; and Professor Zeph Stewart generously put the support of the Department of the Classics behind the book, so that our long and partly erratic labors should not be entirely wasted. At Harvard University Press, Margaretta

Fulton and Margaret Anderson offered their extraordinary skills at editing, pruning, and controlling the English language, to make with great patience a presentable book at last, out of what started as piles of unsorted photographs and tattered notes. Other colleagues have been particularly helpful: our thanks to S. Iakovides, E. Porada, E. Touloupa, and to H. and V. Hankey not only for expertise but for the drawings, including the Mycenaean tennis players, that brought such pleasure at grim moments. We wish that the work had appeared in time to thank others who helped and have gone before us: Piet de Jong, S. Charitonides, V. R. Desborough, P. Dikaios, N. Firatli, J. Papademetriou, D. Theochares, and N. Verdelis.

Readers will notice omissions, imprecisions, and probably wrong interpretations. Some known pieces may have slipped out in the course of many reorganizations and renumberings; we hope not and hope even more that the same vase is not in twice in two different periods. We decided from the start not to try to include two matters that are normally found in catalogues, the dimension of the vase and notes on its color and clay. The catalogue is not a full one, but a guide to earlier publications, and not all of those. The text, too, is not so much an archaeological publication of pictorial vases as a running commentary on points that have interested us. We have been more drawn to subject matter than to attribution to artists and have left many areas of potentially great interest unexplored. Our hope is that collecting this material in one place will be of service to other excavators and students of Mycenaean art.

V. K.
E. V.

CONTENTS

Short Titles and Abbreviations

BOOKS

Åkerström, "MykKrukVerk"	Å. Åkerström, "En Mykensk Krukmakares Verkstad," *Arkeologiska Forskningar och Fynd* 1 (1952) 32–46
Alexiou, *Katsamba*	S. Alexiou, *Hysterominoiki Taphoi Limenos Knōsou (Katsamba)* (1967)
Benson, *HBM*	J. L. Benson, *Horse, Bird, and Man* (1970)
BMCatV	Catalogue of the Greek and Etruscan Vases in the British Museum, vol. I, part 1 (1925) and part 2 (1912)
Buchholz, Karageorghis, *Altägäis*	H.-G. Buchholz, V. Karageorghis, *Altägäis und Altkypros* (1971)
Catling, *Bronzework*	H. Catling, *Cypriote Bronzework in the Mycenaean World* (1964)
Coche de la Ferté, *Essai*	E. Coche de la Ferté, *Essai de classification de la céramique mycénienne d'Enkomi* (1951)
CMS	*Corpus der Minoischen und Mykenischen Siegel*
CVA	*Corpus Vasorum Antiquorum*
Dussaud, *Civilisations*	R. Dussaud, *Les civilisations préhelléniques dans le bassin de la mer Egée* (1914)
Evans, *Palace of Minos*	Sir Arthur Evans, *The Palace of Minos* I (1921), II (1929), III (1930), IV (1935)
ExcCyp	A. S. Murray, A. H. Smith, H. B. Walters, *Excavations in Cyprus* (1900)
Furtwängler-Loeschcke, *MV*	A. Furtwängler, G. Loeschcke, *Mykenische Vasen* (1886)
Furumark, *Chronology*	A. Furumark, *A Chronology of Mycenaean Pottery* (1941)
Furumark, *MP*	A. Furumark, *The Mycenaean Pottery* (1941)
Graef-Langlotz, *VA*	B. Graef, E. Langlotz, *Antiken Vasen von der Akropolis zu Athen* I (1925)
HST	P. Åström, D. M. Bailey, V. Karageorghis, *Hala Sultan Tekké I, Excavations 1897–1971. Studies in Mediterranean Archaeology* 45 (1976)
IEE	*Historia tou Hellēnikou Ethnous* I (1971)
Karageorghis, *Kition*	V. Karageorghis, *Kition: Mycenaean and Phoenician* (1974); in the U.S., *View from the Bronze Age* (1976)
Karageorghis, *Kition I, The Tombs*	V. Karageorghis, *Excavations at Kition. I, The Tombs* (1974)
Karageorghis, *MycArt*	V. Karageorghis, *Mycenaean Art from Cyprus* (1968)
Karageorghis, *Nouveaux Documents*	V. Karageorghis, *Nouveaux Documents pour l'Etude de l'Âge du Bronze à Chypre* (1965)
Karageorghis, *Treasures*	V. Karageorghis, *Treasures of*

x

	Mycenaean Art from Cyprus
Lang, *Pylos* II	M. Lang, *The Palace of Nestor at Pylos. II, The Frescoes* (1969)
Lorimer, *HM*	H. Lorimer, *Homer and the Monuments* (1950)
Mercklin, *Rennwagen* I	E. v. Mercklin, *Der Rennwagen in Griechenland* I (1909)
Montelius, *GP*	O. Montelius, *La Grèce Préclassique*, with O. Frödin (1924–1928)
Popham, *DestrKnossos*	M. Popham, *The Destruction of the Palace at Knossos. Pottery of the Late Minoan IIIA Period. Studies in Mediterranean Archaeology* 12 (1970)
Rodenwaldt, *Tiryns* II	G. Rodenwaldt, *Tiryns* II, *Die Fresken des Palastes* (1912)
SCE	*The Swedish Cyprus Expedition* I (1934); IV I C (1972)
Schaeffer, *Alasia* I	C. F. A. Schaeffer, *Alasia* I (1971)
Schaeffer, *Enkomi-Alasia* I	C. F. A. Schaeffer, *Enkomi-Alasia* I (1952)
Schaeffer, *Ugaritica*	C. F. A. Schaeffer, *Ugaritica* I (1939), II (1949), V (1968), VI (1969)
SIMA	*Studies in Mediterranean Archaeology*
Slenczka, *Tiryns* VII	E. Slenczka, *Tiryns* VII, *Figürlich Bemalte Mykenische Keramik aus Tiryns* (1974)
Staïs, *MycColl*	V. Staïs, *La collection mycénienne du Musée Nationale d'Athènes* (1909; 2nd ed. 1926)
Stubbings, *MycLevant*	F. Stubbings, *Mycenaean Pottery from the Levant* (1951)
Sjöqvist, *Problems*	E. Sjöqvist, *Problems of the Late Cypriote Bronze Age* (1940)
Vandenabeele, Olivier, *Idéogrammes*	F. Vandenabeele, J.-P. Olivier, *Les Idéogrammes Archéologiques du Linéaire B* (1979)
Vermeule, *GBA*	E. Vermeule, *Greece in the Bronze Age* (1964)

JOURNALS

AA	*Archäologischer Anzeiger*
AAA	*Athens Annals of Archaeology*
AAS	*Annales Archéologiques de Syrie*
AJA	*American Journal of Archaeology*
AnatSt	*Anatolian Studies*
Annuario	*Annuario della Scuola Archeologica di Atene*
AntJ	*Antiquaries' Journal*
AntK	*Antike Kunst*
ArcRep	*Journal of Hellenic Studies, Archaeological Reports*
ArchZeit	*Archäologischer Zeitung*
AthMitt	*Mitteilungen des Deutschen Archäologischen Instituts, Athenische Abteilung*
BABesch	*Bulletin van de Vereeniging tot Bevordering der Kennis van de Antieke Beschaving*
BASOR	*Bulletin of the American Schools of Oriental Research*
BCH	*Bulletin de Correspondance Hellénique*
Belleten	*Belleten Türk Tarih Kurumu*
BICS	*University of London Institute of Classical Studies Bulletin*
BJV	*Berliner Jahrbuch für Vor- und Frühgeschichte*
BSA	*Annual of the British School at Athens*
CJ	*Classical Journal*
CR	*Classical Review*
Deltion	*Archaiologikon Deltion*
EphArch	*Archaiologikē Ephēmeris*
Ergon	*To Ergon tēs Archaiologikēs Hetaireias*
FastiA	*Fasti Archaeologici*
IstMitt	*Mitteilungen des Deutschen Archäologischen Instituts, Abteilung Istanbul*
JdI	*Jahrbuch des Deutschen Archäologischen Instituts*
JHS	*Journal of Hellenic Studies*
MDOG	*Mitteilungen des Deutschen Orient-Gesellschaft*
MonAnt	*Monumenti Antichi*
JNES	*Journal of Near Eastern Studies*
OpArc	*Opuscula Archaeologica*
OpAth	*Opuscula Atheniensia*
PEQ	*Palestine Exploration Quarterly*
Praktika	*Praktika tēs en Athēnais Archaiologikēs Etaireias*
ProcPS	*Proceedings of the Prehistoric Society*
QDAP	*Quarterly of the Department of Antiquities of Palestine*
REG	*Revue des Études Grecques*

RevArch	*Revue Archéologique*	*Wissenschaften, Wien*
RDAC	*Report of the Department of Antiquities, Cyprus*	*TürkArkDerg* *Türk Arkeoloji Dergisi*
SBWien	*Sitzungsberichte der Akademie der*	*UnivMusBull* University of Pennsylvania, *University Museum Bulletin*

MYCENAEAN PICTORIAL
VASE PAINTING

I
INTRODUCTION

MYCENAEAN PICTORIAL VASE PAINTING is a curious strand in the art of the Greek world between 1400 and 1150 B.C. About seven hundred whole or broken vases survive, painted with a variety of chariot scenes, bulls, birds, fish, goats, stags, warriors, poets, and fishermen. Enough of this odd painting has come down to us to encourage an attempt to treat it in terms of stylistic development and to offer some observations on the kinds of scenes that appealed to potters and customers in different regions of the Aegean at different times. Half a dozen scholars have already attacked the problems of identifying workshops and hands among the painters and trying to locate the principal workshops. We hope that publishing as much of this material as possible for the first time will make these aesthetic pursuits easier. A broad view of pictorial painting by chronological period, theme, and style may be useful to excavators and to scholars generally interested in the range and quality of Mycenaean art.

Mycenaean pictorial painting means, essentially, the images painted on large vases: kraters and bowls in Cyprus and the East and a greater variety of shapes in Greece. In the East, the scenes are fairly standard. The fourteenth century produced chariots and men, bulls, birds, a few fish. In the thirteenth century the repertory was enlivened with the addition of archers, boxers, sphinxes, griffins, more hunting scenes. On the Greek mainland the thematic ideas were more diverse from the start. Chariots and bulls were not so common at first, but there were scenes with human figures dancing or fighting and birds in various moments of display. After the middle of the thirteenth century the painting became more adventurous and exciting, with war scenes and hunts. Crete was separate in style and develop-

ment; the usual motifs were birds and fish, very like those on larnakes, the clay coffins common in Late Minoan III. In the thirteenth century there was an invigoration, with chariots, bulls, and human actors in cult scenes. Cretan styles, however, are not included in this survey. Rhodes, Kos, and Naxos had distinct minor schools, and some of the most interesting pictorial vases have been found outside the strict limits of the Mycenaean world, in Near Eastern harbor towns like Ugarit, north to Çandarlı and Troy, south to Palestine and Egypt. (See Map 1).

The "inspiration" for such paintings, which is discussed in Chapter II, is generally assumed to come from frescoes in palaces and rich houses, and to some degree perhaps from gems. Although there are no frescoes in Cyprus and no Aegean gems, our constantly expanding knowledge of the themes in the wall paintings of the sixteenth and fifteenth centuries, especially in the Cyclades, allows us to see fresh connections for such images as chariots, animal hunts, women in windows, processions, bulls, birds, and fish. Certain links are evident, like the spotted bulls of the Ramp House paintings at Mycenae and the early bull vase found there (VII.3). Although the principal mainland frescoes of processionals and hunts are often later in date than the comparable vases, the contributions of Akrotiri on Thera and Ayia Irini on Keos, both of which have Cypriote pottery, suggest that images for painters, and possibly handbooks, were circulating through the Aegean at an early date. It would be desirable to develop a new view of how persistent images were established in the minor arts, and how they were modified in accordance with the internal dynamics of each medium.

1

It is apparent that pictorial vase painters selected from the general repertory of Mycenaean art figures that suited the shapes of their vases; that each set of images engendered its own appropriate style for swift execution and decorative impact; and that these styles quickly moved on a divergent course from the general styles in wall painting. In individual cases it may be possible to discern direct copying or inspiration from particular classes of gems and ivories; in some cases the influence of lost textile work is apparent. On the whole, however, the pictorial painters used a professional idiom that was not simply a reflection of styles in the other arts.

Their interest, and profit, was in adapting a general imagery to the special decorative demands of putting active pictures on both sides of a large luxury or funeral vase. Possibly the workshops possessed sketchbooks of standard scenes, which helped fix both the iconography and the finer details.

Because such vases were painted rather quickly and because so many have survived (principally only in fragments from Greece), pictorial pottery offers a greater range of views into the Mycenaean imagination than almost any other class of their art, apart from gems. In understanding what the Mycenaeans were like and how they conceived of the world around them, the evidence of these vases is often crucial. It helps protect us from the clichés that arise from seeing the Mycenaeans primarily in the architectural terms of palaces and tombs or through frescoes and other expensive, palace-oriented arts, which were partly colored by Minoan traditions. Many pictorial vases were used in the tombs of quite ordinary people, and fragments have been found in the remains of modest houses. One supposes that these vases were moderately expensive, compared with ordinary abstract Mycenaean wares, but they were clearly not restricted to the rich. We cannot tell how often customers commissioned vases; probably they usually selected from whatever the workshop specialized in, but the kinds of scenes most commonly found in each region are informative in their own limited way. These are scenes chosen by people outside the palaces, whose tastes were partly independent of the fashions in aristocratic circles. Especially in the Late period, they may reflect the real interests of the ordinary Mycenaean.

Private taste, however, had to contend with the fixed, often stereotyped images of workshop tradition. Mass production, most visible in the Ripe period on Cyprus and in the chariot scenes of the Middle period, was made easy by the formal compositions of most pictorial vases. There is almost never any strong narrative tone or illustration of particular events. This is true of Mycenaean art as a whole, and of most arts of the Late Bronze Age in the Mediter-

ranean. Action is reduced to a decorative stillness. Horses pulling a chariot seldom gallop, and their legs are often so deeply mired in the ground line as to assure us that showing motion was not the painter's primary interest. Boxers seldom plant a fist on the face of an opponent, archers never release an arrow, hunted animals never die. More bulls sniff flowers than fight, or if they do fight, it is a graceful interlocking of curved horns without muscular thrust. Birds squat or walk slowly as often as they fly; fish on their blank waterless spaces may seem to dive but they never splash and rarely eat. This static conceptual record of "action" permeates Mycenaean art from the sixteenth to the thirteenth century, from the galloping motionless lions of the Shaft Grave dagger at Mycenae to the battle frescoes at Pylos. Exceptions, however, come early and late in all media. Early, there are occasional flashes of true observation and empathy: the stumbling fawn on the ivory pyxis from the Agora at Athens, the crumpled bull on the Dendra hunting chalice. Late, after the disruption of the palace world and economy, there is new activity, recorded on vases especially, because gold and ivory were no longer widely available to craftsmen. Then the rowers really pull at the oars, the warriors bend their knees in the swaying chariots, the griffins tend their fledglings; on sarcophagi the mourners weep and tear their hair. On the mainland, at least, the twelfth century is the most vital period of painting, after most external models have been lost. The period has not been well studied for its artistic expression, but there is increasing interest in its relation to the arts which inherit Bronze Age themes and principles, in the Geometric world of the eighth century.

The development of Mycenaean pictorial vase painting is presented here in terms of the traditions in design. Comparatively few vases have a firm archaeological context or have been recorded on stratified floors. Many come from tombs that were in use over several generations, particularly in Cyprus. The early records of those tombs do not indicate closed burial contexts or tomb groups. On the Greek mainland many interesting figured sherds were discovered in Heinrich Schliemann's big trench through the top of Mycenae, and, while one supposes that most of them are late thirteenth or early twelfth century in date, there is no written mention of most of them, nor any additional information in the trays in the basement of the Athens National Museum. When precise stratigraphic information is available, it is mentioned in the catalogue, but for the most part the material has been ordered by its own internal development.

Arne Furumark's stylistic analysis of Mycenaean pottery has been followed in general, although it does not always work for pictorial pieces unless their shapes have been preserved. A glance at Furumark's drawings of birds or fish demonstrates that there is seldom any chronological consistency for the outlines of animals, so much depending on the hand, taste, and training of the individual craftsman. Filling ornaments and subsidiary designs are often a better clue to the date, and the shapes of the vases develop according to standard rules.

We are not, of course, entirely certain that we have classified this previously disorganized material in precisely the correct way because of the lack of connected groups or identifiable hands in most of the fourteenth and thirteenth centuries, but we believe that the general sequence will prove to be somewhere near the truth. On the other hand, the division into phases may be slightly arbitrary. There are no clear lines separating, for example, the Early III phase from the Middle I, or Middle I from Middle II; for Greece we have inserted an entire Transitional period between the canonical phases Late Helladic III B and III C. In a few cases, when a group which may be chronologically or stylistically later is so small as to make separate discussion difficult, it has been attached to the end of an earlier group. This happens to bulls and birds in Chapter IV. Another departure from standard procedure is found in Chapter VI, where the style formerly known as Rude has been rechristened Pastoral; it corresponds to the Ripe II phase in Greece. We are aware that the internal divisions of periods may seem more precise than they are in fact. Early and Middle Pictorial in Cyprus and the Levant have been divided into three subphases, each lasting only twenty to twenty-five years in absolute terms. Such distinctions, suggested because of certain stylistic shifts that seem to correspond to chronological breaks, may be premature and are possibly too stiff and exact. The sequence is probably right; the absolute dates or phases may not be. Future stratified finds will surely shed welcome light.

The sequence we have followed generally matches Furumark's phases. We have not tried to follow recent suggestions for raising Late Helladic III B to the Amarna period in Egypt. A rough table is put forward with the proviso that absolute dates are used as a convenience and not as a matter of conviction:

Early Pictorial: Late Helladic III A:1

I	1410-1390	LH III A:1 early
II	1400-1370	LH III A:1 early
III	1375-1360	LH III A:1 late

Middle Pictorial: Late Helladic III A:2

I	1365-1340	LH III A:2 early
II	1345-1325	LH III A:2 late
III	1330-1300	LH III A:2 late

Ripe Pictorial: Late Helladic III B

I	1300-1270/60	LH III B:1
II	1275-1230/20	LH III B:2

Pastoral Pictorial: Late Helladic III B (Cyprus and the East)
1250-1220

Transitional Pictorial: Late Helladic III B-C (Greek mainland)
1230-1200/1190

Late Pictorial: Late Helladic III C

1200/1190-1165	LH III C:1a
1170-1140	LH III C:1b

As a matter of principle, the pictorial vases found in Cyprus and the Near East have been treated separately from those on the Greek mainland. This is not meant in any way to prejudice the reader's judgment on the difficult question of where these vases were made and what the commercial connections between east and west may have been. Probably the situation was more flexible and accidental than partisans have been willing to admit; there are certainly vases by individual painters on both sides of the Aegean (see Chapter XIV). The Cypriote material is presented first, because it is so much more extensive and offers a chance to observe changing styles. Near Eastern finds of pictorial vases have been included in the Cypriote section for obvious reasons: we do not know of any independent workshops in the East before the Late period, except possibly at Ugarit, and when Mycenaean pictorial appears in the Levant it is normally accompanied by Cypriote exports.

It has not been possible to illustrate every piece, for reasons of expense and the probability of losing the thread of the argument in a mass of broken material. Most of the mainland pictorial is in sherds, and a lot of it is not easily recognizable—a bird's wing, a fish's tail—unless one is familiar with the whole series. Much of this smashed evidence has been merely identified, or its qualities suggested in line drawings, enough to help excavators—who have been known to publish their pictorial sherds upside down. The more complete vases in the Cypriote series present a different problem, that of not being able to give as many views and details as one would like. There are, however, fairly complete photographic archives in Nicosia and Boston for further consultation by scholars in the field.

Pictorial vase painting offers some exciting evidence for reconstructing Mycenaean culture. It has not been possible here to take full advantage of the evidence for discussing such matters as hats, shoes, sword belts, weapons, agriculture, and ships. The real chariot, as reflected on vases, is discussed by M. A. Littauer and J. Crouwel in the Appendix, but other fruitful lines of inquiry are left for other scholars. The two most obvious omissions are the pictorial world of Crete and the relation between vase painting and sarcophagus painting. The issue of the pic-torial vases' funerary significance is also left to one side. Connections between the vases and gems would prove exceptionally interesting, but that is a separate topic. The major aim has been to show what Mycenaean pictorial painting is like and to suggest how it may have developed.

II
SOURCES AND DISTRIBUTION
OF PICTORIAL PAINTING:
A Historical Sketch

FROM AN ARCHAEOLOGIST'S POINT OF VIEW, Mycenaean pictorial painting links ideas and imagery to foreign travel in a way that no other Bronze Age form of expression has really done. Ivory and gem carving are equally interesting, in different ways, for their signs that ideas from other cultures were quickly absorbed by Aegean craftsmen and that Aegean fashions had a reverse influence on neighbors; but the distribution of ivory and gems is more erratic and the exchanges of ideas harder to interpret.

It is not yet clear how the Mycenaean pictorial style really came about. The usual idea, that the painted vases are copies of frescoes, is theoretically attractive although not directly proved. Many themes from frescoes are popular on vases, especially horses and chariots, bulls and stags, women in architectural settings, processions, and decorative ensembles of birds and fish. There are rarer correspondences too, like fishermen, bull jumpers, and boxers, and certain wall paintings on the mainland, like the Tiryns stag scenes, have fairly close replicas on painted vases. In general, however, the two media are linked more by subject than by style.

Fresco prototypes for the subjects of pictorial vases are better known now than when Furumark justly pointed out that the vases have standard subjects "which belong to the common stock of Minoan and Mycenaean art." While some themes are shared by metalworkers and gem carvers, they are more concentrated in the fresco workshops from the late sixteenth to the early fourteenth centuries. The standard repertory at Knossos includes women in architecture, a chariot, bulls and bull jumpers, processions, griffins, sacral scenes, birds, and fish. Theran painters also

are at home with architectural facades, hunts, boxers, fishermen, ships, lions, griffins, goats, and birds. Ayia Irini on Keos contributes horses and chariots, as well as architectural facades, women in windows, processions, hunters, stags, dogs, ships, and vases. The Ramp House fragments at Mycenae include bulls, bull jumpers, architecture, and women. It is the geographical spread of these subjects, just before the start of pictorial vase painting, and the realization that they were once far more widely distributed, that makes the connection between the two traditions attractive. We need to know more of the connections among workshops and craft guilds, of the existence of inherited handbooks of design, and the momentum of particular images among painters. It is obvious that some painters and workshops specialize in bulls or chariots or birds, and whole areas of imagery popular in wall painting are ignored by the vase painters with their outline technique and somewhat limited range: no landscapes, for example, no monkeys playing and hunting, no women picking flowers, and, only rarely, convincing scenes of sacrifices or priestesses. Conversely, goats and boars are quite rare in wall painting.[1]

If subjects were introduced by wall painters and selectively borrowed by vase painters, they did not "copy" di-

1. Furumark, *MP*, 430; for frescoes in general, as they relate to particular pictorial vases, the connections are made in the text for each piece. The Knossos frescoes, A. Evans, *Palace of Minos* I-IV; S. Alexiou, *AA* 1964, 785; M. Cameron, S. Hood, *Sir Arthur Evans' Knossos Fresco Atlas* (1967); M. Cameron, *BSA* 63 (1968) 1 f.; C. Doumas, ed., *Thera and the Aegean World* (1979) 579. For Thera, S. Marinatos, *Thera* II-VII (1968-1976). For Ayia Irini, K. Coleman, *Hesperia* 42 (1973) 284 f.; K. Abramovitz, *Hesperia* 49 (1980) 57 f. For the Ramp House frescoes, W. Lamb, *BSA* 24 (1919-21) 189 f. For the megaron, G. Rodenwaldt, *Der*

rectly any more than classical vase painters did. Since they were trained to work only in glazes and outlined forms, an initial figure or composition would be transformed into a series of patterns suitable to the work at hand. They were under different commercial pressures, to turn out vases quickly for daily profit, while a wall painter was probably commissioned and took the desires of his patron more seriously. Once a vase workshop developed a set of images, it might also adapt motifs from other professions. It is characteristic of Mycenaean art that similar designs appear in a broad range of materials and are shared by fresco painters, goldsmiths, bronzesmiths, and stone, ivory, and gem carvers. In the present state of our knowledge, it does not seem likely that pictorial vase painting depended strictly and uniquely on another single craft such as wall painting but that there were, rather, "ideal" compositions reflected in various arts as excerpts or distortions suited to the medium.

The swift development of a Mycenaean pictorial style in a previously unpictorial culture is no more surprising than the equally impressive development of work in ivory and gold, silver and gems, marble and bronze. The Shaft Graves of Mycenae show the process of developing a vocabulary for the representation of natural and human activity in a number of precious materials. Contemporary endeavors in other provincial capitals between 1600 and 1450 suggest the role of traveling craftsmen in disseminating techniques and themes, and also the receptivity of patrons, whose earlier traditions had involved abstract ornament on inexpensive materials. There is no need to look for influence from other pictorial traditions, except, as always, in relation to Crete and the Cyclades; the specific forerunners are discussed in the appropriate chapters (III and VII). A general survey suggests that most Mycenaean inventions in pictorial compositions are independent, not developed out of earlier work in other cultures.

In the Middle Bronze Age and the opening years of the Late Bronze Age, there were sparse flashes of an "illustrating" tendency in Crete, the Cyclades, the Greek mainland, and the Near East. These are so rare and local, except in Crete, and so nearly restricted to birds and fish that they seem to be the work either of single artists or of local workshop schools without major influence beyond their areas. The round red and black birds of Melos, the swallows of Thera, the face-ostrakon or the dolphins and partridges of Crete, the fish of the Argolid, the birds of "Palestinian Bichrome," or the bulls of the Tell el-Ajjul Painter are mostly conventional in design and limited in distribution through the Aegean.[2] In terms of style, it is not possible to link early Mycenaean pictorial compositions like the Zeus Krater (III.2) or the Pyla-Verghi krater (III.13) directly to any of those earlier schools. Some pic-

torial vases seem to draw on similar traditions, like the birds-in-a-tree theme of the W Krater (III.1) and the mother-and-child birds of the Louvre ewer (VII.6). From the beginning there may be a distinction between the impulse to make scenes with some kind of narrative content, which are related to Mycenaean pleasure in military and hunting themes, and the decorative impulse, using generalized birds and fish already available around the Aegean. Consequently, the strains in Mycenaean pictorial painting are mixed from the beginning; the forms that develop in particular places must depend partly on the market, and partly on the painter's experience and contacts.

As soon as Mycenaean pictorial vases were made anywhere, they appeared in Cyprus and its major trading harbors in the Levant, like Ugarit and Alalakh. This happened around 1400, near the time of the destruction of Knossos in Crete. One might suppose that Cretan craftsmen were somehow shaken loose into the East by political events and contributed to the formation of the pictorial style, yet from the start the style has a specifically Mycenaean tone and content. The shapes of the early pictorial vases are related to those of the fifteenth-century Palace Style, which was current in both Crete and Greece, and sometimes the organization of the ornament recalls the principles of the Palace Style (III.A, B). On the other hand, whenever the Palace Style went pictorial, it avoided human figures and animals, concentrating on marine scenes or on decorative birds and fish in settings of plants (III.1–2). It lacked the element of humor that marks some of the earliest Mycenaean pictorial, displayed no interest in chariot scenes, bullfights, or armed soldiers. These themes are much more in keeping with the arts of the Shaft Grave period on the Greek mainland where from the beginning the horse, the bull, the lion, and the soldier were attractive elements in the Mycenaean expression of male excellence.

When the Mycenaeans started to develop an artistic vocabulary to express these ideas, they were of course deeply influenced by the Cretans and certain Cycladic peo-

2. Aspects of Cycladic and Minoan pictorial painting are discussed in connection with the Forerunners and Early pieces in Chapters III, VII, and XII. For Near Eastern pictorial painting and schools see, among others, R. C. Thompson and M. E. L. Mallowan, *Liverpool Annals of Art and Archaeology* 20 (1933) pls. 55-59; W. Heurtley, *Quarterly of the Department of Antiquities of Palestine* 8 (1939) 21 f.; V. Seton-Williams, *Iraq* 15 (1953) 57 f.; C. Epstein, *Palestinian Bichrome Ware* (1966); J. Margueron, *Syria* 45 (1968) 83 f.; R. Amiran, *Ancient Pottery of the Holy Land* (1969) 152-165; J.-C. Courtois, in Schaeffer, *Ugaritica* VI, 110 f.; P. Åström in Schaeffer, *Alasia* I, 7 f.; K. Sams, *AnatSt* 24 (1974) 169 f.; V. Karageorghis, *RDAC* 1979, 198 f. The beautiful Hittite graffito published by K. Bittel, *RevArch* 1976, 9, suggests that there was much more quick sketching and painting in Anatolia and the Levant than we are currently aware of; cf. *MDOG* 78 (1940) 57, fig. 14.

ple, both in figure drawing and composition, and after two or three generations they had integrated these Aegean fashions with their own rather stark and fantastic weightless styles, which appear on some of the metalwork in the Shaft Graves.[3] But there is always an abstract element in Mycenaean art, even in the most ambitious scenes of narrative, which accords with but is not allied to the abstraction in Syro-Palestinian or Cycladic vase painting. Abstraction in pictorial painting may seem to be a self-contradicting judgment; it is meant to express a fundamental self-contradiction in the style. Abstraction is poetic in one way; even in the most vigorous scenes of noblemen, horses, chariots, and birds there is a meaningless quality to the narration, which never reaches its goal and seldom shows people in contact; it is poetic in the sense of total freedom from temporal accident, in the stability of clear images, in always being in process, never concluding. In another way it is harsh and formal, expressionless, strongly patterned and decorative, but without the surface grace of lyric painting from nature. There is an ambition in Mycenaean pictorial painting that is not sensed in Syro-Palestinian or Cycladic, an infusion of religious or feudal themes (where the links to wall painting have been most strongly sensed) that lifts it far above the decorative bird compositions of Palestine or the stick-figure soldiers of Thera, yet it necessarily shares with them a respect for the vase's function and restricted space, the need for borders and for balanced compositions — the syntax of vase painting.

Given the blend of mainland and Cretan styles in Mycenaean art at the time pictorial painting was "invented," and the different economic and political situations surrounding the vase painters in separate regions, it is not surprising that no single analytical or stylistic theory about this class of vases will suit all the surviving examples. The differences in local schools and periods are taken up in each chapter, but the historical development and distribution of pictorial vases may be summarized as follows.

On mainland Greece there are two or three local schools of pictorial painting from at latest the early fourteenth century. From the present scattered evidence, there is very little relationship to Middle Helladic pictures of birds and fish. Attica, Boeotia, and the Argolid have produced early pieces, each different in style. Attica, with decorative birds and fish, seems most influenced by the Cretan Marine and Palace styles. The earliest human figures appear on the Circus Jug at Mycenae and on the cutaway jug from Melathria in Lakonia (VIII.6, 8); both have been placed in the fifteenth century by some, but they seem to us more likely to have been painted around 1360. These human figures have no relation to the fat static figures in spotted robes, which occur from about 1400 in Cyprus and the East; they are more lively, informal, and direct. In the Middle period, corresponding to the Amarna Age, the mainland becomes more active; good animals and birds are painted in more places (Chapter VIII) and the products of known painters are found at Mycenae, Tiryns, and Nauplion in Greece, and at Enkomi in eastern Cyprus. Most of the vases now known were found in tombs; it is not yet clear how far their subjects may have had funerary significance, though horses, chariots, birds, and fish certainly have symbolic overtones in many cultures. Apart from a partly published group of vases in the Argolid and the extensive unpublished material from Berbati in the hills east of Mycenae, the material surviving from the Early and Middle periods is scanty and idiosyncratic in comparison to the material in Cyprus and the East.

In Cyprus the first pictorial vases appear in the period referred to with compression as that of the fall of Knossos; the vases themselves may have been made as early as 1410, and Knossos flourished until 1380 or 1370, but for both it is the opening of the new Late Helladic III A:1 style. This style is, in general, created by craftsmen who are less dependent than before on older fashions and more conscious of new possibilities; there is more space in the design, which allows the characteristic pictorial processional and combat forms to develop. At this period Cretan domination of trade with the East has relaxed, and Mycenaean Greeks are more active in Cyprus than before.

The evidence from Cyprus matches that from Rhodes, Miletos on the Asia Minor coast, and Ugarit in Syria. Minoan exploration of the eastern trade routes had established some coastal footholds, emporia rather than full-scale colonies, as at Trianda and Miletos; in Cyprus there are sparse but significant artefacts of Late Minoan I and II from Morphou Bay (Toumba tou Skourou) in the west to Pyla-Verghi and Hala Sultan Tekké in the south. Mycenaean Greeks either accompanied Cretans on some of these voyages, or made contemporary expeditions through the Cyclades by themselves; their wares are found at Ayia Irini in the west, possibly at Enkomi in the east. Probably Greek and Cretan explorations were designed to develop friendly relations with the Cypriote entrepreneurs of copper ores. The Greek connection began in the Shaft Grave period, continued sporadically through the fifteenth century (Enkomi, Pyla-Verghi, Hala Sultan Tekké, Maroni) and expanded dramatically after the fall of Knossos as though freed of some previous constraint. Early Mycenaean pottery at first appears near or with Minoan pottery, as at Ayia Irini, and then replaces it entirely until a

3. E. Vermeule, *The Art of the Shaft Graves at Mycenae* (Semple Lectures, University of Cincinnati, 1975).

renewal of trade in Cretan octopus jars in the thirteenth century. The reverse trade, especially in White Slip I milk bowls, is a sign of preliminary acquaintance between Cyprus and harbor towns like Zakro, Phylakopi, Thera, and Trianda, probably a thin souvenir trade accompanying the basic commerce in copper.

From the Late Helladic III A:1 phase onward, Mycenaean pottery comes in quantity to Cyprus, and in III A:2 and III B it occurs at almost every major and minor site. Although pictorial vases are only a small percentage of the whole, they far outnumber pictorial vases in Greece. The situation in Cyprus, the only Late Bronze Age territory to exhibit this density of trade with Greece, must consequently be distinguished from contemporary situations elsewhere. There was no question in the fourteenth century of a Mycenaean program of immigration into or colonization of Cyprus. The vigorous Cypriote culture expanded without check, integrating Mycenaean pottery and a few other exports like razors into its own repertory of crafts. Cypriote architectural styles, tomb designs, pottery, textile weaving, cylinder seals, and terracottas continue without any sign of disruption and with a kind of independence symbolized by refusal to replace the cylinder seal with the Aegean gemstone, or the continuing use of the Cypriote language and script. The situation is thus in direct contrast to Rhodes, where only Mycenaean material is found and native culture vanishes. It is also in contrast to Egypt, the Levant, or Anatolia, where Mycenaean wares represent casual informal trade through a variety of hands from the coast to the interior.[4]

The number of early pictorial vases, in contrast to mainland Greece, must reflect some happy interaction of Cypriote consumers, organized in small kingdoms, and interested in foreign fashions, and Mycenaean entrepreneurs, who may have been encouraged by the wealth of Cypriote funeral gifts and who fed an appetite for a range of wares that were not available to any other inhabitants of the Mediterranean world outside the Argolid. While the new discoveries in the Argolid suggest that our knowledge of pictorial painting on the mainland is still very defective, the present evidence is that Cypriote customers offered a strong demand for pictorial vases from the beginning of their close contact with Mycenaeans and that the patrons who commissioned pictorial kraters and the mourning families who bought them for tomb gifts had a large choice of vases in front of them.

It is this point that has caused controversy in the past and has led to a quickening of clay analyses in the quest to determine the local origin of the pictorial vases.[5] One group of scholars has come to believe that all the Mycenaean vases in Cyprus were imported from the Argolid by ship. The discovery in 1936 of the potter's kiln at Berbati in the Argolid strengthened that point of view, especially since there were defective pictorial pieces in the kiln debris, although published pieces do not seem earlier than the Middle period (VIII.1–3). Others believe that this position is too inflexible; that certainly pictorial vases were made in the Argolid and often shipped abroad; that craftsmen from the Argolid may have traveled to Cyprus to make certain pieces; and that there must also have been Mycenaean potters resident in Cyprus who knew their customers personally and made their wares with an eye to Cypriote tastes and customs. These potters may have lived in prosperous harbor communities, like Enkomi and Hala Sultan Tekké, where cultures mingled and where so many pictorial vases have been found; they may have traveled in the interior of the island and sold at fairs.

Obvious signs of the resident Mycenaean potter in Cyprus are bowls made in the shape of Cypriote Base Ring wares and decorated in Mycenaean style as early as the fourteenth century, and the reverse influence, for example a Mycenaean three-handled jar of the Amarna period made in Cypriote Base Ring fabric.[6] A fine strap-handled krater covered with scale pattern and birds was so deceptively Mycenaean-looking in photograph as to deceive even the great scholar Arne Furumark into thinking it a mainland piece of the mid-fourteenth century; in fact it is a Cypriote vase belonging to the White Painted tradition.[7] Such exchanges of ideas among Cypriote and Mycenaean potters and painters assure their mutual enthusiasm, but the mechanisms are hard to imagine if scholarly theory keeps them five hundred miles apart throughout the Late Bronze Age.

4. Mycenaean trade and colonization in Cyprus are discussed in *The Mycenaeans in the Eastern Mediterranean* (1973). Positions in earlier standard works, like Stubbings, *MycLevant*, and H. Catling and V. Karageorghis, *BSA* 55 (1960) 109 f., still seem valid; see also *Acts of the International Archaeological Symposium "The Relations Between Cyprus and Crete ca. 2000-500 B.C."* (1979).

5. J. F. Daniel was one of the first to propose a mainland origin for most pictorial vases (*AJA* 47 [1943] 252 f.); then the Granary style sherds from Tarsus were thought identical in clay to Argolid examples (H. Goldman, *Tarsus* II [1956] 206). The elaborate work of the Oxford laboratories under the archaeological supervision of H. W. Catling (see Select Bibliography) seems to point in the same direction, although questions have been raised about the neglect of silver as a trace element and the lack of clay bed samples; *RDAC* 1978, 80 f., discusses problems with the method. F. Asaro and I. Perlman (see Select Bibliography) have tried to distinguish local fabrics in the Peloponnesos and how they differ from some Cypriote samples; the analysis is apparently delicate enough to suggest, for example, that Mycenaean sherds from Tell Abu Hawam correspond in makeup with those from Tiryns and that only about one quarter of Mycenaean vases from Enkomi in LH III A have typically Argolid clay patterns. Some pictorial pottery seems to come neither from Greece nor Cyprus. The clay itself may have been an article of commerce, as now. Laboratory findings seem to favor a rather flexible view of production centers and commercial relations, as sketched here.

6. *CVA* British Museum I, pl. 1.32.

7. *ExcCyp* 40, fig. 68, 1103; Furumark, *MP*, 252, FM 7.31 (III A:2).

The view adopted in this book is that trade between Greece and Cyprus, manifested in pictorial vases and in many other spheres, occurred on a variety of levels, with all kinds of channels and private adventures. Ships surely came from Greece with cargoes of painted pottery; potters may have roamed abroad as freely as architects and metalsmiths, some spending a few months and some settling overseas permanently. The simplicity of a potter's equipment makes him exceptionally mobile. He needs only a supply of clay he is happy working with; he makes his wheel, builds his kiln, fires his pots, sells them, and moves on or settles in as he wishes. Some of the pictorial vase makers may have used local clays, some may have had sacks of clay brought from the mainland or one of the islands, as potters today often import clay.

Modern views of Bronze Age trade are often stereotyped and filled with anachronisms. Because the tradition of the itinerant craftsman has nearly died out today, his role in earlier times may be neglected. Nowadays channels of import tend to be fixed, and mass production is common, so it is easy to think of an Argive merchant monopoly of pictorial kraters, with shipping and agents prearranged, and Cypriote customers' taste inexorably formed by fashions emanating from Mycenae. The facts do not suit such ideas, nor do they accord with what we know about the small scale and personal enterprise of Bronze Age trade.

A more flexible view helps bring to the foreground some characteristic qualities of pictorial painting. It may be easier to see which series of animal pictures show fresco influence and which do not, which parts of the Aegean are more influenced by Minoan pictorial themes and which are more independent, which schools are interested in cult scenes and human figures, which are content with standard animal friezes.

When one sees even a fragment, one has an instinct about it — that it is close to what is being done in Tiryns or in Athens or, on the other hand, that it fits realistically into the Cypriote and Eastern series. Such feelings are no doubt primarily subjective and would not necessarily match laboratory clay analyses precisely, but since the clay specialists have not found the clay beds, it does not yet seem to be a field from which connoisseurship must retire before the thermoluminescence machine. The hands of individual artists are distinguished so far as possible in Chapter XIV, where it will be seen that some sell their vases exclusively in Greece, some exclusively in Cyprus, and some in both places as well as the Levant. Beyond identified artists (and it is amazing that most pictorial vases do not easily lend themselves to attribution), there are links that are hard to describe. A fragment of a chariot krater from Berbati may look quite at home in the Cypriote sequence, or similar papyrus blossoms may appear both in the Argolid and in Rhodes. In general, however, idiosyncrasies of ornament and style flourish in each locality of the eastern Mediterranean.

Although the origin of the local forms of pictorial style is not yet clear, once the traditions are launched the continuity is easier to follow. The limited number of subjects may suggest a limited number of ateliers, even though fewer than forty convincing attributions to individual hands have been made. Some painters seem to specialize in birds, some in bulls, some in chariot processions. Within these genres the formulas are easily recognized, and within the formulas the individual flourishes and the passage of time, which changes style, are visible.

It would be impossible to reconstruct all the influences on Mycenaean vase painting or all its vagaries of circulation through the Aegean. The evidence of interaction with frescoes, metalwork, ivory carving, and sarcophagus painting is too disturbed by accidents of time and catastrophe. An occasional oddity may suggest a link or a tradition in images that lasted a century or more, then died away, for example the Maroni fisherman (III.30) and the Thera and Phylakopi fishermen in fresco and polychrome paint a hundred years earlier, or the Homage Krater (III.29), the gold ring from Tiryns, and the painted stele from Mycenae (XI.43). A bird scene may recall a Cretan larnax; a helmet or weapon form may be the single surviving illustration of a curiosity known otherwise only in the text of Homer. In most spheres the connections are faint, and historical and artistic reconstruction not yet possible.

What remains, a vivid and fascinating class of Bronze Age art, is the series of scenes transmitted from generation to generation, from 1400 to nearly 1150, on the grand painted vases of the Mycenaean world, from Olympia and Pylos in the west to Miletos and Ugarit in the east, the most complete corpus of old Greek imagery we have.

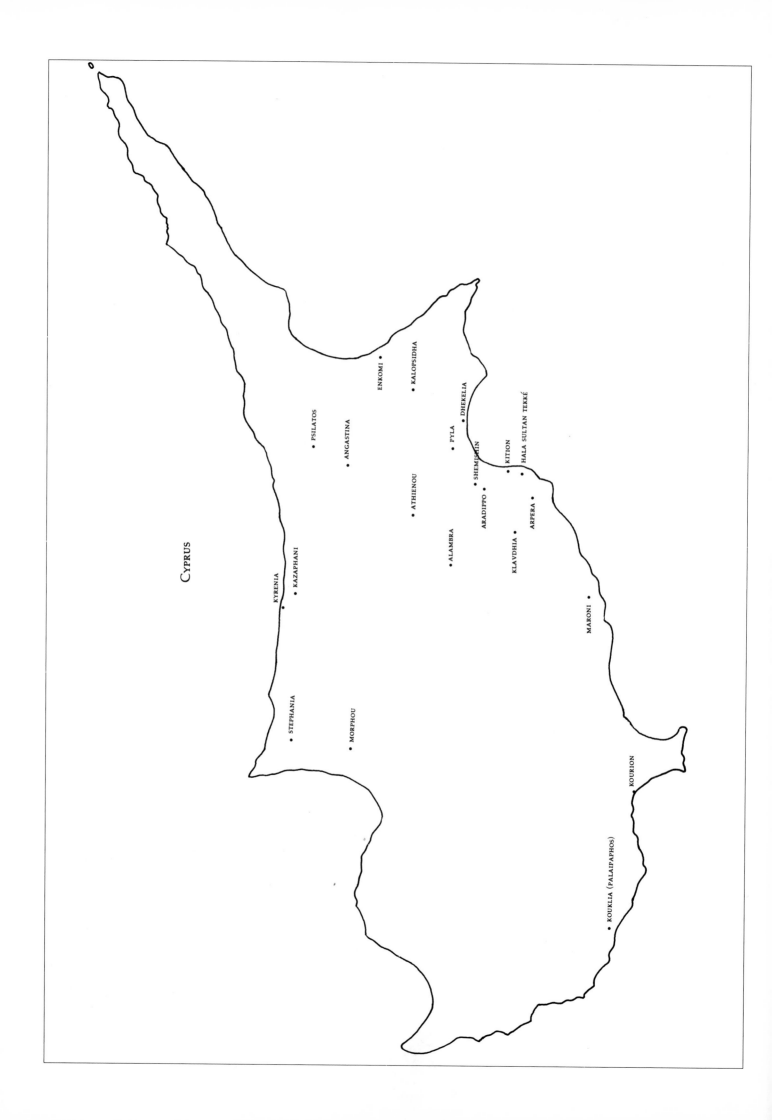

III
CYPRUS AND THE EAST:
Early Pictorial

A N ARTISTIC CLIMATE suitable for the creation of a genuine pictorial style seems to occur toward the end of the fifteenth century. By the second quarter of the fourteenth century, the idiom is already established. The Early Pictorial material appears more richly in Cyprus than anywhere else. The reasons for this are partly artistic, partly economic and have been discussed briskly by a variety of scholars. Because the fullness of the material in Cyprus permits a more useful examination of the initial stylistic tendencies and the development of pictorial painting, we survey Cypriote vases first without, we hope, prejudicing future arguments about their origin.

The craftsmen who started the fashion of putting human and animal pictures on vases may have been partly trained in the traditions of the Palace Style in Crete. In the fifteenth century, marine scenes, birds, goats, military images, and even human faces were part of the Minoan repertory of designs.[1] Yet the first genuine pictorial vases outside Crete are not Cretan in style, not even to the degree one would expect of transplanted or refugee Minoan artists; nor do they reflect a style emanating from the Greek mainland in any detectable way. Cretan vase painters who tended toward pictorial imagery were probably partly conditioned by themes in wall paintings and in the delicate minor arts. Their imagination created richly filled and whirling designs of birds and fish in motion, or birds feeding in blown foliage, or even modeled crabs and barnacles.[2] There is usually a delight in the setting and in the intimate connection between the figure and the landscape. Human narrative did not appeal until later, nor was the stately formal processional or ceremonial scene congenial. The painted human faces of Knossos and Thera are exceptional, perhaps functioning as ostrakon sketches rather than full-scale vase designs.[3]

The chariot may illustrate the disjunction between themes in wall painting and vase painting. The chariot fresco painted at Knossos in the fifteenth century did not seem to inspire any Cretan vase painter to pick up the theme and develop it, and the chariots and horses at Ayia Irini on Keos, standing still in a processional context, apparently did not influence any Cycladic or Mycenaean painters to try the scene, before they fell in the destruction debris of LM I B/LH II. The gap may be accidental, but the simple sequence from Aegean fresco to Mycenaean vase is nowhere documented, even though fresco inspiration often seems plausible.[4] The early mainland material (Chapter VII) looks quite different from the Cypriote, with one exception (VII.1); there is a greater variety of shapes, more birds and fish, fewer chariots, and an aesthetically distinct repertory, which does not seem to be the source of inspiration either. In Cyprus, pictorial painting reaches a degree of authority around 1400. The Early Pictorial documents must be regarded in terms of style rather than archaeological context, however risky this may seem.

The history of archaeological exploration on Cyprus makes it a sad but accepted fact that the vast majority of vases discussed in this and the next two chapters have been

1. See Chapter VII, section on "Forerunners in Greece and the Islands," and note 3 below.
2. S. Alexiou, *Katsamba* (1967) pls. 20-22; Evans, *Palace of Minos* IV, 329 f.; I, 521; Popham, *DestrKnossos*, 71 f.
3. S. Alexiou, *Charisterion Orlandou* (1964) 112; S. Marinatos, *AAA* 4 (1971) 74, fig. 25; *Thera* IV (1971) col. pl. G; see also P. V. C. Baur, *AJA* 13 (1909) 429.
4. IX.48 and following (stags); Furumark, *MP*, 141, 436.

found in tombs that were not carefully excavated and that do not yield a sound chronology. The rich material from the 1896 British excavations at Enkomi on the east coast has never been published in terms of context, although individual vases are famous. Some of the finds are published as "tomb groups," but the stratigraphic evidence from the tombs has been lost.[5] The Swedish excavations at many sites in the 1920s and 1930s produced important material, but the dating was based mainly on the general contents of the tombs, all from the Late Cypriote II period, for which there are as yet no exact chronological subdivisions.[6] Three recent tombs at Kition on the south coast were carefully excavated, but two of them had been disturbed in antiquity, like so many other Cypriote tombs.[7] In general, evidence for absolute chronology is meager, for the material associated with pictorial vases is often scanty and too fragmentary to serve as a reliable guide to the development of successive stylistic stages. Even pictorial sherds found in stratified contexts in habitation sites often have the appearance of heirlooms or intrusions, and since pictorial style itself is individual, any ordering into an intelligible sequence is necessarily tentative.

We have tried to classify the pictorial vases by period through the several ingredients of "style," which include the shape of the vase; the area and composition of the picture; the forms of human figures, animals, chariots, or plants; and particularly the filling ornaments and patterns. There is an attempt to suggest how one phase of painting and image making leads into the next. Other eyes may come to other conclusions, and there will certainly be new scientific and stratigraphic evidence.

Early Pictorial falls almost entirely before that fixed point in the development of shapes and patterns offered by the thirteen-hundred-odd fragments of Mycenaean vases found at Tell el Amarna or Akhtaten, Akhenhaten's city founded in the 1370s in central Egypt.[8] The litter of Mycenaean commercial enterprise at Amarna should be used very cautiously for chronology, like the sporadic finds in the Near East. It belongs to a limited period in which special techniques and certain abstract or floral motifs were popular. There are no pictorial sherds at Amarna, nor even fragments of the kind of krater on which pictorial painting was normally done. One can use the evidence from Egypt only by comparing its patterns with those on Mycenaean vases found elsewhere in context with pictorial vases. This is a roundabout method, complicated by ignorance of the total composition on the vases from which the Amarna fragments survive. However, the evidence from Egypt is still a chronological cornerstone in its own restricted way. Amarna was built toward the end of our Early period and abandoned in, roughly, Middle II; its absolute dates may be about 1375-1345.

On Cyprus, the Early and Middle phases have each been divided into three successive parts, although certain themes at each end that are scantily represented are grouped together for convenience.[9] The dividing line between the two is roughly the start of the Amarna Age. Again, we emphasize that these pictorial stages are not absolute. The careers of painters and the development of themes may overlap or shift from one stage into the next at historical points that we do not yet know. Historical events are rarely linked to changes in style because the vases may be found in strata of widely separated towns whose histories do not correspond or in tombs used over several generations. We stress those links we know about, urge excavators to be more diligent in providing reliable contexts for pictorial vases in the future instead of extracting them as showpieces, and depend on a diagnosis of stylistic sequence that has stood firm for more than twenty years.

FORERUNNERS

The earliest pictorial vases in Cyprus are tall oval kraters for mixing or storing liquids. They have a broad low neck, a flat or ledged rim, and two wide strap handles from rim to shoulder. These amphoroid kraters owe their form, ultimately, to the large jars of the Palace Style that were so popular on Crete and the Greek mainland in the later fifteenth century. The early kraters clearly were influenced by a tradition of metalworking in their profile and the treatment of rims and handles; a close counterpart is the silver "pictorial" krater with fighting warriors from Shaft Grave IV at Mycenae.[10] As on the Palace Style three-handled jars, on the early kraters the neck ornaments are often reserved in negative, light on dark. The body decoration tends toward

5. *ExcCyp*, passim; *BMCatV* I.2; *CVA British Museum* I; D. M. Bailey, in *Hala Sultan Tekké* 1 (1976) 1f.

6. *SCE* I, 467 f.; Sjöqvist, *Problems*, 127 f.; V. Karageorghis, *OpAth* 3 (1960) 135 f.; P. Dikaios, *Enkomi* (1969-71) II, 441-496.

7. V. Karageorghis, *BCH* 87 (1963) 364 f.; 88 (1964) 346 f.; *Kition* I, *The Tombs* (1974) 16 f.

8. V. Hankey and P. Warren, *BICS* 21 (1974) 147 f., and V. Hankey, "The Aegean Deposit at El Amarna," in *The Mycenaeans in the Eastern Mediterranean* (1973) 128 f.; Furumark, *Chronology*, 57, 113; W. F. Petrie, *Tell el Amarna* (1894) pls. 26-30; *BMCatV* I.1, A 990-999; H. Frankfort, J. D. Pendlebury, *The City of Akhenaten* II, 110; W. Helck, *Die Beziehungen Ägyptens zu Vorderasien*[2] (1971) 168; P. Åström, *OpAth* 4 (1962) 221, n. 6; Popham, *DestrKnossos*, 94.

9. For example, some bulls that might be Early III are placed in Middle I; all Ripe chariot scenes are in Ripe I (V.26, horseback rider, should probably be in Late, cf. XIII.28 and following).

10. A. Sakellariou, *I°Congresso di Micenologia* I (1968) 262 f.; *RevArch* 1975, 195 f.; Karageorghis, *Nouveaux Documents*, 222 f.

vertical strips of architectonic, marine, or floral ornament, another metallic trait. The earliest examples suggest that their makers were trained in or influenced by that older palatial tradition, although the results are subtly different.

Two forerunners show the type to come, even though they have no pictorial imagery.

A. The krater from Qatna (El Misrifeh) in Syria stands among the earliest because of its shape and stratigraphic context. In form it is comparable to the silver krater from Shaft Grave IV except for the position of the handles on the rim. It uses the massive spiral guilloche of the Palace Style horizontally around the shoulder, with heavy paint imitating a reserved or relief effect; a broken running spiral is in reversed color on the neck. Found with a Cypriote bowl and a Rhodian jar, it may have been exported from Cyprus, like so many later pictorial vases in the Levant.

B. Like the Qatna krater, the early krater from Pyla-Verghi in southern Cyprus uses the heavy architectural spiral pattern of the Palace Style, but vertically down the body, forming strips like metallic compartments, punctuated by bands of chevrons and oblique leaves. The neck also bears the characteristic reserved wavy band common on jars of the late Palace Style. The broad decorated zone, which occupies the whole body of the vase except the foot, conveys a formal and grandiose spirit reminiscent of palatial Crete. Yet because of the shape and fabric, it is difficult to regard the Pyla krater as a Cretan import into Cyprus,[11] and it is unlike the earliest mainland pieces. It is quite possible that this handsome vase was made in Cyprus, where it was found.

In form and decoration, these vases of about 1400 herald the coming of the genuine pictorial style. The grand formality of the Palace Style, still sensed here, had to be dissolved before the pictorial style could really develop. Surviving memories of the Late Minoan Marine Style, with its marine creatures floating entirely around the surface of a vase in an artful, seemingly unplanned manner, may have been an aid in opening up the "free field" of decoration that naturalistic imagery needs. Such changes from a formal geometric style to a free style are often abrupt, as at the start of Cypriote pictorial free-field painting in the seventh century or the contemporary transition from Attic Geometric to Proto-Attic.[12] At the beginning of such a style there may be a rude burst of energy, an urge to paint fantastically without much discipline. This reaction against formal convention may be seen in Crete, too, after 1400, as architectural control gives way to exuberant and cluttered space filling. In the eastern Aegean, the pictorial style shifts swiftly from odd experiments to the full-scale introduction of human and animal compositions.

EARLY I

The W Krater (III.1), the Zeus Krater (III.2), the Stockholm Bullfight (III.3), and the Roc Krater (III.6) are the key pieces in this group. They share a bold sense of narrative, some humor, a vivid splash of drawing on a large field, bizarre elements, and, at times, some faint links to fresco compositions, although the intervening links cannot be found. Perhaps for this reason, many Early pieces have titles, as though they were pictures on a wall.

1. The W Krater, found in a tomb at Dhekelia near Pyla in southeastern Cyprus, illustrates the transition from formal to pictorial decoration. It has a broad shoulder, low neck with reserved band, and a wide decorated zone that covers almost all of the body except the foot. This zone is divided into vertical panels, as on the Pyla Krater (III.B), alternately filled with strips of scalloped lines like wave crests (a looser version of the chevrons on III.B) and with long thin scenes of birds in a tree.

The tree is painted as a tall flower; it may be a palm, with pairs of neat spiral fronds on the lower stem and two or three spear-shaped fruits erect at the top. The birds sit in facing pairs on the lower branches or hover below the blossom-fruits in air that is incongruously filled with seashells. The heraldic design and crowded filling ornament recall certain traits in contemporary Minoan painting and on later larnakes and vases, but neither the sketchy, symmetrical trees nor the lightweight, spotted birds are exactly like Cretan types. Simple Near Eastern painted versions of the same scenes are found in Cyprus;[13] perhaps a combination of influences produced a local version of a widespread Aegean and Near Eastern theme.

The birds are small in scale, with oversized feet thrust forward for balance and ineffective little raised wings. Their tails are barred or fringed. Some seem to have a crest. The general impression is that the figures have not yet acquired their full importance, because floral and abstract motifs predominate and the birds are nearly lost in the busy surface. This is an early appearance of the seashell filling ornament, which is more characteristic of Early III; it also derives from the Palace Style.[14] It is fitting that birds should appear at the beginning of the pictorial tradition

---

11. H. Catling and V. Karageorghis, *BSA* 55 (1960) 113.

12. V. Karageorghis and J. des Gagniers, *La Céramique Chypriote de Style Figuré de l'Age du Fer* (1975).

13. Dikaios, *Enkomi*, pls. 57.20, 64.3; C. Epstein, *Palestinian Bichrome* (1966) fig. 2; V. Hankey, *BSA* 62 (1967) 125 (Tell Abu Hawam 306 o); R. Hamilton, *QDAP* 4 (1935) pl. XIX.

14. Evans, *Palace of Minos* IV, figs. 238, 260, 269, 270.

(cf. VII.F, G, 5, 6); they are the most popular subject until the very end.

2. The first true vase in the pictorial style is one of the most famous, and has attracted many interpretations and suggestions. Found at Enkomi, it is sometimes known as the Zeus Krater, or "Zeus with the scales of Destiny," a probably misleading title that may no longer be separable from the vase. Recently an effort has been made to rechristen it the Talent Krater, on the grounds that it is a scene of weighing copper ingots, but that title has yet to win wide acceptance.[15] It is a tribute to the new-formed style that we should want a title for a vase at all.

The krater is of moderate size (0.375 meters high), with the typical broad low neck of the Early style; reserved neck ornament, wide shoulder, and big picture zone. Evidently it began as a marine scene, with a large flabby octopus at the center of each side. The human, animal, bird, and tree elements are crowded into the narrower spaces under the handles, which may reflect an experimental stage when new pictorial images were introduced rather cautiously. In one handle zone there are two flying birds, three palm trees, and a form like a spotted fringed snake. In the other handle zone there are a chariot with two passengers, a bull, a nude bearer, a robed figure holding scales, two palm trees, a flower, and an upper border of hanging rocks.

The significance of the odd imagery on this vase has been much discussed. Disputants either concentrate on the chariot scene or try to establish a wider imaginative relationship between the fertile emblems of the sea on front and back, the dry-land chariot scene, and the airy realm of birds. The disjointed composition makes it very difficult to establish any meaning with even a fair degree of certainty.

The octopods (or rather, polypods) are liberally spotted with white, a sporadic feature of the first two pictorial stages. They have less tension or elegance than those on contemporary pure octopus vases (III.7,8). One has a baggy configuration and an extra split arm stretching toward the other, which has suggested that the pair may be in the process of mating.[16] The combination of marine fertility symbolism and chariot or animal scenes occurs also in Crete and on the mainland. Although the octopus is normally considered a Minoan symbol, it took an early place in Mycenaean warrior mythology, as the numerous gold cutouts in the Shaft Graves at Mycenae demonstrate. The persistence of the connection, with funerary overtones, is illustrated by the fourteenth-century bathtub larnax from Mycenae with an octopus inside and a chariot outside (VIII.5.1), and the Episkopi larnax of Late Minoan III B,[17] on which the chariot drives over octopus tentacles as though voyaging with dry wheels over the waves of the sea, with hunting and animal figures adjunct. The larnakes tend to suggest a nexus of fu-

neral imagery, in which the chariot is the vehicle for the journey to the other world, the octopus a symbol of the sea that the person must cross to the west, and their marriageable state an expression of continued fertility. Whether any of this nexus can or should be applied to the Enkomi krater depends partly on whether one conceives of chariot vases as funerary or simply as expensive vases from ordinary life that were put in the tomb as fine gifts, and partly on whether one judges pictorial vases as disjointed patterned compositions or whole units of imagery.

Most analyses of the vase have considered the parts as though the imagery were as disjointed as the scale and composition. There are, of course, two separate pictures. On the smaller, the two round-bodied birds with long necks and short legs, flying right between the polypods, may be unidentifiable water birds; later the type is sometimes called a swan. The birds have the heavy outlines of the Early period (cf. III.6) and are filled with a simple pattern of small curved strokes. Two trees grow from the tentacles, the other is centered on the ground line. They have curved, barred leaves on a bending, barred or spotted stem, light on dark, like the polypods. The spotted, fringed undulation from the handle over the head of the leading bird may be a bizarre filling ornament rather than a snake or worm. Oblique loops from the upper border suggest a simplified rock pattern as a framing device.

In the larger scene the painter poses the chariot in the air on the left, moving right over a tree whose spiral fronds are filled with arcs and fringed on top. Driver and passenger in spotted robes are shown from the waist up in the "dual" chariot box, whose spots spill over into the space inside the four-spoked wheel. Since this early chariot sets a standard, from our limited point of view, for generations of chariot pictures, it is interesting to note how schematic and conventional the drawing already is (see Appendix). The box is waist-high, apparently covered in oxhide, although the spots that conventionally suggest cowhide are not distinguished from those on the robes. The box is loosely connected to the horse by a curved pole stay with a Y attachment, perhaps a conflation of the L-shaped pole brace with its short vertical member, which should be seated in the pole. Although the painter is indifferent to the second horse, all Mycenaean chariots are pulled by teams. (The double tail is not helpful here, since it is repeated on the single bull.) The yoke has a prominent rein-guide for three reins, which pass through and terminate on the horse's muzzle without

15. Dikaios, *Enkomi*, 918 f.

16. J. Wiesner, "Hochzeit des Polypus," *JdI* 74 (1959) 35.

17. E. Vermeule, *JHS* 85 (1965) 136; *A Land Called Crete* (1968) fig. 35; B. Rutkowski, *BSA* 63 (1968) 226; *IEE* 336; P. Warren, *Aegean Civilizations* (1976) 108.

a headstall. The rear of the main chariot box is balanced on the axle; the rear-axle design was an innovation for hunting and war chariots to eliminate see-sawing.

The passenger has no arms or hands — this will be standard — and the driver has only two triangular projections, which merge into the reins. Although the krater is very early in the sequence, judging from its shape, reserved neck, white arcs on dark at the base of the neck, and broad pictorial field, it is clearly not the first pictorial vase in the ancient sequence, because the standard conventions for drawing human figures have already been developed. The human head has been reduced to a scheme suitable for quick pictorial rendering: a basically oval form with jagged solid outlines of hair, a large oval eye with the pointed duct at the rear (and a stripe beneath, making it seem set in hair), jutting angles for the profile with emphasis on the nose, a thick triangular neck. There are many later variations on this convention, which persists until the Ripe period. The figures are thick and unresponsive, the spotted robe substituting pleasure in surface pattern for any interest in anatomy and motion; this too persists for dressed figures until the end of pictorial, while active figures are shown nude.[18] It is this standardized quality that has led scholars to believe that pictorial scenes were taken over from older fresco compositions, though free variation in composition argues against direct copies.

Surely no fresco ever looked like the main scene here; versions on finer metal vases might be credible. Over the horse's back there is a simple palm with barred leaves; under his belly a nude figure facing back, holding a curious object in the form of a double triangle. On the upper right a bull charges through the air, his long horns penetrating the upper striped rockwork border. The bull, like the horse, exhibits developed conventions in drawing, such as the reserved face with circular dotted eye (reserved faces become fashionable again two hundred years later), the elongated, dark spotted body, the short bent legs suggestive of rapid flight or exertion, the long horns bent forward sweeping the rocks.

On the right below the bull is a thick figure in a spotted robe, standing footless on an octopod tentacle. His one grotesque arm, sprouting from his belly, holds a disputed object that is more like a pair of scales than anything else. This figure has been thought of as the god Zeus judging the destiny of the charioteers before a battle or as a seer taking omens before a hunt (with a portable altar?) or as a steward waiting to weigh the bull meat when it is caught, or as a commercial official ready to weigh a copper ingot (carried by the nude man below). Although the spotted robe indicates superior social status, there is little likelihood that the holder is a god. The scales are appropriate for a funerary scene, but the general tone of the picture is not funerary.

Neither is it a battle scene; it is more like a hunt. The nude man and the bull must be fitted into the interpretation.

The nude figure retains vestiges of anatomical accuracy in the long legs, knobby knees, and swaying balance on pointed toes. The face is reserved, the body a dark silhouette with white spots like the bull and the octopods. The curious object he holds appears twice more in pictorial painting (III.13 and IV.16); it seems to be an open frame of hourglass shape, a snare, a kind of bow (the crossbow was never Mediterranean), or something wooden that does not survive materially. In the Near East the shape may represent a stool.[19] The recent interpretation of it as an ingot is attractive, although it does not seem solid or heavy enough and is the wrong shape.[20]

The free-field scattering of figures and fillers over the whole available surface is a sporadic feature of pictorial painting; it does not seem to indicate an attempt to render front and rear planes in perspective, any more than when the same system occurs in the Pylos frescoes two centuries later. It does, perhaps, preserve the older feeling for bird's-eye views, traditional in both fresco and metalwork. In this system figures are normally given equal visual weight, without emotional or psychological emphasis through changes in scale or centering. When it comes to interpreting the scene, therefore, the composition does not often give a clue to the intention of the narrative.

The picture is loose, disjointed, ill proportioned, ambitious, and ambiguous. Its predecessors in ceramic art are lost but are inferred from the high degree of conventionalization here. There is little sense for structure but much for color contrast and detail. Considerable bold invention unites elements of land and sea, symbol and genre, and relates the figures to some degree through glances and gestures. Whatever the scene means, it probably has a narrative intention. The ingredients have not been combined before in just this way. Perhaps the urge to illustrate an exciting story of heroes known in song or the adventures of the dead, is part of the explanation of the origins of pictorial painting.[21]

3. A similar experiment with figures loosely strewn over a tall field appears on an early amphoroid krater frag-

18. V. Karageorghis, BCH 83 (1959) 193.

19. Cf. A. Furtwängler, ArchZeit 1885, 142, for an Oriental cylinder on which men with swords bring a captive to a lady on an hourglass-shaped stool; tables of the shape are commoner, S. Laser, Hausrat, in Archaeologia Homerica F (1968) pl. III f.

20. Dikaios, Enkomi, 918 f.

21. The difficult question of the relation between sung narrative and narrative pictures is discussed positively by V. Karageorghis, AJA 62 (1958) 383 f., and T. B. L. Webster, From Mycenae to Homer (1958), negatively by L. Banti, AJA 58 (1954) 307, and E. Vermeule, CJ 1958, 97 f. There are at least stock genre scenes and formulas in both media.

ment from Enkomi. On the right the horns and forelegs of a heavy bull explode in motion toward the left; above the bull's horns is a pair of silhouetted human feet pointing left. The drawing combines fine contours and balance of dark and light areas with a slight gaucherie. The scene must reflect some kind of toreador composition, although in frescoes the human figure normally faces the bull to vault over his horns or leaps down behind him.[22] Here it looks as though the bull has just tossed the man from behind so that he flies through the air. Without other fragments, interpretation is insecure—the man might be vaulting another bull—but there are views of comic lapses in the bullring in the Ripe period (V.48, 50).

The human figure wears striped boots as in a wall painting. The bull's horns are expressively sharp and striped along their length; its legs, reserved above the dark hooves, are striped with flesh folds. These stripes may be displaced upward from the hooves, which are striped in such frescoes as the Ramp House fragments at Mycenae. The fragment should be associated with two other fine bull fragments from Enkomi (III.4, 5).

4. Two fragments of an open krater with strap handles, to which perhaps six more fragments belong, show two bulls in procession against a background of zigzag lines and rayed rosettes. The animal on the right is in double outline, filled with scalloped edging and large spots; behind him is a pair of dark, sharp horns, possibly belonging to another animal turning his head back over his shoulder. On the other fragment is a cruder, stocky animal with short weak legs, dark hooves, and a dark wavy scallop along the lower edge of his belly; the upper body and front legs are filled with slashes; there are striped flesh folds above the hooves. The other fragments are enigmatic but suggest silhouetted human figures with striped legs playing bulls; one figure is below the bull's front legs, the other is overlapped against the animal.

5. Part of the shoulder of an open krater with vertical strap handles seems to show two bulls goring each other, one charging from the right with raised horns, one twisting low from the left to slash the underbelly of his opponent. A dark rounded bulk on the left may be the hindquarters of a third bull, suggesting that the goring pairs occurred twice on each side, but the state of the fragment makes all interpretation uncertain. The dark silhouetted forms are elegant and precise. These three sets of sherds (III.3, 4, and 5) are worth noticing for their free handling of active, even bloody, scenes, and for the early introduction of the open krater as a vehicle for imaginative painting.

6. The same narrative vigor and perhaps gross humor as on the Zeus Krater is displayed in the scenes of huge birds and chariots on an open krater with strap handles from Enkomi. This is the earliest chariot scene preserved on an open krater. The shape makes a slightly more constricted zone for painting than on the Zeus Krater, although the field is still broadly spread from the rim to the bands below the greatest diameter. From this time on the field of imagery narrows progressively into horizontal strips.

The krater has one large chariot on each side, speeding to the right over conventional patterns that may be interpreted as either rocks or waves. A bulge of obliquely veined rock hangs down from the upper frame, perhaps suggesting a closed valley in a rocky landscape—or perhaps it is merely an inheritance from Minoan tradition. Behind each chariot a huge bird pursues and attacks with open beak and flailing wings. The charioteers gesture in agitation and despair, on one side waving their arms in the air, on the other (more damaged) side whipping the team on to greater speed.[23] Within its conventional terms the picture is filled with originality; it suggests narrative or myth. The painter is evidently not reproducing a common genre scene but a specific incident. What the story may be, of a chariot chased by monstrous birds flying over the mountains, can only be guessed at; perhaps it was a version current in Cyprus of one of the Old Babylonian tales of the Anzu or thunderbird fiercely resisting divine capture,[24] the prototype of Sinbad and the Roc.

The thick, white-dotted outlines of the birds' oval bodies are characteristic of the Early period. On one side the outline is filled with a central "backbone" of chevrons, from which dark white-dotted "ribs" radiate, on the other with a more normal series of vertical strips enlivened with bars and spots. Their necks are long, like those of ostriches or bustards.[25] On the better-preserved side the wings are three unconnected rows of pinions rendered by bars; on the other, the more menacing bird has jagged batlike wings, and the front wing follows the chariot contour as though enveloping it in skin. The chariot bodies are odd: one is dark with a reserved panel filled with dotted scales on the box, the other

22. Evans, *Palace of Minos* III, 204 f.; A. Sakellariou, *Les Cachets minoens* (1958) 85-89; A. Ward, *Antiquity* 42 (1968) 117; O. Lendle, *Marburger Winckelmann-Programm* 1965, 30 f.; J. Younger, *AJA* 80 (1976) 125 f.

23. A. Furumark, *OpAth* 1 (1953) 61, believed a whip was never shown on Mycenaean vases, but always the *kentron*, or goad; however, a good whip is shown on the Knossos chariot fresco, S. Alexiou, *AA* 1964, 785 f., figs. 1, 4, and similar whips are represented in Egypt, for example, in the Tomb of Useramon, Thebes 131, J. Vercoutter, *L'Égypte et le monde Égéen Préhellénique* (1956) pl. LXII, no. 468. At least one ancient (Roman?) whip made of copper rings survives, Boston 18.1971.

24. The Anzu bird, the Akkadian version of the Sumerian Imdugud, has a variety of adventures in which he is pursued and pursues in turn. The tales include the theft of the tablets of fate from Enlil and their recovery by Ninurta, and the chained bird and the lord of Arata, which involves a chariot with pictures of vanquished enemies; T. Jacobsen, *The Treasure of Darkness* (1976) 132 f.

25. S. Benton, *JHS* 81 (1961) pl. 3.1-2.

has white overpainted arcs on the rear section, spots on the box, and accents on the wheel rim, spokes, and axle. The men are also in solid dark silhouette, with reserved faces and thick, emphatic eyes tilted on end. On the better side, their agitated hands, outspread fingers, bending bodies, and angled whip, the horses' feet clear off the ground and sprinting, the nervous outline of the rocks—all seem marks of a painter who has tried hard to invest his figures with emotion and his theme with drama.

Some of the later conventions are present here. The chariot is detached from the horses. The pole stay seems to project from the driver's belly and is ornamented for the first time with slim pendent triangles like leather flaps or tassels, which are decorative but do not support the pole. These are the pictorial painter's version of the leather thongs that lashed the stay and the brace, often converted on vases into a dripping arcade (see V.4). The rein-ring is framed by spirals and looks metallic. The horses' manes are dressed in neat, striped plumes, as though they were ornamented with ostrich feathers, an Egyptian fashion. Most Aegean horses sport such plumed manes, the hair not brushed loose. The legs are painted with reserved areas, presaging the reserved inner hind leg that is later a standard method for suggesting the paler color there. In front of the team a vertical ripple, emphasizing the border of the scene, is a loose version of later "rock pillars" or streams (III.16). A rock (or wave) beneath the team's bellies will later be hardened into an abstract or spiral form; above it, an elongated striped lozenge may offer a link between the seashell forms of the Palace Style and the later conventional type with rounded end.

The style of drawing illustrates a transition from Early I to Early II. It is more sober than the Zeus Krater, richer and firmer in ornament. The discipline of composition and interest in color contrast are new. The imaginative narrative shows that pictorial idiom, now well established, can be used to illustrate tales.

MARINE SCENES

The other vases belonging to this opening phase of the pictorial style have marine scenes derived from Minoan tradition. No attempt is made in this survey to describe the mass of octopus vases; they are omitted deliberately, being too numerous and having only marginal pictorial significance. However, two early octopus kraters are interesting in technique,[26] and the fragmentary Maroni fish vase certainly deserves wider recognition.

7. An amphoroid krater from Enkomi with a broad shoulder and short neck has a thick, white-spotted octopus displayed all over the decorative field, which is ornamented with fine palm designs. The animals are similar to those on

the Zeus Krater, perhaps from the same workshop, a sample of the kind of work done when narrative pictorial is not attempted. An amphoroid krater from Alalakh (III.8), of fine fabric, illustrates the same style with liberal white overpaint and provides an early example of export to the East from Cypriote workshops.

9. Three fragments from a large vase found at Maroni provide a fine example of how wall painting affects the pictorial style. Parts of five large fish, sharklike predators rather than dolphins, cover the greater part of the surface, scattered in torsional diving arrangement as on frescoes. The massive bodies are shaded to indicate color change, and the outlines are beautifully drawn. The fish have open, narrow mouths filled with sharp teeth; the eyes are round, as usual on fish, the jagged fins prominent, the tails forked. Contour and mass are suggested by dilute glaze. Double wavy lines floating from the jaws and fins suggest both the trailing weeds among which they feed, and water rippling with their passage. Several Minoan vases have this trait, a natural development from the "seascaped" Marine Style, but the Maroni vase does not fit conveniently in the Minoan style (cf. VII.J,K, 7).[27] On later fish vases this motion in water is omitted, like most other aspects of environment or landscape.

EARLY II

The uncertainty and looseness of the new Mycenaean pictorial style is soon overcome. The next phase is characterized by neat drawing and carefully balanced, almost rigid, compositions. The first four pieces still have originality and charm. It is symptomatic of the disorder in the study of pictorial painting, however, that the first two may as easily belong in the late thirteenth century as in the early fourteenth (see VI.2).

10. A fragment found at Kition bears part of the head, breast, and arm of a Minoan-looking woman. The head is in profile to the right while the body seems frontal. The hair is worn in long loose waves, as in Late Minoan frescoes, with a reserved space for the ear, like *"La Parisienne."* There is a marked disproportion of scale between the small head, with its deep but delicate chin, and the thick triangular neck, apparently a difficulty in transition from one viewpoint to the other. The lower neck is draped with three strands of

26. See the white-spotted octopus and bird fragments from Amman (LH II?), V. Hankey, *BSA* 62 (1967) 137, fig. 8, pl. 31 c.

27. D. Levi, *Annuario* 43-44 (1965-66) 336, figs. 30 a, b; *Festòs* (1976) pl. LXXIX; Evans, *Palace of Minos* IV, fig. 239; Popham, *DestrKnossos*, fig. 8.3; *Ergon* 1971, 223, fig. 272.

necklace, the bottom strand having round pendent beads. There may be a bracelet on the right wrist. Personal jewelry is not normally seen in vase painting, as it is in fresco, which makes the fragment seem even more like a copy from fresco.

Only the right breast and arm are preserved. A large round nipple is painted on the breast (cf. V.2, XII.18); the breast is not necessarily naked, for a faint line below the necklace may indicate a fine, transparent blouse as on the Miniature Frescoes at Knossos. The arm is drawn in a full boneless curve, held well out from the side, perhaps a dancing position. On the left is the vertical convention for an architectural facade, a checkerboard strip indicating ashlar masonry, closer indeed to fresco conventions than the striped partitions on the Window Krater (III.12). The fragment evidently belongs in the same artistic climate as the next two; how such strong apparent connections with Minoan painting were maintained in the absence of known frescoes on Cyprus is a present mystery. The possibility that this fragment is of very late date is in a way encouraging; instead of the fresco connection, it may reflect the imaginative revival of the Late period (XI.50).

11. The fine fragment from Kouklia (Palaipaphos) is by a different painter and is variously dated from Early to Pastoral. It may come from an open neckless krater like the Window Krater (III.12). A woman moves to the left in a curious position, with her head in profile left, her body frontal, her right knee lifted, and her right arm held out straight before her. A horizontal band of paint at waist level may indicate an architectural setting, perhaps the railing of a balcony, and a vertical line by her left leg may be the post.[28] The band has also been interpreted as a spear; from its tapered shape, she would be protecting a warrior behind her.

This lady wears the most elaborate version of Minoan costume to survive on pottery. The bodice is V-shaped, with ornamental sliced ovals on the border by the collar and a pattern of dashes on the border by the arm. The narrow belt is barred. The skirt swells out below the waist but still clings to the contours of hip and knee; it is sewn in V-shaped flounces that are alternately blank and spotted. This may be the closest a pot painter could come to the polychrome embroidery of fresco, and recalls the sharp diagonals on a fresco skirt at the Ramp House, Mycenae.[29] The conventions are all part of the pot painter's repertory. The dancing position in motion, held in by architectural framework, and the elaborate details of clothing suggest inspiration from a large-scale work in color. It is unlikely that the shoulder pattern represents wings.

12. The famous Window Krater from Kourion is a major curiosity in Mycenaean painting, although not entirely unparalleled. The same painter's hand is also detected on the next three pieces (see Chapter XIV, Painter 1). The large

open krater has vertical strap handles and a low offset rim. The picture fills only the upper half of the vase; each side has a chariot group between groups of human figures framed in stripes or empty striped boxes with fringed fillers. The background is almost blank. The artist is neat, organized, and accurate. He is the first to distinguish the two horses in each team, separating the heads and the well-jointed legs. The composition seems planned, perhaps from a sketch; the instinct for vertical frames, stopping the flow of action within the picture before the handles, also occurs on the next vase and is noticeable in the following period.

The "windows" are simple striped rectangles, more pattern than architecture. On side A there are four windows, set two and two in a block on the left. Each is filled with a short woman in a skirt striped to match the frame; the women face each other in pairs and seem to be talking. The "floor" between them slants haphazardly. The set of four squares on the right has dark, fringed segments of circles in the corners rather than figures. On side B there is one tall window on the left, containing a single slender lady who sniffs a lily; on the right are two tall windows with a woman in each, facing each other with raised hands. The design is thus unsymmetrical on both sides, interestingly askew.

The windows are usually interpreted as a simplified architectural facade. They derive at least in part from the conventional notations in fresco to indicate palaces or houses, either for ladies on balconies or for views of shrines and ceremonies. There are well-known examples earlier at Knossos, Thera, and Keos and later at Orchomenos, Tiryns (see XI.50) and Pylos.[30] Late Mycenaean larnakes also exhibit mourning women in patterned (often checkerboard) frames or panels or show them peering over the tops of windows.[31] A nearly contemporary Hittite version in ceramic relief appears on the Bitik vase.[32]

As so often on these Early vases, a narrative is suggested, but the point is not clear. Each chariot has the nor-

28. H. Catling, *AA* 1970, 26, n. 11, compares the Pylos sealing (C. Blegen, M. Rawson et al.; *Pylos* I [1966] 317, figs. 311.8, 312.6) but notes that the line may be caused by the ring's bezel being made in two pieces.

29. Cf. Lang, *Pylos* II, pls. 1, 32. Ramp House fresco skirt, W. Lamb, *BSA* 24 (1919-1921) 189 f., pl. VIII.9.

30. Evans, *Palace of Minos* I, 443 f., II, 600 f., III, 46 f.; S. Marinatos, *Thera* VI (1974) pl. 9; K. Abramovitz, *Hesperia* 49 (1980) 59-60; H. Bulle, *Orchomenos* I (1907) pl. 28; G. Rodenwaldt, *Fries des Megarons von Mykenai* (1921) 35 f.; W. Lamb, BSA 24 (1919-21) pl. VII; W. S. Smith, *Interconnections in the Ancient Near East* (1965) figs. 95-96; Lang, *Pylos* II, 131 f.

31. T. Spyropoulos, *AAA* 3 (1970) 191, figs. 9-13; *Connaissance des Arts* April 1971, 77 (soldier in checkerboard "window," *ibid.*, 76); S. Marinatos, *AAA* 3, 62, fig. 20.

32. T. Özgüç, *Anatolia* 2 (1957) 57; E. Akurgal, *The Hittites* (1962) pl. 14.

mal complement of two figures in spotted robes, departing slowly (the horses stand still on one side, move briskly ahead on the other) for a destination that is not hinted at because the teams are trapped in boxes: war? a hunt? the tomb? The ladies watch from their houses, raising their hands in subdued gestures of farewell (made antithetic and thus not directed at the chariot group), or sniffing flowers and talking. Scholars have thought of a farewell to soldiers, as on the Warrior Vase (XI.42), or of Homeric *teichoskopiai*, women watching their defenders from the walls, or of mourning, even of "an act of adoration" (of what, one wonders).[33] Of course, the scene may be pure genre, a sketch of how the two sexes spend their time, the women gossiping and the men driving about.

The heads are finely drawn, with aquiline profiles. The women's hair is dressed in spit curls over the brow and long, wavy tresses halfway down the back. The horizontal eye is a large oval pointed at both ends. The ear is suggested only by a curve in the hair; neither wall painters nor pot painters normally put it in. The hands are broken ovals, with one side fingers, the other side thumb. The dress is a conventional reduction of Minoan fresco costume; it was probably worn rarely on Cyprus or in Greece but persists in artistic convention. The women wear a close-fitting jacket with long sleeves and a rolled collar; the belt is a prominent roll; the horizontal stripes on the skirts partly represent embroidered flounces and partly match the frames. The tall women on side B have a willowy grace and authority that set them among the finest figures in Mycenaean painting; the short ones on side A are less attractive.[34] The preconceived image is partly spoiled by artificiality and the painter's inexperience.

The chariot groups on either side are badly smashed. Each dual chariot is covered in spotted hide; the down-curved end of the pole projects behind; the felloes of the four-spoked wheels are exceptionally solid. The horses' manes are dressed in separated plumes of triple sprays; the four ears, two eyes, and separate muzzles are clear for the first time. They bend their front knees to indicate a willing pace; the hind hooves are curiously elevated off the ground. The drawing of the men's profiles is better seen on III.13, by the same painter.

13. A large open krater from Pyla-Verghi may be slightly later than the Window Krater, illustrating the transition from experiment to established practice, perhaps about 1370–1360.

On each side two chariots move right against an uncluttered landscape consisting of an undulating strip of barred rock-pattern, which forms a road under the horses' feet. Similar striped rocks hang from the sky (cf. III.6). At the right end of each panel is a striped rock barrier from top to bottom like a pillar, the same as the frames on the Window Krater.[35] The composition is similarly closed, balanced, and rigid.

Early vases without filling ornaments in the field offered enough space for two chariots in each picture. Here, there is also a small figure of a nude man on each side, probably a huntsman or archer rather than an ingot bearer. On side A he is in the air between the two chariots; on side B he marches before the front team, presaging the *rhab-dophoroi* of the Ripe period (Chapter V). These men carry the same lightweight double-triangular frame as on III.2. Each has the same long legs, knobby knees, pointed toes, reserved face with ruffled hair, and stripe below the eye.

The chariots are large, with heavy-rimmed wheels (one six-spoked, two four-spoked) and very high boxes divided into three spotted sections. Possibly the third, extra section tries to show the front, but perspective is usually alien to the pictorial style. The down-curved pole-end sticks out behind. In front the pole curves up from near the bottom of the box but does not seem connected to the pole; the brace and stay are a thick striped ribbon decorated with hanging tassels. The horses are long-bodied, with short legs; their hooves are raised off the rocky road for clarity, as on III.12. Their male sex is indicated. The harness is engraved after firing, with barred strips for girth and neckstrap. This technique of incision is extremely rare.

Driver and passenger appear above the chariot box from the breast up, wearing softly striped robes. They have the aquiline profiles and large pointed oval eyes of the ladies in the windows, and their hair flows long down the back. The top of the hair is a row of jagged triangles, not real curls, perhaps hats; the driver on side B wears what seems to be a rolled striped fillet. On later vases odd hair effects may sometimes indicate a headband or hat meant to keep the hair out of the eyes while driving (III.14, 15).

This procession through the landscape is quieter than that on III.2 and 6, with less narrative interest but more deliberate grandeur. One cannot tell if it is a genre hunt or a magisterial procession; the only clue to such a still scene lies in the nude men and what they carry, at present an in-

33. A. Evans, *JHS* 21 (1901) 111; Furumark, *MP*, 445; T. B. L. Webster, *From Mycenae to Homer* (1958) 59; cf IX.13, 15.

34. Side A is so called because it is less damaged, but side B was probably painted first.

35. S. Benton, *JHS* 81 (1961) 49, suggested tentatively that such "veined rock" motifs might represent rivers, similar to widespread conventions in Egyptian painting, Assyrian reliefs, or even the column of Marcus Aurelius, but the rock motif is traditional in Aegean fresco and minor arts, while the rare rivers are sinuous; the Thera ship fresco clearly contrasts the round veined rocks on the river bank with the weed-rimmed water, S. Marinatos, *Thera* VI (1974) col. pl. 8.

soluble problem. The hooked ends of the frame on side A and the way it crosses the bearer's face seem to rule out the possibility that it is an ingot, and the interpretation that the "ingot" is destined for the occupants of the foremost chariot is far too precise or fantastic for so imprecise a scene.[36] The painting is interesting, is on a large scale, and has good contrasts of mass and space, and of texture in spots, stripes, solid, and blank areas—a true showpiece.

14. A fragment of krater from Enkomi preserves two heads, driver and passenger, to the right, in a very similar style and probably by the same painter as III.13. The driver again wears the fillet over his brow, with jagged hair above. The field is filled with rows of vertical dashes, in contrast to the blank grounds of the last two.

15. Alalakh yielded a fragment of another chariot krater by the same painter, with parts of two or three heads. The front head is very similar to those on the Window and Pyla kraters, with a striped fillet, jagged hat on hair profile above, large pointed eyes, and long tresses down the back. Behind, however, are wild arrangements of vertical, waving rippled lines sprouting from horizontal barred rectangles, very like the feathered "Philistine" headdress seen on sherds from Kos painted nearly two hundred years later (XII.29-31).

EARLY III

The Early III group has a greater variety of themes, including chariots, swordsmen, scenes with men and vases, scenes of homage, a fisherman, bulls, goats, and birds. The chariot kraters are characterized by the frequent use of neatly striped seashells as filling ornaments. The painters seem to have acquired *horror vacui* and are impelled to fill in blanks in the picture with any suitable arrangement of shells. The effect is not one of exuberance and confusion, as happens in the Middle period, but is neat and symmetrical without much imagination.[37]

CHARIOTS AND HUMAN FIGURES

16. An amphoroid krater from Maroni, now in New York, has a new tall, slender form. The neck is higher. The handles have metallic ribs and knobs. There are two chariots on each side, separated by a vertical striped rock barrier as on III.12 and 13. The drawing is elegant and conventional, without narrative interest. A kind of finicky mannerism has set in. The armless driver and passenger in each chariot wear standard spotted robes that match the chariot body. The hair is now short and curly, with the eye

set in it; the faces are beaked, the necks painted solid. The chariot body rides on very high four-spoked wheels; one is painted with large irregular spots as on a bull's hide. The horses' bodies are still too long, but their legs are in better proportion, though the affected curve of the front legs is annoying. The harness is richly rendered in white paint with ornamental bows drawn through the breastband and girth. The neat drawing and symmetrical composition recall group II, but the seashells underline a detectable shift toward purely decorative patterning. In all four chariot groups the shells occupy almost identical positions; they fill the space between the horses' legs and seem almost to be part of the harness between the reins and the brace. The separation of the chariots by vertical striped and banded rock patterns emphasizes the painter's disinterest in an internally coherent composition. Everything is static. A pointed rock between the tail and rump of one team seems particularly arbitrary and tasteless. This abstraction from observed image to pattern will increase. The neatly banded lower body and contraction of the picture field also look forward to the Middle period.

17. Two parts of a krater from Enkomi show a very similar style, less neat in execution and more interesting in iconography (Chapter XIV, Painter 2). It may be slightly later. Again there are two chariots on each side, with sparser seashells separating them and forming a row above the reins. The rocks no longer grow from top and bottom, but are shrunk to a small striped hillock under the bellies and between the teams; this motif continues for generations. The spotted robes of the pair in the chariot contrast with the heavier spots on the box on side A; on side B irregular marks on the box have spread both to the robes and to the air inside the wheels (cf. III.2, 20). The striped brace goes directly to the yoke, while the rein-guide is high up on the necks. The horses' manes are dressed in a crested fashion, perhaps with ostrich plumes tied in the hair.

On side A a slender nude figure stands behind the second chariot, the reserved face in profile and the dark body frontal. His right hand is on his hip, and he holds a small shallow bowl in the left, toward the chariot. This may be a phiale for libation if the chariot procession is ceremonial; if this is a genre view of aristocrats, the figure may be a cupbearer. It connects with similar scenes on III.21, 22, by the same painter.

18. The scheme is somewhat different on the De Clerq krater: on each side a single chariot moves left (the normal

---

36. Dikaios, *Enkomi*, 922.

37. Seashells on Amarna fragments, isolated in rows, sometimes picked out in white paint, W. Petrie, *Tell el Amarna* (1894) pls. 27.32-34, 28.63, 30.122, 125; *BMCat V* I.1, A993, fig. 262; by this criterion Early III must overlap the start of the Amarna period.

direction is right, although there are several exceptions) at a full gallop toward a robed human couple. Another robed figure and a tree are set behind each chariot. These act as framing devices, a substitute for striped rock barriers, and they are themselves framed by vertical rows of seashells bordered with U-pattern. The conventionally galloping horses are completely arrested by these barriers, and the human figures are isolated. The composition is thus triple, with quiet ends and a rushing center.

The chariot is lightweight and abbreviated. The horses' hindquarters are low, hind legs stretched out, to emphasize speed; their bellies scrape over a long rippling rock pattern, their manes are dressed in ostrich plumes. Seashells float over the reins, tassels dangle from the (disconnected) pole brace. The heads of driver and passenger are well drawn, with strong profiles, and smaller eyes than before. The passenger's neck is barred, as if he were wearing a torque necklace or a set of metal rings.

The human couples face each other over a plant that is really a lozenge-shaped seashell on a multiple stem. (Plants and flowers are a hallmark of the next period.) Both figures are apparently male, one with a helmet curled up in a crest over his brow and the other with long tresses down the back. The helmeted man has a torque neck. The robes are spotted to the waist, with embroidery indicated below by stripes or chevrons. Both figures are armless, and the bodies have an artificial curve in their antithetic scheme, like standard Mycenaean flowers. There is no positive indication of sex; from our distant point of view, the pairs might be couples saying farewell before war or a helmeted male and a stay-at-home robed wife, but the painter has not clarified the meaning. For a similar male hairstyle, see the next.

19. A fragment of an amphoroid krater from Minet el-Beida, the harbor of Ugarit, has similar but more dramatic robed figures. The style is slightly later; the bending trains of chevrons and dotted circles in the field are transitional to the Middle period, and the feet sink down through the framing bands, as they do so often later.

Two soldiers stand stiffly in profile to the left; on the right, on a much smaller scale, is the rump of a bull walking right. Perhaps he is tucked under the missing handle, and the soldiers are at the end of a chariot scene, or perhaps it is a foot procession to a sacrifice. Their long spotted robes are embroidered with two rows of dashes at midcalf level, while the double outlines reach the ground line. The costume suggests a peaceful situation, and the large swords in tasseled scabbards hanging at chest and waist should be a sign of officer rank in an ambassadorial or ceremonial scene. The baldrics are not drawn in (cf.

III.21). The swords are an unusual type with broad-horned handles, crescent pommels, and short tapered blades (cf. IV.50, 62). The hair is worn in long tresses, as on the last. The chinless profiles and high-set eyes are more common in the Middle period.

20. A similar, interesting scene of men in elaborate robes, with animals, appears on a series of nonjoining fragments that may come from Enkomi. The surviving pieces do not show a chariot, but other mysterious adjuncts suggest a sacrificial ceremony. On side A there are parts of three tall robed figures. The robes have embroidered bands (reserved wavy lines on dark) at waist and hem; as on the last, the double outlines touch the ground while the lower hem is raised inside to show the feet, which sink through the framing bands). The rest of the robe is neatly spotted. On side B there is one robed person on the right, with a confusing design behind him that might be the head of an animal lowered to the ground; it has no convincing parallels. Another robed person is seen on the second fragment of side B, with lines to the left that may represent a staff of office and the curved legs of an animal; a robed person walks toward an object with a curved bottom and flaring sides bending left, its interior filled with spots and crossed by diagonal lines ending in hooks. This has been interpreted with hesitation as an altar or a chair.

21. A famous fragment, known as the Sunshade Krater, unites several elements of the preceding pieces, with a chariot scene to the right by the same painter as III.17; there is a robed figure with sword, a nude attendant, and small vases in the air. It has been published extensively, sometimes identified as a mythological scene because the sunshade in the attendant's hand is misunderstood as a pickaxe poised for murder.

As on the previous fragments by Painter 2 (III.17), the chariot is painted with trefoil and irregular large spots like a bull's hide; there is a down-curved pole-end behind. The driver and passenger wear the usual spotted robes. The driver has arms now, bent at the elbow to grasp the reins at waist level. Pendent loops of striped rockwork hang from the upper border.

A tall, armless figure in a spotted robe paces behind the chariot; he is armless and wears a long sword on a baldric over his right shoulder; the sword has a crescent-shaped pommel and a tasseled scabbard, as on III.19. (The sword ought to hang behind his left hip but is set in front of his waist for clarity.) The striped hem is raised above the feet as on III.19 and 20. Like the passenger in the chariot, he is a massive figure, and even with too small a head he seems a princely or commanding warrior whose rank deserves the comfort of the sunshade held by the attendant behind him. In Egypt and the Near East this protection is usually reserved for kings;[38] at Mycenae later it also appears in normal chariot scenes (X.4). The tall, active attendant recalls the juxtaposition of lithe nude and static robed figures on the Zeus (III.2) and Pyla-Verghi (III.13) kraters, but there is new authority and pictorial cohesiveness in the procession here.

Five vases are scattered over the field, a multiple version of the shallow bowl held by the attendant on III.17. In front of the robed man's chest is a striped "sacral ewer" of LH III A:1 form; at the level of his knees, a striped chalice with slender stem of a type known in both fine stone and clay; toward the ground line between the robed man and attendant, a striped two-handled kylix of pre-Amarna Mycenaean shape; above it a little cup with one high-swung handle; higher, just under the sunshade, a conical rhyton or filler with loop handle on the rim. These are all reflections of real contemporary vases.[39] Because two are for pouring liquids and three are for drinking, the suggestion of ceremonial libation is strong. The ewer and the rhyton often, but not exclusively, have ceremonial functions; the chalice usually has. This painting encourages an idea that one function of chariot kraters is funerary, with illustrations of the ceremonial cortege to the tomb and of gifts like vases that are suitable for libation and offering (cf. III.23).[40] Such illustrations are relatively rare, although painted vases are used as background fillers on vases from Rhodes, Karpathos, Thera, and Crete (V.19, XII.17, 28).

22. A fragment that may be from the other side of the Sunshade Krater preserves the head and shoulders of a man in a spotted robe with a baldric over the right shoulder. A striped loop of rockwork hangs over his head. The rim of the chariot he follows is visible on the extreme right. Framing his head are the upper part of a spouted ewer on the left, a crosshatched hemispherical bowl with loop handle on the right. The form of the ewer occurs in both bronze and clay in Cyprus. One must imagine a near replica of the last scene, with slightly different vases, and near replicas scarcely exist in pictorial except on opposite sides of the same vase.

BULLS AND BULLS' HEADS

Three bull vases that may be placed in the latter part of the Early period are neither so dramatic as those of Early I nor so standardized as those of the Middle group.

23. An open krater from Enkomi in fragmentary condition had vertical strap handles and an uninterrupted decoration of facing bulls' heads. They carry double axes on shafts between their horns and are separated by horns

of consecration with double axes on shafts inside them. The motif is adopted from Minoan religious symbolism; there are slightly earlier fresco versions and contemporary ceramic versions in Crete.[41] The heads have exaggerated long oval eyes set vertically and framed loops on the muzzle; they look almost like octopods. The ears show that these were not intended as skulls, which are not used in Mycenaean painting or other media as funerary symbols; these are the painted counterparts of bull's-head rhyta, which maintain the (probably sacral) power of the living bull. Few pictorial vases have such a clear cult character (cf. V.102, 103) or so strong a connection to themes on painted coffins. However Minoan the imagery, the krater is not likely to be a Minoan import, on grounds of shape and design. The bulls' striped horns and the neat seashells separating the horns of consecration from the heads are characteristic of this phase of painting in Cyprus but not on the mainland. The composition is formal but decorative, with its balance of high and low, dark and light, mass and line (cf. IX.27, XII.27).

24. A fragment of amphoroid krater from Enkomi has two spotted bulls (or bull and cow) facing each other across a scalloped mound; there are rows of neat seashells in the field. The quiet heraldic scene is charming. The bulls' bodies are short, heavy, well proportioned; their hides are covered with large spots (the inner face of the hind leg is reserved); the faces are expressive, with full oval eyes, curled lips, pricked ears, and long sharp horns clicking against each other. The stillness of the scene suggests that it may derive from a cycle of bull episodes that are not all preserved to us; or it may be the precursor of the family scenes in Middle and Ripe, a prelude to mating (the tail held high by the left animal suits this); or it may be the start of a fight, immobilized by the mound. This looks like a rock, with a double undulating outline; the dotted circles inside it are not proper for rockwork, however; if they are not automatic, misplaced pattern, they may be intended to suggest a pile of hay in a meadow, or even a pile of manure. For comparable pictures of bulls and cows at leisure in a meadow, see IV.32, V.40, 41. For birds at mound nests, see IV.38.

38. Cf. J. Crouwel, *BSA* 68 (1973) 344.

39. On the "eastern" character and possible metallic fabric, Furumark, *MP*, 436, n. 1-3; Catling, *Bronzework*, 147 f.

40. Lorimer, *HM*, 48; E. Vermeule, *JHS* 85 (1965) 141; Benson, *HBM*, 20 f.; H. Catling, *AJA* 72 (1968) 45.

41. Evans, *Palace of Minos* II, 475; III, 40; IV, figs. 285, 287 b, c, 289 c; Furumark, *MP*, 247; G. Karo, *Greifen am Thron* (1959) fig. 67; M. Popham, *AAA* 3 (1970) 94; R. C. Bosanquet, *BSA* 8 (1901-1902) pl. 18; M. P. Nilsson, *The Minoan-Mycenaean Religion*² (1950) fig. 71.

25. A rim fragment of an open krater from Enkomi shows the rear of a dramatically positioned bull charging right. His body is covered with a large scale pattern, and the lower left leg is banded. The flowing tail hairs and spear of legs suggest high speed, the forward slant of the back perhaps indicates a scene of goring.

GOATS

26. The Maroni Goat Krater is one of the most handsome and sensitive of all pictorial documents, although it is worn on the surface. It is so much finer than other Mycenaean goat pictures that one may be justified in sensing a special link to wall paintings like the Thera antelopes, or to stonework like the Zakro goat-and-shrine rhyton.[42] Yet the composition is fully adapted for pottery with characteristic ceramic filling ornaments.

The krater is the new taller shape with metallic ribbed handles, like the Maroni chariot krater (III.16). On each side are three slender wild goats or antelopes in a rocky landscape. The two sides seem connected in narrative sequence. On side A the small herd is shown at peace. Center and left, two goats are painted haunch to haunch in a mannered heraldic stance, stretching their heads around over their backs to feed on the upper shoots of a tree growing between their hind legs. This Near Eastern motif is more common on Mycenaean ivories and gems than in painting (V.109, 110; VI.8, 9; IX.73, 74, 78; XI.83, 84). A third goat on the right stands sentinel with his bearded head raised, sniffing the wind among the rocks. On side B an alarm signal has been given, and all three goats begin to sprint right among the jagged rocks.

The mannered heraldry of A and the repeated frieze of B do not make the vase dull. The expressive outlines of the animals, the smooth stippling of their hides, the darker masses of tufted beard and forked scut, the understated clarity of interior markings on the breasts and legs combine decorative patterning with a talent for tone and shading. Sharp, striped rocks bend or hang from the upper border, more tastefully placed than on III.16; on A they form a defile through which the sentinel goat watches, on B they give an impression of the dangerous crags of their habitat. Low scalloped, striped rocks on the ground line are centered under the bellies in the quiet scene, but on the running side the rock under the middle goat slants to indicate the speed of his passage. Even the upright sprays of the conventional tree ripple with life. The drawing is dryer than on the slightly earlier polychrome sherd from Phylakopi;[43] there is the pervasive neatness of the period (and perhaps of Maroni workshops), but it preserves an

empathy with nature that will soon fade away. The quatrefoil rosettes and striped seashell fillers secure the date.

BIRDS
The bird motif, at least as an independent theme, is not nearly so common in Cyprus in the Early period as it will become in the next, in contrast with Crete and Greece (VII.5, 6). The small birds in trees on the W Krater (III.1) and the big round birds on the Zeus (III.2) and Roc (III.6) vases are parts of larger compositions. From Middle I on, the tendency will be to set a frieze of birds rather statically around the vase (IV.40–45).

27. The London-Manchester bird krater, consisting of two nonjoining fragments in two collections, originally had a continuous frieze of birds in the zone between the handles, without any filling ornament. The birds have long necks with bars, round eyes, and gooselike beaks, a faint derivative of the same, ultimately Minoan, tradition that inspired the Argos duck vase (VII.H). The body is smaller, filled with conventional barred triangles for feathers; the barred fringed wings lifted for flight are too small, too, but preserve a suggestion of action that will be discarded later in favor of pure ornament. There is a bird fragment (III.28) of the period in Ashdod.

TRANSITION

Two interesting vases from Cyprus seem to be drawn in a style transitional between the Early and Middle periods. The Homage Krater from Aradippo and the Fisherman sherd from Maroni both have narrative scenes, one of cult and the other of daily life. The surroundings begin to grow cluttered, and the friezes are narrow.

29. The Homage Krater, an open vase from Aradippo, has an ambitious religious scene on the principal side, whose message is slightly dimmed by the crudity of the figure drawing. It seems clear that the subject, men in procession to a seated divinity, was borrowed from or influenced by a composition in another medium. Precise fresco prototypes have not been preserved,[44] and the best

42. S. Marinatos, *Thera* IV (1971) col. pl. D; N. Platon, *Zakros* (1971) 164 f.; see also the basket vase with leaping goat, IX.77.

43. C. Edgar, *Excavations at Phylakopi* (1904) 145, 176. The many leaping goats from Thera are not usually comparable in quality; S. Marinatos, *Thera* VI, col. pl. 11.

44. Lang, *Pylos* II, 83 f., the goddess seated facing left, row of worshipers approaching from left; cf. Karageorghis, *AJA* 62 (1958) 386, n. 41,

analogues, the gold ring from Tiryns and the top of the Painted Stele from Mycenae (XI.43) are, of course, later. The procession of votaries or soldiers toward a seated goddess is a familiar one on Near Eastern cylinder seals and on Cypriote seals influenced by them, and the seated bronze goddesses of Enkomi, among other sites, are evidence enough for the familiarity of the iconography in Cyprus. The Homage Krater may not represent a regular scene of offering, but an occasion suggesting the blessing or transfer of strength from goddess to warriors.

The principal side shows two scenes, not quite identical. On the left two robed swordsmen and a spearman approach the goddess, on the back of whose throne a bird perches, looking toward the next scene; on the right are three spearmen, a smaller goddess, and no bird. Evidently the painter began the scene from the left and was cramped by the time he came around to the right. The left side has filling ornaments of dot-rosettes, which will be popular in the next phase,[45] and the robed figures are separated by narrow, flame-shaped tongues; on the right there is no space for dividers, except for loose trains of bars separating the goddess from the mortals. The dividers are even more pronounced on the Tiryns ring. On the fragmentary reverse side of the vase, a pair of nude un-armed men steps right toward a tree divider of chevrons (cf. III.18); then two isolated men, each within a panel made by chevron trees, step right, and on the far right a standing robed figure (the head is gone) faces left in front of a tongue-shaped divider. The filling ornaments are dot-rosettes, quirks, and trains of bars. There seems to be an increasing *horror vacui*, with new assortments of fillers, and this phenomenon, together with the lack of symmetry, heralds the new style of the Middle period.

Both types of male figures, robed and naked, are drawn in the style that has been developing in the early fourteenth century. The armless robed men are increasingly curved in outline (cf. III.18) as though to compensate for lack of anatomical decision; they have small heads, curly short hair, beaked noses, and long curved necks striped with horizontal "torque" bars. This feature, first seen on III.17, will have a long life in Mycenaean pictorial and revive strongly in the Late mainland style. (Chapters X–XI). These men wear long swords at the right hip, suspended from a baldric indicated by a simple stripe down the front of the neck. The scabbards are not tasseled. The nude men are a development of the long-legged gangling attendants of III.2, 13, 17, and 21; now the torso is not merely schematically contracted but, on side A, disappears altogether between collarbone and waist, where the obliquely held spear substitutes for flesh. This dissociation

of parts of the body is perhaps meant to clarify the figure, as though the painter feared that a spear carrier rendered in monochrome silhouette would seem to be pierced through by his weapon. In ivory, gold, or polychrome fresco, such problems are easily solved by relief planes, another indication that this scene is imitated from a different medium. On side B, where no spears are shown, there is a thin, curved chest line; the thinness and curve will be exaggerated in later vase paintings.

The dumpy little goddesses or queens on their thrones with footstools beneath their feet look like badly stuffed pillowcases in their spotted robes. The Mycenaean vase painter, unlike the seal carver, had little practice with seated figures. Their buttocks are lifted off the throne seats to keep the outline intact. The heads are small, eager, and beaky. The feet are omitted as on many robed figures (cf. III.2). One footstool is a dark bag, the other a more recognizable striped rectangle, without the handles shown on the Tiryns ring or the comparable ideogram on the Pylos tablets.[46] The thrones are simple three legged chairs with high backs; furniture is unpracticed in pictorial painting because normal themes do not demand it. See the man on a campstool, IX.11.1.

30. The Maroni Fisherman fragment is similar to the Homage Krater in general style. On the surviving fragment a nude silhouetted man walks right between tall, striped rock barriers characteristic of the Early period. He holds a fish by the tail in his left hand. The body is broad-shouldered, narrow-waisted, and long-legged; the chest is frontal and V-shaped. His kneecaps are sharply pointed, and the flat line of the foot well marked, as on the Homage Krater. The subject was unusual in Aegean painting before the two fresco panels of young fishermen were found on Thera, although the Maroni fisherman is clearly related in theme to the four fishermen of the Phylakopi stand, to the octopus fisher on a gem from Knossos, and to another Cretan gem on which a man holds large fish upright on a cord, a scene familiar in Egypt and analogous to the bunches

and below, XI.43. E. Porada, *AJA* 52 (1948) pl. IX.17, shows a comparable but demonic offering scene on a Cypriote cylinder seal.

45. Furumark, *MP*, FM 27.16 (LH III A:1); *BMCatV* I.1, A 991.

46. M. Ventris, J. Chadwick, *Documents in Mycenaean Greek*² (1975) 332, 346; S. Iakovides, *Perati* B (1970) 271 f.; Vandenabeele, Olivier, *Idéogrammes*, s.v. Tabourets, 161 f.

47. The two Thera fishermen, Marinatos, *Thera* VI, covers, pls. 85-88, col. pl. 6; *Kreta, Thera und das mykenische Hellas* (1976) pl. XXXIV. Octopus fisher gem, Knossos, Oxford CS 205; Evans, *Palace of Minos* I, fig. 497; IV, fig. 440, suppl. pl. 54 C; J. Boardman, *Greek Gems and Finger Rings* (1970) pl. 62. Fisherman with fish on string, *British Museum Catalogue of Gems* (1888) 80; G. Perrot, C. Chipiez, *Histoire de l'Art dans l'Antiquité* (1894) VI, 851, no. 4; *CMS*, VII.88. The Phylakopi

of corded *skombros*, or mackerel, on Thera.[47] The Maroni fisherman seems to be naked like the Thera youths, while the two Minoan fishermen wear kilts. This kind of genre illustration of ordinary activity is extremely rare in Mycenaean pictorial painting (hunting scenes are regarded as aristocratic, not pictures of daily life); the theme is Egyptian and Minoan, though the style is not. That such a vignette should spread from fresco and gem cutting into pottery seems natural, as for the Homage Krater. The Maroni vase evidently once presented a series of fishermen isolated in compartments by vertical, striped rock barriers, as the Phylakopi men are separated by ivy leaves. At least one of the Thera frescoes was made as a real panel that could be plugged into any wall, so there is an intriguing possibility that wall paintings could travel through the Aegean more easily than has been thought. With this piece and the Homage Krater, we are dealing with a school, or a painter, ambitious to try subjects outside the normal repertory.

31. Fragments from Hala Sultan Tekké of a once-beautiful scene of a bull jumper vaulting over the long flat back of a bull with deeply scalloped hide also look forward to the athletic vignettes of the next phase, like the archer on IV.16. The vaulter is in the act of somersaulting, not falling stupidly as in V.48 or posed miraculously in the air as on IX.18.1. His head hangs down, brushing the bull's back; his long arms are spread on the bull to propel his flight, and his exceptionally long legs, with sharply contoured knees, may be flipping up in the air, one on either side of the bull's back. The jumper's face is reserved, with a rounded chin and thick neck reminiscent of the ivory bull jumper at Knossos,[48] although the curious angle of flight seems to have displaced the eyebrow, which should be over the startled round eye, to the middle of the cheek. There is ambition and skill in this picture, which may with good fortune become still more complete.

fisher vase, C. C. Edgar in T. D. Atkinson, R. C. Bosanquet, et al., *Excavations at Phylakopi* (1904, *Journal of Hellenic Studies* Suppl. Paper 4) 123, fig. 95, pl. XXII; C. Zervos, *L'Art des Cyclades* (1957) figs. 312–315, and often elsewhere.

48. Evans, *Palace of Minos* III, figs. 296-297.

IV
CYPRUS AND THE EAST:
Middle Pictorial

Fewer vases of this period have been selected for discussion, because the types become more standard. More are listed in the catalogue, because the popularity of pictorial kraters evidently increased and the geographical distribution is broader. Pictorial vases were never really mass produced; they remain the finest and most ambitious Mycenaean pottery, made for a relatively limited but rich market. Even so, almost from the beginning there are noticeable signs of contentment with a formula that can be rapidly drawn and painted, as in the more common Mycenaean vases. The quality of both classes, in shape and fabric, remains high in the fourteenth century.

The Middle period begins at roughly the same time as the founding of the city of Amarna, about 1375-1370; as a stylistic phase it extends down close to 1300. In terms of mainland pottery as a whole, this is Late Helladic III A:2, a period when many centers of pottery making have developed and are not yet all alike; Mycenae and Berbati in the Argolid, Athens in central Greece, and Rhodes in the eastern Aegean are manufacturing centers especially to be noted. Once again the majority of pictorial kraters are found in Cyprus, and their circulation in the Levant is increasing.

The pottery of the Middle period in Cyprus is again divided into three phases, a pattern of development supported by the tomb contexts.

In the first phase the compositions, particularly chariot groups, acquire a standard form. They continue the neat drawing and balanced arrangement of the Early period, but the popular use of long-stemmed, highly stylized flowers against the background tends to distract from and overshadow the main image and to deprive it of vigor.

The blank spaces around the chariot, which earlier had often been filled with human figures or rows of shells or rocks, are transformed into a uniform meadow, which, ironically, has lost all power to suggest landscape. The same mannerisms are seen on nonpictorial vases. The seashell persists for a while as a subsidiary filler, and there are rows of parallel chevrons or chains of dashes, as on the Homage Krater (III.29). Bulls are becoming more popular too, and like the chariots, appear in a profusion of long-stemmed flowers.

In the second phase the filling ornaments become more abundant and varied, while the figure drawing tends to lose the neat outlines and even the awkward, diagrammatic, but recognizable proportions of earlier times. Some human figures of the Middle II period are the worst ever drawn (IV.12, 14). The rich floral and abstract designs in the field create a stifling atmosphere that contains the elements of its own rapid disintegration. Chariots tend to be swallowed up by the filling ornament around them, and usually there is only one group on each side, because the minor fillers have taken all the space. White paint is used on occasion to try to correct or clarify the tangle.

The third and final stage may betray signs of degeneration, but it also represents a genuine shift in style. Exuberant filling ornaments are still used, but they slowly die out. The long-stemmed flowers become more schematic than ever, then gradually give way to the new decorative motif of the whorl shell.[1] The shape of the amphoroid krater also undergoes certain changes: the neck becomes higher and the handles flat, discarding the older

---

1. Furumark, *MP*, FM 23.

metallic knobs and midribs and thus breaking the last faint link to the Palace Style. The reversion to emptier, clearer compositions, through distaste for Middle II excesses, permits once more a clarity of drawing and design that at times is almost like bas-relief (IV.49, 50). The new space brings back an interest in subsidiary human figures, which will continue in the Ripe phase.

MIDDLE I

CHARIOTS

1. An amphoroid krater from Enkomi, with two chariot groups on each side, shows unbroken development from the Early period. The chariots are well drawn, with wheels on massive rims and the axle set close to the rear of the box. The passenger is in a separate section; the pole projects at the rear of the floor to form a step, as on III.12, 13, 17, 21. The figures in the chariots have the beaked noses, large eyes, solid short curly hair, and massive bodies of the New York and Homage kraters (III.16, 29), with the exaggerated curve of the De Clercq couples (III.18). The vase's early shape and ribbed handles, and the seashells and interior stippling on the pole brace (as on the bodies of the Maroni goats, III.26), indicate an early date.

What makes this krater different, however, and brings it clearly into the Middle group, is the nature and spread of the filling ornament. Long-stemmed flowers with spiral leaves and a fat calyx on the stem isolate each chariot group even more abruptly than the rock barriers of the Early period. The remaining blanks, which might have set off the firm outlines of the main images, are instead cluttered with seashells (sketchier than before), vertical rows of horizontal strokes, groups of framed chevrons, U-pattern, and dotted circles (as on the Homage Krater, III.29) in the air of the wheels. The effect begins to be suffocating and distracts from such otherwise effective details as the plumed manes, the fetlocks, and the drivers' bunched fists. There is more interest in the ornamental character of the composition than in representation.

2. The fragments of an amphoroid krater from Cyprus show this tendency gone wild. It too has two chariots on each side; the plumed manes, pendent rocks, jagged rock barriers, seashells, and the driver's "torque" neck all connect it with the earlier idiom.

Interspersed in an almost desperate way with these elements are the new fillers—chevron groups with dotted borders, trains of dashes, and the big flower-palmette that scrapes the horses' bellies. Outlines and emphases are no longer respected—a rock design pierces the horses' necks,

extra circles clutter the spoke areas of the wheels, as though the spokes splayed at each end. Dashes are used to create a double contour, for example behind the charioteer's back or along the horses' backs and bellies, but the idea is better than the execution. If the background were eliminated, one would see some fine touches in the drawing, the horses' long nervous heads with indication of muzzle and nostril, the jointed raised forelegs, the fresco technique of whitening the inside of the hind leg, where in nature the hair grows paler. In drawing, though not composition, this piece is a definite advance on the New York krater (III.16).

3. A chariot krater from Enkomi is a fine illustration of the developing new style. Four strong chariots with heavy-rimmed wheels are driven right across a plain studded with palm trees. There is a special touch of naturalism about the groups of stately, bending palms, which are drawn partly behind the teams with some suggestion of depth. The pendent rocks above have taken on a U-shaped, ladder-striped form, neat and economical. The long-stemmed flowers are tucked out of the way under the handles. There are subsidiary striped ornaments like outlined boulders under the horses' bellies, however, columns of dashes or thin curved rocks between tails and legs, and extra motifs such as dotted circles inside the wheels, a palm knocked down by the passing wheel of one chariot, and lozenges and rosettes in the field. This is an expression by a skillful painter of the new desire to combine strong outlines with a dense background, using white for harness details in the old style.

BULLS

If few chariot kraters are assigned to the opening of the Middle period, it may be partly because of a new theme that immediately caught on as a popular fashion. There was one example of quiet bulls on a krater in the Early period (III.24); from now on, bulls in a meadow nearly rival chariots as a subject. Bulls are, of course, common in Cretan art, charging or standing, being brought in from the meadows or engaging in toreador games; they occur in fresco and stucco relief, on crystal and ivory, on stone vases, gems and sealstones, as full figures or isolated heads in sacral contexts (cf. III.23). In the Middle period, bulls usually appear isolated or in couples, rather statically, in a landscape setting.

4. On an amphoroid krater from Enkomi the handles are still ribbed and knobbed, and the picture zone is spacious. The panels are decorated with two bulls on one side and two cows(?) on the other. The bulls are stalking through scattered and blown long-stemmed flowers, more

suggestive of real trees or flowers than mere ornamental fillers. The flowers, palmette fans reminiscent of frescoes, also grow down from the upper border in diagonals or curves, replacing the older pendent rocks. The rocks persist on the second side to create a landscape, as on painted floors at Amarna.[2] The naturalistic setting is matched by the powerful and detailed rendering of the bulls in their full masculine pride. There seems to be an intentional contrast with the cows on the other side, whose bodies are rather clumsy, bloated, and elongated, though the filling patches representing spotted hide and the rippled hair of the tails are the same as on the bulls. There are enough filling ornaments but not too many: U-patterns, dotted circles, and large flower rosettes with dotted centers, as well as the striped patches of undulating rock on the cow side. The landscape is arranged in a disciplined way to frame the bulls but not obscure them, and certain flowers are overlapped by the bulls' bodies. This should be compared to the bull vases by the Papyrus Painter on Rhodes (XII.7, 8).

A suggestion of mild narrative accompanied by earthy humor may be detected in the relation of the two sides of the vase, as on the Maroni Goat Krater earlier (III.26), and, in a grander and more subtle way, on the Vapheio Cups. The bulls stand magnificently among the swaying flowers, staring to the right, as though they had caught sight or scent of an interesting possibility, while the cows on the other side stand tail to tail with heads turned back, gazing at each other with expressions of mild surprise and anticipation. In Cyprus, at least, the Mycenaean artist has a sense of humor.

BIRDS

Birds were rare in the Early period and not all of a type. They had some affinities to Minoan art, but the birds of the W, Zeus, Roc, and London-Manchester kraters were clearly not Cretan imports (III.1, 2, 6, 27). In the Middle period the bird begins to acquire a standard form; the painters have lost their uncertainty about how the body should be designed and filled. The new figure has a curved outline with heavy borders, usually divided into vertical bands within, decorated with various patterns like designs on embroidered textiles: U-patterns, dots, hatchings, parallel chevrons, in fact all the standard background filling ornaments of the contemporary chariot and bull compositions. The necks of these birds are long and curving, like swans or ostriches and are most often painted solid. Bird kraters generally have small decorative motifs in the field such as flowers and concentric segments.

6. An amphoroid krater from Enkomi has three birds facing right in a frieze on either side of the shoulder. The double outline of their bodies is already considerably removed from the original fresco prototype, where the form is brought out by contrasts of color or by polychrome handling. The vertical divisions of the birds' bodies are filled with "embroidery" ornaments: dashes, chevrons, and dotted circles. The birds cover almost all of the shoulder zone and are set so close together, beak to rump, that there is space for little filling ornament except a flower bud. One tall flower, concentric semicircles, and some U-patterns at the handle link this vase to others of the first phase. The birds' feet, where drawn in at all, are fleshy and have a pronounced curve like some contemporary mainland birds,[3] but the artist does not bother about consistency here: his "type" varies from bird to bird. The wings are so tightly folded along the body that they do not show as separate elements, in contrast to IV.7.

A vase so close to this that it must be by the same painter was found in a potter's storeroom at Mycenae (VIII.14). This is the first case that raises the question directly of where pictorial vases were made. Trade was brisk in both directions, copper and other resources attracting mainlanders to Cyprus from the sixteenth century on, and it is not difficult to imagine shiploads of vases, some pictorial, traveling in either direction. The outlines and inner decoration of the birds and the field ornaments on the Mycenae or "Petsas' Krater," belong to the same phase and hand as the Enkomi krater; both were probably made at Mycenae, although the workshop was not fully explored. The bird vases from Koukounara near Pylos (VIII.15-17) fall in the same general period, but the individual style is quite different.

7. A fragmentary amphoroid krater in New York belongs to the same group as the Enkomi and Mycenae vases, by a different painter. Mrs. Immerwahr has described well the "two plump, long-necked water birds moving to the right in a luxuriant floral setting liberally strewn with small filling ornaments" and has placed it in the Amarna period while sensing a close connection to the Palace Style. The birds have the same heavy outline and oval body as on IV.6, with the interior divided vertically and filled arbitrarily with lines, dashes, and spots. The heads and necks are painted solid, the eye is a large circle and dot, the beaks are open. One feature that recalls the earlier phase is the extended wing rising from the back, rendered almost like a fin with long pinions.

2. Perhaps an Aegean fresco of bulls in a meadow may still appear; the pictorial quality of the Vapheio cups or the Katsamba ivory pyxis might suggest a painter's tradition, as on the floors of the palace at Amarna; cf. E. Davis, *The Vapheio Cups and Aegean Gold and Silver Ware* (1977); W. F. Petrie, *Tell el Amarna* (1894) pls. III, IV; F. von Bissing, *Die Fussboden aus dem Palaste des Königs Amenophis IV* (1941); J. D. Pendlebury, *Tell el-Amarna* (1935) 126 f. Cf. XII.7-8.

3. VIII.15-17.

MIDDLE II

In this stage, the full development of the style, floral and abstract filling ornaments increase, and varieties of long-stemmed flowers are frequent. Chariot kraters, again the most common type, are almost choked with flowers. What space is left is dotted with smaller, more flexible fillers. There is usually a single chariot on each side, with the horses' feet tending to overlap the framing bands. The potter often banded the pot before handing it over to the painter, whose designs refused to be limited by the available space.

12. An amphoroid chariot krater from Enkomi has the earlier shape and ribbed handles, but the shoulder zone has narrowed and is more strictly framed by vertical bands at the ends. The composition has changed, and the drawing is disastrous. The chariot wheel is half below the base line, thus avoiding the problem of connecting the box to the axle. The box is lower and longer to accommodate three persons, a crowding that is more common in the next phases. In fact it is the wing that is extended, over empty air, not over the floor of the box. Of the three figures, only the driver's arms are fully drawn, and the way each hand holds two reins is an attention to detail unusual in such a bad picture. The two passengers are armless and strongly curved backward. The spots of chariot and robe have spilled upward on to the men's clearly defined necks like high collars; this takes the place of the tall "torque" necklaces of earlier vases (III.18, 29; see also IV.2, 13). The faces are in paler solid glaze, the hair and beard darker, accentuated with looping rows of white dots. The hair is dressed in an unusual fashion, short curls with one long tress like a pigtail hanging down below the shoulder. The noses are long and aquiline, and lips and chin are well indicated. The rear passenger's beard has slipped upward and runs straight across the face below the ear to the lips (cf. III.2, under-eye stripe).

Behind the chariot marches a footman who is a candidate for being the worst-drawn figure in Mycenaean art. This kind of marching groom now becomes more common and is to be distinguished from the accessory hunters and attendants of earlier vases (III.2, 13). The head is the same as the passengers', the body is rendered solid as earlier, but the arms are split open into frames filled with dashes (right), dashes and a forearm bone (left); the torso and legs are enlivened with crude white chevrons and dashes; a row of white spots emphasizes the contour of the chest and small of the back. The anatomy is extraordinarily crude and ill proportioned, with the stable right leg far shorter and thicker than the forward-swinging left leg. The hands (three fingers and a thumb) are empty. The horses' manes

are enriched with ostrich plumes (probably), as in Egypt; their bodies are enlivened with white dashes, curving rows of spots, and white harness.

The ground of the vase is filled with trains of crooked chevrons and typically Cypriote-Amarna interlocking quirks, which form lines above and below the reins. Tasseled triangles drip from the high-set brace, now a common feature. The large flower in front of the team is a cross between a lily and a palm with spear-shaped fruits.

14. A recently discovered fragment may belong near here in the sequence. It is broken in a way that makes it look more dramatic than it really was, and it has been published as possibly a mythological subject. In fact it is clearly one of these poorly drawn but vigorous attendants walking behind the chariot; the arms are split and striped, and the chest is filled with chevrons, the outer leg contours with spots, as on IV.12. The rendering of the eye, vertical in the head with a shape like a collapsing balloon, is reprehensible.

15. An amphoroid krater from an unknown site in Cyprus, in a private collection, is heavily and deceptively restored.[4] It has some archaisms common in the Early phase, like the reserved band and low ridge on the neck, but the style places it here. Again the drawing is bad but vigorous. On the first side the chariot team stands still; the feet are neatly on the band, the inner side of the hind leg reserved. The chariot wheel has quirk fillers; the spotted box is a curiously dismembered "dual" type with air between box and wing, perched on the top rim of the wheel instead of on the axle; the brace runs from the front rim of the box to the yoke, and the pole has disappeared, except as its rear projection may have become a dot-and-circle ornament.

The armless driver and passenger have large beaked noses, negligible chins, heavily outlined eyes. The groom standing behind is peculiar for his spotted upper body like a blouse; he is naked from the waist down. The loose gestures are like those in IV.14. The trails of chevrons, dashes, wavy lines, palmette stuffing under the horses' bellies, and row of seashells are all Middle-type fillers.

On the second side the team is represented in full gallop, a rare motif. Their curved, kneeless front legs recall III.16. The hind feet kicking up and knocking the wheel do not appear elsewhere, but one may compare the galloping single horses from Mycenae (IX.5, 7) or a team from Rhodes (XII.6). Chevrons, dotted circles, tall flowers and flower heads, lozenges, dashes, and a crosshatched chariot pole give the whole composition an air of looseness and confusion.

4. Restored areas include: side A, forelegs and heads of horses, the filling ornament next to them, the torso but not the head of the figure at the back of the chariot box, part of the box itself, the upper part of the attendant's body, head, arms, and the filling ornament around him; side B, the horses' heads, chariot box, and figures.

16. An exceptionally small amphoroid krater from Enkomi shows a progressive simplification of the style, with crude effects. The chariot moves right among sparser ornaments (chevrons, flowers); the wheel is on the ground line, the horses' legs sink through to the bottom band, and the archer(?) facing the team stands even farther below the picture frame. The spotted chariot wraps itself around the axle in dangerously shifting positions. The striped, short, curved chariot pole brace on side A is so drawn that it seems to pierce the horses' rumps and reappear as their genitals. The long-legged, slack-postured archer holds one of the hourglass shapes of the Early period (III.2, 13), but it is under his arm; the hands (a curl and a dash) in front of his chest are empty. On side B he is replaced by a stylized flower. The same tomb produced a second vase with archers and boxers (V.28).

18. A final illustration of this style is an amphoroid krater from Klavdhia. Against a ground almost solidly filled with vertical chevrons and U-patterns, one side has two confronted chariot groups with a groom between, the other a single chariot with two adults and a child in front. Both compositions are unique.

The groom between the facing teams has a spotted blouse as on IV.15; otherwise naked, he is one of the rare figures in Mycenaean art whose genitals are depicted. Nose and neck are outlined and reserved, but the face and hair are filled solid dark with a round eye in the middle. The hands, one of which is attached directly to the shoulder, have six fingers. In the chariot the driver leans well out of the box with the small passenger huddled close to him (forced forward by the framing band). Each has the same black face and reserved nose and neck but they are less bizarre.

The interesting scene on the other side of the vase, which is fragmentary and worn, may be the only one in the Middle period to deserve consideration as a possible illustration of mythology. Two adults stand side by side facing left, supporting between their short outstretched hands a little child whose arms are spread broadly in the air. Illustrations of daily life, such as parents taking their son for a drive in the chariot, are almost unknown in pictorial art, but so are heroic illustrations, the leave-taking or murder scene in an epic context, which later became so poignant in Homeric poetry. Is it Hektor saying farewell to Andromache and Astyanax? Or, by parallel with the composition on a Geometric sherd from Athens, is it Neoptolemos taking the child Astyanax from his mother to kill him? A mythological interpretation prompted by memories of Homer or the Epic Cycle demands, however, a belief that these famous episodes were already stock scenes in whatever poetry circulated in the mid-fourteenth century.[5]

BULLS

Bull scenes still hold second place to chariot scenes, but their numbers increase in the Middle II stage, and they have considerable vivacity. One (IV.32) has the feeling of a poetic landscape, in spite of its very sketchy drawing, and others make lively decorative use of the patched and dappled hides of the fresco tradition. This contrasts with the embroidery fillers of the Ripe period.

32. An amphoroid krater from Enkomi combines human figures with bulls, cows, and calves in a breeding scene, a naively endearing composition that recalls some of the ideas of the Vapheio cups. Side A has two cows, a calf, and two attendants. Side B has three leaping bulls and one small figure almost lost in the stampede.

On side A the cows are set in a rocky landscape made by a striped crag hanging from the upper border and semi-circular boulders on the ground. The air is filled with chevrons, lozenges, trains of dashes, and weak plants on spiral stems. The middle cow, looking back over her shoulder in surprise, is lifted clear of the rock under her belly because she has been gored in the rump by her calf. This kind of humorous prodding appears on a few other bull vases, both in Cyprus and on the mainland in the Ripe period (V.40, IX.19). Between this cow and the leader stands a long-legged attendant, patting the neck of the gored cow and grasping the tail of the one in front, whose muzzle is being caressed by another man. The attendants are drawn in the new way, with a thin, very curved torso rendered by a single line, without mass. The center one has a torque neck. The cows' full bodies are covered with dappled patches, tails lifted high (as so often in scenes of the prelude to mating); their well-drawn hooves are too large for the short legs, and wrinkles of hide are shown on their necks. The scene has a fine sense of composition, nearly unique in Mycenaean painting, and evokes something of the Cretan spirit of joyful genre, though stiffened and cluttered; the air of tranquil delicacy and friendliness between man and animal, with gentle humor, is special.

On side B, three massive bulls leap from left to right toward the waiting cows. The filling ornament is denser, mostly chevrons, seashells, and spiral plants. As on the other side the last figure is much smaller, suggesting that the painter may have worked by habit from right to left with-

5. Cf. C. Aldred, *Akhenaten* (1968) fig. 55, sketch from the tomb of Ahmose: Akhenaten and Nefertiti kissing in the chariot while Princess Meryt-Aten waves on the horses. On the difficulties of the Astyanax motif, see E. Brann, *AntK* 2 (1959) pl. 17.1, versus K. Fittschen, *Untersuchungen zum Beginn der Sagendarstellungen bei den Griechen* (1969) A.12, fig. 11. Vermeule is doubtful that any Mycenaean scenes are genuinely mythological or can be identified with any Homeric episode of the eighth century; Karageorghis is more open-minded.

out leaving enough space. This little bull is thus made to rear up and mount the rump of the bull ahead of him, whose tail streaming high over his back toward his horns suggests haste to reach a love-object. All the bulls are shown in almost a caricature of the flying gallop, and their scrota and pizzles are drawn with particular attention. The first and last bulls have stippled necks and large, energetic trefoil blobs on their bodies. Between the first two, a little figure who must be herding them toward the cows seems about to be knocked down in the rush. He is running forward and looking back, his outstretched arm caressing only chevrons.

The pleasant atmosphere and the loose, disorganized filling ornaments may suggest that the painter specialized in figure scenes in some other medium and had not yet adapted his skill to pot painting, where fillers play such an important role in the composition.

The other bull kraters of the period generally have two bulls on each side, facing each other or in line as a frieze. At first elaborate dapples are the rule, but occasionally more abstract lines and chevrons are substituted. One (IV.34) may show bulls fighting over a cow; another (IV.36), a bull and a cow nuzzling. On a fragment from Enkomi (IV.37) two black bulls gallop headlong, one after the other; there are white painted seashells on their hides.

BIRDS

Birds do not follow the same pattern of development as chariot and bull designs, for reasons noted above (at IV.6). There is less variety in composition, the outlines of the bodies are static and heavy, and because the surfaces of the bodies are filled with ornament, there are fewer fillers in the field. It is thus harder to be precise about dates. All the rest of the fourteenth-century birds are grouped here although, as in the case of bulls, the last few may be later.

38. An amphoroid krater from Maroni has a family scene handled in the rare white-on-black technique, like IV.12 and 37. On each side of the vase two long, fat water birds, probably swans, nuzzle each other over a tall mound nest on which their babies perch. The drawing is absolutely symmetrical but anatomically lifeless. The parents' bodies are divided into a number of vertical compartments; the chest and tail sections are broader, and there are up to four differently filled strips in the midsection. The fillers are cross-hatching, concentric arcs, U-pattern, chevrons, dashes, and stripes. There are flowers in the corners of the picture and dotted circles over the birds' necks. The heads conserve some of the long elegance of the older image, and the oval eye is better than before. The nest between the parents is built up tall, straight on one side and with spreading top corners on the other. The spotted baby birds

on top do not seem to be feeding, as they do on the later Leukandi pyxis (XI.91), which may depend on this kind of tradition, but simply to be enjoying their parents' protection. Concentric arcs cleverly suggest the interlaced straws or grasses of the nest. An agreeable, quiet picture.

On an amphoroid krater from Klavdhia (IV.39), with two vertically ornamented birds on each side in a frieze, the nest of IV.38 reappears as a rock-filled divider between the birds. Most bird scenes have no story to tell and easily become decorative "wallpaper" with repeated bodies in a frieze. Sometimes the monotony is broken by heads turning alternately forward and backward or by an introduced bird of another feather, like the little dark one with white outline who feeds under one handle of IV.40. This vase has birds so bloated as to engender feelings of repulsion rather than gourmet lust; the wings are a row of quirks or a thin streamer quite unable to lift the huge carcass, even if the wizened legs could kick off. On many bird kraters the animal is elongated to fill the space. A handsome solution occurs on IV.41; the frieze of birds is set off by a broad, handsome checkerboard belt filled with chevrons, an unusual design that will reappear in Late revivals of the Palace Style on the Greek mainland. In the bird frieze, the chevrons are converted into flowers, and the birds open their beaks to feed on them. A remnant of the extra lifted wing (cf. IV.6) now begins to look more like a plume attached to the back of the neck. The pictures in this group (IV.41-45) are not graceful like the older designs, but they have a handsome simplicity that looks forward to the Ripe period.

MARINE SCENES

These are surprisingly rare in Cyprus and the Near East in the later fourteenth century. Apparently the octopods and fish of the Cretan tradition were not as much in demand as chariots and bulls.

The best is the Hubbard amphoroid krater (IV.46) from an unknown site in Cyprus. The ten-tentacled polypods on each side are almost identical, the long tentacles becoming formal wavy lines that nearly meet under the handles. Chevrons join the top tentacles over the eyes. The body is mannered in the Cretan fashion, a broad upper part, tiny "waist," and bulbous pointed "snout." The painting is authoritative, and the whole vase extremely handsome in effect.

MIDDLE III

The final stage of the Middle style begins a dissolution of older practices and a shift toward a simpler, bolder idiom.

31

Exuberant filling ornaments begin to disappear; the whorl shell becomes popular. The higher neck and flat handles are good indications of a vase's place in the development.

CHARIOTS

General simplification and exaggerated awkwardness are typical. For the first time, chariot kraters are found on Rhodes (XII.3-6), and there are several in the Near East (IV.49, 50, 71-77). While some of the Rhodian examples may belong to a distinct school, at least one (48.1=XII.3) is by the same painter as three other vases from Cyprus and one from Ugarit (see Chapter XIV, Painter 10).

48. An amphoroid krater from Kourion shows one chariot moving left on each side. The ground is filled with schematic, desiccated flowers, rocks, lozenges, and good whorl shells. There is a striped ogival rock under the team's bellies. The passenger stands in the elongated wing; the box itself curves around the rim of the wheel, no longer related to the axle. The pole brace joins the pole high in front of the box, awkward but clearly defined. The figures have double-outlined bodies (cf. III.20), beaked profiles, and little hands without arms. The horses have shrunk at the chest and grown at the rump. Their rubbery front legs are drawn in a new way, solid to the curve of the knee, then split in two lines (cf. IV.29). The general elongation and mannerism recalls the affected drawing of III.16, in an earlier transitional phase; like that painter, this one on occasion uses elaborate white paint for the harness. This group can be very crude, but here the painting is neat and hard.

48.1(=XII.3). A krater from Ialysos by the same painter substitutes rosettes and whorl shells for the dry rocks, and dotted circles for the chains of lozenges above and below the reins. Altogether it is a freer and more interesting piece. The painter seems to have worked mainly in Cyprus, and the vase to be an export to Rhodes; there are two more from Rhodes in the same group (XII.4, 5). The details of chariot box, passengers, thick brace and split-legged horses with the inner surface of the hind leg reserved are much the same. The harness is white.

49. A complete amphoroid krater from Tel Dan in Israel is a very fine specimen with links to a number of vases from Cyprus, Rhodes, and Ugarit. The low concave neck and ridged handles make it relatively early; the abundant flower fillers connect it to the Middle II stage, but the split legs of the horses, the voluted rock or plant under the bellies, the striped pole brace with a sharp downward prong, and the legs sunk deep through the framing band look forward to the following group.

One team on each side moves left, which is rare in the East. The team's heads, lower legs, and tails are split apart, the inner face of the hind thigh reserved. Driver and passenger, in spotted robes, have well-drawn faces with round eyes and reserved ear-spaces, short curly hair; on one side they are both in the front section of the dual carriage, on the other side the passenger overlaps the chariot wing. The spotted box rests on the axle. The fillers are tall flowers growing upright on stems composed of blocks of vertical and horizontal stripes. The leaves form an arcade under which appear little flowers. There are tilted flowers near the wheels and handles, U-patterns under the reins and curved dashes over them, chevron groups with top hooks, quirks in the wheel space and under the tails, trefoil rosettes, and dotted circles. This profusion, in rather stiff design, is the end of the true Amarna style.

50. A most interesting amphoroid krater from Ugarit is very close to the Ialysos krater but has three figures in the chariot box (a tendency that increases in the Ripe period) and four robed men on the ground. As the laden chariot moves right, the three men facing it, perhaps the armed chiefs of the city, seem to greet it; one follows the chariot. These personages wear the long spotted robe with double border (cf. III.20) and barred hem at the bottom; on two of the figures small feet seem to be suggested. There are "plumed crowns" or feather bonnets on their heads as on the charioteers' (cf. III.14, 15), and long swords in tasseled scabbards hang across their breasts. With so many figures, this is an ambitious picture, but the stiff arrangement of the personalities in two groups and the lack of gesture rob the scene of explicit narrative. The team, with sway backs, thin bodies, and stiff, split legs, has begun to reach the silly stage. The headstall, bridle, and harness are richly picked out in white paint with zigzags and loops. The pole brace is the new heavy type, decorated with white zigzags attached to a triangular yoke-saddle in back of the withers, with hanging stripes that now may really represent leather thongs to cradle the pole. The fillers are broad palmetto flowers framing the scene, tilted flowers over the reins and under the box and tails, and one on its side under the bellies, as well as quirks and dotted circles.

Several more chariot kraters from Cyprus belong to this group.

51. On a krater from Enkomi there are three figures in the chariot box and two other nude, silhouetted figures facing the team, with their arms stretched forward as if in greeting. In the field there are diamonds and stylized long-stemmed flowers. This may be thirteenth century in date.

52. A fragment from Enkomi shows the team going right with a nervous toss of the head; a robed figure stands in front of it. The harness is white, with spots on the broad girth tied with looped ribbons, and the fillers are dashes above the reins and a lozenge chain beneath.

55. Another krater, known as the Sèvres amphora, shows a different facet of the period. On each side there is one chariot; the fillers are long-stemmed flowers, flower heads, quirks, and dotted circles. Side A has two little nude men, separated by a huge flower, in front of the team. These mannequins are oddly drawn: legs like stilts with a sharp triangular "knee" coming out the back, a short, fat torso mounted directly on the thighs without hips or waist, curled arms without hands, a square reserved patch for a face inside a dark shape that looks rather like a conical helmet with cheek-pieces or a stiff straw hat. However crudely rendered, hair could hardly make such a tall spike on top of the head. Bronze helmets of a comparable type are known in the Aegean even earlier.[6] Many attendants in chariot scenes have weapons, usually swords, but body armor is rare. There are four other famous examples from the East, two from Enkomi (one unpublished and V.113) and two from Ugarit (XIII.28, 29). The hunter of V.60 may also wear it. On the Greek mainland "after the Trojan War," the new pictorial style is often meticulous in such military details (see Chapter XI). On side B one helmeted "scout" is leading the team with a little spiral hand.

In general the Sèvres amphora illustrates a phase in which the people in the chariot are shorter in relation to the box, and the horses disproportionately long in heads and legs. There is a good deal of elaboration hanging down from the chariot pole brace, in this case dripping wavy lines, probably rendering the leather straps that attached the brace to the pole. Some vases in this group use triangles, which will be more fashionable in the next period. White paint, previously used to make a complicated harness stand out against the dark silhouetted horse bodies, is now used to decorate them in a continuous spiral. This happens at Mycenae later in a more emphatic style (X.1 and following). The pendent striped genitals of one team look like a similar decorative impulse.

56. Fragments of a chariot krater from Hala Sultan Tekké show the team on one side at a sprightly gallop, with hind legs on the lower framing band and front legs with split knees sharply bent, suggesting fast action. This sense of speed is increased by the way the triangles on the pole brace blow backward. It is most unusual for a Mycenaean painter to take into account the effect of environment or activity upon his forms; wind blowing, or the strain of muscles are elements of direct observation alien to the style until the twelfth century. The horses are well proportioned. The people in the chariot are drawn in a peculiar bold style, with long hair, rippling to the shoulder, forming a black mask over the face. The eye of the driver is reserved in two concentric semicircles, and a

narrow strip at the front of the chin and neck shows pale; the passenger behind has a slightly more open face.

Behind the chariot wheel is a form that looks very much like the head, crested bristles, and forepaws of a boar; a loose wild boar would not be expected like a carriage hound in this position, so one should think of a hunting dog. In the thirteenth century on the mainland there are several pictures of dogs running with carriages (X.1, 2; cf. XI.70-74), but in the East in the fourteenth century, this is a unique appearance.

The other side preserves part of the team and box, flower and quirk fillers, and a great swordsman facing the horses' heads with uplifted blade. His face is masked by hair to the nose, with lips and neck reserved. His robe is spotted, with a heavy dark border. The sword in his right hand has four sharp projections from the front of the hilt—not fingers, for the other hand, which can barely be made out flailing high in the air, has apparently only the usual thumb and one finger. The figure looks tall and menacing, as though trying to halt or challenge the chariot rather than hail it. This is a true vignette of Bronze Age military watchfulness.

62. An amphoroid krater from Enkomi has a team right on each side with tall flowers before and behind, flowers over and under the reins, and a small flower upside down behind the box; the "rock" under the bellies is now an antithetic spiral pattern outlined with dots. The style is sketchy but vivid. In one box are a driver and passenger with long thick faces, jagged hair, and a row of dots below the hair, conceivably representing hats or helmets. In the other box the driver is alone, and what looks like the hilt of a sword(?) is outlined with dots behind him. This is probably a displacement, for clarity, of the sword hung on the box rails of Egyptian chariots and on the chariots of the Shaft Grave stelae at Mycenae. The bottom of the box sags down to fill the top half of the wheel, resting on the axle. In front, a man on foot faces the chariot, the body in dark silhouette but the face and feet reserved. The arms and neck are outlined in dots. The man wears an odd conical helmet or hat with a forward curl on top; a jagged row of triangles bordered by dots down the back possibly represents a crest and leather flanges. The nude footman becomes more popular in the Ripe phase.

69. From Klavdhia comes an interesting fragment with the team right. The horses have a clear yoke-saddle and a white harness of ladder pattern rising in a V from which hang looped ribbons ending in arrow points; they have

6. S. Hood, *BSA* 47 (1952) 256, pls. 50-52; H. Hencken, *ProcPS* 18 (1952) 36; *The Earliest European Helmets* (1971); A. Snodgrass, *Early Greek Armour and Weapons* (1964) 3-4; J. Borchhardt, *Homerische Helme* (1972) pl. 37.

white spots around the eyes and along the muzzles. There are dots and crosses on the chariot, concentric ovals under the reins, and a tall flower and hanging flower in front of the team.

70. A chariot fragment from Kition may belong to this phase, though it is too small for certainty. It shows parts of the neck and head of a team with mane plumes, the head drawn partly in outline, perhaps with a bit fastening the three reins. Over the backs of the horses is a frieze of plump birds like partridges; beneath the reins is a row of leaves. This kind of filling ornament parallel to the reins is more common in the next phase, but the oddity of the birds in this position may suggest an earlier experimental stage. They can hardly be vultures joining a war campaign.

Fragments of chariot kraters of this period are also found in the Levant; apart from those already listed from Tel Dan (IV.49) and Ugarit (IV.50), they occur at Ain Shems, Amman, Tell el-Ajjul, Alalakh, and Sarepta.

73. From Amman come fragments of an amphoroid krater in a thin, hurried style. The driver, with a cap of dark hair, faces right, alone in the chariot, his body a curved, spotted triangle. There are quirks above the reins and flowers under them, flowers under the handles, and chevrons in the field. The chariot wheels are totally filled with spots; the horses' legs are very far down through the framing bands.

78. A pilgrim flask from Sarepta, near Tyre, in Lebanon has an unusual subject: a single horse or a team in a field of flowers on each side. Pilgrim flasks rarely carried pictorial images, because the shape was poorly suited for it: either a tondo on the front and back or an elongated figure on the narrow ends (XII.18) would be cramped. The flask, poorly preserved, is one of three from this Late

Bronze Age tomb, which contained a total of thirty-four Mycenaean vases, mostly III B; this and three others are of LH III A:2 date. Although the fillers are crude, the combination of flower, whorl shell, and train of dashes seems to set the date. On one side there may be a single horse, maneless, the body reserved and the outlines bordered by dots inside—an unusual design before the Ripe period on the mainland. On the other side one can make out the divided heads of the team, dark with applied white chevrons. The horses are small and lightweight, with winds blowing their manes in a meadow.

There are four other examples of single horses rather than teams on Mycenaean pottery in the East (VI.60, XII.42, XIII.28, 30).[7] The subject is more common on the Greek mainland, but this kind of pilgrim flask has Oriental and Cypriote prototypes; the Sarepta flask seems fairly certain to be an Eastern creation. Because of the spotted horse (a bull tradition) and the freedom of design, one may suppose that this vase was made in the East by an artist who had seen a chariot krater and wanted to use the theme differently.[8]

---

7. XII.42, XIII.28-29; cf. also XI.40. Although the III C material from Cyprus is only lightly touched on here (VI.59-62), see the Late horse from Sinda, VI.60.

8. Many pieces may have been omitted inadvertently from this chapter; an omission we regret is the group of five pictorial fragments given by the British Museum to the University of Otago in New Zealand. They are well published and illustrated by J. H. Betts and J. R. Green, "Some Levanto-Helladic Krater Fragments in the Otago Museum," *BICS* 11 (1964) 70 f., pls. 1-3. Four of them (nos. 1-4) have scraps of chariots and horses, with chevrons and loose spirals in the field; one (no. 5) has a pair of sketchy bulls with striped legs crossing one another, and a tri-curved arch under the belly of the right-hand bull. Since the authors suggest that their no. 2 is by the same hand as IV.29 (BM C346) and may even be from the other side of the same vase, it is possible that the whole set of fragments comes from Enkomi.

V
CYPRUS AND THE EAST:
Ripe Pictorial

THE USE OF THE TERM "RIPE" for pictorial vases made in the first two thirds of the thirteenth century (1300-1230) is not meant to suggest that these are better vases than before. There is no single phase when the vases are "best"; some of the Early ones are excellent, and many in the Middle phase. Ripe means, rather, that the mature Middle period has brought several stylistic mannerisms to the point where they must change or die out. Both trends can be followed.

By 1300 the chariot composition had been popular for over a century in the East and perhaps was beginning to lose its appeal or seem "old-fashioned" to Cypriote customers. Chariots are no longer the most common theme; in the East, at least, there are more bulls, and birds and fish begin to be painted on new vase shapes, as they were earlier on the mainland. There are just over two dozen chariot kraters, plus odd scraps, that seem to belong to the first half of the thirteenth century, and then chariots as subjects fade away. Although the absolute chronology of these pieces is not known precisely, of course, it is difficult to believe that any vase listed here could be put later than the third quarter of the thirteenth century, and most of them probably belong before 1250.

This withering of an old tradition does not occur on the Greek mainland, where chariot scenes had been rare before, but gain new popularity in a demonstrably mainland style toward the end of Late Helladic III B and emerge in an extraordinarily vigorous series of fragments in the twelfth century (see Chapters IX-XI). One difference may have been that thirteenth-century Greece witnessed a considerable revival of the art of fresco painting, as local kings ornamented their new palaces with scenes of war, hunting,

and processions; visits to these palaces may have stimulated vase painters to experiments with a more ambitious repertory. On Cyprus no frescoes are yet known from the Late Bronze Age, so this source of new iconography was denied to workshops established in the East. Natural processes of change, boredom, and even shifts in social and economic patterns may all have contributed to dissolving the chariot tradition.

Potting in the Ripe period develops those changes that were incipient at the end of the Middle period: the new taller, top-heavy amphoroid krater with flat handles is at first the rule, and slightly later comes the rival bell krater (see V.19), which competes with the older shape for perhaps two decades and then replaces it. The amphoroid krater had, in the course of its evolution, become quite an awkward, ugly shape (V.18, 23), while the bell krater offers a much simpler and more consistent relation between the picture field and the vase form.

The tendency to reduce and control filling ornaments, observed at the end of the Amarna period, is now carried further. Sometimes the ground is almost completely blank, sometimes the old flowers, straightened and simplified, persist under the handles; in one group, antithetic spirals under the teams' bellies replace the ogival rocks of the last phase. There are usually lines of ornament above and below the reins, commonly quirks, sometimes chains, N-, or U-patterns, which came into fashion in Middle III. The manner is often sparse and hard, with exaggerated or careless renderings of horse and man. A row of dripping triangles as an arcade from the brace becomes commonplace. The absence of filling ornaments leaves more space in the picture: this may be filled by lengthening the horses, by adding more passengers (three or four) to the chariot box, or very often, by reintroducing men on foot. These may be "grooms" holding a staff (*rhabdos*), or new and interesting specimens, like riders, boxers, belt-wrestlers, and archers. The robed personage wearing a sword is now rare. To compensate, fantastic figures like griffins and sphinxes enter the repertory; they had been used slightly earlier on the mainland in a different manner (VIII.30, 31).

RIPE I

CHARIOTS

Criteria for splitting these late chariot kraters into groups or phases are detectable but not entirely persuasive. There is a break of a kind around the time of the Suda Bay (Aptera) krater in Crete (V.19), but because the two krater forms overlap so considerably and the material is relatively limited, it seems best to present all the III B examples together in a stylistically coherent order that may correspond roughly to a chronological order.

1. An amphoroid krater from Cyprus, now in Rochester, New York, has a dry formality of style that suggests why customers got bored with chariot scenes. The old Middle flowers are tidied up and set in stiff rows in the handle zones; they do not interfere with the composition, except to fill in the blank in front of the horses, which is more commonly filled by "grooms." The horses' bodies are long, weak, and mannered; the hooves are on the lowest band. The heads of the two people in the chariot are in dark silhouette, which was unusual before. Only the circular eye shows, the hair and beard of earlier times are eliminated; there is a curious bulge at the back of the neck. The long drooping nose will become increasingly familiar. Each of the driver's hands turns into two reins. It is particularly interesting that the same artist painted a near-twin krater found at Nauplion in the Argolid (IX.1.1); both are close to V.2. The Rochester vase has three Cypriote signs painted on the lower body.[1]

2. On an amphoroid krater from Haghia Paraskevi near Nicosia, the main scene, a chariot with driver and passenger left, is framed by very formal flowers — almost unrecognizable hybrids of palm, papyrus, and lily — that are clearly thirteenth century in type. The only other fillers are the quirks above and below the reins and a single lozenge behind the chariot like a beauty mark. There are also lozenges on the rim.

On one side the flower has been converted into a curious "goddess" figure with upraised arms and spiral breasts.

This detail is often reproduced (sometimes reversed). The "goddess" wears a straight ankle-length tunic decorated with chevrons below the breasts and horizontal stripes from the waist down. The curled arms raised toward the cheeks have splayed fingers, a gesture sometimes found in figures and paintings of mourning women who tear their cheeks in grief.[2] The lady may have been created in sport through analogy to a voluted flower, and some scholars have taken her to be a meaningless filler in the scene, but a nearly identical fragment from Ugarit (V.3) shows that the scheme was not entirely accidental, *hapax*. Other occurrences of females waving good-bye or sorrowing at the departure of warriors are certain, and with the increased interest of this period in introducing new human types, there is nothing remarkable in a woman being among them. The Window Krater was a precedent (III.12), the Warrior Vase is an aftermath (XI.42). She seems more likely to be a woman than a goddess, however much she may approximate the type of goddess with upraised arms, or *psi*-figurines; one does not turn one's back on a goddess.

The chariot pole brace is thick as in Middle III. It hangs straight down, either a misunderstanding of the vertical member or because the pole is missing. The outlined faces of both passengers and the woman have the new exaggerated nose, which almost touches the chin while the mouth is ignored. The profiles are remarkable also for the flying forelocks, columnar or triangular necks with a bump in back, and flat skulls with scalloped hair. On the "goddess" side the team is at a terrific angle, with front legs on the upper band and hind legs on the lower.

3. On a fragment of a bell krater from Ugarit, parts of two figures, one with spiral breasts, are preserved, but no chariot. The figure on the right seems to have the same straight frontal stance and spiral breasts as the lady on V.2, though the arms are down in a loose curve, and the head is turned right. A strong line from temple to base of nose seems to indicate the jawbone; it is like the facial style of the robed male figures on a rhyton from Tiryns (IX.15), but in their case the line may be a beard. To the left of the lady is perhaps the chest and raised fist of a "boxer" (cf. V.28B and IX.18).

4. Another amphoroid krater from Cyprus, now in Rochester, reduces the conventional flower fillers even further to palms under the handles. The painter experiments with a surface enrichment of elaborate chains and triangles of dots that ripple from various parts of the harness to the ground like a bead curtain. The transformation of the re-

1. O. Masson, *BCH* 93 (1969) 172.
2. E. Vermeule, *JHS* 85 (1965) 128; S. Iakovides, *AJA* 70 (1966) 43; M. Andronikos, *Totenkult, Archaeologia Homerica* W (1968) 9 f.

lations between the pole brace, pole, leather connecting-straps, and box into pure decoration have been discussed in detail elsewhere.[3] The dissolved connections of vehicle parts had already begun in the last period (IV.49 and following), but here the pole brace springs up in a high arc to the level of the horses' upper necks, and the lower pole has risen to rump level. Both are insubstantially drawn with dotted lines. The leather straps, which should connect the two, are transferred to the pole as wavy-line triangles and hang to the ground. There is no connection between the axle and the pole. The effect was contrived after the horses were painted, as the chains drip across their bodies; it is a delicate, interesting effort to connect all the parts by tracery, perhaps a parallel instinct to the embroidery style of contemporary bull kraters.

The charioteer and passenger are in dark silhouette again, as on V.1; the reserved eye is larger, the hands on the reins have a thumb and finger and stretch high with animation, as though to indicate travel at full speed, although the team is stationary. The composition actually has a backward pull in the bent, lithe figure of the groom who precedes the chariot on each side, an excellent rendering for this phase of figure drawing. Though there is marked disproportion between the long muscular legs and the wizened arms and small head, there is genuine grace and movement in the backward sway, the downcast head, the legs, shown pushing off (rear) and receiving weight (front). This ornamental ballet is heightened by the slender wand, the *rhabdos*, which looks like an elongated finger in the right hand.

Between the team and the groom is a newly invented filler like a formal tree in section, a festooned circle supported on wavy lines, a lollipop. This does not seem to occur elsewhere.

5. An amphoroid krater from Enkomi is by a different, interesting painter of the same period; this has painted signs like V.1.[4] The horses are extremely elongated, one of the ways of filling space when filling ornaments go. The traditional flowers are now almost gone—there is one spray with concentric arcs for buds—and are replaced by antithetic spirals under the handles. This will be a recurrent motif in the next group. The chariot sides are no longer merely spotted but covered with dark dotted circles like a desiccation of older bull-hide markings (cf. III.21). The striped, curved pole runs right up the front of the box; it seems to be joined properly to the undercarriage but then tails away behind into the spirals in a whimsical flourish. Triangles, standard by now, hang from the pole brace, which doubles as reins; there is N-pattern above, where the reins should be. The driver and passenger have shrunk down inside the box so

that only their heads and angular shoulders show; the hair is interestingly treated as curls in joined loops, reminiscent of a much older style (cf. III.14), but the new pronged noses are evident. The horses' heads have gone even a stage beyond V.4, since the separate muzzles are beginning to merge and the eyes are still enlarged; when the muzzles join completely, the "facing head mirage" will begin.

The groom in front of the chariot on either side is a picturesque figure clad in a knee-length tunic, something new in pictorial costumes in III B.[5] It seems to appear first in the East and rapidly becomes the standard clothing in late Mycenaean frescoes and vase painting on the mainland in the thirteenth century. Perhaps Mycenaeans had worn this costume for a long time, but it made its way into art only when the older veneer of Minoan fashion finally disappeared.[6] The tunic has horizontal ripples across its surface and a deep fringed lower hem. The figure of the groom is graceless compared to the last, but such is always the case when clothes are worn, because outline substitutes for structure. He too holds the *rhabdos* high in his right hand.[7]

6. An amphoroid krater from Cyprus, now in Bonn, shows this stretched-out, whimsical, sparse style in a later phase. The horses are extremely long and sway-backed, legs well down through the framing bands, with quirk guilloches above and below and triangles hanging from the high arch of the reins. The horses' muzzles split below the large eye. There are fancy plumes but no ears on the crest. Where V.5 turned the chariot pole into a spiral for fun, this painter turns the spiral into a dotted circle with a tail (like a headless bird) under the handle (cf. V.14). The instinct seen on V.4, to connect distinct parts by ornamental tracery, is carried further: the driver and passenger, who raise their arms, are connected by triangles to suggest a third person between them. They have thin bodies, a stroke for a nose, hands like circles, and a curve from the head for a pigtail or helmet crest (cf. V.19), mannerisms that illustrate how the III B painters reduce traditional designs to fluent shorthand without considering the shapes of the original subjects.

3. V. Karageorghis, *BCH* 93 (1969) 165.

4. Painted signs on Mycenaean vases, from Cyprus and elsewhere: C. Schaeffer, *Missions en Chypre* (1936) 119 f.; Stubbings, *MycLevant*, 46 f.; O. Masson, *Minos* 5 (1957) 9 f.; *I° Congresso di Micenologia* (Rome, 1968) I, 417; *Archeologia Viva* 2 (1969) 149; J. Raison, *Les vases à inscriptions chypriotes peintes de l'âge mycénien* (1968); P. Åström, *OpAth* 9 (1969) 151 f.; E. Vermeule, *Kadmos* 5 (1960) 142; E. Vermeule and F. Wolsky, *Kadmos* 15 (1976) 61, n. 1; J. Crouwel, *BABesch* 47 (1972) 28-29.

5. *BCH* 83 (1959) 193 f.; Vermeule, *GBA*, pl. 35 B.

6. Lang, *Pylos* II, pls. M, N, 121-123; Vermeule, *JHS* 85 (1965) pl. 28.

7. Cf. C. Picard, *Journal des Savants* 1955, 103.

The formal palm, filled with chevrons and arcs, in front of the teams has reached a hybrid stage, with the spray of upper leaves turned into opposed tongues like the horns of pictorial altars (VIII.33, XIII.29).

The next group of chariot scenes, several by the same painter, is characterized by antithetic spirals under the horses' bellies, a peculiar and easily recognized facial style, and some imagination.

7. On a fragmentary krater from Enkomi, the horses are contracted so that two grooms can march before them. The filling ornament is restricted to the chariot area: dense rows of chains, reins, and triangles above the team, lozenges in the wheels, and a large antithetic spiral pattern connected by chevrons below the bellies. The peculiar chariot box seems to be split in three parts, somewhat in the manner of the box on the Pierides krater (IV.15), but in fact it is a single long box with a vertical panel filled by wavy lines beneath each of the three figures above the railing. Only the different ornaments, crosses (usually reserved for stag bodies) on the men's robes and zigzag waves on the box make it clear that we do not see the whole figure, as though in transparent cross-section, standing on the floor of the box. That development will take place in later mainland painting (XI.1 and following, VI.52). The rim line of the box continues across to the horses' rumps, with the decorated pole stay springing from the stomach of the driver, the curved vertical member of the brace dissociated and hanging down like an extra tail, the pole itself another thin line from the axle of the wheel to the rear hock of the horse. Lozenges in the wheels deny the expected space. After this the further disintegration of the chariot is predictable; it reaches one of its ultimate forms on the contemporary chariot krater found at Corinth (IX.1), where the first two figures are shown down to the feet, standing on the pole stay.

Although the vase is quite badly broken, it seems as though the horses' muzzles may now be joined solid, so that the right eye of each horse, side by side in a dark mass, suggests a single facing horse. Four ears, distinct from the blowing mane locks, correct the impression quickly.

The grooms have the long-legged slenderness of V.1 and V.4, and in the schematic face the nose descends in a long line to the base of the throat. This mannerism will be imitated by others, sometimes with the nose connected by extra lines to the rest of the face and neck: see V.14, 19. The grooms seem to twirl their slender staffs like batons, as on the next piece.

8. An amphoroid krater from Ugarit by the same painter has become famous for Professor Schaeffer's discussion of it as an illustration of Ugaritic mythology. The neat horses with double hooves, the three people

in the chariot box on the major side (one pushed out to sit on the dangling pole brace, as though a solid sapling could conceal half a body), the flat skulls and long dripping noses, the slender groom, the applied white harness so rare in this phase, the condensed fillers and showy palmette spiral combine to make this one of the finest vases in a period of distorted and attractive images.

The "mythology" is centered on the bird who replaces the more standard groom on one side, facing the team. The bird, partly under the handle (cf. V.14), is dark, footless, with one folded wing and a lifted wing added as a kind of crest (cf. IV.41), a long ostrich neck, and curved beak.

A chain of quirks, like those so often used above reins in this period, seems to tie the bird to the ground, so that Professor Schaeffer associated him with old stories of the capture of a giant bird in the mountains who is thus chained and tamed (cf. the Anzu bird, III.6). Birds under handles become increasingly common; best known are the "geese" of the Warrior Vase (XI.42). The spray-with-lozenge rising here between wing and neck is also seen at Enkomi and in modified forms on Rhodes (V.61, XII.12-14); plain or dotted lozenges, later on, are especially characteristic of Ugaritic pictorial.

In pictorial painting, a juxtaposition of images may suggest narrative ideas, but the narrative itself is never made explicit through action. To be sure of the story, one would have preferred to see foot soldiers attacking the bird. The dissociation between bird and groom on a krater from Minet el-Beida (V.21) and the birds dividing boxers (V.32) argue against this being an explicit illustration of myth, though the painter may have remembered childhood tales while making his static design.

13. An ambitious krater from Enkomi has three grooms in each picture, two before and one behind, forming an impressive cortège or military expedition. Parts of the drawing are terrible, such as the broken knees on the horses' front legs to suggest spirited prancing, but the slender-bodied grooms on long stilt legs are the most elegant in III B painting. They typify the new convention, with the torso arched backward in a single curve from waist to elbow, extremely long legs with muscular thighs, bony knees, and slender calves, and hands reduced in scale and function until eventually they become mere fingers springing from the chest.

The headdress or hair of the charioteers and grooms is rendered in a series of outlined circles, forming a cap with ruffled edges across the top of the skull. If this is meant as a feathered headdress, it is fairly conventional, not like the curious fork-shaped feather crowns from Kos in LH III C (XII.29-32), yet it is different from the usual representation of hair. In the fourteenth century something similar had appeared at Enkomi and Alalakh (III.14, 15) and, less clear, perhaps curls bound by a fillet, on the Pyla-Verghi krater (III.13) and the Middle krater from Ugarit (IV.50). Since a new, almost anthropologically descriptive interest in armor and helmets entered the pictorial style in the Amarna Age (cf. IV.21, 50, 55), it would not be totally surprising to find the feather headdress here already; it will be notorious among the Sea Peoples in a generation.[8] Or it may be a simple wool cap or beret like those the Archaic Cypriotes delighted in.

14. An amphoroid krater thought to come from Cyprus, now in Boston, is one of the latest intact chariot vases. It exhibits some new grotesquerie and marks the first appearance of a new subsidiary subject, belt-wrestling. This is part of the late interest in various types of pedestrians, such as archers, boxers, and spearsmen (V.28B and following). Many comments have been offered on the "degeneration" of this vase, particularly because the chariot wheels are not round but oval and the faces are so oddly drawn. The Middle period flower motif is conserved as a filler, now springing out of the horses' backs; the pole stay drips handsome rippled triangles, the pole brace drops two vertical members to the ground, and there is no pole; the field fillers are opposed U-patterns repeated in the "horseshoes" around the wrestlers' waists. Under each handle hovers a long, awkward bird with short neck, curved beak, folded wing, whalelike tail, and semicircles for feet. The hard consistency of style on this vase makes the total effect more impressive than the awkward details might suggest. A comparison with the queerer contemporary krater from Corinth (IX.1) suggests that all tradition is not yet discarded in Cypriote ateliers.

Belt-wrestling is an Oriental sport that one might expect to find sporadically in the Levantine Aegean.[9] The two opponents are strapped together around the middle and try to pull each other off balance. Perhaps the massive angle of the projecting buttocks here is meant to indicate the strain on the hips and legs, but the arm gestures are those of sparring boxers (V.28B-33). The convention of drawing the hand as a curl with an opposed thumb began in the early fourteenth century with the Window Krater (III.12); it is now standard. The faces are queer because of the bent line joining the nose to the shoulder, apparently meant to serve as the profile of the lips and front of the neck, but confusing because the face is glazed solid and the neck is in outline. The effect is like a runny nose, but might conceivably represent a face protector. Similar awkwardness marks the krater from Suda Bay, Crete (V.19).

15. An interesting group of fragments from Hala Sultan Tekké suggests, by the antithetic spirals festooned with rock pattern, that it belongs in this series; the two

passengers in the chariot and the groom have faces very like those on V.14, and the robes filled dark with a reserved border connect it to V.17. There are lozenges and dotted circles in the field. The groom is the usual long-legged fellow with feet sunk to the lower band; the long-nosed face with front line from chin to shoulder mirrors the faces on the Boston krater. The passengers are squat in the box, which is covered with an unusual pattern of stripes bordered by loops, a more typical filling for birds. The spokes are drawn for both wheels, as on V.14, as though they showed through from the far side. In spite of the grotesqueness characteristic of this whole period, what survives of the drawing is rich and neat.

16. A very fragmentary amphoroid krater from Stephania, Cyprus, now in Sydney, Australia,[10] with two "grooms" in front of each horse, is especially interesting for the sherd that preserves the dark silhouette of a Naue Type II sword worn at the left hip.[11] A baldric does not show; perhaps these late Aegean swords with their European(?) connections were carried in waist scabbards (but see V.26). It is clearly a change from the long swords worn by robed figures in the Middle period (IV.50) and an added indication that the "grooms" of these vases are not there merely to take care of the horses,[12] that they may on occasion be infantry accompanying the charioteers to war. The whorl shell filler connects this to V.13 and to the Middle period (IV.28, 48, 72), but the figures of the "grooms" assure it a late place in the sequence. There are elegant seven-petaled rosettes as groom-dividers.

17. An amphoroid krater from Cyprus, now in Amsterdam, is like a bridge between the Enkomi groom krater (V.5) and the Suda Bay bell krater (V.19). Again new military habits are represented. The ground is empty of fillers, except for the wavy triangles hanging from the pole stay and thin antithetic spirals under each handle. Three people ride in the chariot, with a groom behind on one side and a horseman in front on both sides. The figures in the chariot are exceptionally well rendered in dark silhouette with a reserved outline, as on the Suda Bay krater and in many thirteenth-century frescoes, a rarity in

8. Cf. XII.29-32; K. Galling, in Schaeffer, *Ugaritica* VI (1969) 247 f.; E. Porada in P. Dikaios, *Enkomi* (1969-71) 801 f.; N. K. Sandars, *The Sea Peoples* (1978) 117-137.

9. C. Gordon, "Belt-Wrestling in the Bible World," *Hebrew Union College Annual* 23/1 (1950-51) 131 f., pls. 1-5. We owe this reference to E. Porada.

10. Illustrated by kind permission of the late Professor J. Stewart.

11. Cf. H. Catling, *Antiquity* 35 (1961) 115; *ProcPS* 22 (1956) 102 f.; *Bronzework*, pl. 12; N. K. Sandars, *AJA* 67 (1963) 117; J. Lagarce, in Schaeffer, *Ugaritica* VI, 349 f.; *Syria* 45 (1968) 271; and in Schaeffer, *Alasia* I (1971) 381; J. Bouzek, *ibid.*, 433; N. K. Sandars, *The Sea Peoples* (1978) 89.

12. But see V.21.

vase painting before the Transitional period about 1200 (Chapter X). The hairstyle, a mass of neck-length curls, is new. The "groom" is quite standard, if unusually thin and tall, except that he wears a long sword at the vest, horizontally under his bent elbow.

The two horse riders in front of the chariots are early Aegean examples of an iconography that was fairly well established in the Near East and Egypt by the thirteenth century. The practice of riding is documented from at least the early second millennium onward, when the skills of the seminomadic tribes of southern Iraq, who rode both onagers and horses, spread into Mesopotamia and eventually to the Levant and Egypt. The reliefs depicting the critical Battle of Kadesh of 1286 B.c. show at least four mounted Egyptians and as many as seven mounted Asiatics and Hittites. Both armies apparently used the riders as lightly armed mobile scouts. There is one other Mycenaean picture of riders, from Ugarit (V.26), and slightly later terracotta riders at Mycenae, but riding as a general technique or a military asset did not, apparently, develop in any widespread way on the Greek mainland until after the Bronze Age.[13]

In this early picture all the horses are emphatically male. The ridden horses are shown as much smaller than the teams pulling the chariots; this is surely a problem of space and the relation between horse and rider, not a real distinction. There is no reason to call any Aegean horses ponies, and no practical purpose for horse breeders to develop a special mount. Chariot horses themselves were likely to be small, for quick maneuvering.[14] The painter must contract the horse in order to get the rider's head even with those of the men in the chariot, near the top of the picture. On one side the ridden horse is almost too low, and a pyramidal crosshatched cap was added to the rider's head to raise it. The painter, working within the conventions or imaginative limitations of his chariot tradition, did not pause to consider the true relationship of man and horse, but simply set the rider's torso on the horse's back, as he would on a chariot box. Both riders are distinguished from the dark charioteers by spotted robes. The man in a cap sits better than the bald one; both hold the reins short and tight. The painter has drawn chariot reins, four for each horse, high to the poll and low from the bit. For the suggestion that ridden horses in thirteenth-century pictures may sometimes be teams cut loose from damaged chariots, see V.26, but the painter probably really intended single ridden horses here and simply neglected to adapt the harness he was so used to drawing. However awkward the details may be, the vase offers one of those rare glimpses of adventurous life in the Late Bronze Age, which the pictorial style can occasionally contribute to enrich archaeology and history.

18. An amphoroid krater from Enkomi is another famous piece of the Ripe period. Formal tall flowers, flower heads, and whorl shells recall the Middle III period; the spirals under the horses' bellies and the dripping ornaments fastened through an elaborate yoke from the reins place it in early III B. Intentionally or no, this is one of the funniest vases in the Cypriote pictorial style, as a huge beaked fish swims out from beneath each handle to pursue the pair of travelers in the chariot; on one side the fish has leaped high enough to prod the rear man in the back, and the habitual backward bend of bodies in this phase is given a cause at last. The bend is accentuated by a wide belt of pale spotted cloth bisecting the black silhouetted figures from chest to hip to form a parti-colored tunic. On one side the passenger clutches the charioteer, on the other he gesticulates in horror.

The fish itself is not the usual pictorial type but a special creature. The stocky, undulating body with four fins and a straight tail resembles a manatee; the large round eye and pointed striped beak like a toucan's suggest a deliberate hybrid, such as the later *ketoi* in Homer, who sport about Poseidon's gold chariot wheels as he drives across the waves (*Iliad* XIII.27). The *ketos* is more usually compounded with a dog's or lion's head, something that could bite, fanged rather than beaked; it appears so already in Hittite art;[15] from the beginning of Greek literature the *ketos* is feared because he can eat sailors: something more than a shark or tuna, less than an underwater dragon. The beak looks powerful enough to inflict substantial damage; its closed striped form is more congenial to this vase painter's repertory than the open teeth so common later.

Because the painter has automatically employed flowers and whorl shells as fillers, the setting for the scene is not specific. The chariot passengers are not necessarily driving along the shore; the painter may have thought that a fish looked better under the handles than a bird, and then

13. We owe much to Mrs. Littauer for her discussion of V.17 and V.26 (see Appendix). For early riding, see P. R. S. Moorey, "Horse-riding in Iraq before the Kassite Period," *Iraq* 23 (1970) 36 f.; A. R. Schulman, "Egyptian Representations of Horsemen and Riding in the New Kingdom," *JNES* 16 (1957) 263 f.; J. K. Anderson, *Ancient Greek Horsemanship* (1961); M. A. Littauer, "Bits and Pieces," *Antiquity* 43 (1969) 289 f.; D. Levi, *Studies Presented to David M. Robinson* I (1951) pl. 4 a-c; M. S. F. Hood, *BSA* 48 (1953) 84 f.; E. French, *BSA* 66 (1971) 164; H. Catling, *RDAC* 1974, 95 f.; Vermeule is grateful to Timothy Kendall for his *Warfare and Military Matters in the Nuzi Tablets* (Ph.D. diss., Brandeis University, 1974).

14. Mrs. Littauer notes that the horses buried in the Iron Age tombs at Salamis were, although small by present standards, in fact rather large for their period; cf. P. Ducos in V. Karageorghis, *Excavations in the Necropolis of Salamis* I (1967) 154 f.

15. E. Vermeule and S. Chapman, *AJA* 75 (1971) 288, n. 10; D. G. Hogarth, *Hittite Seals* (1920) nos. 155, 161; K. T. Shepard, *The Fish-Tailed Monster* (1940) 8.

in good humor may have made his picture a decorative joke without necessarily thinking of myth.[16]

19. A bell krater found at Aptera, Suda Bay, Crete, is an oddity from several points of view, and perhaps should be discussed in another chapter, except that it fits into the Levantine series and not in the Greek mainland or Cretan pictorial style. Chariot scenes are known on Cretan frescoes and sarcophagi,[17] and surely other chariot vases will be found in Crete, perhaps again around Kydonia, which was such a flourishing port in Late Minoan III B. For the moment, however, there is only one other chariot composition on a vase before the III C period, and that is an endearingly miserable panel on a pyxis by a local Kydonia painter who otherwise specialized in birds and made the extraordinary lyre-player pyxis.[18] The Late Minoan style of those pieces is perfectly clear and has little to do with the Suda Bay vase. Until its further connections become more certain through excavation, its style seems perfectly at home near the last two vases.

The Suda Bay krater is an early form of bell krater, perhaps among the first with a chariot scene, although bull compositions occur on the shape even earlier.[19] The bell krater becomes fashionable in Greece at about the same time.

The bell krater opens up a broader field for composition than the late amphoroid krater, on which the framing bands by the handles had begun to encroach on the picture. Perhaps because there is more space, all the solutions for filling blank ground that were tried in the thirteenth century are employed simultaneously here: longer horses, three attendants and, for the first time, four people in the dual chariot box on one side (three on the other). Minor filling ornaments are rare, as in all this class: quirks above the reins, pendent triangles, antithetic spirals tied with chevrons under the horses' bellies, filled lozenges. A rarity is the one-handled jug suspended in the field in front of the first foot soldier on side A, a filling ornament that occurs mainly on Early pieces, the Sunshade Krater and the Enkomi Ewer sherd (III.21, 22). As in that case, people have speculated whether the vase represents funeral gifts, and the chariot procession a cortège to the tomb.[20] Vases painted on vases also occur in cult scenes in the Ripe and Late periods (XI.65, 66, XII.17) and by themselves in ceremonial contexts in Early Pictorial (XII.28).

Side A is less well preserved, slightly more elaborate. A "groom" leads the way with the jug hanging before him. As on V.16, he is a military man, carrying a spear awkwardly under his arm with the blade behind him, so that he appears struck through. The interest in weapons and military escort for chariots is typical of this phase of painting (V.16, 17); it increases in the Late period (X.1 and

following, XI.1 and following). Two unarmed grooms follow the carriage. The double box holds four people, the last armless, the two center figures gesticulating at chest level like the grooms. Their bodies are dark with a pale border, as on V.17. The figure style is that of several examples in this period, with the torso sharply bent back, elongated legs, the calves placed symmetrically—one bulges front, one back—elbows bent up, two-pronged fingers. The facial structure is even odder than on the belt-wrestlers of V.14; on some figures the nose drops straight from the hair in front of the face, and on side B it even angles down under the chin, as though it were the nose-guard of an unusual helmet. Except for the spearman, all the characters wear a kind of snood with a long curled pigtail hanging behind. Long hair like this has not been popular for some time (III.18); it may be a concession to Minoan taste or an odd form of cap-helmet with a hanging plume.

On side B there are only three men, flat-headed and short-haired, in the latticed chariot, followed by three unarmed grooms. Here the footmen's faces seem more clearly boxed in, and the "hair" is crosshatched, as it often is on caps and helmets (V.17, IX.18.1, X.32).

The interpretation is difficult as always: a military scene in which only one of thirteen men is armed, or a funeral cortège where the hanging vase suggests a gift or libation and the spearman will engage in a ceremonial throw or contest.

Of the remaining chariot kraters that can be placed in the III B series, the fragmentary late amphoroid krater from Minet el-Beida (V.21), with the groom soothing the muzzle of a startled horse, is perhaps most interesting. V.23, by the painter who did paired boxers without a chariot (V.32), seems to be one of the latest of all. It is noticeable that bell kraters rarely carry chariot compositions; V.19 and V.22 are exceptions; so is the Griffin Chariot (V.27) in its own way. The shape comes in while the subject is dying out. There are fragmentary kraters of the first part of the thirteenth century from Kourion in Cyprus. Tell Abu Hawam, Byblos, Gezer, Alalakh, and

16. For fish in perhaps comic or unusual intrusions, especially with bulls, see V.42, 43, 58, and Slenckza, *Tiryns* VII, nos. 32, 106.

17. S. Alexiou, *AA* 1964, 785; M. Cameron, *AA* 1967, 330; J. Nauert, *AntK* 8 (1965) 91; *AJA* 76 (1972) 437; E. Vermeule, in *A Land Called Crete* (1968) fig. 35; *IEE*, 336; A. Evans, *Prehistoric Tombs at Knossos* (1906) 28.

18. H. Drerup, in F. Matz, *Forschungen auf Kreta* (1951) 82 f., pls. 3, 50; Benson, *HBM* (1970) pl. VII.1; cf. I. Tzedakis, *AAA* 2 (1969) 365, figs. 2, 3; *AAA* 3 (1970) cover, figs. 1-2; S. Marinatos, *Kreta, Thera und das mykenische Hellas* (1976) pl. 128.

19. The late bell kraters have an angular profile and a sharply angular rim; cf. Furumark, *MP*, FS 281-282.

20. Lorimer, *HM*, 48; Furumark, *MP*, 451; E. Vermeule, *JHS* 85 (1965) 142 f.; H. Catling, *AJA* 72 (1968) 45 f.; Benson, *HBM*, 20 f.

Troy (V.25.3-10, XIII.19-21); all belong to this Eastern Mycenaean series, though they are so scrappy it is difficult to put them in a stylistic sequence. More will certainly turn up both in Asia Minor and in the Levant as excavation proceeds. It is worth noting that none of the Eastern cities seem to contain any recognizable mainland pictorial compositions until the Late period.

21. The fragmentary amphoroid krater from Minet el-Beida shows, for the first time, contact between an attendant on the ground and the horses pulling the chariot, recalling the bull-petters of IV.32 (cf. V.10). The bird under the handle must be considered when the "chained bird" krater (V.8) is discussed mythologically; this one turns its back to the attendant but seems attached to his shoulder by a wavy line terminating in an arrow point, like a feather shot from between wing and tail. This connection does not attract the attention of the attendant, who appears on one side in a long robe, on the other in a knee-length tunic (cf. V.5). In both cases he has his left hand on the team's bits, and his right is raised to check them or fondle their foreheads; the flying mane and the sharp forward slant of the front legs show that they have been traveling at a terrific speed and are skidding to a halt. The man's face is painted solid with a low ridged brow, a squashy nose, and little chin; one wonders if the tradition of the African skilled with difficult horses begins this early. But then, anthropologically, the figures on the Boston and Suda Bay vases (XI.14, 19) would be hard to diagnose.

22. On a bell krater from Klavdhia the newly opened, broader field is abruptly closed by a double wavy line rising in front of the horses, separating them from a stiff plant beyond. The painter may not have been used to the bell shape. Both parts of the box are shaped like mudguards or wings, and the riders are sunk to the breast inside, so the reins must flow from the driver's thorax; the men wear checkered clothes instead of the usual spotted robes. The vertical member of the pole brace has become an extra tail waving free. The horses' hind legs are dotted inside the outline, a novel variation, and the fillers are also odd: horseshoes over the reins, an S below the belly, and an old-fashioned whorl shell.

23. The worn, late amphoroid krater from Aradippo, now in the Louvre, is rather standard, though the flat-headed grooms' rear arms are curled pleasingly to fit in the gross curve of the small of the back. This is by Painter 18, who is sketchy and simple but full of ideas (cf. V.32). The chariot is divided into two or three boxes (a second "wing"?), with the center perched directly on top of the wheel. The bellies of the three riders are thrust forward, their robes striped (A) or spotted (B). The wheel spokes splay into Y-shapes at the rim. The grooms' caps have little curled plumes behind, more like the curious headgear on the Suda Bay krater (V.19) than sphinxes' caps.

24. A sherd from an amphoroid krater was found at Tell el-Muqdâm (Leontopolis) in the central Delta of Egypt, along with a group of fragments of faience vases. The faience pieces are decorated with flying ducks, vertical sprays of ivy leaves, tassels, lotus buds, and cartouches that probably represent Ramesses II and Merneptah. On the krater the chariot is simplified, with the front part in three high concentric arcs, the rear wing an oval with dots, high over the wheel and impinging on the team's rump. The driver, with a flattened head and a possible tassel or ribbon down behind, is typically Ripe; the armless passenger wears a clearer, soft striped flat cap with a ribbon in the back. The isolated seashell in the field is now a rare filler. Chariot kraters were apparently not particularly popular in Egypt, but this one is an encouraging sign of the Cypriote-Mycenaean contribution to the trade that brought so many Egyptian goods to Enkomi and Kition.

HORSES AND RIDERS

26. Fragments of a bell krater from Ugarit do not seem to include a chariot, but illustrate a row of riders; parts of three are preserved. The style seems late, perhaps close to 1200; the parti-colored faces of the horses and the filled lozenges in the field are characteristic of Transitional and Late drawing on the Greek mainland (XI.16, 21, 23). The riders are in dark silhouette, small in proportion to their mounts, of whom one at least is emphatically male, as on V.17. One rider, standing up high (of course without stirrups) so that his legs are visible to below the knee, wears a short sword at his waist; there may be the loop of a baldric behind his shoulder. The other riders sit far forward; all of them hold four reins, as though driving a chariot team. Comparable horseback riders in Egyptian battle reliefs of the same general period seem to be either messengers or scouts, or, sometimes, fleeing chariot crews mounted on the harnessed teams they have cut loose from the chariot (see V.17). The two eyes on the side of the preserved horse face may indicate a team. The excavator, Professor Schaeffer, thought that the krater might be a local late product, which would not be surprising in view of the connections in style to the Late soldier kraters of Ugarit (XIII.28, 29), and that the pronounced genitals on the horse were characteristic of Ugaritic art. Possible influence from Egyptian battle reliefs would be understandable in turbulent late-thirteenth-century Ugarit, and these fragments show the same readiness as on the Greek mainland to incorporate new developments or war imagery into a style which had previously been self-perpetuating and often removed from real observation.

GRIFFINS AND SPHINXES

So far, these monsters appear on only two Eastern Mycenaean pictorial vases in the early thirteenth century, and on three in the Pastoral style (VI.16-18), which is surprising considering their Oriental affinities and their popularity on seals, ivories, goldwork, frescoes, and painted sarcophagi. Perhaps more will be found. The sphinx, but not the griffin, entered the pictorial repertory on the Greek mainland slightly earlier than on Cyprus, but in a different form, as a protome, sometimes associated with men (VIII.30, 31). While both griffins and sphinxes carried a cult significance at the beginning of their popularity in Aegean art, this seems to wane slightly in the thirteenth century, as, in an ironic way, ivory carvers and painters begin to observe them as though they were real animals, eating and sleeping; by the twelfth century (XI.65, 91) they are mated and feeding their young. Both Levantine Ripe Pictorial representations are crude.

27. A bell krater from Enkomi, of good shape and fabric, combines the two kinds of monsters, as on the later Leukandi pyxis (XI.91). On one side two griffins face across a schematic "palm" whose stiff shoots at the base look like miniature horns of consecration, a sacral tree; the right-hand griffin is attached to a two-man chariot. On the other side sphinxes in plumed crowns face across a tree in the same way.

The style here is not indebted to other media in which the griffin was popular, where it is usually a full-bodied, heavily muscled animal with a proper lion's body and eagle's beak. These griffins seem to have an underfed horse's body and bull hooves, both more natural to a vase painter than rendering a lion. Lions in general puzzle painters (V.114, VI.4, 22, 24, IX.82, XIII.27). The head looks like that of a bald buzzard or vulture with a ruff around the neck as though in display. The shoulder is ornamented with reserved "eyes," perhaps a simple attempt to reproduce the more usual spiral scroll-lock on griffins' breasts in other art, though the true spiral is managed for the sphinxes on the other side. The pointed wing is lifted, as on frescoes, and overpainted with white spots. It is not clear why the outside of the legs is reserved below the knee, like golf socks; the inner surfaces of legs have been reserved for a long time under fresco influence (IV.17 and following). The chariot, whose tall double box is painted with π marks, has a well-drawn wheel with white spots and stripes on the rim and axle; its attachment to the unharnessed griffin is curious, for the pole and support are somehow fixed under the griffin's tail, and the tail itself is raised erect and grasped by the driver to serve as "reins." Whether the theme has funeral connotations, as on the

short end of the Haghia Triadha sarcophagus, is a matter of individual opinion; considering the long connection of the griffin and sphinx with death in Greek art, it is not unlikely.

The plumed sphinxes on the reverse have the same bodies as the griffins, but the left-hand one has human forelegs, like later centaurs. White spirals mark the breasts, white dots outline the wings (see X.42). The heads, less odd than the griffins', are almost the standard "human" type seen on ivories and repoussé gold diadems; the necks are reserved, as though to emphasize the drawing of the profiles. Where caps on ivory sphinxes are sometimes fluted, these are striped, and the floating plumes are short.

28A. An amphoroid krater from Enkomi has sphinxes on one side, archers and boxers(?) on the other, and a running dog under one handle. The sphinx side (A) is unfortunately very fragmentary, but what survives exhibits a delicate, sketchy style with interesting filling ornaments. The head and lifted wings of the left sphinx and the rear of her body and tail are preserved. There are flowers and quatrefoil ornaments in the field, and a row of spirals under each animal's belly, as in chariot scenes of early III B (V.7 and following). The sphinx has the long horse body, dark at the rear, and the crude bull hooves of V.27, with long tail erect. The pointed wings are raised, framing the head on each side, and filled with lines of triangles for feathers. The head, which does not look especially feminine, has short curls or a cap but no plume. She may wear a necklace of dots. The breast and shoulders seem to have been reserved; there is at least the start of a reserved patch at the waist. The sphinx on the right has a long striped neck, a reserved front body, and legs that look like bent folded wings (cf. V.72) by which she laboriously pulls herself forward toward a flower.

Under the handle between the left sphinx and the men on side B, a dog leaps over a tilted flower, as though to attack the sphinx from the rear. The head and lunging front legs are reserved. Dogs, like hunting scenes, are slightly rarer in Eastern pictorial than on the mainland, cf. V.60, 73, 113.

ARCHERS AND BOXERS

The new interest in human figures, in new costumes and attitudes, is one of the pleasures of the Ripe Pictorial phase: grooms, *rhabdophoroi*, horseback riders, spearmen and swordsmen, even women. A few vases show people in action or processions as the main themes, not subsidiary to chariot or bull compositions. There are archers, who had appeared in both previous periods as scouts or minor figures in chariot scenes; boxers, who seem to be new in III

B both in the East and on the mainland; simple marching men; and officers and sailors in a ship.

28B. Side B of the sphinx vase shows four men moving right. Two archers in the rear carry a simple (rather crooked) bow; the two men in front, who are separated by flower motifs, make menacing gestures with their left arms, like boxers warming up for the punch. All the figures are in the late, bent, balletic style characteristic of pictorial painting around 1250-1240, with arched chests (the archers thin, the boxers thick, as Homer later suggests they might be), the knees bent athletically (the rear boxer even bends his backward), and the schematic outline face with a thick neck but no grotesquerie. The archers have a smooth hairdo, the boxers a jagged outline of curls.

It is not immediately apparent why these two figures should be combined on a single vase, with sphinxes on the other side; one guess would be that this is a funerary vase showing the sphinx-guardian and devourer of the dead on one side and those who participate in the funeral games on the other. The vase comes from the same tomb as the earlier archer vase (IV.16), but one cannot always extract precise chronological value from the contents of a Cypriote tomb. Often the material ranges through fifty or a hundred years, and this is valid for objects other than pottery. Whatever the vase was designed for, whatever images pervaded the craftsman's mind, it is a new departure in the pictorial style and looks forward to other boxing scenes that are more popular, by the available statistics, than bowmen. The Mycenaean archer motif is surprisingly rare, considering that it is the only human theme to be attested in the Dark Ages, both in Cyprus and on the mainland (cf. XI.58).

At least five other vases from the East illustrate boxers, usually shown sparring in pairs (V.29-33). The bold but static gestures and the formal pairing make this subject congenial to the rhythms of the pictorial style. Whether they represent funeral games, as in *Iliad* XXIII ("I will rip his flesh and smash his bones," 673) is problematic but not unlikely. There are two other boxing scenes from mainland Greece (IX.17, 18). Some attempts are made to isolate the boxers by pairs when they are arranged in friezes. On V.29, now in London, a flower separates the chinless fighters, and they are also framed by flowers; they are active and spring to their work with big round reserved fists. V.30, now in Brussels, may be part of the same vase, judging by the well-drawn flowers and interlocked U-patterns, although there are chevrons in the field; the lithe figure is in an active pose with a long lunging leg, but little is left (it may belong to V.9). On V.31 a series of dejected palms(?) divide the very mannered pairs (one arm up, one down, thumbs projecting from fists); on V.32, sketchily filled

birds are the dividers. Generally speaking, the legs are emphasized for length and thrust, the chests are relatively thick, the heads are held straight up, and the fists curled.

On V.32, by the painter of a chariot krater from Aradippo (V.23) a long lock of hair springs and falls in a curl behind the neck. This headdress, reminiscent of those on the Suda Bay krater (V.19), is an oddity, hard to diagnose either as a helmet plume or as a "plumed crown"; perhaps it was stimulated by some intermediate reflection of an older style, such as a gem or a cylinder seal dependent on the Boxer Rhyton from Haghia Triadha in Crete, where the opponents wear both helmets and long hair, or on the strange locks of the boxing children from Thera. On a boxer by the left handle the genitals may be indicated (cf. IV.18).

33. Fragments of a deep bowl with boxers, from Kition, exhibit a later style that is not unlike some mainland pieces (X.8, for example): the chest is just a thin stripe, the flat-topped heads and long noses recall V.7-9, 14-19. The gestures of antagonism are purely symbolic; the thick legs are jointed backward.

It is possible that the two kylix fragments from Kourion (V.34, 35) also illustrate boxing scenes, for which the gesture of V.34 at least is appropriate. The shape is an odd one for pictorial scenes, but Ugarit has parallel oddities (V.36, 37). V.34 may be by the painter of the chariot scenes V.8-10.

Two vases from indeterminable contexts at Ugarit seem to belong to the same Ripe phase, with designs of simple, mannered human figures on a nearly blank ground.

36. A rhyton from a corridor outside a temple is banded in good style in the handle zone and lower body, and at first sight might seem earlier in design than the figures upon it, who look III B.[21] There are at least two spearmen (the publication does not specify the number) marching right, the spear held in both hands at the diagonal, right hand high behind the shoulder, left hand forward and down. This is the ballet posture of grooms and boxers in the Ripe phase. The drawing of the outlined torso is unusual, with a double contour and reserved interior but silhouetted legs. The necks are very long; the hair has a curl in back.

36.1 A rhyton fragment from a tomb at Minet el-Beida was designed in zones; only part of the top zone survives, with a standing man to the right between vertical dividers.

---

21. The other two rhyta found seem to be LH III A:2 late, but their association with this one is not clear; C. F. A. Schaeffer, *AAS* 13 (1963) fig. 29; J. -C. Courtois, in Schaeffer, *Ugaritica* VI, 116.

It is not clear from the published drawing what the figure is doing; he may simply hold a short vertical staff before him with both hands. The head is a rectangle with a ruffled top for hair, a dent in the profile for a mouth; all its affinities are with the odder grooms of this phase. Scrappy heads in this arbitrary form are known from Gezer and Tell Abu Hawam (V.25.6-8). The body seems pregnantly swollen, which is very curious if true; could the bulge be a small round shield?

37. A fragmentary large bowl, perhaps of Cypriote shape, preserves parts of four men marching right, separated by filled lozenges suspended on vertical wavy lines, reaching from rim to base, an Ugaritic idiosyncrasy. The men are painted entirely in dark silhouette with only the eye reserved, which makes an odd impression. The right arm is a simple loop in the curve of the back, the left is represented in front of the chest only as a circle with two very long fingers sticking straight up. Too little is known of Ugaritic habits to invest this gesture with its later international significance. This formally decorative piece with its quiet, interrupted frieze recalls similar compositions with fish at Ugarit (V.131, 132) and may be characteristic of a local pictorial atelier.

OTHER HUMAN FIGURES

38. A fragmentary amphoroid krater from Enkomi has long been famous for its elaborate representation of ships and two classes of men: the huge warriors with spotted robes, helmets, and swords, who stand on the deck or the shore, and the little nude men who toil below the decks. This is the first full naval scene in the history of Mycenaean pictorial painting (as opposed to isolated Middle Cycladic or Helladic pictures of ships, or the naval fresco from Thera), and this in itself is surprising, since ships must have been as highly regarded as chariots.

Only one other Mycenaean ship picture, from Kos, has people attached to the vessel (XII.33) or combines class distinctions with a cross-section in a way that anticipates the Arkesilas cup in Paris. Professor Stubbings, who linked this scene through the birds on the stern to a bird jar from Hala Sultan Tekké (V.69) where the bird's body is partly vegetable, says, "After seeing his almost satirical portrayal of the upper and lower deck, we begin to know our man; as we look again at his plant-birds we can detect the streak of whimsy, and if we have any taste for such things we have achieved the supreme aim of archaeology as we share an instant of the Late Bronze Age."[22]

Although three fragments have been added,[23] the picture is sadly incomplete. The scene seems almost the same on each side: the ship, with three or four lilies on the stem, a mast with stacked rigging rings or deadeyes, and a bird prow, supports two large figures on the upper deck, facing each other across the mast, and four small figures on the lower deck, facing each other in pairs across the mast-step. These busy nude dark men with reserved faces and necks are essentially boxer types, their arms held forward with curled fingers, but since the gesture is borrowed from other compositions there is no way of knowing what work they do; not rowing, at least, but perhaps hauling on ropes(?). It is equally unclear whether the vertical striped box structure to the right of the little men is part of the interior structure of the ship, a cargo hold perhaps, or an instinctive decorative frame. A comparable box interrupts the painted frieze of lions and dolphins on the hull exterior of the Parade ship in the Thera fresco, slightly closer to the mast. Internal braces and frames are commonly represented in clay ship models and in selected ship pictures from Egyptian to Geometric. It has also been interpreted as a ladder leading from the deck to the interior. Considering the schematic shorthand for familiar objects characteristic of the period, the ship is remarkably faithful to Aegean traditions.

The robed figures standing on the deck are standard, footless and armless, with long hair, fat bodies, and the long swords in tasseled scabbards which were characteristic of the Middle period (IV.50), to which the whorl-shell fillers under the handles also link the vase. It should be set fairly early in III B. That the shipboard soldiers wear no helmets is not surprising, now that the custom of hanging helmets up on hooks for sea voyages has been demonstrated by the Thera fresco. The flanking soldiers on the shore wear the conical crested helmets also familiar from the Middle period (IV.55, 56[?], 62).[24] The complete robed figure on the right wears the long sword with a pronounced crescent pommel and guard; the naked figure on the left seems unarmed in spite of his helmet, and is also a boxer type, hands high with curled fists. The distinction may be purely decorative or may continue the contrast between the armed Mycenaeans and the unarmed Minoans in the Thera fresco; or it may imply a distinction in status, the grand admiral or aristocrat who raised the fleet and commands the contingent of each ship, and his lieutenant or second-in-command who organizes a departure or guides the ships to new coasts. It is clearly a military scene, not a pure commercial venture, nor a festival voyage as on Thera, and it fits well with the recorded Sea Peoples raids of the thirteenth century, a prototype for ship-raiding scenes in Homer.

22. *BSA* 46 (1951) 176; cf. Dikaios, *Enkomi*, 925, n. 789.
23. V. Karageorghis, *OpAth* 3 (1960) 146, pl. X.
24. See Chapter IV, note 6, and H. Hencken, *The Earliest European Helmets* (1971) 20 f.

39. A very fragmentary amphoroid krater from Enkomi has been published as a crude mythological representation, perhaps a forerunner of the classical story of Herakles fetching the golden apples from the Garden of the Hesperides, perhaps an Oriental story concerning the tree of life or gathering of magic fruit. The drawing is as crude as anything in Mycenaean pictorial and offers few clues to any wonderful imagination behind it. On the shoulder is a disorganized tree, which has features of a palm but also drooping branches with dashes for leaves; on the left a dumpy figure with a violent stripe for a nose reaches out to seize an upper branch with his left hand and brandishes a twig which he has already picked with his four-fingered right hand. The figure, very worn, seems to be clad in an unusual tunic that flares out at midthigh, and is further odd for the torso being in frontal view. Two plumes or locks of hair sweep back from his brow (cf. V.32). The general composition recalls Oriental scenes of a genius stroking a date palm, and perhaps some corrupted Oriental idea is better able to account for this creation than a genre scene such as striking olives or plucking apples.

BULLS

Bulls are great favorites in the Ripe period. In many ways these pictures show a finer sense of design than the chariot kraters. The most common type is a frieze of bulls to the right or a single long bull on either side of a bell krater. Birds and fish are popular in the background, and very often the bird performs some service for the bull, such as picking ticks off his head.

Occasionally the bulls are placed facing each other peacefully over a flower, or fighting. They may be simple protomes, single or in continuous zones. Rare types include facing bulls, toreador scenes, and hunts with dogs.

In most bull scenes the filling ornaments have nearly disappeared from the background, and are absorbed into the bulls themselves, in rich decorative designs which suggest embroidery. This happened earlier to birds. The large body of the animal offers an ideal surface for the new trend. It is often divided into three sections with contrasting fillings in each. The naturalistic blobs and trefoils of the earlier period have given way to arrows, π shapes, stripes, dots and dotted circles, crosses, semicircles, wavy lines, scale patterns—a richer variety than for any other animal. Some of these designs appear in thirteenth-century frescoes too, but most seem indebted to textile patterns or are derived from the ordinary designs on nonpictorial Mycenaean vases.

Bull scenes in the thirteenth century link Cyprus and the mainland closely. There is suddenly a greater range of vase shapes, which had been traditional on the mainland; now bulls in Cyprus appear on amphoroid kraters, bell kraters, jugs, stirrup jars, shallow bowls, and saucers. The decorative use of bulls is more versatile than that of chariots, or they are less restricted by function. Works by individual painters, on these varied shapes, are found both in the Argolid and in Cyprus, and the workshops of Tiryns may be influential in setting the new styles (see V.44, 45, IX.19, 20; V.73, 74, IX.21). Attributions to painters may be arguable when the mainland pieces are so fragmentary (see Chapter XIV) but there can be little doubt that these bull kraters are closely connected among themselves and to the contemporary pieces at Tiryns (IX.19 and following). They are also close to the bull vases here set in the second phase of the Ripe style (V.73 and following). Those have been put "later" in the sequence because, often, a certain looseness of line and impressionism seem to lead into Pastoral painting (Chapter VI).

40. An amphoroid krater from Enkomi serves as a link between the old and new styles. On each side of the vase there are two bulls with a little calf surrounded by a wonderful array of birds, as though sketched live in a meadow. By convention the animals are called bulls, but once more, as on IV.4 and 32, there is a contrast between the two sides. One is a family scene, with a proud quiescent bull watching a cow, who lowers her great horned head as though to lick the tiny calf standing between them. On the other side two less massive, perhaps younger, bulls butt each other in a playful way with tails raised high over their backs. Between them a miniature bull mimics their attitude. On both sides the little bull in the middle seems to gore the legs of the great bull on the right, without doing damage.

Underneath the animals, between their legs and under their necks, comes a series of large and small birds—there are eleven altogether—who may have begun life as filling ornaments but are skillfully converted into actors in the scene. On the bullfight side they climb legs or pick ticks from the charging bodies; one little bird has been scared off the miniature bull by the lunging above him and flies up into the mêlée. A fat bird under one handle is reserved and striped, a conventional and uninteresting type as on the boxer vase (V.32), but all the other figures are dark silhouettes with expressive feet, beautifully balanced on the light ground, exhibiting a better sense of the harmonies of mass and diagonal motion than any chariot scene.

Even the abstract filling ornaments, filled and solid lozenges, on occasion have tails raised out horizontally to match the bulls' tails. The bulls are elegant animals, stippled with white dotted circles in even rows all over; the horns and tails are long, thin, and curving in contrast to the body mass, and the small neat-hooved legs are striped, with the inner hind leg reserved as on frescoes and horse vases. In spite of its broken and slightly worn condition, this vase is one of the finest illustrations of the strengths and potential of the pictorial style: impressive figures with motion suggested but not exaggerated, mild narrative implied through a careful choice of attitudes, minor lilting currents of humor, blended into a bold and elegant decorative monument, spirited and animated in a happy rural scene.

41. An amphoroid krater from an unknown site in Cyprus makes the transition to the more static, fully embroidered style. Two bulls on each side face across a formal palm tree design; the field is filled with flowers reminiscent of the Middle period, from which it may indeed be transitional (cf. IV.30). Yet the abstract decorative drive of the early III B phase seems to have taken over fully. The bulls are loosely drawn and arbitrarily divided; the three principal sections—shoulders, belly, and rump—are further subdivided in the center (like Middle II birds), and each part has a separate filler: dot-necklaces for older dewlap wrinkles (one with pendants), crosses on the shoulders, vertical stripes and quirks on the belly, dotted circles on the rump; the effective consistency of V.40 has gone. The eye is made smaller or greater by adding circles, the lines of the clacking horns lack authority, the muzzles and hooves droop. There is a bird under each handle.

42. An amphoroid krater from Klavdhia illustrates a different stylistic tendency, to stretch a single bull body as far across the surface of the vase as possible. Some of these will contend for the prize title of "the longest bull in art" (V.51). It is a neat design but made clumsy by the elongated cylindrical body, which has none of the usual anatomical curves in back or belly, and by the legs, which look unduly short because they are hidden in the framing bands. The body outline is enriched with very even, dark "waves" inside, a pattern ultimately derived from older trefoils and scallops (cf. IV.32) seen earlier on the hind legs of the toreador fresco at Knossos. The interior is filled with simple vertical wavy lines. The desire for pure decoration is emphasized by the intrusion of a great fish just under the bull's nose, oddly drawn as though seen from above, with two flounder eyes, two "ears" (fins) and "beaks" (jaws). A striped bird follows the bull. The blank field makes the whole construction stand out as though in relief. The single-bull-in-panel composition will become more frequent in this and subsequent stages.

43. A bell krater from Enkomi offers an interesting variant, with a single fine bull *en face* on each side, and on one side a fish in the air over its back. The bulls' stretched-out shapes harmonize better with the low clean lines of a bell krater than with the complex profile of an amphoroid krater. This too is an early piece, to judge by the floating flowers and formal palm trees in the field, while the hatched lozenges and dotted circles belong in Ripe. On the fish side the bull has a plain cross-stitched pattern from the rippled dewlap collar to the tail. The horns are huge, set on a pillar above his skull like architectural horns of consecration, making the narrow face seem to bend to the earth with the burden. On the other side the bull is beautifully painted with a dark head and great pale eyes, the horns branching out in a fine lyre curve from below the ears; the massive forequarters are covered in cross-stitch like a shawl, the rest of the long body accented with more traditional trefoil blobs along the contours and light quatrefoils down the center, finely spaced.

The fish has an open mouth and fangs; its body is filled with wavy lines, as so often later. Perhaps the association of land and sea animal has no more symbolic meaning than such juxtapositions do on peasant pottery and textiles of many cultures (see V.58).

Bull and bird compositions are common to Cyprus and the mainland, and it is frequently difficult to distinguish the two schools in terms of style. The typical design is one bull on each side of a vase (usually a bell krater) moving right, with the bird in front of him either feeding or pecking at his neck or nose. V.44-46 are characteristic; 44 and 45 are nearly twins and have a good parallel at Tiryns (IX.20).

44. A bell krater from Enkomi offers a very neat, massive charging bull, head lowered and horns almost scraping the ground, with the bird rising in the air as his long bill sticks into the bull's neck. Miss Benton identified the bird as a cattle egret, who is known to savor ticks and relieve animals of them.[25] The painter seems to show a moment when the bull has become irritated with the bird's jabs at his hide, and moves suddenly, shaking his head to dislodge him. The bird is thus represented in a double movement, still feeding but kicking his feet to fly up and away. His odd tail has been compared to an electric light bulb.[26] There are no filling ornaments to blur the bold design. The bull's solid dark head and horns stand out against the lighter parti-colored body: scale pattern on the shoulders, a belt of zigzags, wavy lines across the belly, and ⋀ and dots on the rear. The big eye of concentric circles is emphasized by interior fringes of dots. The triangle representing hair at the end of the pizzle is pronounced and neat.

45. The companion piece to V.44 has a strong bull

25. S. Benton, *JHS* 81 (1961) 44.
26. J. L. Benson, *AJA* 65 (1961) 340.

running with bent knees and trotting hind legs; his horns curve up at the end to scrape the framing band, and he seems to switch his tail. He is covered with dotted circles on the shoulder, dotted scales at the belly, and an effective wheel pattern of dots on the rump. The bird pecks peacefully at the ground, unaware of the rush behind him. On V.46 the bird works on the bull's horns on one side and turns back to commune with him on the other. There is a new handsome pattern, a crossband filled with ripples, on the belly, with good trefoils above and below; the rest is cross-stitched around the contours, fore and aft, very neat and stylish. The lozenges, filled at the corners, herald the next stage.

BULLS AND HUMAN FIGURES

Human figures are rarer in bull scenes than in chariot scenes, and the pastoral friendliness of the Middle period (IV.32) has gone. Three versions on bell kraters merit attention and suggest a rising interest in bullring scenes in the East.

48. A bell krater from an unknown site in Cyprus shows a cow followed by a smaller one, perhaps her calf, on one side, and a toreador scene on the other. The highly patterned animals with bold outlines have a good deal of charm, and the flexible treatment of the nose and lips—three circles with openings, perhaps in "false perspective"—look forward to the Pastoral (Rude) or ivory-carving style (Chapter VI). The fillings on the body are in four panels of crosses, dots, crosses, and solid glaze; the forelegs are correctly heavy to the knee; the horns curve back at the tip; there is ruffled hair to mark the vertebrae. The bull, however, has grown impossibly long, as space-filling problems override common sense. One wonders that the clumsy toreador managed to travel the full course from horns to tail without resting for the night. He is posed frontally at an awkward angle, with his head at the level of the bull's tail, simply to fit the space, and so seems to slip off the bull's rump rather than spring to the ground; the outspread fingers and slightly parted lips also suggest panic as much as tense striving for balance. There is a great distance in style and tautness between this and fresco scenes, and one should not blindly believe it is derived from paintings or from *taurokathapsia* gems, both unknown in Cyprus. Yet it is not more awkward than a mainland fragment (IX.18.1), made at a place and time when both sources were available to look at. It is not clear whether the human actor has a pointed head with curls in the back or is wearing protective headgear as at Mycenae; the legs are thick and straight at the ankles, like trousers. This is a decorative and humorous painting in spite of occasional clumsiness.

50. A bell krater from Enkomi has two ornamental bulls on each side, their legs poked forward in a mannered way, tails high and split at the ends in three forks (tassels), in a field of filled lozenges with spirals beneath the handles. On one side, in front of the larger bull the angled figure of a man falls on his back in profile; the head is there, although it looks missing in the drawings, brushing the bull's chest. The position is not a standard one in bullring scenes, where the leaper should face the bull to grasp his horns and vault over his back; this looks as if the jumper has made an accidental slip, although the very posed silhouettes of the bulls undercut any message of charging and goring. The man may wear a conical helmet, as on the last vase. The neat outlines, clear fillings of dots and crosses, and even distribution of lozenges in the background make an exceptionally attractive surface that robs the narrative of vigor.

51. A bell krater from Pyla-Verghi wins the prize for "the longest bull in art". The animal is so stretched out across the surface, he should need an extra pair of legs under the belly to support him. This quadruped is divided into at least four panels filled with π designs, wavy stripes, double and single dotted circles, and πs again at the rump. (The π design first made its appearance on the leather sides of chariot boxes in this phase, V.27, presumably made from the hides of similarly marked bulls.) A squat and awkward human figure behind the bull holds the tail in his left hand. He is drawn in a crude but expressive way with his head to the right, his left leg frontal, and his right leg bent to the left; the right arm is bent high. Perhaps this too represents a toreador who has leaped to the ground behind the bull and catches hold of his adversary to steady himself in a moment of precarious balance. Judging from the bull's clearly drawn pizzle hair, it is not the prelude to a milking scene.

52. The transition to the second stage of the Ripe period in bull design is illustrated by the wonderful bell krater from Arpera with a facing bull. In the field are handsome swaying palms and a few lozenges and filled circles. The frontal head is in a way more successful than on V.43, but simpler and more schematic, like isolated bull's heads on some III B vases (V.102, 103, IX.27, XII.27). The small, close-set eyes are filled with wavy lines, the muzzle is broad and hard-edged. The shift toward Ripe II is marked by the restriction of filling in the belly section to four horizontal rows (scale, dotted circle, chain, and scale), though the front and hindquarters are decorated in the earlier way, with dotted circles and a dotted wheel pattern on the haunch (cf. V.45). In the second stage the filling of the center section will get progressively sparser and more linear or will sometimes be left out altogether. The bent forelegs and ominous stare make the great bull seem to charge off the vase toward the customer.

STAGS

Wild animals reappear in the Ripe stage after being absent from the pictorial repertory for decades, since the time of the Maroni Goat Krater (III.26). It is hard to say why they are favored in the early thirteenth century: perhaps because they form an element in the fresco cycles at palaces like Pylos and Tiryns (where, however, the wall paintings may be slightly later than the vase paintings); perhaps through that restlessness with chariot scenes which also encouraged the invention of new human designs and the use of griffins and sphinxes; perhaps because hunting was a more popular sport among a broader class of people than before.

Stags and goats are the common quarries in pictorial painting, and they are comparatively rare on Cyprus, more numerous on the mainland. Cypriote sites are filled with the bones of fallow and roe deer, sometimes in such numbers as to suggest domestication, so that their rarity in painting is an artistic, not an environmental, problem. Full hunting scenes are extremely scarce. Usually the animals are abstracted from the chase and from the landscape, set in decorative friezes to the right, around a bell krater. Birds may appear as minor elements, as they do with bulls. The body fillings are of course more schematic than on frescoes, where artistic tradition commands the use of crosses for markings on stags, or the real hues of red and buff. On vases, wavy lines or arrowheads are as common as crosses, or there may be reserved patches as on bulls. The bodies are less richly embroidered than the bulls', and there is less fantasy or variation in the designs.

53. A bell krater from Enkomi has three stags trotting right on one side, two stags sniffing or feeding on the other. The convention in pictorial painting is to put antlers, the distinctive mark of the animal, on females as well as males. This convention persists in classical painting and bronzes as well. Genitals are not normally drawn for either sex, as they usually are for bulls and sometimes for horses. Representations of wild animals do not normally illustrate the kind of herd or family behavior one sees with bulls. An exception is formed by those mainland vases showing the deer's young on her back (IX.48).

Here there is perhaps a dim reflection of the kind of sequence seen on the Maroni Goat Krater, peaceful grazing on one side and alarmed departure on the other, but the decorative principles are again too strong to encourage natural vignettes. The animals are filled with wavy lines and T-patterns; the ground is lightly sprinkled with delicate dotted circles and occasional lozenges. One notes particularly the alert carriage of the heads of the trotting stags, with antlers branching up through the framing band. The long muzzle is still narrow here; soon it will become a standard bulbous bottle. The strokes inside the muzzle, which at first look like teeth, are the "ingrowing hair" that marks most wild animals in the Pylos frescoes.[27] It is curious that the Mycenaean artist almost never ruffles his outline with hair on the outside where it should be; the recognizable outline is sacred, not to be blurred by impressionistic details. On the grazing side the branching antlers of the second stag cross the first one's rump, so that he seems to be in a closer plane; this overlapping of figures was not generally liked, and many stag vases have the animal's head back over his shoulder so that each outline stays intact.

54. Another stag bell krater from Enkomi is duller and quieter; on each side there is a frieze of three almost identical stags with three almost identical birds pecking the ground under their bellies. Animals and birds, filled with the same vertical wavy lines, bend their heads back in curves; the stag bodies form a closed composition with the scuts turned up over the rump like parentheses. The strong repeated forms on a totally blank ground have a bas-relief quality that is highly successful as decoration. This is close to several mainland designs (IX.49).

55. A third bell krater from Enkomi, slightly more vivacious and abstractly patterned, seems somewhat later. Three stags prance with bent knees on each side; on one side the third animal is little and climbs up on the back of the second with his pointed hooves. The bodies are striped in groups of wavy lines, leaving reserved patches; an abstract lozenge is inserted in one. The hindquarters are dark. The noses are now long bottles, and the branches of the antlers have been converted into decorative circles like bubbles on a stick. Handsome rosettes hang in the field over each back, and under the handles a scale pattern in the style of Oriental mountains forms a stiff remnant of landscape. This hillock from the deer's natural wilderness refuge continues sporadically on wild animal vases till the end of Mycenaean painting (IX.77, XI.82, 83).

GOATS

Mycenaean painters seldom draw the true ibex or moufflon of the high rocks (V.59), but a long, thin dark animal with sprightly legs and short horns swept back, sometimes bent or angled (V.58). Like stags, goats are fairly rare in the East, more common on the Greek mainland, where they may sympathetically be shown skipping in a high

27. Lang, *Pylos* II, 17, 33, and s.v. "in-growing hair" in index.

field. In Cyprus and Rhodes the tendency is, of course, to make decorative patterns out of them, swirling in antithetic designs or prancing in a frieze. Goats by nature almost never stand still.

58. A rather hastily drawn bell krater from Hala Sultan Tekké presents a goat with a bull's head and a dog's tail, two on each side, followed by a big lunging fish with fanged jaws. All the figures are at oblique angles, the goats springing right from the bottom of the lower framing bands to poke their horns through the top, the fish standing on its tail just under the handle. The fish is all dark with a round eye, the goats in dark silhouette with reserved muzzle and funny rosette eyes—two circles with ingrown lashes. The legs seem awkward because the flat feet stick out in front as though there were an extra "knee", and the long tail over the back is surely misplaced. Painters often distort established anatomy but seldom invent it; the extra length may be whimsy, like the juxtaposition with the fierce fish, who would not normally be seen in a goat pasture even by the Salt Lake, but who is clearly chasing the animals. Here is the same light-hearted attitude to reality as on the *Ketos* krater (V.18); the fish teeth threaten, and the goats look back in surprise.

59. A bell krater with proper moufflons, from Enkomi, is more sedate, yet made lively by the expressive goat faces and their delicate placement in a field of circles filled with quatrefoils. The animals stand lightly on tensed or bent legs; some are bearded, almost all open their mouths; they are dark with almost completely reserved faces so that the drawing of the parted lips and the large almond eyes is well shown. The dark horns sweep back in a full curve past the neck again. It is an attractive vase, with perhaps some reminder of the leaping goats on the Maroni krater (III.26), but the difference in style and quality over a century is immediately apparent, with life and motion lost for the sake of formal pattern.

HUNTS

Hunting scenes are rare on Cyprus in comparison to the mainland, where pictorial versions are found at the principal palace sites containing fresco cycles of boar and stag hunts. In general there are two forms of Aegean hunting scenes: the small extract of a predator leaping on the back of a bovine, such as a lion on a bull or stag, which prevails on gems and ivories; and the strung-out form of huntsmen urging their dogs on against deer, boar, or goats. Hunting pictures on vases normally adapt this second, fresco pattern, but in a condensed style, which suggests that the painters may never have seen such frescoes with their own eyes (XI.70 and following).

There are three Ripe hunting vases from Cyprus so far: an exciting chase of mixed animals in the early Ripe period (V.60), a huntsman and bull in the second phase (V.73), and a hunter in chain mail (V.113).

60. A bell krater from Aradippo shows a huntsman, two animals, and two hounds on each side. The surface is not in good condition. On the first side the huntsman, in the rear, armed with a sharp hunting javelin and wearing a peaked cap, launches his weapon into the mêlée before him—a boar or lion and a goat each trying to shake off a hound that has sprung onto its back. Pictorial vases usually show only a single huntsman, for economy of space. The second side shows the huntsman leaping off the ground (only his legs are preserved, painted in front of the rear animal's haunch and hard to see), while two stags are brought down by hounds on their backs.

In his quest for new pictorial themes, the painter has tried for a dramatic atmosphere of violent action. The picture has a great deal in common with mainland pictorial versions, yet they have a vigor and clarity, a sense of noise and rush, or even pain in the bitten deer (XI.78), which is confused here because the figures are jammed in together and the drawing is awkward. The effect is not bad, however, for one senses the jostling and overlap that would emanate from the real scene.

The extraordinarily mixed bag of game may be an expression of Cypriote largesse. The left-hand animal on the better-preserved side is usually reckoned to be a boar; wild boar were prime objects of the chase, as in the Tiryns and Orchomenos frescoes, and they still are in parts of Turkey. It may be that a desire to connect all hunting scenes with the Tiryns cycle has "created" the boar here, for the animal has a long body, deep chest, long tail, and talons. The head does have a boarlike crest of bristles, however, and a pointed snout unlike a lion's (cf. XII.17). One dog, tail curled in a neat spiral, legs tensed and bent, lands with a spring on the shoulders. Another hound uses the boar as a springboard to climb onto the next animal—probably a goat rather than a doe—which looks around in surprise, nose to nose with its nemesis. The goat's legs are short and crooked for such an elongated body, but they help suggest panic and bounding over the terrain. The whimsy of the confrontation between dog and goat is not an undertone in mainland pictorial versions, where fear and pain are more common, but the Ugaritic version (XIII.27) may be playful. Behind the animals the huntsman in a short tunic and cap launches the special thonged spear called *aiganeé*, used for goat hunting in the *Odyssey* (cf. XI.77).[28]

---

28. Cf. Lang, *Pylos* II, 16 H 43, pls. 12, 121 B, and H.-G. Buchholz, V. Karageorghis, *AAA* 3 (1970) 391.

The stags on the other side are better drawn, perhaps because the form was more established. Their heads are slightly lifted, with neat, branching horns, their feet clear of the ground line as though they were bouncing stiff-legged to shake off the dogs.

BIRDS

Bird compositions of the Early Ripe period share with bull scenes a preference for embroidery-filled bodies set against a relatively blank ground and outlines frozen into repeated ornamental forms. When birds are the principal decoration of a vase, they are of course less lively than when they flit under bulls' legs or pick ticks (V.40, 44). A brief description of three examples may illustrate different facets of the style.

61. On a bell krater from Enkomi, two birds with huge raised wings appear on each side; the only filling ornament in the field consists of a few lozenges that spring from the birds' bodies. These are attached on wavy lines to the interstices between neck and wing, and wing and body, and so fill the same function as the "extra wings," like crests or plumes, on subsidiary birds on chariot kraters (V.8). The outlines are extremely conventional; the attenuated "body" is a separate semicircle hitched on behind the wing, more like a tail; the very small feet stand on four toes under the wing. The large flat curves of wing and body provide ideal spaces for embroidery filling, stripes, crosshatching, dotted circles, and running arcs in separated areas, as on bulls of the period. This painter is known from fragments of two other vases found at Enkomi and one at Ugarit (V.63-65). A jug from Enkomi (V.66) shows a weaker, more contracted version of the same tendencies.

67. A bell krater from Enkomi has the more powerful curvaceous style of the moufflon krater (V.59). Four birds on each side are drawn as though alighting from the middle air or hovering in perfect formation; this lightness is unusual for the period. The chest and body lines are in thick dark outline, the body recurving under itself; the neck and a wing-shaped patch on the body are reserved and filled with wavy lines. The brushwork is skillful, and the formal birds are very graceful in their bold curves; perhaps it is another work by the moufflon painter.

Several bird pictures of this phase are by artists whose handling of other scenes has already been discussed: a jug (V.68) with a frieze of birds by the painter of the bull-and-bird scenes (V.44-45), a three-handled jar with sketchy "plant birds" (V.69) by the painter of the Enkomi Ship Krater (V.38). One artist's birds are so queer that one ought to be able to recognize parallel queerness in other scenes, but so far the attempt has not been successful; he may be a beginner in the field (V.72).

72. The Fitzwilliam bird krater is a fine specimen of potting, an amphoroid krater (which in this period is rarely decorated with birds). On one side is a frieze of three long skinny birds, each with a great raised wing and a long "foot" coming out of the middle of the back. On the other side there is only one bird, the rest of the space being occupied by a variety of filling ornaments, which are unusual in pictorial compositions of this stage. This single bird has three wavy "feet" coming out of his back and the added feature of a pair of front legs, like extra wings or furled umbrellas, with which he pulls himself along in a manner recalling the curious sphinx of V.27. The first bird in the frieze of three has one such extra leg. All the bodies are tubular, and the single wing rises up in a sharp triangle like a sail. The interior filling of simple groups of stripes or wavy lines is about all that this painter has in common with his contemporaries. The field ornaments are like weak and ill-drawn reflections of Amarna fillers, such as chevrons, debased flowers, palm trees without trunks, triangles, spirals, lozenges, isolated wavy lines, and tentacles. It certainly never occurred to the artist to look at a real bird, nor even really to imitate an established type from another vase. One may be surprised that the potter gave him such a good piece to decorate, but it is not without a certain childish and disorganized charm.

RIPE II

In the later part of the general pottery style called Mycenaean III B, several trends break up pictorial vase painting into schools or styles. A number of vases found in the East continue the patterns of the earlier thirteenth century but in a still more isolated and static fashion, and this stage represents the end of the orthodox pictorial style as such. Having flourished for over a century and a half, it began to be repetitive and dull. In the Levant the chariot scenes have disappeared almost entirely; a few very late examples such as the warrior kraters found in Ugarit were probably not made in Cyprus (XIII.28, 29). For this reason all the chariot vases were discussed in a group above, although the later ones may be approximately contemporary with the characteristic bulls and birds of this second phase. At the same time in the latter thirteenth century the mainland is a center for a great revival of pictorial painting, with a vigor and fantasy that continues into the twelfth century. The same is true of Crete, where pictorial styles were never exactly popular, but where the later Late Minoan III B period produced some extraordinary images of cult and culture on both vases and larnakes. The long-standing and excellent ateliers of Rhodes seem to fade away like the Cypriote ones, but their place is taken by the late painters of Kos; certain Cycladic islands like Naxos also develop local fashions.

Above all, in Cyprus and the East a new free style springs up, much influenced by ivory carving, with a loose and poetic line. This was formerly called the Rude style, because some of its effects no doubt seemed rude compared to the neat if unimaginative drawing of the earlier thirteenth century; but Rude is a poor term, since it denies much of the interesting impressionism and vitality of the style, and we would like to rechristen it the Pastoral style, for its subject matter and its countryside freshness and observation. This style forms, in effect, the third stage of the Ripe period. Stratigraphically it is found in both LH III B and III C contexts, bridging the thirteenth and twelfth centuries. Because it establishes new values it is treated separately in Chapter VI.

The chronological extent of the second Ripe phase may be roughly the third quarter of the thirteenth century, with a few later continuations. The repertory of pictorial themes is limited mainly to bulls, stags, goats, birds, and fishes. The association of different animals in a single scene is rare, and when it happens, the figures are not actually interrelated but are treated as separate decorative motifs. It is more usual to find the same animal or bird repeated in a frieze or facing across a triglyph or checkerboard pattern. On small jugs a single design may be painted on the shoulder.

The background is rarely decorated, except for a few lozenges. Embroidery effects become less exuberant, and there is an increased tendency to contrast "embroidered" and blank spaces inside the outlined figures. This practice started during the previous stage, and now becomes frequent, especially with the introduction of bull protomes as a popular image. The outlines of these protomes are usually edged with dots, joining semicircles, or scalloped lines, leaving the rest of the figure empty.

Bell kraters and a few persistent amphoroid kraters had been the dominant shapes in the previous stage. Now the amphoroid krater is almost completely superseded by new forms, although the bell krater survives. Shallow bowls with repetitive interior friezes and small jugs with single motifs on the shoulder were particular favorites.

BULLS

73. One of the finest late painters, Painter 19, made a "bull hunt" krater and a very decorative bull jug, both found in Cyprus, and a krater at Tiryns (IX.21). This is one of the few times the same hand is detectable on both sides of the Aegean, although the bulls, birds, and stags of Tiryns are more closely related to the Cypriote series than are those of the other mainland workshops.

The "Aktaion" bell krater from Klavdhia, sometimes so labeled because fond classicists connect the huntsman and leaping dogs with such classical illustrations of the myth as the Pan Painter krater in Boston, is unusual in the Ripe II period for including a human figure at all. Perhaps it still belongs to the end of Ripe I, when subsidiary grooms and archers were so popular; occasionally there are other human actors in these later pictorial scenes (V.113), but they are exceptional. This very pretty vase, of late shape with its contracted underbelly and foot (wrongly restored), is one of the most elegant manifestations of the end of the proper pictorial style. It is a pity that it is so broken; and one should notice that a good deal of the upper part of the dog handler and part of his right-hand dog are restored.

The principal side shows a bull low on the ground with one front leg stretched out and one bent under his chest, in a field of delicate lozenges filled at the corners, as on the Pierides jug (V.74). The hindquarters of the bull are not preserved, but one may imagine them kicking out behind in a lively version of the "flying gallop," as on the other side. The head with long curved horns bends back in easy curves over the shoulder, and the lozenges follow the twisted contour. The eye is three concentric ovals as on the Pierides jug, and the muzzle is a similar circle. The lines of the horns and the back are nearly parallel with the upper framing bands and harmonize with the curves of the forelegs; there is a fine sense of design at work. The body is filled with a consistent series of little arrowheads, as on stags of the Ripe period, both early and late, a welcome change from the arbitrary divisions inside the body practiced by other contemporary painters.

The strong backward turn of the bull's head and his collapse toward the ground suggest that this may be a unified hunting scene, although no sign of weapon or wound is preserved. The decorative intention is playfully underlined by the way the left-hand dog climbs the bull's foreleg to reach his master better. The dogs are delightfully clumsy, with big feet like puppies, reserved heads, and open yipping mouths; the prancing motion is a rarity this late. Too little remains of the human figure to make a direct comparison to others of the thirteenth century except in the very sharp backward curve of the chest and shoulders, and the two-line claws holding the light leashes.

The damaged reverse side preserves one of the finest flying gallops in pictorial painting, with the long bull's body skimming over the field, the slender neck twisted back in a higher curve and the feet well off the ground, not grazing or resting. Traces of little paws in front suggest that he is hurtling unwittingly into another dog.

74. The jug by the same painter, in the G. G. Pierides Collection, of a peculiar Cypriote shape with metal ancestors, has dramatic sunburst rosettes on the body between dark bands enriched with white crosses (white paint is rare in this period in general); on the shoulder, opposite the handle, is a short dark bull filled with white crosses. The rosettes are repeated by the handle, and the field is filled with careful lozenges filled at the corners. The painter has distorted the bull's back to harmonize with the curve of the jug's neck, and his horns curve backward to follow, more like a goat's than a bull's; this anxiety to subordinate anatomical form to decorative charm is a hallmark of the period. The bull has a solid quality, with heavy hooves. Its massiveness is created by a white contour line just inside the border of the dark silhouette, but is partly negated by the even distribution of white crosses over the hide, not clustered to suggest bunched muscle in motion. The head is formed of harmonious curves—the triple oval eye with dots under the lower lid and sure closed loops for brow and muzzle. A white collar, a ladder pattern like a choker, representing the wrinkled dewlaps, appears also in the mainland pictorial style (VIII.12, IX.38). The front legs are finely curved without knees, though the hind legs retain proper hocks. Although the fabric of this jug is coarse, the painting is both perky and bold, and it stands out among the later Cypriote tableware of its time. A fragment (V.74.1) found at Tell Sukas south of Ugarit, of a bull with a dewlap collar and crosses on the hide, may be by the same painter.

76. A more characteristic specimen of the Ripe II stage is a bell krater from Enkomi. A bull and a bird are painted on one side, without any interaction, the bull plodding right, the bird behind him with head turned back and feet off the ground; there are three boring lozenges in the field. The other side has a single bull, quite a good palm tree behind him, and loose spirals in front. The wavy-line filling covers all of the bird and the front and rear quarters of the bull; the belly section of the bull is nearly empty, with two dot-rosettes neatly placed in the center and an edging of semicircles. This lightening of the center had begun in the Ripe I stage with V.46 and V.52, and is carried further here. The drawing is poor, and it is against such bland faces as this that the Pastoral style reacts.

80. A bell krater sometimes known as the Gjerstad krater introduces the first bull protome in company with a complete bull. It is by a painter who specialized in such protomes (Painter 21, Protome Painter A), with about a dozen pieces identified as from his hand, and many more related works by artists whom he influenced (V.76-97, Painters 20, 22; cf. IX.19 and following).

The protome quickly becomes popular, perhaps to help fill small surfaces with an abbreviated form of a favorite subject. It is better by itself; when it appears along with a complete bull it looks merely fractured or buried in the ground. The protome usually extends below the animal's shoulders in a triangle or cuts him off at the "waist." The bull is painted in sections, with an almost empty center, and when the front and rear quarters are indicated, they get lighter, with small decorations of joining semicircles or dot-rosettes; a rosette or lozenge may be inserted in the protome. There is a faint memory of the older naturalism in pictorial painting; the circle clusters are not a bad imitation of dapples, the legs are striped, the genitals indicated, but it is a weak picture compared to those of Ripe I. There are, however, good bold curves in the jaw and horns, and the parted lips anticipate the Pastoral style.

As the painter's style becomes settled, he explores and varies his theme: two bulls with a calf betwen them (V.86), bulls walking around the inside surface of bowls (the distortion necessary to paint them on the outside proved unsuccessful, V.84), protomes on the shoulders of jugs of a Levantine shape (V.82, 83), where the protomes face and lock horns, or are seen as charging, the two lowered heads all that is necessary on such a small surface (V.85). The Protome Painter's lines can be thick, authoritative, and highly ornamental; if one divests one's mind of the earlier grandeurs of the pictorial style and looks at these designs as new decorative inventions, they are very good.

Single bulls on bell kraters and protomes on bowls and jugs can be monotonous, and the freshness of the Pastoral style will be a marked relief. One very late bull design on a bell krater illustrates some of the features transitional to that new vitality.

101. A bell krater from Haghia Paraskevi, Nicosia, now in Berlin, presents two strongly marked bulls on each side, with an apparent effort to indicate perspective. The bulls are in limp attitudes, with unhooved hind legs hanging in the air and the front legs through the framing band; the head is lowered, so that the whole animal seems to slip dejectedly forward. The outline is bold and simple, with curious interior contours so that both hind legs are shown separately up to the tail socket and the front left leg shows through the chest from the shoulder down. There are two lower belly lines, which at first suggest that the belly was drawn twice, once too narrowly to accommodate the central filling ornament and then expanded; yet the variety of these contours suggests that the artist was really concerned with three-dimensional effects, with developing a technique to render mass. He has abandoned the former flat grand form for a more supple one, less arbitrarily divided. The split circle filled with stripes like an accordion on the center of the belly gives a dramatic touch. There is a beginning of impressionism in the arcs used to show neck wrinkles, in the missing lower jaw line framed by a parenthesis, the quick hook of the muzzle, the pricked ear before or behind the horn at will, the shading and heavy outline of the tail hair. An intact outline is no longer paramount; it is being broken up to gain new qualities.

FACING BULLS' HEADS

The facing bull's head occurs sporadically in the pictorial style (III.23), but it remains a rare subject, often related to other media. There are two Ripe II versions in the East, very different from each other; the first perhaps was copied directly from silver-and-niello work, the second is in a simplified ceramic style that looks forward to the Late or Mycenaean III C stage.

102. The famous fragmentary stirrup jar from Enkomi is hard to date precisely, because only the top is preserved and because the subsidiary motifs are unusual. The neat drawing and spacing of the ornaments are typical of the best III B painting; the rough treatment of the curls of hair on the bull's brow and the bold symmetry combined with experiment may well be among the more original products of Ripe II. This is, as usual, a head, not a skull, with the texture of hair rendered on the muzzle and crest in a manner that originated on stone rhyta in the Late Minoan I period in Crete, a texture usually omitted in pictorial painting. It has long been observed that this painting is a near copy of the bull's-head metal bowls of Enkomi and Dendra,[29] closer to the former, the stiff compartments of black inner contour corresponding to the niello inlays on the gold faces of those farouche masterpieces of metalwork. The context of the Enkomi bowl would suit the tentative date of this stirrup jar — not necessarily when it was made, for the Dendra example, far more formal, is probably a hundred years earlier — but the period when it or others like it may have been on exhibit, somehow available to influence the images of pot painters in search of new themes.

103. A late bell krater from Aradippo develops a new, very formal pattern that is characteristic of late III B and early III C pictorial in areas as distant as Athens, Mycenae, and Kos. This is the broad band of checkerboard in the center of a panel forming a triglyph-and-metope effect, in which the "metopai" may be filled with antithetic animals or an interrupted frieze. Here the checkerboard is wider than the bulls' heads, like a wall; the architectural use of the design is seen in contemporary frescoes from Orchomenos and Pylos and on the late painted mainland larnakes.

The thin forms of the solid-painted heads suggest they may be proper boukrania, not full bulls' heads. There is a narrow panel of crosshatching on the muzzle; the round eyes are small like sockets; the horns spring out broadly and then rise to touch the upper band in thin points. The two skulls are suspended by a chain or cable.[30] The whole design is unique, handsome, a little macabre.

STAGS

Wild animals and hunting scenes continue to appear in the Ripe II period, although they remain uncommon. Sometimes the traditional frieze is used, sometimes the animals are set off from each other by vertical dividers, triglyphs, or checkerboard. This is a more emphatic version of the disjunction of figures on contemporary bell kraters. Perhaps the influence of ivory carving is already at work, favoring single figures within marked borders. The appearance at this time of such new designs as goats feeding in symmetrical pairs at a central tree is surely due to the popularity of Oriental ivories.

104. A krater fragment from Ugarit seems powerful in the drawings and may be transitional between the first and second Ripe stages. The forms of the stags are those of the earlier period, with short, well-branched antlers, well-bunched bodies with humped backs, and a not-too-prominent bottle nose. On the other hand, the bodies are drawn partly in dark silhouette and partly in outline (dark chest and rump, arrow-filled reserved bellies, reserved noses) and are divided from each other by vertical fillers ultimately descended from palm trees. An odd streamer — two wavy lines enclosing a chain — springs from their necks to flow over their backs almost like reins. This sense of staccato division is perhaps more in keeping with the second stage.

105. Another difficult piece, from Minet el-Beida, is a rhyton of the figured type so beloved there, with what seems to be a stag right, filled with spots and U's, with perhaps a smaller one skipping to the left; Professor Schaeffer believed them to be horses (who do not usually have such an interior filling); if the tails were long they could well be "une jument avec son poulain qui bondit . . . la race des chevaux de pur sang arab."

106. A fragmentary bell krater from Enkomi recalls the earlier period in its large, handsome rosettes hung over the backs of a frieze of stags moving right, some looking back (cf. V.55). The later style is evident in the vertical wavy lines that separate and box in some of the stags, in the

29. Schaeffer, *Enkomi-Alasia* I, suppl. pl. D; A. Persson, *The Royal Tombs at Dendra* (1931) pls. 1, 12-15.
30. Contemporary hanging bulls appear on an unpublished Minoan larnax in Germany, suspended back to back with thongs around chest or foreleg, in a hunting context.

clumsier sagging bellies of some of the animals, and in the variety of treatment of the heads: here an open mouth, there a solid head, there a caricature bottle nose filled with a wavy line. Some forelegs are dark and split at the knee, others reserved, with the normal arrow fillers of the hide. There is some confusion about how to organize a large number of animals in a frieze without monotony—an effort that in itself suggests a late stage—and the way some deer bump into each other, rump against chest, perhaps suggests a refreshing lack of planning.

GOATS

A shallow bowl in the Pierides Collection has a playful pattern on the interior, two opposed goats attached by their hooves to a series of concentric circles in the center. The goats whirl around belly to belly, each filling half the bowl, hind legs floating free and horns running into the rim. Their long bodies are in dark silhouette except for a patch in the muzzle that is filled with stripes on one and broken lines like ingrown hair or teeth on the other (cf. V.58). Certain sportive inaccuracies of anatomy may again anticipate the Pastoral style: the double tails, and the genitals of one goat hitched on backward. In its much simplified form, this bowl recalls goat and bird designs on Rhodes (XII.10, 12) and a fish bowl from Ugarit (V.133).

Twin bell kraters (V.108, 109) by the same painter, both from the rich side-chamber of Tomb 18 at Enkomi, make a successful composition of dark goats rearing up against a central, bordered checkerboard panel. The openmouthed silhouettes are graceful in their compensating curves and well placed in their blocks; there is an effective contrast between the rhythmic movements of the animals and the tall static checkerboard. These approach the borderline of the Mycenaean III C:1 style (XI.84).

Rhyton fragments from Ugarit (V.110) show how, in the last pair of vases, the central motif with rearing goats was adapted from the older Oriental motif of a central plant, usually a short tree, with goats standing on their hind legs to nibble the leaves in a familiar heraldic pattern. In these designs the goats may be hoof to hoof or back to back with everted heads, so long as they match. The image of the goat eating the tree, which has a long history in the Near East, appears at this same stage at Mycenae (IX.73, 74). A goat in a field of arrowhead pattern (wishful thinking?), V.111, is amusing as the painter draws the head from above, loops the ears and muzzle, and pops the eyes.

112. A very fragmentary amphoroid krater from Enkomi, one of the last specimens of this type, is another transition to the Pastoral style, although the fabric excludes it from that class. There is a frieze of sketchy animals, apparently goats and kids, around the shoulder. Their outlined bodies are filled with horizontal and vertical lines, and there are crude N-patterns and spirals filling the background. The painter may have been attempting a vivacious scene of life in the flock, but the composition is of inferior quality, not so much because of the traits of the period as because he was a bad painter.

"HUNT"

113. Fragments of a bell krater with an unusually narrow picture zone illustrate a hunting or pastoral scene on the right half of one side; on the other, all that remains is a diving fish by the right handle. The drawing is bad but strives for liveliness. This curious "hunting" scene is not the usual huntsman and hounds but something like a perversion of a master of animals or an image of a cowherd trying to protect his bulls from a predator. A small man occupies the center of the right half of the picture; he is dressed in a calf-length tunic patterned with scales like chain mail and has a grotesque doglike face with curly hair falling down his neck. In spite of his scale-corselet(?), the man seems unarmed; he faces right and tries to hold the leg of a fleeing animal with his right hand, its tail in his left. The animal in question is rather doglike but seems to have horn-buds on its brow, as well as hooves. A triangle hanging from its belly is probably the hair at the end of a bull's pizzle, not an udder, but the animal is probably domesticated. The face is reserved, the legs long and awkwardly flexible. Behind the man, another animal comes rushing through space with its front legs kicking up in a cat-spring, perhaps a mountain lion drawn like a dog, with a sharp muzzle, pricked-up triangular ears, and a ruffled outline along its back like a ridge of hair. On the missing left part of the picture there must have been other animals and perhaps human beings; perhaps the more usual hunt has turned into a general mêlée with a threatening confusion of hoofed game and taloned predators. The little hunter seems overwhelmed by the size of the animals around him, an expressive touch not out of place for the clumsy but congenial experiments at the end of Ripe II.

The fish on the other side compares with other diving fish of this stage (V.128, 130); the body is filled, with reserved borders, wavy scallops for dorsal fins, and two streamers from the mouth.

LIONS

114. One of the very latest of all pictorial amphoroid kraters, from Shemishin near Aradippo, is the only Ripe Cypriote piece to bear genuine, incontrovertible lions, and is one of the funniest and most handsome of all (cf. VI.4, 22, 24). Whenever one talks glibly of pictorial vase painting as an imitation of scenes in other arts, frescoes or gems, one should look again at this piece and reflect. It illustrates almost perfectly how a subject well liked by all kinds of Aegean craftsmen may be changed and distorted to fit on a pot, and how decorative distortion is regularly used, regularly desired, to create something new and suitable. Many observers will not find it "suitable" to turn heraldic lions into dachshunds and pull out their sausage bodies right around the vase from the center to the handles; this is perhaps caricature, but it is grand pottery.

These lions remind everyone of the Lion Gate at Mycenae, if it had no rearward limits, and of the related gems.[31] A pair of heraldic lions opposed over a flower topped by horns of consecration is just what is needed to prompt reveries of Minoan cult and Mycenaean aristocratic spirit. That it belongs in the Ripe II period is clear. The rosettes in the field over the backs of the animals link it to V.74, 90; the bold outlines and back-turned heads with open mouths to V.58, 80 and following, 106; the separation by a flower and the disjunction of figures turned to heraldic advantage link it to V.110. The whole composition is a symphony of circles and cylinders: the tubular bodies, the rosettes reflecting the large round eyes made of several circles or filled solid, the circles in the field, small editions of the beautifully drawn row of circles filling the lion bodies from eye to tail, with all pretense of interest in real anatomy gaily abandoned. These circles have given birth to a row of little circles under three of the bellies, and others rise up like bubbles from the backs.

On one side the lions are more formal, separated by a stiff flower, like a lily with holy horns for its bud; on the other side they stumble into a dance and cross their forepaws. An extra rosette between their necks keeps them apart. After these grand centerpieces, the wizened haunches rubbing themselves on the handle framing bands cannot fail to amuse, and the tails doing a pas de deux are a charming inanity. The legs and feet come in all different shapes, some like hooves, some like human feet under the split knees; on the dance-step side the disparity in length between the two sets of front legs reminds one of that childhood monster, the "side-hill grampus."

BIRDS

There are two kinds of bird designs at the end of the Ripe period: a full-bodied traditional type with rather dry, formal interior filling, and a new elongated, schematic type seen as though from above, with the whimsical ornament of V.69 reduced to an arbitrary series of dotted shapes or quick open lines. There are protomes, too. Few of them are interesting.

115. A bell krater from Klavdhia uses the checkerboard centerpiece to separate two birds in the style of the goat kraters, V.108 and 109. On one side the round addorsed birds twist their heads back to touch the checkerboard with their bills and by a curious and not unpleasant device, the raised wing is converted into a sheet of striped membrane between the back and the head. The bodies are divided in two and filled with wavy lines or scales. On the other side the birds are darker, one solid and one with a heavy outline filled with diagonal waves; on both sides they stand tiptoe on arcs of claws. There are two large rosettes in each panel.

116. Inside a bowl from Cyprus, now in California, six small spotted birds jump along around the outer edge, their crooked knees poking forward at a sharp angle from the inner ring. The birds' bodies are reduced in size and weight, and the raised wing is a simple curved line.

118. The beginning of the new reduction to linear form appears on a fragmentary bowl from Hala Sultan Tekké. Two birds without feet or wings chase each other around the rim, the bill of the follower sticking into the tail of the leader. The split tails are those of swallows seen from above or below. The oval body is contoured with spots, as on Minoan birds of the late thirteenth century.

119. A bowl from Kition takes a further step by opening up the body of the bird behind so that there is a single line from neck to forked tail; the wings become a bracket near the head. There are seven birds on this bowl, four partly corporeal with broad wings, three in schematic outline form. The figure takes only four brush strokes. This is one of at least five bowls by the same painter: two with very fine-lined forms and triangle tails (V.120, Ugarit, and V.121), one with the wings turned back again to the head (V.122, Ugarit), and a lovely cup from Enkomi (V.123) with seven swallows darting in free patterns in the air, turning in two circles and skimming around the bowl.

124. A very dull bowl from Cyprus has bird protomes in the outer circle, counterclockwise for a change. If bull protomes look silly, these eleven spotted shapes with linear beaks look worse. A purely abstract ornament would have been more effective.

125. A miniature conical rhyton from an unknown site is another crude attempt at making images on a shape that is rarely pictorial except at Ugarit. The rim, handle, and bottom are missing. A zone of five "flamingos" deco-

---

31. P. Åström, B. Blomé, *OpAth* 5 (1965) 159; G. Mylonas, *Mycenae and The Mycenaean Age* (1964) 17 f., 173; the Shemishin krater has elements in common with the Late hunting krater at Ugarit, XIII.27.

rates the upper body between the usual bands. Three of the birds are dark, one has a striped neck, one is hatched inside. The birds have very long legs turned to the right, with well-jointed knees and three claws. The heads are turned to the left, and by some misunderstanding of the usual silhouette, the body seems to be put on backward with the tail in front. The effort to create a regular decorative frieze on a rhyton is praiseworthy; one should compare it, however, to the fine fish rhyton from Ugarit (V.131).

FISH

In the late thirteenth century birds and fish are often combined, either by themselves or set in the coils of an octopus. The combination was made popular by Cretan vase painters in the fifteenth century and may well have had a specific symbolic meaning to Cretan minds, but in the late pictorial style in the East there is rarely a sense of significance in the juxtaposition of creatures from different elements, except perhaps on the famous island stirrup jars (XII.23, XIII.8).

126. An oddly drawn fragmentary bowl from Hala Sultan Tekké must have had pictures in sections separated by crosshatched blocks. In the one preserved section, a distorted bird seems to be chasing a swimming fish. They are penned between very broad zones of concentric circles in the interior and at the rim. Both fish and bird are in dark silhouette, with added white spots; white overpaint is rare in the normal Ripe style but continued to be used for marine subjects like octopods and is revived in the Late period. The fish seems to be an ordinary dolphin, but the bird looks as though it has a goiter in the tail and is wearing galoshes; its fish tail flips far out behind the round body, and one may wonder whether the painter intended a little fish here, made an error, and covered it up by extending the splashed paint into a bird. The head and chest are perfectly well drawn in the old full-bodied style; the soggy feet must be accidental.

The other fish vases of Ripe II follow the patterns already observed with goats and birds: fish in checkerboard panels, in whirling friezes inside shallow bowls, and on rhyta.

127. The checkerboard-panel pattern used so successfully for goats and birds (V.109, 115) is also used at Enkomi for fish, though to interrupt a sequence rather than as a heraldic centerpiece. A bell krater from Enkomi has a rather broad, open-bodied fish swimming right in each panel; like the birds of the period, the fish is made with a quick, thick outline in two single curves from jaw to tail, the interior empty, but with an eye of concentric rings blocking the gullet between belly and jaw. It is a simple design, much worn.

128. One of the most interesting of all late kraters is a bell krater of unattractive fabric with a school of eight outlined fish on each side, diving at free angles down to the right. Two are large predators who have each swallowed two smaller fish as they rushed into the school; two other small ones got away. The fish are nicely drawn with rows of fins, solid or filled with triangles along their backs, and flaring tubular snouts; there is no distinction of species between the two sizes. The little fish are striped along their length in a characteristically casual way; the big ones are of course left plain so that we can see inside them.

This interior view of a solid fleshy object is matched by a different painter on the next vase, where the fish's skeleton shows through the skin. It is an extremely rare technique in Mycenaean pictorial, though some scholars have tried to call it a common characteristic of "primitive" painting, which pictorial painting is not. There are two comparable pieces from the mainland, the Koukounara birds with eggs (VIII.17) and a Tanagra larnax with a corpse inside the image of the larnax on the end. The two Cypriote specimens are different in intent, scarcely "X-ray" painting; V.128 twists the need to find an attractive filling ornament for the big fish into a vivacious study of life under water, and V.129 is an equally comic demonstration of prolepsis or wishful thinking in the manner of a Roman mosaic, like "the unswept floor."

129. A very fragmentary bell krater from Cyprus shows three fish of common Mediterranean form, perhaps *mavromates*, who seem to swim around the shoulder, but since the backbone of one is hurriedly but precisely drawn, perhaps they are a beautiful memory or a happy anticipation of luncheon in the potter's workshop. The fish on the right still has his striped skin. They are piquant forms, with noses turned slightly upward and the lines of fins and tails carried out in sweeping brush strokes. The backbone fish bumps the bottom band as if on shallow bottom or near the edge of the dinner plate.

130. A beautiful hydria or one-handled jug in the Pierides Collection has eight fanged fish swimming at different angles on the shoulder. They are rendered in silhouette, with round reserved eyes and open jaws, the teeth shown as small bumps along the inside of the long parted jaws, matching the fringe on some tails. Some have two, some three dorsal and ventral fins; in style they recall V.126, and here too white paint is used to draw three zigzag lines along each body. Most of the fish are diving down to feed on the bottom, not in the strictly patterned composition of old Minoan fish vases (cf. III.9, VII.J) but loosely colliding; one comes up to jab a companion under the neck. The view of this vase from the top is fine, though

it must have been an awkward tilt to draw at. The style is close to that of the next.

131. On a conical rhyton from Ugarit, five fish in silhouette stand upright on their tails in a regular pattern around the upper zone. This is an excellent and original way of treating a vase shape that in the marine sphere had previously been decorated almost exclusively with octopods. Ugaritic taste for the rhyton shape with unusual pictures is well documented.

The fish are separated from each other, two pairs and a singleton, by wavy lines like weeds, concentric circles, and a remnant of a flower. The oval bodies are ridged with as many as four pairs of fins; the sharp heads are filled with diagonal stripes like a decorative simplification of teeth. The usual feeding posture is reversed, probably because the painter held it upside down to draw; this is seen on the next rhyton (V.132) also.

A series of shallow bowls with fish swimming around the interior forms a parallel to the bird series. The finest is a bowl from Ugarit with two opposed fishes, V.133. Their tails are hitched to the central circles in a style very reminiscent of the goats on V.107. The fishes are built solidly and simply with fine recurving tails; their mouths are sharp, open beaks with a line undulating inside, a tongue or a small fish. This elegant pattern is also known in the west (IX.120, X.85, 100).

The other bowls are simpler and rougher, with the fish in a circular frieze, in silhouette or in outline filled with chains (V.136) or crosses (V.132). A late bowl (V.137) of good fabric but crude drawing seems to represent some combination of sea slug, snail, and monster; perhaps they were meant as fish, though one depressed creature uses his "fins" to creep along weakly, like a prehistoric organism emerging from the waters to dry land.

138. The transition to the Pastoral style is illustrated by a bowl from Kition in the later fabric, no longer good hard Mycenaean red on buff, but matt red, washy paint on a light brown surface. It preserves a quasi-Mycenaean pictorial style, in a row of four fish swimming left, three spotted, one striped "herringbone" fashion (see V.129); the fish are now crowded into an interior circle, the outer rings being given over to crosshatched lozenges and zigzags. At the center, instead of concentric circles there is a spiral, which will be a standard feature in the Late period. It has lost the flair of earlier bowls, the very last gasp of a tradition that shortly before had produced such handsome pieces as the Ugarit bowl, V.133.

The next phase of painting in the East still falls within the thirteenth century at the start and lasts well into the twelfth; for historical reasons there is a clear break in the line of pictorial style changes; the latest expressions of image making in Cyprus are considered in the next chapter.

VI
CYPRUS AND THE EAST:
Pastoral

SCHOLARS HAVE LONG DISTINGUISHED a style in vase painting, coinciding with the last phase of Late Helladic III B, confined to Cyprus and occasionally the Syro-Palestinian coast, which they called Rude. This name signifies the inferior quality of the style compared to other Mycenaean vases.[1] Vases painted in the Rude style are usually bell kraters of angular profile and of a fabric clearly inferior to the true Mycenaean.

Furumark described this style as "a derivative Mycenaean ware, based on the Levanto-Mycenaean III B style." He emphasized the "rudeness" both in shape and decoration and concluded that "these vases cannot have been made by the same potters and painters who manufactured the genuine Levanto-Mycenaean ware."[2] On the basis of this argument he formulated the theory that this style was produced in a place where genuine Levanto-Mycenaean pottery was well known but not manufactured and was decorated by painters who were also familiar with the indigenous Palestinian style.

Stubbings recognized the obvious weakness of this theory and defended the Rude style as forming an original stylistic group, which could be subdivided.[3] He recognized two groups of vases (his III and IV) in the Rude style that he attributed to two individual painters, but he also underlined the homogeneous character of the style.

Mrs. Immerwahr categorically rejected the idea that the Rude style could form an original stylistic group. She put forward the suggestion that the kraters decorated in the Rude style (Stubbings's groups III and IV) are not strictly Mycenaean but rather Levantine imitations of the Mycenaean style.[4]

The chronological aspect of this problem has been treated by Catling, who attributes the *floruit* of this ware to Late Cypriote II C, that is, he considers it contemporary with the last phase of Late Helladic III B.[5]

The most recent commentary on this style, by Benson, distinguished a painter of the Rude style who painted bird kraters. He simply mentioned the various problems connected with the style without attempting to solve them and concluded that "until all the painters active in the Rude Style have been considered individually, it is too early to discuss it as a total phenomenon."[6]

It is clear from this short survey that the Rude style cannot be excluded from a study of the Mycenaean pictorial style, whatever one believes about its origin, and that it represents an artistic phenomenon of exceptional importance for the development of Mycenaean art in the East during the last phase of the thirteenth century.

This chapter reproduces, to a great extent, Karageorghis, *Nouveaux Documents*, 231-259. Since 1965, however, more material has been discovered, and we have included it here to make the study of stylistic development more effective.

1. The most complete study of this style was made by Furumark, *MP*, 465-470.

2. *Ibid.*, 470.

3. F. H. Stubbings, "Some Mycenaean Artists," *BSA* 46 (1951) 173, Note.

4. S. A. Immerwahr, review of Stubbings, *MycLevant*, in *AJA* 60 (1956) 140, n. 25; "Mycenaean Trade and Colonization," *Archaeology* 13 (1960) 12. M. Popham suggested that Rude style kraters "indicated some difficulty in obtaining the genuine article," in *Acts of the International Archaeological Symposium "The Relations between Cyprus and Crete ca. 2000-500 B.C."* (1979) 190.

5. H. W. Catling, "The Bronze Age Pottery," in J. du Plat Taylor, *Myrtou-Pigadhes* (1957) 42 f.

6. J. L. Benson, "Observations on Mycenaean Vase-Painters," *AJA* 65 (1961) 342 f.

Furumark attempted an analysis of the style, mainly the specimens that had been published up to the time when he wrote his magnum opus.[7] So far as possible, we have made a particular point of studying the style from the original vases and not from illustrations, because of its peculiarities in the use of paint and its varying qualities.

After long reflection, we have decided to propose a new name for this style, the name Rude being admittedly most unfortunate. Based on the frequency of pastoral scenes, we propose the name Pastoral, which is descriptive without any aesthetic prejudices about its qualities.

EARLY PASTORAL

During the last phase of Late Helladic III B, one may observe a definite deterioration in quality of the fabric. This is obvious in the shallow conical bowls with two horizontal strap handles at the rim, of which large numbers have been found in recent years at various Late Cypriote sites, such as Enkomi, Kition, and Palaipaphos. This fabric, a development of the normal Mycenaean, has a characteristic clay that is not well refined and a paint that is semiglossy or, when thinly applied, matt. One must distinguish it, however, from the rough, painted pottery of Late Cypriote III. The fabric is what Joan du Plat Taylor called "Apliki B" in Late Cypriote II C with a possible slight overlap with Late Cypriote III.[8] It is interesting that Furumark, in a note on the fabric of Apliki B, declared that the category he called Rude style "is analogous but different." He observes that this "general category of local imitations of Myc. III B pottery . . . with simplified and carelessly executed Myc. III B patterns in more or less lustreless paint occurs on the Greek mainland, in Laconia, Messenia, and Thessaly, etc. as well as in Rhodes and Phylakopi."[9] He gave references to a comparable fabric from Troy. It is evident that the degeneration in Mycenaean fabric quality is not an isolated phenomenon, and one may not speak, with Catling, about an "imitation" of the pottery of Late Helladic III B.[10] It is simply a development of it, just as Hellenistic matt glazed pottery is a development of Attic glazed ware.

Apart from the degeneration in fabric, there is also a limitation of vase forms toward the end of Late Helladic III B, so far as one can judge from the material already published from Myrtou, Apliki, Enkomi, Palaipaphos, and Kition. The most favored shapes are the bell krater, bowls of various forms, and the jug. These shapes, a development from the greater range of the Ripe style, were traditional on the mainland.

It is in this atmosphere that the Pastoral style developed. The Ripe pictorial style had already had a life of nearly a century, and toward the end, it showed signs of degeneration.[11] The bull motif, drawn in outline and filled with small embroidery-like designs, had known great popularity but was then forgotten.[12] The creation of the new Pastoral style may be partly a reaction by the vase painters against the old Ripe style, with its embroidery effects and conventional character, and an effort to revive the Mycenaean pictorial style by creating a kind of revolution in the art of drawing. The artists were inspired, apparently, by the art of engraving on ivory, which was flourishing toward the end of the thirteenth century.[13] Its characteristics were bold outlining of figures and rendering of anatomic details by thin and thick lines. This influence is detectable in the earliest specimens of the Pastoral style.

1. On a bell krater from Enkomi the two panels between the handles are decorated with a pictorial scene.[14] Side A is bordered on the left by two vertical parallel lines with oblique strokes between them. Side B is flanked on either side by one straight and two wavy lines respectively. On side A a goat walks left, turning its head back to reach the foliage of a bush or tree with curving stem. In back of

7. See note 1. The material has doubled since 1950, and more specimens from the reserve collections of the Cyprus Museum have been studied; they were discovered mainly in the 1896 British excavations at Enkomi.

8. J. du Plat Taylor, *Antiquaries Journal* 32 (1952) 157.

9. *Ibid.*

10. Catling, "Bronze Age Pottery," n. 5, 47 f.

11. One may mention here vases like the krater fragment from Enkomi, BM C370 (*BMCatV*, 73, fig. 119) or the lion krater from Shemishin (V.114).

12. There are several representations of bulls in the last phase of the thirteenth century with embroidery-like ornaments inside the outlined body, already showing signs of degeneration (V.51, 99-101).

13. Among other works on Mycenaean and Eastern ivories, see E. Decamps de Mertzenfeld, *Inventaire commenté des ivoires phéniciens et apparentés découverts dans le Proche-Orient* (1954) (*IvoiresPhén*); R. D. Barnett, *A Catalogue of the Nimrud Ivories in the British Museum* (1957); *PEQ* 71 (1939) 4 f.; and *Archaeology* 9 (1956) 87 f.; G. Loud, *The Megiddo Ivories* (1939); H. Kantor, *The Aegean and the Orient in the 2nd Millennium B.C.* (1948) 98 f.; *JNES* 15 (1956) 153 f.; and *Archaeology* 13 (1960) 14 f.; J.-C. Poursat, *Les Ivoires Mycéniens* (1977) (*IvoiresMyc*); H. Gallet de Santerre, J. Tréheux, *BCH* 71-72 (1947-48) 148 f.; S. Symeonoglou, *Kadmeia* I (1973) 44 f.; A. J. B. Wace, *Archaeology* 7 (1954) 149 f.; J. Schäfer, *AthMitt* 73 (1958) 73 f.; B. Freyer-Schauenburg, *Elfenbeine aus dem samischen Heraion* (1966); M. E. L. Mallowan, *Ivories from Nimrud 1949-63* (1967-74); I. J. Winter, *Iraq* 38 (1976) 1 f.; D. Collon, *Iraq* 39 (1977) 219 f.

14. The form of this krater corresponds to Furumark, *MP*, FS 281, under which this vase was listed, but it has several characteristics corresponding to FS 282, like the conical profile and the straight vertical upper part of the sides. The straight sides provided a flatter surface for the painter to draw on. The clay is hard, buff-pinkish, with a buff slip, orange to light brown paint, semiglossy when thickly applied, but matt and washy when thin.

the goat a bull walks left. The animals are rendered partly in outline and partly in silhouette. The goat's head is painted solid, as is the upper part of the bull's body and his neck. This recalls the realistic touches on certain Early and Middle pictorial vases, but the changes in texture come from the Ripe II style. The goat's body is filled with vertical wavy lines, indicating the animal's hair.

The bull's body is more elaborately rendered, with very thin lines for details of the head, especially the forehead. There is an effort to show the folds of the dewlap with small strokes along the outline. Thick and thin lines are used for the veins on the legs. Curved lines inside the body indicate the folds of the hide at the forepart and midsection of the body. A bold, thick curved line is used for the stem of the bush, terminating in the foliage, represented by one single large outlined leaf, with details inside shown with strokes. On side B a bull (or cow?) walks left; there is a leafy bush on the extreme left, with branches springing from the band that frames the panel near the handle. The animal's body is similar to that on side A. The bush is more elaborately drawn than on side A, with large leaves and veins indicated by thin lines. The animal is treated even more naturalistically, especially the eyes and the mouth. We have here a bold and competent painter who, unlike his predecessors, did not decorate his vase with a static representation; he tried to create a lively pastoral scene. Life is represented not by violent action but by the expression and movement of one specific moment, as in certain works of art of Minoan Crete: the moment when the animal approaches the foliage, more precisely when he eats the leaves with mouth open, or the moment when the goat turns its head back to reach the foliage while the majestic bull looks on. The artist is a master of his brush, using it boldly and precisely, just as a modern artist would.

The influence on this painter of the technique of ivory carving is obvious. The use of thick and thin lines is well known in ivory engraving, where the artist has only the thin line for rendering details of animal bodies and the thick line for shading. In bull representations on ivory, the artist makes a special effort to render anatomical details inside the outlined head and legs; these same characteristics are observed in the treatment of the bulls on this vase.[15] The subjects on both sides of the krater belong in the ivory repertory, where walking or galloping animals with the head turned back are common.[16] Also common is the representation of two animals walking in the same direction, one turning its head back to look at the other, as on side A of our krater, but more often they are represented in violent action.[17] In ivory carving a bull is often associated with the tree or bush motif, so popular in the ivories of the

Near East, particularly in the thirteenth century.[18] This theme will be adopted by the vase painters of the Pastoral style as a favorite composition. Finally, the fashion of preparing a framed rectangular panel to receive the picture may also have been inspired by the rectangular engraved ivory plaques. Though some of these features were inherent in the pictorial tradition, ivory work may represent a new stimulus.

The following specimens also suggest the influence of ivory carving.

2. On the fragmentary upper part of a bell krater from Kouklia (Palaipaphos),[19] the panel is decorated with an outlined bull walking right, with a bush or tree motif in front. Only the forepart of the bull and the tree survive. On the extreme right are traces of a vertical line that flanked the panel as on VI.1. Vertical curved lines indicate the folds of the bull's dewlap, as occasionally in ivory carving.[20] The painter was particularly careful in rendering the details of the advancing foreleg, especially the knee. The tree is identical with the so-called olive trees with pointed leaves on ivories, usually in association with bulls, suggesting the country setting.[21] The same parallels may be found in ivory carving for the attitude of our bull, with lowered head, curved neck, and advancing foreleg.

3. On a fragmentary bell krater from Kition the panel is decorated with a bull facing right and a tree in front. Only the forepart of the bull and part of the tree survive. The animal's body is rendered in thick outline, thicker near the upper part of the neck. Thin curved lines show the dewlap.

There are some striking similarities with the bull from Palaipaphos, VI.2, in style and in subject matter. The details of the head suggest that the two fragments may have come from the same workshop.

15. H. Kantor, *Archaeology* 13 (1960) 19, figs. 10 A, 15-17; de Mertzenfeld, *IvoiresPhén*, pls. 1, 5, 7, 4.17 a, 21.1186, 27.315, 25.305 c, 39.391, 65.704, 66.744, 69.70; Poursat, *IvoiresMyc*, pls. XV.5; XVII.3; L.453.

16. de Mertzenfeld, *IvoiresPhén*, pl. 69.788 c: ivory box from Enkomi with a goat galloping left, turning its head back in the opposite direction.

17. de Mertzenfeld, *IvoiresPhén*, pl. 70.791, from Enkomi; H. Kantor, *Archaeology* 13 (1960) 19, fig. 10 A; Poursat, *IvoiresMyc*, pl. XIX C; Vermeule, *GBA*, pl. XXXVII C.

18. de Mertzenfeld, *IvoiresPhén*, pl. 39.391, from Megiddo; pl. 69 d, from Enkomi; Kantor, *Archaeology* 13 (1960) fig. 15 right, from Matmar in Middle Egypt; Poursat, *IvoiresMyc*, pl. XIX C.

19. Enough survives to show that the krater was of the same shape as VI.1; the clay is buff-pinkish, well baked; thick smooth pale slip covers the surface; the paint of the decoration is dark brown, semiglossy.

20. de Mertzenfeld, *IvoiresPhén*, pl. 79.788 b, the ivory box from Enkomi, on which even the attitude of the bull is identical with that of the Kouklia fragment; cf. also the attitude of a charging bull with a tree in front of him in Kantor and in Poursat (see note 18).

21. H. Kantor, *Archaeology* 13 (1960) figs. 15 right, 16, and 17; and *JNES* 15 (1956) 170 f.

4. On a fragmentary bell krater from Palaipaphos, part of the outlined body of a lion is preserved, including the neck, part of the head, the forelegs, and the body. The mane is rendered with oblique wavy lines, in the same fashion as the bulls' dewlaps on VI.1-3. There is an attempt to show the anatomical details of the legs in the same fashion, with thin lines. The ribs are shown by parallel vertical, curved lines. A blot of paint for the hide may recall the older fashion for bull figures, a tradition also seen on vase VI.1. The lion must have been in action with both forelegs stretched forward, as in a flying gallop. The mouth seems to be half open, with the tongue showing. It is not clear what the whole composition looked like. The two curved lines springing from the lion's chest may be the horns of a bull, in which case this may be the well-known composition of a lion attacking a bull, which was so much in vogue in ivory carving and gem cutting in the Late Bronze Age both in the Aegean and in the Near East[22] and also in the Iron Age at Nimrud. Though this fragment is inferior in quality to VI.1-3, it shows clearly the influence of ivory carving both in subject matter and in style.

These four vases demonstrate how ivory engraving influenced the naissance of a new style in vase painting. The art of ivory engraving may also have influenced low-relief stone sculpture, as represented on the well-known contemporary relief fragment from Mycenae, on which a charging bull is represented in front of an olive tree, and on the relief of the Lion Gate at Mycenae.[23]

5. A bell krater from Ugarit has a bull on one side and a group of spirals on the other.[24] The bull walks right with his head lifted to reach the foliage of a bush springing from the side of the vertical frame band by the handle. On the ground below the animal's belly is a row of scallops; behind the bull by the handle, a framing band takes the form of a ladder pattern. The bull's body is drawn in outline of uneven thickness. The upper and front parts of the body are thickly outlined. The painter was particularly careful in rendering the legs, especially the hind legs, with thin lines indicating anatomical details. Small blots of paint are scattered inside the outlined body; three vertical curved lines in the middle indicate ribs. Though one may observe in the figure drawing the influence of ivory carving, as above, the Ugarit bull is inferior in realism and exactness of drawing; the head and forelegs are too small compared with the body, and the body is too long and thin in the middle. Nevertheless here is a painter who used his brush boldly and freely.

GOATS
The goat is another favorite pictorial motif of the Pastoral style, again recalling ivory carving in style and subject.

6. A fragment of a bell krater from Ugarit is decorated with a goat walking right. The goat is drawn in outline, thick at the upper part of the body and neck and thinner elsewhere; small, thin curved lines indicate the ribs of the body. The goat does not have the exactness and realism of VI.1, but the elongated body, vertical neck with the proudly uplifted head, and long back-curving horns make it particularly pleasing. With very simple means the artist created a bold, elegant drawing.

7. On a bell krater from Enkomi the panel between the handles is flanked with vertical straight and wavy lines. The main decoration consists of a lion chasing goats in a forest. The lion runs to the right; in front of him a goat also runs right with his head turned backward. On the extreme right a second goat runs left, turning his head back to eat from a branch of a tree. Branches of trees with rich foliage spring from the ground behind each goat. The stems are oblique so that the top of the foliage should reach the goats' mouths; there are smaller stems below their bellies. Below the lion is a conical "hillock" made of horizontal zigzag lines, evidently to show rough landscape in the forest. The upper part of the lion's body is drawn in silhouette, but the fore and hindquarters are outlined and filled with irregular parallel wavy lines. The goats are rendered in silhouette, except the hindquarters and the legs. The pointed leaves are drawn with thick and thin lines.

The aim of the artist was no doubt to represent a scene of violent action with a lion chasing goats, which is very familiar in thirteenth-century ivory engravings of the Near East[25] and on a few contemporary vases from the Greek mainland and the East (XI.70, 75, XII.27). But this aim did not succeed. The goats, in their heraldic attitude, with heads turned back, recall the attitudes of animals on ivories, gems, and cylinder seals of the same period. The tree branches with their rich foliage, symmetrically distributed, add to the harmony of the composition but fail to create the impression of wild nature. The lion, in spite of his ferocious look, with a wide open mouth showing his teeth, is quite apart from the rest of the composition and does not seem to have disturbed the grazing goats.

The treatment of the figures, especially the lion's outlined body filled with wavy lines, and the rendering of the leaves with thin and thick lines recall the techniques of ivory engraving that we have already seen.

22. H. Kantor, *Archaeology* 13 (1960) figs. 10 A, 11, 13, 17 above.
23. H. Kantor, *Archaeology* 13 (1960) 23.
24. Buff-greenish clay, imperfectly baked, covered with a smooth pale slip. Orange matt paint on the side of the bull, dark semiglossy on the other side. Form of the krater like that of VI.1 and 2.
25. de Mertzenfeld, *IvoiresPhén*, pl. 40.389 a.

8. An amphoroid krater from Maroni[26] has four goats on the shoulder, two on either side between the handles, walking right with their heads turned back to reach the foliage of trees whose trunks are purposely curved toward the animals. Two of the goats are in outline and two in silhouette. The subject, the figure drawing, and the rendering of the foliage recall very closely VI.7. Stubbings was the first to associate these two vases with one another. In fact, one may go so far as to suggest that they are by the same painter.

9. To the same group we may attribute an amphoroid krater from Kazaphani. Both sides of the shoulder between the handles are decorated with groups of grazing goats, the same favorite subject. On side A there are three goats (one male). The male goat on the left walks right but turns his head to reach the pointed leaves of a long-stemmed bush that springs from behind his back. Not only does the animal make an effort to reach the bush, the bush also bends forward to reach the animal's mouth. The other two goats are antithetically arranged, with a tree between them, and trees bend over their backs.

On side B there are also three goats. The one on the left (a male) walks right to touch the leaves of a bush in front of him; the stem of the bush, however, bends over the back of the second goat as he walks to the right to eat from a bush in front of him. A third goat, on the right, eats from the same bush. Thus the second and third goat are arranged in heraldic fashion, facing each other on either side of a bush motif.

The animals are boldly rendered. The bodies are in silhouette in the full elegant posture of the wild goat in earlier periods of the pictorial style (the Maroni krater, III.26), though with more freedom in the figure drawing, which the Pastoral style permits. The painter often leaves reserved spaces within the body and renders anatomical details, especially the legs, with thin lines of diluted paint (orange, whereas the silhouette is in thick matt red). The heads are reserved, with the open mouths well indicated. In one case a leaf is right in the animal's mouth, a touch of realism. The long, back-curving horns recall the Cretan wild goat.

The neck of the amphoroid krater, unlike the usual kraters of the thirteenth century, is reserved, with a frieze of upright double spirals all round it. The form of the krater is very depressed, recalling some of the Late Minoan III amphoroid kraters rather than the Late Mycenaean.

The composition is perhaps one of the most pastoral of all the kraters in the Pastoral style. The painter, freed from the stylization and static embroidery limitations of the Ripe style, is able to render his animals forcefully and in realistic attitudes, creating a country atmosphere that is realistic and satisfactory as a decorative composition.

MIDDLE PASTORAL

Although we cannot fix absolute chronological limits to the various phases of the Pastoral style, we can trace the succession of stages in its development. The middle Pastoral style has the same general characteristics as early Pastoral, including the limited repertory of subjects and the influence of ivory engraving on figure drawing. Now, however, the drawing is less exact, and the rendering of anatomical details with thin lines is often unintelligible. The influence of ivory engraving is more indirect: the painter now follows the style of his predecessors in vase painting and has no direct contact with the art of engraving for inspiration. Figure outlines lack their elegance, and the painter loses his ability to draw bold, firm lines. The fabric also degenerates; the clay is coarser and the paint as a rule is matt.

The bull continues to be the principal pictorial motif, frequently associated with trees or bushes and once with a bird. We describe below the most representative specimens.

BULLS, SPHINXES
10. A jug from Kouklia (Palaipaphos), which may be classified as the earliest specimen of this phase, has two bulls and three birds around the shoulder, a scene already popular in Ripe (V.40 and following). There is an attempt to render the anatomical details of the bull's body, but the artist does not succeed in the same way as his predecessors. The body is divided into three parts, again in the tradition of Ripe Pictorial. The birds' bodies are outlined and filled with arcs and crosshatching, with vertical striped belts.

11. A bell krater from Klavdhia has a bull right in each panel eating from a bush in front of him. The panel on side A is flanked by groups of vertical straight and wavy lines. On side B, instead of a flanking band on the right there is a tree. The bull is drawn in outline, thick in the upper part and thin in the lower. There is an effort to suggest anatomical details like the dewlap, the ribs, and the muscles above the forelegs, but the rest is unconvincing. The painter now uses thin and thick lines and small scattered blots of paint without any particular purpose. The bush is reduced to three large pointed leaves springing from the ground. The bull feeds on them, but his attitude lacks the realism and movement of the early Pastoral bulls.

To the hand of the same painter we may attribute four more vases (VI.12-15) that closely resemble one another.

---

26. Late form of amphoroid krater; cf. a similar vase of the Pastoral style, M. Dunand, *Fouilles de Byblos* I (1937) pl. 157.444.

All are painted with a bull to the right, eating from a small bush in front of him.

16. A bell krater from Enkomi is decorated on side A with a bull to left with lowered head. The bull is in outline, thick on the upper part and thin elsewhere. The body is filled with irregular blots of paint, with no effort to give anatomical details, and the vertical wavy lines across the neck separate the head from the body rather than indicate folds of the dewlap. The large eye is characteristic of this phase of the Pastoral style. The attitude of the bull is lively and could certainly have made a satisfactory drawing if the painter had shown more care for details within the body. But apparently his main preoccupation was the other side of the vase, two male sphinxes confronted in a heraldic position on either side of a palm tree.[27] They are in outline, thick at the upper part and forepart and thin elsewhere. The midsection, hindquarters, and wings are filled with scale pattern. The forelegs are filled with transverse strokes. The sphinx on the right has a protruding pointed nose; he wears a tall striped cap; two wavy lines, evidently locks of hair, fall to the shoulder. The head of the sphinx on the left is missing. Though this composition is rare in vase painting, it is common in other arts, in the Aegean and the Near East.

Details such as the position of the wings, the cap, the locks of hair, and the scale pattern are known from similar representations on engraved ivories and on gold diadems decorated in repoussé, such as have been found at Enkomi.[28]

17. A fragmentary krater from Minet el-Beida has a bull on one side and two confronted sphinxes on the other. The bull, walking right, is in outline, thick at the upper part and thin elsewhere. Thin lines are used for anatomical details of the legs and for folds of the hide near the forelegs (missing, as is the head). Along the upper part of the neck is a horizontal row of paint blots. The drawing is of good quality, with naturalistic tendencies in the rendering of hooves and genitals. One may compare this bull with those of the preceding phase, when the influence of ivory carving was more apparent.

The other side of the vase is decorated with two sphinxes confronted in a heraldic attitude on either side of a tree, as on VI.16. Here, however, there is more freedom in the drawing and a tendency to imitate more directly the techniques of engraving. The upper and hind parts of the bodies are rendered in thick outline; the forepart is solid. There is an attempt to divide the body into sections to indicate anatomical details. Strokes fill the different sections; the wings are filled with lattice pattern. The painter seems to have confused the body sections as they appear on ivory and metal engravings, where anatomical details are shown

by thin lines or relief, with the actual parts of the body.[29] The tree, with its pointed leaves, recalls the trees of ivory engravings as in early Pastoral.

The sphinx compositions on these kraters belong to the same stylistic group, though the sphinxes of the Enkomi krater are more static, in the Ripe tradition, whereas those of the Ugarit krater possess all the vigor of the Pastoral style.

18. A fragment of a large bell krater from Enkomi(?) is decorated with a sphinx similar to those of VI.16 and 17, though it is too fragmentary to say for certain that it formed part of a similar composition; there are, however, traces of a tree in front of the sphinx. The figure is drawn in outline of unequal thickness and is filled with groups of straight and curved lines. As in Ripe vase painting, the animal is divided into three parts, each of which is filled in a different manner: the hind part with horizontal lines, the midsection with straight or curved vertical lines, and the forepart with lattice pattern and solid paint. The wing is divided into several parts filled with groups of lines in various directions. The style recalls that of a number of Pastoral bird kraters discussed below, VI.28 and following.

20. One of the best bull representations in this phase is on a bell krater from Enkomi. Both sides are decorated with almost identical compositions of a bull to the right approaching a short bush. One side also has a spiral ornament next to the bush near the handle. The panels are flanked

---

27. It is regrettable that A. Dessenne, in his monumental work *Le Sphinx, étude iconographique* (1957), confused two kraters from Cyprus with representations of sphinxes. On p. 159, where he is supposed to describe BM C417, he describes in fact C397, which is also decorated with sphinxes. On p. 159 n. 3, he refers to the sphinxes on C417 as if they were on the other side of C397, as follows, "Un taureau ailé à tête humaine, coiffé de la tiare à cornes, et pourvu d'une barbiche filiforme, figure sur le cratère même où sont dessinés nos sphinx . . . " It is obvious, however, that we do not have a winged bull but two confronted sphinxes wearing tiaras, as they are correctly described in *BMCatV* I.2, 86.

28. For representations of sphinxes on metallic and ivory objects from Cyprus, see Dessenne, *Le Sphinx*, 154 f. The sphinxes on our krater may be compared with those on BM C 397, on which they are rendered far more carefully with their curly hair falling on the chest, recalling the prototypes in Mycenaean art. But the sphinxes of BM C417 also form a distant echo of this art: the circle on the chest of both sphinxes is nothing else but the curly lock of hair, which was misunderstood by the vase painter; the *kalathos*-cap also recalls the well-known headdress of Mycenaean sphinxes. The tree motif between the two sphinxes may, however, be of Oriental origin (Dessenne, *Le Sphinx*, 159). Furumark (*MP*, 467) points out that the palm tree between our sphinxes is "identical with a tree design common in Palestinian LB II and EI I vase-painting."

29. Dessenne, *Le Sphinx*, commenting on the style of these sphinxes, makes the following remark: "Délibérément, le peintre a rejeté toute ressemblance avec la nature, comme s'il voulait faire une caricature d'un type déjà simplifié à l'extrême. Il s'est amusé à combiner des lignes tout en gardant à la représentation un aspect général tel qu'on pû reconnaître un sphinx ailé."

by two vertical stripes near the handles. The bulls are drawn in unequal outline (thicker for the upper and hind part of the body), and the interior is filled with irregular blots. Vertical curved lines on the neck separate the head from the body. The line of the forelegs is projected up within the body to form a raised curved line, probably the muscle above the forelegs. The figure is well drawn and lively, and there are touches of realism in the drawing of the tail and genitals.

22. A deep bell krater from Angastina might be slightly earlier than this phase, but its curious scene of lions playing or fighting, or a dog attacking a lion, is in such an untraditional style that it may as well be dated by the other pictorial krater in the tomb, a Middle piece with a bull and spiral on one side, two sketchy goats and a tree on the other. The lion krater has a narrow painted zone, with a scale-patterned animal prancing to the right, crossing forepaws with a smaller animal prancing left. Both have open snarling mouths and tails curled high over the back. The right-hand animal is divided into hatched forequarters, a striped belt, and dark hindquarters. If it is meant as a distinct species, the scene should be an extract from a hunt, with the lion at bay, the hound threatening. It is a lively sketch, and the lion's large eye and protruding tongue are nicely done. The schematic patterns seem linked to those on the equally curious Protogeometric bell krater at Knossos, with lions devouring a man, and prancing sphinxes.[30]

24. In the original publication of this fragment of a bell krater from Maroni, the two animals in a heraldic position are described as bulls, with heads turned back toward the shoulders. Later they were recognized as lions. The rendering is awkward, perhaps because this motif was rare in pictorial vase painting and the artist was unfamiliar with it. He tried to copy a composition that was common during the thirteenth century in other arts, where lions were represented with the forelegs lifted higher than the hind legs and with the head turned back. The obvious parallel is the Lion Gate at Mycenae, which may also be considered to have been influenced by ivory carving.[31] The inexperience of our painter is seen in the eyes, rendered as if the head was represented *en face*, and in the teeth(?), a series of small semicircles pointing outward. The mane is shown as if it were a pair of horns (hence the wrong interpretation in the first publication of this fragment). The animals' bodies are in outline, with vertical lines in the middle, obviously to show the ribs; curved lines separate the head from the body. The paws of the forelegs, represented by two circles each, are placed on groups of concentric arcs springing from the ground, as if they were trees or bushes with symmetrical branches.

GOATS

Goats are a favorite pictorial motif during the second phase of the Pastoral style, as they were during the first phase, in association with other animals.

25. On a fragment of a bell krater from Hala Sultan Tekké, only the hindpart of a goat is preserved, in silhouette, in the Ripe tradition, with a high degree of realism. The hooves are reserved.

26. On another fragment of a bell krater from Enkomi, two goats gallop right; originally there may have been four in the zone between the handles. Between the two goats is a tree, which the goat on the left feeds on. The drawing is awkward and careless. The outlined bodies are divided into three main parts, filled with horizontal or vertical lines.

Well-drawn goats appear on side B of VI.23.

BIRDS

Benson has already grouped a number of Pastoral vases decorated with birds, six of which he attributes to his "Long-beak Painter."[32] In all cases the birds are drawn in outline; their bodies are divided into three or more parts (neck, main body, tail, wings), each part filled independently, usually with groups of parallel lines.

29. A fragmentary bell krater from Enkomi(?) has two birds with gracefully curved outlines; their bodies are divided into two parts, each filled with parallel lines and dots. They have fan-shaped tails and long beaks. The spreading wings, filled with scale pattern, give the figures grace and a birdlike sense of movement, different from the rather heavy, static attitude of some Ripe birds. Here at least the figures are drawn more correctly. The painter is conscious of the bird's anatomy and tries to treat the various parts separately. The wings, for instance, are never confused with the rest of the body, and the tail has its own "feathers."

35. A bell krater in the G. G. Pierides Collection, mentioned by Benson, is described as an imitation of the Long-beak Painter.[33] The vase itself, with its buff-pinkish clay, smooth, lighter-colored slip, and normal bell-shaped outline, does not have any characteristics of Pastoral pottery. The association with the Pastoral style comes

30. H. W. Catling, *JHS ArcRep* 1976-77, 15, fig. 33; H. Sackett, *BSA* 71 (1976) 117 f., 123, fig. 5, 124, fig. 6, pls. 15-16.

31. H. Kantor, *Archaeology* 13 (1960) 23; Vermeule, *GBA*, 215; Poursat, *IvoiresMyc*, 201.

32. J. L. Benson, *AJA* 65 (1961) 342 f.

33. J. L. Benson, *AJA* 65 (1961) pl. 106, fig. 26.

through the representation of two birds on each side, walking left. The neck is in silhouette, but the rest of the body and the spreading wing are outlined and filled with straight or oblique parallel lines; the large fan-shaped tails are filled with splaying lines.

36. The fragmentary bell-krater from Enkomi with goats (VI.28) is decorated on the other side with confronted birds on either side of a very schematized tree. The legs of the bird on the right are on the tree trunk. Both birds are drawn in thick outline, with oblique or vertical lines as fillers. The long, slightly curved beaks touch the top of the herringbone tree. Birds arranged symmetrically on either side of a tree or flower were particularly favored on Late Minoan III vases[34] and larnakes and were also favored in the East (XIII.26).

39. From Enkomi comes a rare example of a three-handled jar decorated in the Pastoral style. Apparently the space between the handles was decorated with one bird, drawn in outline and filled with groups of parallel lines. To the same stylistic group we may assign a fragment of a bell krater from Maroni (VI.40). There are traces of two long-beaked birds confronted on either side of a tree with large pointed leaves. Only the heads of the birds survive.

LATE PASTORAL

The final stage of the Pastoral style comes when the "rudeness," of which signs were already observed in the middle stage, develops even further, and the figure drawing becomes more careless and sketchy.

BULLS

43. A bell krater from Enkomi belongs to the transitional phase between middle and late. One side is decorated with a bull to the right, the other with a goat to the right. The bull is in outline, thicker at the upper part of the body. The neck is filled with lattice pattern, the rest of the body with irregular blots. There is an effort to represent the anatomical details of the legs by means of thin lines. One may compare this bull with those of VI.15 and 23, but here the figure drawing is of inferior quality, especially the forepart and head. In front of the bull stemmed spirals spring from the ground, replacing the bush motifs of the earlier stages. The goat on the other side of the vase is more carefully drawn, with a lively and correct body.

45. A bell krater from Enkomi has two confronted bulls in the zone between the handles, flanked on either side by narrow vertical bands. Only the foreparts of the bulls are represented, recalling the bull protomes of the Ripe style (V.80 and following). The drawing is sketchy, the composition very lively and expressive.

47. On a bell krater in the Cyprus Museum, both sides are decorated with a bull to the right, with sketchy trees in front and in back. The animal is supposed to be feeding on the tree, but is now far from the correct and naturalistic compositions of the early stage, where similar subjects were treated. The figure drawing is summary, with the legs and head proportionately too small, recalling children's drawings in many ways.

48. On a bell krater from Enkomi a very awkwardly drawn bull faces right between the handles, with a conical pile of fodder(?) in front of him, filled with lattice pattern. The head and forelegs are poor, and the outline of the body is in general very sketchy and awkward.

49. A krater fragment from Enkomi shows the forepart of a bull to the right, feeding on a tree in front of him. The animal is drawn in silhouette, with a large reserved eye. Except for the horns, it would be difficult to identify the animal, because of its beak-shaped mouth. The tree is drawn like a palm.

50. On a krater fragment from Enkomi two bulls are represented on either side of a tree, with horns interlocked. The painter probably intended to represent the animals fighting, in violent action, like his Ripe predecessors, but we have here neither realism nor grace.

GOATS
51. A bell krater from Enkomi is decorated on each side with two goats running to the right. The animals' bodies are drawn in thick outline on the upper part, thinner elsewhere. The fillers are transverse strokes and dots, with no effort to render anatomical details in thin lines as in the previous period. Though the goats lack a lively attitude and the composition no longer presents the "pastoral" atmosphere of the previous period, the drawing is more or less correct. The rendering of the head and horns may recall those of VI.7 and 8 from the early stage of the Pastoral style and the goat on VI.43 of the late stage.

MISCELLANEOUS
52. A fragment of an amphoroid krater(?) from Morphou-Gnaftia has attracted discussion. The vase to

---

34. This hypothesis cannot be strongly supported, although Late Minoan III vases, some decorated with birds, were known in Cyprus in the late thirteenth century, H. Catling, V. Karageorghis, *BSA* 55 (1960) 116, fig. 5, pls. 26 d, 27 d.

which this fragment belongs must have been decorated with a chariot scene; the surviving piece shows the upper part of a ten-spoked wheel of an open-frame chariot, the charioteer, and the hind part of a horse. Unlike the earlier chariots, this one has no proper box with sides; only the breast is represented, allowing the whole body of the charioteer to appear down to his feet. This is not an accidental innovation by the vase painter. Toward the end of the thirteenth century a similar light vehicle was introduced to Greece and is often represented on vases and in other arts (XI.1 and following). This type of chariot was not much favored by the Cypriotes, who continued using a chariot with a traditional box, as one may see on Iron Age vases, but it is possible that some of these new chariots were introduced to the island by the Achaian colonists in the western end at the very end of the thirteenth century. The appearance of this chariot coincides with major political changes on Cyprus.

A number of late vases are decorated simply with trees or bushes, probably pastoral, sometimes stiff and once (VI.55) engagingly informal.

55. On a bell krater from Pyla-Verghi the painter attempts to represent naturalistic trees with a trunk, branches, and foliage and to create an open-air landscape by adding a conical mound with scale pattern among the trees. This is one of the most successful tree compositions in the Pastoral style.

The Pastoral style is principally pictorial, with few basic themes, sometimes distinguished, more often hasty. An important contemporary group of nonpictorial vases is decorated with abstract motifs, mainly spirals. However, the proportion of pictorial to nonpictorial painting is much higher than on the Greek mainland.

CHRONOLOGY

The date usually given for the Pastoral style is the Late Cypriote II C period, 1275-1200. Very recently it has been characterized as belonging to a derivative school of pictorial painting in the Mycenaean manner dating toward the end of the thirteenth century. Considering recent stratigraphical data, we suggest as an initial date the period between 1250 and 1240, with the style lasting a few decades more, extending into the very end of the thirteenth century and perhaps the beginning of the twelfth. In a perfectly sealed layer of sherds discovered in Nicosia, Pastoral fragments appear side by side with Late Helladic III C:1 pottery.[35] Furumark remarked that several spiral motifs of the Pastoral style could be compared with Late Helladic III C:1,[36] and the form of the bell krater used for both Pastoral and III C:1

is the same, with a biconical outline and an angular profile.

The relation between pictorial Pastoral and the pictorial III C:1 pottery of Cyprus has not yet been fully studied, but the abundant new material from Enkomi and Kition is instructive. A number of pictorial motifs in both these styles resemble one another very closely, like the bull protomes on a fragment of a III C:1 jug(?) (VI.46), which from the point of view of style, are unmistakably "pastoral." The Pastoral fragment from Morphou, VI.52, with a chariot scene, also has chronological significance. The ten-spoked wheel of this open-frame chariot has been interpreted by Catling as characterizing a "custom-built chariot made in Cyprus for one of the newcomers (Achaean colonists), combining the light Egyptian type framework by then in favour with the Mycenaeans with a wheel of local pattern."[37] This shows that Pastoral painted pottery was still produced after the arrival of Achaian immigrants, who introduced the III C:1 pottery in Cyprus, close to 1200.

Pastoral constitutes a style by itself, rather than a second-rate artistic production or an imitation of any other style. It may have its origin in the art of ivory engraving, and the impetus for its creation may be the painter's desire to produce something new and different from the Ripe style, which was already nearly a century old. In its early stage it gave real masterpieces of draftsmanship but it degenerated very rapidly, owing to the sketchy and careless drawing.

Though Cyprus was the center of production of Pastoral vases, the inventors of this style were imaginative Aegean artists like those who painted the pictorial vases of the earlier periods, with a high degree of artistic ability and inventiveness, who were able to adapt the style of engraving to the requirements of vase painting.

A similarly bold and free style, with a tendency to render anatomical details within silhouetted animals, may be observed on the Greek mainland toward the end of the thirteenth century (X.42 and following). This is yet another proof that the styles of vase painting created by the Mycenaeans in the Aegean and the Near East continued to influence one another down to the very end of the thirteenth century.

LATE HELLADIC III C:1

It is not the intention of this survey to include the styles of Late drawing in Cyprus, since the general tendencies have

35. V. Karageorghis, *BCH* 83 (1959) 354; *Nouveaux Documents*, 257.
36. Furumark, *MP*, 467; P. Dikaios, *Enkomi* (1969-71) 266 f., where fragments of Pastoral vases decorated with spirals are compared to III C:1b.
37. H. Catling, *AJA* 72 (1968) 48.

been fully discussed by others, and most pictorial pieces are of minor interest.[38] The usual compositions with antithetic spirals and loops are so connected with developments at Mycenae and elsewhere in the Argolid that they can be explained by no theory other than direct immigration of Achaian settlers from the mainland on a fairly large scale, "in the time of the Trojan War." The fortifications at Sinda, east of Nicosia, and at Maa-Palaikastro on the west coast are reminiscent of the architectural styles of Mycenae and Tiryns, and the pottery is equally "homeland" in style. Enkomi and Paphos were two of the major sites, while on the south coast both Kition and Hala Sultan Tekké received new Mycenaeans.

The curious chariot scene of VI.52 demonstrates that new fashions in armaments and military technology came to Cyprus at the end of the thirteenth century and the beginning of the twelfth, and a sherd from Hala Sultan Tekké (VI.59) may show one of the warriors who brought them. It is a simple, worn piece but seems to have the same embroidered tunic with interior lines, running loops, and a fringed hem as on the Late pieces from Mycenae, Tiryns, and Leukandi. It is difficult to decode the piece, except that the soldier seems to be in a posture of strong motion.

With the chariot and the warrior comes the horse, represented here by a fragment (VI.60) from the third period at Sinda, with a small dark leaping horse in a panel flanked by spirals and trumpets. He rears on his hind legs over a triangular "rock" and raises both front legs, a dashing silhouette. The field is filled with floating dotted circles like suns or dandelion heads. A beautiful head and neck of a horse from Sinda has been too poorly published to illustrate.[39]

The Late birds are the usual mainland types, filled with stripes or dots or incorporated into spiral and trumpet designs, like a sketchy bird from Sinda (VI.61). Fish are also used sketchily as subsidiary decoration; a good example from the Cesnola Collection in New York (VI.62) has a confronted pair standing on their tails and sharing a meal of a drooping weed; the frieze of the low open bowl is dominated by filled spirals and trumpets.

The fine drawing of these Late pieces and the establishment of the Mycenaean repertory of pictures on Cyprus in a vein totally different from the long preceding traditions of chariots, bulls, other animals, and fish, undoubtedly protected the artistic continuity of image making in Cyprus through the Dark Ages. It is one of the few regions where people continued to draw and sketch from the world around them after the big disruption of the political and economic world in the twelfth century. The Protogeometric archer krater from Enkomi may be weak in comparison to what had gone before, but it is a sign that Mycenaean drawing never really disappeared.[40]

38. A. Furumark, *OpArc* 3 (1944) 194, 232; *OpAth* 6 (1965) 99 f.; for the general historical problems see also F. Maier, *The Mycenaeans in the Eastern Mediterranean* (1973) 68; V. Desborough, ibid., 79, and *The Last Mycenaeans and Their Successors* (1964) 197 f.; N. K. Sandars, *The Sea Peoples* (1978) 144 f.

39. J. H. Young, *AJA* 52 (1948) 531, pl. 58 a.

40. Schaeffer, *Alasia* I, 269; G. Kopcke, in *The Dark Ages in Greece* (1977) fig. 31.

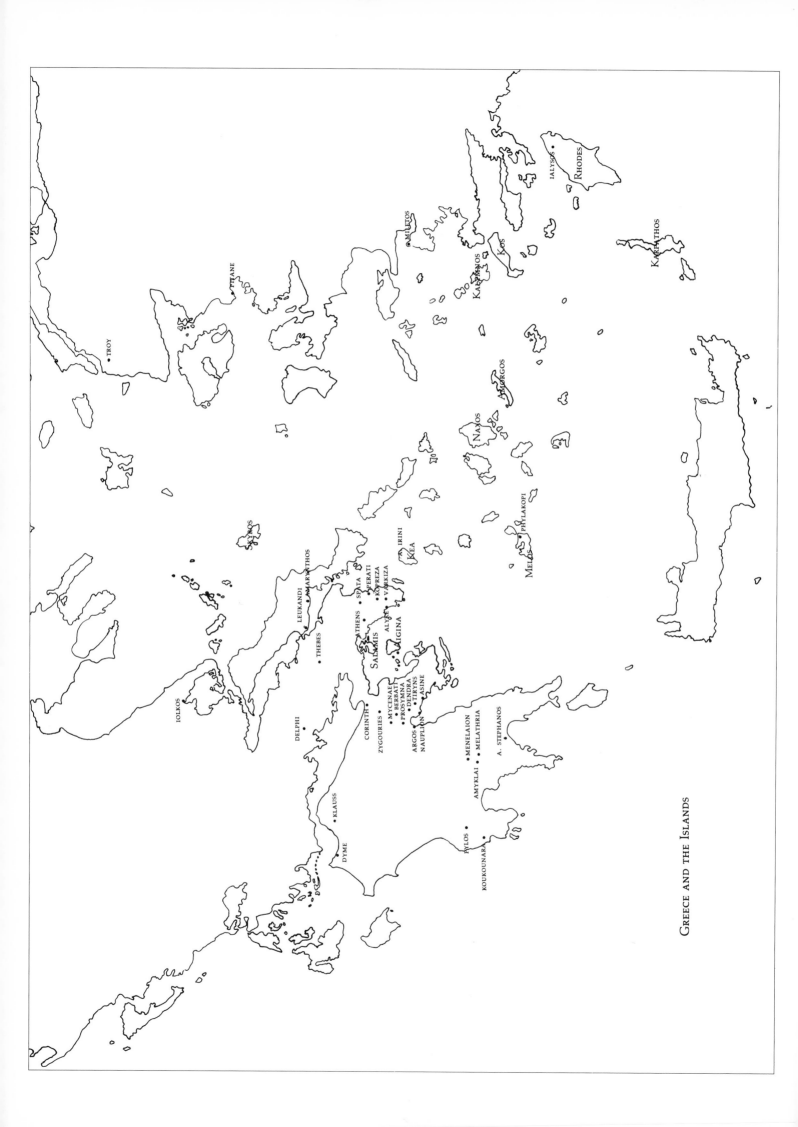

TROY

PITANE

MILETOS

IALYSOS

RHODES

KARPATHOS

KOS

KALYMNOS

AMORGOS

NAXOS

PHYLAKOPI

MELOS

IRINI
KEA

SKYROS

LEUKANDI

AMARYNTHOS

SPATA
PERATI
KOPREZA
VARKIZA

THEBES

ATHENS

IOLKOS

ALYKE
AIGINA

SALAMIS

DELPHI

CORINTH

ZYGOURIES

MYCENAE
BERBATI
PROSYMNA
DENDRA
TIRYNS
ARGOS
NAUPLION
ASINE

MENELAION
MELATHRIA

A. STEPHANOS

KLAUSS

AMYKLAI

DYME

PYLOS

KOUKOUNARA

GREECE AND THE ISLANDS

VII
THE GREEK MAINLAND:
Early Pictorial

I N THE INTRODUCTION, reasons were given for looking at the pictorial vases found in Cyprus before surveying the fewer pieces found in mainland Greece, but the order of presentation should not influence observers who wonder where most of these vases were painted.[1] The abundance of the Cypriote material and its generally good preservation allow a more secure analysis of developments in pictorial styles. The mainland material is usually sadly fragmentary, and from the sherds it is nearly impossible to judge principles of composition. Even so, the fragments often give wonderful detail and glimpses of vivacious scenes, and make it clear that the mainland has its own sequences of styles and its own tastes. Half a dozen to a dozen vases found in the Argolid were painted by artists whose works are also found overseas, especially in the Middle and Ripe periods, and in those cases there is no obvious difference in the taste of the two Aegean areas. In general, however, mainland workshops decorate a wider variety of vase shapes than is found in Cyprus, prefer much less filling ornament in the field than on many Cypriote vases, and display a higher degree of fantasy and imagination.

The general homogeneity of Mycenaean pottery in the fourteenth and thirteenth centuries, the period of the "koiné," complicates the difficult arguments about the origin of pictorial vases.[2] Ordinary patterned ware in Cyprus often looks as though it might have been manufactured in the Argolid or Attica for the export trade, except for some "seconds," dented and bent vases, among them. There are also clearly Cypriote Mycenaean pieces, Cypriote shapes like chalices, shallow bowls, and bowls with wishbone handles, decorated in Mycenaean tech-

niques by potters working on the island.[3] Technical analyses have not yet solved the problems surrounding the rarer pictorial vases. Certainly Mycenae, Tiryns, and Berbati were strong centers of production, and Lakonia, Attica, and Boeotia have their own styles, but the styles of these known workshops do not in general correspond to the often cluttered and stereotyped Cypriote pictures of chariots and bulls. The next three chapters illustrate how different mainland pictorial vases seem from many of those found in Cyprus; they stand apart, as the vases from Rhodes stand apart (XII.1-20). Tiryns and Mycenae are most influential for Cyprus.

Mainland painters put pictures on the cutaway jug, the ewer, the pyxis, the alabastron, the bottle, the stirrup jar, the rhyton, and the bowl, as well as on the krater which is so standard in Cyprus until the Ripe period. The pictures are often patterned compositions of birds and fish, with a few interesting human figures, rather than the large set pieces of Cyprus, the chariot processions and embroidered bulls. The rhythm of development is also different, for according to the excavation record, which may be accidentally faulty but must be respected, mainland pic-

1. See the select bibliography; the argument has flourished for thirty years. See, for example, J. F. Daniel, *AJA* 46 (1942) 289; Stubbings, *MycLevant*, 25; S. A. Immerwahr, *AJA* 49 (1945) 555; V. Karageorghis, *Kypriakai Spoudai* 1961, 7; *Nouveaux Documents*, 201; H. Catling, A. Millett, *BSA* 60 (1965) 212, *RDAC* 1978, 70 f.; Å. Åkerström versus J. Crouwel, *Iº Congresso Internazionale de Micenologia* I (Rome, 1968) 48, 42; F. Asaro and I. Perlman, in *The Mycenaeans in the Eastern Mediterranean* (1973) 213.

2. Furumark, *MP*, 462, 521.

3. Karageorghis, *Nouveaux Documents*, 201; A. Furumark, *OpArc* 6 (1950) 267.

torial painting is quite rare in the early fourteenth century, and there are still only some thirty-five pieces of the Middle period.

It is during the Ripe period, and especially toward its end, in the latter half of Late Helladic III B, that mainland painting really comes into its own, just as the Pastoral style is giving a new look to the increasingly repetitive themes of Cyprus. This is really the third phase of the Ripe period; on the mainland it is chronologically transitional between Late Helladic III B and III C and is a remarkably vigorous phase (Chapter X). The biggest surge of painting comes in the Late period (Chapter XI), with a remarkable combination of fantasy, military adventurousness, and styles both bold and delicate. The largest number of mainland fragments, and the best in quality, were made when pictorial painting had practically died out in Cyprus, either because political and economic changes were taking place on the island with the Sea Peoples and new waves of emigrating Greeks or because the aesthetic energy had run its course. Late Helladic III C painting on Cyprus is, for the first time, practically indistinguishable from mainland work (Chapter VI, end).

FORERUNNERS IN GREECE AND THE ISLANDS

Mycenaean pottery in general represents a fusion of disparate traditions, the Middle Helladic and the Minoan. In the case of pictorial painting there also seems to be a major influence from the Cycladic islands. Middle Helladic matt-painted wares, usually starkly linear and abstract, were occasionally decorated with small sketches of birds and fish. Minoan painting, when it began to influence Mycenaean in the sixteenth century, offered a range of grasses, flowers, and ferns, and in the fifteenth century added marinescapes and symbols of religious cult; fish and birds and some rare human studies became part of the standard repertory in Late Minoan II and III A:1. On the islands, especially Melos and Thera, there is more adventurous, awkward, and colorful painting in the sixteenth century. There are two styles, the graceful curvilinear studies of nature allied to Minoan painting, used so effectively for flying birds, diving fish, prancing goats, and meadow flowers; and the more active, less poetic and dreamy series of stick-figure soldiers. For the soldiers, or griffins, or ship scenes, there was no established Minoan tradition, so that outlined figures in active poses with hourglass bodies and simplified weapons were directly invented to suit a need that would surface on the mainland as

well.[4] Because mainland taste also runs to soldiers, a few ships, and some monsters, Cycladic "forerunners" have been included to show the island tradition; its influence on the mainland is still not fully understood.

SOLDIERS

A. A pair of fragments with outlined stick figures from Akrotiri on Thera, in matt brown paint, show soldiers in action and at rest or on guard. One is running right, with very long bent arms and a raised front knee, thrusting out a sword at waist level. A long plume is attached to his head, although the helmet is not shown, and he wears the dark knee-length tunic of mainland soldiers. The other man stands quietly, with a spear at rest vertically in front of his shoulder, and his large hand is raised with spread fingers. The pose may recall the quiet guard of the Town Mosaic from Knossos, but these armed figures are more in keeping with the temperament of the military and naval fresco from the West House on Thera, narrative and active vignettes of a kind not generally popular in Crete.

GRIFFIN

B. A sherd with the head of a griffin, right, must share in the tradition of occasionally demonic birds or griffins on the Melian bird vases of Phylakopi. The griffin has a feathered crest, a large eye, and perhaps a protruding tongue; in front of him may be the lashing tail of another "bird" creature. It is not clear yet how influential these Cycladic flying demons were for the griffin iconography of the Shaft Graves at Mycenae, but since one Cycladic griffin vase was found in Grave VI, and the marauding griffin of the West House fresco is so like the metalwork griffins of Mycenae, the connection is probably closer than used to be imagined.

---

4. It is interesting that the Minoan-looking pieces from the Cyclades, like the Fisherman Vase, the goat, and the ducks from Melos (C. Edgar, *Phylakopi in Melos* [1904] pl. 22, figs. 95, 114, 115, 149) should have received so much more attention than the stick-figure types, such as the soldiers from Melos (*Phylakopi*, pl. 13, nos. 14, 16) or Thera (S. Marinatos, *Thera* II [1969] 44, fig. 30; *Praktika* 1968, pl. 114 a); the contrast in traditions, or the presence of a subsidiary tradition, is important in itself. For Thera pictorial animals, see S. Marinatos, *Praktika* 1970, pl. 294 b (horse or ass?); for the male head, *Praktika* 1970, pl. 294 c; *AAA* 4 (1971) 74, fig. 25. The dolphins, swallows, and other birds are far more common: see *AAA* 2 (1969) 66, fig. 2; *Praktika* 1968, pl. 78 a-b; *Thera* II, col. pl. C 7-8, p. 14, fig. 5, pls. 11.2, 17.2; *AAA* 5 (1972) 2, fig. 2, col. pl. 2; *Praktika* 1970, fig. 313; A. Furtwängler, G. Loeschcke, *Mykenische Thongefaesse* (1879) pls. 8-10; A. Wace, *BSA* 25 (1921-23) pl. 30; *Mycenae* (1949) pl. 97 c; C. W. Blegen, *Korakou* (1921) 28; Graef-Langlotz, *VA*, 16, pl. 1.17.

SAILOR?

C. The well-known fragment of a large matt-painted jar from Aigina preserves a paneled design with a silhouetted stick figure riding left, balanced on a fish-prowed ship, or perhaps on a real fish. Although the panel seems small for the rest of the ship (or fish) unless it was oblique, this style does not permit shorthand or incomplete figures. The man has a round head, duck-billed lips, and what may be a helmet, curled fore and aft; the arms are bent sharply, as on the Thera figures. The ship's prow or fish has barred teeth, a filled oval eye, and strong outlines. This sherd and the next give a small glimpse of early narrative pleasure in describing the adventures of seafaring along the coast and through the islands; it is more likely to be a crude counterpart to the themes of the Silver Siege Rhyton or the West House fresco than an early version of the dolphin or *ketos* rider.

SHIPS

D. The Iolkos ship scene is restored from three small fragments; there are perhaps two ships, no people. The polychrome design shows a short vessel, thickly outlined, the reserved interior filled with zigzag pattern; there is a stout curved ram on the prow, and a steering oar. The polychromy is in the Cycladic tradition.

FISH AND BIRDS

E. Middle Helladic fish appear on a fragment of a large vase from Argos, which may be a local imitation of Minoan octopus vases. Two thin black fish with open mouths dart around the hairy tentacle of an octopus; there are ornamental crosshatched lozenges in the background. The style of drawing predatory fish in solid silhouette remains almost the same until the end of Mycenaean painting.

In the Shaft Grave period, between the Middle and Late Bronze Ages, the Cycladic tradition impinged on the mainland development in a variety of ways; the most conspicuous pictorial imports are the bird jugs, from Marathon in the east to Samikon in the west.[5] Almost immediately, Mycenaean painters begin to essay their own bird designs, which are generally heavier and stiller. A contrasted pair from Grave Circle B at Mycenae illustrates the different styles.

F. A bird jug from Grave *Nu* may come from Melos; it is related to a series from Phylakopi and Thera. The ewer form with back-tilted neck is a good shape for decoration with flying birds, and the Cycladic treatment is at once more dramatic and more decorative than most Minoan birds. The bodies are outlined in swift curved strokes with simple curves filling the necks, breasts, and wings; they have a three-plumed "pheasant" tail. The fillers are arbitrary; their delicacy suggests ruffled areas and feathers, but there is no attempt to render separate pinions as in Crete. The light-bodied bird with long, lifted wing and feet dangling behind will have a four-hundred-year life in Mycenaean art.

G. A local spouted jug from Grave *Gamma* is an obvious contrast, one of several awkward bird designs from the Shaft Graves. The bird, heavy-bodied, walking rather than flying, is cramped on the neck of the vase, the gross body filled with dotted scale pattern for feathers, the raised wing barred like a ladder, the small round "turkey" head drawn with a simple dot eye and a short hooked bill. This round-bodied type also endures throughout the Mycenaean pictorial tradition and may be closely matched at the end of the thirteenth century (X.66 and following).

After the Shaft Grave period, the earliest pictorial vases on the mainland are either imported from Crete or indebted to Cretan Palace Style traditions; at times the contrast between the imports and the local pieces is startling. On present evidence no authoritative independent pictorial style flourished in the Argolid in the early fourteenth century, when the big early kraters began to circulate in Cyprus (except VII.1). Excavation has not supported the theory that all early pictorial Cypriote vases were made around Mycenae. Attica and Boeotia do have early vases, but the style is quite unrelated to developments in the Levant.

H. The most beautiful and striking vase of the early period in Greece is the big three-handled Palace Style jar from Argos, painted with ducks. The design is clearly related to seal designs and vase painting at Knossos, and the vase is either an import from Crete or made by a painter who trained in Crete and worked in the Argolid. Deshayes made a strong case for Argive creation.

The vase has one "major" and two "minor" panels set off by the three loop handles high on the shoulder, although the composition unrolls freely below them. The major panel holds two fat ducks entwined in conversation, bodies right, the one in front turning his head back to caress the second. The other panels each have a single duck, body right, one with head turned back, as though the rear of the vase were an expanded version of the front. The ducks are set in a "meadow" of trailing background garlands of elaborate rosettes connected by foliage lines to form spirals with papyrus blooms in the angles, and a spray of flowers in the Egyptian manner, which will become a Mycenaean mannerism in the Middle period (Chapter IV).

5. Cf. J. Davis, *AAA* 9 (1976) 81.

The ducks are like their Egyptian counterparts, the Nile waterfowl (*chenalopex, anas Aegyptiaca*) often painted in sprays of papyrus. The motif, filtered through Crete, found early favor in Greece and the islands, with such surviving witnesses as the dagger from Shaft Grave V, the riverbank hunt of the West House fresco at Akrotiri, the two bathtubs from Phylakopi on Melos, the ivory comb from the Rutsi tholos, or the Arsenal sealing from Knossos and related mainland gems.[6] Technically the Arsenal sealing is closest to the Argos vase, employing excerpts from the same composition and the same decorative engraved fillers of scales, ripples, and crosshatching.

The ducks' heads are extraordinarily lifelike, with more grandeur and detail than any other bird picture in Greece. Yet, even so early in the development of pictorial imagery, the foliate background has been converted to formal ornamental pattern, and although the ducks are beautifully marked with stippled breasts and bellies, there is considerable abstraction and unnatural variety in the markings of the wings folded along the backs. Plain stippling, dotted scales, rippled lines, dashes, and crosshatching are all combined in severe divisions, anticipating the arbitrary body filling of birds in later stages (Chapters IV, VIII); the heavy, rolling lower border of the wings, if not indebted to gem carving, has a metallic look. This emphasis on dramatic patterning partly abstracted from nature is a basic element in the pictorial painter's idiom. It is a reminder that themes may often have been transmitted to the painters' workshops through media requiring different techniques, through gems, metalwork, ivory, or textiles, so that sets of images that later become self-perpetuating among painters, with their own inherent rhythms of development, may have originally arrived there with a bias toward particular forms of execution. The Argos duck vase is so big and elaborate that it also suggests some indebtedness to wall painting, although prototypes have not yet emerged from the earth in Crete or Greece; later versions of duck scenes are found at both Tiryns and Pylos, in fragments too small to show the original composition.[7] While the section of the Akrotiri West House fresco that has ducks along the river is too crude to serve as a model, its very existence suggests that there were other Aegean studies of the subject.

Whatever its inspiration, the Argos duck vase stands by itself, apart from normal Cretan vase styles, an unusual naturalism for the end of the fifteenth century. It may be compared to the elegant spouted jar painted with swirling birds and fish, from Katsamba, which retains the oblique design of the Marine Style without the massiveness and clarity of the Argos vase, or to the fragmentary fourteenth-century jar with ducks "swimming" in a field of flowers,

from a private house west of the palace at Knossos.[8] The scale of the bodies in proportion to the height of the frieze, the intense counterpointed detail of tone and texture, the expressive heads and skillful evocation of an atmosphere of gentle attraction make the Argos vase the bird equivalent of the quiet Vapheio Cup.

I. A lidded pyxis from Tsountas' Tomb 7 at Mycenae is a Cretan import of the next phase, Late Minoan III A:1. It is almost certainly by the painter of the similar pyxis from Gournia and a pyxis lid from Knossos.[9] Just over half of the body and lid are preserved. Four full-bodied birds, perhaps partridges, fly right with outspread wings through a crowded field of flowers and arrow-shaped leaves. As in Cretan frescoes, the flowers hang from the upper border, interspersed with stripes representing blades of grass in a field, matched by grasses springing from the lower ground line. The rich clutter of filling ornaments suggests that the pyxis is already approaching the Middle period, in the second quarter of the fourteenth century, although the powerful reserved rosette on the lid and the dotted flames around the edges are links to the older Palace Style.

The birds' bodies are divided into four clear sections: dark heads, outlined barred wings raised or lowered from the barred collar, spotted oval bodies, and tails of four striped feathers with rounded tips. This division still echoes natural markings, as on the Argos duck vase, and has a harmonious consistency-in-variation of full and broken lines, dark and light areas, held within strong curves. The insistence on a landscape setting for birds is a Cretan trait affecting the Early period in Greece; sometimes it degenerates into clutter.[10] The sculptural solidity of the Argos vase has thinned out into quick pattern, but

6. Dagger: G. Karo, *Die Schachtgräber von Mykenai* (1930-33) figs. 54-56, pls. 93-94; E. Vermeule, *The Art of the Shaft Graves* (1975) 21; bathtubs: Edgar, *Phylakopi*, figs. 114-115; Evans, *Palace of Minos* III, 115, fig. 65; IV, 332, fig. 274; comb: S. Marinatos, *Crete and Mycenae* (1959) fig. 222; J.-C. Poursat, *Les Ivoires Mycéniens* (1977) no. 410, pl.XLI; Buchholz, Karageorghis, *Altägäis*, no. 1278; Arsenal sealing: Evans, *Palace of Minos* III,117, fig. 67; IV, 615, fig. 602, cf. fig. 597 B; V. Kenna, *Cretan Seals* (1960) 58, fig. 122.

7. Rodenwaldt, *Tiryns* II, pl. 1.5, cf. pl. 16.1; Lang, *Pylos* II, 17 C Sw, pl. 52.

8. S. Alexiou, *Katsamba* (1967) pls. 20-22; Evans, *Palace of Minos* IV, 335, figs. 278-279; the latter already approaches the Middle period with its standardized flower sprays, more schematic division of the birds' bodies into vertical panels with zigzag and crosshatching, and the opening of a light oval panel with dark flower heads on the bird's side.

9. Gournia: H. B. Hawes, *Gournia* (1908) pl. X.40; C. Zervos, *L'Art de la Crète* (1956) fig. 741; Buchholz, Karageorghis, *Altägäis*, no. 1042 (detail); Knossos: Popham, *DestrKnossos*, fig. 6.3, pls. 7 e, f, 46 k; cf. fig. 5.2.

10. As on the alabastron from the Tomb of the Mace Bearer, Evans, *Palace of Minos* IV, 357, fig. 300; most Cretan III A bird sherds reflect the style.

the pyxis retains a charm and vivacity that will soon be lost in mainland painting, as in Cretan.[11]

J. The most impressive early Cretan import with a marine scene is the Varkiza tunny basket. Full-scale marine scenes are not popular in mainland pictorial painting until the middle of the thirteenth century, although there are always isolated fish in decorative use. The Varkiza basket is probably a direct import into coastal Attica from Knossos, where sherds of similar vases are known.[12] Four fish dive toward the bottom of the vase, obliquely twisted in a torsional pattern, separated by seabed rocks with trails of drifting seaweed. The composition is formal, simple, and bold. Such vases were the models for pieces like the Maroni fish vase (III.9) and the fine fish krater from Mycenae (VII.8). The open mouths of the feeding fish and the bending weeds that adapt to the stir of their bodies give a sense of environment and mild action. Pendent rocks from the upper border continue the Marine Style tradition and are often a hallmark of the Early period, occasionally revived in the thirteenth and twelfth centuries. Like the bird pyxis from Mycenae, this vase is Late Minoan III A:1, the first quarter of the fourteenth century, and is thus contemporary with the first true mainland pictorial vases, which display a markedly different style.

K. A fragment of a large vase, possibly even a larnax, appeared on the surface of a plot on Pindar Street in Thebes. It was connected to the Palace Style of Late Minoan II, but is unusual for that or any period. It represents a purse fishing net—the twisted rope of the mouth of the net is visible at the upper right—in which four open-mouthed fish swim eagerly toward another that seems somehow attached to the rope, while a sixth fish swims away right, perhaps escaping. The attractive fish on the rope may be a lure rather than a live decoy, and is flanked by three swelling, leafshaped patterns, like fish without the eyes and gills drawn in. These may be spinners meant to attract the living fish by dancing in the water as the net moves; they are related to the foliate band ornament of fifteenth-and early fourteenth-century vases. The marine scene is attractive and energetic, with the highlit silver ribbons along the fishes' flanks reserved, like the bright eyes and pale gills; it is perhaps ultimately indebted to netting scenes in Egyptian painting but makes an original impression.

EARLY PICTORIAL ON THE MAINLAND

The forerunners and imports differ so much among themselves that there is no clear matrix out of which mainland

pictorial painting might develop. From the beginning there are dissonant styles, and painters are harder to connect than in other periods of Greek painting. The earliest chariot krater in Greece seems to be a fragment from Aigina, but the main series does not start until about 1360. Most Early paintings are on one-handled jugs and ewers, in contrast to Cyprus but in accord with Cretan habits. An early human figure from Lakonia on such a jug has been placed tentatively in the Middle period (VIII.6) for reasons discussed there. The other Early pieces are mostly birds and fish, as among the forerunners.

HUMAN FIGURE

1. A krater fragment from Aigina probably comes from a chariot composition, although only the head and shoulders of the "passenger" are preserved. It is in a big, fluent style, like the Window and Pyla-Verghi kraters (III.12, 13). The man has ruffled hair, a very large eye, a sharp nose, a good deep chin, and bent neck, and he wears a simple robe embroidered with large circles; this is an Early characteristic, like the striped, bulging pillow shape behind him, perhaps a pendent rock.

QUADRUPED?

2. A one-handled alabastron from Mycenae may be an accident. It seems to have a zone of bizarre quadrupeds humping left around the shoulder. Wace thought they might be cats, Zeuner thought of a dromedary and cat. Neither animal occurs on later Mycenaean vases, although the spotted cat is known in metalwork and on ivories. Perhaps a chance splotch of paint helped the painter make animal shapes for amusement, the kind of imaginary childish creatures one sees shortly on the "Circus Pot" (VIII.8). It is possible that a simple jug from Aigina, painted with a goatbird and a flying shmoo (VIII.10), also belongs in this Early period.

11. There is a fragment of a bird of this stage from Mycenae, in what may be a local style: A. Wace, *BSA* 25 (1921-23) 107, fig. 25a. The legs are preserved with parts of the wings and neck, in solid silhouette with a floral filler. It was found with earlier and later sherds in the subsidiary supporting wall of Grave Circle A; Wace dated it to LH II, but it is unlikely to be any earlier than LH III A:1. The bird, soaring left with curved wings spread on either side, has five-toed feet; the flight position and fine swooping angles are rare.

Three fragments from the Athenian Acropolis are possibly Middle Helladic birds or fish, very fragmentary: Graef, Langlotz, *VA*, nos. 16, 17, 219. The first two, in matt brown-purple paint on coarse clay, seem to represent pinion feathers of birds; the third is described as the forepart of a fish.

12. For example, Evans, *Palace of Minos* IV, 304, fig. 239; Ashmolean Museum 186, 1910 (M. Theochares, *Antiquity* 1960, 269 fig. 3); Popham, *DestrKnossos*, pl. 47 c, cf. fig. 8.3, or the later Herakleion Museum sherds from Knossos, nos. 4443, 5183.

BULLS

The bull is never so popular in Greece as he is on Cyprus. There are two Early fragments from Mycenae.

3. A large, very thick sherd, possibly from a larnax, preserves part of a dappled bull's head to the right, with a bulging eye and the start of a flaring muzzle. The head is tossed upward as on the Vapheio Cups or in fresco design. The combination of large-scale outline and richly varied interior markings gives a free and daring effect; this is the closest of all the Argolid vases to wall painting. The color spots on the bull's hide are not patterned, rounded blobs, as later, but free arrangements of projections and hollows with minor dots between, rather like the incised patterns on the faces of steatite bull rhyta. The impressive scale of the fragment suggests that it may have come from an elaborate scene of bull catching, as on two much later larnakes, but the pictorial style would not have accommodated the multiple human figures of the Katsamba pyxis.[13]

4. A fragment of a krater seems to belong to the close of the Early period, the same stage as the Maroni Goat Krater (III.26). A simple striped rock pattern with curved border hangs from the upper framing band over the bull's back. Only a triangular fragment of the body is preserved; the hide is rendered with a disciplined combination of trefoil-shaped blobs and regularly spaced spots. There is some similarity to the leaping goat on a basket vase from Nauplion (IX.77), but an Early date is likely enough.

These two sherds show that well-painted bull compositions existed in the Argolid in the first third of the fourteenth century; complete kraters may well be found. Then the subject seems to lose popularity, with few illustrations (VIII.12), just as it is gaining ground in Cyprus; it fades away until a revival in the Ripe period, in styles often difficult to distinguish from those of the Levant.

BIRDS

5. A one-handled jug with a cutaway neck from Thebes bears on the front a broad lily whose stem is tied with a ribbon like spreading roots. On either side a small bird in solid paint flies with open wings toward the plant. The principle of design is the same as on the octopus-and-fish ewer from Athens (VII.7), and the action is a simpler version of the birds feeding in a tree on the W Krater in Cyprus (III.1), a motif that also appears on Minoan larnakes of this period. The broad pictorial sphere with free-field decoration is an Early sign; the lily is close to one on a contemporary bowl from Athens.[14] The bird has short wings like curved ladders attached at each side of the base of the neck; later birds are less likely to fly, more likely to

have both wings, raised or folded, behind their backs.[15] The type owed nothing to Crete but is not inconsistent with earlier styles in Greece. The body is a slender curve, the tail a triangle with fringes, the curved feet seem to push forward as though walking; the head is all eye with a central dot, and the beak is open for feeding. The whole is an unusual and cheery design in a Mycenaean center that did not care much for pictorial painting.

6. A spouted ewer, said to be from Attica, in the Louvre, should, by its shape, be placed at the beginning of Late Helladic III A:1. The body is low and globular, the arched handle has a pronounced knob, the plastic ring and foliate band of the Palace Style still appear on the neck. The base of the handle is ornamented with a fine painted floating ribbon in three strands. On the front of the vase three parent birds fly right in an uninterrupted field, each with a baby bird sporting over its back. The large birds are drawn in an idiosyncratic outline style, the long thin necks and long curved raised wings forming a triangle to which the body and tail are appended on the left, the small hooked feet on the right. The bodies are filled with rows of dots (elongated to bars where necessary), following the contour of the outlines and separated by inner contour lines to form strips. The tail is a fan filled with oblique dashes. The legs are short for the period, tensed under the belly in landing position.

The habit of mounting a small animal on the back of, or in the air over, a large one becomes more common in later stages of mainland painting (IX.48, XI.91). It raises the question, already discussed in connection with Cypriote vases (V.40), of whether the painter intended a scene of family interplay or was simply using a reduced version of the larger animal to fill space. The family interpretation seems truer and more attractive; the painters were not robots, nor were they cut off from imaginings about nature. Here the baby birds mimic the position of the parents, one wing out behind and feet skidding in front, as though taking flying lessons. This free and whimsical design, strongly outlined, spare and pale, is the most curious surviving example of an experimental period of Attic painting in the early fourteenth century. There may be some connection to the Cycladic bird style (VII.F) and the picture cannot in fact be as isolated as it seems.

13. T. Spyropoulos, *Ergon* 1969, 10, figs. 6-7; I. Tzedakis, *AAA* 4 (1971) 216 f., figs. 4, 7; cf. S. Alexiou, *Katsamba*, pls. 30-33; cf. also Chapter V, note 30.

14. H. Thompson, *Hesperia* 21 (1952) pl. 26; *Archaeology* 4 (1951) 224; S. Immerwahr, *The Athenian Agora* XIII, *The Neolithic and Bronze Ages* (1971) 205, T. XVI.1, pl. 47.

15. Ladder wings in a bird-and-plant scene, Crete: Popham, *DestrKnossos*, 108, fig. 14.80, but with pinions rendered in normal Cretan style.

FISH

7. A spouted ewer from a tomb in the Athenian Agora is close to 1400 in date. Its plastic neck ridge, foliate band, and pierced knob handle are signs of the ebbing fifteenth-century tradition; it may be slightly earlier than the Attic bird ewer (VII.6).

There is a broad lopsided octopus on the front, with a symmetrical but not yet rigid display of tentacles, filled with ornamental dot-and-curlicue designs, remnants of the older seaweed pattern. High on each shoulder a fish swims toward the octopus, like the birds toward the lily on VII.5. They have curiously blunt heads and splayed tails, more like sharks or whales than the usual dolphin.

The Agora ewer relates to its Cretan predecessors in the same way that the bird vases do, although the Marine Style ancestry is much more direct and influential. The plain background and simpler organization of forms are obvious distinctions; there is also greater disregard for the real aspect of animal bodies and a lack of interest in the visual representation of motion. Occasional "gestures," like a raised wing, a split tail, or a tensed claw may imply that the painter had motion in mind, but his principal concern is to adapt a satisfying pattern to his form. A similar design of this period was found at Karpathos (XII.26).

8. A fine though fragmentary early fish krater from Mycenae has a scene of chase with open mouths. There are parts of at least two fish on three sherds. In the field are spiked, double wavy lines and framed chevrons of Early III type. The fish may be from opposite sides of the krater, for on two sherds the body and tail of the leading fish and the head of the pursuing fish are in dark solid paint, while the third fragment shows a reserved tail with interior stripes. The bodies are large in proportion to the frieze space, with the massiveness and activity of the Maroni fish krater (III.9); the head of the predator is impressive, with sharp jaws parted to show a rippling tongue. The fins are drawn in sharp blocks filled with stripes, effective against the dark bodies, suggesting an increased transparency of flesh, as on the Phylakopi flying fish fresco. The tails are broad with neat fringes. One cannot tell the species. The trailing spiked lines may be neatened seaweed sprays, not adapted to the motion of the bodies as on the Maroni and Varkiza vases (III.9, VII.J).

Two fragmentary fish vases from Pylos (Englianos) show a loose organization of simply designed swimming or diving fish in a style that may ultimately be Cretan but is much modified and abstracted.

9. A wall fragment of a strap-handled open krater has one preserved fish diving down to the left; the back is dark, the belly light, and a wavy stripe undulates along the flank from a circular eye. This is a simplification of the contrasting color schemes in dolphin frescoes and on dolphin vases, later repeated in floor patterns in the palaces of Tiryns and Pylos.

10. From the shoulder of a stirrup jar or sharply profiled jug: a solid dark fish in streaky paint with reserved oval eye (fish eyes are usually round), short open beak, dorsal and ventral fins. Fish are rare on stirrup jars in Greece (IX.115, X.117) and are so far unknown on Cyprus; they are popular later in the Dodekanese (XII.40).

Furumark placed two undistinguished vases from the Argive Heraion at the start of the mainland fish tradition; both may be later.

11. A poor alabastron with three fish swimming right, separated by the handles, gives a scheme that will be widely used later. The crude fish are reduced to pattern, with an oval body, a spray of tail, and no separate head but a point on the front of the body.

12. The inside of a very large bowl has spotted fish alternately rising and diving at angles, against a background filled with thick waving lines that may represent seaweed. This composition is in the tradition of the Varkiza vase (VII.J), crudely reflected to be sure. The thick bodies with multiple arcs to set off the reserved faces from the spotted skin recur in all periods of Mycenaean painting. The pleasant conceit of placing them inside a bowl, swimming in liquid, is further developed later (IX.120); there are early fourteenth-century examples of the same scene in Crete.[16]

This survey of examples of possibly Early pictorial painting found on the Mycenaean mainland is not intended to be complete,[17] but may serve to illustrate the wide variety of shapes and styles that carried pictorial imagery. It would be hard to deduce development, let alone local schools. The lack of Early chariot scenes may be accidental; little of the material is well preserved. The evidence shows that pictorial vases in Greece come from both houses and tombs, but the better pieces are normally from tombs, as usual, in contrast to Crete and the Cyclades.

16. Popham, *DestrKnossos*, 102, fig. 8.3, inside cup type C.

17. There may be Early fish sherds at Delphi, L. Lerat, *BCH* 59 (1935) 359, fig. 15.1-2. There is certainly material from other sites either unpublished or unavailable for discussion.

The fine shield krater from Mycenae, Athens NM 1295, is not included here because it is not strictly pictorial, like the LM I shield jug from Vari, Attica (Buchholz, Karageorghis, *Altägäis*, no. 903) or the piriform jug with shields and rockwork, LH II (G. Säflund, *Excavations at Berbati 1936-1937* [1965] 25, fig. 10).

VIII
THE GREEK MAINLAND:
Middle Pictorial

I N GREECE, very little pictorial painting can be placed with certainty in the period from the founding of Amarna through the end of the fourteenth century. The LH III A:2 phase is a prolific one in other ways, but the pictorial style seems still tentative, and the material does not yet justify a division into three separate chronological phases. When the Berbati pictorial fragments are published, the sequences of styles, and local schools, should become far clearer. Already one may guess that the workshop of Painter 9 was located there.

Between 1360 and 1300, mainland painters continue to decorate a greater variety of vase shapes. In Cyprus and the Levant in this period, pictorial vases are almost exclusively kraters, generally amphoroid kraters. In Greece kraters are dominant, too, because the broad decorative field encourages this kind of painting, but pictures are also found on bowls, jugs, rhyta, and stirrup jars. This makes it harder to establish direct links in style with pieces found in Cyprus, although certain chariot, bird, and bull kraters on both sides of the Aegean are related. The mainland fragments also suggest a preference for stronger contour with less florid filling ornament; the ground is less cluttered than in the East, and there are, for example, no seashell filling ornaments on surviving pieces of the Middle period (but see IX.83).

CHARIOTS

There may be nearly twenty fragments of amphoroid kraters with chariot scenes from the "Potter's Quarter" at Ber-

bati in the Argolid. Three have been published, and at least one belongs to the Middle period. All three are grouped here for convenience, because the chariot scenes of the following Ripe phase from Mycenae, Corinth, and Nauplion are quite different in style. It is clear that the style has already been formed, that the painters can do good quick schematic work, and that one can expect earlier chariot scenes to be excavated in the future.

1. A fragment of shoulder and rim from an amphoroid krater preserves two men in the box of a (missing) chariot moving right. The long-stemmed flowers in the field behind the chariot are a typical Middle III variety (IV.48 and following). Both men have curved torsos draped in spotted robes; the driver's hands jut from his breast as thumb and finger circles, the passenger is without hands. The painter makes a cap of dark hair, a dotted circle eye, a prominent nose, and a receding chin; the style recalls the Tel Dan krater and its associates (Painter 9, IV.49) and opens the interesting question of Berbati as a major exporting center. A sherd from Mycenae (VIII.5) may come from the same workshop. See Chapter IX, note 1.

2. A slightly later fragment from near a handle has two schematic armless men in a chariot moving right. The front of the box is spotted, the wing is ornamented with large circles. The men's heads are drawn with dark caps, hair or berets, quick sharp triangles for nose and lip, and a simple dot eye.

3. A fragment of an amphoroid krater preserves part of the team's necks. The locks of the manes are in outline, like IV.59; there is an accented rein-ring with four reins like those used by Painter 6 (IV.19 and following), and

rows of alternating V-pattern above and below the reins.

4. From Nauplion, from the Palamidi, comes a small, well-known sherd with the undercarriage of the chariot moving left, drawn in a simple style. The wheel has a thick rim and four spokes, the lateral one apparently projecting through to the rear of the wheel (it may be confused with the projection of the pole behind the box); the carriage body sits along the curve of the wheel and is neatly spotted. A rather high proportion of early pieces from the Argolid have the chariot moving left (VIII.5, IX.1, 1.1, 2, 4?). Nauplion must once have been a good market for pictorial vases. (IX.1.1).

5. Mycenae, which would shortly become such a major center of pictorial art, has apparently yielded only one Middle chariot fragment, and an interesting larnax. The fragment of an amphoroid krater, with a driver in a spotted robe going left, holding the reins in rounded hands with vertical slashes above the reins, is a valuable document. It seems closely connected with the Berbati workshop (VIII.1) and with three vases in the East, one from Tel Dan (IV.49) and two from Maroni in Cyprus (IV.63, 64), as well as with the head of a charioteer from Miletos (XIII.2) and possibly a chariot from Tell el-Ajjul (IV.74). It is symptomatic of our ignorance about the trade in pictorial vases that this small sherd from a capital town in the Argolid and the Berbati fragment are at present the only links between Painter 9 and the mainland, but the distribution of his works in coastal sites of the Levant is well suited to the increasing tempo of commercial voyages in the Amarna period.

5.1. Larnakes are not normally included in this survey,[1] but the coarse bathtub larnax from Mycenae demonstrates the further familiarity of local painters with the chariot schemes so well known in the East in the Middle period. A larnax is so bulky and fragile that it is almost always locally made. This one is decorated with a schematic octopus inside, as so often in Crete. Only two important fragments survive. On the outside the chariot and team move right; there is a flower in front of the horses and one under their bellies. Two crude thick lines at the extreme right might conceivably be the remains of the groin and legs of an attendant. The horses are dark, with fused bodies but two tails; the inner face of the hind leg is pale, as on vases. There are four reins to the rein-ring; there seem to be both pole-brace and stay as well as a pole curving up behind the hindquarters. The larnax is too fragmentary to discern on it any special influence from fresco; in monochrome silhouette it is more like a chariot vase scene transferred to a larger, coarser shape. The connection between the chariot scene and the octopus is interesting in general for explorations of funerary iconography as they are linked both on vases (III.2) and on Minoan coffins.

HUMAN FIGURES

The isolated human figures in the opening phases of mainland painting do not at all correspond with human figures in Cyprus. The Cypriote grooms and attendants are part of the chariot-scene tradition, whether nude or robed. They are not isolated and are seldom engaged in specific action. In Greece, the three or four fourteenth-century attempts to paint men have no connection with chariot traditions and for that reason, perhaps, strike us as extraordinarily clumsy and artless. They may exhibit features seen earlier in Cycladic paintings of soldiers (VII.A), but any real connection would be surprising, beyond the shared primitivism in drawing subjects outside the court tradition. Since these scattered earlier pieces are outside the pictorial conventions, they are difficult to date except by shape and subsidiary ornament. The large group of Late pieces, which can be fixed in the flux of styles by context and interrelationship (Chapters IX-XI), offer fewer problems. It would be hard to predict from such beginnings that paintings of human beings in action will become one of the prime strengths of later Mycenaean art.

6. A jug with a cutaway neck from Melathria in Lakonia has an uneasy warrior floating between two of the vertical curved stripes on the body. This odd sketch cannot be dated precisely in itself, and the type of jug has contexts ranging from III A:1 to III B:1 early — that is, most of the fourteenth century. It is not likely to be fifteenth century, as thought at first, but to join the small group of the "Circus Pot" (VIII.8), the Zygouries bowl (VIII.9), and the Menelaion sherds (VIII.11), in early LH III A:2, probably in the second quarter of the century.[2]

The warrior hovers halfway up the vase, facing right, with an outlined helmeted head; the body is composed of irregular dark borders with a stacked-chevron interior, recalling the attendant on the Cypriote krater of this period, IV.12, although those chevrons are white with added spots (cf. IV.14). There the chevrons are matched by

1. The relation between larnax painting and pictorial vase painting was discussed in a tentative way by E. Vermeule, *JHS* 85 (1965) 123 f.; since then many more larnakes have become known, at Tanagra in Boeotia, where several hands are distinct, at Armenoi near Rethymnon, and at other Cretan sites like Gazi. Scenes of the dead and their mourners remain the explicit preserve of the larnax painters, but both vases and larnakes illustrate bull jumping, chariots, hunts, ships, and robed figures.

2. This is suggested by the spiral tentacle with filled arcs on the shoulder, as well as by the contexts of the best parallels, for example,

chevron filling ornaments, so characteristic of the early Amarna Age in the Cypriote series; since mainland pictures usually have no fillers, such a cross-check cannot be made (but see VIII.12). The top chevron forms the chin line, and its outer angles form extra "elbows" (or shoulder-guards?) below his arms. The edges of the chevron stack are blurred by the wavering forms of the "corselet." The groin seems to be just under the collarbone. The figure is no doubt meant to be armored or clothed in some fashion, and the head is clearly topped by a floating triple plume from the helmet crest. The extended left hand holds a bent line, a club or knife. The four fingers and thumb are stroked on with considerable accuracy for a period when most figures have an uneven number of digits, and each long flat foot is equipped with the regulation five toes (see VIII.11). The figure resembles the stick soldiers of Thera (VII.A) in its slapdash quality, but the bulkier chevron-filled body and the hint of action may suit the beginnings of a long tradition of warrior imagery lasting from the mid-fourteenth century to the early twelfth.

7. A small krater fragment from Ayios Stephanos in Lakonia, of indeterminate date ("LH III A-B"), has a dark silhouetted figure left with a curved shape in front of him, which the excavators thought might be a fish. A cross-hatched insert across the chest and up the right side could be a baldric, or an arm treated in a peculiar manner to distinguish it from the chest it crosses. The sherd could as easily be thirteenth century. If the figure is wearing a baldric (and therefore is not a fisherman), it would help establish Lakonia as a center of early military pictures, but it does not illuminate the style of the period.

8. The little jug from Mycenae, sometimes called the "Circus Pot," is mid-fourteenth century by shape and context, an instructive and curious manifestation of what Furumark called "styleless" painting. Most scholars judge it an early example of picture making by an untrained artisan who was not concerned with traditions in fresco or on pictorial vases, who rendered an idea or a scene quickly and crudely, independent of any model. His motive — to amuse himself or a child? — and his meaning — odd ritual (Nilsson, Stubbings), myth (Marinatos), or ribald genre (Dow) — cannot be judged with any more certainty than a child's drawing when the artist is not at hand for questioning.

The "Circus Pot" is a small jug, a miniature hydria, with an upright handle at the rear and two loop handles at the sides. The developed drawing usually published makes the picture center under the rear handle; if one reads the scene in the normal way, centered on the front of the vase, the two human figures come together. It is not certain that they are women. The one on the left wears a knee-length

kilt or skirt; the boneless legs are spread with the feet curved upward; the unequal arms wave in the air; the body is frontal, and the "chicken" head with protruding lips turns right. From the front of the vase, this is the principal figure. To its right is a figure painted solid with a reserved face and protruding lips, armless as on chariot vases, hunched in on itself, swaying right. Below on the left a fine goose with inner markings and solid beak strolls left on branch-toed feet; below on the right, a goat (headless but horned) chews toward the right at a little tree. Its fillings are less firm than the goose's, M's and lazy connecting lines. Above the goose are two four-spoked wheels. Above the goat is one of a pair of larger wheels held aloft by a creature beneath the rear handle, the "juggler" who names the vase. This dumpy figure lofting his wheels on either side of the handle has a plump striped body, a round head facing right with long beak lips and spike hair; he sits down, for lack of space or for narrative reasons, with his bumpy legs stretched before him. Flying at his stomach is a large dark bird seen from above, with railroad-track wings swept back in an oval to frame the body.

Many interpretations have been offered. Wace, the excavator, thought of a juggler-entertainer in a dance scene. Nilsson considered that sun-wheel symbolism might be linked to ritual dance. Marinatos thought the little man under the handle was in a smashed chariot, relic of heroic myth, gesticulating with despair at the onslaught of a frightening bird (cf. III.6). Dow caught the image of a scene in the courtyard of a chariot maker's workshop, with the body of the chariot represented by the "bird," complete with shafts and train with lashings; the farm animals are wandering casually through. Stubbings thought it an adaptation of the old Near Eastern goat-and-tree motif, certainly ritual, a miniature replica of a sacred vessel. None of the explanations has a rational niche for each figure, except as a generalized fertility dance with people and animals.

Furumark stressed the point that such a scene ought to have a meaning, simply because the design lies outside the ordinary ceramic series.[3] Doodling is not often attested on

A. Wace, *Chamber Tombs at Mycenae* (1932) pls. 20.2, 45.1. Slightly earlier examples are *Chamber Tombs*, pl. 56.19, and, from Karpophora in Messenia, *Deltion* 23 (1968) B, pl. 111 B.

3. Furumark, *MP*, 459; the point is theoretically strong, but not enough is known about impulses toward pictorialization in the Bronze Age to be sure that an untrained person making a picture needed to have a "significant" purpose. A similar "styleless" kind of drawing in the thirteenth century occurs on a Cretan larnax in Herakleion, with worn figures, cousin to the "Circus Pot" figures, spread all over the surface. These include chariot and horse, bull's head with "suns," a ship, birds, fish, argonaut, palm tree, wheels, a dog chasing an *agrimi*, a vulture eating a corpse, and women, with their hands on their heads, watching a bull jumper. Aside from summarizing all the major themes of Bronze Age funeral iconography, the larnax suggests that the line of style illustrated in

Mycenaean pottery. He felt that the painter wanted to try something different because it had significance for him; in the absence of known models he relapsed into a common primitive manner with marked differentiation of the parts of the body and jumbled organization of the elements. Certain features of "style" do connect with earlier habits: the ladder wings of the bird, both in Crete and Greece (cf. VII.5), the dancing lady(? III.10,11) and the flower-sniffing lady of Alyke (IX.13); spike hair, used in LH III C (XI.1,2), is the simplest way to draw hair. Other tunics are filled with wavy lines, other dark birds are drawn from above. These are solutions that any child can invent for himself; childlike also is the interest in fingers and toes, which are different in number on each foot. Of all the figures the goose is best, firmly outlined, with a good gait and head.

9. The design on a fragment of a deep bowl from Zygouries was immediately seen by the excavator to belong to the "school" of the "Circus Pot." Its surviving figure, left of the handle, might be a long-horned goat with two short ears, a reserved body, and a forked tail, browsing to the left. It is harder to see as a bird, but it may be a goat-bird (see VIII.10, IX.87). The tremulous outlines and weak two-toed legs recall not only the preceding vase but certain earlier Cycladic attempts to draw animals from inexperience. The date could shift as much as a century.

10. The same problem is set by a simple one-handled jug from Aigina. On the left of the shoulder frieze are a flying goat and a goat-bird heading airily toward a degenerate octopus pattern or a set of waves culminating in an open sac with tentacles. The goat may be recognized by his two horns curving back and two jaunty forelegs, although the hind legs are fused into a drooping fish tail, like sea-goats on later Island gems. His companion, with a horn, three legs, and a fat fantail like a bird's, hops with bent knees toward the octopus waves with an air of happy anticipation. Both figures are charming, if not "art." The jug is dated to the later fourteenth century or the thirteenth on grounds of shape, yet the shape also appeared at the end of Middle Helladic; these errant figures may belong here, and in style they are certainly linked to the last piece. However, there are other goat-birds in the thirteenth century (IX.87), and the jug could descend in date.

11. Three sherds from a krater have been published (upside down) in connection with the Mycenaean house near the Menelaion at Amyklai outside Sparta. The figures are set in panels divided by a column of framed circles, which might ordinarily suggest a late LH III B or early III C date.[4] Yet the shapes of the head, long arms, fingers, and toes are very close to the primitivism of the "Circus Pot" and the Melathria jug. Of one figure on the left there re-

mains an outspread hand with four fingers and thumb at the end of a long horizontal arm. The other figure, broken in two, has a round head with protruding beaked lips, a circular eye without a pupil, a frontal body, a long, double-curved arm flung out like the dancer's arm on the "Circus Pot," a hand rendered as a spiked fist with the thumb down. The legs are on a separate nonjoining sherd; they are thick with symmetrically everted knees like horse hocks, the feet drawn frontally and upright on tiptoe, perhaps suggesting nimbleness in the dance. One senses a connection to the figure of the Melathria warrior (VIII.6).

The "sea fight" from Phylakopi (X.39) and two sherds with splayed hands from Athens (X.41, 41.1) are similar in style but apparently chronologically later; without the precedent of the "Circus Pot," these Menelaion sherds would no doubt be set later too, almost automatically. They need not be, however.

BULLS

On present evidence, bull scenes on vases are not nearly so popular on the mainland in the Middle period as they are on Cyprus. This is surprising in view of the number of bull gems and bull frescoes. The only vase that resembles contemporary Levantine pictures is the fragmentary bull-and-flower krater from Mycenae.

12. A group of seven fragments of an open krater from Mycenae preserves parts of two bulls, or a bull and a cow, gamboling right through a field of long-stemmed flowers and scattered double chevrons. The foremost bull raises his hind legs off the ground in a checked gallop (cf. IV.32), the second is sniffing a flower. There are tendencies that will become stronger in the Ripe phase, such as the comparatively small scale of the head, the reduction of the wrinkles in the dewlap to a collar of arcs or striped ladder pattern (cf. IV.36, V.74), further arbitrary division of the body by a patterned belt behind the chest, zigzags on the breast, and stripes on the legs; there is a pleasure in beginning to group the marks on the hide more neatly along the exterior contours of the body. The hind legs are reserved, the tails are long and drooping with a splayed tassel-end. The leading animal has striped genitals (cf. IV.32, 55). There may have been bulls on one side and cows on the

an early phase by the "Circus Pot" is not really aberrant and has a duration of at least a century.

4. It is not clear whether the sherds came from inside the house. The majority of sherds have a context of LH III A:2 to late LH III B. See H. Waterhouse, R. H. Simpson, *BSA* 55 (1960) 72, n. 33; Furumark, *MP*, 540.

other, or a pair on each side. The fragments exhibit the same happy carelessness as IV.32, though by a cruder painter, who has difficulty drawing hindquarters and forelegs reasonably. Some scholars feel that this is a crude imitation by an unpracticed artist of a composition that was currently fashionable in the East; others contend that since many Eastern pieces are equally awkward in drawing, there is no need to place the Mycenae krater in an inferior category. This is one of the few Middle pictorial vases to show any link between the two regions at all (cf. VIII.13). In the next phase, bulls are often indistinguishable in style on both sides of the sea.

13. A rim fragment of an open krater from Mycenae may also be fourteenth century. It has a facing bull's head on the flat top of the rim, set among loose quirks. Like facing bulls from Cyprus, this is painted with flesh and hair, not as a skull (cf. V.102, 103). The head is rendered solid with reserved and dotted round eyes; the ears and horns jut symmetrically from a flat poll; the broad muzzle seems to flare into nostrils. The prototype for such placement may be in metalwork.

BIRDS

Bird designs remain popular on a greater variety of shapes than in Cyprus: kraters, ewers, bottles, and jugs. As in Cyprus, the painting shows static composition and pleasure in the arbitrary patterning of the body. Birds flying or feeding are rarer in Middle and Ripe pictorial than in the Early and Late phases; decorative considerations have primacy. The first krater is of particular interest because it is by an artist whose work is also found in Cyprus.

14. An open krater from Mycenae, sometimes called "Petsas' Krater," is almost surely by the painter of IV.6, from Enkomi. The krater was found smashed in Room D of a building not yet fully explored, lying in a layer of so much excellent broken pottery and lumps of red coloring that the excavators supposed they might be nearing a potter's workshop. This was never verified, which is more the pity since "Petsas' Krater" is such an invaluable link to the East; if it were actually in a workshop, it might have illuminated the discussion of where pictorial vases were made.

The published picture of the vase is poor. A drawing gives a clearer impression of the likeness to IV.6: the continuous frieze of heavy-bodied birds right, with the thick outlines of head, neck, and breast changing to an open double line contouring the back and drooping tail. The body surface is divided into vertical slots filled with cross-

hatching, chevrons, dashes, and dots; one bird has an elaborate rosette on its breast. The background is filled with the same palmetto and U-pattern on both vases. The Mycenae vase also has a dotted spray of three branches rising from the junction of one bird's neck and back, either foliage or a weak rendering a raised wing plume. The Enkomi vase has undulating stripes like grass or weed before the beak of the leading bird; the Mycenae vase is too damaged to show whether the birds are feeding (cf. VIII.16). In their physical type the birds may be swans, rocking on their bellies with feet pushed out behind as though swimming, although the filling ornaments are land plants.

A group of three Middle pictorial bird vases found in a tomb at Koukounara near Pylos, on the west coast of Greece, illustrates a different aspect of mainland style that is not matched in Cyprus. The group consists of two kraters and a ewer. Although they cannot be the prototypes of Cypro-Mycenaean bird kraters (the excavator proposed that they were the earliest pictorial vases made in the heartland of the Achaians before they moved eastward to show the Cypriotes how to paint), they do fall fairly early in the mainland sequence. The tomb context ranges from LH I to III; shape and ornament place the three pictorial vases in LH III A:2 late, in the final third of the fourteenth century.

15. An open krater with argonauts on one side has two swanlike birds to the right on the other side. A small bird perches on the tail of the first, a fish swims over the tail of the second. The picture zone is narrower than in the Early period. Filling ornaments are sparse; this is generally true of mainland pictorial and particularly true of bird vases both on the mainland and in the East. In this case the ornaments are idiosyncratic: a double spiral, a four-spoked wheel,[5] a filled triangle like the crest of a wave. The birds have heavy, round bodies with broad contours and inconsistent markings. Bands of chevrons and diagonal stripes form irregular quadrants inside the oval bodies, and the interstices are filled with branches, rock pattern, palm leaves, arcs, and dots. The first bird has a bristling crest at the base of the neck, and both have fringed tails. They are placed in a swimming position, as on the last, long necks lowered to the ground line as though feeding on the surface of the water, feet paddling behind. The fish adds to the waterside atmosphere. Perhaps he is meant to be seen in perspective farther off. The thick outline with two dorsal and two ventral fins is open at the tail; there is a double

5. See XII.28 from Karpathos. Wheels or crossed circles are surprisingly rare as filling ornaments until late LH III B, except on the disks of stirrup jars; Furumark, *MP*, FM 41.21.

ribbon of color along the upper and lower flanks and a branch pattern in the right place for a backbone (cf. V.129). One supposes that the bird on the tail of the leader is a little cygnet perched dry on its parent's back, either a direct observation from nature or a pattern drawn from tradition (VII.6); it is useful for space-filling.

16. A second krater has two elongated "swans" on each side, crowded together on an almost empty ground. The outlines are thick and contorted; the necks are looped back so that the heads fall above the breasts; the wings are mere oval loops behind the tails. The whole design is compressed and airless. On one side the birds' bodies are filled with split, fringed footballs,[6] separated on the leader by a banded hourglass. The excavator suggested that these ovals are eggs, as they may well be on VIII.14. On the second side the long and awkward bodies are split into panels, the first with typical fillers of dashes and arcs, the second with a more unusual arrangement of vertical chevrons in the center flanked by solid-centered fringed concentric arcs.[7] The curious wings are drawn as narrow tubes, striped or solid, projecting forward over the heads and backward to the tail, each pair tied by chevrons at the juncture. It is rare to see both wings on a profile bird. The filling ornament is antithetic U-pattern over the heads only. Each bird holds a long filament with multiple stems hanging down, like dripping weeds.[8]

17. The ewer has three scrawny birds in a frieze around the shoulder. The long body of the leader has a filling of four dark, jagged ovals, perhaps eggs (it is too much to hope that the adjacent dashes are the cilia of the egg-laying tract). The other two birds have thicker bodies carelessly filled with stripes and dashes. All have raised wings. This amusing piece does look like an attempt to describe the reproductive value of a goose or, less likely, a hen. Hens were not yet domesticated in Greece but were known to the Egyptian army in the East in the fifteenth century.[9] Marinatos interpreted the scene as two males following, and disputing over, a desirable female. This would harmonize with the implications of the livelier bull scenes (cf. IV.32, 36), but for a dispute the frieze composition is static.

These are the best-preserved Middle Pictorial bird scenes from Greece, but fragments from several sites may be assigned to this period. Mycenae produced the most; others have been found at Asine, Athens, Delphi, and Eleusis. Some are too fragmentary to be sure of the date. Four may serve as illustrations.

MYCENAE

18. A fragment from an odd shape is perhaps the bottom of a pierced egg-shaped rhyton with a nipple. Beside the

nipple is preserved the long dark neck of a twisted bird with a long triangular beak and a dot eye. There is a dot-rosette in the field.[10]

19. The top of a small bottle, rhyton, or jug has two long-necked birds raising their heads toward the spout, on a field of S-pattern. Below is apparently an outstretched wing with a thick border and inner crosshatching, fringed at the lower edge. The quality is good. The sense of upward dancing or flying motion contrasts with the heavy Cypriote style of the period (IV.38 and following); this sprightliness of dancing ducks is occasionally seen elsewhere on smaller vases (IX.95, X.64).

ASINE

25. An interesting but worn and fragmentary amphora(?), late fourteenth century, shows a bird identified as a hoopoe (*Upupa epops*). The crested bird, right, is feeding on an arc of dots like seeds or grains of corn, among standard Mycenaean flowers. When intact, this must have been an attractive vase with alternations of firm dark silhouette and open sprays of curving dots.

DELPHI

27. A fragmentary open krater from Delphi has the usual frieze of heavy birds right, but in a distinctive style. Parts of two birds are divided into multiple vertical slots that are filled, as in Cyprus, with bars and U-pattern; the neck is solid, the tail fringed. The beak is enormous, like a toucan's. These birds combine the folded and the raised wing, with the raised wing held far out in front of the body like a walking aid (cf. V.72). The only surviving filling ornament is a double circle fringed with sunburst rays over the back of the leading bird; the second bird opens his beak at it. This was once an impressive vase, though constricted by

---

6. Cf. an LH III A:2 jar from Mycenae: J. Papademetriou, P. Petsas, *Praktika* 1950, 210, fig. 9.16, and the pattern in the bull, V.101.

7. Superficially this seems like an anticipation of the Close Style, but a version has already appeared on the Window Krater, III.12.

8. S. Marinatos associated these on a grand mythological scale with exotic spices of the East such as cassia, cinnabar, or the magical moly plant, *Ergon* 1963, 85 f.; *EphArch* 1964, 7.

9. Domestic fowl are generally regarded as an introduction from the East fairly late in the Bronze Age: J. H. Breasted, "Annals of Tuthmosis III," no. 483 in *Ancient Records of Egypt* (1907) (Eighth Campaign, Year 33); H. Carter, *JEA* 9 (1923) 1 f.; W. S. Smith, *Interconnections in the Ancient Near East* (1965) fig. 39; more recently a specimen has been reported at Lerna, in Lerna IV, "The first appearance in European prehistory," as well as two from the surface and mixed layers; N.-G. Gejvall, *Lerna* I, *The Fauna* (1969) 49 and n. 1. Cf. F. Perdrizet, *RevArch* 21 (1893) 157.

10. Cf. E. French, *BSA* 59 (1964) pl. 70.d.4, 5; *BSA* 60 (1965) pl. 51.c.6; pl. 52.e.2, LH III A:2. A recent discussion of French's chronology of pottery at Mycenae, *BICS* 24 (1977) 136 f.

the narrowness of the picture zone. Delphi is not noted as a pictorial center.

BIRDS, HUMAN FIGURES, AND SPHINXES

An intriguing group of vases from Mycenae is partly connected with the bird series but has more interest for its expression of cult or demon imagery in the fourteenth century. The group combines birds with human protomes or with sphinxes.

30. A large piece of a low alabastroid stirrup jar without context from Mycenae may be late fourteenth or early thirteenth century. There are lateral flowers in the spout zone and bands enlivened with white zigzags framing U-pattern on the shoulder. The picture field has, from the left, an oblique, chevron-filled papyrus, the head and part of the breast of a human figure or a sphinx facing right, a striped bird with one raised sharp wing whose beak crosses a long curved object with a barred upper border, and a flower pendent from the upper border. The flowers are characteristic of the late Amarna period. The bird is not unlike the one on VIII.18 from Mycenae, above; another like it was recently found at Thebes (VIII.29).

The head may belong to a sphinx as easily as to a human being. The brushwork does not clarify whether it has ruffled hair or the flat cap sphinxes often wear, usually plumed. The outlined face is rectangular with a simple dot eye, and an ear is drawn in on the back of the neck, an unusual feature. The pattern on the shoulder may be the start of a spiral coil, a common motif on sphinx breasts. It is possible that the curved lines by the bird's beak are the tips of the backswept wings of a sphinx in front, as on the next vase. (Another possibility is that they represent the curved horns of an altar.) The association of birds, sphinxes or human figures, and plants is unusual in this period; the fragment has a sacral, idyllic aura, which recurs on the next example. The quality is excellent.

31. Two low, compressed stirrup jars were discovered in a corridor of a building southwest of the Lion Tomb. One has been partly published. There are flowers in the spout zone, bands and fine stripes on the shoulder, white zigzags on the handles. In the narrow frieze, parts of three couchant sphinxes are preserved, interspersed with flying and resting birds, papyrus flowers, and dotted circles. The drawing is neat and sober, with a good balance among solid, striped, reserved, and blank areas.

The sphinxes seem to be all the same type. The one complete sphinx wears a flat cap with two long plumes streaming in the air behind, the usual iconography in ivory carving. The face is outlined, with a flat forehead, long nose, receding chin, and a loop ear drawn inside the head contour at the back of the crown. The body is long and thin in a horizontal crouch. The breast and haunch are painted solid, the central body reserved. One forepaw is curled forward, balanced by the tail curving upward to terminate in a spiral. The wings are raised on either side, thin and pointed with undulating edges, the surfaces finely crosshatched. A small papyrus plant crosses the front wing.

To the left of this sphinx a bird, drawn from above, flies almost into her chest, with striped wings outspread. Beyond are visible the raised wing of another sphinx and two papyrus plants. To the right is a standing bird and two papyri, then the raised wing and curled tail of a third sphinx, perhaps one of an antithetic pair.

The clean lines and abstract fantasy of these vases, with their quiet undertones of sacral imagination, distinguish them sharply from anything found so far in the Levant and give them an important place in the history of Mycenaean painting. The type does not seem to be transferred to vase painting from any other field of minor art; ivory reliefs with sphinxes naturally make great use of contours and internal musculature, but not of strongly contrasted surface patterning, and in other fields of the late fourteenth century, such as gem carving, sphinxes are surprisingly rare. The sphinx form has been so well adapted here to the decorative needs of the pictorial style, one suspects that there may be an anterior tradition that has not yet been discovered. The juxtaposition of birds and these demonic attendants of divinity, or divine surrogates, harks back to the Minoan nexus of imagery, here stabilized into quiet pattern.

[32. It is in many ways a pity that the attractive three-handled jar from Mycenae, now in Munich, with a painted decoration of sphinx protomes, should have proved to be a forgery. It is an ingenious forgery, certainly one of the earlier examples of the art in the Mycenaean field, done with considerable authority and wit. The sphinxes were applied in washable paint to the lower body of the jar, one on each side. The long-nosed females wore ruffled flat caps with three plumes; they had slim oval eyes, slanting, five-strand beaded necklaces, and raised wings bent sharply to frame the face. The wings were filled with (un-Mycenaean) scale-net pattern.]

ALTAR AND DOUBLE AXE

33. An open krater with strap handles, from a mixed nonsepulchral deposit in the Agora of Athens, has an ele-

gant design of an altar with horns of consecration framing a central double axe. The motif is of course Cretan and not often used on the mainland except for burial larnakes; it appears sporadically in Cyprus (III.23), Rhodes (XII.2) and, in the Late period, at Ugarit (XIII.29). The Athenian vase has a pair of tall palm trees on either side of the altar, the two on the right separated by vertical lozenge chains. The altar has three rectangular supports ornamented with chevrons and reserved wavy line, with antithetic U's filling the air like fillets. The thick horns are striped white and outlined with a zigzag border; there are white chevrons on the altar table and white lines around the three spear-shaped fruits of the palms. The context does not help with the problem of whether it was a ritual or funerary vase, but it was evidently an important krater, finely drawn. The nearest analogy for the subject is the Late krater from Ugarit (XIII.29).

HELMETS

34. Helmets, like shields, are not generally regarded as pictorial motifs because they are so close to abstract ornament. A kylix from Nichoria on the west coast is included because figure painting in the southwest is relatively rare and because it illustrates a fourteenth-century habit of converting ornament to picture, a trend that will increase later. The kylix has a frieze of ducklike "helmets," baggy shapes with double contours, filled with vertical slashes, with a knob for a plume socket, and two plumes floating left and up. Cretan painters had long used the motif, more elaborately.[11] The pictorially decorated kylix is more common on Rhodes (XII.11, 13, 15) than on the mainland.

11. Cf. A. Wace, *BSA* 49 (1954) pl. 35a, d; M. Popham, *BSA* 73 (1978) 179f., fig. 1a.

IX
THE GREEK MAINLAND:
Ripe Pictorial

THE MOST INTERESTING Mycenaean pictorial compositions on the Greek mainland seem to fall into three principal periods. The first is Late Helladic III B, the first three-fourths of the thirteenth century; second, a long and productive Transitional phase, LH III B-C, which may be placed roughly between 1230 and 1190; last, a surge of new design in LH III C proper, the first half of the twelfth century. It is clear that these phases do not correspond precisely to the sequence of styles in the East.

Some scenes in the Ripe phase, in LH III B, have fairly close parallels in Cypriote Ripe I and II, although there are too few complete vases in Greece to justify a matching subdivision. The correspondence is closest in pictures of stags and bulls; the chariot scenes seldom correspond in detail. There is no developed Pastoral style (Chapter VI) in Greece, but one horse composition at least (IX.8) is drawn with a similar free vigor; a leaping goat (IX.77) and a lion among bulls (IX.82) show analogous styles. The latter part of Ripe painting in Greece is chronologically parallel to the Pastoral epoch in the Levant without sharing its developments. The differences between mainland and Levantine Ripe consist mainly in the greater variety of vase shapes in Greece, the more daring and experimental compositions, and the restraint in use of filling ornament. Since jugs, bowls, and rhyta are also being painted pictorially in the East, the first difference is not critical; since the material is mostly fragments, the second two may have been diagnosed subjectively. The differences are subtle but not entirely elusive.

Some fragments that might perhaps be classified in the Ripe period have been set aside for the Transitional group (Chapter X). This seems justified by the divergent courses of painting in west and east. Cyprus exhibits neither Transitional nor Late (III C) features that can be distinguished from mainland Mycenaean. The renewed unity of style reflects the political and economic situation of the island in Late Cypriote II C and III. The wave of Mycenaean emigrants who established themselves in Cyprus in the late thirteenth century brought a more clearly mainland fashion in pictorial painting, so that LH III C is generally the same at both ends of the Aegean bridge (Chapter VI). The Transitional period falls during this emigration, and it should not be surprising that the best examples of the period are restricted to the stabler towns of the Argolid and a few coastal sites. There is no hard division between Ripe and Transitional, only a series of experiments. The whole classification must remain necessarily tentative until the publication of the pictorial fragments from Berbati (VIII.1-3). The recent publication of the Tiryns pictorial sherds has been of great value.[1]

1. The small site of Berbati in the hills about an hour east of Mycenae was investigated by a Swedish team in the mid-1930s; Professor Åke Åkerström has been particularly interested in the potter's workshop, which produced perhaps two hundred fragments of Mycenaean pictorial vases. Some of the other material from the site has been published, by G. Säflund, *Excavations at Berbati 1936-1937* (1965), and samples of the pictorial material have been illustrated by Åkerström: "Das mykenische Topferviertel in Berbati in der Argolis," *Bericht über den VI. Internationalen Kongress für Archäologie* (Berlin, 1939) 296f.; "En mykensk Krukmakares Verkstad," *Arkeologiska Forskningar och Fynd* I (1952) 32-46; and "A Mycenaean Potter's Factory at Berbati near Mycenae," *Atti e Memorie del I° Congresso Internazionale di Micenologia* (Rome, 1968) I, 48-53. References to some material are found in Furumark, *MP*, and V. Karageorghis has seen the material. Most sherds are said to be LH III A and B, most published examples are III B, and none seem demonstrably earlier than the Middle period on Cyprus. The potter's quarter is said to have been in operation from Middle Helladic until the late thirteenth cen-

CHARIOTS

The first major chariot kraters in the mainland series are the odd examples from Corinth, Nauplion, and Mycenae. The virtual certainty that chariot kraters were painted earlier than this at Mycenae was discussed in connection with the chariot larnax there (VIII.5.1). That Argolid workshops provided kraters for the Cypriote market seems certain (IX.1.1), but the Corinth and Mycenae vases have unpracticed distortions not seen in Cyprus.

1. The amphoroid chariot krater from Corinth is a big, top-heavy piece that should belong to the early stages of LH III B both in style and by context.[2] On each side an oddly designed chariot moves left carrying three people, preceded by a groom between two elaborate, stylized palm flowers. On both sides there are running broken spirals above the reins; on the more battered side there is also an antithetic spiral under the horses' bellies, and a row of pendent triangles dripping from the reins. These features are characteristic of the Ripe I stage in Cyprus (V.1, 2, 5, 6, 7). The practice of putting three persons in the chariot starts later in this series in the East (V.17 and following).

The design is bold and clear, yet some details of the drawing are so curious that the vase has sometimes been considered the work of an artist who had never tried a chariot scene before.[3] It may be equally possible that the disregard for pictorial conventions in favor of shorthand represents an impatience with the conventions by one who is all too familiar with them.

The bodies of the long, weak horses are joined, their heads separated; their legs go far down through the triple ground line so that their hocks are between the second and third bands, and the chariot wheel rides just above the lowest band. The heads are long and thin with bulbous Roman noses. The far horse has two pricked-up outline ears; there are three plumes of mane locks. The four reins are attached to a large rein-ring of ladder pattern outlined with dots, then start again at the front of the necks to pass up to the lower muzzle at a sharp angle. It is an effective expression of harness, though inexact. The vase suggests, in company with a few others from the Argolid, that some teams were driven not with bits but with dropped nose bands.[4]

The dual chariot is rendered as two arcs (pole support and brace), attached to the team's rump, so that the tail is converted into part of the carriage, and to the rim of the high wheel with double spokes. The box is reduced to two spotted fan-shapes nestling in the angle between pole and wheel, supported at the rear by an outlined form that may derive from the old convention for the pole jutting be-

hind the box. A thick, curved framing band by the handle of the vase takes up too much space to permit the passengers to be placed inside the chariot box properly; one very small passenger stands on the upper rim of the front of the box, and two taller men stand on the pole brace. This habit of bringing the human figures out of the chariot, perhaps to maintain the clarity of their outline, will become more established in later vases (cf. XI.15); it is matched to a certain extent in late-thirteenth-century frescoes where animals and people are detached from the ground line and is a commonplace in Geometric chariot scenes.[5] The driver and passengers are thus represented as footless cylinders in spotted robes, like the Kopreza dancers and the men on the Tiryns rhyton (IX.12, 15). The style of drawing is close to that of V.2: a long line for the nose, a bump for the chin, ruffled dark hair drawn flat across the crown of the skull. The double-spoked wheels and running broken spiral bands are also close to the forms on that vase; the reserved inner face of the horses' hind legs and the split front legs are common to the majority of Ripe I chariot scenes in the East. The representation of the chariot is so odd, however, that one hesitates to attribute this vase to Painter 30.

The groom leading the team, also a common figure in

tury. The excavator points to a number of misfired pieces from all periods as evidence for a long pot-making tradition in the town. The typical pictorial themes are said to be chariots, bulls, birds, fish, hunting scenes, antithetic animals, and boxers.

There is no doubt of an interchange of painted vases between the Argolid and Cyprus, and several vases by individual artists have been found on both sides of the sea; for example, "Petsas' Krater" at Mycenae (VIII.14) and the bird krater from Enkomi (IV.6), the chariot krater from Nauplion (IX.1.1) and the Cypriote krater in Rochester, N.Y. (V.1), the Pierides Painter's vases from Klavdhia and elsewhere in Cyprus (V.73, 74) and at Tiryns (IX.21); see the list of painters in Chapter XIV. The Berbati material, when published, should add many new facts in this sphere. In the meantime we are fortunate that the Tiryns pictorial material formed the subject of Slenczka's dissertation, published as *Tiryns VII: Figürlich Bemalte Mykenische Keramik* (1974), which collects and analyzes the unpublished sherds from the older German excavations (previously best studied in the photo archives of the German Archaeological Institute in Athens) as well as new German discoveries and the important group found by Verdelis in the water channels and "Epichosis," and already partly published in *AthMitt* 82 (1967) 1-53 with two color plates. We had already tried to arrange much of this material within our own system, and although our sequence does not always correspond with Slenczka's, there are no serious differences of chronology. In general Slenczka starts the sequence of the wonderful Tiryns pictorial material slightly earlier than we do.

2. The context, including cups with antithetic spirals, paneled and metope bowls, is illustrated by S. Weinberg, *Hesperia* 18 (1949) pl. 22, fig. 35.

3. Stubbings, *MycLevant*, 33, "the chariot groups appear to be drawn by a painter unused to such subjects."

4. Cf. the Appendix and M. Littauer, *Antiquity* 43 (1969) 291 f.

5. Cf. Lang, *Pylos* II, 43 H 6 (pl. 125), 7 C 20 (pl. 132), 50 H nws, soles of feet (pl. N).

the East, has a similar reserved head; the body is solid silhouette from mid-cheek down. The new torso form of broad shoulders and hollow chest with a single thin line down the front of the breast is seen in contemporary examples from Cyprus and Crete (V.17 and following). The thick buttock and long, thin legs are severely patterned, with pointed knees like horse hocks (cf. IV.55).

The Corinth krater is distinguished, by its taller neck, apparently more contracted foot, and shorthand chariot, from most of its contemporaries in Cyprus, but there are enough similarities to the style of Ripe I Cypriote vases to raise the question whether it was not made in a workshop that exported some more conventional pieces. The issue of origin is illuminated by the next krater.

1.1. A contemporary chariot krater, at the start of the Ripe series, has the same general contours as the Corinth krater, with a slightly lower neck and broader foot, and is far more conventional in style. It comes from the same hand and workshop as V.1, now in Rochester, acquired in Egypt, but once certainly in Cyprus, and marked in Cyprus with dipinto signs, perhaps a merchant's mark. V.2, with chariots and a lady, from Haghia Paraskevi near Nicosia, is probably by the same man, Painter 30. This mainland krater, which was sold only as far from the workshop as Nauplion (and found in the same tomb as IX.77, cf. IX.14.1), provides another fixed point for discussions of the origins and circulation of chariot vases in Late Helladic III B. As on V.1, the team moves left toward a grove of three palm trees (there are flowers on the other side). The horses have Roman noses, puffed chests, awkward flat feet shoved deep through the framing bands, and reserved inner hindquarters. The pole brace jabs through the horses' tails and hangs loose. The spotted chariot has the driver in the box, the passenger between the wings; they are eager, dark-faced men with prong noses. Rows of quirks frame the reins, there are two circles (one dotted and one plain) inside the high wheel, and two more palm trees behind the chariot.

It may prove in the end that V.1, V.2, IX.1 and IX.1.1 are all from the same shop, but at the moment it seems safer to exclude the Corinth krater from the series.

2. The third of the major chariot vases from the Peloponnesos is really no more than a large sherd of an amphoroid krater found at Mycenae, in the area of the poros wall between the tholos tombs of "Aegisthus" and "Clytemnestra." Wace judged it to be quite early, because it is well drawn and has no filling ornaments in the field; mainland vases rarely have elaborate fillers, however, and quality of drawing is no criterion for dating. Some of the mannerisms of the Mycenae vase, like the lavish use of white paint, the backbent groom filled with white slashes,

the irrational rosettes on the horses' bodies, and the disintegrated representation of the chariot, are hallmarks of the Transitional period (X.1-20). The heads, particularly the groom's, and the authority of drawing suggest that the Mycenae krater is a herald, rather than a member, of the Transitional group, in the third quarter of the thirteenth century.

Chariots move in each direction from the surviving handle, so that they are back to back; most vases found in the East have a uniform direction, normally toward the right. The horses' bodies seem too long to allow space for a second chariot and groom on each side, whether duplicates or facing inward in a symmetrical composition. To the right of the handle the dual chariot is represented by two spotted semicircles with a man in each, raised high above the wheel, supported on a thin line that may be a reminiscence of the pole stay now severing the box from the wheel, while an arched line connecting the two may be a conflation of the pole brace and the horses' tails, swung through to the back of the wheel in the newly created space. This dislocation of the parts of the chariot is attractive in terms of design, and probably comes about, not because there is no space to draw it in the full traditional way, but because the painter wants to emphasize the highlights of the scene and dispense with static elements.

To the left of the handle the chariot box is omitted entirely. Driver and passenger emerge from the pole stay, from the waist up; the driver alone had perched here on V.8 and IX.1. The whole undercarriage is replaced by the horses' tails, which curve back over the wheel and flick the felloe at the rear. On both chariots a thickening of the "pole stay" line at the end may recall the traditional projection of the pole behind the box. The distortions are those of the Corinth krater, taken further. They convey an impression of the eager merger of the chariot masters and their horses without the distraction of the chariot itself. The wheel is retained, naturally; the painter likes the impressive moving parts. He draws well and has certainly seen chariots; it is his purpose that has changed, from representation to expression.

The human figures are also different on each side, which emphasizes once more the need for caution in the game of attributing vases to particular painters from fragments. On the rear, where the figures appear only from the chest up, there is a thickly outlined round skull, reserved face, long pointed nose, bar for the body, and loop for an arm. On the front the hair (or hat) is solidly emphatic, the beak profile tops a massive triangular neck, and the bodies are striped with applied paint. The rear arm, crooked at the elbow, encircles a hollow space, but the body is a substantial tube below the arm; evidently the new Ripe "thin-line" torso (as seen on the groom of the Corinth krater) is being combined rather awkwardly with the traditionally solid bodies of drivers and passengers. The tube form will win out in the Transitional period. The driver seems to have one tasseled rein in each hand; actually one is the pole stay, the other the pole brace, with traditional ornament, each converted to a rein beyond the team's necks. This team may be driven with a bit.

The horses are elongated and mannered in gait; the manes are elaborate with five curled locks; the necks are tensed as though braking pressure were being applied, and the curve is accentuated by a white ladder pattern down to the shoulder. The bodies are bordered internally with a white stripe and adorned with seven white dotted circles. This enriching use of applied white occurs sporadically in the East, usually for harness, but the embroidery effect here is closer to patterns used on bulls (cf. V.40, 41). The interior outline is also effective in suggesting highlights on moving legs; it recalls the bull on V.73, or the fish on V.130.

The groom is a masterpiece of Mycenaean vase painting. The full head may be wearing a hat with soft folds rendered in U-pattern (cf. V.13); the arched, slender neck echoes the curving horses' necks; the body leans affectedly backward with the staff in the left hand gesturing the horses to hold and the looped right arm signaling to the lost part of the picture. The full muscular forms of the body are emphasized by the interior patterning of stripes, which create a lattice effect. A tassel floats forward at the knee, the top tie of the greave or legging; this is a fresco mannerism,[6] adapted for at least one other good contemporary vase (IX.8).

Two fragments of open chariot kraters were found in the dromos of the same tomb at Kopreza in Attica that contained the dancer krater (IX.12); they may be from two separate vases. IX.4 is apparently lost.

3. A rim fragment preserves the head of a team moving right, preceded by a foot soldier. The horses are drawn in a standard Ripe manner with distinct heads and joined bodies, dot-circle eyes, pricked-up ears, three flying mane locks, and forelocks (unusual). The figure in front is not an ordinary groom but an infantryman with his right arm drawn back to throw a long spear, in the manner of the Tiryns fighters (X.37) or the Amyklai sherd (X.36). Perhaps the double wavy line at the extreme right is the tail of the helmet crest; the silhouetted form like an axe blade at the shoulder is difficult, perhaps some part of the armor, a shoulder guard or shield (cf. XI.57). The fragment may be already Transitional, for until that time foot soldiers in chariot contexts are generally peaceable, while war excerpts become more frequent after about 1220; the siege

fresco from the megaron at Mycenae is a parallel thirteenth-century combination of chariots in motion with battling infantry.[7]

4. The second fragment has the wild head of a driver in a left-moving chariot. The two hands gesticulate agitatedly in the air; three reins grow from six fingers on the right hand. The head has bold bumps for nose and chin in solid paint, but a hat(?) is simply outlined and filled with U-pattern as on the groom's head of IX.2; the huge eye is also reserved, in two compartments, with a dotted oval above like a true eye and a square with a dark patch in it below, like a tongue in a mouth; this "window" effect in parti-colored faces is increasingly common in the later periods. Three lines parallel to the bent upper arm give a curious effect of rapid motion through the air but may be the relics of another feature, such as chevron ornament. Seven fingers are preserved on the upraised left arm, with a line below that might be part of a whip (cf. III.6).[8]

HORSES WITHOUT CHARIOTS

This category does not exist on Cyprus so far as we can tell, though it does appear at Ugarit and Sarepta (IV.78, V.105?, XIII.28). Perhaps some of the fragments are deceptive, but enough are certain that we can be sure the Mycenaeans occasionally painted horses running free or being led by their grooms before harnessing to the carriage.

5. An unusual set of fragments from Mycenae shows a free dark horse galloping on a blank field marked with white paint like a gate or a sign. Wace understood it to be Mycenaean rather than Hellenistic; it was found close to the surface west of the poros-rubble retaining wall of the Treasury of Atreus.[9] Scholars have doubted that it is Mycenaean, yet a date in the Ripe period might be upheld on both stylistic and contextual grounds. The horse is thrusting himself forward with his hind legs just leaving the ground, his forelegs apparently outstretched, his head

---

6. For example, Lang, *Pylos* II, 21 H 48 (pl. 116, pl. 122 upper soldier), 16 H 43 (pl. 121); Rodenwaldt, *Tiryns* II, pl. XIV.10.

7. G. Rodenwaldt, *Fries des Megarons von Mykenai* (1921) Beil. I, IV; Lang, *Pylos* II, 26 H 64 (pls. 18, 123).

8. The hands compare with those on some Athens vases (X.41, 41.1); the material is too scanty to allow a sure contrast between Athenian and Argolid tendencies in painting.

9. Cf. A. Wace, *Mycenae* (1949) 119, 129; *BSA* 51 (1956) 116 f.; Wace thought the fragment might be LH III A, but the general agreement that the tholos was built about 1270-1250 may make the later date preferable.

and neck pulled far back, his muzzle lifted. The dark brown body is highlighted with pale overtones, as on the fine animal on IX.6; perhaps it is from the same workshop. The fragments come from a krater; there may have been a single horse on each side, a new departure in pictorial composition, like an adaptation of the old Ephyrean style. Alternatively, the horse may have escaped from his groom; there seem to be flapping white straps of harness at the breast, but since they do not encircle the belly, perhaps they are intended to represent bunched muscle. The white grid behind the horse has not yet been interpreted; it is neither script nor a horse jump. The freedom of the tossing head and sensitive nostril, the power of contour, and the unusual recording of light playing on a dark hide merit Wace's judgment that the fragments are a Mycenaean masterpiece; the style is odd for classical painting.

6. At Tiryns Schliemann found a sherd with the rump of a horse painted with similar highlights, pale streaks rather than applied white paint to render muscles and lines of light along the haunch and groin. This is a fine, thin-walled piece from a markedly curved vessel, not a krater. The separated hair strands of the lower tail are done in dilute glaze below the darker stub of bone. Such shading and gradation of color through dilution and concentration of glaze are not characteristic of ordinary Mycenaean pictorial but do appear on a few select pieces from the Argolid in Ripe and Transitional; the III C painters use color or starker contrasts for similar effects. This is one of the rare artists who exploited the possibilities of tone to suggest solid form (cf. IX.67, 79). The penis projects as a narrow oblique stripe. A goat from Mycenae (X.52) may be by the same painter.

7. The galloping composition of IX.5 receives a curious variation on a krater fragment from the northeast extension at Mycenae, a piece that may be Transitional but suits the Ripe group of free horses. Two pairs of horse legs are crossed on the striated surface. Aegean animals do not normally gallop with their own legs crossed. Perhaps it is the remnant of a pair of horses in the flying gallop, the hind legs of the leading horse and the front legs of the rear horse. This would suggest that there were no chariots in the picture. The long, lean outlined legs and unusual action recall the more vivid aspects of natural observation in the Pastoral style in Cyprus (Chapter VI).[10]

Horses in a natural state, not controlled by grooms or charioteers, occasionally appear in surviving frescoes, especially at Pylos. The horse-and-nautilus frieze in that palace is mere static decoration; the horses-on-the-rocks are a stiff superposition of animals on landscape. On other occasions horses, generally white, are associated in an outdoor setting with deer, boar, women or goddesses, and

shrine facades.[11] Cretans had put wild ibex or antelopes in such contexts. The few free-running horses on vases, supported by the Pylos imagery, may illustrate an aspect of Mycenaean sympathy toward their most valuable animals that the stereotypes of chariot painting have concealed.

Another group shows horses with their grooms or on leading reins.

8. The best of the Ripe horse compositions from Mycenae consists of three open krater fragments that might be associated with the wild, blown animals of the Pastoral style. The naturalism of drawing and free use of the brush led previous scholars to give the krater a very early date, perhaps on the mistaken principle that "earlier is better."[12]

The main fragment shows a single horse being led to the left by a soldier in a "hedgehog" helmet.[13] The horse's head is sketched freely and rapidly with bold curves and marks of the turning brush. The head is raised; there are five long, dressed mane locks, but the hair also lies thick on the neck; the ears are pricked up; two forelocks blow on the brow. The animal wears a bridle with a low nose-band; there are three reins to the neck, two lead lines dropping forward (to the missing soldier's hand). Evidently the horse is wearing chariot harness and is being led up to the carriage as on the Mycenae frescoes. There are contrasts of thick and thin lines on the head and a thick bulge of muscle in the breast. The eye is offset in an enlarged socket with a contracted pupil and a stripe below the tear duct. This is the most spirited horse study in mainland painting. It can be associated with a few other scenes that capture the companionship between horses and the warrior-masters or grooms who gentle and train them. The rest of the krater suggests the working relationship in a fragmentary way. The soldier leading the horse is preserved only in the back rim of his spiked "hedgehog" helmet; he was walking left with the leading reins. Another fragment preserves the tasseled legs of a soldier or groom striding left with a considerable spread of leg, with a horse moving away behind him to the right (only one hind leg is preserved). A third fragment has both hind hocks of a standing horse facing right.[14] Perhaps there were

10. In hunt scenes, deer or antelope legs may overlap this way.

11. Lang, *Pylos* II, 1 F 2 (pls. 79-81, J, R); 7 C 20, 8 C 21, 10 C 27 (pls. 47-49, 132).

12. For example, Furumark, *MP*, 243, the "earliest phase of mainland style represented only by a few fragments."

13. This seems to be a single animal, in spite of what might be taken for two extra ears on the top of the head, which are apparently ruffles of hair on the brow, forelocks.

14. The position of the legs of the striding soldier may suggest he is moving right, a simpler composition, but the tassels on his greaves must surely be on the front of his legs. The fragment with hind hocks was pub-

two horses on each face of the krater, with a soldier by each, one following the other toward the chariot.[15] This would be a more patterned reflection of the harnessing scene on the Mycenae megaron fresco[16] and analogous to the late horse-and-soldier krater at Ugarit (XIII.28).

A groom gentling a horse appears on a fragment of an amphoroid krater at Berbati, and a man fondling his horse's muzzle was noted at Ugarit (V.21). In the Late period there are several scenes of men walking beside their horses or leading them along (XI.7, 8). There are two pictures of small horses on leading reins (cf. X.25, 28). The men who pat bulls in the fields, in Cyprus, express a different attitude, that of a farmer or livestock man (IV.32); in Greece the kinship between the light-armed soldier and his chariot horse accords with that respect and affection conveyed in epic poetry, a distinctive quality in military aristocracy.

HUMAN FIGURES

Half a dozen fragments of vases from the Argolid and Attica portray human beings without chariots. They include the boxers and figures in spotted robes already seen in the Levant and some variant types. Some of these vases (IX.12, 16) have been placed in the fourteenth rather than the thirteenth century by the scholars who published them; they are presented here as a group that contrasts to known fourteenth-century figure drawing.

11. The fragmentary base of a tall jar from the Argive Heraion has a nude man in silhouette, facing a tree on his left. The figure is an exaggerated development of the type used for grooms and attendants on Ripe chariot kraters. The torso is reduced to a stripe, bent violently backward so that it sinks below the hips; the start of a neck(?) may be made out at the level of the groin. Two thin curved arms of unequal length seem to meet in a circle before the man, one from behind the neck thrusting up across the chest, the other looping down to meet it. The thighs bulge in ovals, the long legs are accentuated with pointed knees. A thin tree rises from the base of the vase, with irregular slashes for branches; both man and tree are well below the four stripes of the ground line. Perhaps the scene is an unskilled version of a traditional dance before a sacred tree.

11.1 A curious fragment from Tiryns has a more substantial silhouetted man seated on a folding campstool. The sherd is not easy to understand, because the figure is set in a narrow box framed by a pair of verticals on each side, a compartment style not common in this period, unless they represent the kind of dividers used on the

Tiryns gold ring and on the Homage Krater (III.29), pairs of javelin shafts, or slender trees as on the Tiryns rhyton (IX.15). In the Aegean a seated person is usually a cult or ceremonial figure accepting worship or offering it, as on the "Palanquin" and "Campstool" frescoes at Knossos or the procession frescoes of Thebes and Pylos. The man here is in the convention of nude or lightly armed people such as grooms and spearmen; he has an apparently enormous chest and shoulders and powerful arms lifting from his sides; the thin legs are splayed, as though the whole figure were restless, swaying and swinging on his seat. In the compartment on the right is a sharp leaflike shape—a shield seen from the side? Though worn, this is a powerful, enigmatic fragment.

12. It is more common in this period for human figures to wear the long embroidered robe known also in Cyprus and Crete. The varieties of robes and their decorations are becoming better known as more of the Tanagra larnakes are published; this is clearly one of the common mainland costumes in the thirteenth century. A formal, static scene with two pairs of robed figures has long been known on an open krater from Kopreza in Attica.[17] The reverse is filled by three great palm trees with ridged trunks and spiral-volute branches. The vase is badly damaged and worn, and has been in sherds for years but is now mended; the figures are faint. The two sets of robed figures face each other; each has only one arm, bent up to clasp the partner's hand. The figures are squat, cylindrical, naive; the robes reach the ground, eliminating any sense of action and emphasizing the formal, ceremonial nature of the scene. The robes on the two figures in the center are ornamented in horizontal tiers, like a reduction of flounced Minoan or Mycenaean skirts, but sex is otherwise not indicated. The two figures on the right have the breast area filled with U-pattern and dots, and dots also fringe the oval, silhouetted heads, which have large, reserved irregular eyes. These dots are not helmet crests, any more than the filling ornament suggests cuirasses; they are simple sprays of hair and are used also to fringe the palm trees on the reverse.

lished by Furtwängler-Loeschcke, *MV*, pl. XLI.429 a, b, in a position wrongly suggesting that they were the front legs that belong with the head.

15. The composition might have been basically symmetrical, with the horses back to back, one soldier following his horse, one leading him, or there may have been a soldier in front of each horse and a groom behind.

16. G. Rodenwaldt, *Fries des Megarons von Mykenai* (1921) Beil. I, no. 4 or the upper part of no. 5.

17. Most of the "Sphettos" (Kopreza) vases were not published; V. Staïs, *EphArch* 1895, 257, felt that they added little to general knowledge of the period. Those illustrated (pl. 10, nos. 8, 10, 11) are LH III A and early III B.

Suggestions that the scene represents pairs of boxers, dancers, or warriors greeting or parting do not seem substantiated either by the costume or the still poses. It may indeed be a scene of funerary leave-taking, since the vase was found in a tomb; if so, the gesture of clasped hands to salute one departing or being reunited in another world may be the Mycenaean prototype for the gesture so familiar on classical grave stelai and loutrophoroi. The Tanagra larnakes have shown that many other ceremonial funerary gestures were transmitted practically unchanged to later Greek times, so the salute with clasped hands may also represent real behavior in a long powerful tradition.

13. A small jug from Alyke (Voula) in Attica is painted with a single lady in a long robe; she stands between palm trees and sniffs a flower or drinks from a cup. This interesting, inexpensive piece has certain iconographic connections to older traditions, as represented on the Window Krater (III.12) and to contemporary experiments on thirteenth-century larnakes. The picture is sketchy but emphatic. The woman is presented frontally like the female on the Rhodes pilgrim flask (XII.18); her head is turned to her left, her right arm is stretched up to the sky, and she holds a flower(?) to her nose with her left hand. The simple robe is ornamented only with an interior line from the neck that splits down the skirt, suggesting folds. The face is all nose and eye framed by an open circle; the hair or cap is painted solid with a dangling plume, like those worn by sphinxes. The flower is drawn as a cup with curling sides filled with dots like seeds; perhaps it is a cup. On the Window Krater, women combine the gesture of sniffing flowers with saying farewell, and this may be a simple farewell to the dead; the other possible interpretation is that she is a priestess in a "sacral" cap holding a chalice, as on the Thera and "Campstool" frescoes. The two palms splaying out from the woman suggest an outdoor setting, and the excavator thought of a picturesque genre scene, picking flowers in a garden and rejoicing at their fragrance; but palms occur on IX.12 with its possible funerary gesture, and a ceremonial interpretation should not be ruled out here.

14. A sherd from the Acropolis at Athens has part of a robed figure with heavy outlines and a crosshatched surface, preserved from hip to foot. A peculiar feature is that the figure is raised above the ground line, as on contemporary larnakes and a few Tiryns pieces. It is not levitation, of course, but Mycenaean insistence on intact outlines in the later periods.

14.1 Another figure in a scratchily crosshatched robe is the attractive, expressionist lyre player on a fragmentary krater from Nauplion (cf. IX.1.1, 77). The decorated zone is blocked in panels, the side ones covered with filled scale patterns, framing the musician. He stands, or levitates, at the left facing a giant lyre or concert kithara with seven strings, as tall as he—the size to suggest the grand sound that comes from it? For a less desirous man it would be hopeless to try reaching the strings on such a broad instrument, but the passion of music extends the player's arms beyond his own height, the left thrust through the central strings and turning back to pluck with a desperate agility of wrist, the right sunk to stroke a chord at the bottom of the string cluster. Tuning pegs are shown on top. The thin angled feet are off the ground as the kitharist puts himself into his work, while his robe supports him, touching the ground on either side (cf. III.19, 20). A slightly later musician plays a smaller phorminx (XI.69).

15. A conical rhyton from Tiryns, in a number of fragments, has two registers of robed male figures and trees, interspersed with open trefoils. The painting is bold and simple, with borders of fine bands, N-pattern, and chevrons.[18] Parts of about ten men are preserved, although only two are nearly complete; two are set close together nearly touching, but the others seem more spaced out. They face right and raise both arms, the left arm touching a bent tree. They are authoritatively outlined, with fine strokes, in long robes descending over their puffed chests to the ground line, hiding their feet. Lines of dots follow the outer contour of the robes, as on charioteers' robes. The faces are stark and curious, with a triangle for the region from brow to nose, another for the chin, and curly ruffled hair at the back. The hieratic attitude of raised arms and the gesture of touching the tree recall some tree-shaking episodes on Minoan gems or Eastern priests in front of "the tree of life"; the shape of the vase is ceremonial too, and perhaps they are priests or feudal leaders invoking blessings or giving strength to the people.

16. Many fragments of a tall trick rhyton from Ayia Irini on Kea are the remnants of a most interesting processional scene with a little bull and men in spotted robes marching in rank. From its shape, decoration, and context (it was found inside the temple on the site), the vase is evidently ceremonial or ritual, like the last. Mrs. Immerwahr first understood the shape; it had two or more hollow ring handles on the shoulder so that fluids could be manipulated for surprise appearances and disappearances. This class of trick vases is known at different periods in Crete, Melos, Thera, Karpathos, on the mainland in Attica, and on the west coast.[19] The ring handles are sometimes mounted with

---

18. The fine quality of such ornamental borders is often seen in luxury wares at Mycenae and Tiryns toward the end of III B; cf. E. French, *BSA* 64 (1969) pl. 17 b, c; LH III B:2.

19. S. A. Immerwahr, "A Mycenaean Ritual Vase," *Hesperia* 46 (1977) 34-35. Mrs. Immerwahr dates the vase a little earlier than we had thought, to the mid-fourteenth century, pp. 38-39.

modeled animals' heads, which have not survived here. The painting is surprisingly crude. Perhaps as many as eight or nine figures are preserved on slightly more than a third of the frieze; six are fairly clear. Their rounded shoulders and bodies overlap in a way strange for Mycenaean painting, as though a crowd had been reduced from a processional fresco. The heads and shoulders rise above three bands that originally served as the lower frame of a narrow picture zone; the lower bodies extend below this "ground line" in coarse bulbous arcs. The spots or slashes decorating the robes are repeated on the upper shoulder of the vase, interspersed with hard lines like flower sprays. The men are drawn in variant inexpert ways, with beak-nosed profiles, large oval, dotted eyes (the oval frame sometimes omitted), and smooth caps of dark hair. The eye frame sometimes runs into the hair or is attached to it by a line like a tear duct. One man wears a tall spotted collar, as in Cyprus (IV.12). Only two men have arms; one seems to hold an object. The little bull is tilted up through the framing band at the shoulder level of the marchers—accompanying them to an altar or shrine? The theme is known from the "Palanquin" fresco at Knossos and from the marchers with the bull in the Pylos vestibule;[20] soldiers and bulls are connected in the fourteenth century in the East (III.19, 20?).

This small group of vases with robed figures in apparently ceremonial scenes, found in tombs, a temple, and miscellaneous contexts, suggests that there was more "ritual" painting on a popular level than most students have been aware of. Robed and nude men and women, the dance, the procession, the gesture in front of a tree, are all aspects of a long Aegean tradition known also in fresco, on gems and gold rings, and to some extent in the Linear B texts. They appear here in the last uninterrupted phase of ordinary painting before the social and political way of life associated with palace control was disturbed.

BOXERS

The theme of boxers is less fashionable, apparently, on the mainland than in the Levant. It appears in two contrasting styles from Mycenae, which bracket the Ripe period. One is early, in a style recognizable also in Cyprus (V.29 and following); the other may be Transitional and is bizarre.

17. A fragment of a krater(?) from Mycenae preserves parts of a pair of confronted boxers. The left figure exists from head to waist, the right is only curled fingers reaching out. The action is conceived statically, as on V.29; the fighting or sparring stance is conveyed only by the hori-

zontal position of the short arms, each curling up into two fingers. The head and shoulders sway back; presumably the knees were bent in an attitude of vigor. The head is reserved, with dark hair coming down to the framed eye; the nose is a fluent point, the mouth a slight indentation in the sloping chin. The body is painted in silhouette with liberal streaks of (gray-)white overpaint along the contours, especially highlighting the arms. A dotted circle-rosette fills the air above the point of contact between the two opponents. The inclusion of this sport in regular competitions, funerary or other, is welcome evidence for the continuance on the Greek mainland of the old Minoan athletic vogue.[21]

18. A curious sherd from the Citadel House on the acropolis at Mycenae has a boxer in helmet and uniform, sparring left. The context is said by the excavator to be pure LH III B, in a layer of fierce destruction. The fragment is small and contains lines that are difficult to read. The boxer is drawn in outline with disjointed interior details. His low, domed helmet has vertical stripes; his eye is attached as a circle to the front profile; the head is very broad with a pointed nose; the stout neck is crossed by a pair of lines, suggesting a stiff collar or protector. The torso sways forward, as in the old pictures of Tom Molyneux; it has four stripes at the waist like a high belt and dotted circles above and below. The thin arm, bent up to guard the face, has lumps of muscle in both parts; the fist is a circle with the fingers not separated. On the left may be traces of the opponent's nose and muscled forearm, with spread fingers. The style is harsh and fanciful.

BULL JUMPER

18.1. The famous sherd from Mycenae with a helmeted bull jumper may be Ripe or Transitional—toward the latter part of the thirteenth century, at least.

20. Cf. Evans, *Palace of Minos* II, 770 f., figs. 502-503; IV, 397 f., fig. 332; S. Alexiou, *AA* 1964, 785 f.; M. Cameron, *AA* 1967, 330 f.; S. Immerwahr, *Hesperia* 46 (1977) 37; a bull follows a chariot and robed figures approach a shrine(?); Pylos procession, Lang, *Pylos* II, H 5, pls. 119-120. For robed figures with (sacrificial?) axes, P. Demargne, *BCH* 70 (1946) 148 f., and cf. V. Karageorghis, *BCH* 83 (1959) 193 f.

21. Aegean sports, except bull jumping, have not been deeply studied, but E. Homann-Wedeking, *Sport und Spiel* in *Archaeologia Homerica* T (forthcoming) must correct that. Boxing is now best known from the Boxer Rhyton from Haghia Triada (R. Paribeni, *Monumenti Antichi* 12 [1903] 331; F. Halbherr, *Monumenti Antichi* 14 [1905] 365; G. Karo, *JdI* 26 [1911] 265 f.; K. Müller, *JdI* 30 [1915] 247; Evans, *Palace of Minos* I, 668); the related fragment in Boston (J. L. Benson, *Bulletin of the Museum of Fine Arts, Boston* 64 [1966] 36 f.), and from the fresco of boxing children from Thera (S. Marinatos, *AAA* 4 [1971] cover, 407 f.; *Thera*

The fine banding at the rim recalls the Tiryns rhyton (IX.15), and this may be a rhyton rather than a bowl. The only mainland fragment yet known with this theme, it is perhaps a reflection of the same revived interest in Minoan sports that produced the boxers (IX.17, 18), the contemporary bull jumpers of the Levant (V.48), and bull jumping on gems and coffins. There is a closer connection to the awkwardness of Cypriote bull jumpers than to such mainland frescoes as survive at Mycenae, Orchomenos, Tiryns, and Pylos; even the less skillful Tanagra larnax shows the leapers face down in a more canonical vaulting position.[22] The larnax has bulls head to head and tail to tail; it may be that the hero of this fragment is falling feet first between two bulls.

The bull is quite plain, as in the later thirteenth century everywhere, the body surface broken by three groups of three lines bordered by dots, as a collar on the neck and two belts on the body. He stands right with head lifted (the horns brush the frame), short and stocky in proportions suitable for a rhyton, the ear pricked back as though listening for the leaper's crash, a circle at the muzzle matching the eye (it is probably not a nose ring). He recalls work by Painter 21.

The jumper is nearly horizontal, with his back to the bull's back; he has completed his somersault and comes down with broad gesticulations for a supple landing (between two raised tails?). His head is protected by a tall cap, crosshatched and looking like wickerwork, with spiral horns sprouting from the conical upper part. This kind of crosshatched headgear comes both flat (X.32) and in a tall curved cone (XI.70); the horns may be decoration by the painter or part of a general series of innovations in headwear at this time, like the horned and "hedgehog" helmets of the twelfth century or the hunter's horned headdress (cf. XI.42 and following, XI.80). The Cypriote bull jumpers' heads are also protected (V.50). The right leg kicks up level with the chest, its energy emphasized by three toes; the left leg dangles down in startling curves punctuated by a pointed knee; there is no torso, properly speaking, but as in many Ripe figures the active parts take over from parts that merely shelter organs, so that the legs join the arms, which are spread out balanced as for a swan dive, with curled fingers forming two hooks as on IX.1, 17. The outlined head has a Ripe straight brow; the inside of the neck is bordered by dots as on the bull, whose eye is also reflected in the man's.

These last two athletes may both be Transitional, but they have not yet acquired the particolored energy and mass of III C figures.

BULLS

The great majority of bull compositions in Greece were painted in LH III B. Their rarity in the fourteenth century was discussed above (VIII.12). They are practically nonexistent in the twelfth century, when the chariot is dominant. Of all mainland images, the bulls correspond most exactly to types and compositions in Cyprus, especially those at Tiryns. There are the same quiet friezes to the right, the same antithetic bulls either at peace or fighting, the same family scenes with little bulls or in combination with birds like cattle egrets; there are bull protomes and facing heads. The trend noted in Cyprus, of bull compositions having progressively blanker backgrounds as the filling ornaments were absorbed into the bulls' bodies, merges with what has already been standard practice on the mainland; but one may contrast the simpler bulls of the thirteenth century with the flowery, awkward scene on VIII.12.

As usual, the mainland material is very fragmentary. This means that one criterion used to distinguish the two phases of the Ripe period on Cyprus, the progressive emptying of the center section of the bull's body, is difficult to apply in Greece, where most bulls are preserved as either horn and muzzle or haunch and tail. Consequently, the group is treated as an unbroken sequence, with the minor fragments grouped by site. Tiryns and Mycenae are the most productive centers for this kind of painting.

19. A handsome krater from Berbati has a family scene with close parallels on Cyprus. It is a bell krater with wishbone handles, of good fabric and quality. Two larger animals face in from the handles toward the center, with horns locked in a typical fighting pose. The painter has inserted a small bull between them, below their heads, so that the big animals are portrayed as nuzzling their calf affectionately, and the locked horns are converted to mild contact.[23] The composition is a simpler, more informal version of V.40, is close to V.44 and 45, and is a near-replica of the scene on V.86, by Protome Painter A

IV (1971) 47 f., pls. E, F). The formal, playful aspect is demonstrated by the use of gloves, thongs, and head protectors. Boxing, wrestling, jumping, bull jumping, javelin throwing, and perhaps running and swimming races may be part of the Minoan contribution to Mycenaean athletic life.

22. Rodenwaldt, *Tiryns* II, 162 f., pl. 18; Lang, *Pylos* II, 36 H 105 (pls. 24, 116, 124,C); W. Lamb, *BSA* 24 (1919-1921) 192 f., pl. 7; H. Bulle, *Orchomenos* I (1907) 79 f., pl. 28; T. Spyropoulos, *AAA* 3 (1970) 196, fig. 16; for the steatite vase from Athens, M. Mayer, *JdI* 7 (1892) 80.

23. V. Karageorghis believes that small animals are adults reduced in scale to serve as space fillers; E. Vermeule thinks they are real infants or adolescents in family scenes, drawn like miniature adults, as Greeks continue to do in classical times.

(Painter 21), except for the finer filling. The faces are reserved, with large round eyes (two circles and pupil for the adults, one circle for the calf). The body surfaces are in three divisions with stippling on the forequarters and haunches of the adults and dotted circles in the center section, the young one filled all over with vertical wavy lines, with arcs on the neck and stippling on the inner face of the hind leg. The bodies are full and deep, sunk low on splayed legs, the curves ample and authoritative, the stippling neat, drawn into finger-whorl patterns on the right to break monotony. The small bull, with genitals, charges so fast that his forelegs are flattened to the ground, his horn grazes the mother's chest, and his tail is flung up in his father's nose. This is the best of the mainland bull vases, by an experienced, decorative painter.

On present evidence, Tiryns is the palace town with the greatest interest in bulls (and stags, to match its frescoes); it is an extraordinarily productive center with several workshops all through the thirteenth century. Most of the painted material is sherds, much from the "Epichosis" and from the water channels, as well as many individual pieces from the old German excavations, which have now been published and catalogued by Slenczka. A glance through the plates of *Tiryns* VII will show the rich variety of partial bulls and the preferred styles of filling their long flat bodies, including scallops, U-patterns, dot-rosettes, and dotted circles; quartered haunches and dotted haunches; bellies with vertical ripple strokes and fluent zigzags; there are arrow patterns, as so often on stags (and the same workshops produced both kinds of scenes), little triangles filled with scale pattern, and occasionally a harking back to the old Cretan tradition of trefoil dapples across the hide. The scenes are rarely animated; most of them are dull, yet the large forms and ingenious filling ornament lend them a handsome enough aspect. Slenczka segregated about six workshops, probably centered at Tiryns, in the Ripe period.

It has long been known that five krater sherds (IX.21) from the old Tiryns excavations were painted by the same hand as the "Aktaion" krater in the British Museum and the Cypriote jug in the Pierides Collection (V.73, 74) found on Cyprus (Painter 19, Chapter XIV). Clay analyses have also tended to stress Tirynthian connections, although the evidence is not yet satisfactory. It is notable that equally productive sites, like Mycenae, do not yet show this linkage in pictorial painting across the Aegean; however, there are fragments from the same workshop at both Mycenae and Tiryns in this period and the next, and one cannot be absolutely certain where the wheel and kiln were physically situated. It has been suggested that a single merchant ship from Tiryns could have contained nearly all the painted kraters of the mid-thirteenth century found on Cyprus, and this argument has strong attraction for those who maintain the cultural priority of the Argolid over a "province" like Cyprus. This cannot be the complete or wholly correct answer to the problem of origin. We have seen that the Pierides bull jug (V.74), by the artist in question, is of typically Cypriote shape; nothing like it is known in the Argolid. Many painted vases in Cyprus have themes that do not occur on the mainland, and we take it for granted that there were workshops in both places and that mainland artists also traveled to Cyprus for a season or two. It is particularly in the scenes of bulls and stags that Cyprus and Greece are clearly in step.

20. A fragmentary krater from Tiryns is very like the bull krater from Enkomi, V.44 (Painter 15). Rim and wall fragments survive. A long bull, to the right, lowers his head while a cattle egret picks at his horn. The bird is smaller in relation to the bull than on most Cypriote versions of this scene and flies down obliquely from the upper right rather than climbing up the bull's flesh as usual. The bird's wings are not drawn; the oval body is filled with vertical wavy lines. The bull has a thin face and oval eye with elongated pupil; the body is divided in three, with U-pattern on the forequarters and a blank center section whose contours are reinforced with U-pattern (cf. V.44).

21. The sherds of the krater by the Pierides Painter (Painter 19) show on each side a large bull with a tasseled tail and dappled hide, facing right toward a long-necked bird in a field of lozenges. The bull's eye is rendered as concentric ovals with a row of dots bordering the lower lid like lashes. The haunch is patterned with trefoil dapples within a dotted contour border; the dots spread down the lower leg. The bird has a long neck flexed downward, filled with a column of diamonds. The lozenges, spread evenly over the field, are filled with dark arcs at the corners and so have a reserved quatrefoil center.

A separate fragment must be the haunch of the bull on the other side of the vase, and the recently found head and neck of a bull must belong. The Tiryns sherds come from a dump-deposit by the north edge of the west stairs, and the vase was apparently in use at the same time as the procession fresco in the palace, whose pieces were found discarded in the same general area.

22. The worst of Argolid painting is illustrated by another fragmentary krater from Tiryns with a ridiculously long bull, right, in a field of lozenges and dotted circles. The hindquarters and a narrowing stretch of body to the shoulder survive. The drawing is incompetent but prettily patterned. The bull seems about to squat on his hind legs, with his tail tucked under his rump; the pizzle is a bump, way forward, where the foreleg ought to be. The dotted circles of the field are echoed in the body, which is also decorated with scale-filled triangles attached to the contour lines at various points. One lozenge in the field under the hindquarters has corner filling of solid-centered concentric arcs, looking forward to the richer filling style of LH III C.

Of the other Tiryns fragments, one would single out for special mention a very pretty jug (IX.23), of which only the neck partly survives, with two bulls right, filled with arrow and scale patterns; the head is dark with a reserved eye. This is also evidently by Painter 15, who decorated the Cypriote kraters V.44 and 45, bulls with birds, and the Tiryns fragment, IX.20. A curiously weak-legged bull (IX.24) shows the ornamental possibility of embroidery patterns, which are seldom well handled in the Argolid: the chest and legs are filled in with solid dark paint, but a window is opened in the center of the body, contoured with rippling wave pattern outlined by neat dots, with a dot-rosette on the shoulder.

Protomes of bulls appear sporadically in the Argolid, and Tiryns produced the most depressed of them. On a fragmentary jug (IX.25) a long, swaybacked bull, with weak hindquarters and the bulbous nose more common in the next phase of painting, is framed by two protomes filled with vertical ripples which, as they drain down through the framing bands, empty the protomes of life and energy. The bull has weak ripples down his chest and along his flank, with lozenge fillers and the traditional ringed and dotted collar to indicate dewlaps; both scrotum and pizzle are meticulously indicated. He is earless, though the protomes have ears. This is nearly as sad as the protome bowl from the Argive Heraion (IX.44). Tiryns also has a protome bowl (IX.25.1) with faint white bulls' heads painted on a dark band around the inside of the bowl; this technique is usually Late and is seen in a few examples at Mycenae and Athens (X.99, XI.74, 91, 121, 135).

Most of the principal sites in the Argolid have one or two examples of vases painted with bulls; there is nothing so special about any of them that one could detect a different school of painting. Probably most were made in Tiryns and Mycenae. Argos has two one-handled jugs, Berbati a fragment of a fine krater with bulls and a bird, Dendra has a pair of hooves, Mycenae has fifteen or more rather simple, undistinguished pieces in fine fabric; there is one each from the Argive Heraion, Nauplion, and Athens.

ARGOS

26. One of the few complete mainland bull vases is a one-handled jug with a bull walking right on the shoulder. It is less rich than painted jugs in Cyprus; the paint is worn and light, the style dry, the outline weak. The bull is cramped in the frieze so that his legs sink through the framing band below the knees; the body is divided into three clear sections, each filled with evenly spaced crosses; the short tail starts tasseling at the haunch. The lowered head has an enlarged oval eye and a quick line for the muzzle that leaves the nostril open, as happens often in the Pastoral style. The date should be Ripe II, as for the counterparts at Enkomi (V.96-100).

27. Another one-handled jug with a broader body and slimmer neck carries the isolated pattern of a dark facing bull's head on the front. The scheme is rare on mainland pottery (see VIII.13) and represents a thirteenth-century survival of the design on the Karpathos ewer (XII.27) and the Enkomi krater (III.23). It seems to be a simplified imitation of the bulls' heads on the silver-and-niello bowls from Dendra and Enkomi; it abstracts the pattern from the floral surroundings, which persist on the contemporary Enkomi stirrup jar (V.102). One may note a similar starkness on the Dendra silver bowl compared to the luxurious Enkomi bowl. The bold schematic outline is enlivened by bulbous light eyes and branching horns tied by an ogival loop pattern; the ears point down beside the eyes. The worn face may have been patterned. The absence of subsidiary ornament is refreshing; the emblematic design makes a handsome pattern except that it is slightly lightweight for the size of the vase. The similar stark head on the Aradippo krater (V.103) is approximately contemporary. Another thematically related piece is the kylix from Amorgos (XII.21) with stags facing across a bull's head. One may wonder whether the bull's head has a constant significance in these cases, funerary or symbolic of sacrifice, or whether it is merely decorative.

BERBATI

28. One of the more-publicized sherds from Berbati is a fragment from under the handle of a bell krater, which preserves the rumps and tails of two bulls from opposite sides of the vase and a bird as filler between them. This is contemporary with the Tiryns group but has no precise analogues on Cyprus. The bulls' hides are filled with arrow pattern. Since they are so fragmentary, the links to Cypriote vases have been seen more in terms of the bird, yet its wonderful slim, pointed-oval body filled with N-pattern and its large, curved beak are not matched on Cyprus; it is a new, abstract type to be regarded in the context of a number of other mainland birds, like the one from Dyme in Achaia (IX.112). There may have been birds in the main scenes too; the bird beneath the handle appeared in this phase in Cyprus (V.14).

MYCENAE

Fifteen or so fragments of bull compositions from Mycenae are placed in the Ripe phase. They illustrate the standard spread of types: friezes, bulls with birds, fighting bulls. None is distinguished.

30. A fragment of a bell krater with an embroidered bull moving right on short legs and soft "paws" is poorly drawn but richly patterned: solid arcs around the rim of a circular haunch with a crosshatched circle in the center; the center section bordered by open semicircles below, alternate open and solid ones above; the characteristic mainland ladder pattern behind the shoulder and rows of dashes for hair on the forequarters. This front section seems to be joined on backward, with the off foreleg walking toward the tail.

30.1 The fine bull's head from Mycenae probably belongs to the same period and a related workshop, but it is more distinguished because of the natural markings on the hide, the reserved streamer giving energy to the forward thrust of the horn, the dots fringing the outline of the eye with its deep tilted tear duct, and the loose U-pattern defining the wrinkles of the throat. The filled lozenges in the field recall the Pierides Painter (IX.21), but the fragment itself is finer and more pictorial.

31. Two fragments from opposite sides of a large krater each have part of a long stiff bull; on one there is a bird below the belly. The bulls have nearly flat backs and belly contours. The bellies are vertically striped with wavy lines. One bull has arrow pattern on the shoulder, N-pattern on the haunch; the other has arrows on the haunch. The inner faces of the hind legs are barred. The bird is inactive, simply placed as decoration under the belly. It has an oval body with a central row of spots, and a long neck and beak, probably a wading bird like a heron or cattle egret. Similar birds appear at Tiryns (IX.109).

36. A rim fragment of a krater has the head of a bull right and a circle with an interior border of dots in the field. This is contemporary with the work of Protome Painter A, close to V.76; the lip line is left open in the same way, the eye is a dotted oval, the body filled with rippled wavy lines.

37. A rim fragment of a krater has the horns of two bulls locked in a fight. Overhead is a circle bordered on the outside by dots and on the inside by circlets. The shoulder of the bull on the left is filled with vertical rippled lines and π-pattern on the torso. The long horns sweep in reverse curves, the ears are pricked up. It is close to the work of Protome Painter A. Possibly the scene involved a small bull as on IX.19.

39. A rim fragment of a bell krater has heads of two bulls approaching to fight(?). The animals wave curled horns at each other but do not lock. The horns are striped (rare), the shoulders are filled with N- and arrow pattern on the right, trefoil blobs(?) on the left; the faces are reserved, the eyes different in each head.

Protomes are not so common on the mainland as in Cyprus, although some of the fragments listed above are in the general style of Protome Painter A (IX.36, 37). However, the two Tiryns protomes (IX.25, 25.1) and two fragments with protomes, from Mycenae and the Argive Heraion, are not by that painter.

43. A shoulder fragment of a jug(?) has the solid red protome of a bull or goat from the breast up springing from the framing band. The body is a simple curve, as on works by the Protome Painters. The drooping head has the typical thin muzzle of a bull, with a large, reserved dotted eye; the horns, however, seem to branch just above the roots, as on a stag or goat.

ARGIVE HERAION

44. The rim fragment of a bowl from the Argive Heraion with two bull protomes was originally published as "the upper part of two fishes." One can see why, for the bull on the right has no muzzle, and the way the pointed top of his horned head disappears into the framing band makes him look like an aquatic creature. The body, filled with crosses, has a scalloped interior contour along the back. The bull on the left has the same scalloped contour and a muzzle shaped like three noses or lips down the chest. These bulls seem like crude imitations of a model set by the Protome Painters, again raising the question of ateliers.

NAUPLION

45. A once-famous bull composition, originally published as rams, has been known so long it is often forgotten. The inscribed three-handled jar from Pronoia, Nauplion, about half preserved, apparently had a larger animal walking away from each handle, nudging a smaller one in front of it. The animals do indeed look like rams (which do not otherwise occur in Mycenaean pictorial), with very short legs awkwardly attached at the rear, but when placed in the bull series they fit. The bodies are drawn with the standard Ripe triple division; the filling is limited to rows of dots following the contours and stripes on the inner face of the hind leg. The eye is a large tilted oval, the lips drawn as though slightly parted. The rump of a little animal appears by the nose of the larger, as though a cow were nudging her calf to move along. This form of vase is not normally decorated with bulls, although there is an earlier example from Rhodes (XII.9), but the delicacy of this scene is successful. It is rare on the mainland for incised marks or inscriptions to accompany figured pottery; perhaps this vase should be taken into special account in considering the trade with Cyprus, where potters' or merchants' marks are frequently incised and painted on pictorial vases.

Bull compositions outside the Argolid are very rare and presumably were not often made elsewhere in Greece; there are two from Attica.

ATHENS

46. A small curved fragment of a closed shape from the North Slope of the Acropolis preserves the lowered head of a small bull with richly marked hide in the old tradition, so rare in the Argolid. The horns curve forward and down; two stripes serve for pricked-up ears, the eye is a dotted oval.

47. A krater of unknown provenance, said to have come from Athens, is painted in an odd style, with two bulls on each face. They float on air among scattered fillers of dotted circles. The bodies are painted solid, the faces reserved and spotted all over. The lips are parted, the eyes oval, the horns project in a double curve upward and forward. The bodies are long and powerful, with curiously bent legs and well-defined hooves; the long tails are tasseled at the very end. It is possible that such a vase may have been found on Salamis, although in its handsome decorative flair it is superior to most Salaminian pieces (X.82? 102? XI.41).

STAGS

No stag scene survives complete in Greece. This is a special pity, for the fragments are lively and elegant, and scholars have felt the influence of the stag fresco at Tiryns as a model for mainland vase painters.[24] Since many fragments have only the hooves and legs of leaping animals, it is not always easy to distinguish stags from goats. As a general criterion, we have classified as stags those light-colored animals that have interior markings, branching horns, and short upright tails, while dark animals with horns swept back are considered goats. Stags and goats are similar in body, stance, and hoof; the painters concentrate more on their leap and dash as hunted victims than on their anatomy and scale. On a few vases the two kinds of animals are mixed (IX.49, 51).

Stag scenes found in Cyprus share certain traits with bull scenes (V.53-55, 104-106) and are rarer than on the mainland. In the East the stags are often placed in schematic decorative friezes to the right; on the mainland they are more often shown in motion, with their feet off the ground in lively intimations of a dash through a blank landscape. Hunting scenes with stags or goats pursued by men and dogs are discussed separately (XI.70-80); some of the isolated stags and goats from Mycenae and Tiryns may have been part of larger hunting compositions also.

Stags continue in the Transitional and Late periods. Examples from Tiryns and Mycenae show the standard Ripe characteristics.

TIRYNS

48. A krater fragment from a vase that was once apparently decorated with a frieze of stags and does to the right, their heads turned back, preserves part of a mother with her fawn. The animal has the long tubular body and thin legs of the Cypriote series (V.54) with a similar but denser filling of vertical rippled lines. The drawing here is firmer and more authoritative. The doe is endowed with horns, as so often, since horns are visually characteristic for the species; she turns her head over her back to look at a yearling or fawn perched on her rump. Animals riding on their parents' backs seem more common in Greece than in the East, and the young normally face away from the adult, perhaps for better decorative balance between the two heads. The motif appears on Late Minoan coffins as well. The doe's face is reserved, with a long tubular snout and parted lips; the round eye is typical (unlike the arched eye of fresco deer); the horns branch symmetrically in simple curves with short bars as decorative "velvet" on the inner sides. The filling is consistent all over but varied in direction, with vertical ripples on body and neck, horizontal on haunch and leg. The little animal is more loosely rippled; its forelegs have three-toed hooves like bird claws far out on the mother's tail. The chest of another deer with neck turned back appears following closely at the left, so that the fawn bridges the two animals. Although the outlines are formal and the frieze composition static, there is an unusual expressiveness here of watchful concern; this empathy with the animal is also apparent in the Tiryns stag fresco, though generally missing at Pylos. The influence of the fresco is clearer on a

---

24. For example, Furumark, *MP*, 442; Evans, *Palace of Minos* IV, 580; Rodenwaldt, *Tiryns* II, 140 f., 151, n. 1. One should note, however, that fighting stags are not attempted in vase painting so far as we know; fresco influence is not so strong as to produce direct copies in vase painting, but rather develops thematic material that is passed on in a general way and controlled by the principles of pictorial painting.

Transitional piece from Tiryns (X.44). Here a more general formula is evident, totally comparable to the series found on Cyprus except for its more delicate whimsy; the formulaic aspect is emphasized by the antithetic spiral ornament under the deer's belly.

MYCENAE

49. Two, or possibly three or four, fragments from a krater show a looser, livelier style in spreading small-scale deer broadly across the surface. The animals are mixed dark and light; some may be goats, although there is evidence (IX.51) for parti-colored deer too. The effect is very like that of the goat fragments, IX.67-69.

The first pair of nonjoining sherds shows, from the left, a dark body with thin striped legs and pointed hooves leaping above the ground line, then an animal with hind legs still on the ground, its rump filled with arrow pattern, its body lightly striped, a striped bird sitting on its shoulders. On the right a striped animal with chevrons filling the legs prances forward and up, the motion accentuated by a long neck curving high. The legs all have curved triangular upper parts, sharp knee joints, and linear lower parts with a triangular hoof.

51. Another fragment shows a dark head with branching horns, a reserved tubular face, and dark neck, following a light-colored animal with a thick contour line around the haunch, which is filled with arrow pattern. The dark head evidently belongs to a stag, for goat horns would sweep back; the mingling of light and dark areas on the same animal occurs on Cyprus (V.55). The slender nose is indistinguishable from goat profiles. IX.52 and 53 may belong.

It is a misfortune for our appreciation of Mycenaean views of nature that so many excellent scenes of stags are now represented only by single sherds. Many show points of contact with wall painting, many are lively or beautiful. At Tiryns one can see a Schliemann sherd (IX.54) with an exceptionally sharp pointed hoof, like the stags of the Pylos frescoes;[25] wonderful elaborations of branching horns, unlike the regular symmetries of Cyprus (IX.55); and numbers of angular legs and round eyes. Mycenae has the same types, pronged antlers, galloping legs, bodies filled with arrows and crosses. One cannot guess how many Mycenaean families owned such stag vases, but the numbers of single sherds from different vases suggest they were popular.

GOATS

There are always fewer goats than stags in Mycenaean painting—less noble and admired animals perhaps, as in

Homeric similes later—and they are often more light-hearted. Thirteenth-century goats are characteristically dark and lean, with legs either dark or striped, backswept horns, and a short scut. They appear in hunting scenes, in friezes skipping and swaying along the ground line, or in antithetic compositions, nibbling leaves from a tree in an old Near Eastern motif (see V.110). They are rarely bearded in hunting scenes, more often when they eat.

A series of six fragments from Mycenae (IX.66-70) may come from a single large krater and are almost certainly painted by the artist of the stag-krater fragments IX.49-53. The fragments do not join, but taken together they give parts of four dark goats, two with their forelegs on the ground, two prancing in the air, with a rising and falling rhythm whose organization is sadly unclear. There may have been a pair going quietly on one side, a pair agitated and starting to run on the other. This is a traditional rhythm from at least the time of the Maroni Goat Krater (III.26), implying at least a mild narrative, a change from peace to the scenting of danger or approaching hunters. The goat's nose is slender, the eye reserved in a minimal circle, the horns sweep back in a flowing double curve; on the body fragments there is a deliberate modeling in streaky glaze paint, making highlights on the chest and flank; the thin legs have sharp knees and fetlocks above the hooves. One should compare the fragment from Amarynthos, X.51, and the fine Mycenae dog(?), IX.79.

The stag painter made his goats in harmony with his stags, but other goat fragments have a different style. One large krater (IX.71), preserved only around the handle area, shows dark hunted goats scattered at different levels over the field, two high in the air by the rim and one lower by the root of the handle. The attitudes of the animals suggest that they are being hunted rather than frisking in a meadow, although no dog or hunter is preserved. Hunted animals are often smaller in scale than animals in friezes, to allow for the hunter's tallness. The action springs outward in both directions from the handle, one goat going left and two right, their hooves bunched up under their bellies and their tails curled up over their backs like dogs'. They are painted in simple dark silhouette with dilute orange modeling streaks. The reserved eyes are dotted, the drawn-up legs well marked with hooves and fetlocks, the horns a simple back-curve. The stance is in contrast to the more usual adaptation of the flying gallop for hunted animals, but there are earlier

25. Lang, *Pylos* II, 16 H 43 (pl. 121); cf. the fuller hoofed deer, one with genitals, 2 C 2, pl. 131. The depiction of genitals is more common in wall painting than in vase painting, except for bulls, whose pizzles are so impressive and who are often involved in preludes to mating scenes, and the rare copulating goats of Leukandi (XI.85). Stags are seen in a different light, of speed or escape, but cf. Rodenwaldt, *Tiryns* II, 147, fig. 62.

models for the crumpled pose of potential victims, like the stumbling fawn on the ivory pyxis from Athens.[26] The silver hunting chalice from Dendra[27] shows not only that the general scheme antedates the hunting frescoes at Tiryns but that the forms of moving animals were conventionally set to suggest winning or losing, so that the victor hounds are in the flying gallop pose, while the victim deer have a broken or crumpled stride. Such symbolic conventions, already fixed in the metalwork of the Shaft Graves, are here combined with the free-field scattering characteristic of later frescoes and other thirteenth-century vases, like the battle scene from Tiryns (X.37). It is perhaps an urge toward symmetry that has caused the front hooves to be put on backward.

Two sherds from Mycenae, of the later thirteenth century, correspond with a type better known in the Levant, the goat eating leaves of a tree, sometimes considered a tree of life. This antithetic Near Eastern scheme usually arranges the goats heraldically facing the tree and climbing with forefeet up into it, as on ivories.[28] There are unpublished examples from Berbati. In the next phase it is not uncommon for the goat to nibble at an ornamented panel instead of the tree, as in Cyprus (cf. V.109, VI.9, XI.84, 85.1).

73. A fragment of a bowl or cup has a dark goat with a pale face, small beard, dotted eye, and parallel backswept horns. It stands upright left of the tree, probably bracing its forehooves on the trunk. The lips are drawn in, slightly parted, as it ingests one of the outlined triangular leaves. See also IX.78.

74. A similar scheme on a cup fragment has an outlined goat filled with wavy stripes to the left of a tree with outlined leaves. The goat stands on his hind legs and lets his forelegs hang down. The face is reserved, with an oval dotted eye and a small beard; the lips are drawn in, and probably the lips of the goat on the other side of the tree appear at the right.

75. The cemetery at Prosymna produced a ewer decorated with three goats on top of the shoulder. The position is unusual; it may be compared in style to the prancing goats from Ialysos (XII.10). There were four children in the tomb, only one adult; perhaps the animal jug was a child's favorite. The three goats are arranged in a frieze, neatly spaced on the sides and front. The dark bodies are long and dachshundlike, with short legs, the tails rather long, one curling under itself and the others anchored to the ground line. The muzzles are bottle-shaped, like those of LH III C stags, with a double contour, double-circle eyes, and short back-curved horns. The beards are schematically drawn as a straight line under the chin with diminishing cross-bars to the tapered point.

It is a little surprising that Tiryns, otherwise so prolific in animal vignettes in this period and with such a taste for hunting scenes in its wall paintings, is not renowned for its goats. This may be because most Tiryns animals are set in quiet friezes, while goats are too small and active to maintain such a role with dignity. There are two fragments of small dark animals running (76.2, 3), which might be goats, or the second may be a dog from a hunting composition. The prettiest piece (76.1), which must be late, is from a paneled composition like the moufflons and birds from Enkomi (V.109, 115). The panel is checkered, with light-bordered dark triangles ruffling the edge, treated as leaves or branches that the animal paws. Only his head, chest, and forelegs are preserved, left; the face is reserved and striped, with a neat beard under the chin; the body is contoured with dark scallops, like a bull from the same site (IX.24), and perhaps belted; into the chest is set a pattern like a four-spoked wheel. These static paneled compositions are relatively rare on the mainland but increase in popularity toward the end of pictorial painting, like the stag from Mycenae (X.48) and the goats and birds from Leukandi (XI.84, 141). See also XI.85.1.

Creatures resembling goat-birds will be found under IX.87.

A basket-shaped vase from Nauplion (IX.77), with flat bottom, incurved sides, and two loop handles upright at the rim, is decorated with an elaborate leaping goat in a landscape of undulating striped rocks, a bush, and a fruit tree, probably a date palm. It is hard to date. From the same tomb as the chariot krater IX.1.1, this kalathos has unusual features. The goat is launched right in full flying gallop, hind legs kicked high, but the front legs stop just before landing on the ground, as though the animal, attracted by the fruit of the tree, abandons his journey. A chevron-filled panel at the right under the handle reinforces the tree and blocks any forward motion. Smooth, striped border rocks press in on the scene above and below, in the old Minoan tradition used for fresco and gold work, as sharp rocks were used in the earlier goat scene from Maroni (III.26) or with bulls in a pasture (IV.32). The rocks, and the bush which sprouts up under the goat's groin leave little room for passage; this cramped effect appears in thirteenth-century frescoes at Pylos, like the Blue

26. T. L. Shear, *Hesperia* 9 (1940) 274 f.; Vermeule, *GBA*, 219; S. A. Immerwahr, *The Athenian Agora* XIII (1971) 166, pl. 32; Poursat, *IvoiresMyc*, pl. I. For the influence of ivory carving on later pictorial styles, see Chapter VI; Karageorghis, *Nouveaux Documents*, 232 f.; and Poursat, *IvoiresMyc*, 217 f.

27. A. Persson, *The Royal Tombs at Dendra* (1931) 51, fig. 30, pl. 17; W. S. Smith, *Interconnections in the Ancient Near East* (1965) 72; cf. E. Vermeule, *The Art of the Shaft Graves at Mycenae* (1975) 22 f.

28. Cf. Poursat, *IvoiresMyc*, pl. IV.4; pl. XLIX, p. 85, s.v. "Bouquetins."

Birds. The rocks are very like a rock on a bull fragment (VII.4), tentatively placed in the fourteenth century; that bull has trefoil dapples and spots like this goat and could conceivably be by the same hand, underlining the uncertainty of dating pictorial material. The theme of the feeding goat is generally thirteenth century. They are often in heraldic pairs on the mainland (IX.73, 74), often feeding in flocks in the Pastoral style of Cyprus (VI.8, 9). The bush on this vase is like most Pastoral bushes; the reserved face with fluid drawing of lip, eye, and ear also has a Pastoral quality, though the dense spotted coat and hairy profile do not; the striped legs are those of contemporary stags. This vase, like the horse of IX.8, may represent the mainland counterpart of the Pastoral style, rather earlier in date, but surely post-Amarna.

"MINOTAUR"? (GOAT AT A TREE)

78. An enigmatic animal figure inside a bowl from Mycenae was published as a Minotaur, painted at a moment when Mycenaeans no longer feared the power of the monster in the Knossos labyrinth. It has the dark body and bent horns normally associated with goats. The large break by the hind legs has perhaps obscured the true identity of the animal, which, it was observed acutely, has difficulty in standing upright. It is sadly less imaginative to identify it as one of those goats that stand upright to eat leaves from trees (IX.73, 74), yet the rear animal hocks, the lips indicated on the snout, and the bent horns are suggestive. Neither bulls nor men are drawn this way by Mycenaeans. The leafy bush or tree, an oval filled with wavy lines, is placed conveniently in front of the lips. There are two weak, disjointed spirals behind the animal's back.

DOGS

Some dogs may have formed parts of hunting compositions (see XI.70 and following). There are examples in the Transitional and Late phases; only two are clearly Ripe.

79. A fine "dog" from Mycenae, on a krater fragment, might be seen as a horse or a goat, but in the absence of confirming traits and considering the canine proportions, Furtwängler's identification should continue. It is painted in solid silhouette with strong modeling through dilute washes of pale orange, in the manner of the best horses (IX.6). The attitude is borrowed from stag compositions, with the body to the right and the head turned back over the shoulder (no

other surviving dog does this); the tail is curled up. The animal may be springing in midair. The dilute strokes emphasize the contours, following the long axis of the body but curved in symmetrical ovals on the haunch, a technique apparently invented and favored only at Mycenae for suggesting muscle and three-dimensionality.

80. A puzzling sherd from Argos may show the dark silhouetted head of a dog or a boar to the left, facing the outer fringe of a standard Mycenaean flower. Overhead is a dotted circle spraying arcs of dots to each side. The animal has two short sharp ears or horns curved back, a small reserved eye with a dot-circle pupil, a protuberant narrow loop extending obliquely from a jut in the nose, and a square muzzle (unless the surface is broken). Perhaps a boar is more likely to be painted among flowers. Boars are extremely rare; see XII.17.

SHAGGY DOG?

81. A krater fragment from Mycenae has a long hairy animal body moving right on dark crooked legs. It is as though a bull's body were mounted on stag's legs and covered with lion's fur. The pelt is textured by diagonals, slashed consistently in rows, pale yellow with a dark droplet at the lower end. Perhaps the thicker slashes on the neck represent a collar, as on the Leukandi dog-lion (XI.79), or the ladder pattern indicating dewlaps on some bulls (IX.20, 23, 38). Hair texture is rare in this form.

LION AND BULLS?

82. Two fragments of a finely made krater from Mycenae preserve parts of three animals in an enigmatic and dispirited scene painted by an unsure hand. It seems to show a snarling lion in a herd of cattle. The forms are outlined in firm curves of varying thickness, recalling the contemporary Pastoral style in the East (VI.3, 4, 19). There is a Pastoral sketchiness and lack of conviction, too. Though the bulls have no horns, their bulging faces, loop ears, and collars (dewlaps) identify them fairly well; the scene does not show a pride of lions, but a more traditional predator versus grass-eater conflict in which the enemies are reasonably companionable. The lion, at the left of the rim fragment, walks to the right with his head turned over his back; he has pricked-up ears, a bumpy brow, a round eye, and open mouth; his "mane" is reduced to a slim swirling fillet with a pointed end. The bull to his right seems to

sit, like Ferdinand, and contemplate the future; the painter has drawn in a simple collar and a strong shoulder muscle. The other bull, on a separate fragment, lowers his head and stretches his body, like one determined to protect his herd; the weak single lines of his front legs suggest that he may collapse from nerves before he can charge. The hind legs are inserted with loops into the body, like the handle of a vase through the clay wall; Pastoral painters do this too (VI.4, 19). The extra leg under the bull's neatly banded waist may have wandered down there from the front or, possibly, may represent the traditional tassel of hair hanging from a bull's pizzle.

DUNG BEETLE

83. The fragmentary top of a three-handled jar, painted early in the thirteenth century, is one of the rare mainland pictorial vases to employ the seashell filler. By one handle, a dung beetle in dark silhouette, seen from above, with six legs and a five-pronged tail, rolls a ball of dung along with his front legs. This sight on the floor of his workshop may have caught the painter's eye and appealed to him on the spur of the moment.

QUADRUPED BIRDS?

84. A four-legged bird on wheels occurs on a jar fragment from Mycenae. It looks like a child's toy quail to be pulled along on a string. The long, low body is filled with vertical rippled lines; the eye is a dotted circle, the beak a short curve, the claws twist under to form circles with central dots. Some bird askoi also have four legs.[29]

86. A parallel of a kind exists on a krater fragment from Delphi, with a thin dark body, right, outlined in spots; it has an oval head, tilted eye, long neck, claws on the four feet, and a triangular striped "sail" sticking out behind. It may be simply a badly drawn wingless bird.

GOAT-BIRDS?

87. Krater fragments from Makrysia near Olympia show dark horned animals with bird bodies and tilted legs between rows of running spirals. The long oval heads and parallel backswept horns are those of minor goats. This is not a genuine composite animal like a griffin or sphinx so

much as a humorous sport, of a type familiar earlier on Aigina and at Zygouries (VIII.9-10). See also XII.34, 35, 37. The goat-bird reappears in the seventh century on Island gems.

CRAB OR SHIP

88. A fragment from Mycenae has a shape that might be interpreted as a crab or a seashell, painted in pale wash tones of yellow and brown. It has also been published as an oared cult ship.

The category of miscellaneous animals is practically restricted to the mainland, especially to Mycenae; the Levant has a more limited and standardized range of subjects. Since there are not many of each kind and often only one, they look like experiments that never caught on to the point of entering workshop tradition; many may be playful, like the "Circus Pot" (VIII.8). Later periods add serpents, hedgehogs, and scorpions to the repertory (XI.86-90, XII.23). The rarity of lions and boars is most surprising in view of their regular inclusion in wall painting and on gems. The lack of griffins and sphinxes may be accidental, in view of the contemporary examples in the East (V.27, 28, VI.16 and following) and earlier and later specimens in Greece (VIII.30, 31, X.42, XI.65, 91); they must always have been rare. The exclusion from the standard pictorial repertory of subjects more often treated in wall painting, on ivories, or on gems is another cautionary signal against viewing figured kraters as direct reflections of painted palace walls.

BIRDS

As in all periods, most pictorial fragments are painted with birds and fish. Mainland birds of LH III B are generally standard types without much elaboration or fantasy. Some may have belonged to bull kraters (IX.99, 109). There are friezes of water birds and symmetrical antithetic arrangements. Birds in panel designs may be contemporary but have been put in the Transitional phase, Chapter X, where panels are increasingly common. In the East, paneled scenes also come toward the end of the Ripe tradition (V.115). Styles in body filling match those of the East:

29. Clay duck askoi often stand on four legs or three; E. Vermeule, *AJA* 64 (1960) 12, no. 45, pl. 4, fig. 31; V. Desborough, *The Greek Dark Ages* (1972) 54; *The Mycenaeans in the Eastern Mediterranean* (1973) 85; *Kretika Chronika* 24 (1972) 245 f.; A. Pieridou, *The Protogeometric Style in Cyprus* (1973) in Greek.

ripples, stripes, crosshatching, dots, plain dark silhouettes; the fillings are simpler than in the Middle phase, and there is less flight or swimming motion, until LH III C. A few examples illustrate the range.

ATTICA

89. The most magnificent bird design of the period is spread around a conical rhyton said to come from Attica, now in Berlin. It is painted in an elaborate floral and fringed style that has no good parallels yet and may indicate a strong local school. The lower part of the rhyton is covered with neat rising wavy lines like twisted blades of grass, from which tall, stemmed flowers emerge. The six birds are either rising up out of this meadow setting or clashing in the air. The bodies have double contours and are filled with arcs, chevrons, and semicircles, looking forward to Close Style patterns (also used earlier, VIII.15, 16); the long necks are painted solid, the curling legs have spiral or claw toes. It is fanciful and rich for the period. There is a faint connection in style to the krater without provenance, X.82, which might be Attic.

Other Attic paintings are so far less good than this that the desire to find skilled Athenian workshops is still unfulfilled. There is a kind of bustard on the Acropolis (IX.90), as well as spotted birds that are more like the standard Argolid bird (IX.91), and a fat round-bodied bird in the countryside at Spata (IX.92), which somehow recalls Early forms like the Roc Krater (III.6) because it is in a stance of attack, flying high with its bill and feet forward as though hissing and stabbing.

ARGOLID

In the Argolid almost every site has a bird or two, although it is clear that Mycenae and Tiryns are again the most prolific in the dull kind of bird usually attached to static bull compositions. This bird normally has an oval body without much wing and is filled with spots or wavy lines; some are nearly reduced to the role of filling ornament. The Argive Heraion has two such ordinary pieces (IX.93, 94), but something more amusing too, a pretty spouted cup from near Prosymna (IX.95) with four dark, ladder-winged birds flying or swimming in a circle around the interior in a crudely drawn but pleasant design. The composition is more common for fish, set swimming in the liquid of the bowl, though it is also used for goats and birds in the East (V.118 and following, XII.10, 12). Since most Mycenaean birds, from swans and flamingos to bus-

tards and egrets, are drawn with two or three claws, the lack of webbed feet should not deprive these specimens of swimming talent. The wings grow from the back of the head like a crest, and three of the bills are corkscrews.

96. At Argos a handsome, two-handled globular flask from a tomb on the Deiras has a frieze of heavy-bodied birds walking right on the tips of their claws. Pictorial decoration of the central register of a bottle or pilgrim flask is not done in the East, where ornament of the whole facial surface on each side is more common (IV.78, XII.18). There are nine birds in the frieze, of equal size except for a little one crowded in near one handle, perhaps the last one to be painted. The oval, drooping-tailed bodies have a thick contour line within which the fillings vary in groups, crosshatched or solid dark, in both cases set off from the contour by reserved stripes. The birds are "failed swans," in the sense that the characteristic long bent neck has become absorbed by the body contour. The little bird, through exigency of space, is rendered more as an egret with a spotted body and long legs. The lack of surrounding space in the frieze adds to the heaviness of the design, but this is one of the better thirteenth-century Greek compositions.

97. Mycenae has several bird vases of the period, handsome kraters or smaller pieces with amusing designs. A two-handled jug with a strainer spout is a shape not usually painted with figures; a light, round-bodied bird flies toward the spout to drink, a conceit more familiar on the later snake hydriai where the snakes rest their heads along the strainer spout.

98. A krater that is nearly complete illustrates the quiet, handsome style, two big birds set tail to tail on each side. The heads bend back so that the birds face each other across a pair of ornamental circles (not eggs) in the field. Inside the double contours of the bodies the painter has set solid circles rimmed with dots, contrasting with the circles in the background, which are light with dots inside or have dotted borders with inner solid arcs. This is not the egg-laying fantasy of the Koukounara vase (VIII.17) but a light, decorative formal scene.

Of the others, some birds filled with rippled lines may come from bull-and-bird compositions (IX.99-104), not often an exciting scene on the mainland; one of these (IX.100) has been associated with pieces from Tiryns and Enkomi. They may walk away from the animal's hind legs or horns (IX.101, 102); the usual fillings are spots, ripples, and crosshatching.

105. One fragmentary shallow bowl had a frieze of round-bodied birds with long legs and ladder wings around the inside; this is neither the swimming composition of the Argive Heraion bowl (IX.95) nor the fine flying-swallow scenes of Cyprus and Ugarit (V.119 and following), although it is contemporary with them; it is an excellent illustration of the static and sometimes coarse level of the usual III B pictorial.

Tiryns has a number of ordinary krater fragments of friezes of water birds. They are characteristically drawn with a contoured oval body, a drooping tail that often drags on the ground line, sharp-kneed striped or dark legs, a long neck held swan fashion in a graceful curve above the body, a small round head and round eye, and a long straight bill. The workshop specializes in these wading birds—herons, cranes, or egrets—and likes to emphasize their light-colored bodies, using only a neat row of spots just inside the body contour and, usually, a single straight row across the center of the body like machine gun bullets. While such a bird may occasionally sit on the rump of a bull or stag (IX.109.1), the conventional scheme is to set a flock of waders at a stately gait to the right against a blank background (IX.109.2, 3). There is also a bird, usually called a flamingo, with a round body filled with ripples, a head held more upright, and a short, curved bill unlike the jabbing beaks of the herons. Once again, from the meager evidence, although many fragments at Mycenae and Tiryns have elements in common, such as plain oval bodies and rippled fillings, it is clear that there are workshops in each town. From the Tiryns group one would single out the following.

107. A fragment from the rim of a krater has the neck and upper body of a bizarre bird flying left in "air," a passing breeze painted as a slanting wavy line and broken arcs. Even if this is the kind of compartment frame seen on a slightly later bird krater from Mycenae (X.74), its light, interrupted curves suggest that the painter was trying, for once on the mainland, to introduce the kind of "environment" first seen on the Maroni fish krater (III.9). Soft fringes like sawteeth hang from the bird's bill. The neck outline has a double contour with a reserved effect to set off crosshatching inside; the body commences with an extremely round shoulder broadly outlined in dark paint but hollowed or pale in the interior, with a long bar; it may be, in effect, the model for those hollow, open "swallow" bodies toward the end of the Ripe period in Cyprus (V.119 and following), at a moment before the disintegration of the forms has reached full abstraction. Dot-rosettes in the field link the handsome piece to certain bull kraters and to the flamingos of IX.110.

108. Fragments of a shallow bowl with a frieze of spotted birds inside (heading left) recall the bird bowls of the Argive Heraion and Mycenae, but the style harks back to an older tradition, with a single angled wing rising from the middle of the back; unusually for Greece, there are good filling ornaments in the field, filled lozenges and dotted triple circles; this stands apart from the norms of Argolid painting. Yet such bowls with four birds circling left have a local older model in the silver bowl from Dendra with its densely filled ground, and however great the descent in style, there may be a continuing tradition of bird bowls of which we are still ignorant.

109.1 A small fragment showing a spotted marsh bird sitting on the spotted rump of a bull (more likely than a stag) is interesting as another demonstration of the predilection of mainland painters for mounting one animal on another, a theme rare in Cyprus. While it is obviously related to the usual abstracted but pleasant scenes of bulls being serviced by cattle egrets (V.44 and following), the rump-perched bird is not yet known in Cyprus, and one thinks of the Tiryns doe-and-fawn vase (IX.48) and others to come in the next two periods. The motif is apparently not used in wall painting either, although well known on Minoan larnakes; once more the practical independence of pot painters from other artisans may be intuited.

Unfortunately, flamingos survive nearly always just as heads, close to krater handles. Yet two more spacious fragments from Tiryns suggest that the migration paths of flamingos over Greece (then, as now, to Hala Sultan Tekké on Cyprus?) brought the large admired birds into the repertory of Argolid painters. These form a link to the fine fragment from Achaia (IX.112). One is a quiet frieze (IX.110), the birds in two directions marching in close order, the bodies humped and rounded, the curved necks held back, the beaks rounded under. On the other (IX.111) the birds may be in a more restful posture, squatting after flight or at least with the legs shortened; the bodies are painted like Easter eggs, with a quadruple rippled belt, dot-rosettes at breast and stern, and a narrow, rippled tail.

ACHAIA, TEICHOS DYMAION

112. The elaborately fortified citadel at Dyme on Cape Araxos, facing the western seas and marshes, has produced unexpectedly fine III B pottery. A broken large krater has a frieze of water birds right, probably flamingos, who may have been seen in the marshes on their way south in December. The bodies are the long pointed ovals typical of the Argolid, filled with vertical ripples; the birds have no wings and drag their tails on the ground. The long thick-thighed legs suggest a thrust of forward motion as the birds walk on their toes. In the absence of other figured pottery from the site, one might think of the krater as an import from the Argolid, but there is a fine fish bowl further east near Patras (IX.120).

FISH

The rather puzzling rarity of early fish compositions on the mainland lasted through the Middle period. It is possible that a few of the examples listed here as Ripe might fit in style into the latter years of the fourteenth century, but the forms are so schematic that it is hard to be certain of precise dates. At any rate, there is a marked increase in the popularity of fish designs in the thirteenth century, reaching a high point in the early twelfth, with fish tangled in octopus tentacles on stirrup jars and as isolated or paneled motifs. The Ripe versions are of two basic kinds, predators chasing each other (but almost never chasing schools of other fish species) and more succulent round fish. The backgrounds are normally blank, without weeds or other suggestions of marine environment. There is a preference, seen in other aspects of III B painting, for setting rows of identical fish in friezes, like stags or birds; there is relatively little interest in scattering their forms freely over a broad surface as in the older schools of marine decoration. As with the numerous Cretan fish of the thirteenth century, bodies are outlined and filled with parallel wavy lines like ripples in the water or occasionally with zigzags; a few fish are drawn in solid silhouette. There is not much relation to the patterns on real fish. Both types may be shown with teeth or a tongue in a gaping mouth. Paneled compositions of fish, as of birds, are treated in the next chapter.

ATTICA

115. A fragmentary stirrup jar from Spata in Attica offers a clear illustration of the predator frieze. Parts of three dark fish are seen swimming right in a narrow zone around the belly of the jar, with large reserved eyes, open mouths, and protruding tongues. It seems to be a pursuit scene. The flowers on the shoulder of the vase may place it early in III B, or it may still be fourteenth century. Cyprus does not favor stirrup jars with fish friezes, but they are popular in Crete and the Dodekanese. The pursuit theme may also be more typically mainland and Cretan.

DELPHI

116. A fragment with a fish feeding among flowers recalls the interest in setting of earlier pictorial days and looks forward to the playful elaborations of patterns into fish and birds about 1200. The fish cruises low along the ground line, as on a river bed, and swallows a crooked line resembling the bent stem of a weed. The teeth inside the

outlined jaws are rendered as low zigzags. The worn flower pattern in front of the fish may be automatic, as on the shoulder of the preceding stirrup jar.

Most fish, and the finest ones, come from the Argolid as usual. South of the main production centers, there is a fine fragment from Amyklai.

AMYKLAI

117. Fragments of a rounded, closed vessel preserve parts of three fish swimming up toward the neck of the vase in oblique or nearly vertical positions. The bodies are filled with close-set, fine wavy lines along the length of the fish as usual, broken by cross-striped belts just below the greatest thickness. These fish are the long, lean predator type with open mouths and small fins. On contemporary rhyta from Ugarit and elsewhere the shape of the vase makes similar compositions pleasing; here the fish are surfacing for food rather than diving; it is a good design for a bottle of liquid.[30]

ARGIVE HERAION

118. A fragment with two obliquely swimming fish was described by the excavator as part of a more thrilling scene: "Two fishes advancing toward a monster of some sort, whose head and forelegs are alone visible." These appendages are not visible in the publication. Monsters are extremely rare in Aegean marine contexts; the "Scylla" on the Silver Siege Rhyton has not been seen since Gilliéron drew it,[31] and other queer apparitions like the "sea slugs" at Berkeley (V.137) seem accidental. However, the "monster" might have been a bull or goat (cf. V.42, 58; IX.121). The fish have filaments or whiskers from their lips and are roughly filled with wavy lines; one is large, the other a different species or an infant.

MYCENAE

Mycenae will have a fine series of fish fragments in the next phase of pictorial painting: there seems to be only one that may be Ripe, and that is not certain.

---

30. This is from the Mycenaean house near the Menelaion, with mixed contexts; see Chapter VIII, note 4. A companion sherd with striped seashells may be before 1300, but the fish do not seem earlier than others in this chapter and are close to Transitional pieces from Mycenae. See H. Waterhouse, R. H. Simpson, *BSA* 55 (1960) 72, and in general H. W. Catling, *JHS ArcRep* 1974-75, 12; 1975-76, 13; 1976-77, 24.

31. The famous "Scylla," Evans, *Palace of Minos* I, 698, or S. Marinatos' hippopotamus, *Deltion* 10 (1926) 78 f., is no longer visible: Vermeule, *GBA*, 100. A. Sakellariou, *RevArch* 1975, 195 f., 201, figs. 6-7, has found the head of a man swimming in this fragment.

119. A fragment of a krater has a round-bodied fish like a sunfish or puffer fish, cruising low along the ground line on a tall blank field. Two strokes at the top are almost surely the fins of another fish high above; the composition must have been curiously free and spacious. The fish is all dark with an open mouth drawn nearly round, the jaws almost touching to form a hollow circle, fringed with interior teeth, in which the circled eye floats. The thick body has four thin fin stripes top and bottom.

ACHAIA-KOUKOURA

120. A fine bowl with an upswung handle from the tombs at the Klauss-Koukoura site near Patras is the most "Eastern"-looking of these Ripe fish vases. It is a real rarity in the western Peloponnesos, where pictorial styles are so limited (IX.87, 112). About one-fourth of the bowl is missing and has been partially restored and repainted. The outside is decorated with scallops below the rim. Inside the bowl two larger fish form the framework of a tondo pattern, curving their backs along the outer circle of the bowl and enclosing a small fish between them. The bodies are dark, with large reserved circular eyes and long open mouths fringed with teeth. Small fins sprout at irregular intervals along the back and belly. The forked tails nearly touch one another. This dancing composition recalls the Cypriote jug in the Pierides Collection (V.130), and of course there are simpler bowls in Cyprus with fish inside (V.133 and following) analogous to the bird bowls. The "family" atmosphere is created by the exigencies of the tondo composition. If this is in fact an imported piece, it may be one of the fruits of Rhodian trade along the west coast.[32]

TIRYNS

Tiryns has a few fragments of fish from the Epichosis that may belong to this straight III B phase, but nothing as interesting as the fish of the next two periods. One small but refreshing fragment (IX.121) is a shoulder vignette, possibly from a jug, which has the same amusing confrontation of a small bull and a great fish as on the Cypriote kraters with bulls and goats (V.42, 58). The bull's head is in the general style of the Protome Painters, so familiar in Cyprus; the lips are quickly sketched so as to seem slightly open, and the eye is a lozenge, tilted, as though in apprehension. The fish, whose heavy dark contours and light interior stripe look forward to the particolored effects of the next period, is seen from above like the fish on V.42, so that he seems to have two ears but one Cyclopic eye in the top of his head, an uncomfortable fusion of viewpoints. He is equipped with an exceptionally long snout, like a swordfish's, perhaps to give him the aggressor role, lunging at the grazing animal in a waterside meadow.

UNKNOWN PROVENANCE

122. A one-handled jug sold at a Swiss auction is decorated with a series of eellike fish around the shoulder and bands below. It is a simple, inexpensive design. The eels are set at an oblique slant, as though growing like simplified flowers from the ground line. The heads are sharp triangles with a dot-eye, fins projecting on each side; the bodies are three waving curves for top, bottom, and spine.

32. W. Taylour, *The Mycenaean Pottery in Italy* (1958) 186 f.; in general, see P. Åström, *OpAth* 5 (1965) 89 f.

X
THE GREEK MAINLAND:
Transitional

THE LATER DEVELOPMENT of Mycenaean pictorial painting is really unbroken from the chariot-and-groom krater at Mycenae (IX.2) to the last bad chariot scene at Salamis (XI.41). The fluidly shifting lines of growth in local schools and ateliers do not break into distinctive phases easily, particularly in the absence of strict stratigraphic information. Now a new archaeological interest in the end of the thirteenth century and in the developments of the twelfth has helped provide fixed chronological points, not only for some destruction levels on the mainland in late III B but also for a more meticulous record of the position of pictorial fragments in these often complex levels. The best new information comes from Leukandi, Tiryns, and, at last, Mycenae itself. It is gratifying to note that the period already called, in terms of style, Transitional from LH III B to LH III C has been confirmed chronologically by recent developments at Mycenae.[1]

The Transitional period produces a class of pictorial kraters and bowls decorated with the same themes as earlier, but in new stylistic experiments that sometimes seem bizarre or weak, and are often more chromatic than before, the surface enriched with white paint. Figures are often more slender and active. Some fragments used to be considered Late on stylistic grounds because of their apparent incompetence, but the incompetence may now be seen in other terms, as a gradually increasing freedom from copies of canonical compositions and as a search for a new idiom and authority, especially in the drawing of men and horses. Transitional painting differs from pure III C painting, which often has more definition and austerity and a higher technical level.

The absolute chronology of these phases is not yet agreed upon. The division between Late Helladic III B and III C partly depends on the histories of individual sites: whether they were involved in destruction at the end of III B or whether there were new foundations or cemeteries at the start of the twelfth century. Some excavators prefer to call this period, which we regard as a significant transitional phase, III C:1a, although it is often difficult to distinguish their ordinary material in such strata from III B:2. Even when this phase is thought to start in the twelfth century, it contains items that were also current in most palace towns before their destruction.[2] For these scholars III C:2 (III C:1b) is the source of the major pictorial pieces, as at Leukandi and Perati. For excavators of settlement sites in the Argolid, however, there are rich deposits of pictorial associated with the end of III B and slightly different types in III C. This chapter makes no technical attempt to align the different strata at different sites or to link them to

1. G. Mylonas, *Praktika* 1970, 120 f., pls. 168-169; N. Verdelis, *Deltion* 20 (1965) 137 f.; cf. E. French, *BSA* 64 (1969) 71 f.; *AA* 1969, 133; *BICS* 24 (1977) 136; K. Wardle, *BSA* 68 (1973) 297 f. The stratigraphic division of LH III C settlement phases at Leukandi in Euboia is illustrated by M. Popham, E. Milburn, *BSA* 66 (1971) 333 f.; they stress the lack of connection between pottery types in Leukandi's stratified levels and those at other sites. See also S. Iakovides, *Perati* B (1970) 393 f.; *AJA* 83 (1979) 454 f.; P. Grossman, J. Schäfer, *Tiryns* V (1971) 72 f.; *Tiryns* VIII (1975) 96, fig. 75.

2. The Perati stirrup jars (XI.145 and following) are dated to Phase I of LH III C, about 1190/85-1165/60 (S. Iakovides, see note 1), although such jars are in general clearly later than Mycenae and Tiryns destruction-level pottery; a similar problem appears at Ugarit with the date of the Late kraters (XIII.27-29). Because there is no general agreement on either the stratigraphy or the internal stylistic developments of mainland pictorial pieces, we can group similar pieces here only on a tentative basis, with the expectation that they will be rearranged by other scholars with better information.

tomb groups at other sites except stylistically, although such stratigraphic interpretation is easier now than ten years ago. It tries only to establish the progressive rhythms of later pictorial painting, with criteria for groups heading toward the interesting twelfth-century style and for those already in that idiom.

CHARIOTS AND SOLDIERS

One group of paintings that belongs to this Transitional period both in excavation context and in style centers around the big chariot krater (X.1) from Tiryns by the so-called Painter of the Tiryns Shield Bearers. This interesting and idiosyncratic group has already been discussed in considerable detail by several scholars who have been concerned with the identity of the painter or workshop.[3] More than one painter works in the atelier, whose products are distributed only at Tiryns and Mycenae.

1. The elaborate scene on the fragmentary chariot krater from Tiryns has a chariot team as a centerpiece, with two spearmen marching in front of the horses and two grooms or warriors following behind, preserved only below the thigh. A dog runs under the belly of the team, matched by a dog under one handle and another that may be from the other side. The scene on the rear is being filled in with new fragments, if they are indeed from the same vase; it seems much like the front. The composition is a traditional one in many ways and has parallels in the East both in vase painting and in ivory.[4] It has been suggested that the passenger holds a parasol, like an eastern prince, as on X.4. The format of chariot prince or warrior accompanied by foot soldiers is generalized enough to stand for expeditions either of war or of hunting, although the running dogs are perhaps more at home in a hunting scene, as in the Tiryns boar-hunt fresco or on the ivory box from Enkomi. Yet in epic poetry, dogs accompanied their masters overseas on military expeditions as companions, guards, and extra fighting resources, and the Enkomi hunt is carried on by men in military gear. These late paintings may be general abstractions of the impression made by a military retinue, not restricted in the painter's mind to any specific function.

The krater has many odd details of painting technique, costume, stance, ornament, and elaboration. The chariot and team are directly descended from standard III B compositions; the Mycenae krater (IX.2) was a prelude. The elongated, flattened horses' bodies with legs down through the base lines, the joined heads with eyes as important separate entities, the formal arcaded loops pendent

from the reins (conflated with the pole brace), and the spirals lined up stiffly over the reins were already incipient in Ripe I in Cyprus.[5] The screenlike effect of dripping ornaments on the Rochester krater (V.4) is more formally controlled here, with a playful undercurrent implying that the arcades continue as wavy lines of white down the horses' bodies, with the ornament shifting from spots to stripes (cf. X.13). The restricted use of filling ornament is more charactistic of the mainland than the Levant, but this vase is rich in spirals and white paint, like the Mycenae chariot krater. The spirals over the reins are echoed in isolated ornamental spirals inserted on the chariot body, like scrollwork on a coach, and used again behind the wheels to punctuate the scene between the centerpiece and the following men, as well as in the dogs' scrolled tails.

The liberal use of white paint is typical of almost all pieces in this group. The horses are strongly outlined in white to emphasize the curve of the thick neck into the back; this line breaks up into a stream of dots at the brow, and the whole muzzle is rendered in consistent spots, with large spotted eye circles; spots drip from the lower muzzle strap. The neck is striped horizontally in wavy lines, the body striped in wider-spaced verticals, the upper legs obliquely barred, the lower legs highlighted by a single vertical stripe. The ornamental spirals and arcades are spotted, the two reins filled with a looser wavy stream of white. The wheel rims and solid outlines of the chariot are striped according to the curves, always across the axis. Solid white is used for the six erect mane tufts and the forelock, silhouetted in a formal spray against the upper framing band.

The running dogs are elaborated with the same repertory of white ornaments, restricted to outlining the contours of so small an area, with bars on the front legs (excessively long, with pointed feet, as though borrowed from a fawn), highlighting lines on the rear legs, and dotted spiral tails.[6]

The fragmentary chariot is now fortunately supplemented on each side of the vase by several new pieces from Tiryns. The driver leans back in a smooth curve, and

3. H. Schliemann, *Tiryns* (1885) pl. XIV; M. Mackeprang, *AJA* 42 (1938) 543, 548; Furumark, *MP*, 447 f.; *OpAth* 1 (1953) 63 f.; Å Åkerström, *OpAth* 1 (1953) 10 f.; S. Charitonides, *EphArch* 1953-54 II, 101 f.; J. L. Benson, *AJA* 65 (1961) 344 f.; Slenczka, *Tiryns* VII, 47-48; J. Crouwel, *BSA* 68 (1973) 343 f., *BSA* 71 (1976) 55 f.

4. A. Furumark, *OpAth* 1, 63, fig. 10 and discussion; see Chapter IX, note 26.

5. See V.4, 6, 7, 8.

6. Of the two extra dogs, one is clearly under the right handle of the rear of the vase, running in front of the chariot. The other, preserved only as head and paws, could come behind the chariot on the front or under or behind the lost chariot on the back; cf. German Archaeological Institute photo, Tiryns 583.

the passenger holds his hands level at the height of the reins. The box seems to have a solid body in the old style, with a heavy wraparound frame striped in white like the big round wheel; the inset spirals give the (hide) covering an airy look.

The two foot soldiers in front of the chariot have attracted much attention over the decades because of the peculiar "tails" between their legs and the new, small, round shields they hold high in their left hands like dishes. Such small shields are used by some of the Sea Peoples—the Shardana and Pulesati (Peleset) among others. This shield is recorded on the Pylos frescoes and may have become popular on the Greek mainland as the result of Eastern contact in the thirteenth century. It implies a shift in fighting tactics toward mobility, away from set standing duels. The shield's normal accompaniment may be the single throwing spear, as here (no one with a round shield carries a sword in Greece, although the Shardana do), a simple tunic perhaps of reinforced linen or felt (cf. X.9), and often greaves.[7] It represents a different stream of innovation from the "moon" shields of the Mycenae Warrior Vase and stele (XI.42, 43), or those with recessed segments at Iolkos (XI.57).

The shields are painted with the outer face toward the viewer, the hand passing behind it so that the handgrip is concealed; this one-handed grip is the most characteristic aspect of the new defensive armor, which the artist portrays without concern for correct military stance. The handgrip is clearly implied by the absence of telamon or baldric. Other shields of this type are recorded in XI.1, 22(?). No boss is shown, and because of the profusion of white spots on other parts of this vase the spots around the rim can scarcely be understood as reinforcing metal discs.

The spread of added white paint across these foot soldiers does not accent different parts of the surface but reduces the odd silhouettes to consistent ornament, with wavy stripes from waist to knee, spots outlining the heads and "tails," slash bars between white outlines on the lower legs. These are not greaves, since they match the patterns on the horses' and dogs' legs; the groom on the Mycenae krater (IX.2) has genuine tassels to indicate greaves. The pointed crests on the heads may represent a cap-helmet of some kind (cf. X.5, 9). The puzzling "tails" may perhaps be understood, with Åkerström, as late, exaggerated reminiscences of the peak of the old Aegean kilt, which, although not fashionable after 1300, still occurs in some late Pylos frescoes, but in more bizarre costumed contexts.[8] The "tailed man" in the Tiryns fresco is in a different, cult context and costume.[9] Perhaps the simplest conclusion would be that an intended kilt was formalized and exaggerated into a design in keeping with the pointed arcades above the horses, impelled by

pattern rather than interest in costume. The two footmen behind the chariot seem to be painted in the same costume and stance, although the spears are held at a different angle, more at rest, judging by the bent elbow of the rear figure (cf. X.6, 9).

2. Two sets of fragments from a single(?) chariot krater at Mycenae are evidently by the same Painter of the Tiryns Shield Bearers, not just from the atelier like some Mycenae pieces. They are perhaps slightly cruder but have the exact mannerisms: the horses' mane locks in white against the upper band, the big round facing eyes outlined in white spots, the spots on the muzzle contour, the spotted arcades, the rippled bars on the bodies forming vertical compartments, the white spots contouring the dog who runs under the team. What is preserved shows the team's heads, chests, reins, part of the box with bent-elbowed driver and passenger with empty hands extended in front of his chest; the groom leading the way (the back of his head and one hand are preserved) reaches back to touch the horses' chests, where there is a white streak. Where the Tiryns vase has spiral filling ornaments above the reins, the Mycenae vase has a second twisting rein line (or pole brace) filled with white; from the groom's gesture it is clear that the vase is not an exact replica of the Tiryns vase, and that the spearmen leading there have been rearranged. The fragments are extraordinarily interesting for demonstrating the existence of nearly identical scenes at Mycenae and Tiryns, in a stratigraphic context at the end of III B in the complex south of Tsountas' House, not far from the Citadel House with its chariot krater (X.4) and the House of the Warrior Vase. This quarter is extremely productive for pictorial painting, like the houses close to the Perseia Fountain on the other side of the palace. The levels indicate that this whole group is properly separated from the Ripe style as a Transitional phase, which was already evident in artistic terms.

3. On a chariot krater fragment from Mycenae, Charitonides noted the similarity to the better preceding pieces,

7. The best discussion is still Lorimer, HM, 148 f.; see also A. Snodgrass, Arms and Armour of the Greeks (1967) 32; Early Greek Armour and Weapons (1964) 38-48; H. Hencken, The Earliest European Helmets (1972); N. Verdelis, AthMitt 82 (1967) 1 f.; J. Borchhardt, Homerische Helme (1972) 37 f.; J. Bouzek, RDAC 1975, 54; N. K. Sandars, The Sea Peoples (1978) 106; see also XII.29-32.

8. Å. Åkerström points to the Knossos fresco, "the Captain of the Blacks," OpAth 1 (1953) 16, fig. 4, but there is considerable discrepancy in date and the length of the kilt peak; short-peaked kilts at Pylos: Lang, Pylos II, pls. N, 24, 124, 129; bizarre tailed costumes: pls. A, M, N, 16, 23, 117, 129; pointed black lappets over a kilt: pls. 16, 117, A, M. If an exaggerated kilt form is intended, the exaggeration may spring from the pleasure in arcading decorations in this period. S. Marinatos believed it a skin-costume in a sacral context, Archaeologia Homerica A (1964) 32.

9. Rodenwaldt, Tiryns II, pl. II.7.

as well as the difference in quality: the lack of stability in the outlines, coarser ripples and arcades, and generally sillier appearance of the chariot driver with his chin in the air and weak hands held high. Only the spread fingers of the passenger are preserved. If this is by an apprentice in the workshop of the Painter of the Tiryns Shield Bearers, he is copying a popular master model, though how far one should speculate on the number of painters working in small ateliers, each represented by one piece of vase, is problematic.

4. Fragments of a krater from the Citadel House at Mycenae belong in the same group but differ again in detail. At the left is preserved a tall-necked man, spotted white, who holds, apparently, a large umbrella against the upper framing band to shade the head of the personage driving the chariot, emphasizing his princely status. The Eastern motif of an attendant shading the king in this way was already alluded to in the early-fourteenth-century Sunshade Krater (III.21). Its revival here may harmonize with a general late revival of Palace Style reminiscences or may be another effect of the increased late-thirteenth-century ivory trade. The spirals dotted in white over the reins, the liberal added white, and the outline of the surviving faces indicate that the fragments are from the same workshop.

Three sherds with white-striped soldiers or attendants, from Mycenae, have been associated with the Tiryns chariot krater and its relatives, and although there is no present evidence for chariots in these scenes, they are certainly suitable in style.

5. A figure from a krater, wearing a peaked cap-helmet, raises his left hand high in a conventional gesture of command. The forms of the body are the same as those on the preceding chariot vases; he is neither a spearman nor a driver but might be a passenger (the head passes over the upper framing band) or possibly a groom leading a horse. The main features are a sharp pointed nose and chin, with white spots, a reserved face and neck, broad shoulders striped vertically with white wavy lines, and the circular form of the thumb (as on X.3). The face is identical with the others in this group; the fragment may belong to one of the other Mycenae kraters. See X.8.

6. A krater fragment from Mycenae preserves the arms, torso, and groin of "a man with a bustle," like the Tiryns spearmen—a straight line of chest and leg from which a haunch and rear leg spring in an arc from the small of the back. This is a foot soldier, the lance or spear held vertically at rest, the rear leg drawn back in a thick curve as on X.1, the front leg more columnar and straight. The massive right elbow is bent in the normal way, not in toward the waist as on the throwing spearmen of X.1. Ob-

servation of the effect of different muscular activities on the external forms of the body was rare earlier, but will increase in the Late period. The left arm curves upward smoothly; it may have been supporting a small shield. The whole body is striped across the axis of the curves, as before, while the spear is spotted. Two horizontal lines behind the right arm recall the fingers on X.2.

7. The fragment of a krater from Mycenae has a smaller part of another bustle-man, following a round form that may be the wing of a chariot. The figure would then correspond to the first attendant behind the chariot on the Tiryns krater. The white lines again curve across the axis of the forms.

8. The rim fragment of a krater from Mycenae(?) preserves part of a man making a commanding gesture with circled thumb, a close counterpart to X.5 in every way except for the lack of white overpaint. The gesture is also associated with boxers, but general likenesses suggest that this figure belongs in a chariot scene where the white was for some reason not added.

A whole group of fragments from Tiryns (X.9-15) belongs to two or three kraters[10] representing a second or lower level of the same school of painting—clumsy, bright with white dashes, spots and ripples, and egg-headed chinless men. Schliemann seems to have discovered them at the same time as the name piece by the Painter of the Tiryns Shield Bearers. While some students have wanted to place them in full III C for their crudity, the Late period is in fact seldom crude, and these are clearly related to the first group. The practical advantage of retaining a generation of transition is demonstrated not only by the evolving style with its blocks of color contrast but by the newer form of chariot that appears on X.9. It is the lightweight open-railed chariot, which will become increasingly popular as the thirteenth century gives way to the twelfth. Like the new round shields on X.1, it reflects real changes in armament and military practice, whether inspired by acquaintance with Egyptian vehicles or another foreign contact in this generation of Sea Peoples, when so many innovations, from sword types to cremation, are appearing in the Aegean world. Since the krater with the Shield Bearers portrays one of the last solid-sided chariots and these kraters are by an apprentice, the connection in date is interesting.

9. There are two people in the open chariot: a driver wearing a soft cap, slinging his thick hands up and forward to suggest speed or that he is urging on the horse (which

---

10. Unfortunately it was not possible to have the fragments out of the case to compare interiors, but the Athens National Museum kindly gave permission to photograph the interiors of NM 1507, 1508, 1512, and 1654; the first three may be the back of 1509.

causes the reins to be drawn too short), and a "bald" passenger. A footman in a latticed tunic or breastplate, with his right hand bent negligently at the waist, uses his left to prod the passenger in the small of the back, helping him onto the chariot or keeping him in place as it lurches off to a fast start. This kind of subcomic observation appeared occasionally in the Cypriote series and, while no one could accuse the Mycenaeans of being a humorous people, there will be an increasing number of small gestures, distributions of weight, swinging arms and legs, lurching postures, and other hints that a new phase of painting, with original motifs, is emerging. The profuse added white is more careless than on the earlier series, with changes in texture and design — bars on the team's crown and neck, which will be characteristic of animal patterning in early III C, crosses on the forequarters and barrel of the body (these had been reserved for stags and bulls before), panels of inserted spots, and concentric arcs filling the corners, a typically Late design. The footman's arms are barred, his corselet made of openwork diamonds with a spotted border, his legs outlined in white and spotted; the additional paint is no longer wanted just for clarifying outlines or creating a uniform enriched surface but for reorganizing bodies and objects in a disjunctive contrasted style, looking forward to the alternating blocks of tones normal in III C. Proportions are disjointed too, the horses' heads shrunken and bodies elongated, the men's heads large and the bodies squat, symbols rather than drawings of figures. The picture frieze is narrower and more drawn out. Both men and horses have diamond-shaped eyes, a feature of the Late period at Mycenae for men and stags. In fresco painting the eyes of human beings and animals were usually differentiated by shape, but here there is an increasing sense of arbitrary pattern that will obliterate the traditional distinctions.[11]

Of the other fragments in this set, one might point to the nice Adam's apple of X.10, and the amusing pair of feet on X.14. They belong to one of the drivers and suggest how precarious the footing could be in the new open chariot.[12] The wheel is sunk deep through the base line as usual in this series, the spotted rail curves up in front of it, and behind the rail two feet kick wildly in the air. The driver evidently wears boots barred with white, and a white ankle contour may be the loop into which he inserts his foot on the chariot floor. Perhaps there is so much air between the feet and the chariot because of Mycenaean insistence on intact outlines — the particular problem had not occurred before the sides of the chariot were opened up — or, considering the other funny touches in this group, the painter may have shown him off balance at a bad turn or a bump in the road.

HORSES

Apart from the elaborate chariot kraters, there are a few paintings of horses alone or with their grooms, as there were in the Ripe period. These are judged slightly later in style. Mycenae has two fragments (X.20) of a little horse who may be eating a flower that waves in front of his head, pendent from above, as though he were in a grove. The body is thin and insubstantial, with feeble legs splayed forward. The new love of white paint appears in the spotted contour, with two trails of spots crossing at chest and withers. Another walking horse (X.21) has a curved highlight along the back edge of his hind leg, rendered by a reserved stripe. A pair(?) of fine sherds (X.23, 52) has the hindquarters of a horse and of a goat; they may come from a very large krater or possibly a collared jar, like XI.13 with horses and birds. On X.23 the painter has distinguished the solid bone of the tail from the finer hairs floating down from it, with pale dilute glazes, which are also employed to model dark and light tones on the haunch, as though it gleamed in the light. The pale inner side of the leg is filled with neat arcs, looking forward to the more intensive patterning of Late Helladic III C. The quality of this study is extremely high. The thick curved line covered with a lacing pattern behind the horse is either a distinctive frame within the picture space (see X.52) or possibly a bound pole brace dropping toward the solid-painted chariot on the left (Mrs. Littauer).

24. A lively horse moving fast on the rim of a big open krater is related to the developments of the Pastoral Style in the East, which had one representative at Mycenae in the Ripe period (IX.8). The horse, on loose reins, stretches his head and neck far forward, moving after a footman (the elbow is preserved); its ears are pricked up, and the mane plumes, decorated with loop pattern, wave back and high. The thick stripe of the cheek strap of the bridle seen against the reserved face is transitional to the interest in light-and-dark contrasts of the next period. The dotted eye is set high with a tear duct at the bottom.

There are two Mycenaean ponies, or small horses who seem immature. One is a sketchy red animal pulled left on leading reins (X.25); the mane is a series of upright dashes, and a pinto patch on the shoulder is reserved and filled

11. Miss Lang, in *Pylos* II, pays closest attention to the shapes of animal eyes. The round eye belongs to the bull and the nautilus; the plain oval goes with birds and human figures; the perked-up oval is for dogs (and boar?); the two-pointed oval is for dogs, human beings, and sphinxes; the oval with a point toward the muzzle and a rounded back is for the lion, dog, deer, and boar; the griffin has the point back, toward the crest. Lions have eyelashes.

12. See Appendix and H. Catling, *AJA* 72 (1968) 48.

with loops. A krater fragment (X.26) has a matt black pony to the right, perhaps running, since the mane stands out in separate stripes and curves as if lifted in the breeze; the ears are pricked up.

27. A more pastoral view of, probably, a donkey or ass, comes on the fragment of a small krater from Mycenae; the animal nibbles on a flower as on X.20. The style is different from that, however, and closer to the preceding horses on reins; the body is dark silhouette with a firm contour and erratic filling, the face is reserved with a stripe from the round eye down to the muzzle, the mane is drawn in bent strokes. The front legs, bent forward oddly, are striped like stags' legs. Such stripes are more characteristic of asses than of horses (Mrs. Littauer). The flower is a triangle, with a chevron that may be part of the stem. The idea of painting an entire krater with grazing animals had been used for stags and bulls before but is new for horses (XI.13) or the rarely pictured donkey, part of the more empathetic late Mycenaean view of the animal world.

28. Outside of the Argolid only Athens has produced a horse picture in this period, an attractive fragment of a small bowl or krater on the Acropolis, with a horse on reins to the right. The eye is reserved and dotted, the mane sticks up in stripes, and the ears are pricked. Such studies of horses in action, unfortunately so small and fragmentary, seem to testify to a more intimate observation of animal life, as on the contemporary ostraka of Nineteenth-Dynasty Egypt, although never approaching Egyptian skill and humor.

SOLDIERS

A small group of soldier images may be placed in the Transitional period; they are not yet in the full "black-and-white" style of LH III C but seem more experimental than most Ripe figures. Some of them, of course, may belong in chariot scenes, but they do not suit any of those discussed above.

29. A krater fragment from Mycenae has a soldier in a plumed helmet carrying a round shield. The style is sketchy but expressive. The silhouette head resembles Geometric versions of soldiers whose helmet plumes are thinned out like locks of hair; the interior is almost entirely filled with a reserved dotted eye. Body and shield are blended, as so often in Geometric, rounded at the top with an oblique border in front, reserved and filled with concentric arcs; the bent arm protrudes from it in front. It is conceivable that the figure is a charioteer, like the armed charioteers of the next phase (XI.1).

30. The fragment of a small bowl from Mycenae has a crosshatched panel framing a small soldier walking left with his ration bag. The face is not so bestial as in the Loeschcke drawing; the nose is a pointed beak, the head all thick outline and round dotted eye as on the last, the thick neck simply outlined. The body is painted solid with the legs well spread in the "bustle" style of the Tiryns group (X.6, 7), so that the rear leg seems like a tail. Whether the line behind the neck is a bent staff or an arm is hard to tell; if an arm, it is much thinner than the front one. From it hangs a round bucket or bag with a swinging handle(?), decorated with four spots. This may be a version of the bags on the Warrior Vase (XI.42), for carrying rations of barley or figs on campaign.[13]

31. A tantalizing fragment of a small krater or large bowl from Mycenae has the head of a man in a fur cap or tall peaked helmet, who, by the wheel marks on the interior of the sherd, should be lying face down close to the left handle. If this is correct, it may be part of a battle scene, where falling figures are known as in fresco (X.36, 37). The face is reserved, with good profile drawing and an oval eye with large dark pupil. The dark helmet has a tubular peak, perhaps a crest holder, like some bronze helmets, and it protects the back of the neck to the shoulder; the ruffled stripes along the back of the helmet suggest fur or hair, a shako. There are dilute-glaze modeling streaks. In fresco battle scenes many victims meet no physical resistance to their collapse; this might, possibly, be a large-scale version of a composition like X.37, but it remains perplexing.[14]

A few other fragments from the Argolid in this period have parts of people: a duck-billed man in a crosshatched cap or helmet from Dendra (X.32) and parts of what may have been chariot scenes from Tiryns. Two (X.33, 34) are pleasant sketches of men with long noses, slanted eyes, and parted lips, refreshingly apart from the standard Ripe types and evidence that there was once far more small-scale quick drawing than we usually attribute to the Mycenaeans. Such pieces are too small even to guess the form of the scene, perhaps peaceful or preparatory to war. The chest and arm of a spearman or groom (X.35) suggests that the quiet processionals with decorative stances of the Ripe tradition still prevail and that the new energy of III C pictures has not yet fully stirred the Tiryns workshops.

---

13. Mycenaean rations are discussed in L. Palmer, *Mycenaean Greek Texts* (1963) 96 f., and M. Ventris, J. Chadwick, *Documents in Mycenaean Greek* (1956) 157 f.; see also the Warrior Vase, XI.42, and "the Archilochos connection," W. Schuchhardt, *Opus Nobile, Festschrift U. Jantzen* (1969) 153.

14. Near Schliemann's description of the piece is a puzzling mention of a vase with deer outside, men and women inside—Geometric or Corinthian? H. Schliemann, *Mycenae and Tiryns* (1880) 69.

BATTLE SCENES

However, Tiryns, Amyklai, perhaps Athens, and Phylakopi on Melos have all produced sketches of battles that look as if they belong to the end of the thirteenth century, contemporary with the fresco battles of Pylos, Orchomenos, and Mycenae. The palace wall paintings and the mainland fragments have land battles; Phylakopi, perhaps naturally for an island, has a sea battle; and these themes will again be favorites in Greek Geometric painting. Because full-scale battle scenes are so rare in Mycenaean pictorial, — the prelude of the march to war is the preferred moment — it is particularly hard to discern development in these crude, fragmentary survivals. It is possible that some fragments, like those from Athens (X.41, XI.55.1) or those discussed earlier from the Menelaion (VIII.11), belong in the circle of the "Circus Pot" (VIII.8) or that all belong in the later thirteenth century. The pictorial traditions of Phylakopi are virtually unknown after Late Cycladic I.

Battle scenes began in Mycenaean art with the stone, silver, and gold objects of the Shaft Graves and continued on stone and gems, but were difficult for the vase painter, who liked his forms and contours intact. The two silver vessels from Shaft Grave IV established an iconographical prototype that spread fighters freely over a rocky landscape and used overlapping figures and spears as binding diagonals.[15] Vase painters were disinclined to overlapping, landscape, or tilted axes and usually respected the ground line even when chariots or horses became mired in it. The floating warrior from Melathria (VIII.6) and the stick-soldiers from the Cyclades (VII.A) are isolated on blank grounds early in the sequence, and toward the end the Shield Bearers from Tiryns (X.1) still touch nothing. The late fresco compositions at Pylos and Mycenae may have provided a newer model for pictorial painting, as they spread lunging and toppling figures boldly across the wall surface without anchorage to a ground line, and this is the principle in the compositions from Amyklai and Tiryns. These active, interlocked battles differ both from the static processions of III B and the monumental friezes of III C, although the Late period also instills a life into charioteers and soldiers that was earlier unknown.

36. The battle fragment from Amyklai comes from an archaeological context of late III B, early III C, and some mixture of Geometric. Parts of three figures survive, drawn on different scales and spread over the surface on different levels. At the left a crouching or fallen figure lifts his arm up vertically with the fingers spread; a long dark diagonal spear is falling from the finger tips. In the center a

naked man (the phallus is indicated) strides or leaps over him to the left with bent knees; he holds a spear or branch level in front of him like a pike-fighter. One cannot tell if this figure has just dispatched the last, or if he is crouching to take a blow, avoid attack, or indeed, is dying. The spread-legged stance with bent knees seems to be used for dead warriors at Pylos, as it had been in Egyptian painting, a limp starfish pose. (An enigmatic line slanting up from the back of the left calf and curving down again to form a "tail" might recall the winged appendages on the hunter's legs on the faience rhyton from Kition or may be a careless streak of paint).[16] On the right a figure on a comparatively huge scale strides off, perhaps in another duel. The discrepancy in scale occurs again at Leukandi in III C (XI.66). It was used in the Siege Scene among the Mycenae frescoes and may have an expressive function, as in Egypt, the victor leaving infantile victims behind, or it may focus on a central pair of duelists flanked by smaller, staggered groups of fighters.[17] The legs and thighs are not ill drawn.

37. The best battle sherd comes from Tiryns and is arranged in a composition close to the Pylos fresco battle scene 22 H 64.[18] At the top is a horizontal spear held by an arm from the left; the remains might be interpreted as a figure either hurling his spear to the left with his arm drawn back behind his head or jabbing it to the right with his arm thrust forward. Below this a naked man falls forward on a slant to the left, his head upright, the right arm flung up before his face in a swimmer's position, the chest at a strong slant. The figure is in dark silhouette with a reserved dotted eye. Below his chest, the curled fingers of a hand reach up from below. The three levels of composition and the agitated, active stances make the loss of the complete scene a sad one. The head is close to the profiles of one or two soldiers in the Tiryns wall paintings, and the composition is matched in the fragmentary battle fresco from Orchomenos.[19]

15. G. Karo, *Die Schachtgräber von Mykenai* (1930-33) 174 f., 306 f., nos. 481, 605-607; A. Sakellariou, *RevArch* 1971, 33 f.; *RevArch* 1975, 195 f.; W. S. Smith, *Interconnections in the Ancient Near East* (1965) 67, fig. 88.

16. V. Karageorghis, *BCH* 87 (1963) 368, pl. VII; *Mycenaean Art from Cyprus* (1968) pl. XXXIX; *Kition* (1976) pl. III; *Civilization of Prehistoric Cyprus* (1976) 176, no. 135. See E. Porada's suggestion that the appendages may be based on the rhyton artist's misunderstanding of Egyptian representations of demons holding knives with their feet, in *Acts of the International Archaeological Symposium, "The Relations between Cyprus and Crete, ca. 2000-500 B.C.,"* April 1978 (1979) 119.

17. Pylos scenes with two scales of proportion, Lang, *Pylos* II, pl. 119, vestibule procession; with three scales, pl. 125, throne room scene. Scenes at Mycenae with two scales, G. Rodenwaldt, *Fries des Megarons von Mykenai* (1921) Beil. II and col. pl., siege scene.

18. Lang, *Pylos* II, pls. 16, 117, A, M.

19. Rodenwaldt, *Tiryns* II, pl. XI.5. The new Orchomenos frescoes, T. Spyropoulos, *AAA* 7 (1974) 320 f., col. pl. II; *Deltion* 28 (1973) Chron., 262, 263, fig. 4.

38. From Phylakopi, a spear thrower appears at the left edge of a paneled scene; the frame is filled with overlapping arcs, which would date the fragment close to 1200 in the circle of the Amyklai battle.[20] Only the arm and the spear remain of a man facing right with his right arm drawn back for a long cast. This is the stance on the Tiryns sherd in reverse. There would have been space for a duel at least, if not a more ambitious scene; it is less likely to be a hunting composition.

39. Another fragment from Phylakopi shows a dark silhouetted man walking left in front of a dark irregular mass that may be the prow of a ship with a ramming beak. There is no effort to coordinate the man and the ship spatially. The large thighs, long flat feet, and narrow stride are typical of later III B. This can be considered a battle scene only in a marginal sense, since the "ship" might possibly be the accidental distortion of a ground line. Yet marine battles are part of the Mycenaean tradition in iconography since the time of the Silver Siege Rhyton or the Epidauros fragment, and historically many of them must have occurred in this period. The legs on X.40, from Naxos, might conceivably suit such a scene; the splay-fingered hands from Athens (X.41) might belong to feeble or desperate victims. The leaf-bladed spears at Tiryns (XI.55.1) and Athens are too stationary for active war.

The distinction between the Transitional and the developed LH III C styles is slightly harder to draw in the realm of animal compositions, because there is no central group to which marginal fragments can be attached. The hunting scenes and related dog chases are all discussed together in the next chapter (XI.70 and following) although the context of XI.71, at least, in the rich layers that straddle III B and III C around "Tsountas' House" at Mycenae, might suggest that it is still thirteenth century. It seems more profitable to study the whole group of Late animals together. A few selected examples, however, demonstrate that the same currents of stylistic change are reflected in animal as in human compositions; the juxtaposition is instructive in the case of stags.

SPHINX

42. The wonderful pyxis with vertical loop handles from the "religious center" of Mycenae, painted with a sphinx facing two "trees" of stacked chevrons, is very close to the work of the Painter of the Tiryns Shield Bearers (X.1) and is perhaps from his hand. The sphinx's legs frame a "sleeping" bird with head turned back, and both are en-

riched with liberal, finely controlled white paint in sweeping lines and rows of spots. The sphinx's head is not really like the soldiers' on the krater; she has a long nose, receding chin with thin lip, small circular eye, forehead slanting back, and ruffled hair or cap, although the inner hair contour has the same shape as their outer skull contours. The spotted spiral tail curled high and the spotted hind legs recall the hounds on the krater, and the white lines defining the muscular legs and strong hooves recall the definition of its soldiers' legs and horses' hooves. The sphinx is thin, with weak hindquarters, but a high plump chest and alert raised wing, which has a line of dark spots as a ripple up the center; dark spots are also added to suggest ruffled feathers on the S-curve of the bird's body. The pyxis comes from the deeper levels of the transitional period III B to III C and so seems precisely contemporary with the chariot vases of the group. The religious associations are not yet so clear as on the Tanagra larnakes or the Leukandi vases (XI.65, 91), but this is one of the finest late distillations of a theme so long known on gems and ivories (cf. VIII.30, 31).

BULLS

Bull scenes have generally lost their popularity, just as in the Levant. There are one or two fairly late examples, the Mycenae bull jumper for instance (IX.18.1), but the richly embroidered static bodies of the Ripe period have disappeared from the pictorial repertory. The rise and fall of popular subjects is probably dictated as much by internal rhythms in the pictorial arts as by external circumstances, so it would be false to interpret the fading away of the bull theme as reflecting the change from the stabler palace period, with its records of large herds and flocks, to the more precarious twelfth century, when chariots and hunts dominate. Yet it is clear that most painters' attention was more vividly devoted to scenes of action than to generalized views of grazing animals. The big bull krater in Munich (IX.47) and some of the odd horn fragments might be viewed as Transitional, but there is no clear group. One particolored bull from Tiryns, with dark shoulders, spotted belly, and crosshatched haunch may illustrate the disintegration of the old habits of patterning and a new arbitrary sense of "color."[21]

20. C. Edgar, *Excavations at Phylakopi* (1904) pl. XIII, nos. 14, 16; pl. XIX, no. 8; cf. 147, fig. 124.
21. Slenczka, *Tiryns* VII, 49, no. 103, fig. 13, pl. 16.3.

STAGS

In contrast, stags increase in favor, whether under the influence of the Tiryns stag-hunting fresco or the increasing interest in hunting scenes in general. They occur both as isolated animals and as victims.

43. A head with curving horns from the rim of a krater from Mycenae has been associated many times with the group of the Tiryns Shield Bearers (X.1) from the patterning of white spots around the outline. The head is turned back decoratively over the dark body, striped with white wavy lines as on the horses of this group; the antlers are simplified, without branches; the round eye outlined with spots and reserved face also reflect the painter's practice in drawing horses.

44. The handsome stag sherd from Tiryns, from the rim of a large krater, is one of the clearer examples of influence from the Tiryns stag-hunt fresco. The surface is badly worn. The stag moves right with his head turned left over his back as so often, but here the head is raised and the lips parted as though in alarm. This is the new empathetic style seen even better in the doe hunt from Tiryns (XI.78). Again the composition is apparently a repeated frieze; a mark at the right edge of the sherd may be the remains of the scut of the deer in front. The horns are arranged in elegant symmetry with the branches drawn as spiral curls bending toward the outer tips. The heavy contour line, characteristic of Transitional pieces, allows a slender reserved tube to be opened in the face, where a pointed oval eye adds to the impression of alertness; stag eyes in vase painting are usually round, but in fresco they are pointed. The body is covered in solid brown wash instead of the normal texturing of crosses or stripes; there are plain red deer in wall paintings both at Tiryns and at Pylos.[22] Perhaps some painters distinguished fallow deer from roe deer for color contrast. The hairs along the back of the neck are stiff separated bars, as on donkeys and ponies (X.25-28), and are drawn paler than the hide in dilute glaze. The ears are pricked up in a natural, urgent way; the whole pose and attitude reflect the informed alarm of the wall painting.

The sherd is useful for emphasizing the differences between wall painting and vase painting, too. The attitude of the alarmed animal is older in pictorial painting than the Tiryns fresco and was superbly handled on the Maroni Goat Krater (III.26). Even when one senses the influence of fresco, the vase painter clearly handles his subject in his own way, making a more isolated and patterned scene; there is none of the overlapping of bodies, which the wall painter can manage through patches of color, none of the anguish of deer scraping their heads along the ground or

trampling each other in fright. The combination of ornamental and expressive elements is further developed in III C in formally beautiful studies.

45. Another Tiryns krater is already on the III C side of the Transitional borderline. A frieze of bottle-nosed stags (one and a half) marches right; the faces are parodies of the tubular snout of Ripe Cypriote and Greek stags, the whole animal bulbous, crude, and disjointed but not without weak-legged charm. The curves of brushwork are clear on the haunch of the leading stag; the artist is not incompetent. The new III C style is evident in the abrupt changes of body pattern, bars on the neck, arcs and chevrons at the shoulder, a patch of chevron pattern at the groin, a solid dark haunch and pale legs. This bulbous-faced stag is quite like the neater hunted stag of Mycenae (XI.77.1), a contemporary vase, although it is treated later with the other hunts, and both are contemporary with the delicate stags X.44 and XI.76. These illustrate the poles of pictorial in relation to the palace frescoes.

47. At Mycenae, a stag with branching horns on a deep bowl is a charming small study of an alert, short-legged animal like a dog. The fabric is the finest. The animal occupies the full height of the frieze, with generous space around it. The nose is square, the head short and thick, the body lean and rectangular; the outline contours are firm, and the interior diversified with bars on the muzzle, a three-stripe collar at the neck, a spotted body, and barred haunches. The front right shoulder is drawn on over the body as though it were a separate attachment in clay, as happens in the Pastoral style. The antlers are ornamented with leaf patterns slanting diagonally inward. The animal retains some of the alertness of hunted or sentinel deer in wall painting, though motionless.

48. A handsome paneled krater recalls the paneled kraters from Enkomi, though the stag is a pure mainland image. He faces left toward the broad checkerboard-and-loop divider, magnificently disproportioned, partly rearing, as though skidding to an unexpected halt with braced front feet. The Ripe forms are gone; the new bottle-nosed and variegated animal is less mobile, more broadly decorative. The muzzle is an elongated sack with a small nostril hole, the little round eye serves as a base for the symmetrical antlers, branched as a tree is branched, scraping the framing band. The body is covered with graduated ornament, dense dots on the neck and spaced open circles on the flanks. There is neither muscularity nor sufficient air. It is surprising to see a seashell filler under the belly; the motif was never popular on the mainland and not in general use since the fourteenth century.

22. Rodenwaldt, *Tiryns* II, pl. XI, nos. 1, 10; Lang, *Pylos* II, pls. 131, 136.

Two further fragments complete the group; both are early III C. A stag (X.50) from an unknown place in the Argolid (which may be Tiryns) is part of the usual frieze marching right; he preserves the slender bottle nose and the strongly branched antlers of the tradition, but the weakly drawn body has been opened up and divided into segments by blocks of vertical ripples, and the crown of the head is adorned with jutting hairs, like the fringes beloved by III C pattern makers. A sherd from Amarynthos in Euboia (X.51) with the dark chest and striped legs of a stag is interesting for the distribution of this style in Greece and for the handsome rosette in the field, dark with double reserved contours.

For other stags that are partly of this period but involved in hunting scenes, see XI.70 and following.

GOATS

52. A goat sherd from Mycenae may belong with the fine rump of a horse (X.23), or at least come from the same workshop, judging by the decorative zigzag border and the use of concentric arcs as filling on the leg. It is best restored as one of a pair of goats standing at a tree to eat. There is a faint possibility that another fragment (X.55) with a goat's head and a similar decorative band may come from the same workshop although not the same vase. Paneled compositions are becoming more frequent, as at the end of the Ripe period in Cyprus. What is odd about these three fragments is the way the paneling device curves or slants, as though forming an arbor around the figures. The goat is painted dark with dilute modeling streaks, and the pale face of the inner leg is filled with good close arcs, repeated at the base of the tree or mountain on which he climbs; the pointed, rather thick hind feet are below the ground line; the tail is curled up behind the back in an outline loop. There is the trace of a horn or a circle filler over the back. The antithetic goat composition was noted above in the Ripe period (IX.74) and continues in III C, although with a panel substituted for the central tree (XI.84). The fragment is of high quality.

There are two more interesting goats from Mycenae; by the handle of a bell krater (X.53) a goat surges left with lifted head, and color contrast is clear in the reserved face, thigh, and scut set against the dark body; the eye is the new diamond shape that appeared in the Tiryns chariot group (X.9). The ears are pricked forward, perhaps to suggest the role of sentry goat in a hunting scene; the striped horns bend back at a sharp angle, and again the body is modeled with streaked highlights. A curious unicorn goat

or antelope (X.54), dark with a large round blank eye, is finely drawn in smooth abstract curves. The muzzle is square, the brow and crown rounded with two drooping forelocks and two neat curved ears, framing a single, spirally twisted horn growing upright from the back of the head. It looks like a true *strepsikeros*, an oryx or addax horn, perhaps a souvenir from North Africa. The animal rocks along on broadly curved legs in a stiffened flying gallop. The tail is exceptionally thick, like a kangaroo's, arching up in a strong curve for symmetry. Other goat fragments from Mycenae are remarkable chiefly for the practice of painting "ingrown hairs" along the contours of reserved areas (X.55, 56), a trait in a surprising number of animal representations in the Pylos frescoes and harmonizing with the interest of III C painters in fringed borders. Another fragment is not very different in style from normal Ripe goats, with violently curved horns and alert loop ears (X.57), but was found in a stratigraphically Transitional position with Late chariot fragments.

BIRDS

There are many trends in drawing birds at the end of the thirteenth century, and dating by style is a little uncertain. In general, the principal forms of composition are the traditional processional frieze to the right, the newer paneled scenes, and a few experiments at showing tangled flight. The standard spotted interior filling of the Ripe phase has given way to triangles, hatching, streaks, and bars, with some solid dark bodies. In full III C, by contrast, most birds are light colored and filled with concentric arcs or other typically twelfth-century ornaments, or their bodies are formed of spirals, or their heads are attached to spirals and triangles as abstract designs. There are clear III C groups of birds in the Argolid, Attica, and Euboia, as well as the birds that fill spaces on III C octopus stirrup jars. These can be differentiated from the birds grouped here, some of which are Transitional in their stratigraphic context.

TIRYNS

59. Schliemann's fine goose krater, published along with the stag sherd (X.44) and certainly contemporary with it, has been supplemented by two new big fragments. The frieze is narrow, the procession stately on a blank ground, the geese following closely, so that one's tail is under the next's bill. The simple filling of inward-pointing dark triangles and the barred tails are a relief both from the monotonous spots of the Ripe phase and the dense ornaments of Late. The designer has set the legs directly under the breastbone, but the birds are dignified enough to keep their balance. A more disintegrated bird (X.61) is filled with irregular spots and a jagged inner contour like the ingrown hair on goats; it is stratified on the border of III B and III C. Disintegration is even more apparent on a set of at least fourteen krater fragments (X.62) from the water channels, on which a series of low-squatting, dark quail-like birds are hissing with open beaks; the spots have been displaced to the outside of the body, for which they form a broken contour line and flow like feathers between two stripes of trailing wing. The staccato rhythm of the spots lends the scene a clumsy atmosphere of outrage and disturbance.[23]

63. The most decorative of these late III B pieces is the fragment from Sir John Beazley's collection in the Ashmolean: a dark-bodied "flamingo" under the handle of a krater, perhaps in one of the last of the bull scenes. The long neck is striped in groups of bars, a late feature, and the round head and hooked bill are matched on Transitional birds at Mycenae.

MYCENAE

Mycenae has produced a number of single bird sherds from the end of the thirteeth century, almost all simple and schematic. A new feature is the bird enclosed in a paneling frame, often bordered by filled loops or concentric arcs. Some of the birds are crosshatched (X.67), some dark with barred necks (X.66) or filled with loose ripples or spirals; the beaks are often hooked. One dark duck on a bowl (X.68) has bars inside his bill, as though he had teeth or were swallowing grain; this might be the reflex of a painter who draws goats or fish with fangs. The coming abstraction of III C is present in a fragment from the Citadel House (X.71), on which a duck's head with upturned bill seems to be set as a protome on a crosshatched triangle; the trick is typically III C, but the excavation context seems to require a Transitional date.

74. Two fragments of a large krater with flying birds exhibit a fondness for dividing the surface of the vase into curved segments formed by wavy lines inside stripes, the kind of arched frame noted on the horse and goat sherds (X.23, 52, 55). This is much cruder, in a bold way, and is probably over the border into III C. The sectors of the field seem to form rounded triangles, with circular ornaments like flower spirals containing "blossoms" of a filled triangle bordered by dots. On the larger fragment two dark birds fly right, each in a separate compartment, one close to the ground line on the left, one awkwardly dangling its legs in the air on the right, perhaps feeding on a flower. The lower

bird has ears and a fringe of bars on its neck and back like a horse. A reserved oval panel may be set in its side, as often in III C. On the smaller piece a bird goes left near the ground line, tucking his feet up, fringed along his humped back.

ATHENS

Athens is the only place outside the Argolid with any concentration of pictorial fragments at the end of the thirteenth century; these are mostly scraps of birds and fish. The new paneled style is suddenly popular here too (X.77-79) and must be made locally, to judge from the rough style and the fabric, which is generally coarser than in the Argolid. A water bird (X.77), a flamingo type, filled with wavy lines in the Ripe style, walks toward a ragged checkerboard panel filled with dotted circles and fringed with loops; a rippled bird (X.78) with a fringed fantail has a wing like a long, fringed fish fin curved below the body. From the Fountain on the Acropolis comes quite a fine duck's head (X.80) on a closed shape, which is increasingly rare; two little dark birds (X.81) with open loop bodies rollick right in a pursuit pattern.

82. The only complete vase of this period is an intact krater of unknown provenance with vertical strap handles. It is likely to be a mainland rather than a Levantine vase and might come from the site that has produced other intact kraters of the later thirteenth and early twelfth centuries, one of the Mycenaean cemeteries on Salamis in the Saronic Gulf.[24] The vase has rather squat proportions and a biconical profile; the pictorial frieze is narrow, as on many Ripe vases. Three birds fly right as well as they can without wings; they are at least lifted off the ground line, with the end birds looking back and the center one tilted down in a dispirited plunge. The fillings are all different: wavy lines at the left, concentric triangles and spots in the center, overlapping scales of double arcs filled with spots on the right. It is a handsome decorative piece, really the end of the Ripe tradition of controlled ornamental friezes.

FISH

Fish designs follow the same general principles of development as birds and often share the same filling ornaments,

---

23. Miss Benton remarked of these fragments, "In archaic art, birds with dots are having a family quarrel. Could this be a ruff or reeve?"

24. A series of pictorial kraters was rumored to come from Salamis in the late 1950s; see IX.47, X.82, 102; a small jug with a weak bird on the shoulder, of this general phase, was sold at Sotheby's in London on March 27, 1972.

although it is more natural for a fish to have the lateral wavy lines along his sides that are traditional in marine scenes. This suggests that the fish is usually drawn as though in water, gliding through ripples, rather than in the kitchen, for he is almost never equipped with scales or bones. As with birds, the Mycenaean artist tends to blend species or at least is not concerned to distinguish them; most fish are simply long and lean, with a pair of arcs at the gill area to set off the face from the body, an irregular number of sharp and usually symmetrical ventral and dorsal fins, and an open mouth. There are some rounder, slower fish and one or two attempts to revive the dolphin type so expertly rendered in earlier Minoan and Mycenaean art. Most fish swim to the right, some are set in paneled scenes like birds, or, when set in friezes, seem to chase each other around the circumference.

MYCENAE

Mycenae shows the general, narrow range of such pictures. A fragment of a small rounded vase (X.83) was discovered by Tsountas in the same tomb as the fragment of the warrior with helmet and shield (X.29). The fish's contours are bordered by dark semicircles outlined in arcs, and the center is filled with undulating lines, standard elements of design well organized to give the impression of the body stripes and clusters of denser color seen on a fish sliding through shallow water. Like all late fish pictures, it is quick and schematic, and none of these fragments differs markedly in concept from contemporary fish on Minoan coffins. The rim of a banded bowl (X.85) has two fish in pursuit, with two different kinds of stripes, more decorative than predatory; a similarly open-mouthed fish (X.87) swims gaping toward a panel.

Sometimes a predator swims after a school of an apparently different species, as on the shoulder of a fine jar (X.86), where the pursuer has a squared tail and the fish in front have longer-fringed, more delicate tails. One krater fragment (X.88) shows a heavier fish surfacing toward the rim and set in a field of scale pattern, like bubbles in water. The whole vase would have had a series of such diagonal rising bodies. The usually blank ground is filled to suggest the rippling surface broken by a school rising to feed. One cruder fragment of a bowl (X.95) is clearly in the III C style, included here because the Argolid has no separable III C stylistic groups.[25] The scene is inside the bowl as so often in Cyprus; a broad, diagonally striped fish is upside down at the rim, right side up for the person drinking. There are fringed concentric semicircles in the water, like seaweed-covered rocks, and a crude streamer perhaps suggesting seaweed; the impression is of a late revival of a

total Marine Style seascape. The bowl is banded, and striped patterns toward the center may represent rocks or shells.

Fish are even rarer at other sites in this period, and it is not easy to tell how they should be classified. One Athens example and one or two of the Tiryns fragments seem to be mature III C.

ARGOS

96. Argos is not a big pictorial center, which is surprising in view of its proximity to Tiryns. A dump produced a fragment of a large paneled krater showing a big fish, like a dolphin in type, swimming left toward the panel divider, which is made of vertical stripes with loop borders. The fish is dark with reserved contours, a feature characteristic of III C in the Dodekanese that also occurs in the later thirteenth century on Cretan larnakes. The snout is turned up and reserved, with a fringe of slanting teeth inside the lower jaw; again the predator equipment and the arched leaping body are schematically decorative, since there is no space for an opponent. One assumes there was a facing fish on the other side of the panel.

ATHENS

Athens, like Argos, is not a productive source of pictorial sherds, but there are enough in all periods to assure us that the Argolid styles were known in both town and countryside and that some were imported, some made locally, none at the highest level but almost all competent. Of the four fish scenes known in this period (and X.99 is full III C), two are only scraps of kraters dropped in the Fountain on the Acropolis; the other two are the rarer *lekane-kalathos* shape, which is slightly more common as a bearer of pictorial in the Dodekanese. Trade east through the islands is natural enough at this time, although the evidence for it is more obvious at Perati on the coast than in Athens itself.

99. One of the lekanai is in the early twelfth-century technique of light-on-dark painting, a matt cream design on a dark grey to black ground. White-on-black pictorial is extremely rare on the mainland, usually limited to full III C, but there is a fish from Tiryns in the same technique. The rim of the lekane is ornamented with concentric arcs, and the preserved fish inside the rim has heavy white contours and fine gill arcs, with a delicate wavy line filler set

---

25. An "inaccessible" sherd with a fish (from Mycenae?) was published from J. F. Daniel's photograph by J. L. Benson, *AJA* 72 (1968) pl. 67, fig. 17; the reserved contours and fangs are probably LH III C elements.

obliquely across the body; the varying strengths of the lines seem the work of a well-trained painter.

100. The second lekane, from the Agora, is far cruder, almost a parody. It was the latest vase in its tomb, on the border around 1200. Three fish, or two fish and a water bird, roughly rendered, swim around the top of the inside of the flaring rim as on the last, so that the lower body of the vase holds a pool of liquid beneath them. The two rough outlines that are clearly fish are blowing bubbles, a feature not seen since the Maroni fish krater early in the fourteenth century (III.9). The third creature may have started as a fish, as on the last, and through an accident of paint, coming too close to the tail in front, have been converted into a long-necked water bird, with extra lines added to frame the body and serve as wings. The finest example of such mixed designs is the bowl from Kalymnos in the Dodekanese (XII.22).

SALAMIS

Perhaps one should consider the meager pictorial pieces found in late-thirteenth and early-twelfth-century tombs on the island of Salamis along with the Attic group, but there are so far no connections of style and not enough pieces to allow forming a clear opinion of Salaminian work. Some of it is obviously provincial, but if the big kraters rumored to have come from there are in fact local, some of it is extremely good. One small cup (X.101) with concave sides and a raised base was properly excavated; it has a crude fish (not a cruder ship?) at the waist. A late worn krater (X.102) is said to have come from the island. The illustrated side has three heavy-bodied fish swimming right in a standard frieze composition, a clumsier version of the bird krater, X.82, which may have the same source. The fish have thick arched backs and nearly flat bellies, a triple "girdle" at the waist, the bodies filled with normal wavy lines and spots. A triangular fin is painted directly against the body surface instead of outside the contour, a rare device, but understandable in a period when triangular filling ornaments were so popular. There are also wispy striped fins above and below. Despite dullness and uncertain provenance, it is possible to infer that Salaminian painters were interested in pictorial themes at a time when many Mycenaean communities were not.

TANAGRA

103. A ring vase with an arched basket handle and a spout, from the Tanagra cemetery that produced the painted larnakes, is the only mainland vase of this shape with a pictorial theme so far, although a similar piece bears whorl shells. The original design sets a row of dark-bodied fish swimming left around the top of the ring, a row of light striped fish swimming right below them, and two more dark fish swimming along the curving handle away from the spout. Since ring vases are meant for circularly swirling liquid, the design is a happy one. Two species are evidently intended, more for decorative contrast than for observation of sea life. Both dark and light fish have the same long bodies, squared tails, and fringe fins. The light-stripers, however, have long sharp beaks, while the heads of the dark ones are mostly eye cavity (two fish part their mouths slightly) fringed all around with internal fangs. See X.96.

TIRYNS

Tiryns has a few rather ordinary fragments, one piece from each of about ten or twelve vases in a variety of shapes. The most interesting fish (X.105, 106) are, like the Argos vase (X.96), dark with a broad reserved contour and a streak of light along the bodies, as in the Dodekanese and Crete. These have more life than most fish designs of the period because they are set at oblique swooping angles as in fresco or on Cretan larnakes, with simple massive forms. The reserved outline makes the mouth more effectively open, providing musculature for contracting lips, and the eye seems brighter and more focused in a dark body. Another all-dark fish (X.108) is rootling along the ground line with massive head bowed down; the handsome open trefoil rosette seems like another revival of the seaweed forms of the Marine Style. Two well-drawn, rather flat fish (X.112) with delicate rippled interior filling behind a striped gill crest are set under the same kind of bowed arc filled with zigzag as on the superior horse and goat sherds from Mycenae (X.23, 52). A fish inside a lekane(?) (X.113) is painted in the white-on-black technique seen at Athens (X.99). The bottom inside of a cup fragment (X.115) has a dark fish and a crosshatched fish swirling in a circle, like the Cypriote examples or the slightly earlier cup from Achaia (IX.120); this must have been a handsome design.

It is clear that a number of these late fish scenes are painted in the early part of III C, but they are in a variety of styles that hark back to the Ripe tradition of body filling and general organization; they do not display the novelty of invention that is more surely the contribution of the twelfth century.

XI
THE GREEK MAINLAND:
Late Pictorial

PICTORIAL PAINTING IN THE TWELFTH CENTURY is a fascinating field for exploration. Many of the star pieces have been known for generations, but neglected, because they seemed difficult to interpret when the pictorial tradition was not well understood. The various attempts in the twentieth century to treat the Warrior Vase from Mycenae as a seventh-century example of Orientalizing painting illustrate how little attention has been paid to available material.[1] Painting in the pure LH III C period has more definition and interest, in the active artistic centers, than some preceding pictorial work. The quality is often very fine and is accompanied by a new high level of technique in both potting and glazing. The Warrior Vase is in some ways a touchstone for this admirable level of twelfth-century painting, even though it is not the best vase; many fragments are superior to it in line and conception, but it is the only major piece to preserve the relations between composition and form. There is a new richness of repertory and ornament in the Late period, even apart from octopus stirrup jars, with which we are not primarily concerned. The groups of soldiers that go with the Warrior Vase are only a small segment of the surviving material; hunting themes, birds, and fish are also wonderful.

It has often been said that the homogeneity of Mycenaean pottery dissolved after the destructions on the Greek mainland at the end of the thirteenth century, that with a loss of central control or fashion many more individual local schools began to flourish. This belief is true to the extent that one finds few exact connections among shapes, fabrics, and ornaments at different III C sites and that there are distinct styles, easily recognized, in distinct geographic areas like the Argolid, Achaia, Euboia, the Cyclades, Crete, the Dodekanese, Cyprus, Asia Minor, and Ugarit. On the other hand, we are not faced with a wild spectrum of local potters doing local experiments independently of the tradition. The twelfth-century centers that flourish continue to exhibit general cross-links in their art, as they did in the Palace age, so that the label "III C" means something vivid as a general term, in spite of local variations. In the realm of pictorial painting these links are surprisingly strong. Even at sites where the stratigraphy is not clearly published, one is immediately confident of the date when looking at a III C piece, whether at Ugarit or Sinda or Leukandi or Asine. This unity of idea and execution in the twelfth century is worth historical reflection.

The most conspicuous features of the new III C style on the mainland are: increased fondness for diversity and counterpoint in handling surfaces, a rather arbitrary modulation of ornamental textures or color contrasts, a light curvilinear elegance of scrollwork and filling (especially in the Close Style). Polychrome painting and the "black-and-white" style are related expressions of this surface enrichment. Changes in composition take several forms. Some reflect real historical and social changes, like the dwindling popularity of the stately chariot procession,

---

1. The instinctive aesthetic feeling of connection between Late Mycenaean painting and the seventh century was fully discussed by G. Becatti, *Studi in Onore di Luisa Banti* (1965) 33 f.; see also W. Schuchhardt, *Opus Nobile, Festschrift U. Jantzen* (1969) 155. Doubts that the best-known piece, the Warrior Vase (XI.42), could be Mycenaean were expressed early: F. Dümmler, *AthMitt* 13 (1888) 288; cf. E. Pottier, *BCH* 31 (1907) 247. See note 18 below.

the increased illustration of foot soldiers, and particular changes in dress and armor. In other cases the hallmark is fantasy, whether in the combination of sea and land worlds on the finer octopus stirrup jars, or the new kinds of animals in the repertory, from scorpions to griffins, or the way pictorial elements are hooked onto ornamental patterns. It is an imaginative period on the whole, and one in which many vases seem to reflect new confidence among the painters. Perhaps there was a consciousness that such artists were now the principal guardians of the pictorial tradition, since there was no more demand for the talents of fresco painters, and the workshops in ivory, gold, blue glass-paste, and metal vessels had generally faded away. The older tradition is not in any way oppressive, however, but is freely and creatively turned in new directions, toward recording daily life, expressing emotion or humor, and establishing a quasi-mythical iconography, with a continuing insistence on clarity in detail.

Mycenae and Tiryns continue as the major centers of painting. Athens is active but on a poor level. Leukandi and Naxos are strong competitors on the east coast and among the islands. Perati, in eastern Attica, never developed a strong pictorial tradition, except that it shares with many other III C centers a fondness for richly controlled octopus stirrup jars with inserted birds and fish, a common type. In the East the painters of Kos are distinguished, eclipsing the earlier, rather imitative compositions of Rhodes (Chapter XII). Crete is rich in pictorial images, although its best productions still are largely within the bounds of the thirteenth century. In Cyprus there is a clear distinction between the Pastoral style of the late thirteenth century and the III C style, which is almost indistinguishable from Greek mainland styles and reflects the arrival of the new "Achaian" settlers.[2] Asia Minor and the Levant share this invigoration in pictorial painting and other spheres (Chapter XIII).

The problems of both relative and absolute chronology were alluded to at the beginning of Chapter X. Where stratification is partly clear, the middle III C levels are the most productive. If they are called III C:2 (III C:1b) one should remember that this is not the same label as the conventional III C:2, which used to mean "sub-Mycenaean"; it is rather the most prosperous economic and artistic phase of the twelfth century, preceded by difficult beginnings and followed by greater poverty. An increasing number of sites are showing three principal levels of III C, including Mycenae and Leukandi, and, as one might expect, it is the central cluster of levels, the stable phase between foundation and disappearance, that most encourages pictorial painting as well as other types of creativity.

CHARIOTS

On the whole, chariot scenes are less fine than they were in earlier periods, perhaps because the theme is overworked, perhaps because, with the expense of horses, chariots were no longer so widely used. There are innovations in the type of carriage (see X.9), and a new attention to the way the human body is affected by chariot-driving techniques. Many scenes are summary. A few are beyond the pale. Mycenae and Tiryns continue to be the most productive sites in this sphere.

MYCENAE

1. Two krater fragments, divided between the museums in Athens and Nauplion, do not join and may come from opposite sides of the vase. The scale is small enough in relation to the vase surface, however, to permit two complete chariots on each side, a reduced and silhouetted scene that seems more active than the standard earlier processional. One fragment shows the bodies of two soldiers inside the chariot, the other has the heads and bodies of two soldiers in the chariot followed by a horse.

The chariots are the new open-carriage type with a curved rail at waist height. Each vehicle carries a driver and a spearman, with implications of war rather than ceremony. This suits the twelfth-century interest in scenes of action. Both the charioteer and the fighter carry round shields, rather small; Mrs. Littauer has wondered whether, on gusty days, such a pair of shields might offer so much wind resistance that the light vehicle could turn over; the "Dipylon" shield, with its narrow waist, of comparable Geometric chariot scenes might be an inventive improvement. The chariot, in contrast to most earlier scenes, is moving fast as though to the battlefield. Several chariots of this period are drawn as though moving at top speed; earlier, galloping horses were the exception (IV.15). The drivers hold the reins high, as in the Transitional group (X.1 and following), and the spearman holds his weapon at the diagonal over his right shoulder. The men's knees are bent in response to the swaying of the vehicle.

The solid silhouette of the figures, with a large oval reserved eye and a head rayed with spikes, gives a rather

---

2. The problem is discussed extensively by H. Catling, V. Desborough, S. Hood, and F. Maier in *The Mycenaeans in the Eastern Mediterranean* (1973); see also P. Dikaios, *Enkomi* (1969-71) II, 527 f., 907 f. (Palaikastro-Maa); Schaeffer, *Alasia* I (1971) 505; E. Gjerstad, *OpArc* 3 (1944) 73; A. Furumark, ibid., 194 f.; V. Desborough, *The Last Mycenaeans and Their Successors* (1964) 196 f.

Geometric appearance. Apparently the soldiers wear the "hedgehog" helmet, which has been known since the thirteenth century (IX.8) and becomes more common in the twelfth.[3] A nose guard or cheekpiece is suggested by the hair under the nose, like an escaping beard. The tunics are short, flaring out at mid-thigh. There are no strong contours, and the rather slapdash brushwork with dilute tones adds to the sense of curves and elasticity in the bending knees and wind-blown fringes on the tunics. The horse, which follows the leading chariot closely, presumably pulling a second chariot, has a reserved eye, outlined ears, and a mane rendered in single curved hairs, as on the Tiryns chariot krater, XI.14. There is always a "single" horse in this period, but one must assume that a regular team is meant as before; there seem to be two reins.

2. Two fragments of a krater, with a pair of chariots in swift motion to the right, are painted in a purer III C style. There is a strong contrast of light and dark, and the horse's rump is filled with typical solid and concentric arcs. On each piece there survive the hind legs and tail of the horse, part of the chariot rail and the knees of the driver. The angle and push of one pair of hind legs suggest rapid careering. As on the last krater, one may imagine two chariots on either side of the vase. They are not drawn exactly in the same way, for on one sherd the open rail curves up in a high outward arc at least to the waist of the driver, and on the other it bends left and down at an angle between his thigh and knee. Since these chariot parts are simple stripes, it is easy for the painter to make a careless pattern of them without observing the realities. Part of the wheel is preserved on one fragment; it must be sunk through the lower framing bands, since it is lower than the hocks of the horses, and on the other piece it must be on a level with their hooves, as though they rose in the air. The drivers seem to stand on the axle between the wheels, again a minimal-frame chariot, with little to protect the men or help them balance. Their knees are again bent, in silhouette, perhaps clad in greaves lightened by reserved bars below the kneecap. The filling ornament on the horse's hide, outlined fetlock, and thin separated strands of tail hair underline the III C painter's interest in surface variety.

3. A krater fragment with a driver(?) or groom(?) to the left is puzzling to interpret. The man himself is clear, wearing a dark belted tunic to the buttocks, with bare thighs and dark greaves lightened by a reserved slash below the kneecap. His arms are apparently lifted, causing the shoulders to bulge, as at Leukandi (XI.39). Behind the shoulder two faint semicircular lines may represent the rim of a small round shield, perhaps worn on a telamon to leave the hands free for driving. In front of the bony knees, a curved line may be the chariot rail, rising excessively

high as on one fragment of XI.2; it seems less likely to be the tail of a horse. Behind the figure three sets of barred arched lines with outline loops (ears?) and a diagonal above may be the remains of a handle ornament; it does not suit known versions of horses' heads or chariot wheels (but see XI.7). Perhaps this is a chariot into which the soldier is backing a horse; the line in front of the man would then be a hanging rein. The "black-and-white" style is well handled and recalls similar pieces from Tiryns, Leukandi, and Naxos (XI.18, 59, 63).

4. The rim fragment of a small krater or bowl from the III C levels at Mycenae has a poor design of a driver, right, clutching a bunch of reins over a horse's back; below his fist the reins fall into an elaborate triangle, partly doing duty for the horse's tail. Everything is in unrelieved dark silhouette; the driver's head is a blob with a pointed nose, his torso sways backward, and his right arm is flung out behind him (did it hold a goad or whip?) while the left arm is lifted to drive. The poor blobby style appears at both Mycenae and Athens in this phase.

5. The rim fragment of a bowl from the same levels preserves the outlined face of a driver(?) right, with a deep chin and a near-smile, arm stretched out before him to grip a diagonal line equipped with two bent cross-hooks like a goad, the *kentron*. There is no certainty that this is a chariot extract, yet it agrees with a few other Late compositions.

6. The rim fragment of a bowl has a more bizarre chariot design best matched in Athens (XI.32, 33). Technically it is a fine piece; only the painting fails. The drawing is in outline, with an open-rail chariot moving right, holding one man, a ghostlike creature whose head is set off from the body but barely defined as human, a simple loop above the torso. His right arm is drawn back as on XI.4, and his left arm, a wavy line, is bent forward to drive. The chariot has a waist-high rail curving up and back, a striped floor, and part of the wheel rim, a tall wheel for once. The man holds a T-shape upside down in his rear arm, again perhaps a whip or goad rather than a weapon. Behind him are apparently the heads of a team with ruffled manes drawing the following chariot; this looks like a blasted tree. The bowl is one of a class of drinking vessels that reduce war scenes to a small scale, in this case rendered without finesse.

---

3. The conventional rendering called the "hedgehog" helmet is probably two halves of a leather or metal cap clapped together to hold a bristle crest along the top seam; see the discussion in J. Borchhardt, *Homerische Helme* (1972) 39; Lorimer, *HM*, 228 f.; D. Gray, *JHS* 74 (1954) 6; H. Hencken, *The Earliest European Helmets* (1972) 8; the term "hedgehog" is used throughout this chapter in quotation marks. The fragments IX.8 may be the earliest appearance of the type.

The following fragments illustrate the same sphere of horse skills but do not include chariots (except XI.10), either because of the way they are broken or because they focus on the horse being led by his groom to the chariot or simply tended; there are a few isolated horses.

7. A famous polychrome krater fragment shows an elongated horse with his attendant soldier behind him. The technique is good, and the applied orange color is an interesting new development in the twelfth century. The sherd comes from a very thick krater that must have had space for a many-figured composition, perhaps reflecting the same activities as in the chariot-harnessing fresco in the megaron at Mycenae.

At the extreme right a vertical striped pattern may be part of the chariot into which the horse is being backed for yoking (cf. XI.3). The attendant groom, clearly a soldier, has the horse by two reins and is applying pressure to back him into position. The soldier's costume is the typical short tunic reaching to just below the hips, striped across the shoulders, and dark greaves with reserved stripes at the knees. This man has an impressive nose and a beard, and his long neck bulges in the back, another III C characteristic. Two spikes at the back of the neck suggest he is wearing a "hedgehog" helmet. The new fashion for beards is equally handsomely recorded on the Warrior Vase, to which this fragment has been connected stylistically, not the same hand but a shared atmosphere.[4]

The horse is a long thin tube on feebly bending legs, wonderfully divided into sections. The neck is outlined and filled with zigzag, and the outlined mane plumes are prominent. The body is in six parts with emphatic changes of surface pattern: arcs at the shoulder, a vertical zigzag, an orange-yellow "saddle" area, three vertical zigzag bands, then the rump and left rear leg in applied brown-yellow, while the inner face of the other leg is covered with arcs and stripes. The tail starts high on the back (cf. XI.3) and falls in thin wisps from a long stump. Considering the decorative imagination, the soldier's lively stride, and the attempt to show a difficult operation in this medium, no one cares if the horse's legs are far too short; he is not the first to suffer so.

8. A fragment of a large-sized krater shows a groom-soldier with a staff leading a horse to the right. These studies of grooms and horses began in the thirteenth century (IX.1) and seem always military. The late date of this fragment is assured by its contrasts of dark and light, the arbitrary filling ornament, the man's diamond eye (see X.10, 53). The horse has the weakness of outline often observed in this group, but the man is strongly contoured and dramatic.

The horse is led by a nose strap and a lead line (see

Appendix). The muzzle is crossed with stripes, which may represent the strap- or basket-muzzle sometimes worn by stallions in archaic painting, a device to prevent their biting (Mrs. Littauer). The eye is two large circles, the neck is patterned with weak wavy lines, the pricked-back ears project into the frame. The groom carries a staff or goad, not a spear, but he is not the old *rhabdophoros* type; his helmet is plumed, and the dark neck under the outlined face may represent a protective collar, as on some Tiryns fragments. The triangular torso has strong dark contours and a light interior. The eye is a latticed diamond below curls escaping from the helmet band. Again a fine piece technically, it may be another extract from a chariot-harnessing scene.

9. A horse with a hanging rein is a weaker version of the last horse on a paneled(?) krater of fine quality. There are the same loose outlines and insistent fillers. The long muzzle has a triple outline within which the dispirited oval eye is set at a slant; the neck is filled with concentric arcs and curves. The ears may have been painted solid for color contrast. Two lines drooping from the face may be the reins, without a human grip on them. Above the horse's neck to the right, a spray of spikes may belong to a "hedgehog" helmet of the attendant soldier, who would have to be walking on the far side of the horse, as on XI.7. At the left two vertical stripes are bordered by short-stemmed circles, part of a tree or paneling frame.

10. An ornamental horse, left, on a large fragment of a krater is apparently still attached to the chariot, to judge by the two rows of hook-spirals over his back, which have usurped the place of reins. The long body is sectioned off as on XI.7, but less elaborately: crosshatched center part, dark rump and legs. Under the belly a suspended chevron-and-shell filler forms a plant ornament in a revival of the Middle style, recrudescing in an age that enjoyed fillers generally; the spiral reins also flourished earlier. At the extreme right there may be a hand and the chest front of a driver.

12. A charming bowl fragment essays the impossible, a facing horse. Even the far more skilled archaic black-figure vase painters were to discover how difficult this view is. The horse seems caught in a moment of turning, perhaps as he backs into the chariot, for the neck is twisted as though the body extended to the left. The head is lop-sided, with a reserved broad brow fringed by mane hairs, two bulging dot-circle eyes, and a full square muzzle with a splaying dark V-shape upside down to suggest spreading (slit?) nostrils and a triangular blaze on the nose. Some

---

4. G. Rodenwaldt, *Fries des Megarons von Mykenai* (1921) 65, n. 72; J. L. Benson, *AJA* 65 (1961) 346.

bulls' heads in clay spread out at the muzzle this way, but the animal seems equine. Color partitioning sets the head off well against the dark neck and chest with their hair fringes and gives the lugubrious expression a sympathetic emphasis. The study seems to be framed by large multiple arcs pressing on the animal's cheeks, probably not a bird's-eye view of the reins.

13. The only fairly complete horse vase of this period from Mycenae is a handsome collared jar from the rich area around the Citadel House, one of the finest examples of the Late pictorial style, with a scene of horses and birds. The shape is rarer on the mainland than in the Dodekanese but persists at various mainland centers until the end of sub-Mycenaean. Here the drawing is authoritative, the spacing of the composition generous and stately, the details spirited. The lifted heads of the horses with sparse bristling manes are connected with the small horses on leading reins discussed in Chapter X (X.25-28).

The published side of the jar has two full-grown horses with a foal between them, all sniffing the wind to the right, with six birds above and below them. The horses are in dark silhouette with round reserved dotted eyes and flowing tails of separated strands. Four of the birds, in contrast, are light colored, outlined with typical III C fillers of stripes, stacked triangles, and zigzags, and accented blank body areas; the bodies of these pale birds are drawn out to give more space for filling, while two dark birds, above and below the horse on the left, have rounder, more collected bodies.

The suggestion of shared meadow life recalls the bull-and-bird vases of the Ripe phase (V. 44 and following) and is presented equally formally, with the light birds turning their necks back in heraldic stances while the dark birds stoop and plunge. Arranged tiers of animals are popular in III C, better known in designs that place young animals on their parents' backs (XI.83, 91), which also appeared in the Ripe phase. Each adult horse carries a light bird on its rump and encloses a bird between its legs; a huge bird apparently is trying to settle on the small foal's head, while another swoops down on its rump. One cannot tell if agrarian tales of vultures picking out foals' eyes influenced the design; these birds seem more at home in a marsh or water meadow. The horses are well articulated, with an emphatic separation of the hind leg profiles so that the far leg is drawn up under the belly in order not to overlap the near one. The hooves are picked up off the ground line, the forelegs bent in a static run. The noses are squared and raised, the manes rendered in straight, fine parallel fringes like the fringes on the birds' tails; the flowing tails are drawn in fine lines from a solid stump (see X.23). The jar does not necessarily carry funerary symbolism, as has been

maintained;[5] it may have traditional associations between predators and pasturers but is of particular interest for its sophistication and fine technique.

TIRYNS

Tiryns has an impressive series of late chariot and horse scenes, expanding with the recent excavations in the water channels and the lower town; more should be expected. There is a surprising variation in quality. The two big chariot kraters (XI.14, 15) may be earlier than full III C. The beginning of this group undoubtedly overlaps with the group of the Tiryns Shield Bearers (X.1 and following), and it is quite possible that the first bizarre example was painted in the thirteenth century. Yet the filling ornament, hard contrasting outlines, herringbone hair, and eye-drips make it consonant with the rest of the Late group. Some of the following fragments come from the water channels, some from the Epichosis (joins are possible between the two groups); new fragments from the lower town are not included.

14. The central portions of a large open krater preserve the team, chariot box and wheel, four passengers, and a groom in front of the team on one side, the chariot wheel, rail, and part of the horse on the other. The proportions and the details of the drawing are pathetically awkward, but there are quick firm brush strokes, and a certain self-confident bravado rescues the vase from the limbo of totally untalented productions. On the principal side the horse body is long and symmetrical fore and aft, like Geometric bronze horses. It has massive forequarters and rump, a thin tubular body, and legs bent at matching angles. The large space under the belly is filled with four crooked concentric arcs. The team's face is heavily contoured with a reserved interior, the oval eye is elongated by a dripping tear duct (see X.27), and a sharp line at the muzzle results from quickly slashing the reins across the muzzle; the lower lip droops down. The hair is neatly arranged in two forelocks, three abstract curling mane plumes, and a five-stroke mane. The double reins are ornamented with a row of pendent loops, as occasionally in earlier periods (IV.49). The chariot itself is a joke, in the manner of the first chariot krater from Mycenae (IX.2). The wheel is very high, apparently off the ground as on the reverse; a pole projects from it to support a double chariot box with double contours, the old-fashioned kind with solid sides. Out of the box emerge four little heads on necks made of stripes. Since he is more handless than

---

5. J. L. Benson, *AJA* 72 (1968) 207; *HBM*, 26 f.

usual, the driver is forced to hold the reins in his teeth (cf. XII.6). Under the driver, the edge of the box rests directly on the horse's rump; there is no practical or mechanical connection. The elimination of harness makes room for a good long horse tail with herringbone hair wisps at the end. The frontal groom "leading" the team holds nothing (there may be a round shield floating in the air in front of him); he has a minimal body, with broad shoulders seen *en face* and a crotch starting at the level of the armpits. His head is reserved with a tilted oval eye, and his thin arms hang down straight with splayed fingers (see X.41.1); he has a sharp knee, high on the right leg, low on the left, and swollen feet raised off the ground. The more damaged secondary side gives a good four-spoked wheel, the high side and projecting floor of the box, and a horse like a curved slug held up on toothpicks. The odd quality of this vase lies in its combination of boldness and formlessness, perhaps more expressionist than primitive.[6] However odd the painter, he seems to have impressed a customer in Tell Abu Hawam (V.25.8 u).

15. A more fragmentary krater by the same painter has several stylistic oddities in common with the last. There is ample room on each side of the vase for two chariot groups, as on the small kraters of this period from Mycenae (XI.1 and following). Through a miscalculation, however, the painter did not leave enough space for the second chariot, although he had already drawn the horse, so he has been forced to transfer the passengers out of the missing box onto the horse's back. This error is assisted by the excessive elongation of the horse's body. The human figures are the same bird-headed types with striped necks as before, but their bodies had to be adapted for "riding," so there is something more below the neck, not much. They clutch the reins that pass beside them. The horse is like the one on XI.14, with the same head, long tail with herringbone spray, and arcs filling the space below the belly, but he is longer-legged and less articulated. This equipage is followed by another team, and another splay-handed swollen-footed man hovers in the air between the two. This is a far more childish work than the last, and speed has betrayed the artist into thoughtlessness, not expressive of anything, except perhaps a lingering feeling for the splendor of chariots and a love of horses. It is also interesting for the suggestion that the painter worked from left to right but drew his horse before his chariot. That this miscalculation was habitual is demonstrated by a third piece (XI.15.1) by this artist, with better paint, with two men on the team's back. The suggestion has been made that these vases are not mistakes but represent the Tirynthian cavalry preceding the chariot forces.

16. The most magnificent of the Tiryns chariot kraters, from the water channels, shows the richness of the III C style at its best. It is a large thick piece, in several fragments (see XI.16.1). Again there are two chariots in procession, or even three, with a driver and a spearman who wears a round shield slung on a baldric. The chariot is a good illustration of the new low-slung open-bodied racing car with a high front rail, designed for mobility not defense. The two soldiers balance on the level of the axle and on a webbing of leather straps. The rail curves as high as their waists in front and then bends down to hip level, a streamlining detail. The driver seems to be unarmed, left arm bent forward and up, right arm gripping the rein (or rein and whip) just above the rail. The warrior behind him carries a round shield, possibly of dappled oxhide, and a long spear with a leaf-shaped point, resting diagonally, point up, over his right shoulder. Both men wear the short flared tunic that ends just below the hips; an embroidered or punched metal surface is suggested by ornaments of chevron pattern across the shoulders, concentric filled semicircles facing in at the waist (the war belt or *mitra?*), and zigzags and lateral stripes at the lower hems. The driver wears standard dark greaves with reserved stripes like ties above the knees. The warrior's legs are striped in clusters along their entire length, probably arbitrary patterning more than a rendering of long linen leggings.

The horses are in real motion in a fresh way, the hind leg swinging forward with the point of the hoof set in the ground, an outlined fetlock emphasizing the action. The front hooves of the following horses are also delicately raised and drawn back under the forequarters. Although the corresponding bend of the knees is a trifle clumsy, at least observation is at work in coordinating the moving parts of the body under muscular stress. The bent knees of the chariot riders, less awkward than on XI.1, also suggest the swaying motion induced by the pace. The patterning of the horses is in the most ornamental III C manner: a reserved face with filling of arcs and wavy lines on cheek and muzzle, two dots at the lips perhaps representing rein-rings, although the reins do not pass through; the body painted solid but broken open at the center for a belt insert of a pale pattern with wavy borders, filled with a wavy line on one; the rear leg dark on the outer face with pale fetlock, light on the inner face with collected groups of transverse stripes; the long dark tail set off by an added rippling contour line.

---

6. The frontal groom shares certain late features with frontal figures on the Tanagra larnakes because the canons are loosening, but this kind of representation remains rare and is used more often with robed figures than with nudes.

The other fragments show two dark feet braced on three curved leather thongs that seem to attach directly to the team's tails as before, with part of the vertical chariot rail; parts of two slender men, the driver in a dark tunic and the soldier behind in an embroidered or metallic one, both bending their knees behind the chariot rail; possibly the soldier wearing a bonnet, of XI.16.1, belongs here. He has the striped neck of other Tiryns figures and herringbone slashes across the shoulders of his tunic. The horse of XI.16.1 has a more consistent ripple pattern along his body, fine mane locks, and the kind of added shoulder, drawn over the body, that appeared earlier in Pastoral painting.

In some ways this krater is the most potent ancestor for Geometric chariot scenes, a brilliant Late version of a theme that began more than two centuries earlier. As a vignette of armed warriors on the way to action, it is a splendid twelfth-century document.

17. Two fragments of a paneled krater preserve only the part of the scene immediately to the right of the zigzag-filled panel on each side. In each a driver holds a bunch of reins very high; there is no soldier or passenger with him. This is an odd quirky style, the better driver drawn with a fringe of striped hair like a cock's comb, which may indicate a schematic "hedgehog" helmet, and with a striped "torque" neck like many Tiryns soldiers. The second driver is painted as though he were enveloped in a dark hooded cloak blowing back in the wind; the hood also has a striped crest and frames an enormous round eye, like a ghost's.

18. Parts of two warriors in an open-railed chariot, on a krater fragment said to come from Tiryns, are in the strong "black-and-white" style. This handsome sherd reflects the same composition as XI.1, 2, and 16, the battle pair equipped in short flaring cuirasses or tunics and greaves, riding right, the driver apparently unarmed, the warrior holding a pair of spears or javelins diagonally, blade up, over his shoulder. The chariot rail is outlined, pale, rising above the waist and curving down again to hip level. The warriors' legs are also left pale, even though the greaves are indicated by ties at the knees to contrast with the dark tunic shaped in two triangular sections with a reserved belt, as on the Warrior Vase (XI.42). The proportions are rational, close to fresco painting, with some of the stiffness of fresco and no patterned flourishes of ornament.

19. A fragment of a round bowl has a vivid representation of overlapping chariots speeding right. It is of fine quality and poor drawing, like other reductions of chariot scenes onto small surfaces (XI.2, 5, 6). It is interesting that the painter has set one chariot group higher in the field than the other, a fresco composition, so that the hind feet of the higher horse are stepping on the arm of the driver of the lower horse. Although this kind of field-scattering was used in thirteenth-century wall painting for hunts and battles, normally in vase painting the chariot seems weighty enough to demand a ground line. An exception, of course, is the "Egyptian" composition in the megaron at Mycenae, where the chariot may be seen speeding left over the palace roof (though the reconstruction has been doubted).[7] The impression given by this fragment is more like a perspective view of a race, perhaps at games, than a war or processional scene.

At the lower center, one man in an open-railed chariot tugs on the reins with his right hand and possibly uses the two-pronged goad, the *kentron*, with his left. He is the long-headed clumsy type seen also on XI.4, his eye a triangle slewed toward the front of the face, bald head reserved (with the mouth open?), body dark; he leans forward in a motion that suggests either whipping the horse or turning a post. The chariot rail arcs up to neck level; the upper rim of the wheel is at waist level. Three strands of the horse's tail curve back as though blown in the wind of his speed. Above this the dark hind legs of a horse with thick hooves impinge on the driver's arm; this horse pulls a chariot by the pole, his tail blowing against the thick rim of the wheel, but his legs at a standstill. The indication of the chariot pole is rare now.

20. An even worse scene occurs on the shoulder of a small collared jar. There is a reduced, clumsy team to the right, painted solidly in silhouette; the head is only a long shape like a deflating balloon. Two reins attach to the back of the head, ornamented below with a row of pendent drops. Another pair of reins runs obliquely from muzzle to withers. On foot in front of the equipage one sees three desperate soldiers(?) with open mouths, who are probably carrying spears at the diagonal. The man nearest the horse wears a striped hat or crest; the next has spikes of hair or bristles on his crown and a long double tress of hair rippling behind his neck in the old Minoan way; the third man is perhaps curly-haired. The drawing is so bad, one cannot make out details well, except for the open howling mouths as on some larnakes of this period. There seems to be good will on the painter's part, urging him to make an expressive little battle scene, but he is almost completely untrained.

21. One of the finest "black-and-white" fragments from Tiryns corrects any impression of deterioration in this period; there are just good painters and bad ones. For

---

7. M. Littauer, *AJA* 76 (1972) 150, raises doubts about Rodenwaldt's reconstruction, in *Fries des Megarons von Mykenai* (1921) Beil. II; cf. W. S. Smith, *Interconnections in the Ancient Near East* (1965) 84, fig. 120. However, there is a long tradition of showing soldiers falling downward, head first, from their chariots, from the Shaft Graves; W. Heurtley, *BSA* 25 (1921-23) 134, fig. 30, stele IX.

once both heads of the team are indicated, with two eyes with tear ducts and three reins, although the brow profiles are skillfully mirrored lines blending into a single muzzle. Every line is crisp and bold, and the bridle shows well on the reserved faces, a dotted brow band above the eyes, a striped cheek strap, a nose-band, enlarged (slit?) nostrils where two of the reins terminate, the third being attached to the back of the nose-band. The dots and stripes may represent the same interest in suggesting metal studs or bosses as the "metallic" ornament on the armor of XI.16. The tall dark slim arched neck and the ears pricked sharply forward are vigorous, but the total impression is one of abstract ornament.

Of the other Tiryns fragments, some only scraps, a small Schliemann fragment (XI.22) deserves notice as a reduction of the soldier scenes on bigger vases, a figure holding a small round shield by the hand-grip in front of a horse. Some horses develop a disfiguring saclike face almost exactly like an octopus (XI.25); the eye may pop out of this bulge, or the head may disappear altogether, leaving a disconnected fringed eye floating in front of the neck (XI.29). As the animal becomes disjointed, so does the chariot, leaving only two disconnected wheels. Fragments with the open-railed chariot may show the old "personnage en robe" type as well as the newer dark athletic driver (XI.26, 27). There are animated gestures, hands with splayed fingers, hooves tilted digging into the ground or lifted altogether in the air.

The best of these isolated figures (XI.28) are the eager driver and soldier going left, both with long-bristled "hedgehog" helmets and round shields, their tunics laced in loops down the sides and fringed with tassels across the thigh, the driver's arms high and urgent, the passenger nicely balanced with his spears over his shoulder, the outlines firm and the picture authoritative. Evidently there was a considerable range of workshops dealing with spirited military themes; in a period of which we know so little, it is especially unfortunate that the Tiryns material should be so fragmentary, yet nearly every fragment is interesting. See Addenda, page 229.

30. Finally, there is one chariot scene on what seems to be a larnax, from the water channels. It preserves the long, thin rear legs of the team, lightly spotted, with a lank tail of three long hairs, a drooping straplike line, probably a pole drawn with a quickly turning brush, and the rim of the wheel. Chariot larnakes are so rare that the iconography must be of interest, but this was clearly not in a funerary context any more than VIII.5.1.

31. Another fine piece of pinax, larnax, or other flat clay object, not a vase, preserves one of the best of all Tirynthian heads, the driver with his hands raised to the

reins. The face is boldly outlined, with angular nose, lip, and chin, while the rest of the figure is a mixture of ornamented reserved areas and dark silhouette. He wears a low dark rounded helmet or cap beneath which a row of curls decorates the brow and temple, and a long club-tail of hair swings out behind the neck to the shoulders. The back of the head is flat, but the striped torque neck bulges in back as on so many other III C pieces. The interior of the chest is reserved to show off the driving arm more clearly; a rare feature is the pair of nipples painted on the chest, which suggested to Verdelis a molded metallic corselet. The lower arm is opened and filled with arcs, like the wrist-cuffs on the Warrior Vase. The body is a thin tube laced with zigzag, reflecting the framed zigzag at the top of the sherd. The scale, clarity, and latent energy in the painting are remarkable.

This collection of rather poorly preserved fragments from Mycenae and Tiryns at least demonstrates that a variety of painters and workshops continue into the twelfth century; few of the painters are talented, but they are interested in trying some new versions of the traditional chariot composition, with such innovations as views of the open racing chariot, the single horse being led to work or harnessed, the active soldiers poised with spears, round shields, or spike helmets, and the effect of motion on the body. These experiments temporarily infuse a new life into a scene nearly extinct and probably guarantee that the chariot is still being used in "horse-pasturing Argos" in a period crucial for the formation and transmission of epic poems.

Other parts of the Greek mainland, apart from the old royal Argolid centers, have sporadic chariot imagery or views of horses; there is scarcely enough from each site to form a series that might illuminate principles of style, but enough to show that both the theme and the military fact existed throughout Greece.

ATHENS
Four oddly drawn fragments of small bowls and kraters from the Acropolis recall the crudest Mycenae and Tiryns specimens. They are in local clay, apparently, with a farouche quality. One might not care to distinguish these sherds as coming "from an Athenian atelier" (too complimentary a word), but they signal that the pictorial ambitions of Athens at the end of the Bronze Age have not vanished.

32. The rim of a small krater preserves a charioteer driving vigorously to the right. The drawing is all thick lines, without blocks of color. The driver, head up through the framing band, has an oval head with tilted eye at the back, a beaked nose, an outlined round body with traces of stripe-filling, and a long curved arm reaching high and forward with three fingers toward the double rein, which stops short of his grasp. Lines below may be the pole and the tail of the horse.

33. A charioteer on the rim of a krater clasps both hands to his head. This is a characteristic mourning gesture, not too useful in driving, but not impossible in contexts of amazement or distress. The whole interpretation is uncertain, but it is possible that the scene reflects the Egyptian habit of tying the reins around the waist to leave a soldier's hands free. Head and chest are painted solid, the chest frontal and triangular as in Geometric art; there are two stripes vertically below—"legs" or the kind of substitute for a body seen on the Tiryns chariot krater, XI.14.

The other two fragments show what might be the remains of the body of an open chariot (XI.34), and a gesturing man (XI.35) who seems to be seated or riding in a chariot whose rail conceals him from the waist down. The head is up through the framing band, spiked with three lines (nose and two lips). The body is a solid rectangle, the upper arm very thin, and the lower, bent up, very thick, with four splayed sharp fingers like shoots on a palm tree. If it is in fact a charioteer, there are no reins.

36. From the Fountain in the north wall of the Acropolis come fragments of a paneled krater with a standing horse and a running man(?). The light zigzag panel frame and traces of large concentric arcs or spirals in the field suggest a III C rather than Transitional date. Only the rear quarters of the horse are preserved, facing left from the panel frame, sunk through the framing bands as deep as the thigh, very lightweight with well-separated thighs and a thin tubular body in silhouette, like XI.11.

LEUKANDI

The number and high quality of pictorial fragments from the little site of Leukandi-Xeropolis, between Chalkis and Eretria on the inland coast of Euboia, remind us that our general views on Late painting can be changed at any moment by fortunate excavation. It is the most productive site after Mycenae and Tiryns, even though it has been probed only in small areas. Most fragments are stratified in the second Late Helladic III C group of levels. This suggests that the first III C levels are still Transitional from III B (although perhaps with newcomers) and that the productive levels correspond with the general III C:1b strata at other sites. The style has more in common with Tirynthian painting or with the Argolid at large than with Attica, as one might expect geographically; the sea trade into the

Gulf of Argos may be partly responsible, or possibly the origin of the settlers. There are more distant links to Naxos and Iolkos. Some of the figures discussed in the section on human figures (XI.59 and following) may once have been in chariot compositions.

37. An interesting krater fragment with a charioteer was a surface find. The peculiar chariot type, discussed by Catling, seems to be a development of the Argolid light racer. The front rail is apparently abandoned, and the driver looks as though he rides the flat platform with the aid of thong-loops on his feet and safety straps around his calves, a dangerous, unstable device at such a low point of gravity. All is in solid silhouette, which obscures details one would be grateful for, such as whether the driver wears greaves for battle or is unarmored for country travel, and how the pair of diagonal straps really attaches to his legs. The man's knee is bent (cf. XI.1) and the leg thrust forward; possibly he has one foot out front on the pole for balance, as is occasionally attested in Egypt. This position lowers the hands from the usual high reach forward to a looser grasp centered between team and man. The two short reins seem to be held in the left hand (drawn like an arrow with three fingers). The "goad" in the right hand, suggested by Catling, is rare now (XI.5, 6); this is unusually long and prods the animals in an excruciating place. The team is dark, with a long tail enlivened by parallel strokes of loose blown hair. There are streaks of added white on the haunch and tail and the driver's calf. From the scale one assumes there were two vehicles on each face of the vase, as on the examples from Mycenae and Tiryns (XI.1, 2, 16).

38. An even more puzzling sherd from a krater may possibly be interpreted as part of a chariot battle scene. From the illustration it seems polychrome. The lower body and legs of a man, left, float in midair behind the rump and tail of a dark horse; this suspension may be caused by a barbed spear entering his midriff at a slant from the left or, by some shorthand, he may be the driver, with arrow-fingers holding a slanting rein, jumping forward from an unrailed car like the last. Both moves are known in the battle scenes of the *Iliad*; so Agamemnon "pushed Peisandros from his chariot to the earth, striking toward his chest with his spear" (*XI.142*); or "Oïleus striker of horses leaped down from his chariot and stood against him" (*XI.93*); or a combination, as Odysseus "struck Chersidamas with his spear on the navel as he leaped from his chariot" (*XI.423*). The costume consists of a fringed thigh-length tunic split at the groin so that the leg contours appear, with greaves tied below the knee and above the ankle. The legs are fat, as on the Naxos and Tiryns sherds (XI.49, 63), the outlines firm, the contrast between pale (whitened?) flesh and dark tunic, boots, and horsehide well planned.

39. Another krater fragment may illustrate the soldier-groom walking ahead of a team of horses, but again the scene is uncertain. The man strides right in a dark tunic and greaves, the flesh reserved. He wears a short, tasseled sword at the waist, uncommon in this period in painting, though such swords are plentiful in excavations. The head seems to be turned back over the shoulders; the point of the beard shows on the left, the back of the hair or helmet on the right. Both arms are raised, which swells the shoulders oddly (cf. XI.3); the left arm has two stripes like an armlet. He may be pulling on the leading reins of a team, which appears as dark shapes lightened with white stripes on the left, or urging on the troops with a gesture.

PERATI

The III C cemetery at Perati is not far from Leukandi, but it almost totally lacks its rich pictorial style, except for bird and fish motifs on stirrup jars. It is worth noting in this regard that the krater shape, which normally carries pictorial themes in Ripe, Transitional, and Late, is not a fashionable vase in this cemetery; only four examples were found, although skyphoi and deep bowls are relatively common. At most III C sites pictorial vases come from houses, not from tombs. There is only one horse and one man, both on stirrup jars.

40. The short-tailed horse on the shoulder of a small stirrup jar is an isolated image, running left with bent legs. The tail is curled up over his back like a goat's (see X.52), the mane hairs rendered in short bristles as on the Athens and Mycenae ponies (X.25-28), the large oval eye reserved. The muzzle is exceptionally pointed, the legs weak with extra bends; evidently the painter was not skilled with this theme. Over the horse's back hangs an outlined shape like a double axe standing on one wing, or an hourglass; this form is connected to the back of the horse's head by a long line that passes through the "axe." If this is indeed an axe, it is the first example of a symbolic scheme well known in Geometric art; some have tried to connect it with Poseidon Hippios, with chthonic overtones, or with funeral cult.[8] Iakovides thought the line might be the shaft of the axe, drawn crooked, or part of the harness. There is so little overt symbolism or cult connection in Mycenaean pictorial painting that one might also view it as a weak filling ornament attached to the staff of the stirrup jar, and the horse as one of a limited but distinct class of free-running animals (IX.7). The drawing is weak but animated and is not

readily aligned with any known school of painting except, perhaps, the Athenian.

SALAMIS

41. A nearly complete chariot krater from Salamis, from the necropolis at Chalioti, is a distinguished representative of that late, bad, but ambitious school of painting. Unlike most chariot scenes, it is a hunt, with the charioteer running down a quadruped. It may not be as late as it looks; often on Salamis the shapes and technical qualities of the vases are finer than the execution of the painting. This and the goat vase (XI.82) are among the last mainland specimens of the traditional open krater with vertical strap handles; only the narrowness of the pictorial zone and the extraordinary manner of drawing a disintegrated chariot suggest so late a date as III C. It is quite possible that thirteenth-century shapes lingered on in a relatively isolated place; the same strap-handled krater appears in a similarly late context and style at Ugarit (XIII.27f.). There is a nautilus design on the reverse of this.

The hunter in the chariot is reduced to a linear scheme (as at Athens), merged with the chariot box. The box is a high old-fashioned rectangle covered with spots, with a blob on top for the driver's head, one curved line from the rim for his driving arm, and a lower hooked curve for his free arm and finger. Two lines emerge from the framing band across the top of the scene—not the reins, which are attached to the horse's mane and the driver's arm. The traditional aspect of this drawing is evident in the use of a pole brace from the chariot rim to the horse's rump. The wheel is high, four-spoked, with a clear axle, decorated with a row of spots inside the rim. The horse has remarkably clumsy outlines with thick contours along the head and back, a stout body crouching on dog's legs (the front knees are jointed backward). The head is a lifted triangle with long notched mane plumes streaming graphically behind; there is no eye or harness. The line of the shoulder and the division of the hind legs are marked.

Horse and chariot have nearly caught a galloping animal whose long tail with a feathered end waves under the horse's nose. This animal is also spotted decoratively; the markings are probably ornamental, not meant to suggest a deer; the long tail is more usual for horses or bulls. It prances on its hind legs and waves its forehooves in the air near the handle. For people who enjoy bad drawing, this is

8. F. Schachermeyr, *AA* 1962, 230; N. Coldstream, *Greek Geometric Pottery* (1968) 174, 292; Benson, *HBM*, 23; S. Iakovides, *Perati* B (1970) 151.

a masterpiece in its way, and a welcome indication that hunting from a chariot was still practiced against the fleeter animals until the end of the Bronze Age.

(For other late hunting scenes on foot, see XI.70 and following. For figures that may once have formed parts of chariot compositions, see Amarynthos, XI.56; Iolkos, XI.58; Leukandi, XI.61, 62.)

SOLDIERS

There is a vigorous collection of human images in the Late period, mostly sherds as usual. Some soldiers may have been part of chariot scenes as attendants and spearmen. Soldiers in "hedgehog" helmets are the most common types. Hunting scenes are treated as a separate group, and ships are also segregated; only one has sailors in this phase. As one would expect, Mycenae and Tiryns are the most productive centers.

MYCENAE

42. The Warrior Vase, from the House of the Warrior Vase at Mycenae, is by far the most frequently published example of pictorial painting to survive from the Bronze Age, and one of the most commanding. In style it is not superior to many other fragments, but it has the merit of considerable completeness, offering the chance to examine Late composition in some detail.

Complicated interpretations have been suggested for the scenes on the krater; there is still no general agreement on the relationship between the two sides or the origin of the peculiar armor. Studies suggesting that the vase is wrongly dated to the Mycenaean period are usually based on a failure to look at related fragments; many sherds are related in color, costume, facial type, and structure. Problems in understanding the narrative derive from excessive optimism that there is a narrative content; this is a general difficulty with Mycenaean painting.

The shape of the krater is still capacious, deep, and firmly controlled. The frieze is generous in comparison to other pictorial zones of the age, for example the Salamis hunting krater (XI.41); this use of the whole surface is shared by krater painters at Leukandi. The high double-arched twisted handle is a novelty at the end of LH III B and sporadically popular in III C; the "bull's head protome" at the center of the handle, if indeed it is a bull, was used in Crete and at Mycenae before. It is more common on larnakes than kraters; whether this suggests a shared funerary

symbolism or playful modeling may be left to subjective judgment (cf. XI.59).[9]

The front of the vase is generally understood to be the side with a woman standing at the left. This frieze has seven figures: the woman and six soldiers marching right in procession up to the handle, where a bird is framed in the arch. The bird motif is a complication of the type seen in Cyprus much earlier (V.14). The battered rear of the vase has only five soldiers, right.

The woman on the front was painted before the handle was applied; it overlaps her skirt and hides some details. The back of her head and right arm are broken away. She is dressed in a characteristic ankle-length mainland tunic with a dark bodice and sleeves, a particolor contrast with the yellow-gold panel down the front of the skirt. This is part of a mild coloristic effect, seen on XI.7, in which pale yellow, dark brown, added white, and reserved areas are set against each other for a modulated chromatic version of the "black-and-white" III C style. The costume is less used in fresco than in minor arts; it is worn by women on the Tanagra larnakes and terracotta figurines.[10] The skirt is raised in an arc at the bottom to show the ankles, as on some Cretan terracotta figurines. It is possible that the woman is pulling her skirt upward with her right hand, from the way it flares out under the handle; this flare has no tensile relation to the curling hem. The feet are bare. The left arm is lifted in a curve with the hand touching the crown of the head; the gesture is not specific but is often a gesture of mourning as well as meditation, cult respect, and parting. The head may be covered with a cap or low *polos*, which falls in a soft peak over the brow; the two stripes on the brow may represent the contrasting hatband. The raised sleeve has four bars at the wrist like a cuff, a motif that appears on the soldiers' arms too. There is a reserved patch with filling stripes on the upper arm, like the barring on the soldiers' armpits on the reverse; here it is possibly the hand of the right arm crossing the breast and extending a short distance in front of the body. These striped inserts accord with the habit of striping the necks and legs of animals and soldiers in this period. The structure of the arms is not clear; most of the soldiers also lack one arm, the inactive one on the left or shield side.

The woman has the same face and body as the soldiers, with the exaggerated features of the phase (see XI.7):

9. N. Oakeshott, *JHS* 86 (1966) 114; O. Broneer, *Hesperia* 8 (1939) 393; E. Vermeule, *AJA* 64 (1960) 6, no. 8a; V. Desborough, *The Last Mycenaeans and Their Successors* (1964) 100; cf. XI.59 and note 15.

10. Cf. E. Vermeule, *JHS* 85 (1965) pls. 25-27; T. Spyropoulos, *AAA* 2 (1969) 20, and 3 (1970) 184; *Praktika* 1969, pls. 13-14, and 1970, pls. 48-49; E. French, *BSA* 66 (1971) 175 f.; S. Marinatos, *Kleidung, Haar-und Barttracht*, in *Archaeologia Homerica* A (1964) 30.

short lumpy torso with a thick waist, long legs, a long co-lumnar neck, low skull, fleshy nose with the underside rising nearly to the eye socket, oval sharp-cornered eye with a contracted central pupil, arched eyebrow, oval flap of ear, full muffin lips, and receding chin rendered as a small fold of flesh. The initial drawing does not always coincide with the final paint; she has two nose outlines, like one of the soldiers. Some noses on the vase are pointed, some have this trunklike shape. The reserved flesh areas are standard in polychrome painting.

The six soldiers at the right march in uniform step, left leg advanced, nearly identical in face and costume with only expected uncontrollable variations. The helmets are peaked fore and aft — deerstalker caps, Miss Lorimer called them — dark-painted with white spots, peaking into a triangular or cup-shaped socket, from the back of which a reserved plume with a central wavy line floats down to the back rim of the helmet or ear level. (The Warrior Vase is unusual for showing ears and eyebrows at all; the ears are ovals or facing disjointed loops.) A pair of horns curves up from the front of the helmet into the framing band, probably intended to spring out diagonally. Horned helmets of various types increase in popularity in Greece just before and after 1200, either through Shardana influence or through other, marginal tribes of Syria.[11] The painter may have meant to indicate that the helmets were made of leather reinforced by metal discs, yet ornamental spotting for its own sake is so widespread in the Transitional and Late phases that no technical deductions can be certain; the tunics or cuirasses are equally spotted.

The soldiers are bearded; beards are still rare in the twelfth century but come partly back into fashion as they have not been since the period of the Shaft Graves (XI.7, 45-47). The body clothing is in two sections: a stiff corselet standing away from the chest, flaring out at the waist, with long sleeves (not distinguished as belonging to a shirt under armor) and the new hip-length, triangular, fringed tunic skirt noted in chariot scenes. Both parts are framed by ladder pattern, which perhaps indicates lacings at the sides but is also part of the ornamental repertory, like spots. Two reserved stripes form the lower hem of the corselet, and some skirts have a ladder-patterned hem. There is a rhythmic alternation in the skirts, just as the skirt color changes on the Warrior Stele (XI.43) and border patterns change in fresco processions. The first and second soldiers have plain fringed skirts, the third a ladder-hem, the fourth is broken, the fifth is painted yellow and bordered, the sixth is broken. The skirts are loosely spotted in added white. On this side of the vase there is no need to spot the corselets, since their surfaces are sufficiently relieved by the reserved inset patch on the chests, left blank so the

clumsy clenched fists could be drawn in dark lines. Earlier pictorial tended to slice away the torso at this point so that the hand would be outside the silhouetted contour (V.13, 14, 17, 19, IX.1). The emphasis on more solid, massive bodies in III C makes this technique impracticable, and the surface broken by color contrast is just as serviceable and more congenial to the taste of the age. The hands are emphasized by cuff stripes; it is clear that they are intended to grasp the spear shafts but that the shafts actually cross the wrists rather than the palms.

The greaves are the usual dark leggings tied above the knee (see XI.49, 59); the ankles and feet are crosshatched to indicate boots, either wrapped-on cloth campaigning shoes or textured leather. The other campaigning equipment consists of a segmented shield, a thrusting spear with a leaf-shaped point, and a leather ration bag. The shields are pale yellow circles with an arc cut from the bottom edge, ornamented with half-loops around the inside border. They make a fine gold halo-background for the dark complicated tunics. Because the soldiers are reserved, the tops of the shields show through them as a yellow band above the corselet, and the curved lower edges follow the curves of the tunic hems. On the other side of the vase, where the shields are tilted down for hand action, the curve disappears altogether behind the men's backs, so perhaps not too much should be made of its odd cutaway form as ancestral to the Thracian pelta or shields of Anatolian Amazons. The spears are longer, for infantry thrusting, than those carried by chariot riders; the long leaf-shaped socketed blade corresponds to many contemporary excavated examples; see also XI.55.1.[12] The dark leather ration bags or wine sacks tied onto the shafts appear in one or two other Late paintings (X.30); the possible connection to military rations in the Linear B texts was discussed above.[13]

The reverse of the vase is simpler. The five soldiers are in action, their spears (now much shorter for reasons of space) raised high at the diagonal in their right hands, legs well apart, the shields tilted forward and down, all in concerted motion like forerunners of the hoplite phalanx or the occasional massed ranking of foot soldiers in the *Iliad*. Except for the ration bags, discarded for fighting, and the helmets, the equipment is about the same as on the front. Opinion has divided over whether the painter meant to show the same soldiers in different phases of activity, or

11. J. Borchhardt, *Homerische Helme* (1972) 37 f., pls. 12-15; F. Schachermeyr in Schaeffer, *Ugaritica* VI (1969) 451; N.K. Sandars, *The Sea Peoples* (1978) 117-137.

12. Catling, *Bronzework*, 121-122; *ProcPS* 14 (1956) 185; E. Vermeule, *AJA* 64 (1960) 15.

13. Chapter X, note 13.

whether the soldiers on the reverse are a hostile party against whom the others are marching. Or, if the scene is funerary, the first group would be going to the games, the second starting the spear volley in honor of the dead. The attitudes seem more aggressive and practical than ceremonial. The general formulaic principles of Mycenaean art preclude specific interpretation, but we may still note the great number of active military scenes on kraters in the twelfth century and wonder whether they all serve the same function.

The helmets on the second side are the "hedgehog" type, dark and crested with bristles, which began circulating in the thirteenth century (IX.8). These are probably stiff caps of leather or metal, made in two halves from front to back, with a spray crest clamped in the joint. They are not often spotted white, as here.[14] Only the head of the second soldier from the left is well preserved. The helmet rides high on the crown, bagging over its band in peaks fore and aft. On the fifth soldier it fits more snugly. The soldiers again lack their left or shield-bearing arms, even though the shields are lowered for defense; the first shield has an empty handgrip and an interior border of semicircles; the rest are blank. Since the arms are raised and the hands clearly outside the contour, there is no need to reserve blanks in the chest; the corselets consequently have rows of decorative white spots and a white stripe across the chests. The raised armpits are striped white. The first two tunic skirts are washed yellow inside the ladder-borders and fringes, the third and fifth are dark with white spots. Since there are fewer figures, the field is more spacious, and filling ornaments are used: a band of touching semicircles on the upper border over the heads of the third and fourth soldiers and three groups of concentric circles punctuating the blankness above shoulder height.

The pair of birds under each double-arched handle shows little change from the Ripe or Transitional periods; birds are hard to date. They are dark, goose-bodied, with a striped neck and open breast. The wing forms vary, trailing below the body on one, rising thickly above the tail on the other. Some scholars have thought of them as symbols, the bird of prey on the side of the marching warriors attacking a domestic fat goose or duck on the side of the lunging soldiers. Without Homer, such symbolism would probably not occur to anyone.

The ornamental "bull" protomes are natural in an age when plastic ornament proliferated on vases and when new kinds of plastic vases — ducks, horses, and cows — were invented. Stags are also used in this position; any animal with big horns to supply the handles would serve.[15] The bulls have III C concentric arcs at the brow, eyes and ears both modeled and formed by painted ovals, and a stripe down the nose. The better one has fringes at the

brow and semicircles bordering the nose stripe. The effect is as much like a hedgehog or bear as a bull.

The Warrior Vase is still among the most monumental Mycenaean paintings of any kind, with a wonderfully practical and vivid character, the kind of expression that gathers strength only in the Transitional and Late periods, the tentative exploration of mood through external forms, enriched with expert color harmonies, a monument that provokes speculation and lends itself to poetic analogy while eluding precise interpretation.

43. The painted stucco Warrior Stele from Mycenae has seldom been discussed for its most interesting aspect, the broken cult scene that forms the top of the three preserved registers. The artistic connection of the stele to the Warrior Vase was noted immediately upon discovery. It provides the only sure example so far known of fresco-color work on stucco by a pictorial vase painter, enlarging our ideas about the flexibility of craftsmen and their ability to work in different media. The funerary function of the stele is undeniable; it closed the right half of the entrance to a crooked niche or side-chamber in a tomb that had been in use for at least two generations. Since the iconography of the funeral stele has three themes — cult, war, and animals — it must be considered from all these aspects by scholars who debate the funerary significance of large kraters like the Warrior Vase.

The sandstone rectangle is preserved to nearly a meter (0.91 m.). It had perhaps three phases of use: the first when it was carved in registers with simple circles and wheels connected by lines; the second when it was covered with about three millimeters of lime plaster and painted in LH III C:1; the third when, already broken, it was used for the interior niche of the tomb where Tsountas found it. It should be possible with modern techniques to detect the entire carved pattern underneath the paint as a clue to the date of original manufacture.

---

14. The most practical interpretation is that these are metal discs applied to the underlying cap, but Late Mycenaean painters enjoy white overpainted decoration for its own sake.

15. This is an age of modeled plastic experiment in handles and ornaments as well as rhyta. There is a stag's-head handle with chevrons on the brow from Athens, Agora AP 2602, O. Broneer, *Hesperia* 8 (1939) 353, fig. 27 g (cf. P 17251); see *JHS ArcRep* 1977-78, 33, a stag from Ayios Stephanos. There are bulls' heads from Mycenae, Athens NM 1218 lot, on a krater, with painted arcs between the horns, and on a rim flanked by antithetic spirals, G. Mylonas, *Deltion* 18 (1963) B, 85, pl. 100, cf. *Praktika* 1970, pl. 169. A quadruped on a strap handle from Mycenae, Athens NM 1141 (1068.3?), Furtwängler-Loeschcke, *MV*, pl. XXXVIII.396; there is a large plastic bull, Acrop. 2668, and two human protomes, H. Schliemann, *Mycenae and Tiryns* (1880) 69, no. 81; A. Wace, *BSA* 25 (1921-23) pl. 7 c. There is a plastic shield from the Athenian Acropolis, Graef-Langlotz, *VA* I, pl. 3, no. 76. The wonderful tubular monsters on the Alyke trick vase are the best expressions of the wit in plastic ornament of the period, Furtwängler-Loeschcke, *MV*, pl. XIX.137.

The lower part of the stele was meant to be sunk into the earth and perhaps had no more ornament than a simple border below the animal frieze. The three painted friezes are unequal, the broadest being the central one, with five warriors marching right in a copy of the reverse of the Warrior Vase; the lower animal frieze of four deer and a hedgehog is approximately half that height; the upper frieze may have been broad to accommodate the standing figures. These scenes are distinguished by elaborate borders, red and black overlapping concentric arcs on framing bands of red, yellow, black, and blue. Yellow is omitted between the scenes; the bands are red framed by blue framed by black. On the narrow sides of the stele, there are badly damaged patterns of "hourglass" or "altar" shape (really tangent concentric arcs) on the framing bands, tied across patches of alternating red and yellow; the arcs are red, brown, yellow, and black. The alternation of colors in the framing bands is exhibited more subtly in the two lower friezes, much as color rhythms are employed in processional frescoes at Pylos and Thebes.

In the lower frieze four deer, heads raised and alert as on X.44, face right on a blank ground. The three at the rear have symmetrical branching horns fore and aft. The front deer is hornless, perhaps to indicate a female being followed by three males (cf. V.53, IX.49) or because the foremost horn would have overlapped the border in a confusing way. The proportions of the bodies are like those of the ˌ Pylos frescoes, the stances inactive as at Pylos, ˌˌˌˌˌ feet are raised off the ˌˌˌˌˌˌ forward, the mouths ˌˌˌˌˌˌ ce expressiveness. The ˌˌˌˌˌˌ lar eye of fresco rather ˌˌˌˌˌˌ pictorial compositions; ˌˌˌˌˌˌ uct toward the nose (see ˌˌˌˌˌˌ erved, as for white tails. ˌˌˌˌˌˌ lors as the ornamental ˌˌˌˌˌˌ ppling. From left to right ˌˌˌˌˌˌ , red with a blue hind leg, ˌˌˌˌˌˌ yellow. This accent of yel- ˌˌˌˌˌˌ the yellow hedgehog in the ˌˌˌˌˌˌ he too is stippled black for ˌˌˌˌˌˌ have yellow horns, the last ˌˌˌˌˌˌ ge of color on the hind leg is ˌˌˌˌˌˌ ale inner face of the hind leg ˌˌˌˌˌˌ n of the hedgehog is not clear, ˌˌˌˌˌˌ ionic, perhaps; hedgehogs are ˌˌˌˌˌˌ -89), as are small animals over ˌˌˌˌˌˌ I.83, 91).[16] It is often claimed ˌˌˌˌˌˌ d copy of the alert overlapping ˌˌˌˌˌˌ fresco; perhaps it alludes to one ˌˌˌˌˌˌ life being left by the deceased.

In the central frieze the five warriors are proportioned, costumed, armed, and set in motion exactly as on the reverse of the Warrior Vase. The shields are again tilted forward and down, so that the putative cutoff segment is concealed behind the men's backs, leaving a simple half-moon shape. There are the same stiff projecting corselets laced or patterned at the sides, the same short triangular tunic skirts with fringed hems (the second from the right also has a laddered hem and zigzags at the sides) and dark greaves tied at knee and ankle, but the feet are not crosshatched for boots. The shortened spears with leaf-shaped blades are brandished high as before, and the left arms are still missing. The heads are almost entirely effaced, yet the Gilliéron drawing shows traces of beards, a ridge-crested helmet on the second warrior from the right, and traces of plumes on the first and fourth heads, as though both helmet types of the Warrior Vase were used on a single file of soldiers here.

The alternation of colors is even brighter than below. From the left the soldiers wear: a blue corselet with red borders, a red skirt, a yellow shield; a blue corselet with red borders, a yellow skirt, a brighter blue shield; a blue corselet with red borders, a brighter blue skirt, a yellow shield with zigzag ornament around the inner rim; a blue corselet with red borders, a yellow skirt with zigzags at the side and ladder pattern across the hem, a bright blue shield; a blue corselet with red borders, a brighter blue skirt, a plain yellow shield. All the fringes are red, the greaves are dark blue, the spears are red. The colors of the tunic skirts and shields fluctuate around them.

The upper frieze, tantalizingly fragmentary, seems to record a scene like that on the Homage Krater (III.29) or the great gold ring from Tiryns. The outline drawing is red rather than black as below. From the left there is a yellow chair with red bands along the seat in which a woman(?) sits, wearing an ankle-length blue robe, facing right. Before and facing her is the red foot of a male figure.[17] Behind this, a yellow triangular patch may be the lower corner of the skirt of another figure approaching the throne. (Tsountas thought there might have been three seated figures in this scene, in which case the frieze would be lower, matching the deer frieze.) On a tomb stele such a scene should suggest an act of homage or respect to a major goddess or to the shrouded dead.

The scenes on the stele may have thematic connections arranged in a hierarchical manner. Tsountas suggested that it illustrates the three phases of Mycenaean social culture, the seated dignified aristocrats of peacetime,

16. Cf. H.-G. Buchholz, *BJV* 5 (1965) pl. 13.5, fig. 4 h.
17. Tsountas thought of a red trunk of a gnarled tree with roots waving along the ground.

the active middle-class infantry in battle, and the lower natural world of animals of the hunt. A triple division into god, man, and beast is probably too classical a concept.

44. A handsome krater fragment from Mycenae preserves part of a soldier in a checkerboard skirt, marching right with a spear and possibly a bag tied to it. This is a fine example of the "black-and-white" style, which seems so close in spirit to certain types of Proto-Attic painting.[18] It is matched at Leukandi (XI.59). The neck is outlined, the shoulder, arm, and front of the chest are painted solid, while the interior of the chest is reserved as on the Warrior Vase to give a clear view of the inarticulate hand holding the spear. The waist is set off by a thick band, a war belt or the lower part of a waist-length bronze corselet. Bands descend in symmetrical curves to frame the skirt. The skirt pattern is four rows of checkerboard squares with a dangling fringe. The curved line at the small of the back and in front of the skirt may possibly be the remnant of a light shield held low. The left arm is missing, as on the Warrior Vase and Stele. The form at the far left may be a spotted bag or skin, with three outlines. The fragment is very thick; the original krater may have been as large as the Warrior Vase, with a number of figures.

45. "Hedgehog" helmets "with cheekpiece" are illustrated on a krater sherd from Mycenae in Munich. Two soldiers march right; only the heads and necks are left. The surface is badly worn, but the clear reconstruction drawing is probably misleading in supplying a cheekpiece for the second helmet; it is inappropriate for this type of helmet and does not occur on the one in front. The reason for understanding it so was no doubt the row of bristles at chin level. The helmets, snug on the brow, are dark and crested with bristles, lacking the spots of the Warrior Vase. They seem baggier, with a beretlike pouch in back. Pernice hoped at first that this might be a piece of the Warrior Vase, but it is by a different painter, the figures are set closer together, and there is no color, no spears. They share only the general similarities of the period.

46. A krater sherd with a helmeted head from Mycenae is all in fine outline drawing. The helmet has a rounded crown with a fringe of bristles; perhaps it is made of metal, since the forms are more conical and rigid than the usual *pilos* or beret type of "hedgehog" cap; it terminates in a pale brown line above eye level. There seems to be a horn on the brow, as on the Warrior Vase, and perhaps another at the back.[19] The nose and chin are sharp points, less arbitrary than on the Iolkos fragment (XI.57), with the lower edge of the nose serving as the lip line; the eye is a simple dot. Three strokes of hair dangle from the chin. The back of the neck is bulbous; the slender part is broken by crossbars, as at Tiryns and Perati (XI.31, 68).

47. A krater fragment from Charvati has parts of the heads of two soldiers moving right. On the extreme right only a spray of bristles survives, probably from the back of a "hedgehog" helmet. The preserved head has reserved double contours with dark flesh, typically III C. This is another bearded man, with five curved hairs under his chin; three hairs or bristles at the back of the neck seem to escape from under the chevron-patterned band of a hat or helmet. The ear is drawn in, as on the Warrior Vase; the eye is oval with reserved contours, the forehead slopes shallowly, the nose is a blunt triangle, and the jaw curves smoothly from nose to ear, with lips or jawbone. The neck is long and thin as usual now, and bordered. A curve below may be shield or shoulder; the right arm is up, perhaps holding a vertical spear, although a diagonal stroke behind the man could also be a spear. This odd fragment calls attention to the variety of styles of warrior painting in the twelfth century and to the new fashion for beards or moustaches.

48. A difficult krater fragment is tentatively interpreted here as an unusual helmet with a triangular crest-holder, a dotted plume dangling behind, and a single line bordered with spots in front. It may represent the fore-and-aft type of XI.42, 46, and 80, but it is very uncertain.

TIRYNS

The group of soldier fragments from Tiryns is more dramatic and of better quality than the Mycenaean ones; most come from Verdelis's and the German Archaeological Institute's explorations of the water channels and adjacent sections of the lower town. There may be many more that we do not know of yet.

49. Fragments of a large curved, closed vessel, perhaps a rhyton or stirrup jar from the water channels, have an interesting picture of a soldier leaping in air in full armor, brandishing a short sword in his right hand. A better drawing than the leaping man of Leukandi (XI.38), it is in outline except for the dark patches of the bristled "hedgehog" helmet and the greaves tied at knee and ankle. The armor follows the pattern usually found with such helmets: a stiff corselet standing out from the body, with fastenings represented by a simple inner border; a short triangular hip-length tunic skirt flaring from a miniscule waist and patterned with nested triangles. The boots below the greaves have pointed toes curled down. The legs are stout,

---

18. See note 1 above, and B. Schweitzer, *RömMitt* 62 (1955) 82; P. Mingazzini, *Annuario* 45-46 (1967-68) 327 f.

19. W. Reichel discussed this, *Homerische Waffen*[2] (1901) 107, as the only surviving example of the *amphiphalos* helmet type; cf. D. Gray, *JHS* 74 (1954) 6; A. Wace, F. Stubbings, *A Companion to Homer* (1962) 514; see also note 6 above and XI.80, a probable *tetráphalos* helmet.

the calves impressively bulging. The sword is really a dagger, with a leaf-shaped blade, a midrib, and a round pommel below the hand. Sword fighters have been rare in pictorial for a long time, since the stately Ripe versions of the Levant, but are common in late frescoes. This continues the tradition of the Melathria and A. Stephanos fragments (VIII.6, 7) but is far livelier and better.

50. An interesting krater fragment is too small to be certain that it shows a soldier—only the legs are preserved—but it bears an apparent relationship to the Orchomenos frescoes with soldiers walking on checkerboard architecture. At Orchomenos the painter uses checkerboard as shorthand for a masonry palace, court, and altar, and makes soldiers in pale greaves file left in procession. The Tiryns sherd has compartments of checkerboard pattern apparently alternating with blank rectangles containing isolated figures; on the preserved surface a dark man skips or dances left at the top, and another figure or pattern appears at the lower left. Checkerboard often stands for architecture in palace frescoes as on the Tanagra larnakes; this compartmented picture is strange but is at least in the tradition of the Window Krater earlier (III.12).

Other fragments have part of a soldier in a "hedgehog" helmet carrying a spear and snarling with an open mouth (XI.51), part of a particularly bristling "hedgehog" helmet, and two reins or javelins (XI.52), four legs in greaves with ankle ties (XI.53), a soldier in a dark cuirass holding a sword with a round pommel high behind his head (XI.54), a little dark runner in a large panel (XI.55) and part of a leaf-bladed spear (XI.55.1). These active and interesting war scenes are scattered signs of how much has been lost from an energetic period that cannot be irrelevant for the formation of the epic tradition.

AMARYNTHOS

56. The once-promising site of Amarynthos on Euboia, now bulldozed, yielded at least two interesting pictorial krater sherds on a surface survey (see also X.51). The more vivid fragment may represent a charioteer with long flowing hair, followed by a man in a "hedgehog" helmet. The surface is worn, and this follower has been restored as a "golliwog," a round dark face with two staring eyes, yet in the photographs the flat lower edge proper to a "hedgehog" helmet seems visible. The charioteer is drawn on a miniature scale in a charming style. He has a small outlined face with a dot in the center for an eye, a dark triangular torso, and two little loops for arms. Three long ripples of waving hair stream from the back of the head beyond the following soldier, combining playful pattern and the suggestion of speed in the wind; it is simply

the old multiple-stem pattern, filling the blanks and tightening the composition in delicate formal balance.

IOLKOS

57. The "Warrior Vase of Iolkos" consists of a rim fragment of a large krater (the rim is rolled and slashed) and a wall fragment. This is one of the finer, more idiosyncratic pieces outside the Argolid. Some details are not clear; there must have been a number of figures on each side of the vase, marching right, but only three heads are preserved. Both soldiers on the rim fragment wear "hedgehog" helmets and carry spears diagonally over their right shoulders. The drawing of the helmet on the second soldier is valuable evidence that this was in fact a double leather cap with an inserted crest at the seam along the crown, for a reserved area along the top of the head separates helmet and crest; this detail does not appear on the leading soldier. Both helmets have hooks curving down by the ear, apparently part of the apparatus rather than the ear itself. The outline drawing of the faces is very sharp and clear, a low brow and three sharp triangles for features, a big round eye (it is almost always oval in the Argolid in this phase), and a short flaring neck. The second soldier's neck is crossed by a diagonal band where the Argolid uses parallel stripes, perhaps decorative rather than representing a metal throat-protector or sword baldric. The neck seam of the tunic is reserved; the leading soldier's is ladder-patterned, and he may have nipples on the metal corselet, as at Tiryns, or spiral scales (XI.31). The thong of a bag hanging from his spear shaft may be detected. The second man's spear is shorter, held lower, with a short leaf-shaped blade with midrib, perhaps a hunting javelin.

A dark object between the men, shaped like the blade of a double axe with ladder-patterned edges, is difficult to interpret; if a shield, it is not otherwise paralleled in LH III C (but see IX.3), although segmented shields that are not dissimilar appear among the allies of the Hittites on the Luxor reliefs of the Battle of Kadesh.

The single soldier on the second fragment is nearly frontal and gestures left with a long arm, reaching for something round. He too wears a metal corselet with strongly marked nipples; the slashes along the top of it (*Zickzackverzierung*) may represent geometric metallic enrichment ultimately derived from an older leather jerkin tied with thongs (cf. XI.16). The face, published in drawing, is sketchy and crude in comparison with the others; this man also wears a "hedgehog" helmet with reserved crest.

58. A krater fragment with an archer is unique for III C, and rare before (IV.16(?), V.28). The motif occurs next

in Protogeometric.[20] The drawing is confusing. The archer, right, is in silhouette with a worn face, possibly a reserved eye; he probably wears a helmet, is almost certainly bearded, and his squat humped body may suggest that he is kneeling to shoot. Theochares thought he was riding in the back of a moving chariot (the slanting line at the right edge), difficult for shooting but a maneuver often practiced in Egypt and the East. A reserved band on the lower body, filled with bars light and dark, one like a broken lambda, might be a war belt or the chariot rail. The wizened arms are bent with the bow in front of the chest; a double line from bowstring to arc suggests he is fitting an arrow to the cord, not shooting yet. A thin quiver with a pointed end is attached to the neck. The infelicities of painting may be excused in such a rare subject but are not helpful in military interpretation. Archers are surprisingly rare in Aegean painting, in view of the many surviving bronze and stone arrow points, and iconographical models in the East. This bow seems to be the small single-stave "European" type that is drawn back only to the chest and so does not require a full kneeling position;[21] this is easier in a chariot. It may also be that the line in front of the archer is a shelter, a large shield or blind.

LEUKANDI

The figures of soldiers from Leukandi may belong in chariot scenes; others are engaged in odd cult and symbolic performances.

59. A dramatic warrior in a checkerboard skirt appears on a fragmentary krater next to the horned bull's head handle. The hind legs and long tail of a horse are by the handle on the other side, without visible chariot or groom. The krater is stratified in Level 2 a, which is contemporary with LH III C:1b at Mycenae. The vase is clearly related to the sequence at Mycenae in proportions, costume, color, stance, and the horned handle. The soldier wears a dark tunic with a checkerboard skirt like the one on XI.44, greaves, and a sword in a tasseled scabbard. The pose is more active than on the Mycenae fragment, with the legs well spread and the right knee bent, the arms apparently held high and forward. The greaves are tied around the thick calves just below the knee and the muscle of the calf; the feet are apparently encased in striped, cross-tied traveling boots. The sword, with a forked hilt and three tassels at the top of the scabbard, is probably worn on a baldric. The soldier's lifted arms suggest a leader waving his men forward, more vivid than the lowlier spear bearers of Mycenae; this was evidently once a more vigorous and complex scene than the Warrior Vase.

There are parts of three more warrior vases from Leukandi: one (XI.60) has a man with a curly beard wearing a dark (leather?) pilos; another (XI.61), a sharp-faced soldier in a crested helmet with two light javelins and an oval shield; and the third (XI.62), a similarly sharp-faced soldier in a helmet with a single fine waving plume.

NAXOS

63. A sherd from the lower part of the pictorial zone on a krater has a stout pair of warrior's legs marching right. The reserved outline and dark interior filling recall XI.47 and many Naxian birds and fish on contemporary octopus stirrup jars. It is not clear that the man is greaved, for there are no ties, and the feet are the same color as the legs. The stance is active with legs bent, the rear heel raised and the ball pressing on the ground line; the forward foot sinks through the line, a feature less common in the twelfth century than before, because of increased precision. A dark tasseled object at hip height in the field before the man might conceivably be a horse's tail but had better be left uninterpreted.

For a dancing scene from Naxos, see XI.67.

UNKNOWN PROVENANCE

64. A sherd from the rim of a small bowl or krater now in Germany has the head of a helmeted soldier to the right. The helmet is a simple inverted bowl shape with a reserved lower border filled with dots, perhaps a leather band with metal discs. A crest of bristles all around shows that it is a variant on the "hedgehog" type. The sherd is worn; the light face has a dot-eye, high straight eyebrow, and snub nose, with dark hair and beard.

64.1. A pair of more schematic "hedgehog" caps with a spray of bristles around the crown, occurs on a sherd now in Tübingen; both soldiers face right; the rear one has a long thick dark neck as though the painter intended to represent a protective collar, and he may be armed with two javelins.

OTHER HUMAN FIGURES

The high proportion of chariot and soldier scenes in LH III C deserves stress. Images of human beings engaged in

---

20. From Leukandi, V. Desborough, *The Greek Dark Ages* (1972) 192, pl. 42; from Enkomi, Schaeffer, *Alasia* I (1971) 269, fig. 106; G. Kopcke, *The Dark Ages in Greece* (1977) figs. 30, 31.

21. Lorimer, *HM*, 277; A. Wace, F. Stubbings, *A Companion to Homer* (1962) 518.

peaceful activities are sporadic. Even hunting scenes tend to emphasize the animals rather than the hunters, and the ships are usually empty. There is apparently less energy focused on behavior outside of a war environment than ever before. This is not new in the tradition of Mycenaean art but does reflect a shift in intensity, which may accord well with the idea that epic poetry of battle was transmitted with greater interest or power at the end of Mycenaean history.

LEUKANDI

65. An interesting if perplexing broken krater preserves a cult scene of a priest with sphinxes. Part of one side survives from rim to ground line; it is stratified in Level 2 b. There is a vigorous use of enriching white paint on the figures, hats, wings, and robe. The scene consists of a human figure, probably a male priest, dressed in an ankle-length robe and crosshatched boots, walking to the right and holding a libation jug in his lowered right hand. Behind him a tame sphinx and her child form a circular motif, the mother above walking right, the child below to the left, as calves used to be shown with cows. There is long precedent on gems, from Minoan times, for divinities and priests with griffins and sphinxes, and in pictorial painting human heads and birds have already been associated with sphinxes (VIII.30, 31). The robed figure may have a headdress; the face is lost. The dress is decorated in tiers, with a broad belt of white stripes enclosing a row of dots; the lower skirt has stripes, a wavy line, and a triple embroidered hem of slashes and zigzags, suggesting flounces and rich color in the old fresco tradition. The jug he carries is a tall, one-handled vase with a slightly tilted lip but without the long spout that was formerly associated with sacrificial libation. The arm holding the jug is outlined and seems to be adorned with a bracelet. The sphinx following is painted in dark silhouette with an interior contour line carelessly added in white; she wears the characteristic flat cap (without plumes), and her wing is lifted. The blunt face has a big round eye, the tubular body is segmented, with a white horizontal S at the belly and stripes at the haunch; the wing suggests a bony or muscular upper thrusting edge, like a tongue pattern, segmented in stripes, and a lower sheet of feathers in rows, ladder-patterned with scalloped edges; the legs are contoured in white. The young sphinx has no wings yet; unlike the parent, it has a reserved face, but the body is similarly decorated with stripes at the waist and an S-loop at the haunch; the cap is ruffled in two rows, the erect tail a twisting line rising between the mother's legs. It is not known at what age an infant sphinx acquires wings.

The imagination in this fragment is shared by the griffin and sphinx pyxis (XI.91), with its concern for infants, amusing associations, and white paint; it is conceivable that they are by the same hand, so that we are glimpsing an individual fantasy of monsters rather than a temperamental surge of interest in an unreal world that might characterize the whole village of Leukandi. This is not certain, of course; at least the number of animal paintings at Leukandi is unusual, and the imagination is of a quality also glimpsed at Tanagra, in Crete, and at Ugarit.

66. The outlined two-handled bowl in the field suggests that another difficult krater fragment may also represent a cult scene. There is the disparity in scale seen in the Transitional battle fragments (X.36), but so little survives that the scene does not mean much. At the left a pair of tall dark legs with thick calves strides left, with the little bowl outlined between them. At the right a small dark male, with right hand, belly, and legs preserved, extends his hand left as though to tickle or prod the large legs. His own legs are bent, the knees sharp, and the arm is bent at the elbow. It is possible that the big legs are in fact the hind legs of an animal like a griffin, for griffins sometimes have foot-shaped paws rather than claws (XI.91) and that the little man is one of its trainers or associates. The vase in the field usually denotes cult or funeral, however.

NAXOS

67. Men joined in a circular dance are painted on a hydria from Naxos. Such hydriai with strainer spouts are quite common in the islands in the early twelfth century, especially in Naxos and Rhodes, and at linked shore points like Perati. In Naxos they are quite clearly meant for ritual libations connected with funeral ceremonies; many have serpents twining along the sides to lick from the spout. Here the dance should represent a funeral occasion. The stick figures are painted frontally, their hands joined, their heads generally touching the upper framing band and their legs spread, kicking the air in the middle of the frieze, the feet all pointing right to give the direction of the line. The figures are apparently unclothed, so it is a man's dance; women also dance by themselves in funerary contexts on larnakes.[22] There is a "child" suspended between the second and third men from the left, and other streaks hang down from the linked hands as fillers. The scene is evidently experimental, part of the III C interest in scenes of ordinary life; the round dance is of course known earlier in terracotta. The Naxos hydria is no less effective in its own terms

22. For example, the Tanagra larnax, T. Spyropoulos, *AAA* 3 (1970) 197, fig. 17 top.

than similar scenes on Geometric vases and may well be ancestral to them.

PERATI

68. The creeping man sketched on the shoulder of a stirrup jar from Tomb 75 at Perati is the only human figure surviving from that site. Though the posture is an uncommon one, it is the only sensible way to place a man in such an awkward space and need have no relation to frescoes of many centuries before, such as the blue monkey picking crocuses at Knossos. In technique it recalls Tiryns idiosyncrasies. The reserved figure has double contours along the crown of the head and the back, single underneath and around the limbs; the neck is densely striped as at Tiryns, and a group of stripes at the waist recalls animal filling ornament. In photograph the man seems to crawl left on his belly, but this is deceptive because the legs are bent down through the top two framing bands; he is in fact tilted as though rising through the ornament to clearer air. The low brow, long flexible nose, and sharp lips are typical of the era. The flaccid curves of the raised, pawlike right arm are echoed in the ripples of the back; the drawing seems almost deliberately strengthless, less like a crawling dead man than a desperate drinker on his way to refreshment.

TIRYNS

69. A happy chance preserved the sherd of a collared jar(?) with part of a lyre-playing scene—the lyre or phorminx, the hand, and the player's head. The face and the left edge of the lyre compete for space, and the face is obscure. The upper frame of the lyre has triple loops bowing in and out and is tied by two lines across the top—the yoke and the bridge. There are only three strings in this simplified picture, which should not be taken literally. The lyre began to appear with greater frequency in the second half of the thirteenth century; it is familiar in the Pylos fresco, the Chania pyxis, the Menidi ivory lyres, the Amyklai bronze model and the Nauplion musician krater (IX.14.1);[23] it is good to know that it occurred in mainland pictorial in the twelfth, as it becomes a staple of Geometric painting. The Late phase's energy is apparent in the player's fine hand with sharp fingers actively plucking the two strings on the right.

HUNTING SCENES

All the later hunting scenes are considered as a group here, although for reasons expressed earlier some are dated in the Ripe or Transitional phases (see X.44 and following). Perhaps the interest in pictorial hunting scenes was intensified by such boar and stag frescoes as we know from Tiryns and Pylos, but the vases have a different emphasis, lower class as it were, with an occasional helmeted huntsman urging his dogs against deer or, on smaller fragments, the dogs, deer and goats racing for life by themselves. Hunting scenes are rare at all times; two Ripe Cypriote versions with huntsmen were discussed above (V.60, 113) and there are pure animal hunts in Cyprus (VI.7, 22) and the East (XIII.1, 27). The direction is normally left to right, with the huntsman at the left and a stream of animals at different levels flowing and biting right, just as on the old Shaft Grave daggers. The examples from the Argolid have some spiritual and compositional relationship to the Tiryns and Orchomenos boar hunts; a vase fragment from Tiryns (XI.78) may be the finest Mycenaean pictorial image of all.

For hunted stags and goats of the Ripe phase, see IX.48 and following, IX.71; for a lion and bulls, IX.82; for a dog, IX.79(?); for a hunt from a chariot, XI.41.

MYCENAE

70. Three fragments of a large hunting krater from Tsountas' House have been discussed in detail by Åkerström. The whole complex of Tsountas' House and the Citadel House contains strata of later III B (IX.18), Transitional (X.2, 42), and Late (XI.4, 5). Judging by the filling strokes in the animals and the particolored face of the huntsman, this krater is Transitional. It is finer than the Aradippo krater (V.60), more awkward than XI.71, 78.

From the left (if the fragments are all from the same side of the vase) there are two huntsmen, one wearing a tall, curved basketwork hat, the other holding a slanted spear raised in his right arm; the spear has an open cage or set of thongs attached at the midpoint of the shaft.[24] The left hunter is in dark silhouette with two reserved patches in his face, one a long oval eye with the point down, the other perhaps to set off the helmet from the tri-lobed dark patch surrounding the eye. The helmet or hunting cap is latticed; the high peak curves back; it protects the head to below the ear. The construction is like a bull jumper's protective headgear, but simpler in shape (cf. IX.18.1). The hand and spear shaft of the right-hand hunter are also dark.

The second fragment contains parts of a deer and two

23. The Menidi lyres, H. Lolling, *Das Kuppelgrab von Menidi* (1880) pl. 8; the Amyklai lyre, C. Tsountas, *EphArch* 1892, pl. 3; in general, M. Wegner, *Musik und Tanz*, in *Archaeologia Homerica* U (1968) 25 f. Cf. IX.14.1; J. Poursat, *Ivoires Mycéniens* (1977) pl. XLV.426, 427.

24. This seems to be a genuine attachment, not fingers; see H.-G. Buchholz, V. Karageorghis, *AAA* 3 (1970) 391; L. J. D. Richardson, *AAA* 4 (1971) 262; and below on *aiganeé*, XI.77.

hunting dogs. The deer is outlined, the body filled with broken lines like seagull wings and a muscular loop to define the working shoulder; the pointed hooves are high off the ground. The legs, two dark and two light, are attached inorganically to the belly; the hindmost leg kicks violently, horizontally backward as on the Dendra hunting chalice or the Agora ivory pyxis. The dogs are stacked one over the other behind the victim; the dark forepaws of the upper one cross the deer's hind leg, while the lower one snaps at the fetlock. It is drawn in outline, with the same muscular shoulder loops as the deer and miscellaneous markings for hair; the ears are pricked up fore and aft, the snout is long and pointed like a boar's with fangs growing inside the lips; the eye is a diamond. A stiff gallop brings the forepaws off the ground.

The third fragment also has a deer, dark again, and two hounds in changed positions: the deer leaps high in the air, a dark hound with a long curling tail snaps upward at its belly or genitals from below, and the second dog leaps from behind toward its haunch. Only the lower dog is well preserved; it is long and awkward, with a reserved hind leg and flattened ears; the tail starts a spiral, as on the Tiryns Shield Bearer krater (X.1).

If the three fragments are from the same side, the two men, the two deer, and the four hounds were arranged with alternating emphasis on dark and light, not scattered loosely but coordinated by rhythms of snapping and leaping, with the source of energy from the hunters on the left.

71. Two krater fragments of a dramatic "black-and-white" hunt share features of drawing and tension with the Tiryns hunt (XI.78). On one sherd the forepart of a strongly marked stag leaps behind the longer hind legs of another. The stag has dark branching antlers slanting up from the crown of the head, an outlined face filled with concentric arcs at the cheek and bands at the muzzle, a powerful dark neck, spotted shoulder and belly with strong arcs for the shoulder muscles and bands at the waist. The outlined legs are brought up high in front with beautifully marked hooves. The hooves cross the gangling outlined legs of a figure resembling the stag of XI.76.

The second fragment sets a hound over the back of a stag, right. The dog has a pointed snout, barred muzzle, outlined face, strong jawbone, round eye, flattened-back ears, a stripe at the neck like a collar, a dark neck, and a dark body possibly lightened with reserved triangles. Claws on the long legs grate along the deer's back. The deer seems "male" like the other, with traces of the antler at the upper right; the body is ornamented with dark triangles on a light spotted ground. The animals are more powerfully drawn and vigorous than most, in attitudes indicative of greed and fright.

72. An engaging, well-known fragment with a dog chasing a "hare" or fawn to the left is mildly polychrome, yellow and brown on buff, like the Warrior Vase (XI.42). The animals are high up in the frieze; either the pictorial zone was unusually narrow, or there were two or more tiers of animals scattered across the field. The little long-eared spotted victim with a short tail scampering away at the top left has always been understood as a hare, although hares do not otherwise appear in mainland pictorial painting. It may well be a young fawn; the pricked-up ears, scut, spotted hide and diamond eye are equally appropriate, and the image would more readily align with normal hunting schemes on vases as on metal and ivory. In this case the hound would be high over the back of an adult animal in the missing zone below, and the fawn above its mother or stumbling along at a distance. The dog is long and lean, lips parted, oval eye tipped down, with a filling of eight wavy lines on the stretched neck and shoulder and filled triangles tipped in from the body contour. The paws have curling claws. The drawing is simple but expressive of rush and escape.

There are other active and attractive hunting dogs at Mycenae; one (XI.73) mildly polychrome, clumsier than the last, brushes his ears against the upper band, leaping over a frieze of rising and falling animals below. He is dark with a pale face, and the wispy legs have curled claws drawn back under the body for the leap. He is curiously set in an arched panel composition. A bowl fragment (XI.74) painted on the inside in matt cream on a dark glaze was once taken for a crude horse and rider, but Åkerström correctly understood it as a snarling dog descending from the left onto the back of a frightened animal, probably a doe, who stretches her neck up high and flattens her ears back. The dog flexes its outstretched pads over the animal in a huge leap and opens its mouth to show two dangerous teeth. White-on-black painting is favored in the twelfth century for animals, birds, and fish, but the outside of the bowl is normal brown on buff, with the tail and hind leg of another dog.

Two or three fragments with stags must belong to such hunting kraters: a doe (XI.75) running full speed to the right, strongly marked, with dark legs and patches on the body, pale upturned scut, a lightweight active figure, and a tall stag (XI.76) fleeing right on long weak legs with high knees, and the head thrown back.

Two interesting fragments from Mycenae, one from a large krater (XI.77.1) and the other from an amphora (XI.77.2), preserve the pictorial evidence for hunting stags with the *aiganeé*, a spear with a hook on the shaft mentioned in Homeric poetry for hunting goats. Both of these vases may be Transitional in date; the clusters of stripes marking the hide, the bottle nose, and the abstract antlers suggest the later side of that period. Both stags have light bodies with diagonal stripes or wavy lines; the second, a haunch dappled with slight arcs. The symmetrical short antlers are crossed by stripes or loops. The hunting spear descends on their backs from the upper framing band, the end of the trajectory of a distant throw; on the first the dark leaf-shaped blade has a bar above, on the second it is outlined without the bar, and both have a curved hook projecting left a short distance up the shaft. This hook is understood by Buchholz and Karageorghis to be metallic, a Mycenaean predecessor of the leather loop on the Homeric *aiganeé*, the Greek *ankyle*, Latin *amentum*; its purpose is to increase the throwing distance (*Iliad XVI.589* f.) although with some loss of accuracy. In Homer the *aiganeé* is slender and long-socketed or long-shafted, suitable for young men's games of amusement as well as for goat hunting (*Odyssey IX.154* f.); here the shafts are short by the exigencies of the picture space, and the socket is not distinguished. It is possible that the *aiganeé* was also represented in other hunting scenes (V.60, XI.70), but the hooks are not preserved, and the basket arrangement on the spear of XI.70 seems more complex. It is sad to be deprived of the full composition of these picturesque scenes.

TIRYNS

Tiryns has only one good hunting scene of this period, but it is a masterpiece.

78. Four joining fragments of a krater from the water channels preserve, from the handle to the right, a galloping blotched hound biting the leg of a doe who leaps right at full stretch but turns her head back with the lips parted in pain or surprise. The vase has traits in common with the Tiryns frescoes, combined with an original crudity and pathos. The dog, in the flying gallop, has a large misshapen head, heavy for the thin neck, with a full jaw and lumpish snout, the round eye set well back, the lips curved in a grin (but no teeth shown), the dark ears pricked up. The two front legs and near hind leg are dark, the off hind leg lightened inside. The long tail is ringed diagonally, raccoon-style. This black-and-white contrast is emphatic within the body: dark neck and shoulders, pale chest with a dark blotch framed in loops, a dark belt at the waist bordered with loops on either side, pale groin, dark rump. This is evidently influenced in some degree by the unreal dappling of the hounds in the Tiryns and Orchomenos boar-hunt paintings and is congenial with current prevailing tastes among Tirynthian vase painters.

The doe is neatly outlined, elongated in speed and fright, the body filled with parallel dashes, which provide better texture for rough hair than the more traditional fillings, the chest shadowed dark like the spine. The far hind

leg where the dog attacks is also, unusually, dark; the near one has a wavy line streaming down past the hock. The scut, a tasseled triangle with inner triangular filling, is compressed muscularly back for protection. The doe's erect neck is dark and slim, the outlined face twisting up and back, the pupil in the eye sliding toward the hound at her hock, the long lips parted and flexible, the outlined ears flipped straight up. Since just over half of one face of the krater survives, there would have been room for a stag or fawn ahead of the bitten doe.

LEUKANDI

79. Fragments from opposite sides of a large krater with a triple rim, the lower two flanges obliquely slashed, preserve two predators and parts of two victims. If this is a standard hunting scene, it is unusual in two respects: the resemblance of the dogs to lions (see XIII.27, from Ugarit) and the long taloned legs of the victim on the reverse. It might possibly be understood as a parent lion on each side taking its cub out for a frisky stroll; Leukandi is interested in adults and young (XI.91, 141). The composition is in the normal hunting tradition, however.

On the first fragment the dog leaps right with open mouth and hanging tongue, the legs bent up automatically in a springing gesture that has lost vitality. Head and body are outlined, and dark is used for three legs, the tail, and a neck patch growing angularly from the heavy jaw contour; the spotted collar echoes the tubular spotted tail of the animal in front. The left front paw has four talons, the other none, as on the reverse. The scene must be a near replica of the reverse, although there the dog is all dark with an outlined face, leaping left. Both dogs have deep chests, weak hindquarters, and one pale round lion ear, one dark pricked hound ear. The animal in front, victim or parent, is odd enough, with long legs, one dark and one spotted, equipped with claws, and the looped spotted tail tucked between them like a decorative inner tube. The height is proper for a ruminant, the claws for a lion, the tail for nothing that ever pastured in Euboia. The fragments are stratified to the second III C phase.

PYLOS

80. An elaborate hunt in a late and awkward style appears on a deep krater with twisted handles from the dromos of a collapsed chamber tomb near "the palace of Nestor" at Englianos. It was apparently accompanied by another animal vase. On one side a huntsman in a remarkable horned helmet urges on three dogs to the left, or two dogs pursuing a lion. The two dogs closest to the hunter are stacked one above the other, the third leaps ahead in midair. The painting is so clumsy one cannot tell if it is a lion hunt, or if this side is connected narratively with the other, where a large stag stands at bay so that the hounds charge him across the handle. The dogs are lumpily conceived, all dark, with large reserved eyes, thin bodies, and awkwardly bent legs at the trot, except for the leading hound whose legs are thrust forward in midair, as at Leukandi. The pursuers have knees on their front legs, which gives them an odd look but emphasizes their spring and grasping power. The leader has talons on all four paws. The upper dog and this leader also have impressive fangs drawn inside their lips, which part in a snarl. The bearded huntsman is also in silhouette, with a big reserved eye and a spear over his left shoulder. His helmet is a tall conical cap peaked fore and aft as on the Warrior Vase, with two sets of narrow curved horns, a smaller pair at the top and a larger pair halfway down. It is the only surviving Mycenaean example of a helmet that may be equated with the Homeric *tetráphalos kunée* (*Iliad XII.384*) or *korus* (*XXII.314*), an object provocative of considerable discussion in the past.

The reverse shows the fine antlered stag facing right toward the handle and two more rushing dogs. The stag's dark body is more canonical than the hounds'; the antlers curve upward gently with branches on the inner faces, the legs are braced, the scut cocked. The elongated genitals are reversed, pointing toward the hind hocks. This animal may be associated with the rear half of a dark dog leaping in the air, right, even clumsier than those on the front, hind legs under belly and long tail drooping.

In style this vase is not impressive, but coming so late in the series and employing all the motifs of leaping bodies and clashing fangs, it illustrates the end of the traditional composition with an admirable impulse toward narrative vigor and ferocity. Compared to the Cretan krater from Mouliana, it is a masterpiece.[25]

For hunting from a chariot, see XI.41.

PATRAS-ACHAIA

81. Perhaps an extract from a poor hunting scene, two animals are painted on the flank of a three-legged duck askos in Patras. They may both be dogs or a dog and a deer. The stacking of one over the other is typical of hunts, not of simple animal vignettes. The painting is really bad; the idea of putting animals on a duck is odd for the Mycenaeans (though it appears in later Protogeometric art), unless the animals are chasing the duck itself. They are confined in a rectangular panel within an oval panel, the left end filled with arcs and triangles, the right end with wavy lines that might, if interpreted without restraint, be

taken for water in the duck's swamp. The animals themselves are surrounded by miscellaneous wavy lines and a series of loops like the last gasp of Minoan rockwork. A similar misplaced animal appears upside down on a Cretan sarcophagus in Hierapetra; there is another quasi-parallel in Rethymno.

GOATS

Stags and goats whose forms are not well defined, who are static and not caught up in the chase or hunting compositions, were noted in Chapter X. There are probably only four full-fledged goat scenes of the Late period, one bad and vigorous, one neat and ornamental, one paneled, and one sexual. Although many Transitional goats, like those from Mycenae and Amarynthos, are approximately contemporary, they are more conservative. The Salamis(?) krater is earlier than the Perati stirrup jar. The two Leukandi kraters are ripe III C.

82. An intact open krater on a high stem, which may possibly come from Salamis, illustrates the provincial qualities of Saronic schools, like the last chariot krater, XI.41. Technically it is finely made, and the painting retains the echo of vivacious impulses. The rather narrow frieze is uninterrupted on the side with three goats; on the other it is broken into staccato panels.

On the major side three goats prance right in dark silhouette, the paint streaky. The first two are large, the last one little, either through miscalculation of space or to make a family. Only the eyes are reserved, as holes; the center animal is blind. All the bodies are lumpish, with the feet down through the framing bands, the legs slender for the bulk above, forelegs sagging exhaustedly, hind legs staggering. The muzzles are bottle shaped. The horns curve elegantly like a water buffalo's, in opposite directions with varying numbers of curves. Some anatomical lightheartedness is discernible in the leader's long tail, lowered through the ground line, in contrast to the perky short double tail of the fat animal in the center.

On the secondary side a goat in heavy outline, with a blank body, dark head, reserved eye, and horns bent back in a long diagonal wave, is cramped in a panel. The rest of the frieze is occupied by an assortment of motifs, which with good will might possibly be read as landscape motifs but are basically ornamental. On the right is a panel of

25. S. Xanthoudides, *EphArch* 1904, pl. 3; Evans, *Palace of Minos* IV, 374, fig. 312 c; 376, fig. 314 a; V. Desborough, *The Last Mycenaeans and Their Successors* (1964) 177, 188; see also L. H. Sackett, *BSA* 71 (1976) 117 f., and *JHS ArcRep* 1976-77, cover and figs. 33-35.

"mountains" formed by overlapping spotted scales, then an open space with three curling plant spirals and a symmetrical plant form of spirals bordering two vertical spotted stems. At the left is another panel divided in checkerboards, alternately spotted and dark, and a blank spanned by a dark diagonal cross and a spotted upright cross. The inconsistent plan of this side is not otherwise known in animal painting; one would expect an antithetic animal at the right. It suggests a spontaneous way of developing a theme, either lack of practice in setting an animal in a landscape filled with rocks and plants (better executed on the next) or fascination with loose decorative motifs to the degree that the goat becomes subsidiary.

83. On a stirrup jar from Perati the whole shoulder and upper body are covered with a panorama of palm trees, trailing leaves, a cactuslike plant, a fine goat, and at least eighteen birds. So much landscape is unusual, except under water with octopods. The central focus is a symmetrical palm tree with a ridged trunk and eight pairs of curving fronds, the upper seven formed of open parallel lines filled with slanting dashes. The goat or, more properly, ibex, is eating at this tree on the left. Its legs are far down through the framing bands, so that haunch and belly seem to rest close to the ground. The body is dark with reserved ornamental inserts, a porthole filled with a dotted circle on the rump, and a narrow crosshatched slit in the chest. This type of ornamental highlighting is more common in the Dodekanese. The ibex lifts his head to eat, and the magnificent horns sweep back in dark double curves with serrated edges; a legless bird pecks at the tip. His ears are pricked up in outline, a leaf shape like the cactus blossoms on the right; a narrow oval is the controlling form on this vase.

The birds are all dark except for a young one on the left, and drawn in a characteristic shorthand that stresses the beaks, usually open, the pulled-out oval bodies on long necks, and the alert round eyes. They are wingless except for a thin stripe over some backs; some are legless too. They are arranged in three groups as landscape elements and fillers. One bird perches on a palm frond over the goat's head and two float over his back, one settled on his rump and the other just landing. This pastoral arrangement reflects earlier combinations of bulls and birds; it also recalls the contemporary horse-and-bird vase from Mycenae (XI.13) and the more eastern or Cretan scenes of birds in trees in Cyprus (III.1) and at Megiddo (XIII.26). Around the goat the air is filled with lightly dotted circles, like the pattern on the haunch; chains of loops like falling leaves float before him.

On the far left similar chains of openwork leaves trail downward and spread as a thicket on the ground, shelter-

ing four more birds: two legless ones above, one perched on the bush, one picking at the goat's horns, and two below like mother and child, as much earlier on the Louvre ewer (VII.6). These birds settle toward the ground, the large one with a hatched slit opened in her elongated body, the small one, outlined with a fan of tail feathers, in the curve of the parent's back. On the right eleven birds in lively attitudes flutter around the edges of what looks like a cactus growing out of a nautilus.[26] The leaves are ovals with single or double outlines, connected by concentric arcs in the finest III C manner. The birds fly toward the fruits or brake lightly in the air. Two or three have slot openings with hatching. There are two repetitions of the image of the little one on the mother's back. The air is again filled with light dot-rosettes, dotted circles, and dot clusters in odd shapes.

This interesting design seems to be linked more to the Cycladic or Dodekanese schools of III C pictorial painting than to the mainland tradition, where landscape and filling ornaments are still rare in the twelfth century. The stag vase from the Kos Serayio (XII.35) is a starker and more forceful version of a similar theme. Such delicate ornamental designs as this are of course most at home on stirrup jars.

84. A handsome krater from Leukandi is one of the latest examples of the paneled animal picture, which has gone both florid and asymmetrical. The center panel on the krater is broad, consisting of a central row of fringed arc-flowers pointing downward between verticals (and a zigzag on the left only) from which dark leaf shapes with reserved borders spring with an upward twist. Two goats on the right and one on the left stand on their hind legs to nibble these ornaments. This is simply a more vigorous version of the old Levantine goat-and-tree motif and, like the Leukandi birds (XI.141), betrays full awareness of the previous pictorial tradition. The imbalance caused by the single goat on the left is partly rectified by an odd group of hanging fillers like ribbons, zigzags, and wavy lines behind his erect dark body. This (headless) goat has a dark body with two striped, two dark legs; he is ithyphallic. The whole form is more rubbery and flaccid than in earlier versions. On the right the two goats have reserved heads with big round cheerful eyes; their lips smile in the squared muzzles. The bodies are again dark; at least one leg is striped for color contrast. Both seem to eat, not copulate as on the next. This is a happy and colorful piece.

---

26. The deliberate combinations of land and sea life on the Kalymnos (XII.23) and Pitane (XIII.8) stirrup jars and the Miletos beaker (XIII.7), as well as on Minoan larnakes like those from Hierapetra and Armenoi, make this seem less unlikely.

85. A more enigmatic krater from Leukandi may perhaps be understood as a pair of dark goats copulating. Only the hind parts of the animals are preserved; the short curled-up tails are more goatlike than horselike. They stand above a zone of alternating dark triangles with reserved borders; there are fringed concentric arcs and remains of other patterns in a second zone below. The action is toward the right; the rear goat has climbed the back of the righthand animal and inserts a long penis beneath (her) tail; the pendulous scrotum is drawn with considerable attention. Animal breeding and the barnyard habits of animals were themes more delicately handled in the older pictorial tradition, where the love lives of bulls and cows sometimes attracted painters of vases found in Cyprus (IV.32), but this scene is obviously appropriate for the fertile pastures of Euboia.

XI.85.1 At Tiryns the scene of erect goats nibbling at a tree is even added to the hindquarters of a modeled vase in the form of a bull.

There are a few miscellaneous animal scenes outside the standard categories, mostly ornamental. These include caterpillars, hedgehogs, snakes, sphinxes, and griffins. Other animals, like scorpions or crustaceans, occur in larger compositions on octopus stirrup vases; the Kalymnos and Pitane vases are famous for them (XII.23, XIII.8).

CATERPILLAR

86. Seven or more fragments of a large krater from Mycenae are painted in a confusing scheme of major and minor vertical panels with profuse white paint and subsidiary ornament. There are white stripes on the rim and white zigzags below, interspersed with rows of spots; vertical panel dividers are made of three streaks of dense spots bounded by continuous dotted arcs like leaves, framing an inner waving line dotted dark and white over all surfaces. Between these panel dividers concentric arcs on the upper and lower frames are tied together by dark wavy lines with lateral ribbons on the panels. In this spotted and looping chaos, parts of two caterpillars or larvae float in one panel at least. They are no more than broadly curved strokes of the paintbrush converted into living form by the addition of rows of white spots, with dark bars like feelers on the back and belly; the head opens into opposed lips connected by arcs. The better-preserved insect, left, has a double tail or may be two caterpillars mating. For a caterpillar form as a subsidiary ornament, see III.2.

HEDGEHOGS

The hedgehog, like the "hedgehog" helmet, is freshly popular in III C, although rarer in painting than in the rhyton form that circulated in the Levant earlier. Its occurrence in III C is probably caused by the similarity of the body shape to the arc or semicircle, which is so basic in the Late ornamental repertory; it is easy to fringe the arc and add legs, as on the Warrior Stele, XI.43. Whether the helmet was really made of hedgehog hide, or only looks that way, its use by painters of contemporary soldiers may have helped the animal into fashion.

87. The fragment of a deep bowl from Asine shows a design of continuous narrow panels of bordered zigzags with a hedgehog facing right in each blank. One is complete, the second only nose and paws. The animal is drawn in silhouette with a reserved dotted eye and a crest of bristles around the back and tail. The nose is sharper than on most representations, and the lips are parted as though hissing. The long legs bend backward at the knee, and the feet have three claws.

88. Under the handle of a small deep bowl from Mycenae a polychrome hedgehog is drawn with pale yellow outlines and dark brown spots. It is a more snubnosed animal than at Asine, with closed lips; the back bristles are a row of spots, and the body is spotted in diagonals. The tail seems to be rendered twice, once sticking out behind and once curving under the body. Hedgehogs do have a rat tail, and the curving rump here substitutes for the hind legs. Spots on either side of the handle suggest that more hedgehogs may have existed here once.

89. A bowl fragment from Tiryns preserves two of a frieze of hedgehogs strolling right. They are densely filled with parallel wavy lines, successfully suggesting rows of bristles, and short-stroked bristles stand up along their arched backs. The small legs look crumpled, with several "knees." The hedgehogs are close to the base line, and another species of animal may have been higher to the left.

SNAKE

Snakes are used in III C more as rolled, modeled ornaments on hydriai with strainer spouts than as painted decorations. How far the snake's symbolic role as a chthonic or funerary figure is intended is, of course, in doubt. On hydriai, the act of licking from the spout, as most snakes do, is both playful and ritual, a response to the possibilities of the material as well as iconographically significant.

90. On a deep bowl from Mycenae the usual dark broad wavy line between the handles is simply converted to a serpent by adding an eye and substituting a sharp nose for a tongue. The eye is a reserved circle almost filled by the pupil; the inside of the mouth, with a jagged suggestion of fangs, is rendered as on fish. Inner contour lines of white are joined across by diagonal white slashes for a rippling or scaled effect.

SPHINX, GRIFFIN, AND STAG

91. The famous griffin pyxis from Leukandi is related in imaginative fantasy to the sphinxes-and-priest fragment (XI.65). It is perhaps not such a novelty as it seems at first sight.

The decoration is entirely in matt white paint on a gray-black surface (see XI.74, 121). It is a three-handled, straight-sided pyxis, which means a sharp division between shoulder and body as decorative surfaces; the shoulder is decorated with scale-filled antithetic tongue patterns splaying from a vertical divider on the shoulder, tied from the tips by zigzag-filled streamers. The body has an unbroken frieze of miscellaneous animals, not related to the handles or really to each other except as couples with young: two griffins feeding their babies in a nest, a sphinx, and two deer with a fawn on the parent's back.

The griffins face each other across a nest suspended in air, not braced on a mound like the bird's nest of IV.38. An open-beaked fledgling faces each parent for food. The nest is a simple bowl with a wavy line filler. The griffin on the left, perhaps the father, has a knob like an electric light bulb surrounded by dots on his head; the whole flaccid body is bordered by an exterior contour of dots. Like the Leukandi sphinxes, he has a single raised wing with a square tip, merely an extension of his back muscles; the body stripes move down it without change until the solid white tip. The attenuated haunches are high, the tail a tight spiral, the front legs sag in a courteous dance step in which the extended left paw is twice as long as the supporting right leg;[27] the long undulating beaked face is reserved, the rest covered with diagonal stripes and wavy lines. The griffin on the right is plainer, perhaps the female of the pair. The head is crested with two floppy ears or plumes; the long neck is striped, the body solid white, the raised wing with curled tip filled with awkward patches of wavy lines; the tail is a double hanging stripe filled with bars and zigzag. The long front paw reaches out to rest delicately on

the spouse's elbow. Apparently both parents have imparted whatever insufficient food they brought to their infants' mouths, for there is no sign of it in the picture.

In spite of the superficial crudities, the lacy bodies and wings and the elaboration of an affectionate family group make this one of the more charming Mycenaean pictures. Earlier Mycenaean griffins were shown as predators or religious companions or as decoratively abstract symbols. The concerns of raising a family of young griffins are new in the twelfth century. In archaic times a baby griffin suckles like a mammal rather than living in a nest like a bird.[28]

To the right of the griffin family a sphinx in a plumed crown moves up behind a stag or deer who turns back to look; a spotted fawn on the deer's back walks precariously toward the sphinx so that they are confronted, the fawn looking defiant and the sphinx perplexed. The long-bodied sphinx has a decoratively varied hide, the chinless face with ski-jump nose has a dubious expression, the plumes of the cap form a loose spray. A white streak like an extra hand extends from the sphinx's chest to the tail of the deer in front—a thoughtful ground line to catch the fawn if he falls? The long lean deer is in the same stance as the one on the Tiryns fragment (IX.48). The body is filled with diagonal stripes that touch and form triangles; the neck is plainly striped; the antlers in tall curves have triangle points for branches; the scut is held out level as a platform for the fawn to walk on. The fawn's youth is made clear by its lack of horns and its spotted coat. Another deer stands to the right. The Mycenaean penchant for young animals on their parents' backs was noted on several earlier vases (VII.6, IX.48); it is seen more elaborately in antithetic groups on the Hierapetra larnax of the late thirteenth century, where young ibex nibble their mothers' ears.[29]

SHIPS

The painted ship scenes of the twelfth century are all well known because they are so few and of such potential interest for late Mycenaean economics and warfare. The mainland examples lack sailors so far and are not so pic-

---

27. A similar disproportion occurs on the bronze sphinx tripod, Berlin 8947; Catling, *Bronzework*, pl. 36 a.

28. R. Hampe, U. Jantzen, *Olympiabericht* I (1937) 90, pls. 34-35. A seal from the palace at Pylos shows parent griffins teaching their young to fly, A. Sakellariou, *CMS* I (1964) no. 304; C. W. Blegen, *AJA* 43 (1939) 569.

29. *IEE*, 336.

turesque as the rowers from Kos (XII.33) or the Sub-Minoan sea battle from Gortyna.[30]

92. The ship on a pyxis from the Tragana tholos tomb, an advanced III C picture, is one of the more complete specimens, with both ends preserved. New fragments have been found recently. It is a long lean ship with a low gunwale, equipped with a ram as on the Middle Helladic Iolkos fragments (VII.D) but more swift-looking and narrow. It is probably meant to represent a warship or one suited to pirate raids, not a merchantman. The mast is centered, with an oval sail, whose form is more influenced by the filled concentric arcs on the ornamental panels of the pyxis than by marine facts. The same might be true of the curious rigging ring at the top of the mast, which echoes a staff-and-ring pattern in the second panel to the left; however, the Thera ships have as many as five rings, probably halyard deadeyes, and one ring occurs on XI.95.[31] The latticework panels popular in the period are used for the steering platform in the stern, underneath which the steering oar and tiller project on the diagonal, and for the lookout platform or windscreen in the high stem. The fish standard attached to the prow is the open-bodied type with arc fillers and a splayed tail familiar everywhere in pictorial painting, used in this position on ships in the Aegean ever since Early Cycladic times. The double fins wave over the back, as though moving in air as well as water. The ship's stays are curved in low arcs, not the proper taut triangles, to suit the general formal patterning of the vase: a forestay, two backstays, and a mainstay, or halyards or brailing lines. The steering oar is tied to the framing band by two wavy lines in the style of the caterpillar krater, XI.86.

This ship picture has been connected to allusions on the Pylos tablets to "rowers" and "shipwrights," but it was made after the destruction of the palace and its archives. Like all major Mycenaean sites with a good harbor close by, Pylos must always have been involved in shipping, both to Crete and as a way station to Sicily and Italy through the Ionian islands. The late date of the pyxis and the interesting strong Protogeometric remains in the district are assurance of coastal strength here in the worst economic period.

A crude ship is preserved on a bowl fragment from Eleusis (XI.93); it consists of two parallel curves for the hull, seven teardrop oars, a double steering oar, and a double tiller on an oval platform. The ship on the stirrup jar from Asine (XI.94) is miniature and poorly drawn. Most observers agree that it is sailing right, with an incurved bow and a slight ram, a fringed curved screen or relic of the fish standard on the prow, a centered sail, square and crosshatched, with the mast off-center at the left corner,

eleven oars, a tall laddered steering platform, and a steering oar lying almost level in the water. A stirrup jar from Skyros (XI.95) has an octopus on the front, a long bird-headed ship on the rear. Both are simplified. The octopus has a short symmetrical bag body and three tentacles on either side, bordered by dots. The ship is drawn with a long narrow hull made of two lines that angle up as the neck of the bird prow. The thickened lower line has a triangular-bladed steering oar obliquely across it, and the stern curves up and over into a double tail. The mast is centered and surmounted with a ring or halyard deadeye as on XI.92; below it two tautened stays run to stern and prow. No sail is set. The bird's face on the prow is a schematic one, outlined, with an ear, dot-eye, and up-turned bill. How far it is influenced by the bird-headed ships of the Sea Peoples, as shown on the Medinet Habu reliefs,[32] or by "Philistine" contacts in the twelfth century is not clear; Skyros was a natural home for pirates and sea rovers, who would have seen innovative ships in the Levant and across the Aegean. The change from a fish standard to a bird's head is not very great.

Three fragments of a bowl from Phylakopi on Melos (XI.96) preserve parts of two ships on the exterior and an indeterminable picture inside. The ships might be combined into one but for an ambiguity about their direction. One has a curved duck-prow at the left, a centered mast with a single forestay and three backstays (the sail is not set), and a splayed sternpost. The other fragment has a hull with five oars, the root of a mast, and a steering oar at the left. This is as simple as the Skyros jar and may be as late. Possible sea battles from Phylakopi were noted earlier (X.38, 39). A more elaborate sea battle occurs on a sub-Minoan bowl sherd from Gortyna, where the clashing prows are formed as a duck and a stag in a very Viking manner.[33]

BIRDS

Birds are common in III C. They are decorative but not often distinguished. There is little point in describing each one, for most birds are typical rather than individual, and

30. See G. Rizza, V. Santa Maria Scrinari, *Il Santuario sull'Acropoli di Gortina* (1968) 12, fig. 18, no. 5.

31. S. Marinatos, *Thera* VI (1974); C. Laviosa, *Annuario* 47-48 (1969-70) 7 f.

32. H. H. Nelson, *Medinet Habu* I (1929) pls. 37, 39; W. S. Smith, *Interconnections in the Ancient Near East* (1965) 36-37; H. Hencken, *Tarquinia* (1966) II, 537; and note 11 above.

33. See note 30.

the types are formal echoes of earlier designs. They are more passive than before, with rare exceptions (XI.83, 133, 141), and they are more often attached to patterns. The usual types are shown in the accompanying figure. Most twelfth-century birds are small in scale, outlined, filled with concentric arcs or with strips of common designs like zigzags and ladders. Raised wings and folded wings are roughly equal in numbers, but the wings in every case are patterns rather than anatomical structures and could not support the body, which has been true from the Middle period onward.

Birds are found on small bowls, in friezes around the shoulder or body of stirrup jars, and on the shoulder of octopus stirrup jars or nestled among octopus tentacles, often side by side with fish. Mycenae continues to produce birds in significant numbers. Tiryns, usually as productive as Mycenae, does not seem to specialize in bird painting to such a degree.

A key piece is a bird bowl from Korakou (XI.99), which has been attributed to "the Rosette Painter."[34] It can be associated with a great number of fragments from Mycenae, yet it is so fragmentary that a better bowl from Korakou, with no rosettes, may be a more useful model.

One may suppose that the Korakou bowls were made in Mycenae, which has so many comparable pieces, rather than Corinth, which has produced so little pictorial yet.[35]

98. The fine, delicately painted bowl has two panels on each side, with a bird in each panel facing center. The panels are entirely bordered with fine scale pattern, with pointed triangles peaking inward from all sides, framing the birds with the double decorative suggestion of open windows and mountains. The panels are separated by vertical strips of zigzag and ladder pattern, which are frequently used on birds. Most of the birds in the series look like these, with long necks (here dark), curved raised wings drawn as though seen from the underside, and decorative splayed tails; the bodies are filled with fine groups of concentric arcs. The Z-shaped legs are drawn up to skim the scale borders, the curved beaks peck at the scales like berries. This is the Close Style at its most neat and spacious.

99. The fragment of a similar bowl from Korakou has the central divider replaced by a filled rosette with double scalloped border and nine dark petals. The rosette is treated as a living flower, pecked by the arc-filled birds on either side. A scale border around the scene peaks into mountain triangles as before but is less finely drawn.

MYCENAE

With the Korakou bowls should be placed a number of fragmentary bowls from Mycenae, which may all come from the same workshop although painted by several hands. The concentration of fragments leads one to suppose that the workshop was located at Mycenae, somewhere in the lower town. Since there is not much linkage in style to the warrior and animal vases, one should think of several masters with their associates, painting in the fine new manner of the early twelfth century in a town that must have been both prosperous and inventive, still in the lead in ceramic fashion as it has been for so long. Deep bowls are the most common shapes to be painted with birds, but a few stirrup jars are also painted in the same style.

On one example (XI.100) two birds peck at the rosette from the left; this may have been a mother-and-child arrangement to fill the height of the panel; the upper bird's body is very slender. Two more rosette bowls have single birds on each side; the pendent scale triangles framing the

34. J. L. Benson, *AJA* 65 (1961) 342 f.; *JNES* 20 (1961) 73 f.; *HBM*, 60 f.

35. Some deep bowls from Mycenae use the rosette without the birds, substituting an elaborate curved wing pattern, A. Wace, *BSA* 25 (1921-23) 107, fig. 25 c, pl. VII a; *Mycenae* (1949) pl. 82 d; Furtwängler-Loeschcke, *MV*, pl. XXXVI.362.

panels may be close set without "air" (XI.101) or intrude deeply into the picture (XI.102). These scales are on occasion used more whimsically as berries that the bird flies up to peck at (XI.103) or as a leafy setting through which the bird brushes (XI.104). A tree may replace the rosette as a divider between two facing birds (XI.108, 109), as much earlier on the W Krater (III.1), another Eastern motif that developed similarly with goats; the first has a symmetrically decorative tree with a trunk made of circles impaled on a vertical, recalling the ridged trunks of older palm trees, and three pairs of upper branches, curved like ox horns above, the lowest pair a crescent. Occasionally the birds are liberated from the heraldic pose, as on a deep bowl from the east basement of the Granary (XI.110), with a frieze of three "flying swans" under an upper border of triangular scale pattern. One bowl (XI.112) has birds both inside and out, but the inside is superior in quality, two birds right with raised wings and arc filling.

The same workshop made some stirrup jars; the scale triangles may be on the shoulder with alert long-billed birds below (XI.115), more often around the belly (XI.116), or just above or below it (XI.117, 118).

116. A fine stirrup jar from the east basement of the Granary compensates for the narrowness of the frieze around the greatest diameter by stretching out the birds' bodies and interrupting their motion by "rocks" of filled arcs along the upper and lower borders. The birds bump along among these obstacles in a curious reminiscence of Minoan fresco compositions, like the Partridge Frieze or the Pylos Blue Bird Frieze. The wings are squared off and raised like sails, the tails spread in broad triangles with fringes.

117. A tall stirrup jar with a raised disc is associated with the group of bird bowls because the central frieze is a band of dark, eight petaled rosettes with double pale borders, very like contemporary ivory pyxis lids, with filled semicircle ornaments punctuating the design from both borders. The birds are displaced into the lowest band of the four that cover the whole body in a fine display of the aesthetic intentions of the Close Style. (The friezes are all separated by zigzags; there are triangles on the neck and handles, then filled arcs, then the rosettes, then alternating filled semicircles.) The birds are excessively elongated, with two distinct wings and a tubular body; above them, scale-triangles scrape their passing bodies. The bodies are filled with arcs or striped finely, as normal; the tails are fringed; the chests are sometimes black arcs for contrast. This handsome vase shows so many of the mannerisms associated with the bowls that one may think of the Close Style at Mycenae as emanating almost entirely from one workshop; certainly it differs in hand and theme from Close Style vases on the Aegean islands.

118. A burned bichrome stirrup jar has fine scale-peaks on the shoulder, bands set off by chevrons and zigzags below, with dark birds flying right around the upper body, their raised wings topped by streamers floating back in arcs; the necks and tails are barred. At least one turns back to interrupt the direction of the procession.

119. The bridge between the bird vases and the more normal octopus themes of the Close Style is supplied by a fine four-handled jar found by Schliemann in the Granary, with dark outlined octopus tentacles as the major pattern on both body faces, and birds on the shoulder and under the side handles. Dark outlined rosettes on the shoulder link it to the bowl series; the birds are framed in arcades, with scale-triangles curving around their small bodies and lifted wings; they are accented by dark patches on the chest in this elaborate mountain-window setting. The effect is of a series of rocky caves. The birds under the body handles are reduced to protomes with heads turned away from each other, emerging from the top of a tree spray of antithetic spirals; their bodies are chevron patterns. This scheme has some of the features of the birds-feeding-in-a-tree motif, ultimately Minoan (see III.1, XIII.26), and some of the reduced birds among octopus tentacles on normal twelfth-century stirrup jars, but in clarity and density of decoration it is superior to most pieces.

Occasional kraters continue to be decorated with birds, a link with the cup series, but it is not so popular a device as in the thirteenth century. Three from Mycenae use the protome design, and two more subordinate the birds to ornament; only one has a free field with birds in flight. The upper decorative band on a krater (XI.120) is filled with arcades, with chevrons filling in between their peaks, from which quick hooked birds' heads sprout, all facing right. Inside the arcades opposed loops from top and bottom meet at a device like a striped sausage in the center, giving the curious impression that the birds are linking hands, as though skipping rope. The ornament is too frail for the size of the vase and is not used often. The same design made simpler occurs in white paint on a dark krater (XI.121), the birds' bodies made of filled triangles or arcs, and the heads two simple strokes for a curved bill.

The few kraters decorated with birds have abandoned the frieze scheme in favor either of protome birds blended with ornament or playful subordination of bird to ornament. The spiral is another favorite, with the bird's body made of its loops, with a large head and eye tucked in the trailing end (XI.123). A typically III C spiral with an ornamented tube flaring above it like a trumpet is treated as a plant, toward which a subdued striped bird pecks with an open bill (XI.124).

125. These playful pictorializations of birds as ornament contrast with the few free field designs; one krater fragment shows a large bird with an oval humped body, filled with concentric arcs, alighting on the ground line with a thin wing streaming diagonally up behind him to give the angle of flight. In a curious position above him a fish swims left, reversing the usual view but recalling both the decorative disregard for natural roles on octopus stirrup jars and the possible perspective of low foreground land and high background sea on the Miletos beaker (XIII.7). There are no disturbing filling ornaments in the field, but the light clear patterns suggest seashore life unconstricted by registers, in a near-fresco system of decorative scattering.

Mycenae outruns the rest of mainland Greece in the production of bird vases, and it is common sense to suppose that they were made on the spot in one or two workshops. Tiryns has nine or ten fragments, very much in the style of Mycenae, the same arc-filled birds, birds under pendent scale triangles, birds on the shoulder of a stirrup jar, birds with white contours and spots.[36] The most pleasant piece is a krater fragment (XI.126) with a fine Pushmi-Pullyu bird, the two heads rising in slender curves from each end of a long spotted tubular body like a bolster; the middle of the spine supports three sets of rising concentric arcs stacked like a tumbling act. This has been seen as a bird-prowed ship. The rest of the mainland shows one or two pieces at a few sites and slightly larger concentrations at Leukandi and Perati.

A large four-handled jar (XI.136) in Achaia, from the Lopesi site near Patras, shows the same playful conversion of a standard ornament into a bird that the painters at Mycenae enjoyed. There are fringed concentric arcs on the shoulder, and in the main frieze on the belly these have been given bent legs, curved necks at the left end, and broad barred tails with a harmonizing fringe. Similar jars in Patras and Toronto have only the concentric arcs; this is a wittier, handsome piece. Asine in the Argolid has a deep bowl (XI.137) in the style of Mycenae, a bird filled with concentric arcs pecking at a tassel that hangs from the handle. Dendra-Midea uses the Mycenae type of bird protome, with a fringed neck, emerging from a spiral (XI.138). The same design (XI.139) but funnier appears farther north on the Acropolis at Athens, where a chevron pattern mounted with a bird's head climbs precariously up the sloping line linking two spirals.

The other two productive centers, Leukandi in Euboia and Perati on the east coast of Attica, have styles less closely related to those of the Argolid. Leukandi is more independent, Perati more influenced by contemporary island practices, although the usual fine arc fillers are seen in both places as well as on Naxos.

Fragments of a deep bowl from Leukandi (XI.141) give a charming parental scene antithetically arranged on either side of a complex vertical panel bordered with dotted loops. Most panel scenes are Transitional, but the birds are characteristically twelfth-century arc-filled types. The adult bird rushes right toward the panel, striding like an ostrich at full speed, while the baby rises in vertical flight before her breast with open bill and curved wings framing the body as seen from above. The big bird is accented by a dark breast, as at Mycenae; the raised wing is complicated, with four upper plumes joining a broad triangle bordered by loops. Beyond the panel more peaceful birds seem to be feeding on loops. This is in some sense a counterpart to the two family scenes of griffins and sphinxes (XI.65, 91), part of a trend after 1200, which is assisted by the interest in decorative fillers on disparate scales.

Leukandi also uses aggressiveness in such a panel scene (XI.142), as the two birds raise their wings at each other across the panel; as usual the typical scene is here infused with special life. The kalathos bowl, which is usually filled with fish (X.100), here has birds with particolored bodies, striped tubes of wings, zigzag neck and dark body (XI.143).

PERATI

Most of the birds at Perati occur on the shoulders of stirrup jars or are enmeshed among tentacles of octopods. The elaborate scene with birds, trees, and goats was discussed above (XI.83). The bodies show the usual varieties of III C filling: arcs, vertical ripples, crosshatching, or solid dark ovals inside the light, contoured body (a trait more common in the Dodekanese, XII.22, 40, 42). Most interesting are the family scenes and the birds rendered flying downward.

145. Two birds are combined with fish on an elaborate close-meshed octopus stirrup jar; their filling of dark arcs with light borders is a successful rendering of overlapping feathers as scales, like archaic sphinx wings. The bird swooping down on the left is drawn with one wing above the body, one below, the long neck bent below the curled-up claws, an unusual viewpoint suggesting descent on marine prey in the vicinity of the octopus. A less elaborate bird in the center is simply set in midair in normal profile with a raised ladder wing.

Other interesting poses at Perati include birds chasing each other (XI.147), birds facing across a chevron tree as fish swim past (XI.148), and adult birds facing across a young one, the lighter "mother" pushing the fledgling with

36. Slenczka, *Tiryns* VII, pls. 23-33.

her foot to get him off the ground (XI.150). Bird protomes are favorites, but here they grow on chevrons that emerge from octopus tentacles, with a mélange of sea snakes, fish, and rosettes (XI.151). There is only one krater, conventional stripe-necked birds marching left (XI.152); probably this uneven distribution marks a difference between cemetery pottery and that found in town sites.

XII
RHODES AND THE DODEKANESE

THE ISLANDS OF THE DODEKANESE, being situated at nearly equal distances from Greece, Crete, and Cyprus, have the advantage of close contact with all three cultures from the sixteenth century onward. It is natural that island pottery found in the settlements and cemeteries by their harbors should reflect the styles and thematic interests of other Aegean centers. The pictorial material from the Dodekanese has not changed radically in recent years, although it is enriched by the publication of the Late vases from Kos and the Early vases of Karpathos.

Rhodes is the center of vase painting in the fourteenth and early thirteenth centuries and contributes some innovations to the standard series of images. Karpathos in the early fourteenth century produces vases that are partly Minoan in character, as one would expect from its geographical position. Toward the end of the thirteenth century Kos appears more prominently than Rhodes as a pottery-making center with an original local style; echoes of its imagery are found in Tarsus, Ugarit, and Cyprus. Kalymnos, too, has fine pictorial vases of the later period and was apparently in touch with coastal Asia Minor. Most pictorial vases come from cemetery sites, as in Cyprus; the Seragio settlement on Kos is an exception, but the damage done to its recorded finds during World War II has not yet been offset by wider excavation, so that the stratified evidence, which should be most valuable, is not available.

The historical sequence of Aegean "colonization" and influence in the eastern islands is, for the moment, still clearest on Rhodes. The Cretan settlement at Triandha in the Ialysos district, facing Asia Minor, begins in Late Minoan I A, the same period of exploration that brought Minoan traders to Miletos and western Cyprus. The local school of fresco painting that flourished at that time, making decorative patterns of lilies and other plants as at Knossos or Thera, does not seem to influence the development of pictorial vases to any marked degree; pictorial styles must be considered to develop under different influences later on. Apart from a few bird vases in Rhodes and Karpathos that directly reflect Minoan styles of the early fourteenth century, there is no consistent production of pictorial pottery until the Amarna period. From the start, this series is closely tied to Cyprus rather than the Greek mainland, no doubt as a result of the commercial connections maintained by the Mycenaean Greeks who arrived in significant numbers in Rhodes about 1400. They are thought to have had friendly relations at first with the Minoans already there and to have absorbed or ousted them after the fall of Knossos.[1] After a period of consolida-

1. General discussions of the Bronze Age history and sites of the Dodekanese may be found in sources other than those cited below for pictorial painting. Some of the important studies are G. Bean, J. Cook, *BSA* 52 (1957) 116 f.; J. L. Benson, *Ancient Leros* (1963); R. M. Dawkins, *BSA* 9 (1902-03) 176 f.; R. M. Dawkins, A. J. B. Wace, *BSA* 12 (1905-06) 151 f.; P. Fraser, G. Bean, *The Rhodian Peraea* (1954); A. Furumark, *OpArc* 6 (1950) 150; R. Hope Simpson, J. Lazenby, *BSA* 57 (1962) 154 f.; 65 (1970) 47 f.; 68 (1973) 127 f.; G. Jacopi, *Annuario* 13-14 (1930-31) 253 f.; A. Maiuri, *Annuario* 6-7 (1923-24) 83 f.; G. Monaco, *Clara Rhodos* 10 (1941) 42 f.; S. Iakovides, in *The Mycenaeans in the Eastern Mediterranean* (1973) 189; L. Morricone, *Annuario* 43-44 (1965-66) 5f., and 50-51 (1972-73) 139 f.; Stubbings, *MycLevant*, 5. It is quite likely that Minoans led Mycenaeans to these harbors in the late sixteenth and early fifteenth centuries without hostile competitiveness: E. Vermeule, F. Wolsky, "New Aegean Relations with Cyprus," *Proceedings of the American Philosophical Society* 122.5 (1978) 294 f.

tion, the standard scenes of the Middle pictorial repertoire in Cyprus begin to appear sporadically. They are both imported and made locally.

Rhodes

The range of subjects in Rhodian pictorial painting is not great. It includes the usual chariot scenes and bull vignettes; there are some interesting wild goats and birds; the finest of all surviving vases is the Kalavarda rhyton with boars or dancers dressed as wild boar. In the Late period there are octopus stirrup jars, more elegant than in most places. The strongest periods, perhaps by accident of excavation, seem to be LH III A:2 and LH III C:1.

EARLY

BIRDS AND FISH

1. The earliest pictorial vase found so far on Rhodes is a Minoan import, a three-handled jar with birds and flowers. This belongs to the same general school of Minoan pottery as the pyxis exported to Mycenae (VII.I), the basket vase on Karpathos (XII.25), and the many fragments in the destruction levels at Knossos.[2] In this vase the derivation from fresco models is particularly clear in the pendent crosshatched rocks with undulating edges in the upper field, the clear feathering on the raised wing, and the formal swaying lilies. This series begins in the fifteenth century on Crete and lasts until the end of Minoan vase painting, with variations and gradual stiffening.[3] The plump bodies of the two birds suggest partridges, while most Cretan birds of this type are ducks or other water birds, and the way the necks and beaks curve to fit the landscape suggests a general derivation from the principles of composition seen in the Partridge fresco in the Caravanserai at Knossos.[4]

2. A low one-handled cup from Ialysos has a long pedigree of publication for such a sketchy piece. The wall is divided in two zones where the plastic rib had come on earlier "Keftiu" cups. Above there is a frieze of antithetic birds and a structure like an altar or horns of consecration filled with bars. In the lower zone fish dive right, except for one facing pair. A spiral in the upper zone is the only filling ornament. The birds are in outline drawing, the fish are painted solid; both are reductions of contemporary Levantine types, with thin interior markings for the birds' bodies,[5]

the fish with accented teeth and sprays of fins like hair. The idea may be ultimately influenced by Cretan designs, perhaps with a division into the worlds of water and air,[6] but the rigid separation and straight silhouette style are of Mycenaean derivation, far from the whirling compositions of, for example, the Katsamba ewer.[7] The cup may already belong to the Middle phase. It does not qualify to any real degree as a religious image, although such vignettes of birds pecking at altars or horns have a consistent place in the minor religious art of Crete. The fine Rhodian two-handled jar with palms and double axes growing from horns of consecration demonstrates the early spread of Cretan imagery to the potters of the island.[8]

MIDDLE

CHARIOTS

3. A chariot krater from Ialysos was mentioned earlier in connection with the Cypriote Middle III series (IV.48 and following). Its style is closely matched on vases found in Cyprus, Miletos, Tell el-Ajjul in Israel, Berbati, and Mycenae, by Painter 9 (IV.49, 63, 64, 74; VIII.1, 5). It is almost cer-

2. For example, Popham, *DestrKnossos*, figs. 6.1-3, 14, 80, 96, 97; 15.115; pls. 2 a, 7 e-f, 18 a, 19 f, 22 f, 23 b, d, 25 e, 39 d, 46 k(?).

3. There is no general survey of bird vases yet, although an interesting selection was published by W. Heurtley, *QDAP* 5 (1936) 100, fig. 8. Early examples are the splendid bird-and-fish ewer from Katsamba (S. Alexiou, *Katsamba* [1967] pls. 20-22) and the jar from the Knossos Warrior Graves: S. Hood, P. de Jong, *BSA* 47 (1952) 266, I.6, fig. 10, pl. 56 a. There were antecedents in oddities like the griffin cup from the Psychro Cave: C. Zervos, *L'Art de la Crète* (1956) 575-576. The Cycladic swallow and round-bodied bird series are different, but probably in a connected tradition. The bird with folded wings on the alabastron from the Tomb of the Mace-Bearer at Knossos is starker in form, more cluttered in setting, Evans, *Palace of Minos* IV, fig. 300. The alabastra from the Phaistos region share marine symbolism with Minoan larnakes painted at least a generation after the Rhodes and Karpathos vases: C. Zervos, *L'Art de la Crète* (1956) 734, 737-738; *MonAnt* 14 (1904) pls. 27-28; D. Levi, *Annuario* 39-40 (1961-62) 35, fig. 32, cf. fig. 37. This last vase, from Khamillari, with birds carrying or pecking at baskets in a flowery meadow, has iconographic links with the Karpathos vase, XII.25, at the start of a tradition that eventually develops starker sidelines in the Chania poet pyxis: I. Tzedakis, *AAA* 3 (1970) cover and pl. 3, or the birds with horns of consecration at Karphi: *BSA* 55 (1960) 34-35. The thirteenth- and twelfth-century images seem still to be influenced by stonework and by fresco or larnax painting.

4. Evans, *Palace of Minos* II, 110 f.

5. Furumark, *MP*, 251, considered the birds to be a transitional type between Minoan and Mycenaean, perhaps because the bodies are not yet filled with vertical dividers, but Rhodian painters do not normally so divide until very late.

6. *BMCatV* I.1, 150.

7. S. Alexiou, *Katsamba* (1967) pls. 20-22.

8. *CVA* Rodi (Italia) 2, pl. 13.3; *Annuario* 6-7 (1926) 130, figs. 151-152; Furumark, *MP*, FM 36.3, LH III A:2.

tainly an import from the Argolid, not the product of a resettled Levantine potter, although the micaceous clay is also at home in Rhodes.[9] The surface is worn, the painting stereotyped.

Two men in a chariot drive left; one robed figure stands behind the vehicle, and two face it in front. The fillers are characteristic of the period: whorl-shells, rows of dotted circles above and below the reins, a dotted rosette under the team's belly, a swaying palm closing the scene on the right. The horses' legs are deep through the ground line. The harness is picked out in white, and there are rows of white spots beside the mane and across the neck.

Interest is centered on the long-haired figures in their heavily embroidered robes, their arrow-shaped hands gesturing, echoing the arrow shapes of their sword-pommels. The forms of the robes and waving tassels from the scabbards are very close to those on kraters from Ugarit and Tel Dan as well as Enkomi (IV.49, 50). The painter's ambitious but desiccated compositions are marked by a desire to convey a fully narrative scene, an image of captains and charioteers on the battlefield or in procession by city gates, but the scene is too static to suggest whether the motif is one of travelers being greeted or council in battle. Only the braced hind legs of the team, skidding to a sudden stop before the robed men, conveys any sense of energy.

4. In the same general group is the odd krater in Munich from Rhodes. Here the team stalks right through a field crowded with chevron flowers and stemmed flowers, an ogival rock under their bellies, a row of stripes hanging above the reins like a cloud. The charioteer's hands project from an exceptionally swollen breast to grip three reins. The chariot box is divided in two parts, high above the axle; the pale border on the upper box turns into the pole brace, from which an axe-shaped member droops like an extra tail while the pole runs from the ground up into the horses' rumps. The armless passenger, the horses' split legs with pale interior, and the crowded weak flowers are all characteristic of mass-produced Middle painting.

5. An amphoroid krater in the Louvre from Rhodes has companions in Cyprus, like IV.3 and 18. It is thoroughly bad. Two people drive left, the passenger occupying the whole box and the driver far out on the pole, in a mannerism more familiar on the mainland than in the East, as on the Ripe Corinth and Mycenae vases (IX.1 and following). The fillers are Levantine, however: chevrons, a dot-circle rosette, an ornate spiral-triangle rock under the team's belly, a pendent spiral from the pole, and quirks running vertically by the hind legs. The beaked profiles, large eyes surrounded by paint, and ridged hair strongly recall IV.18.

6. The fourth chariot krater of this period from Rhodes is completely different in style and is evidently made locally as a quick version of the more standard Argolid and Cyprus images. The elements are borrowed from such models but are organized differently; there are the chariot, flower, palm tree, whorl-shell, dotted circles, and running quirks in a free arrangement that tends to swamp the chariot motif in fillers. The whole back of the vase is given over to a flower group, four palms and two palmette buds, with hooks and stripes. On the front the chariot is in the center, not attached to the team. The oven-shaped box on the wheel is totally filled by the driver (there is no passenger), who flails bent arms in both directions in a more active pose than most in Cyprus (cf. III.6). He holds the reins in his teeth, while his driving hand is filled with a row of running spirals leading to the team's withers. With charity one might consider this odd design a version of some dramatic scene, with the charioteer both whipping the animals and in emergency transferring his control from the reins to the pole brace, but it is more likely an amateur copy by a craftsman not used to the tradition (cf. XI.14). There is energy in the way the chariot wheel rolls along the rippling stem of an oblique flower caught under it, as along a river bed, and in the disposition of the ornaments to sway and float, framing the slim swaybacked horses. The shape of the vase differs from normal amphoroid chariot kraters, being more like Late Minoan III examples with their depressed bodies, low spreading necks, and splayed handles.

BULLS

7. An amphoroid krater in the Louvre by "the Papyrus Painter" is perhaps from Rhodes, like a companion fragment (XII.8); the provenance is not sure. It suits the Cypriote Middle III bull repertoire. On either side the painter presents a family group (cf. IV.32 and following), a cow following a bull in a rich neat setting of papyrus plants and bordered seashell and chevron stacks. The animals stand out against this dense, formal background because their trefoil dapples are restricted to the inner contour line, with only small dots across the central hide, and because the papyrus plants have been set consciously in a plane behind the animals and seem slightly bent by their passage. The drawing is conventional but neat and forceful; the cow's head tosses eagerly, the bull's is turned back, attracted and commanding; on one side the high tails suggest alacrity for sexual play.

9. The important work at Oxford and Berkeley on the clay of pictorial and other Mycenaean vases has not yet sampled much Rhodian ware: H. Catling, A. Millet, *BSA* 60 (1965) 212; *RDAC* 1978, 70.

Charitonides, in an elegant study of this vase, discussed the feeling for landscape, the rhythmic effect of heavy bodies moving through stems, and the general indebtedness to Egyptian scenes of Hathor cows on boats in papyrus swamps. Dappled bulls and calves are of course a particular feature of Amarna palace painting[10] contemporary with this vase, and there are several Egyptian painters' sketches on limestone ostraka of the later XVIII Dynasty that seem strongly related.

8. A fragment of a krater by the same painter is thought to be a slightly more developed work; the papyrus plants are more articulately placed behind a thinner bull; there are the same dapplings, filling ornaments, rhythms, and firm controls as before. It is difficult, indeed, to postulate "development" in two pieces that could have been made in the same week or even belong to the same vase. There is as yet no evidence for a separate "bull-atelier" on Rhodes; it would be interesting to pursue the cultural problem of how far any of these Eastern painters were personally acquainted with Egyptian imagery.

9. A three-handled jar in the Louvre seems more clearly local Rhodian than the last two. The shape is characteristically Rhodian, seldom treated pictorially in Cyprus (cf. V.69). It is probably on the borderline between Middle and Ripe, close to 1300. A bull is set facing right in each of the three panels, in thin fillers of swaying flowers and grass. The body is not yet divided into three parts, as in Ripe, and strips of rockwork reflect earlier conventions. The bulls are sniffing or tasting flowers, their long bodies filled with pi-pattern, the thick-rooted tails held up in a high curve.

Because Rhodes continues with its fourteenth-century styles in general into the thirteenth century,[11] the following vases are slightly difficult to place; they are of extended Middle character, with sparse and graceful filling ornaments, but it is quite possible they were painted after 1300.

GOATS

Two goat vases, one at least from Ialysos, exhibit pleasant silhouettes and interesting compositions, on local shapes in a style independent of Cyprus.

10. A one-handled jar from the same tomb as the bird oinochoe, XII.12, has a shoulder decoration of two dark goats capering to the right with a flower and crooked whorl shell in the field. The goats are long bodied, with reserved oval muzzles as in Cypriote (cf. V.107) and mainland Ripe painting, one head turned back and one stretched out to nibble the shell, one with a double tail like antithetic spirals and the other with a long dog's tail curled

over his back. The hind legs are sunk through the ground line, the forelegs kick up in action. The jar has a mannered grace and a vivacity in its decorative presentation of wild animals in a meadow, recalling the Thera leaping-goat vases two hundred years earlier.[12]

11. A kylix bought in London in 1907 may be from Ialysos, although it is published as "perhaps Cretan fabric";[13] its peculiar scene of goats rearing up on either side of a papyrus tree recalls the stag kylix from Amorgos in Boston, XII.21. This form of decorated kylix, with a deep capacious bowl and banded stem, is quite common in Rhodes. The goats are drawn with double heads and single bodies; the long back-curled horns have serrated edges like an ibex's; the front legs hook onto subsidiary blooms while the hind legs kick the air. The theme is the same as on the goat-and-tree vases from Mycenae (IX.73, 74), but the style is more carefree and happy.

BIRDS

12. A pretty oinochoe from Ialysos is in feeling very like the goat jar XI.10 from the same tomb, though more heraldic. The two birds are bent, each around half of the shoulder, to join heads and feed at a palm that rises in three sprays from an ogival rock. Palm designs sway on wavy lines issuing from the crevice between wing and back (cf. V.8, 21). The bodies are dissolved to pattern, all in silhouette, so that the necks swirl around to form open loops, and the wing and body are like balanced leaves of a plant. The bills are fringed on top, and a triangle opens in the silhouette behind the reserved eye; the field is filled with floating double-U's. Such lyrical design is not found in Greece or Cyprus.

13. The bill fringed on the upper side is seen again on a kylix from Ialysos, with two birds in a frieze to the right on either side. The drawing is in Rhodian silhouette form rather than Levantine interior division and displays structural peculiarities. Reserved lines break up the silhouette around the borders and form patterns of chevrons, loops,

10. C. Aldred, *Akhenaten* (1968) figs. 34-35; F. von Bissing, *Die Fussboden aus dem Palaste des Königs Amenophis IV* (1941) pls. 1, 8-10; cf. Evans, *Palace of Minos* I, 513, fig. 370.

11. Stubbings, *MycLevant*, 20; Furumark, *MP*, 451.

12. L. Renaudin, *BCH* 46 (1922) 61, pl. 13; J. J. Maffre, *BCH* 96 (1972) 36, no. 80, fig. 23, with references; S. Marinatos, *Thera* VI (1974) pls. 80-81, col. pl. 11.

13. Perhaps thought of as Cretan because of the relation to the amphoroid krater from Ligortino in the Louvre, CA 833: E. Pottier, *BCH* 31 (1907) 118; A. Mavrigiannaki, *EphArch* 1974, 45 f. For a similar sherd, with a bearded goat's head, from the Phaistos district, M. Borda, *Arte Cretese-Micenee nel Museo Pigorini* (1946) pl. 36. The pictorial kylix is more familiar in Rhodian than in Cretan tradition, but there seems to be no way of placing the London vase with certainty.

and bands on the breast and tail. There is an extra "wing," a splayed triangular form between the raised wing and the neck, and plumes ending in chevrons float as long trailers between wing and body. This trait of floating plumes in odd formal shapes should probably be connected with the "chained" bird motif on the chariot kraters from Ugarit (V.8, 21).

14. A Rhodian kylix in Heidelberg also shows two birds in a frieze, right, on each side; the bodies are composed of three silhouetted curved arcs for neck, raised wing, and body. They have long beaks and bulging breasts, and a dotted-circle filling ornament and are close in style to the reduced bird-curves of V.69.

15. A cruder kylix from Vatoi, in Copenhagen, uses two dark humped birds in a frieze, with a mill-sail or lozenge pattern tipped up on top of the back for a wing; the heads are reserved. A spiral fills the space behind the second bird. The style of painting is independent of both Cyprus and Greece; it suggests a swimming procession with some success.

16. A beaked jug from Zukalades has a playful, original design based on a series of papyrus blossoms joined by loops. A long-beaked bird's head sprouts from a loop and turns right to feed on the neighboring blossom. The painter has also inserted eyes in the loops; the lower curve is striped like eyelashes, and there is an oval open eye in the center. There are other fillers of chevron-flowers and drifts of slashes. The painting is excellent, and the sense of humor a rarity, even in Rhodes.

RIPE

Two vases of extraordinary interest, without parallel in other regions, seem thirteenth century in style, although the criteria are not certain. The Kalavarda rhyton and the pilgrim flask with ladies are pictorial in a truer sense than the decorative animal designs already discussed, since they attempt to convey something odd outside the normal tradition, inventing a figure style for the purpose.

17. The Kalavarda conical rhyton with dancing boar-daimons and birds is perhaps the most refreshing piece in the central Aegean. It is of high quality, although now fragmentary with a worn surface. Like some other rhyta, it was painted upside down to give the potter a flat surface to rest it on while drawing, although most rhyton painters solved the physical problem differently. The lower end and part of the side wall are missing. The scene is contained by a broad band of chevrons below the rim and neat bands and stripes at the point.

Three boarlike figures, animals or masked dancers in daimon costume, prance on their hind feet to the right, with three birds rising vertically like punctuation marks between them. The birds are in the usual side profile, but tipped up on their tails, a quarter turn off the usual direction; they may have been painted on while the vase was on its side. Overhead, toward the bottom of the vase, a series of pendent jagged rocks sets the scene in the countryside in the fresco convention, and a flower like a lily floats upside down between the first two animals.

The animal-dancers have been identified variously as lions or wild boar; they have a pronounced crest of bristles rising from shoulder to ear, like a boar's, and the tight spiral curl of the tails is also swinelike. Three feet and four hands are preserved; they look more human than animal, with spread fingers and pointed toes, which has raised the issue of masked dancers in animal hides, but pictorial conventions are not always nice in such details, and the creatures might also be thought of as animals performing human actions, given toes to dance with and hands to grasp with. They are drawn in solid silhouette with only the eyes reserved.

The first dancer, on the left, holds high a dark object shaped like a gourd or a mirror with a handle; perhaps it is a rattle, not unlike the object shaken by priests on the Hierapetra larnax.[14] The second dancer is unfortunately broken from the eye forward. The third reaches out toward a kylix with high-swung handles, by now a rather old-fashioned shape but known in plain wares in the thirteenth century.[15] The birds who fly between the dancers all have raised wings and are filled in different ways. The first has a long hooked bill and a wing of rock pattern; the breast is dark, spotted, set off from the crosshatched tail by filled triangles. The second has an open double-curved bill, spotted breast, and slender oval wing; the third, a dark breast with an inset circle, crossed, and a narrow tube wing filled with chevrons. These filling devices look forward to the twelfth century, and the rhyton should be close in date to the Tiryns rhyton with priests and trees (IX.15). The animation of birds flying among dancers shares the tone of the late thirteenth-century Cretan pyxis from Chania with a lyre player and darting birds.[16]

The musical instrument and drinking cup may seem, superficially, to reinforce Picard's suggestion that the figures are masked human dancers rather than nature daimons or boar totems; yet animals in Aegean art may

14. E. Vermeule, in *A Land Called Crete* (1968) fig. 35; *IEE* I, 336; P. Warren, *The Aegean Civilizations* (1975) 108.
15. See note 43 below; Furumark, *MP*, FS 273, fig. 17; C. W. Blegen, *The Palace of Nestor at Pylos* I (1966) pls. 365-366.
16. I. Tzedakis, *AAA* 3 (1970) 111.

also celebrate, and the discrepancy between animal bodies and "human" limbs is not totally persuasive. The sound of the gourd and the drinking cup held high suggest a celebratory rite rooted in the sympathy and powers of daimons with nature, and the traditional birds, expressing the nearness of divinity, share in awkward but happy flight. The typically ceremonial rhyton joins with other sacral scenes from Attica, Kea, Tiryns, and Ugarit to form a group of late ritual images of special interest (IX.13, 15, 16; XI.65, 66; XIII.29).

18. A pilgrim flask in the Rhodes Museum that has always attracted visitors, although scholars have not cared for it much, has the figure of a frontal robed woman on each narrow side under the handles. The painting is crude but commanding, like some Tanagra larnakes. The women, cramped between the conventional concentric circles on the faces of the vase, differ in detail. One has a faded outline with an interior contour of ragged dots emphasizing the greater divisions of belly and breast (where the nipples are prominent dotted circles); the bottom of the robe is striped in simple bands, representing flounces but looking as though the woman was standing on a pile of planks. A heavy circle in the center of the skirt is evidently meant for genitals. It is odd for genitals to appear in Mycenaean art at all, and odder still under a dress; the scheme is evidently a conflation of the convention of the robed woman and a desire to indicate the working parts, as it were, a common motif in Cypriote and Near Eastern gems and terracottas. A loop on the left squared shoulder may be arm or accident; above it, a column of horizontal stripes rises, and on the other side a column of dots, an abstract rendering of the old image of the goddess with upraised arms. The profile is seen on some charioteers and soldiers: sloping forehead, triangles for nose and lips, columnar neck, and zigzag hair around the crown.

The second woman is more firmly drawn and armless. The long torso has rows of inner dots framing the sides and forming a vertical central seam; the circles of the bosom have no nipple dots and there are no genitals. The flounces start at hip level, interspersed with dots for embroidery. Four rows of dots streak the face from lip to dress, perhaps meant as strands of a necklace rather than the tears or blood drops that are similarly suggested on some larnakes.

These robed women are clearly different from the standard "personnages à robe" in the Levant; they have more in common with mainland iconography although made in a local Rhodian atelier. The frontal body and profile head, the isolation in panels, the dim suggestion of mourning or invocation, are seen on larnakes. Decorated pilgrim flasks are not common; the Sarepta horse flask (IV.78) was an oddity like this. Occasionally a bird is

placed in this position among flowers, or a woman in the Cypriote Iron Age.[17] Since the pilgrim flask itself is often funerary, connoting difficult but imaginary journeys (for in real life wood or leather would be more practical), the images here may intertwine the notions of fertility and mourning with primitive forthrightness.

TRANSITIONAL AND LATE

Most of the intricate and excellent pictorial images from the late periods on Rhodes belong to the series of octopus stirrup jars, which are not surveyed here. There are also octopus rhyta,[18] octopus kylikes,[19] an octopus cut-away jug,[20] an octopus three-handled jar,[21] and an octopus krater.[22] The types of octopus designs on stirrup jars have been surveyed several times.[23] It may be convenient to analyze briefly the forms of fish and birds caught among octopus tentacles on Rhodian jars, for comparison to drawing styles at Kos, Miletos, Naxos, and Perati. The birds and fish are subsidiary motifs, often enlarged in the side spaces, and sometimes drawn with more freshness than the main octopod. They occur in antithetical patterns facing across a tentacle like birds feeding on a plant[24] or set in friezes gliding toward the central octopus body.[25] Occasionally they are placed in a whirling design, rising up in air or waves, vertically or horizontally, to fill space decoratively.[26] When rosettes or other large patterns are used as a stop to the flow of tentacle, the minor birds or fish may be placed back to back, facing the octopus and the pattern, and there may be deliberate variation in the flow of the friezes to both ends.[27]

When the birds have a raised wing, it may be painted in two to four waving plumes or in a long hatched streamer, as in the Middle period. When the wing is

17. Stubbings, *MycLevant*, 20; *CVA* Cyprus I, pl. 30.3; *CVA* Florence 1, pl. 1.10 (Italia, pl. 354); *BCH* 75 (1960) 249, fig. 11 (Bichrome IV).

18. For example, Ialysos T. 4, *Annuario* 6-7 (1923-24) pl. I; Brussels A 1910, *CVA* 1, pl. 3.4.

19. *Annuario* 6-7, 204, fig. 127; 228, fig. 145; Kassel Museum 31.3.66.

20. *Annuario* 6-7, 155, fig. 79.

21. *Annuario* 6-7, 114, fig. 34.

22. *Annuario* 6-7, 226, fig. 143.

23. *Annuario* 6-7, figs. 39, 64, 99; pls. 2, 3; *Annuario* 13-14 (1930-31) 287 f., figs. 30, 31, 35-38, 65, 69, 70, 72, 79, 80, 81; pls. 21, 24, 25; A. Furumark, *OpArc* 6 (1944) 196 f.; V. Desborough, *The Last Mycenaeans and Their Successors* (1964) 152 f.

24. *Annuario* 13-14, 294, fig. 38.

25. *Annuario* 13-14, fig. 36; pl. 21.

26. *Annuario* 13-14, pl. 25.

27. *Annuario* 13-14, pl. 21.

folded, it may be a light insert in a dark body.[28] Bird bodies are normally oval, painted solid, often with a reserved border; if they are in outline drawing, there are several concentric ovals inside or a filling of oval segments and bars.[29] Fish are usually rendered the same way, with a dark body, reserved or striped heads, and a reserved outer border. The outlines are enriched with jagged dorsal and ventral fins; the eye is large, but the teeth not so prominent and menacing as elsewhere.[30] The accompanying figures show typical fish. In a slightly later phase of III C, spiral patterns may be converted to bird protomes with dotted borders, as on the mainland.[31]

SCORPION

19. A stirrup jar includes a scorpion in an elaborate scene of birds nestling on octopus tentacles, fish swimming between them, and filled circles as stoppers webbed to the tentacles. Most of the scorpions in Aegean art do occur in the more elaborate productions and are inorganic additions to conventional scenes. It may be an element taken over from cylinders, or the sign of a school of stirrup-jar painters who felt it appropriate to the superficially bizarre collections of land and sea life that cluster around the octopus as a substitute for seawater.[32] This scorpion is an oval-bodied insect with a solid body and reserved border, as for birds and fish; there are three legs on each side, the

front pair with opposed pincers, and a tail formed of linked ovals in a long chain with a barbed stinger curving up at the end.

BIRDS

20. A late stirrup jar has the body zone filled with rolling spirals on a partly dark ground, clearly echoing the marine imagery of undulating octopus tentacles or waves. The birds and fish are in the shoulder zone in a frieze to the right that tilts the dark bodies up and down, the fish diving and the birds rising with their feet out in front. Dots outlining the birds' heads recall the dotted spiral protomes of the age, and the variations in pattern below seem to suggest some abstract gradation from wave crests at sea to dry land with breaking ripples, above which the marine beasts flourish.[33]

Rhodes also produced or obtained several of the late snake hydriai with strainer spouts that were fashionable in the central Aegean in the twelfth century. The snakes are interchangeably plastic rolls of clay or painted undulations along the sides of the jar, their heads leaning into the strainer and often licking the contents. Pictorially they are simple; in terms of ritual, filled with suggestive interest.[34]

The Other Islands

Even Rhodes has not been excavated systematically, and the other islands of the eastern Aegean are known best through sporadic finds or limited cemeteries. Kos is now the best known. The range, size, and connections of most Mycenaean settlements have still to be learned, but even the finds we have tend to distinguish the pictorial pottery produced in the islands from themes and styles found on the mainland.

28. *Annuario* 6-7, fig. 39; *Annuario* 13-14, figs. 38, 80, pls. 21, 24, 25.

29. *Annuario* 6-7, fig. 39.

30. *Annuario* 6-7, fig. 39; *Annuario* 13-14, figs. 38, 80; pl. 24.

31. *Annuario* 6-7, pl. 2.

32. W. Heurtley, *QDAP* 5 (1936) 94, "The bird within the arms of the octopus has the same wings [as on the Kalymnos stirrup jar], but here the arms are not thought of as branches of a tree, but as crested rolling waves in the trough of which the bird is riding."

33. Miscellaneous bird pictures are not included here, like BM A 932, *BMCatV* I.1, fig. 231; *CVA* British Museum 5, pl. 7.16 b.

34. Snake hydriai are most common in the Dodekanese and Naxos, for example, *Annuario* 6-7, figs. 44, 59; *Annuario* 13-14, 321, fig. 68; *Annuario* 43-44 (1965-66) figs. 195, 259; *Ergon* 1959, 127, fig. 130; V. Desborough, *The Last Mycenaeans and Their Successors* (1964) pl. 7 c, d; the kernos type appears at Mycenae, Athens NM 5427; another, Museum of Fine Arts, Boston, 1971.1.

AMORGOS

21. A kylix said to come from Amorgos, now in the Museum of Fine Arts, Boston, has an unusual picture of two stags facing across a bull's head. It was probably painted in the later fourteenth century, in the Middle period, and recalls XII.11. The given provenance is the more persuasive because of the five Mycenaean pieces from Amorgos acquired by Würzburg in the same year, 1901.[35]

The center is filled with a facing bull's head, a motif well known in Crete, Cyprus, and also Karpathos, but rare on the mainland (III.23, V.102, 103, IX.27, XIII.27). Like most Mycenaean renderings, it is not meant as a skull but still has ears and eyes; the face is drawn in generous double curves with round filled eyes like an octopod's, and the horns are laid on a flat bar across the brow like architectural horns of consecration. The stags are only protomes, from the breast up; a full body would not be possible in such a space. They are in solid paint with long curved necks, reserved oval eyes (the duct in front), parted lips, and horns branching fore and aft with three curved prongs on each branch. The effect is conversational. If there is any symbolic meaning in the scene, it is not clear; in terms of design the bull's head serves as a tree or similar central pattern that might attract antithetic animals to feed.

KALYMNOS

A group of twenty-four Mycenaean vases was acquired by W. R. Paton in 1886; they are now in the British Museum. They came from two different tomb sites buried in pumice along the river bank near the harbor town of Pothia. Many broken vases were discarded; of those saved, some are standard LH III B, some in an interesting III C style. Three are pictorial.[36] The style is close to that of Rhodes and Kos.

22. An open lekane (basin), or kalathos, with two horizontal loop handles outside and two groups of three nipples inside as "rivets" for the handles, is painted inside with birds, fish, and a lily. This is a more elegant prototype for the III C lekanai vases of Athens and Leukandi (X.99, 100; XI.143). On one side two birds peck at crosshatched baskets hanging from the rim, probably their nests; on the other side four fish leap rhythmically in a school. As in Rhodes the birds and fish have dark bodies with light borders; the birds' wings are raised, the fish are jagged with fins. The dividing point between them is

marked by an ornate spiral lily fringed and webbed, like a horizon emblem between land and sea. The whole effect is elaborate and stately, like the best octopus jars that share such themes; the birds may be bringing food to their nests from a shore hunt, in a milder version of the Cypriote swan vases or the Leukandi griffin pyxis (IV.38, XI.91).

23. The famous octopus stirrup jar with birds and animals caught among the tentacles comes from a site half a mile away. This and the elaborate companion piece from Pitane in Asia Minor, by the same hand, are the fullest portrayals of an Aegean marine paradise with, as Heurtley suggested, animals as on Noah's ark roosting in the branches of "the undersea tree." The octopus is attenuated, with a needle-sharp body and a bulbous headknob surmounted by a shape like a vase, a pithoid amphora. The upper left tentacle and the three upper right tentacles are bordered above with dark filled arcs; the area next to the body is closely filled with sharp lacelike ornaments of webbed bands, triangles, lozenges, and loops. Above the spiral ends of the arms two extra wheels spin off like planets, and the undulations of the top arms are tied by fringed and paneled arcs. The spaces around this curious spidery polyp are filled with fourteen birds, four goats, two hedgehogs, two crabs, two "eggs," and a scorpion. They are necessarily small in scale, mostly dark with light borders to stand out in the complexity, arranged in friezes with separate rhythms.

Two light spotted birds with raised two-plume wings and open beaks have just settled on the top octopus arms. On the left, the first of the three lower friezes holds a pair of goats nuzzling or butting, and a bird on the left, whose feet pass below the tentacle-ground line to be caught by a crab below. The crab, seen from above, has six legs, two pincers, and triangular reserved eyes. Next to him, facing toward the octopus' body, a bird with raised wing seems to shriek at a hedgehog who tiptoes up the incline of the tentacle toward a spotted "egg" (not an immature hedgehog rolled up in defense). The hedgehog is dark with a fringe of pricks along the back, as at Asine and Tiryns. Probably the egg is a real egg, which the hedgehog is about to eat, while the bird attacks from the rear with noise and flailing wings. The bird frieze below this is quieter, with four dark birds flying in formation toward the octopus, their splayed toes below the tentacle.

On the right the upper frieze has more active goats than the matching frieze on the left, one running up the

---

35. E. Langlotz, *Griechische Vasen in Würzburg* (1932) nos. 19, 21, 22, 26, 31.

36. BM A1001 to 1024; W. R. Paton, *JHS* 8 (1887) 446; C. Smith, *CR* 1 (1887) 80; *CVA* British Museum 5, pls. 8-9; cf. E. Langlotz, *Griechische Vasen in Würzburg* (1932) nos. 25, 28, 30, 32, 33.

slope of the tentacle toward the octopus with its lips parted, one grazing in the other direction with straddled legs while a bird squawks at it; this goat has two bordered oval inserts in the body, as on Kos. Below this, four birds fly left, all with open beaks as though crying or feeding, and the angles of their raised plumes and drawn-back legs suggesting speed; they are alternately dark with light borders and light filled with spots. In the lowest frieze, another version of the bird and hedgehog drama; the hedgehog, with open jaws, comes out from the octopus web to a spotted egg which the bird, beyond it, may be trying to roll away with its beak. To the right another dark crab tries to catch a bird in the frieze above, and a scorpion with a barbed tail holds the octopus' curled tentacle in one pincer.

The contrast between the formal slender octopus tied in webs of pattern, its irregular bulbousness possibly suggestive of the mating season (cf. III.2), and the active animals caught in its tentacles, carrying on their daily business of feeding, aggression, and defense in this marine world, does not seem incongruous, either in scale or in connection. One may regard the scene as decorative or as symbolic or playful; one must admire the asymmetrical rhythms, the continuing or interrupted flow of frieze, the antithetic or streaming currents of composition, punctuated by open mouths, noise, activity, a pinched foot or a threatened egg. It is a more lively vase than the Pitane jar, which adds fish to the scene according to the conventions (XIII.8).

24. A collared jar with four handles has three decorated friezes on the upper body. The upper two have abstract designs of multiple chevrons and loops; the lowest shows four goats, two at each side facing a central palm tree. Its trunk is made of joined dark circles with light borders (cf. V.4); four long fringed branches bend down in pairs symmetrically. The goats are not identical, though drawn like those on the preceding stirrup jar and on the goat krater (XII.35) from Kos. Their bodies are two slender ovals, spotted on one side of the jar and dark with light borders on the other; two of the dark goats are bearded, and five of the eight have horns swept back in a high arc; the necks are hatched or filled with arcs, the legs are dark, symmetrical, and far down through the ground line. This is a static version of the usual goats nibbling on the tree, expanded to fill a broader field by doubling the animals (cf. XI.84); there is no real climbing or biting, although the lips are parted like birds' beaks, yet the style scarcely deserves the appellation "barbarous" conferred by its owners.

The form of the vase, the twisted handles, and general abstraction of design set it very late in III C (cf. XII.42).

KARPATHOS

Karpathos, like Kasos, forms a natural bridge and harbor station between Crete and the Dodekanese. It is not surprising, then, that the major find of ninety-seven vases of the Early period should show strong Minoan undercurrents of style, and in some cases possibly of manufacture. They come from a chamber tomb near the chief port of Pigadia, with associated objects of bronze and lead.[37] Four are pictorial vases, all early and odd.

25. Half of a double basket-handled vase is painted with birds floating and pecking among flowers. This is a Cretan type of vase, with close parallels at Knossos; another very like it (XII.1) came to Rhodes along the same track. It is not the finest of its class—the major Knossos vase, a three-handled jar with light-on-dark partridges and lilies,[38] is a more controlled production formally recalling fresco design—but it is vivacious and picturesque.

The birds are arranged antithetically, facing toward a checkerboard design with laddered borders, which assumes the form of a stemmed chalice or drinking cup. The upper border of this "chalice" peaks in three curves, over which pendent flowers hang. Other flowers spring from the base of the chalice, waving out toward the birds who feed on them. The birds have thick outlines; the bodies are filled with rows of slashes for stippled feathers; the beaks are open for feeding, the barred tails fan out, the feet are crooked up under to suggest hovering in the air. The conversion of the theme of feeding birds to an apparently sacral scene stresses the Minoan connections, where Cypriote and Levantine versions are straightforward.[39]

26. A related vase, a three-handled jar, very worn, has a principal design of papyrus plants and argonauts, common ingredients of a minor land and sea imagery, which in this case have offered context for an incidental bird above the plant and for two fish flanking the argonaut. The shape of the vase is ultimately Minoan, like the decorative motifs. It has features in common with the fish-and-octopus ewer in Athens (VII.7), suggesting the general matrix of pictorial ideas from which various styles developed. The bird is long bodied with a fat raised wing barely separated from the body, casually barred inside the outline. The fish are sharp-nosed dolphin types, schematically rendered. Such combinations of birds and fish are

37. S. Charitonides, *Deltion* 19 (1961-62) 32-76; R. Hope-Simpson, J. Lazenby, *BSA* 57 (1962) 159.

38. S. Hood, P. de Jong, *BSA* 47 (1952) 264, I.6, pl. 56a; cf. note 3 above.

39. D. Levi, *Annuario* 39 (1961) 39, fig. 37.

common in certain workshops of Late Minoan III A:1-2, as on the Phaistos alabastra and some larnakes; there seems no need to lower the date of this vase to the Middle period.

27. A ewer decorated with a facing bull's head on the front in isolated grandeur is an early example of this relatively rare emblem. The thick outlines and symmetrical squareness of the animal might have suggested a date as late as the Argos jug (IX.27), but the ewer shape cannot be much later than LH III A:1, roughly contemporary with the bull's head krater in Cyprus (III.23). The Karpathos ewer is less simplified and grotesque than the Cypriote krater; in the absence of subsidiary religious symbolism like axes or horns of consecration, it is possible to imagine that the stimulus for this picture was a clay bull's head rhyton, like the example from Karpathos in London.[40] The horns are very short for this type, and sharply curved in; the round eyes and streaming lateral ears are standard, though reserved stripes suggest the furled interior of the ear in an unusual way; the brow has a row of curled fringes, and the face is divided into four compartments filled with short curves in alternate directions, for rough hair. The head is large for the vase, placed crookedly, yet most effective.

28. A fragmentary krater offers a series of designs which have symbolic value in some mute ritual sphere. It is one of the new open kraters with vertical strap handles (cf. III.12 and following, VIII.12). The decoration may have been symmetrical on each face; three-fourths of the front and a fifth of the back are preserved. The frieze is framed by waves above and on the handle, plain bands below.

On the left by the handle there is a long rod-shaped object with a light-centered disc at the top and a knobbed handle at the bottom, like a fan, gourd, rattle, sistrum, or mirror, not unlike the objects carried by the "priests" on the Hierapetra larnax or by the boar dancers on the Kalavarda rhyton (XII.17). Next is an isolated wheel with four spokes, recalling the "Circus Pot" (VIII.8); then a pilgrim flask or globular jug whose reserved body is filled with a central rosette and radiating spokes like a wheel; then two high-handled kylikes stacked one above the other, both in solid paint, and in form like the kylix on the Kalavarda rhyton. On the right, just beyond the center of the frieze, is the start of another pilgrim flask whose dark body is elaborated with reserved ladder-patterned circles around a reserved rosette.

Images of vases on pictorial vases are fairly rare, and usually appear in a human context (the Sunshade Krater, III.21; the Ewer krater, III.22; the Suda Bay krater, V.19; the Leukandi krater, XI.66; the Kalavarda rhyton, XII.17). Bowls and chalices occur on bird vases (XII.25). In Minoan and Cycladic painting there is an occasional holy vase on a vase, like the ewers standing on plant garlands on a three-handled jar from Thera.[41] The pilgrim flask seen twice here is always considered native to the Levant, appearing in the Mycenaean repertory in the early fourteenth century; the particular type with a large rosette is, however, Cretan in design and may be meant for the Minoan globular flask rather than the Levantine flattened flask. Examples from Cyprus, Knossos, and Chania offer good parallels for the designs on the Karpathos krater, with a rosette or wheel at the center and stiff foliate bands here represented as ladders.[42] The kylix with high-swung handles was thought by the excavator to be purely Mycenaean; yet there are examples from Crete, mostly thirteenth century but beginning as a type in the early fourteenth.[43] Since the flask and the kylix are regarded as funerary gifts to important persons as well as objects that play ritual roles, their association with the wheel and the rattle or mirror suggests a fairly elaborated set of funeral images in the early Mycenaean world, whose specific import we cannot yet interpret.

KOS

The island of Kos became an important, original center of pictorial painting toward the end of the thirteenth century, and after 1200 the ateliers seem to have been more productive than on Rhodes. Kos's earlier Mycenaean traditions were quite plain, part of the general Aegean koiné. It is surprising that neighboring Mycenaean installations on the coast of Asia Minor, like Müskebi near Halikarnassos, show no signs of the elaborate pictorial images of Kos, but there are connections with the paintings both of Miletos and of Ugarit (XIII.5, 27 and following).

The three principal sources of pictorial vases on Kos are the settlement site at Seragio (Serayia) in the main modern town and the cemetery groups of Langadha and Eleona just south of the town.[44] There is a much stronger

40. BM A971; *BMCatV* I.1, pl. 15; Vermeule, *GBA*, pl. XLII.C; C. Doumas, *AA* 1968, 381, fig. 10.

41. S. Marinatos, *Ergon* 1971, 201, fig. 241; *Thera* V (1972) pl. 60 a; *Kreta, Thera und das mykenische Hellas* (1976) pl. 158.

42. BM C563 (Maroni), cf. M. Popham, *BSA* 62 (1967) pl. 84 d; R. M. Dawkins, *BSA* 9 (1902-03) 316, fig. 15; I. Tzedakis, *BSA* 66 (1971) pls. 63 b, 64 a.

43. S. Alexiou, *EphArch* 1970, pl. 3; M. Popham, *BSA* 64 (1969) 301, fig. 4; *BSA* 65 (1970) pl. 51 a, b.

44. L. Morricone, *Bollettino d'Arte* 35 (1950) 316; *Annuario* 43-44 (1965-66) 7 f.; cf. also *JHS* 65 (1945) 102; *Ergon* 1959, 131-134; Stubbings, *MycLevant*, 21; V. Desborough, *The Last Mycenaeans and Their Successors* (1964) 156 f.

concentration of interesting pictorial material in the town site than in the cemeteries, which run to octopus jars. Since much of the Seragio pottery was lost or mixed up during the German occupation, and the stratigraphic sequence was lost, one must hope that the excavation of this interesting late Mycenaean town can be developed further.[45] The surviving sherds offer most interesting pictures of twelfth-century warfare and soldiers in curious helmets, which must reflect the historical exchanges and innovations of the last vigorous Mycenaean days in the East.

While the site and cemeteries have a chronological span of about two hundred years, from the fourteenth to the twelfth centuries, the pictorial pieces are all Late. Many of the Seragio sherds are reported to be from a local form of amphoroid krater with a low neck, wide mouth, and comparatively globular body. It is quite possible that the grand III C kraters from Ugarit (XIII.28, 29) are related.

LATE SOLDIERS

29. The rim fragment of a krater has a scene of warriors in tufted helmets marching right; only parts of the heads are preserved. At the left a soldier with a long slanted oval eye and sharp nose like a visor is wearing a tall semicircular helmet with a crest of tongues. The helmet body has a central vertical panel from which diagonal stripes splay upward; the tongues are dark with pale borders. The helmet front has a curved projection like a primitive nose guard; perhaps we should think of a metal crest-holder on a leather or canvas body. The only sign of a weapon is a slender staff with curved double prong, no weightier than a toasting fork, slanting up in front of the soldier. It passes over a curved triangular object, dark with reserved borders, conceivably a shield seen in true profile, or the conical cap of a shorter member of the troop. On the right only part of a helmet remains, a tall bag-shaped cap with straight sides and a curved top, painted in checkerboards, surmounted by a crest of tall rays, possibly a version of a "feathered headdress" though plainer than the next.

30. The wall fragment of a krater has parts of three soldiers in procession to the right, the foremost perhaps climbing a hill or a siege ladder. The only well-preserved figure is the soldier at the left, down to the breast. The body is dark, the head and helmet in outline to show the curious details. The helmet is again shaped like a bag; it seems to enclose the face to the jawbone, slanting down to cover the back of the neck. The oddities of the drawing conceal whether the nose projects from or is covered by the helmet and whether the two lines below are beard or neck. The round eye is conspicuous in the center of this armor.

The flat top of the helmet is crested with a series of tall rays pronged or branching out in Y-forks, more like plants (rushes?) than feathers, although it is difficult to imagine what else could be intended. The soldier's arm is drawn back and perhaps held a spear. A diagonal staff topped by a circle may be a weapon in the drawn-back arm of the next soldier, who wears a similar helmet. Part of a third, at the right, is at a sharp angle high up in the field, as though the head were tilted back, climbing or falling. This kind of picture is not archaeologically useful for determining helmet types but is a vivid sign of the variety of late Mycenaean or Sea Peoples' helmets that artists were inspired to record.

31. The rim fragment of a krater has at least one soldier, right, in a feathered headdress waving above a solid-painted head in which no interior details show. A few feathers toward the front of the crest show the usual Y-fork, the rest are simple curved plumes. The eye stands on end and is reserved. Behind the figure is a circle, like the top of the staff on XII.30. The soldier's arm rises in an awkward rippling arc with a line descending from his hands; either he is making an odd thrust with spear or sword, or he is holding the reins of a chariot.

32. A wall fragment of a krater has a single helmeted head, right, with indiscernible traces of a pale object or figure at the left. The body is painted solid; no arms show, as though they were held straight down from the rounded shoulders. The helmet and face are in outline. The helmet is broken off at the top, but seems to have been a tall bag or turban type, the crest filled with blocks of stripes at right angles, like overlapping leather or bronze plates, or wickerwork. A line from the back of the skull arches over the eye and forms the nose, from which five lines drip as a moustache (cf. XI.45-47). If this line is the lower edge of the helmet, it sat low and broad on the head.

These late helmets from Kos are now becoming better known and figure increasingly in discussions of feather headdresses and the Sea Peoples, for which they have some relevance.[46]

LATE SAILORS

33. The wall fragment of a krater shows the lower deck of a ship being rowed right by two sailors in baggy

The authors have been shown great kindness on Kos by Professor Morricone, Mr. Kontis, and Mr. Nikolaides.

45. *Ergon* 1959, 133; L. Morricone, *Annuario* 50-51 (1972-73) 139-396.

46. For example, K. Galling, "Die Kopfzier der Philister in den Darstellungen von Medinet Habu," in Schaeffer, *Ugaritica* VI, 247; F. Schachermeyr, "Hörnerhelme und Federkronen," *Ugaritica* VI, 451; E. Wente, "Shekelesh or Shasu?", *JNES* 21 (1962) 167; N. K. Sandars, *The Sea Peoples* (1978) 117-137.

turbans. The ship is shown in cross section, as on the Enkomi (V.38) and Phaistos vases.[47] The fragment is too small to yield clear information on some puzzling details. Two bands at the bottom frame the frieze but do not apparently represent the water level. A band in the center serves as the planking between decks. The two rowers brace their feet on this; their rowing benches are not painted in, but they have reached the end of their stroke and from the curved backs and bent legs one understands that they are seated. Each has a single oar pulled with both hands; the oars do not project below the planking. The sailors' bodies are dark, the heads outlined, with simple dot-eyes; their turbans are loosely striped. The lower legs of the man on the left are outlined, possibly to represent greaves, for fighting marines. Facing the sailors on the far left is an enigmatic shape that may be a steersman or timekeeper seated on a bench, one sharp hand gesticulating, the lower legs also reserved. A stripe across the top of the picture must be the deck planking, so low the sailors' heads will crash into it when they lean forward for the next stroke; two lines on the deck may represent the skirts of "officers," as on the Enkomi vase, or part of the rigging. Most pictorial ship pictures are short from end to end; probably there were no more sailors than we see, and the curved line with two crossbars that runs down through the lower planking behind the right-hand sailor may be the stem of the ship.

The revived interest in ship images in the Late period in many media, from terracotta models to graffiti on stone, is understandably most intense in the islands of the Aegean. Skyros, Melos, Kos, and Crete admire this kind of picture, and perhaps the Kos krater is the most sympathetic of all the versions.

GOATS

34. The top of a small stirrup jar from the Langadha cemetery is painted with three goats circling right, one in each of three spaces made by handles and spout. The largest, at the rear, is fairly well drawn in outline, in the style of other Dodekanese goats found among octopus tentacles (XII.23), with a heavy border and an interior made of two reserved ovals. The face is open, the horns swept back. The other two goats are small, cramped, and dark. One bends his head to the ground-line; the other scarcely has a head, only horns.

35. A magnificent open strap-handled krater from the Seragio site has most of the front preserved. The shape is like that of the Ugarit kraters (XIII.27 and following), and the animal drawing has traits in common with those. Three large goats strut right, in grand splayed postures like fro-

zen leaps. The first two have birds on their backs, the third has a bird under the belly and a striped two-petaled flower hanging over his back. The conception is similar to that of the Mycenae jar with horses and birds (XI.13), but less complicated.

The goats are generally dark with long slender swaybacked bodies and short legs, the front pair like human soldier's legs. The thighs are powerful if slightly erratic curves, the slender lower legs are tipped by two-pronged hooves (cf. IX.69). The dark horns make a terrific sweep back to frame or touch the birds. The two front goats have all feet on the ground, landing from a spring; the third, at the left, is still in the air, his lips parted like a bird's beak over an angled six-line beard. The center goat has an opening in his neck, filled with stripes; the beard is shorter, the lips less parted. The small bird on his back raises a single wing and runs fast, with open beak; the center of the body is a dark oval, wing and tail are striped.

The foremost goat is the only beardless one, with a square pale muzzle and a spiral eye; a light crossed wheel is inserted over the front leg, and a pale oval with trumpet-shaped filling in the chest. A long-necked bird, huge in proportion to the goat, flies vigorously between the back and horns; his feet scrabble near the raised scut, and the closed bill bends to peck at the goat's shoulders. The bird's body is filled with concentric ovals, the raised wing and tail with arcs and bars. A vertical column of guilloche fills the space under the goat's belly, a rarity in this period. Although the picture is principally decorative, not narrative, and formally static, there is a reminiscence of the Maroni Goat Krater (III.26) in the way the curves of the silhouettes substitute for explicit action by their boldness.

There are sherds from several related kraters from the town, showing heads and bodies of goats with birds, and it may be that the head on XII.37 is a true goat rather than a goat-bird.

BIRDS AND FISH

Like Naxos, Rhodes, and Crete, Kos has produced fine birds and fish as subsidiary elements on octopus stirrup vases. Many have raised wings, often striped, and fat duck bodies that may be dark with reserved borders or crosshatched. One odd spotted bird flying straight up may be a fledgling following a crosshatched mother. The birds occur in panels with fish or fill the space around the tentacles of octopods; one has a weed in its beak, one runs by itself around the back of a stirrup jar, and one is a sort

47. C. Laviosa, "La marina micenea," *Annuario* 47-48 (1969-70) 7 f., fig. 1 a, b.

of bird-dog at full speed, a filled fringed arc with a head.

The head of a horned goat-bird (XII.37) to the right is a fine example of a rare type more interesting than the Zygouries, Aegina, and Elis versions (VIII.9, 10, IX.87). The creature seems to be in a frieze of pursuit. The parted lips, or beak, are like the goats' lips on the Seragio krater (XII.35), but the rest of the head is birdlike. Instead of a crest, two long horns sweep backward, with arc borders to suggest the serrated edge. Goat-birds will be popular again on island gems of the seventh century.

Two stirrup jars from the Langadha cemetery are handsome examples of the Dodekanese style. On the first (XII.39) fish, swimming among tentacles that are also filled with birds, shells, and wheels, are painted in a variety of styles, some dark with humped bodies and bared teeth, some filled with rippled horizontal lines as so often in Crete, some striped inside strong contours. These are decorative alternations to achieve a balance of dark and light and are not descriptive of species. The whole scene is charged with energy from the dots and stripes that radiate like extra skins from the birds, and there are odd confrontations between the pecking birds and the tentacles, which suddenly turn into lifeless filled circles. The jar shows affinities both with Crete and with the Kalymnos-Pitane school.

The second (XII.40) is a fine paneled jar with a palm tree, like horns of consecration, on the shoulder, and a simple bird. There are four single fish in panels below, two facing across a handsome checkerboard divider on the rear, nearly centered under the palm; the forms are typically Dodekanese, with dark bodies and pale borders, open heads filled with gill-arcs, and blunt snouts striped with interior teeth.

SEAHORSE

41. The interior of a deep bowl, or lekane, has a playful frieze of spirals to which necks and beaks have been attached to make four "seahorse" inventions. They are framed by two fish, one following and one facing. The sea-horses are connected in a running spiral frieze, like elephants holding tails and trunks. The slanted necks are bordered by rows of dots, the beaks are open and toothed with dots and bars. The dark fish are marauder types, springing from a barred panel with loose spiral volutes. The whole effect is messy but cheerful, like the Berkeley sea-slug plate (V.137). As at Kalymnos there are clay nipple-rivets in threes by the handles.

DODEKANESE, UNKNOWN PROVENANCE

42. A collared jar in Toronto, in a peculiar late style, has been identified as a work of the Dodekanese about 1150. On either side are painted two stubby horses with fish over their backs; on one side the horses move right together, on the other they are tail to tail. The shape of the vase, with side handles and shoulder nipples, is at home in the Dodekanese, though not unknown elsewhere, and the use of reserved borders and inserts in the animals' bodies is also characteristic. Horses are unusual in the East so late, except for the grand krater from Ugarit (XIII.28), or the famous little modeled pack-horse from Rhodes. The style here is both sketchy and blotchy, unlike most III C paintings. The outlines are only tenuously connected to the solid paint of the bodies; they run from the tail high across the top of the back and up the mane, to project as an ear; the second ear turns into the front line of the chest. The head is a rectangle or rhomboid, reserved and eyeless. Circles are set in at the chest and the haunch, filled on one side with smaller circles, on the other with tangent arcs or solid discs. Outlined arcs sprout from the dark legs to serve as knees. The manes and tails are fringed. The fish, filled with simple wavy lines, face right over the horses' backs; they have prominent dark fins, fringed tails, and open mouths; three have teeth. There may be an ultimate connection to the horse-and-bird collared jar from Mycenae (XI.13), but the odd iconography is directly linked to Ugarit.

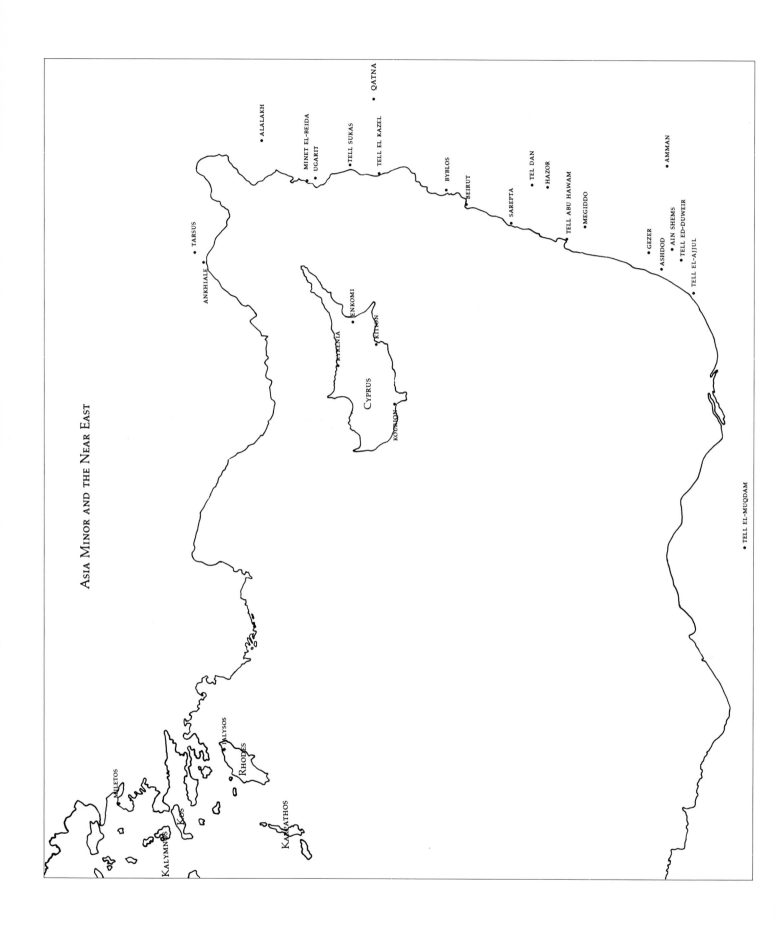

ASIA MINOR AND THE NEAR EAST

QATNA

• ALALAKH

MINET EL-BEIDA
• UGARIT

• TELL SUKAS

• TELL EL KAZEL

• BYBLOS

•BEIRUT

SAREPTA

• TEL DAN

• HAZOR

• AMMAN

TARSUS

TELL ABU HAWAM

• MEGIDDO

GEZER

• AIN SHEMS

ANKHIALE

• ASHDOD

• TELL ED-DUWEIR

• TELL EL-AJJUL

ENKOMI

KITION

KYRENIA

CYPRUS

KOURION

MILETOS

KALYMNOS

KOS

IALYSOS

RHODES

KARPATHOS

• TELL EL-MUQDAM

XIII
ASIA MINOR AND THE NEAR EAST

Asia Minor

With the increasing archaeological exploration of coastal Bronze Age sites in Asia Minor, the body of Mycenaean material is being expanded yearly. Masat, Ephesos, Knidos and Müskebi, Aphrodisias and Milas, and the Burdur region contribute pieces which, along with the earlier finds from Klazomenai, Kolophon, Izmir, Miletos, Pitane, Tarsus, and Troy, create a far more substantial picture of Mycenaean commercial contacts with Anatolia than was available a decade ago.[1] However, pictorial vases form a surprisingly small percentage of the increasing total, except at Miletos. The majority are late thirteenth and early twelfth century. In this Late period one would expect considerable influence from the Dodekanese, which can be traced in places, but not strongly. There is also a series of connections with Ugarit, Enkomi, and Kouklia in western Cyprus. The role of the Peloponnesos as a major exporter, or of Crete, is not yet clear. One lucky find could illuminate many theoretical connections in a period marked by strong commerce and mobile military expeditions.

The earlier commerce, fairly casual, includes surprisingly few of the typical Cypriote scenes one might have expected, such as chariot kraters (found only at Troy and Miletos so far) and bulls (only at Tarsus). This suggests both that traffic may have been limited in comparison with the rich direct trade with Cyprus, and that much of it was in mainland or Rhodian ships; Cypriotes in turn traded farther east, and the Anatolian coastal cities never had an early chance to develop an appetite for Mycenaean images. There is a similar lack of Anatolian imports into Cy-

prus, perhaps for political reasons. The picture is so divergent from that of the rapid early spread of Cypriote material in the coastal Levant (see section on the Near East) that it deserves serious historical consideration.

The sites with Mycenaean pictorial vases or fragments are discussed in alphabetical order.[2]

ANKHIALE (CILICIA)

LATE

1. A sherd from a krater or deep bowl, decorated with an animal combat, was reported long ago with other

1. K. Bittel, *MDOG* 98 (1967) 18 f., fig. 17, n. 25; R. Hope Simpson, *A Mycenaean Gazetteer* (1965); P. Pecorella, *Academia Toscana* "La Columbaria" 25 (1962-63) 3 f.; Stubbings, *MycLevant*, 22 f.; V. Desborough, *The Last Mycenaeans and their Successors* (1964) 160 f. Ephesos: H. Gültekin, M. Baran, *TürkArkDerg* 13.2 (1964) 125; M. Mellink, *AJA* 68 (1964) pl. 50, figs. 10-13. Miletos: C. Weickert, *Bericht über den VI Internationalen Kongress für Archäologie* (Berlin, 1939), 325 f.; *IstMitt* 7 (1957) 102 f., 9-10 (1959-60) 1 f.; A. Mallwitz, W. Schiering, *IstMitt* 18 (1968) 87 f.; W. Schiering, W. Voigtlander, *IstMitt* 25 (1975) 9 f., 17 f.; G. Kleiner, *Alt-Milet* (1966). Müskebi: G. Bass, *AJA* 67 (1963) 353 f.; M. Mellink, *AJA* 69 (1965) 140; Y. Boysal, *TürkArkDerg* 13.2 (1964) 81, and 14 (1965) 123; *Belleten* 121 (1967) 67. Other sites with Mycenaean pottery include Burdur, Cerkeşsultaniye, Dereköy, Erythrai, Fetiye, Fraktin, Gödelesin, Iasos, Kolophon, Maşat, Muğla, Mylasa, Phokaia, Sardis, Stratonikeia, and Telmessos, and increasingly general attention is being given to the historical and economic implications of this spread of trade. See R. Hope Simpson, J. F. Lazenby, *BSA* 68 (1973) 174; H.-G. Buchholz, *AA* 1974, 361; F. Schachermeyr, *SBWien* 309 (1976) 189; J. Jakar, *AnatSt* 26 (1976) 125; M. Mellink, *AJA* 81 (1977) 298; C. Mee, *AnatSt* 28 (1978) 121 f. (thirty-nine possible sites).

2. Two indeterminate pieces from Mersin are not included here, J. Garstang, *Liverpool Annals of Art and Archaeology* 26 (1939-40) pl. LXXXI 4.7.

late Aegean material. The inspiration for the hunting scene seems clearly Mycenaean, rendered in a provincial style that has affinities to Late pieces from Ugarit. The inspiration may, perhaps, come from a gem or an ivory rather than the tradition of vases; mainland hunting scenes ordinarily show dogs or hunters, a tension between domesticated trained hunting animals and wild victims, while this purely wild scene of a lion attacking a bull is far more familiar in carving than in painting. However, it is not unrelated to the Pastoral lion and animal krater from Angastina in Cyprus (VI.22). The filling ornament on the base line, three groups of concentric arcs, suggests a date in the earlier twelfth century.

The fragment preserves only the bodies and legs of the animals and the end of the bull's muzzle, but the suggested restoration of the lion by Evans seems good. The animals are propelled right, the lion on the bull's back, both in solid paint, although the bull's muzzle is reserved with a wavy line running up it; the square tip recalls late Cretan terracottas or Aegean rhyta. The drawing is suggestive of wild action, in the lean crouched hindquarters of the lion slipping on the bull's rump and in the way the bull skids and braces himself on three-toed hooves under the sudden weight, turning his head frontally in surprise. The feet are clearly separated, the bull's from the ground line, the lion's claws from the hide they rake. See XIII.27.

MILETOS

RIPE

2. The head of a charioteer or possibly a boxer, left, on a krater, has affinities with profiles both from Berbati in the Argolid (VIII.1, 5) and from the Enkomi Middle series (IV.49). Without any background, filling ornament, or glimpse of chariot or horse, one cannot judge its affiliations precisely; it may be by Painter 9. If it is, this sherd represents a harbor stop on a very successful voyage to the East (Chapter XIV).

3. A sherd of a dish has part of the body of a dark animal, perhaps a goat, on the outside, and two difficult shapes inside that might conceivably be sea animals. The quadruped is very long bodied, tubular, and crude, with some (lost) painting in the center of the back which made the excavators think of a bird on a pastoral animal, or possibly a chimaira. The interior floaters partly recall the crab-ship from Mycenae (IX.88).

4. The highly ornamental lower body and legs of a bird, right, recalled to the excavators the Enkomi bird krater (III.6), and they placed it in the fourteenth century.

The thick border of the round body and the interest in strong internal division are indeed more typical of Early pictorial than of Late, yet the character of the ornament — rays radiating from concentric circles and stripes bordered by dots — is more like designs at the ends of III C octopus tentacles than normal bird filling.

TRANSITIONAL

5. Part of a bird's head on a krater fragment faces left toward a pointed conical object with symmetrical "horns" curling up along the sides; a vertical row of dots embroiders the center. This has been seen as a cult pillar, a form not otherwise known in vase painting though perhaps connected to such designs as the "maypole" at Pylos.[3]

6. A krater fragment preserves parts of three oared ships, with curved stems and diagonal banks of oars. The painting is very simple, as on the sherds from Phylakopi (XI.96).

LATE

7. The beautiful LH III C tripod-beaker with birds and fish is one of the finest specimens of this style. It is idiosyncratic in detail and cannot be linked directly either to the Dodekanese or to the mainland. Fish are rising and diving through a sea filled with lozenges and flowers; birds hop along the ground line below them. The fish are all slightly different but share a tendency toward dark bodies with inserted zigzags, long necks with multiple gill arcs, the last one spotted, and small open mouths, sometimes containing the eye, sometimes eyeless with snoutlike lips. The fish feed on weeds drawn as string-filaments touching their lips and swelling into floating banner or tongue shapes, seaweed filled with rippling lines. One fish stands on his tail to feed, the others dive rhythmically, drawing the trailing weeds behind them. There are lozenges chained to the borders, also piercing the fish, and isolated floating papyrus flowers on hooked stems. Concentric arcs filled with dark axe shapes, with dotted borders like the flowers, punctuate the lower border. The bird forms are essentially spirals with added extremities, like the Kos seahorses (XII.41); the feet kick back, the wings are raised and bent; one bird has two eyes on the same side. This is a charming scene of shore life which, if the composition were organized in anything more than a decorative way, would suggest little birds skipping on the beach with fish sporting in the waves beyond, in conceptual perspective. The chained lozenge is characteristic of Ugarit, too.

3. Lang, *Pylos* II, 19 M ne, pl. 113.

PITANE (ÇANDARLI)

LATE

8. The renowned stirrup jar with birds and animals among octopus tentacles was made in the same workshop as the Kalymnos stirrup jar (XII.23); it has more birds and fish, fewer mammals.

The tentacles enclose four friezes; one dark bird sits on top of the octopus on the right, with a raised striped wing, long neck, and open bill, stooped low as though feeding on the mucus of the tentacle. On the left the friezes are made up of: a bird walking right and a bird walking upside down with its feet on the tentacle above; a dark fish diving and three dark birds scrambling right; a horse, a fringed rosette, and a quatrefoil flower; and a bird swooping right with elongated neck and hissing open beak. On the right, where the paint is a little stronger, there are: a dark fringed hedgehog with long crooked legs and a Roman nose, facing a fish diving left; a horse with pricked-up ears in a setting of curved stripes like meadow grass, facing left toward a bordered panel; a bird left and a bird right with much space and vertical dividers between; two fish swimming left and a bird with lowered neck, right.

There is less drama than on the Kalymnos vase, no narrative vignettes of birds and hedgehogs; the animals seem isolated and independent even when placed in groups by species; and the forms of activity are really only forms, a raised wing or an open beak, a grin on a fish, decorative reductions of active schemes for ornament. The Dodekanese style is evident in the reserved borders of the fish, the two dark oval inserts in the horse's body, with reserved borders and a pale neck filled with arcs, in the crossed-wheel stoppers of the octopus tentacles, and the loose tongue borders and quatrefoil flowers. The vase has the same carefree attitude toward principles of composition as the Kalymnos vase and is less elaborate in decoration, with more space and lightness, a more general free-floating charm.

TARSUS

Tarsus has produced a bull (XIII.9) and several birds and fish (XIII.10-14), along with fragments of octopods of little pictorial interest except for a fine stirrup jar in island style.[4] The most interesting bird fragments (XIII.10, 11) record a type of humped duck wearing a skirt, by a painter whose work is also found at Tiryns, and at Kouklia and Kition on Cyprus.[5] The Tarsus examples do not preserve

the feet, but the Kouklia sherd at least shows that the duck's body terminates in a kind of skirt or shawl with rippled zigzags. The humped body seems wingless; it is spotted, with a belt of two stripes at the shoulder; the bill is turned up. On a krater fragment (XIII.12) two flying birds with round bodies and raised wings, filled with concentric arcs bordering a dark center, recall the swooping birds of Perati (XI.133) and the elaborate bird from Miletos (XIII.4); the claws are hooked, the long necks bent down.

15. A fish filled with rippling lines dives toward the ground line on a fragment of a large jar; the borders and gills are thick, the inner lines dilute.

18. A fish and a bird recall the forms on the Miletos beaker (XIII.7); it may be from the same source. The bird is made of a spiral with dotted breast, while the fish has the same kind of zigzag inserted into a dark body, and jagged fins.

There are also fragments of octopods, of little general interest except for a fine stirrup jar in island style (Tarsus 1338); other fragments recall Kos. A plastic bull's head is of a type sometimes associated with pictorial kraters. There is no evidence that Tarsus made any of its own Mycenaean wares nor that its trade with places that did was particularly extensive.

TROY

The first pictorial sherds at Troy seem to belong to the end of the Early or beginning of the Middle period, about 1360-1340, in late Troy VI. The scraps are very small, but one at least (XIII.19) shows characteristic seashell fillers of the Middle period on Cyprus, in a chariot scene where the driver wears a spotted robe.

20. Another krater fragment has most of the heads and necks of a team moving right; there are three mane locks, four reins, and fillers of chevrons below the reins and in front of the horses' noses; it is a crowded piece, as happens in Cypriote Middle (IV.13, 18, 20), partly clarified with added white paint and a ladder pattern across the neck and on the upper band.

21. A similar fragment, possibly from the reverse of the same krater, gives the neck and four reins of the team, right; white was used for two dotted rosettes on the neck and a ladder pattern framing the sides of the neck.

4. In general, H. Goldman, *Tarsus* II (1956) 206, 220 f., and the discussion of Argive versus local clay, 206; J. F. Daniel, *AJA* 41 (1937) 281; E. French, *AnatSt* 25 (1975) 53 f.
5. The other humped ducks are Slenczka, *Tiryns* VII, no. 160, pl. 24; Palaipaphos, F. Maier, *AA* 1969, 401, fig. 22, and also at Kition.

MIDDLE OR RIPE

22. An odd provincial animal may be a goat leaping. It is drawn in thick outline, with a back-swept horn and a small dotted eye; the body is filled with parallel arcs curved down.

23. Two dark birds fly right on the rim of a kylix or bowl; details are applied in white paint. This recalls the Rhodian kylix, XII.13, though white overpaint is not very popular in Rhodes. Here it is used for the circular eyes, stripes on the neck, and isolated groups of arcs on bodies and wings. There is a solid-centered rosette in the field. The long bodies and narrow raised wings suggest a III B date.

TRANSITIONAL AND LATE

24. A provincial fragment from a deep bowl, with parts of four striped fish, recalls the Cypriote Pastoral style in its simplicity.

Like Tarsus, Troy produced several octopus compositions, including a rhyton of some importance for dating the famous siege;[6] a hedgehog rhyton and an idol should be very late III B.[7]

UNKNOWN PROVENANCE

25. A handsome one-handled jug in Istanbul may come from an unknown site in Asia Minor; it is very delicate, not in the usual styles. Two birds decorate the shoulder, elongated to cover the whole space on each side of the handle. The drawing is light and clear. The filling ornaments in the field are restricted to open circles like pomegranates. The birds have prominent rounded breasts made of a spiral, like the birds on the Miletos beaker (XIII.7) but finer; their sinuous bent necks are filled with arcs, and the painted raised wings are filled with concentric arcs. The eyes are round with a dark pupil, an unusual effect. A papyrus streamer floats diagonally between wing and tail, as at Ialysos and Ugarit (XII.12, 13, V.8, 21). Concentric arcs ornament the lower edge of the body; the legs are short, with knees crooked forward. The vase is unusual in the Late period for its restrained exaggeration, without contrasts of tone or clutter.

The Near East

At least seventeen sites in the Near East have produced Mycenaean pictorial pottery, and more will appear in new

excavations and in the publication of older excavations. The surveys by Stubbings and Hankey are very thorough and useful, and the principal conclusions are already drawn.

The pictorial vases in the East belong mainly to the Middle and Ripe periods, LH III A:2 and LH III B, with a few pieces of the Late phase (Ugarit, Megiddo). These are the periods of greatest pictorial manufacture; the distribution is a practical result of pot making and trade, without much political significance. In general, pictorial vases are accompanied by Cypriote ware in the East, Base Ring and White Slip, as well as by "standard," or "Argolid," Mycenaean. Almost all pictorial vases in the Levant have closer parallels with vases found in Cyprus than with those found in Greece. While this in itself does not contribute to the solution of the technical problem of where Mycenaean pictorial vases were made, it seems quite clear that pictorial vases destined for the East were at least transshipped in Cyprus, and Cypriote material added to the cargoes. On present evidence there is little support for direct trading between the Argolid, or even Rhodes, and the caravan terminals of the Levant, bypassing Cyprus.

Ugarit has the greatest riches in the pictorial sphere and the longest history of trade, from Early (III.19) to Late (XIII.30). This is natural since it is such a short, direct sail from Enkomi. The other sites show considerable geographical spread; one must imagine various means of transport, and goods filtering hand to hand through the casual networks of commerce.

Sites

'Ain Shems (Beth Shemesh)	Sarepta (Sarafend)
Alalakh (Atchana)	Tell Abu Hawam
Amman	Tel Dan
Ashdod	Tell ed Duweir
Beirut	Tell el-Ajjul
Byblos	Tell Kazel
Gezer	Tell el Muqdâm
Hazor	Tell Sukas
Megiddo	Ugarit (Ras Shamra) and
Qatna (El Misrifeh)	Minet el-Beida

The major pieces of Early, Middle, and Ripe are discussed in Chapters III to V in their place among the vases found in Cyprus, and the few Pastoral examples are discussed in Chapter VI. Here all that is necessary is to mention

6. For octopods, C. W. Blegen et al., *Troy* III (1953) figs. 315, no. 34.713, 407.5, 416.1, 416.34; *Troy* IV (1958) fig. 244.5-7 (D 44); H. Schmidt, *Heinrich Schliemann's Sammlung Trojanischer Altertümer* (1902) nos. 3406, 3436.

7. H. Schmidt, *Heinrich Schliemann's Sammlung Trojanischer Altertümer* (1902) nos. 3562-3563.

briefly the kinds of images found in the East, where they are clustered, and any possibilities of local influence.

EARLY

QATNA

The krater with massive spirals on the shoulder (III.A) begins the pictorial series, although it is not pictorial in decoration; its discovery in context with a Cypriote bowl and a Rhodian jar, and the Cretan elements in its design, suggest the mixed influences that created an interest in products from pictorial workshops.

ALALAKH

The fragment (III.15) of a chariot krater, by the painter of the Pyla-Verghi "archer" krater (III.13), demonstrates the early spread abroad of vases that can be localized as workshop products of Cyprus and of themes that would continue to be popular for a hundred years. The wild rippled lines of one headdress anticipate visually the feathered helmets of the Kos warriors (XII.29 and following), but since the fragment is published in drawing, no local historical conclusions are possible. The octopus krater (III.8) is also closely connected to Cyprus.

UGARIT

The fragment with robed sword bearers and bull (III.19), so close to the De Clercq krater (III.18), is the earliest Levantine example of a subject whose popularity spread in the East in the later fourteenth century. It is not possible to tell whether such aristocratic vases were destined as funeral pieces for Cypriotes or Mycenaeans living abroad or were exported as generally attractive exotica.

ASHDOD

On present evidence Early bird kraters were exported only to Ashdod (III.28), but within a generation their popularity increased.

MIDDLE

There is more material, but not enough to put in chronological series by itself, without reference to the Cypriote series. In Middle I there are bird kraters at Tell Abu Hawam and Alalakh (IV.10, 11). In Middle II there is only the chariot krater from Alalakh (IV.25), for which there are bet-

ter Cypriote than mainland parallels, and fragments(?) at Tell Sukas. The high incidence of robed personages on imported chariot kraters in the East is probably not accidental, but reflects contemporary costume in the Levant as well as Cyprus.

In Middle III the tempo steps up, with chariot kraters at Tel Dan (IV.49), two at Ugarit (IV.50, 77), two at 'Ain Shems (IV.71, 72) one at Tell el-Ajjul (IV.74), and one, with fragments of two more, at Amman (IV.73). There are fragments at Alalakh (IV.75, 76), and the horse-flask at Sarepta (IV.78), so the geographical spread is more extensive than before although the types are still limited. It may be accident that no bull kraters are recorded in the East until the thirteenth century (Tell Sukas), or it may reflect a more intense interest in chariot scenes for their own sake and a disregard for other types of pictorial vases. Perhaps a political loosening at the end of the Amarna age encouraged increased coastal traffic in luxury goods. The mainland series of pictorial vases is still at its tentative beginning (VIII.1 and following) and is probably not the direct source for most Levantine finds. On the other hand, almost all the imports into the Near East show a rather tired spirit, characteristic of Cypriote work at the end of the fourteenth century.

RIPE

Thirteenth-century pictorial imports into the Near East spread farther southward and more broadly into Palestine, while a concentration continues at Ugarit. There are scraps of chariot kraters at Byblos, Gezer, Ashdod, Tell Abu Hawam, and Alalakh (V.25.1-25.10), and more complete specimens at Ugarit (V.8, 20, 21) and Tell Kazel (V.12). Ugarit also has examples of human figures without chariots, the men on two rhyta and a bowl (V.36, 37), and the lady with spiral breasts who may have been in a chariot scene (V.3). The repertory now includes bulls (V.92, 98), stags (V.56, 104, 105), goats (V.110, 111), birds (V.65, 70, 122) and fish (V.131, 133) at Ugarit, and bulls at Tell Sukas (V.74.1) and Tell Abu Hawam (V.79). Ugarit also imports Pastoral style pieces of the later thirteenth century, buying local Cypriote pictorial when the mainland was cut off (VI.5, 6, 17), and continues with octopods. Byblos has a bird, a goat, and a Pastoral bull (VI.23). There is no definite mainland connection yet.

LATE

The situation in the Transitional and Late periods is not yet clear. Older opinion was that Mycenaean III B pottery marked the end of open and vigorous traffic between the Aegean and the Near East and helped to date various destruction levels generally associated with the Sea Peoples or contemporary land raiders. This is ordinarily true, and most sites do not produce Aegean twelfth-century pottery. A little more III C is known than before, however, and it suggests in some limited stylistic or statistical sense that the connections are with the Dodekanese, the Asia Minor coast, and possibly Crete, rather than with Cyprus. How much was contributed by Greek immigrants to Asia Minor and Cyprus is still open to question. The markedly mainland character of the III C style in Cyprus is a graphic illustration of the change in workshop habits. Not much of this normal III C moved farther east. The most spectacular finds are the kraters from Ugarit. There is other late material from Ashdod, distinct from "Philistine" imitations, and sherds at Tell Sukas. A vase with hawks(?) from Megiddo (XIII.26) may belong to the earlier part of the period.

MEGIDDO

26. The pieces republished by Mrs. Hankey, possibly from a four-handled jar, combine into a charming scene of plump birds perched in facing pairs on waving lines, for tree branches, and on the tails of dotted connected spirals. Close Style spotted scales and dotted circles ornament the shoulder of the jar. The style may be local, but it has an affinity to Close Style birds at Mycenae in the playfulness and fine drawing. Parts of four birds are preserved, possibly hawks or partridges; they have short hawk heads, breasts covered with (feather) scales, striped wings with undulating edges, and short feet flexed forward to suggest settling from flight. A streamer, sometimes forked, projects between wing and body, as more often in the east than the west. Mrs. Hankey thought it displayed a Minoan spirit; though no close parallel exists in contemporary Crete, the observation seems just. Similarly the W Krater (III.1) with little birds clambering in branches seemed Cretan; perhaps the tradition lapsed and revived. The theme is common enough on Cretan larnakes, but the execution is different, more orderly and detailed, and the subsidiary ornament is more in the mainland manner.

UGARIT

Ugarit has always been extraordinarily rich in pictorial painting; and the three renowned kraters from its later phases are of exceptional quality and interest. It is arguable how late in the general series these kraters fall. The lion-and-stag hunting krater from the house of Patilu-wa is con-

nected with the end of the Ripe series in Cyprus but has features that would be Transitional in mainland Greece. The two warrior kraters, one with horses, one with fish, are Transitional or Late.

27. A fragmentary open krater with a broad low rim preserves parts of two stags and from nine to twelve cheerful lions of several sizes in a wonderful abstract hunt. The flow of action is generally left to right with subtle interruptions. The lions who leap around and over the stags are spread from the bottom to the top of the picture, while the two stags, at the lower left, are fixed on the ground line. A major fragment at the left of the principal side sets a lion leaping from one stag to the next, his hind feet taking off from the antlers on the left and his front feet landing on the rippled haunch in front, while the stag looks back at him, expressionless. All the lions are painted with huge round eyes made of concentric circles; their bodies are filled with diminishing circles reserved against dark bodies, recalling the dachshund-lions of the Shemishin krater (V.114), which parodies the Lion Gate; that piece is very close to this in atmosphere but not in all details. These lions have small loop ears like the Mycenae lion (IX.82) and thin open laughing muzzles; their feet are sometimes hooved, like deer, and their hindquarters weak in comparison to the massive chests. Most have short tails, but one has a long whiplike tail with a knob two-thirds of the way along, like the fabled lion who lashes himself to fury with the barb in his own tail. The best stag is less original, with the rippled filling and branched antlers of the classic Ripe stags of Tiryns (IX.48) and their Cypriote analogues (V.54, 55). J.-C. Courtois, in his publication of the krater, stressed the links with the hunting scenes of Cyprus and Cilicia (XIII.1), in the Ripe and Pastoral styles, but ultimately placed this piece as coming from a mainland atelier. In this connection one should note the filled lozenge hanging in the upper field, a device very common in if not restricted to Miletos (XIII.7) and Ugarit. It reappears both with and without a tail on the two warrior kraters (XIII.28, 29), as on the spearman rhyton and bowl (V.36, 37), and the Late horseback riders (V.26).

The two Transitional/Late kraters with warriors and animals have a broad low shape with a wide neck, bulging body, two strap handles, and a low ogival foot; this approaches the type used by III C painters of Kos (Seragio, XII.35) or even provincial Salamis (XI.41). It may be a late revival of the traditions of the earliest grand pictorial kraters derived from the Palace Style; there are other revivals of shapes in the same era.

28. The more complete krater has a warrior as the centerpiece on each side. He faces left, holding a horse by the muzzle with each hand, so that they move in toward

him antithetically as though in preparation for harnessing. Side A also has a goat on the far left. Four fish on each side dive to the right over the backs of the animals: on side A there is one fish over the goat, one over the left horse, two over the right horse; on side B there are two over each horse. The scenes are separated by elaborate handle panels with metope construction, vertical framed wavy lines connected by horizontal waves. On the base a branch-shaped sign is painted in red. There is a curiously mixed reminiscence of styles, reflecting practices at Mycenae, Kos, and Miletos.

The horses are painted in dark silhouette, but the silhouette is lightened with elaborate reserved areas, triple arcs on the neck, and triple zigzags on the body, a crosshatched rump, a reserved face with harness sketched in as triangles. This should be a halter with nose-band, represented by a lozenge above the lips, and a strap around the chin, or possibly the kind of basket-muzzle for stallions suggested by XI.8. The lips are not indicated, so the ornament should not represent a bit. The mane is short bars, the tail feathered in herringbone pattern. This manner of enriching interior body surfaces is more familiar on the mainland than elsewhere (XI.7 and following), although there are no exact analogues. The fish, on the other hand, with their long gill arcs and zigzag collars, recall the Miletos beaker (XIII.7) and are positioned as on the Dodekanese collared jar (XII.42). The dark goat on side A has a reserved face with rounded muzzle and eye as on the Enkomi moufflon krater (V.59); the dark horns, backswept, are ruffled on the upper surface, and there are inserted arcs at the neck, hatching on the haunch. Animals and men are separated by diamond lozenges floating on long wavy stems, a pattern conspicuous earlier at Ugarit (see above) and used at Miletos (XIII.7). The stylistic connections among Ugarit, Miletos, Enkomi, and the Dodekanese are not clear yet; the krater is original, possibly local, or reinterprets themes that are more at home in the eastern Mediterranean than we are aware of, with an undercurrent of Argolid pleasure in contrasts of dark and light and dramatic action.

The men holding the horses (Courtois sees them as saddle horses) by the cheek straps offer the first complete view of a scheme that reappears often in Geometric painting and that may be indebted to fresco scenes of harnessing. Their novel armor is treated with the same interest in detail as on the mainland. They wear "Phrygian" caps with the long tail curled in a spiral. Their necks are striped vertically to the nose, as necks at Tiryns are striped (XI.31), with the chin projecting through this flexible protective collar. The chest, arms, and drawn-back leg are outlined in dark paint; the forward leg is reserved on the thigh. The chest is crosshatched like the horses' haunches; it might be an attempt to show chain mail, as on the Enkomi belt-wrestlers or the Aradippo hunt (V.113), but is more likely an ornamental pattern. The soldiers wear greaves with reserved stripes above the knee, as in the Argolid; a dark spiral at the groin against the pale thigh might suggest a cuisse or simply echo the spiral on the helmets. The toes curl up, perhaps suggesting the kind of leather boots with curled toes known in contemporary terracottas. On B, the soldier wears a short sword, hung obliquely at the waist, with a spiral hilt and a leaf-shaped blade; this type is known in Greece at Tiryns (XI.49), but is not the normal type (XI.59) and may be Egyptian.

The composition is clearly eclectic. The horse-and-soldier theme is combined gaily with the horse-and-fish theme, and the goat thrown in as a filler to flesh out a procession on the unusually broad surface. The artist may have been used to painting fish and goats; it seems less probable that there is a coherent narrative or significant image here, a deviation from the sea-and-chariot and wild-goat imagery of the Episkopi larnax.

29. A second very fragmentary krater by the same painter has considerable interest. A warrior stands on the right, facing left, dressed as before with crosshatched chest, greaves, boots with curled toes, and a short leaf-bladed sword with spiral hilt. The forward thigh is reserved and filled with a spiral at the groin. The vertically striped collar is pulled back from the lips, and the mouth seems open; the profile is otherwise the same. The warrior holds a large fish by the tail, so that its head hangs over an elaborate central panel, which resembles a stilted form of broad altar surmounted by horns of consecration enclosing a formal plant. The motifs used to construct this "altar" are all used with purely decorative intent in late Mycenaean painting, yet their assemblage in this fashion should suggest some kind of cult area. The central part is a typical metope of bordered verticals containing a patch of horizontal wavy lines. It is topped by a broad tubular cross-bar that curves down at the sides to the ground line, the flaring lower ends filled with zigzag. A vertical wavy line ties this to the ground under the fish's belly. The horns of consecration are antithetic crosshatched tongues; the plant silhouetted between them may be a form of palm, with spirals springing from the stem and three dark triangles for fruit. Another figure, a fisherman facing right, preserved only as bent elbow, buttock, bulging calves, and upturned toes, has a vertical fish on a string behind him, and a separate fragment shows a vertical fish and a filled lozenge.

The fragmentary bell krater with a row of riders (V.26) must be nearly as late as these kraters, with the horses' faces partly reserved, similar lozenges in the field, and the curious short sword.

Courtois has stressed the links to Miletos, Kos, and perhaps ultimately to Melos and Crete in this rich Late phase. A fragmentary closed vessel (XIII.30) has a curious, weakly outlined quadruped whose rear end terminates in a spiral, with sharp knees on the forelegs, and a pointed head seen from the top with both oval eyes showing; it certainly has affinities with Miletos (XIII.3, 7). There are thin streamers all through the field; one from the lips may be a pendent rein.

XIV
INDIVIDUAL VASE PAINTERS

RECOGNITION OF INDIVIDUAL PAINTERS is of the utmost importance in studying the style of any class of vase painting; it helps to group works by the same person and show them as representative of the stylistic ideas of one man during a relatively short chronological period. By comparing the works of several painters, one gets a better idea of the general stylistic tendencies during a given period. Sometimes one painter can help establish a relative chronology of pictorial vases.[1]

Beazley's attribution of Attic vases to individual painters was facilitated by the fact that Greek painters and potters sometimes signed their vases; after the discovery of two or three vases bearing the same signature, a painter can be recognized by his style. This, however, is not the case with Mycenaean pictorial vases; marks have been found on several of them, either incised after firing or inscribed in a matt washy paint unlike that used for the decoration, but these could be merchants' rather than potters' marks.[2]

The method followed here is based entirely on stylistic criteria. The task has been facilitated by the more or less standard repertory of pictorial compositions used by the various painters in different stylistic stages.

Vase painters were humble craftsmen, probably inferior to goldsmiths, weavers, engravers, and wall painters, at least in regard to artistic initiative and skill. The fragile and utilitarian nature of clay vases dictated their mass production, which naturally affected their artistic merit. An exception to this generalization is found in the case of sixth- and fifth-century Attic vases; they were not merely receptacles but were bought as works of art, both in Greece and abroad, because of their decoration, which was often inspired by mythological subjects, their artistic qualities and the perfection of their fabric and shapes. Some similar appreciation of Mycenaean Greek iconography and calligraphy on vases above the ordinary level may help to account for the numbers of pictorial vases in the Levant.

In some cases a potter was also the vase painter, as in Athenian workshops of the sixth and fifth centuries. One can see that the ware and paint of certain works are identical. In other cases vases whose shape and fabric show that they were made by one potter have been decorated by a single painter.

In attempting to recognize individual vase painters, one must pay attention to the way details are rendered rather than to the nature of the background filling ornaments, though the disposition of the ornaments must also be considered. Each painter had a varied repertory of motifs, both floral and abstract, which he could use as filling ornaments; he would copy different ones from his "sketch book" to suit the requirements of every case; these variations in filling ornament were often intentional, since this was the only way a painter could avoid monotonous standardization.

---

1. Pioneer work in this field was done by F. Stubbings, "Some Mycenaean Artists," *BSA* 46 (1951) 168-176; valuable contributions and a continuing refinement of lists were made by S. A. Immerwahr, "The Protome Painter and Some Contemporaries," *AJA* 60 (1956) 137 f.; J. L. Benson, "Observations on Mycenaean Vase-Painters," *AJA* 65 (1961) 337 f.; S. Charitonides, "A Mycenaean Painter" (in Greek), *EphArch* 1953-54, 101 f., and "The Mycenaean Painter of Papyri," *Deltion* 16 (1960) 84 f. A recent study of stylistic links is in E. Slenczka, *Tiryns* VII, 111 f. V. Karageorghis has studied individual painters, for example, "A Mycenaean Painter of Swallows," *AA* 1967, 162 f.; "A Mycenaean Painter of Bulls and Bull-Protomes," *Alasia* I (1971) 123 f. See the Select Bibliography.

2. Stubbings, *MycLevant,* 45 f.

However, in the Ripe period, when filling ornament was reduced to the minimum, painters tended to vary their subjects. Painter 19, who is known from three or four works, was primarily a painter of bulls, but in one of his compositions he inserted a human figure and two dogs to make a diminutive hunt. The same tendency may be observed in the works of Painter 17.

It was not so easy, however, to introduce innovations in the rendering of details of pictorial motifs. For example, a painter who specialized in bulls would have a standard form that he could draw freehand in a few minutes, with quick, skillful strokes on the curved surface of a vase; to treat the details, such as ears, eyes and legs, differently each time would take longer, and the results might not be successful, so obviously it was to his advantage to repeat his standard version. This being so, one is able to recognize the distinctive style of a given painter and attribute to him vases, or even fragments of vases, on which enough characteristic details are preserved. For example, several works by Protome Painter A (Painter 21) are known; he always drew the muzzles, ears, and horns of his bull protomes in the same way.

Occasionally a painter made changes in his treatment of filling ornaments or the attitudes of figures, the decoration of bodies, or even in the rendering of minor details; this, of course, was inevitable because he was not aiming at a faithful copy of a single prototype. One must also allow for differences in style between a painter's early and late works. Sometimes slight variations can be observed between the compositions on either side of the same vase, although they were obviously painted at the same time by one painter. These differences, however, never affect the general character of a painter's style.

Although pictures of only one subject (chariots or bulls or birds, for example) are usually ascribed to a certain painter, this does not necessarily mean that he concentrated entirely on one motif, or even that his repertory was limited; more likely it is because we find it difficult to see the links between a painter's treatment of one motif and his treatment of another.

Sometimes two or three groups of vases that show similar stylistic tendencies can be attributed to two or three painters; in such cases one can assume that the artists were associated with each other, probably in the same workshop. A comparison of their works may show which of them influenced the others.[3]

In several instances works by the same painter have been found in Cyprus and also in one of the following centers: Rhodes, Tiryns, Berbati, Mycenae, Ugarit, or Alalakh. These raise important problems, which have been discussed briefly in each case.

The majority of the works that have been attributed to individual painters have been found in Cyprus. The fact that some of them belong to the Early stage indicates that the pictorial style was already flourishing then and that there were painters who were directly connected with the Cypriote market. Some of these painters must have been actually established in Cyprus; this is the logical interpretation of the material. Some may have been transplanted Cretans and some Helladic Greeks. It is also noteworthy that products of certain painters have been found at different sites in Cyprus; for example, works by Painter 1 have been found at Enkomi, Pyla, Kourion, along the eastern and southern coasts, and even at Alalakh in Syria. This shows that wherever this painter had his atelier, his products were known both in the island and abroad.

Since the pictorial vases from the Greek mainland are so sadly fragmentary, it is much harder to recognize individual potters and painters. The shapes are often uncertain, and the general mainland distaste for elaborate filling ornaments in the background deprives us of one easy mode of judgment. Even relatively complete pieces may have bizarre differences; for example, on practical grounds it is hard to imagine that more than one artist was painting bird vases in the hamlet of Koukounara in Messenia (VIII.15-17), and yet if these vases were known only separately in museum collections it might be difficult to connect them persuasively. Some mainland cases are obvious: Painter 4, of the bird kraters at Mycenae and Enkomi, Painter 9 with his vigorous overseas pieces, the Pierides Painter, 19, whose fragments at Tiryns remained so long unrecognized, and Painter 30, of the recently discovered krater from Nauplion (IX.1.1.), which so clearly goes with V.1, known for more than a century. Certain painters stand out immediately, and their work should be recognizable the instant any more turn up; these include the painter of stags and goats at Tiryns and Mycenae (IX.48 and following), the Painter of the Tiryns Shield Bearers and his apprentice associate (X.1 and following), and the Painter of the Warrior Vase and the Warrior Stele (XI.42, 43), where the attribution was seen as soon as both came out into the light. The Rosette Painter of delicate birds is also a conspicuous hand (XI.98 and following), like his earlier colleague who drew sphinxes and birds at Mycenae (VIII.29-31).

It is of course much easier to remember these anonymous Mycenaean artists when they are christened with picturesque names drawn from their work, their dis-

---

3. In the case of Painters 21 and 22, it is obvious that the former influenced the latter.

coverers, or owners than when they remain austere and remote in the disguise of a number. It is with a slight pang that we refrain from christening any more of them here, leaving that pleasure to scholars who deal more with the identification of hands than we have tried to do. Wherever possible, associations are indicated in the text, and, where the ordering of the material from different sites made it possible to do so, in the plates as well. The following list of painters by numbers is intended more as a guide than as a thorough discussion.

PAINTER	WORKS	SHAPE	SUBJECT	PROVENANCE
1	III.12	open krater	chariots	Kourion
	III.13	open krater	chariots	Pyla-Verghi
	III.14	amphoroid krater	chariot	Enkomi
	III.15	amphoroid krater	chariot	Alalakh
2	III.17	amphoroid krater	chariots	Enkomi
	III.21	amphoroid krater	chariots	Enkomi
	III.22	amphoroid krater	chariots	Enkomi
3	IV.4	amphoroid krater	bulls	Enkomi
	IV.5	amphoroid krater	bulls	Enkomi
4	IV.6	amphoroid krater	birds	Enkomi
	VIII.14	open krater	birds	Mycenae
5	IV.16	amphoroid krater	chariots	Enkomi
	IV.17	amphoroid krater	chariots	Enkomi
6	IV.19	amphoroid krater	chariots	unknown
	IV.20	amphoroid krater	chariots	unknown
	IV.21	amphoroid krater	chariots	Enkomi
	IV.22	amphoroid krater	chariots	Enkomi
	IV.23	amphoroid krater	chariots	Maroni
	IV.24	amphoroid krater	chariots	Pyla-Verghi
7	IV.41	amphoroid krater	birds	Enkomi
	IV.42	amphoroid krater	birds	Arpera
8	IV.43	amphoroid krater	birds	Enkomi
	IV.44	amphoroid krater	birds	Maroni
9	IV.49	amphoroid krater	chariots	Tel Dan
	IV.63	amphoroid krater	chariots	Maroni
	IV.64	amphoroid krater	chariots	Maroni
	IV.74	amphoroid krater	chariot	Tell el-Ajjul
	VIII.1	amphoroid krater	charioteers	Berbati
	VIII.5	amphoroid krater	charioteer	Mycenae
	XIII.2	amphoroid krater	charioteer	Miletos
10	IV.48	amphoroid krater	chariots	Kourion
	IV.48.1=XII.3	amphoroid krater	chariots	Ialysos
	IV.50	amphoroid krater	chariots	Ugarit
	IV.52	amphoroid krater	chariots	Enkomi
	IV.58	amphoroid krater	chariots	Enkomi
11	IV.53	amphoroid krater	chariots	Maroni
	IV.54*	amphoroid krater	chariots	Maroni
12	V.7	amphoroid krater	chariots	Enkomi
	V.8	amphoroid krater	chariots	Ugarit
	V.9	amphoroid krater	chariot	Enkomi
	V.10	amphoroid krater	chariot	Enkomi
	V.25.1,.2	fragments	chariots	Kourion
	V.34	kylix	boxer	Kourion
13	V.48	bell krater	bulls	unknown
	V.49	bell krater	bulls	unknown

*For V.1 and 2, see Painter 30.

PAINTER	WORKS	SHAPE	SUBJECT	PROVENANCE
14	V.42	amphoroid krater	bulls	Klavdhia
	V.46	bell krater	bulls	Klavdhia
15	V.44	bell krater	bulls, birds	Enkomi
	V.45	bell krater	bulls, birds	unknown
	V.68	jug	birds	Enkomi
	IX.19	bell krater	bulls	Berbati
	IX.20	krater fragments	bull, bird	Tiryns
	IX.23	jug	bull	Tiryns
16	V.38	amphoroid krater	ship, men	Enkomi
	V.69	three-handled jar	birds	Hala Sultan Tekké
17	V.61	bell krater	birds	Enkomi
	V.63	amphoroid krater	birds	Enkomi
	V.64	bell krater	birds	Enkomi
	V.65	bell krater	birds	Ugarit
18	V.23	amphoroid krater	chariots	Aradippo
	V.32	amphoroid krater	boxers	unknown
19	V.73	bell krater	bull, hunter	Klavdhia
	V.74	jug	bull	unknown
	V.74.1	krater fragment	bull	Tell Sukas
	IX.21	krater	bulls	Tiryns
20	V.76	bell krater	bull, bird	Enkomi
	V.77	bell krater	bull	Enkomi
21	V.80	bell krater	bulls, protomes	unknown
	V.81	jug	bull protomes	Enkomi
	V.82	jug	bull protomes	Hala Sultan Tekké
	V.83	jug	bull protomes	Hala Sultan Tekké
	V.84	bowl	bulls	Klavdhia
	V.85	jug	bull protomes	Enkomi
	V.86	bell krater	bulls	Enkomi
	V.87	kylix	bulls	Kition
	V.88	jug	bull protome, bird	Enkomi
	V.89	stirrup jar	bull protomes	Klavdhia
	IX.26*	jug	bull	Argos
	IX.36*	krater fragment	bull	Mycenae
	IX.37*	krater fragment	bull	Mycenae
	IX.39*	krater fragment	bulls	Mycenae
22	V.91	bowl	bull protomes	Klavdhia
	V.92	bowl	bull protomes	Minet el Beida
	V.93	bowl	bull protomes	Pyla-Verghi
	V.94	bowl	bull protomes	Kition
	V.95	bowl	bull protomes	Kition
	V.97	kylix	bull protomes	unknown
	IX.25.1	bowl	bull protomes	Tiryns
23	V.119	bowl	birds	Kition
	V.120	bowl	birds	Ugarit
	V.121	bowl	birds	unknown
	V.122	bowl	birds	Ugarit
	V.123	bowl	birds	Enkomi
24	V.108	bell krater	goats	Enkomi
	V.109	bell krater	goats	Enkomi
25	V.53	bell krater	stags	Enkomi
	V.54	bell krater	stags	Enkomi
	IX.48	bell krater	stags	Tiryns

*Close to the style of Painter 21.

PAINTER	WORKS	SHAPE	SUBJECT	PROVENANCE
26	VI.7	bell krater	lion, goats	Enkomi
	VI.8	amphoroid krater	goats	Maroni
27	VI.11	bell krater	bull	Klavdhia
	VI.12	bell krater	bull	unknown
	VI.13	bell krater	bull	Pyla-Verghi
	VI.14	bell krater	bull	Pyla-Verghi
	VI.15	bell krater	bull	Aradippo
28	VIII.8	hydria	"circus"	Mycenae
	VIII.9	bowl	goat-bird	Zygouries
	VIII.10	hydria	goat, goat-bird	Aigina
29	VIII.29	krater?	bird	Thebes
	VIII.30	stirrup jar	sphinxes, birds	Mycenae
	VIII.31	stirrup jar (two)	sphinxes, birds	Mycenae
30	V.1	amphoroid krater	chariots	Cyprus, unknown
	[V.2]	amphoroid krater	chariots, lady	Haghia Paraskevi
	[IX.1]	amphoroid krater	chariot	Corinth
	IX.1.1	amphoroid krater	chariots	Nauplion
31	X.1	open krater	chariots	Tiryns
	X.2	open krater	chariots	Mycenae
	X.42	basket vase	sphinx	Mycenae
32	XI.14	open krater	chariots	Tiryns
	XI.15	open krater	chariots	Tiryns
	V.25.8 u	krater fragment	charioteers	Tell Abu Hawam
33	XI.42	open krater	soldiers	Mycenae
	XI.43	stele	soldiers, deer	Mycenae
34	XI.98	bowl	birds	Korakou
	XI.99	bowl	birds	Korakou
	XI.100	bowl	birds	Mycenae
	XI.101	bowl	birds	Mycenae
	XI.102	bowl	bird	Mycenae
35	XII.7	amphoroid krater	bulls	Rhodes(?)
	XII.8	amphoroid krater	bulls	Rhodes
36	XII.23	stirrup jar	octopus, animals	Kalymnos
	XIII.8	stirrup jar	octopus, animals	Pitane
37	XIII.28	open krater	soldier, horses	Ugarit
	XIII.29	open krater	fish, man, altar	Ugarit

EPILOGUE

If Mycenaean pictorial vase painting has not attracted much attention in terms of art and style, particularly in its manifestations on the Greek mainland, since the great Furtwängler-Loeschcke *Mykenische Vasen* of 1887, this is surely not because it lacks either archaeological interest or aesthetic charm. It is rather because the mainland material is so fragmentary and the Cypriote vases, in their numbers and completeness, rather repetitive. The only mainland vase that has been consistently illustrated in books on Greek art and history is the Warrior Vase, XI.42, surely because it is nearly whole. The Cypriote vases have fared better, but the same ones are shown over and over, the Zeus with the Scales of Fate (III.2) for its rather spurious mythological interest; the bull and cattle egret krater, V.44, because it is bold, simple, and handsome; and one of the dozens of chariot kraters in London, IV.1, for reasons not altogether clear.

The whole range of Bronze Age painting really deserves better. Mycenaean pictorial vases offer one of the clearest commentaries we have on the activities of the Aegean world between 1400 and about 1150. The other great source of information is the series of carved gems, which survive in about equal numbers. Frescoes and carved ivories are relatively rare, and their range of subjects relatively restricted, although they can also be far superior in quality to the quickly executed painted vases. The vases, however, offer details of costume—armor, hats, bonnets, and helmets—as well as chariots, ships, and the animal world, from cows in heat to caterpillars and dung beetles, that would otherwise be screened off from us nearly completely.

The pictorial style begins in a period of prosperity and exploration when Mycenaean Greeks had been settled in Crete, in the palace at Knossos and no doubt in country towns as well, for two generations or more. Their experience of Cretan painting must have impressed them, but they had their own tastes in art from the beginning, or from the time we can recognize their art as independent and authoritative, at the time of the Shaft Graves of Mycenae, shortly before the end of the seventeenth century. Admiring, flexible, and experimental at the start, they were open to suggestions from Cretan artists in matters of rustic and marine life, but they also insisted that matters they were seriously interested in, like horses and chariots, helmets and shields, be rendered by the palace craftsmen of Crete.

These Mycenaean predilections mark the whole of their pictorial painting, like their wall painting, and although styles shifted, the themes of the soldier in his chariot, the hunter with his dogs, the herds of cattle, persisted for nearly three centuries with enthusiastic customers. Religious ceremonial is rarer than in wall painting, and motifs like the lyre player extremely rare; there is little fantasy or mythology until the very end. On the whole the repertory seems to reflect aristocratic tastes in a medium that circulated far beyond the palaces to middle-class houses and graves; perhaps pictorial vases were one element that gave the Mycenaean culture a sense of cohesion and shared values.

Like all pictorial styles, the Mycenaean developed during a period of prosperity when there were brisk interrelations between the regions of the Aegean and a new cosmopolitan commerce with Asia Minor, Cyprus, Syria, the Levant, and Egypt. It became popular during the "youth" of the Aegean, when there was exuberance in peace and war and adventure overseas, and it may to some degree reflect those adventures, as well as perpetuating the more decorative visions of graceful birds and fish. Once the Mycenaeans were established and became masters of sea commerce and successful traders, more than half the vases have scenes of nature and pastoral tranquility; but by the end of the thirteenth century and the beginning of the twelfth the images of war revive in popularity and take on new nervous energy. Even after the Mycenaean culture became fragmented and dispersed, so that it is traced only with difficulty through the Dark Ages, the spirit is still vivid.

The wonderful Protogeometric kraters from Knossos, with an armed hunter spearing a bearded goat, or two long-clawed lions devouring a bleeding man while sphinxes prance on the other side; the sub-Minoan sea battle from Gortyna or the Mouliana hunting kraters; the Protogeometric archers from Leukandi and Enkomi,[1] are so close in many ways to their Mycenaean predecessors that one may wonder whether the artistic tradition was ever really lost, although renewed influence from goldworkers and other eastern craftsmen is also likely enough in the ninth century. From this first revival onward through Geometric painting, the old Mycenaean themes march on — the lion, the hunter, the deer, the goat, the soldier, the chariot, the ship, and the mourner. Only the dance seems new (IX.11.1, XI.67) and

that was familiar enough in the Bronze Age in gold and terracotta. The possible persistence of both theme and style provides an archaeological artistic analogy to the kind of flexible creative reworking of ancient traditions that is so powerfully displayed in the Homeric epics.

As later poets and painters traveled for their work and their themes, and compositions were carried to the coastal fringes of the Greek world, so one must imagine that Aegean talents and creations were similarly mobile. The questions of where the Mycenaean pictorial style originated, where most workshops were built, what the commercial trade in these figured vases was, whether the rich merchants of the East had the same relation to the Argolid painters as the Etruscans did to Athenian painters in the sixth and fifth centuries, are insoluble at the moment and perhaps of secondary importance to an appreciation of the style itself. Mycenaean vases were always of excellent quality, in wide demand throughout the Mediterranean, and these are the most ambitious and energetic of them. Across the Aegean and around its shores the figured pottery of the Bronze Age Greeks was highly valued and should still be.

1. Knossos: M. Popham, *JHS ArcRep* 1976-77, cover, figs. 33-35; L. H. Sackett, *BSA* 71 (1976) 117, pls. 15-16. Mouliana: see Chapter XI, notes 25, 30. Protogeometric archers: see Chapter VI, note 38.

Appendix
CHARIOTS AND HARNESS
IN MYCENAEAN VASE PAINTING

M. A. LITTAUER AND J. H. CROUWEL

What do chariot kraters tell us of the Mycenaean chariot? Throughout the LH III A and III B periods the vases depict a single type of vehicle, but in LH III C we find a new model, whose difference is chiefly in the coachwork. But to interpret this change we must first understand chariot construction. Unfortunately, the krater representations are extremely schematized, with chariot and harness often converted into pure decoration and even seemingly completely misunderstood by the vase painters. The first part of our task must therefore be to interpret the krater chariots in the light of other evidence. No chariot from this area and period has survived, and most of the other documents are also representations—mainly two-dimensional and in profile, but some in the round. Among the latter are certain murals from Knossos and sites in mainland Greece, a stone signet ring from Avdou in Crete, ideograms on Linear B tablets from Knossos, Mycenaean terracottas, and the Haghia Triada sarcophagus. We shall also use foreign and both earlier and later comparative material from the Aegean where it seems pertinent.[1]

THE "DUAL CHARIOT"

The reconstruction of this chariot type (Fig. 1) is based on information from the sources mentioned above (particularly frescoes), and some of this is admittedly unclear. The parts of the chariot and harness for which we can find modern parallels are labeled according to the modern names, but those parts that appear unique to the Late Bronze Age chariot in the Aegean, for which there are no corresponding elements elsewhere, have been baptized for our purpose, and these terms are given in quotation marks.

The basic parts of the dual chariot were: a box (1), comprising a floor and front and side breastworks of equal height; spoked wheels, probably revolving on a fixed axle and held in place by a linch pin (3); a pole (4) attached to a yoke (5) that rested on the necks of a pair of horses just in front of their withers. Typically Aegean features were the "wing" (6) at the rear of the box, a "pole brace" (7), and a "pole stay" (8); there was a "spur" (10) at the rear of the floor.

BOX

Contemporary terracottas assure us that the box was open behind, as it was on Oriental chariots of the period. The terracottas also indicate a floor plan in the form of a capital D, similar to that of contemporary Egyptian char-

1. In the interests of brevity, notes will be selective. A comprehensive bibliography will be found in J. Wiesner, *Fahren und Reiten*, in *Archaeologia Homerica* I (Göttingen, 1968) and in J. H. Crouwel's forthcoming doctoral dissertation, *Chariots and Other Means of Land Transport in Bronze-Age Greece*. See M. A. Littauer, "The Military Use of the Chariot in the Aegean in the Late Bronze Age," *AJA* 76 (1972) 145 f. Murals: G. Rodenwaldt, "Fragmente Mykenischer Wandgemälde," *AthMitt* 36 (1911) 234-236; *Tiryns* II, 10-12, 97-106, Taf. II.1, 4, 6, XI.11, XII, XIV.3; *Der Fries des Megarons von Mykenai* (Halle, 1921) 24-27, 41-44, Beil. I, IV; S. Alexiou, "Neue Wagendarstellungen aus Kreta," *AA* 1964, 799, Abb. 5; M. A. S. Cameron, "Unpublished Fresco Fragments of a Chariot Composition from Knossos," *AA* 1967, 330-344, fig. 12. Signet ring (the Avdou gem): Lorimer, *HM*, fig. 40. Linear B tablets: Evans, *Palace of Minos* IV, figs. 763, 764, 766-768; M. Ventris and J. Chadwick, *Documents in Mycenaean Greek*, rev. ed. (Cambridge, 1976) 369-375. Terracottas: two important examples from Markopoulo (Attica) and Mega Monastirio (Thessaly), S. Mollard-Besques, *Catalogue raisonné des*

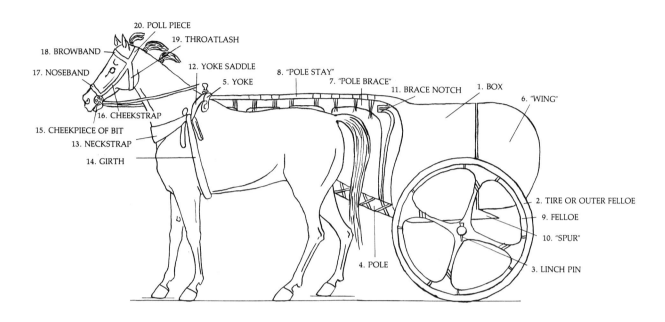

Fig. 1. Diagram of a Mycenaean "dual chariot." (Drawing by Mary Moore.)

iots.[2] There, one or two pieces of heat-bent wood framed the front and two sides of the floor, while a straight beam formed the chord across the rear. The Aegean chariot floor may well have been of woven thongs—again as in Egypt. These would have furnished a lighter and more resilient platform than planks, the resiliency being particularly welcome in an otherwise virtually springless vehicle.

The box, of equal height at sides and front, was probably framed in wood, with a siding of spotted or plain red oxhide or painted linen.[3] The "wings" of the chariot box seem to have been formed of half circles of heat-bent wood, their ends joined by a chord (as on the D-shaped chariot floor), the arc often supported by a horizontal strut, as the Linear B ideograms tell us. They were covered with the same material as the siding. The "wings" were entirely behind the floor of the box and may have served as "mudguards" against flying stones and sand.[4]

The front edge of the box rested on the pole, which passed between the floor and the axle. The rear sill may have rested on the pole also, as on some Chinese central-axled chariots of the western Chou period (1027-771 B.C.), as on a bronze model chariot from Olympia, and as on many chariots on Corinthian and Attic ware.[5] Alternatively, when the axle was at the rear, the pole end, flattened by trimming away at top and bottom, might have lain between the axle and the rear floor bar of the box, in a

horizontal, U-shaped socket that prevented any tendency toward lateral movement. This is the method evidenced by surviving Eighteenth-Dynasty Egyptian chariots.[6] Such a

figurines et reliefs en terre cuite grecs, étrusques et romains (Musée du Louvre, 1954) no. A 1.1, pl. I; *History of the Hellenic World. Prehistory and Protohistory* (Athens-London, 1974) 330. Haghia Triada sarcophagus: S. Marinatos and M. Hirmer, *Kreta, Thera und das Mykenische Hellas* (Munich, 1973) pls. XXXII (below) and XXXIII.

2. H. Carter and P. Newberry, "The Tomb of Thoutmosis IV," *Musée du Caire, Catalogue générale des antiquités* (1904) 24, pl. IX; J. E. Quibell, "The Tomb of Yuaa and Thuia," *Musée du Caire, Catalogue générale des antiquités* (1908) 65-67; H. Carter, *The Tomb of Tut-anhk-Amēn* (New York, 1927) pls. XXXVII B, XXXVIII B; Y. Yadin, *The Art of Warfare in Biblical Lands* (New York, 1963) 191.

3. The box on the fresco at Tiryns is exactly the color of red oxhide, cf. Rodenwaldt, *Tiryns* II, Taf. XII. Some LH III A krater chariots are still close enough to reality to show what is surely spotted oxhide, cf. III.17 and 21, and see IV.4. For painted linen siding, see Ventris and Chadwick, *Documents²*, 366, 367.

4. Rodenwaldt, *Tiryns* II, Taf. XII (cf. also the model from Mega Monastirio); Littauer, *AJA* 76 (1972) 156.

5. M. von Dewall, *Pferd und Wagen im frühen China* (Bonn, 1964) 220, Taf. 19. For Olympia bronze model, see U. Gehrig, A. Greifenhagen, N. Kunisch, *Führer durch die Antikenabteilung* (Berlin, 1968) 31, 01.9215. For Corinthian and Attic ware, see enlarged detail of Chigi vase, P. E. Arias and M. Hirmer, *Greek Vase Painting* (New York, 1961) fig. 17, below; also *CVA* U.S.A. 5, MMA, pls. 551.2, 568.2, 572.2; J. D. Beazley, *Attic Black-figure Vase Painters* (Oxford, 1956) pls. 247.92, 267.7, 307.97 *bis*; M. A. Del Chiaro, "Classical Vases in the Santa Barbara Museum of Art," *AJA* 68 (1964) pl. 31, fig. 1.

6. Personal observation on chariots of Tut 'ankhamūn in Cairo; Carter and Newberry, "Tomb of Thoutmosis IV," 24.

pole would not have protruded behind the box. With the pole between the floor frame and the axle, the floor frame at its sides or rear would have been too high to rest directly on the axle, so small blocks would have been placed beneath it to make up the discrepancy—a practice we have evidence for on both Egyptian and Chou chariots.[7]

Just what the "spur" represented is uncertain. It may have been the protruding end of the pole, as considered above, or the rear of the floor extending in a little sill, as on some Sumerian vehicles.[8] It may have been a strictly profile view of the *two* ends of the floor frame. On Egyptian chariots these ends protruded slightly behind the sides, but the terminals were rounded, not beveled.[9] At a later period in Greece these ends protruded on some documents in the round, where we can tell better what we are looking at than in strict profile views. This feature occurs on at least two bronze models, possibly of the eighth century B.C. from Olympia, and on a probably sixth-century terracotta chariot group from Boeotia.[10] Or the spur may stand for a conflation of two or more of these elements seen in profile.

AXLE AND WHEELS
Axles on krater chariots are in all positions under the box, from central to full rear. (Remember that the "wing" began

Fig. 2. Ladies driving a chariot to the hunt. Mycenaean fresco from the palace at Tiryns, after Rodenwaldt, Tiryns II, pl. XII.

at the end of the floor.) Our most careful documentation, on murals from Tiryns and Mycenae, consistently shows a near-rear position. See Fig. 2.

The wheels are four-spoked, and the spokes widen as they approach the felloes. The earliest evidence of the latter feature is on the gem from Avdou (Fig. 3); it is illustrated

Fig. 3. Charioteer and passenger, with a team of two wild goats, showing good details of structure and harness. Minoan agate gem from a tomb at Avdou near Lyktos, Crete, after Evans, Palace of Minos IV, *823, fig. 803.*

on several Linear B ideograms and on the Tiryns and Mycenae murals. This feature was characteristic of Aegean chariots but is rarely shown on the kraters (for example, III.6, IV.2, IX.2).[11] It also seems possible that the lashings around the spokes on the Tiryns fresco and even in Attic black figure may indicate a composite spoke-and-nave construction similar to that of Eighteenth-Dynasty Egyptian chariot wheels.[12]

The felloe, Fig. 1 (2), so clearly depicted in the Tiryns fresco and also on fresco fragments from Mycenae, seems to

7. Von Dewall, *Pferd und Wagen*, 220, Taf. 19.

8. E. Strommenger and M. Hirmer, *5000 Years of the Art of Mesopotamia* (New York, 1964) pl. XI.

9. Carter, *The Tomb of Tut-ankh-Amēn*, pls. XXVII B, XXVIII B; Yadin, *Art of Warfare*, 190.

10. Lorimer, *HM*, fig. 46 (Athens NM 6128); Gehrig, Greifenhagen, Kunisch, *Antikenabteilung*, 31, 01.9215; P. Perdrizet, *ArchEph* (1896) pl. 3.

11. An exception to the general rule of four spokes on krater chariots, as well as to that of unshaped spokes, is the chariot with a six-spoked wheel on an LH III A krater (III.13) from Pyla-Verghi, now in Nicosia.

12. A. C. Western, "A Wheel Hub from the Tomb of Amenophis III," *JEA* 59 (1973) 91 f.

show a two-part construction with differently colored and radially striped inner and outer concentric elements. See Fig. 4. In the light of contemporary Egyptian practice, this

Fig. 4. Charioteer and foot soldier setting out. Mycenaean fresco from the palace at Englianos, after Lang, Palace of Nestor II, *pl. 123.*

may possibly represent a deep felloe with a differently colored rawhide tire; at least one Egyptian chariot had tires dyed red.[13] Or the rim may have been composed of an inner and an outer felloe (in which case the spoke ends would penetrate both elements) or of a felloe and a wooden tire (which the spoke ends would not penetrate). One chariot of Tut 'ankhamūn's had wheels with wooden tires, the vertical faces of which were flush with those of the felloe, the two elements being held together by lashings of copper wire. In all cases, the main felloe was composed of two lengths of heat-bent wood, overlapping and beveled at the overlap. This double construction permitted a heavier felloe, when that was desired, since there are limits to the degree to which a length of timber of a given thickness and given variety of wood can be bent.[14] The apparently deep felloes of some of the chariot wheels shown on kraters might indicate this double construction.

The linch pin on the Tiryns fresco indicates a revolving wheel and fixed axle, as do the separate wheels listed on Linear B tablets. The fixed axle was already known in Sumerian times. It was superior not only because the nave of the wheel could be greased, thus reducing the noise and friction associated with the revolving axle, but also because this system made it very simple to replace a wheel—a desirable feature wherever the more vulnerable spoked wheels were used and were liable to damage. Equally important, it permitted the wheels to revolve differentially, which eliminated the skidding of the outside

wheel on sharp turns. The assumption that the fixed axle was used in the Aegean is supported by its use on contemporary Egyptian chariots.

TRACTION SYSTEM

As suggested above, it seems likely that the pole either passed under the entire chariot, being attached to the floor frame at front and back, or that its end lay in a socket between the rear floor bar and axle when the axle was at the rear. This supposition appears to be reinforced by those Linear B ideograms that give examples of chariot bodies without wheels but in every case supplied with a pole.[15]

Many vases do not bother to show the chariot pole. Others show it running up obliquely from under the front of the vehicle or making a double curve, upward and then forward, before disappearing behind the horse nearest the viewer. The oblique pole is paralleled on the murals; the pole with the double curve is shown on the gem from Avdou, and possibly also on Linear B tablets and is known to us from the Eighteenth Dynasty chariots on which this part is preserved.

To help prevent splitting and to hold it together if it did, the pole was bound throughout its length with thongs. This detail is not shown on vases but appears on frescoes and on the sardonyx from Vapheio (Fig. 5).

The chariot pole was braced by a peculiar contraption, apparently an L-shaped piece of wood that formed two sides of the triangle of which the pole itself was the hypotenuse. The end of the shorter vertical arm of this L-shaped member was seated in the pole just in front of the box; from its longer, horizontal arm, as this ran forward to the junction of pole and yoke, depended other vertical members that were also seated in the pole—an arrangement that produced an arcaded effect.[16] The short arm of the L rose vertically in front of the box to just below the top of the front breastwork, at which point a rod ran out horizontally on top of the long arm and continued all the way out to the yoke. Except for the Tiryns and Mycenae murals, we would not know that there were two elements,

13. Quibell, "Tomb of Yuaa and Thuia," 67.

14. G. Kossack, "The construction of the felloe in Iron Age spoked wheels," *The European Community in Later Prehistory, Studies in Honour of C. F. C. Hawkes,* ed. J. Boardman, M. A. Brown, and T. G. E. Powell (London, 1971) 149-159. There is no clear evidence yet at this period, however, for the tongue-and-groove construction of a two-part felloe posited by Kossack for one of the hearses found at Salamis and for Assyrian chariots.

15. Evans, *Palace of Minos* IV, figs. 764, 766. One could argue that the axle was present on these without the wheels but was difficult to draw in profile. It cannot be proven either way.

16. Rodenwaldt, *Fries,* Beil. I.1; Evans, *Palace of Minos* IV, figs. 763.c, f, 764.c, e; Å. Åkerström, *OpAth* 12 (1978) 19 f.

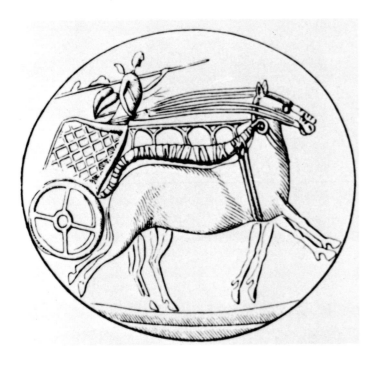

Fig. 5. Charioteer (with whip?) and (partly effaced) passenger with spear, in a wicker-covered chariot, driving a team. Mycenaean sardonyx gem, from the tholos tomb at Vapheio, after Evans, Palace of Minos IV, *820, fig. 799.*

both the "brace" and the "stay." Such other evidence as is furnished by the Avdou gem and the Linear B ideograms, all attesting general use of such an arrangement (which is also shown with an earlier type of chariot box on the sardonyx from Vapheio), does not clearly distinguish the two parts. Nor are the murals themselves precise about how the "brace" and "stay" were connected. On the best-preserved document bearing on this, a fragment from the later palace at Tiryns, we see what appear to be groups of two or three cords hanging from white rectangles on the "stay," falling loosely like fringes, their ends below the "brace." Since they would have served no purpose thus, they must surely represent the means by which the "stay" and "brace" were lashed to each other, with perhaps the cord or thong ends dangling from the knots. On a fragment of mural from Mycenae, showing the yoke end of the pole,[17] they seem to serve this more serious function.

The purpose of the notch, Fig. 1 (11) in the "brace" at its elbow, so clear on the Tiryns mural, is unexplained.

The function of the "brace" and "stay" was to reinforce the chariot pole itself, as well as to reduce the tendency (on a central- or near-central-axled chariot) for the front edge of the floor frame to pull upward and away from the pole when someone mounted or stood to the rear of the axle. It has often been suggested that these features in some way relieved the horses of weight.[18] They could indeed have relieved the horses of the weight of the *pole*, if this were a four-wheeled vehicle with a vertically articulating pole. But the pole and box of a two-wheeled vehicle form a rigid unit, resting at or near one end on the axle and wheels, with the weight in this area, and at the other end on the team's necks. This is a simple lever-and-fulcrum problem. The form of the lever, whether a straight rod or in part a triangle (as the Aegean chariot pole), makes no difference; the downward pressure at the far end is governed only by the distance between this end and the fulcrum (the axle) and the position of the weight in relation to that fulcrum.

Some krater chariots attempt to show the arcading of the connection between "brace" and pole; others render it in garbled fashion (III.6, 13, V.7, 8).[19] On still others there are only meaningless repeated motifs below the reins and also frequently above them. These seem to reveal the painter's uncomprehending efforts to fill a space originally occupied partly by traction elements. Some confused painters either cut short the vertical arm of the "brace" and let it dangle in the air just in front of the box, or they continued it all the way to the ground, which makes it look rather like a prop for an unharnessed chariot. Some doubled this feature.

YOKE, YOKE SADDLES, NECKSTRAP, AND GIRTH

All ancient draught was paired under a yoke, shaped somewhat like a composite bow with the arcs over the horses' necks, and was attached over the pole near its end. There may have been a pin, perhaps with a finial, besides the lashings at the area of junction. That the ends of the yoke curved back sharply upon themselves, as on the Florence yoke and those of Tut 'ankhamūn, seems clear from a fresco fragment from Knossos published by Alexiou. The upper, white, curving object on that fragment is probably the yoke end.

That yoke saddles, Fig. 1 (12), were used, as in Egypt, seems indicated by this fresco fragment, as well as by the Linear B tablets.[20] Both the ideograms and the fresco show the lower ends of the yoke saddle curving sharply upward, and from the latter document we may deduce that they ended in pear-shaped terminals—both apparently exclusively Aegean features. The "handles" of these roughly tuning-fork-shaped objects would have been lashed to the

17. Rodenwaldt, *AthMitt* 36, Abb. 1; *Fries*, Beil. I.1.

18. W. Helbig, in *Homerische Epos* (1887) 134, was the first to make this erroneous suggestion, which has frequently been repeated since.

19. Åkerström, *OpAth* 12, 35, fig. 16.1 (diagram of chariot).

20. M. A. Littauer, "The Function of the Yoke Saddle in Ancient Harnessing," *Antiquity* 42 (1968) 27-31.

arcs of the yoke, as on extant Egyptian examples. These "handles" had spool-like finials. Such a finial is observable on the Knossos fragment; it is white, so it may have been of calcite, like some on Tut 'ankhamun's harness.[21]

The yoke was held on by means of the yoke saddles, which fitted over the necks of the horses just ahead of the withers. To the lower ends of the saddles were attached the neckstrap, Fig. 1 (13), and the girth (14), which went around the horse's chest just behind the forelegs. This extreme forward position of the girth (today the girth is affixed directly behind the withers) caused it to assume an oblique angle, as is evidenced on the Avdou gem, the Knossos fresco fragment, and the Haghia Triada sarcophagus. This angle is also shown on Egyptian Eighteenth-Dynasty monuments, where the concomitant slackness is more apparent.[22] The neckstrap was probably wide, as on the sarcophagus and on the Avdou gem, perhaps made up of several straps, as the Knossos fragment seems to show it. From the area where the girth and neckstrap were attached to the yoke-saddle end, a loop or loops depended, evidently the ends of one or both of these bindings. They appear on both the Knossos and Tiryns murals, where they are decorated with white disks, which may have been of metal or ivory. On the rare occasions when these features are shown on kraters, they may have a decoration of lines or chevrons in white paint (IV.12, 20, 52, 69). The loops and ends of the bindings are also sometimes shown, and even an exaggerated yoke-saddle end.

BRIDLE

The bridle, which is known in some detail only from Mycenaean murals and a few pieces of material evidence, was made up of headstall, bit, and reins.[23] Some complete bits of the period have come down to us, of a type that does not appear on Aegean pictorial documents but that is materially evidenced at this period in Egypt and the Levant. They have long, narrow, rectangular cheekpieces. But at Tiryns a bit with a circular cheekpiece, Fig. 1 (15), similar to those found at Mycenae, is illustrated.[24] This type also occurred in the contemporary Near East. On both types of bits the ends of the mouthpieces passed through the cheekpieces, and the reins would have been attached to the ends of the mouthpiece. The bit was held up in place by the cheekstrap (16) of the headstall. This strap was sometimes decorated with small disks.[25] The headstall also had a noseband (17) at cheekpiece level or just above it, a browband (18), a throatlash (19), and a poll piece (20), really a continuation of the cheekstrap over the poll, as on modern bridles.

Krater chariots make almost no attempt to show the headstall and bit, but there are some interesting exceptions. One is a fragment from Mycenae (IX.8), on which a headstall is definitely depicted, and perhaps the ring of a cheekpiece. On a krater from Cyprus (III.16) in New York, the rings of the cheekpieces are clearly shown.

The four reins, two to each horse, do not seem to have passed through guides at the junction of the yoke-saddle ends and girth on the horses' shoulders, as in Egypt, but to have gone directly back from the bits to the driver's hands, if we follow the evidence of the frescoes and the gems. Only on many LH III A-B vases (especially those found in Cyprus) do they look as though they passed through a guide high up, just behind the neck. This may indicate a rein ring that rose from the pole, but we have no other indication of it, either figured or material.[26]

The horses' manes were bound in varying numbers of tufts, starting at the poll and extending part way down the neck.[27] This is a typically Aegean feature.

THE "RAIL CHARIOT"

In late LH III B and continuing into III C, some vases show evidence of changes in the chariot. (See VI.51, XI.1, 2, 16, 26, 37.) Unfortunately, information about these changes is very scanty, owing to the fragmentary nature of these kraters and their sketchy drawing, as well as to the lack of other sources in the Aegean at this time. The new chariot was open-walled, with only a railing. There was no "wing," but the railing was rounded at the rear—although apparently rather less than was the "wing"—and was probably a single piece of heat-bent wood. We are told nothing of the shape or construction of the floor, but may assume that the box was made for two occupants (the only number shown) standing side by side. The four-spoked wheel continued, but its exact position is not clear.

21. Carter, *Tomb of Tut-ankh-Amēn*, pl. XLII.

22. Littauer, *Antiquity* 42, 30, pl. IV b.

23. Rodenwaldt, *Tiryns* II, Taf. II.4, 6, XIV.3; Fries, Beil. I.2; W. Lamb, *BSA* 25, pl. XXVII. J. A. H. Potratz, *Die Pferdetrensen des alten Orient* (Rome, 1966) fig. 45.g (bit from Mycenae), Taf. XLVIII.111 (one of a pair of bits from Miletos); H. Matthäus, "Mykenische Trensen mit Radknebeln," *Arch. Korrespondenzblatt* 7 (1977) 37 f. (cheekpieces from Mycenae).

24. Rodenwaldt, *Tiryns* II, Taf. II.4, XIV.3; cf. actual circular bits, Potratz, *Pferdetrensen*, fig. 46.a, b, Taf. XLIX.115.

25. Rodenwaldt, *Tiryns* II, Taf. II.4. Disks also appear on a noseband on a fresco from Mycenae; cf. Lamb, *BSA* 25, pl. XXVII.

26. See III.2, 17; IV.1, 16, 18, 19, 20, 48, 49, 56; V.2, 6, 7, 8, 22, 23; VIII.3, 5.1.

27. Rodenwaldt, *Tiryns* II, Taf. XIV.3; Fries, Beil. I.2; Lamb, *BSA* 25, pl. XXVII.

Although there is not sufficient evidence to justify drawing conclusions, it may be suggested that the "pole brace" had also disappeared; at least none of the elaborate arcadings or flying motifs that indicate it on earlier vases are present on the one document that gives us the largest view of the pertinent area: a fragmentary krater from Tiryns (XI.16). Perhaps in the interests of a lightened vehicle the "pole brace" was abandoned, and because the vehicle was so much lighter, it was no longer helpful. Even at this early period the "stay" may have been converted into the thong we know from Geometric and archaic times.[28] Minus the "brace," a "stay" composed of a slender rod would have been more brittle and therefore more fragile than a stout thong. A pole support of one kind or another was a feature of all Bronze Age chariots and would have been essential on these. Had these new chariots evolved under Egyptian influence, one would expect the Egyptian method of support to have been perpetuated in later Greek

chariots. This system consisted of thongs or a system of rods that dropped down obliquely from the top of the front railing to the pole a short distance in front of the chariot. The horizontal thong, running from the top of the front breastwork to the end of the pole, is a more logical descendant of the Mycenaean "stay." Nor did these chariots display, any more than did the "dual" chariots, such other Egyptian features as fenestrated sides and attached bowcases and quivers. In fact, their completely open sides would have made it difficult to attach arms. In their great lightness, they formed a striking contrast to the majority of krater chariots. Their advantage in lightness and maneuverability must have struck all users, since the type is ancestral to all late Greek chariots.

28. For example, Arias and Hirmer, *Greek Vase Painting,* pls. 10 and 11 (Geometric, both perhaps showing "vestigial" brace/stay lashings) and 42 (the François vase).

SELECT BIBLIOGRAPHY

This list does not repeat the original publication of pictorial pieces but concentrates on works discussing style, attribution, and other strictly pictorial problems.

Åkerström, Å. "Das mykenische Töpferviertel in Berbati in der Argolis." *Bericht über den VI. Internationalen Kongress für Archäologie* (1939) 296 f.

———. "En Mykensk Krukmakares Verkstad." *Arkeologiska Forskningar och Fynd* (1952) 32 f.

———. "Some Pictorial Vase Representations." *OpAth* 1 (1953) 9 f.

———. "A Mycenaean Potter's Factory at Berbati near Mycenae." *I° Congresso di Micenologia* I (1968) 48 f.

———. "Mycenaean Problems. I. On the Mycenaean Chariot." *OpAth* 12 (1978) 19 f.

Asaro, F. and Perlman, I. "Provenience Studies of Mycenaean Pottery Employing Neutron Activation Analysis." *The Mycenaeans in the Eastern Mediterranean* (1973) 207 f.

Åström, L. "A Note on a Mycenaean Chariot Krater in Bonn." *OpAth* 4 (1962) 125 f.

Benson, J. L. "A Problem in Orientalizing Cretan Birds: Mycenaean or Philistine Prototypes?" *JNES* 20 (1961) 73 f.

———. "Pictorial Mycenaean Fragments from Kourion." *AJA* 65 (1961) 53 f.

———. "Observations on Mycenaean Vase-Painters." *AJA* 65 (1961) 337 f.

———. Review of V. Karageorghis, *Nouveaux Documents*, in *AJA* 71 (1967) 316 f.

———. "A Mycenaean Vase in Toronto." *AJA* 72 (1968) 203 f.

———. *Horse, Bird and Man* (1970).

Benton, S. "Cattle Egrets and Bustards in Greek Art." *JHS* 81 (1961) 44 f.

Benzi, M. *Ceramica Micenea in Attica, Testi e Documenti per Lo Studio dell' Antichitá* 50 (1975).

Betts, J. H., and Green, J. R. "Some Levanto-Helladic Krater Fragments in the Otago Museum." *BICS* 11 (1964) 70 f.

Biran, A. "A Mycenaean Charioteer Vase from Tel Dan." *Israel Exploration Journal* 20 (1970) 92 f.

Boardman, J. "Iconographica Cypria." *RDAC* 1976, 152 f.

Buchholz, H.-G. "Echinos und Hystrix." *BJV* 5 (1965) 66 f.

———. "Ägäische Funde und Kultureinflüsse." *AA* 1974, 325 f.

Buchholz, H.-G., and Karageorghis, V. *Altägäis und Altkypros* (1971).

Catling, H. W. "Minoan and Mycenaean Pottery: Composition and Provenance." *Archaeometry* 6 (1963) 1 f.

———. "Composition and Provenance: A Challenge." *Archaeometry* 9 (1966) 92 f.

———. "A Mycenaean Puzzle from Lefkandi in Euboea." *AJA* 72 (1968) 41 f.

———. "A Mycenaean Pictorial Fragment from Palaepaphos." *AA* 1970, 24 f.

Catling, H. W., Blin-Stoyle, A. E., and Richards, E. E. "Spectrographic Analysis of Mycenaean and Minoan Pottery." *Archaeometry* 4 (1961) 31 f.

Catling, H. W., Jones, R. E., and Millett, A., "Composition and Provenance Problems in Some Late Bronze Age Pottery Found in Cyprus." *RDAC* 1978, 70 f.

Catling, H. W., and Millett, A. "Composition Patterns of Mycenaean Pictorial Pottery." *BSA* 60 (1965) 212 f.

Catling, H. W., Richards, E. E., and Blin-Stoyle, A. E. "Correlations between Composition and Provenance of Mycenaean and Minoan Pottery." *BSA* 58 (1953) 94 f.

Charitonides, S. "Mykenaios anggeiographos." *EphArch* 1953-54 B, 101 f.

———. "Ho mykenaios anggeiographos tōn Papyrōn." *Deltion* 16 (1960) 84 f.

Coche de la Ferté, E. *Essai de classification de la céramique mycénienne d'Enkomi* (1951).

Courtois, J.-C. "Sur divers groupes de vases mycéniens en Méditerranée Orientale (1250-1150 av. J.-C.)." *The Mycenaeans in the Eastern Mediterranean* (1973) 137 f.

Crouwel, J. H. "Mycenaean Pictorial Pottery in Holland." *BABesch* 47 (1972) 14 f.

———. "A Chariot Sherd from Mycenae." *BSA* 67 (1972) 99 f.

———. "The Parasol Krater." *BSA* 68 (1973) 343 f.

———. "A Note on Two Mycenaean Parasol Kraters." *BSA* 71 (1976) 55 f.

Daniel, J. F. "Late Mycenaean Pottery with Pictorial Representations." *AJA* 46 (1942) 121 f.

———. Review of A. Furumark, *The Mycenaean Pottery*, in *AJA* 47 (1943) 252 f.

Desborough, V. R. *The Last Mycenaeans and Their Successors* (1964).

Evans, A. *The Palace of Minos* IV (1935) 1: 304 f., 335, 374; 2: 534, 659, 818 f.

Forsdyke, E. J. *Catalogue of Vases in the British Museum* I.1 (1925).

———. "A Late Mycenaean Vase from Cyprus." *Essays in Aegean Archaeology* (1927) 27 f.

Furtwängler, A., and Loeschcke, G. *Mykenische Vasen* (1886).

Furumark, A. *The Mycenaean Pottery* (1941).

———. "A Scarab from Cyprus." *OpAth* 1 (1953) 47 f.

Gjerstad, E. *Studies on Prehistoric Cyprus* (1926) 213 f.

Hankey, V. "Mycenaean Pottery in the Middle East." *BSA* 62 (1967) 107 f.

Hankey, V. and Warren, P. "The Absolute Chronology of the Aegean Late Bronze Age." *BICS* 21 (1974) 142 f.

Hüttel, H.-G. "Altbronzezeitliche Pferdetrensen." *Jahresbericht des Instituts für Vorgeschichte der Universität Frankfurt* (1977) 65 f.

Immerwahr, S. A. "Three Mycenaean Vases from Cyprus in the Metropolitan Museum of Art." *AJA* 49 (1945) 534 f.

———. "Some Mycenaean Artists Re-examined." *AJA* 59 (1955) 172.

———. "The Protome Painter and Some Contemporaries." *AJA* 60 (1956) 137 f.

———. "Mycenaean Trade and Colonization." *Archaeology* 13 (1960) 4 f.

———. *The Athenian Agora* 13, *The Neolithic and Bronze Ages* (1971) 121, 145, 248 f.

———. "A Mycenaean Ritual Vase." *Hesperia* 46 (1977) 32 f.

———. Review of V. Karageorghis, *CVA* Cyprus II, in *AJA* 71 (1967) 103 f.

Karageorghis, V. "Two Mycenaean bull-craters in the G. G. Pierides Collection, Cyprus." *AJA* 60 (1956) 143 f.

———. "The Mycenaean Window-Crater in the British Museum." *JHS* 77 (1957) 269 f.

———. "Deux peintres de vases 'mycéniens.' " *Syria* 34 (1957) 81 f.

———. "A Mycenaean Chalice and a Vase-Painter." *BSA* 52 (1957) 38 f.

———. "Some Mycenaean Vases in the G. G. Pierides Collection, Cyprus." *Kypriakai Spoudai* 10 (1957).

———. "Myth and Epic in Mycenaean Vase-Painting." *AJA* 62 (1958) 383 f.

———. "A Mycenaean Horse-Rider." *BABesch* 32 (1958) 38 f.

———. "Les personnages en robe sur les vases mycéniens." *BCH* 83 (1959) 193 f.

———. "Supplementary Notes on the Mycenaean Vases from the Swedish Tombs at Enkomi." *OpAth* 3 (1960) 135 f.

———. "Mycenaean Birds Re-united." *AJA* 64 (1960) 278 f.

———. "Mycenaean Art in Cyprus." *Kypriakai Spoudai* 14 (1961) 7 f.

———. "Le cratère mycénien aux taureaux des Musées de Berlin." *BCH* 86 (1962) 11 f.

———. *Corpus Vasorum Antiquorum*, Cyprus I (1963).

———. *Nouveaux Documents pour l'Etude de L'Âge de Bronze Recent* (1965).

———. *Corpus Vasorum Antiquorum*, Cyprus II (1965).

———. "A Mycenaean Painter of Swallows." *AA* 1967, 162 f.

———. *Mycenaean Art from Cyprus* (1968).

———. "Two Mycenaean Chariot Craters at Rochester, U.S.A." *BCH* 93 (1969) 162 f.

———. in *Prehistory and Protohistory*, ed. G. Christopoulou, J. Bastias (1975) 346 f.

———. "A Mycenaean Painter of Bulls and Bull Protomes." In Schaeffer, *Alasia* I (1971) 173 f.

———. *The Civilization of Prehistoric Cyprus* (1976) 162 f.

Karageorghis, V., Asaro, F., and Perlman, I. "Concerning Two Mycenaean Pictorial Sherds from Kouklia (Palaepaphos), Cyprus." *AA* 1972, 188 f.

Karageorghis, V., and Masson, O. "Un cratère mycénien inscrit de l'île de Chypre." *RevArch* 1956, 20 f.

Kardara, C. "The Itinerant Art." *I° Congresso di Micenologia* I (1968) 223 f.

Kopcke, G. "Figures in Pot-Painting before, during and after the Dark Age." *Symposium on the Dark Ages in Greece* (1977) 32 f.

Leipen, N. " A Clay Alabastron with Shield Decoration." *Annual, Royal Ontario Museum of Art* 1961, 27 f.

Littauer, M. A. "The Function of the Yoke Saddle in Ancient Harnessing." *Antiquity* 42 (1968) 27 f.

———. "Bits and Pieces." *Antiquity* 43 (1969) 289 f.

———. "The Military Use of the Chariot in the Aegean in the Late Bronze Age." *AJA* 76 (1972) 145 f.

———. "The Origin and Diffusion of the Cross-bar Wheel." *Antiquity* 51 (1977) 95 f.

Littauer, M. A., and Crouwel, J. H. "Early Metal Models of Wagons from the Levant." *Levant* 5 (1973) 102 f.

———. *Wheeled Vehicles and Ridden Animals* (1979).

Mackeprang, M. B. "Late Mycenaean Vases." *AJA* 42 (1938) 537 f.

Marinatos, S. "Some Hints about Eastern Mediterranean Mythology." *EphArch* 1965, 1 f.

———. "On the Track of Folklore Elements in Bronze Age Art and Literature." *IV. International Congress for Folk-Narrative Research* (1965) 262 f.

———. "Röntgenbilder in der mykenischen Kunst." *Praktika tes Akademias Athenōn* 1966, 1 f.

Murray, A. S., Smith, A. H., and Walters, H. B., *Excavations in Cyprus* (1900).

Popham, M. R., and Millburn, E. "The Late Helladic III C Pottery of Xeropolis (Lefkandi): A Summary." *BSA* 66 (1971) 333 f.

Popham, M. R., and Sackett, L. H. *Excavations at Lefkandi, Euboea 1964-66* (1968) 18 f.

Pottier, E. "Observations sur la céramique mycénienne." *RevArch* 1896, 17 f.

———. "Documents céramiques du Musée du Louvre." *BCH* 21 (1907) 228 f.

Schaeffer, C. F. A. *Missions en Chypre* (1936) 75 f.

———. *Ugaritica* I (1939) 53 f.

———. "Sur un cratère mycénien de Ras Shamra." *BSA* 37 (1936-37) 212 f.

———. *Ugaritica* II (1949) 131 f.

Sjöqvist, E. *Problems of the Late Cypriote Bronze Age* (1940) 70 f.

Slenczka, E. *Tiryns* VII, *Figürlich Bemalte Mykenische Keramik* (1974).

Smith, A. H. *Corpus Vasorum Antiquorum*, British Museum I (1925).

Stubbings, F. "The Mycenaean Pottery of Attica," *BSA* 42 (1947) 1 f.

_____. "Some Mycenaean Artists." *BSA* 46 (1951) 168 f.

_____. *Mycenaean Pottery from the Levant* (1951).

_____. "Mycenaean Pottery in Cyprus: Some Doubts and Queries about Clay-Analysis," *The Mycenaeans in the Eastern Mediterranean* (1973) 207 f.

_____. "The Circus Pot Reconsidered." *Wandlungen, Studien zur Antiken und Neueren Kunst* (1975) 16 f.

Vandenabeele, F. "Some Aspects of Chariot-Representations in the Late Bronze Age of Cyprus." *RDAC* 1977, 97 f.

Vandenabeele, F., and Olivier, J.-P. *Les Idéogrammes Archéologiques du Linéaire B, Études Crétoises* 24 (1979) s.v. "Chevaux, Chars et Roues," 63 f.

Verdelis, N. M. "Neue Funde von Dendra." *AthMitt* 82 (1967) 1 f.

_____. *The Cuirass Tomb and Other Finds at Dendra, SIMA* 4 (1977) 36 f.

Vermeule, E. "Painted Mycenaean Larnakes." *JHS* 85 (1965) 123 f.

Walters, H. B. *Catalogue of the Greek and Etruscan Vases in the British Museum* I.2 (1912).

ADDENDA

Cassola Guida, P. *Le arme defensive dei Micenei nelle figurazione* (1973).

Catling, H. W. "Panzer." *Archaeologia Homerica* E (1977) 96 f.

Greenhalgh, P. "The Dendra Charioteer." *Antiquity* 54 (1980) 201.

CATALOGUE

CATALOGUE OF MYCENAEAN PICTORIAL VASES

The following abbreviations are used for major museum collections of Mycenaean pictorial vases:

BM   *The British Museum; numbers preceded by* A *refer to E. J. Forsdyke,* Catalogue of Vases in the British Museum *I.1, Aegean vases; numbers preceded by* C *refer to H. B. Walters,* Catalogue of Vases in the British Museum *I.2, Cypriote vases.*

CM   *The Cyprus Museum; many pieces are published in V. Karageorghis,* Corpus Vasorum Antiquorum, Cyprus I.

NM   *The National Museum, Athens; the basic catalogue is V. Staïs,* The Mycenaean Collection² *(1926); the museum authorities kindly permitted us to add the accession numbers of pieces, generally fragments, that were not included there, when they could be ascertained.*

The abbreviation FM *stands for Furumark motive number, and* FS, *for Furumark shape number, in Furumark,* The Mycenaean Pottery.

Because of the extensive cross-referencing in this book, as new vases became known, they were inserted in the catalogue as .1, for example, IX.30.1, in order to avoid renumbering.

Catalogue numbers in bold type indicate vases and fragments shown in the Illustrations section.

Cyprus and the East: Early Pictorial

FORERUNNERS

III.A   Qatna (El Misrifeh), Syria, amphoroid krater, guilloche and spiral. Musée du Louvre. E. Du Mesnil du Buisson, *Syria* IX (1928) 21, no. 110, pls. 17–18; Stubbings, *MycLevant*, 60, fig. 15 b; Furumark, *Chronology*, 56, 112.

III.B   Pyla-Verghi, amphoroid krater, vertical chevrons and leaves. Cyprus Museum. Karageorghis, *Nouveaux*

Documents, pl. 20.1; P. Dikaios, *Enkomi* (1969–71) pl. 232.2; Buchholz, Karageorghis, *Altägäis*, no. 1622.

EARLY I

III.1   Dhekelia, broad-shouldered amphoroid krater, birds in a tree, excavated August 1956 at the site Koukoufouthkia. W stands for I. Williams, then commissioner of Larnaka, and Colonel Willoughby, to whose generosity and vigilance this krater owes its preservation. Cyprus Museum; A. H. S. Megaw, *ArcRep* 1956 in *JHS* 77 (1957) pl. III d; V. Karageorghis, *CVA* Cyprus I, pl. 1; *AA* (1963) 534, fig. 16 a-b. The Mycenaean piriform jars and Base Ring I jugs with tall necks and beak-shaped spouts found in the same tomb support the early date assigned to the vase.

CHARIOTS

III.2   Enkomi, amphoroid krater, "Zeus with scales;" octopods, chariot, figure with scales, groom, bull. Cyprus Museum; Swedish Cyprus Expedition, T. 17/1. *SCE* I, pl. 120.3-4; H. R. Hall, *The Civilization of Greece in the Bronze Age* (1928) 213, fig. 276; Evans, *Palace of Minos* IV², 659, fig. 646; M. P. Nilsson, *Bulletin de la Societé Royale des Lettres de Lund* 1933, 29 ff.; *Homer and Mycenae* (1933) 267, fig. 56; *The Minoan-Mycenaean Religion²* (1950) 34; *Geschichte der griechischen Religion* I² (1955) 343, pl. 25.1; S. Casson, *Ancient Cyprus* (1937) pl. V.1: C. F. A. Schaeffer, *BSA* 37 (1936–37) 220, fig. 10; *Ugaritica* I, 121, fig. 52; V. Karageorghis, *AJA* 62 (1958) 385, pl. 98.2; *Treasures*, pl. 14; *MycArt*, pl. I.25; G. Bjørck, *Eranos* 43 (1945) 58; P. Demargne, *The Birth of Greek Art* (1964) fig. 349; E. Vermeule, *CJ* 53 (1958) 102; Furumark, *MP*, 437, FM 1.7; H. T. Bossert, *Altkreta³* (1937) 265, fig. 483; *Altsyrien* (1951) 72, fig. 234; T. B. L. Webster, *From Mycenae to Homer* (1958) 49; S. Benton, *JHS* 81 (1961) pl. 3.3-5; J. Wiesner, *JdI* 74 (1959) 35 f., figs. 1-3; R. Higgins, *Minoan and Mycenaean Art* (1967) 115, no. 133; *Archaeologia Viva:*

Cyprus (1969) 92, figs. XXXII-XXXIII; T. Spiteris, *The Art of Cyprus* (1970) 73; P. Dikaios, *Enkomi* (1969-71) 918 f., pls. 302.1, 2 and 4, 302 A.3; Buchholz, Karageorghis, *Altägäis*, no. 1621; G. Kopcke, *The Dark Ages in Greece* (1977) no. 26; *The Greek Museums: The Cyprus Museum* (1975) no. 28; V. Karageorghis, *Civilization of Prehistoric Cyprus* (1976) no. 121; *IEE* I, 352, 354; *Cyprus B.C.* (1979) 39 f., fig. 91; Vandenabeele, Olivier, *Idéogrammes*, 291, fig. 201.

BULLS

III.3 Enkomi, amphoroid krater fragment, bull ring scene. T. 7/II, Medelhavsmuseet, Stockholm. V. Karageorghis, *OpAth* 3 (1960) 148, pl. 11.3-4.

III.4 Enkomi, open krater, two fragments, bulls (and men). T. 7/III, Medelhavsmuseet, Stockholm. V. Karageorghis, *OpAth* 3 (1960) 148, pl. 12.

III.5 Enkomi, open krater fragment, bulls fighting. T. 3/IV, Medelhavsmuseet, Stockholm. V. Karageorghis, *OpAth* 3 (1960) 144, pl. 8.1-2.

CHARIOT AND BIRD

III.6 Enkomi, open krater, chariots pursued by birds. Schaeffer, T. 7 no. 4784, Cyprus Museum. V. Karageorghis, *AJA* 62 (1958) 384, pl. 98, fig. 1; S. Benton, *JHS* 81 (1961) pl. 3.1; S. Marinatos, *EphArch* 1964, 8, fig. 6; V. Karageorghis, *Civilization of Prehistoric Cyprus* (1976) no. 123.

MARINE SCENES

III.7 Enkomi, amphoroid krater, octopus. T. 83, BM C377. *ExcCyp*, 48, fig. 74; *CVA* British Museum I, pl. 9.2.

III.8 Alalakh, amphoroid krater, octopus. Ashmolean Museum 1948.465. L. Woolley, *Alalakh* (1955) pl. 128 h, i, j.

III.9 Maroni, fragments of an amphoroid krater(?), fish, T. 2, BM C378.

EARLY II

HUMAN FIGURES

III.10 Kition, fragment, woman. Area II/2512, Cyprus Museum. Karageorghis, *Kition*, fig. 34.

III.11 Kouklia, unstratified pit, 1952, krater fragment, woman. Cyprus Museum. H. Catling, *AA* 1970, 24 f., fig. 1 a-b; V. Karageorghis, F. Asaro, I. Perlman, *AA* 1972, 188 f., fig. 1; J. Boardman, *RDAC* 1976, 152 f., pl. XXIII.1-2.

CHARIOTS

III.12 Kourion, open krater, women in "windows," chariots. BM C391, now CM 1971/XII-6/1; *ExcCyp*, 73, fig. 127; *CVA* British Museum I, pl. 6.9; A. Evans, "Mycenaean Tree and Pillar Cult," *JHS* 21 (1901) 111 f., fig. 6; F. Poulsen, *JdI* 26 (1911) 232, fig. 16; S. Casson, *Ancient Cyprus* (1937) pl. 4; Furumark, *MP*, FM 1.2 (LH III A:1 e), 443 f.; *UnivMusBull* 8 (1940) 9, pl. 4 d; J. F. Daniel, *AJA* 46 (1942) 121; Karageorghis, *Treasures* (cover); *JHS* 77 (1957) 269; *Civilization of Prehistoric Cyprus* (1976) no. 122; T. B. L. Webster, *From Mycenae to Homer* (1958) fig. 18; H. Catling, *AA* 1970, 27, fig. 3.

III.13 Pyla-Verghi, open krater, chariots and groom. Cyprus Museum, CM 1952/IV-12/1. P. Dikaios, *FastiA* 7 (1952 [1954]) 132, fig. 44; *Enkomi* (1969-71) 915 f., pls. 230/1, 231,

301/1,2; V. Karageorghis, *JHS* 77, 2 (1957) 270; *Cyprus*, pl. 72; F. Schachermeyr, *AA* 1962, 367 f., figs. 88 a-b; Benson, *HBM*, pl. 12.7, 32.1; F. Vandenabeele, *RDAC* 1977, pl. 21.4; Vandenabeele, Olivier, *Idéogrammes*, 100, fig. 62 a-b.

III.14 Enkomi, krater fragment, chariot driver and passenger right. Enkomi 1947 no. 2362; Coche de la Ferté, *Essai*, pl. 1.7.

III.15 Alalakh, open krater fragment, chariot and men right. L. Woolley, *Alalakh* (1955) 369, pl. 129, ATP/37/285.

EARLY III

CHARIOTS

III.16 Maroni, amphoroid krater, chariots right, driver and passenger, rock barriers. Metropolitan Museum 74.51.964 (Cesnola); J. L. Myres, *Handbook of the Cesnola Collection of Antiquities from Cyprus* (1914) 48, no. 436; L. F. Bloodgood, *The Horse in Art* (1931), "design resembling the work of American Indians" (M. A. Littauer); C. F. A. Schaeffer, *BSA* 37 (1936-37) 231, fig. 31; S. Immerwahr, *AJA* 49 (1945) 534 f., figs. 8-10; G. M. A. Richter, *Handbook of the Greek Collection*[2] (1953) pl. 4 f; *Treasured Masterpieces of the Metropolitan Museum of Art* (1972) no. 27; *Greek and Roman Art*[3] (1975) 4, fig. 4; G. Kopcke, *Dark Ages in Greece* (1977) no. 23.

III.17 Enkomi, amphoroid krater fragments, chariots right, groom with phiale. T. 12, 1896; BM C344 and C348. *ExcCyp*, 39, fig. 67.832-833; *CVA* British Museum I, pl. 11.14; Mercklin, *Rennwagen* I, 21, nos. 29 (C344) and 28 (C348); Vandenabeele, Olivier, *Idéogrammes*, 135, fig. 91.

III.18 Provenance unknown, amphoroid krater, chariot at gallop left, robed human couples. Formerly Collection A. Barre, Comte de Boisgelin, Paris; now Musée du Louvre AO 22 293; Furtwängler-Loeschcke, *MV*, 28, fig. 16; A. de Ridder, *Collection De Clercq*, 5, pl. 32, no. 516; Dussaud, *Civilisations*[2], fig. 156; Furumark, *MP*, FM 1.5 (LH III A:2 e).

III.19 Ugarit, fragment of amphoroid krater, robed soldiers, bull. Musée du Louvre. C. F. A. Schaeffer, *Syria* 12 (1931) pl. 3.2; H. T. Bossert, *Altkreta*[3] (1937) 270, fig. 502; Lorimer, *HM*, pl. XXVII.3; *Ugaritica* II, fig. 124.9; Stubbings, *MycLevant*, fig. 22; Furumark, *MP*, FM 1.3 (LH III A:2 e).

III.20 Possibly Enkomi, krater fragments, men, animal, and altar(?). CM 1958/VI-20/1; V. Karageorghis, *BCH* 83 (1959) 201; *CVA* Cyprus I, pl. 3.1-3.

III.21 Enkomi, amphoroid krater fragment, chariot, robed figure, groom with sunshade, vases. T. 67, 1076, 1896; BM C339; *ExcCyp*, 37, fig. 65; E. Pottier, *BCH* 31 (1907) 242; H. Hall, *Aegean Archaeology* (1915) 144, fig. 57; Mercklin, *Rennwagen* I, 20, no. 23; Lorimer, *HM*, 315, fig. 45; Furumark, *MP*, 435, fig. 75, FM 1.1, FM 39.1 (LH III A:2 e); V. Karageorghis, *BCH* 83 (1959) 198, fig. 1; E. Vermeule, *CJ* 53 (1958) 104, fig. 10; H. W. Catling, *BSA* 60 (1965) pl. 58.2; M. Davies, *BCH* 93 (1969) 215, fig. 1; P. C. Guida, *Studi Micenei* 12 (1970) 136, fig. 1; F. Vandenabeele, *RDAC* 1977, pl. 21.3; Vandenabeele, Olivier, *Idéogrammes*, 102, fig. 64.

III.22 Enkomi, amphoroid krater fragment, robed figure, ewer. 1896, CM A2024; V. Karageorghis, *CVA* Cyprus I, pl. 3.4; Catling, *Bronzework*, pl. 19 g.

BULLS AND BULLS' HEADS

III.23 Enkomi, open krater, facing bulls' heads. T.12, 1896; BM C401; *ExcCyp* 39, fig. 67.844; *CVA* British Museum I, pl. 11.16; A. Evans, *JHS* 21 (1901) 107; Furumark, *MP*, FM 4.1, FM 35.22, FM 36.4 (wrongly attributed to III B through misinformation that the handles were loops instead of straps); J. F. Daniel, *AJA* 46 (1942) 121.

III.24 Enkomi, amphoroid krater fragment, bulls facing across a "mound." T.93, 1896; BM C366; *CVA* British Museum I, pl. 11.12.

III.25 Enkomi, open krater fragment, bull charging, seashell fillers. T. 12, 1896; BM C406.

GOATS

III.26 Maroni, tall amphoroid krater, wild goats among rocks. T.17, 1897; BM C368. J. Forsdyke in S. Casson, ed., *Essays in Aegean Archaeology Presented to Sir Arthur Evans* (1927) 27, pls. 1-2; Stubbings, *MycLevant*, 34, fig. 6, pl. 7.1; Furumark, *MP*, FM 6.1 (LH III A:2); H. Erlenmeyer, *AntK* 4 (1961) pl. 1.10; G. Kopcke, *Dark Ages in Greece* (1977) no. 6 (part).

BIRDS

III.27 Provenance unknown, krater fragments, frieze of birds. London, BM 1938/11-20/4; Manchester, University Museum.

III.28 Ashdod, Israel, fragment, dark-necked bird with large eye under barred loops. M. Dothan, *Archaeology* 20 (1967) 181.

TRANSITION

HUMAN FIGURES

III.29 Aradippo, open krater, warriors approaching a seated goddess. Musée du Louvre, AM 676; E. Pottier, *BCH* 31 (1907) 232, figs. 10-12; V. Karageorghis, *AJA* 62 (1958) 386, pl. 99.3-4; Furumark, *MP*, 444; T. B. L. Webster, *From Mycenae to Homer* (1958) 53; Vermeule, *GBA*, fig. 36 (wrongly drawn); V. Karageorghis, *MycArtCyp*, pl. IV; cf. the cylinder seal, A. Furtwängler, *ArchZeit* 1885, 142; J. C. Stobart, R. J. Hopper, *The Glory That Was Greece* (1971) fig. 37 a.

III.30 Maroni, amphoroid krater fragment, human figure holding fish. BM C337; H. W. Catling, *BSA* 60 (1965), pl. 60.2; cf. I. Sakellarakis, *AAA* 7 (1974) 370 f.; cf. XIII.29. Octopus fish gem, J. Boardman, *Greek Gems and Finger Rings* (1970) no. 62; fisherman gem, ibid., no. 107; Thera fisherman, S. Marinatos, *Thera* VI (1974) pl. 6.

III.31 Hala Sultan Tekké, two krater fragments, jumper vaulting a bull, right. *BCH* 101 (1977) 753; 102 (1978) 913, fig. 78.

Cyprus and the East: Middle Pictorial

MIDDLE I

CHARIOTS

IV.1 Enkomi or Psematismeno near Maroni, amphoroid krater, two chariots on each side, flowers, seashells, chevrons. BM 1911/IV-28/1; *CVA* British Museum I, pl. 7.4; A. J. B. Wace, F. Stubbings, *A Companion To Homer* (1962) pl. 37 a; V. Karageorghis, *The Prehistoric Civilization of Cyprus* (1976) no. 129; R. Higgins, *Minoan and Mycenaean Art* (1967) no. 132; *The Greek Bronze Age* (1970) pl. 7b; N. K. Sandars, *The Sea Peoples* (1978) 76, fig. 42; Vandenabeele, Olivier, *Idéogrammes*, 118, fig. 79.

IV.2 Kourion(?), fragments of an amphoroid krater, two chariots on each side, rocks, and seashells. CM A2025 a, d; *CVA* Cyprus I, pl. 6.2, 4; Vandenabeele, Olivier, *Idéogrammes*, 68, fig. 32 b.

IV.3 Enkomi, amphoroid krater, two chariots on each side, palm trees. T. 3 no. 257 (Swedish excavations), Medelhavsmuseet, Stockholm; Sjöqvist, *Problems*, fig. 19.1; T. B. L. Webster, *From Mycenae to Homer* (1958) 48.

BULLS

IV.4 Enkomi, amphoroid krater, bulls in a meadow. T. 2 (French excavations), Musée du Louvre; Schaeffer, *Enkomi-Alasia* I, pls. 17, 18; cf. *Syria* 30 (1953) 51, figs. 5-6. Drawing, E. Markou.

IV.5 Enkomi, amphoroid krater fragment, by the painter of IV.4, cow lifting face to smell flower. Coche de la Ferté, *Essai*, pl. I.4.

BIRDS

IV.6 Enkomi, amphoroid krater, frieze of three birds. BM C372; *ExcCyp*, 48, fig. 73.937; *CVA* British Museum I, pl. 9.4; *BMCatV*, 73, fig. 120. See also VIII.14.

IV.7 Cyprus, fragmentary amphoroid krater, frieze of water birds. Metropolitan Museum of Art, New York, 74.51.5850; S. Immerwahr, *AJA* 49 (1945) 535 f., figs. 1-4.

IV.8 Enkomi, fragmentary krater, birds(?) right. Brussels, Musée du Cinquantenaire, A1257; *CVA* Belgique 3, pl. 3.14.

IV.9 Arpera, fragmentary open krater, birds right, chevrons, semicircles. Ashmolean Museum, Oxford, 1953.335; H. W. Catling, *BSA* 60 (1965) 223, pl. 61.2.

IV.10 Tell Abu Hawam, fragments, birds. R. W. Hamilton, *QDAP* 4 (1935) pl. 19.o.

IV.11 Alalakh, fragments, birds. Ashmolean Museum, Oxford, 1948.448; L. Woolley, *Alalakh* (1955) pl. 128 f, ATP/37/284.

MIDDLE II

CHARIOTS

IV.12 Enkomi, amphoroid krater, chariot right, driver, two passengers, groom behind; liberal white paint; palm and chevrons. BM C340; *ExcCyp*, 49, fig. 75; *CVA*, British Museum I, pl. 9.6; *BMCatV*, fig. 111; H. R. Hall, *Aegean Archaeology* (1915) 105, fig. 34; *The Civilization of Greece in the Bronze Age* (1928) 224, fig. 294; W. Heurtley, *QDAP* 5 (1936) 95, fig. 4.9 (described as from Rhodes).

IV.13 Enkomi, fragments, chariot and attendant in torque necklace, right hand raised; chevrons and "rock" with dashes. BM C345; *BMCatV*, fig. 114; *ExcCyp*, 39, fig. 67.836.

IV.14 Enkomi, fragment, attendant behind chariot, chevrons and dashes. CM 1965/VIII-17/3; *BCH* 90 (1966) 305, fig. 16 b; M. Davies, *BCH* 93 (1969) 219, fig. 2.

IV.15 Unknown provenance, amphoroid krater, chariot right, driver and passenger, attendant behind, right arm raised. G. G. Pierides Collection no. 33, Nicosia. *CVA* Cyprus II, pl. 1. (Restored: side A, forelegs and heads of horses, filling ornament next to them, torso (but not head) of figure at back of chariot box with part of box itself, upper part of attendant's body, head, arms, and filling ornament around him; side B, horses' heads, chariot box, and figures.)

IV.16 Enkomi, small amphoroid krater, spotted split chariot, driver and passenger, flowers and chevrons; on one side an "archer" facing team. BM C341; *CVA* British Museum I, pl. 10.8; *BMCatV*, fig. 112 a, b.

IV.17 Enkomi, fragmentary amphoroid krater, by the painter of IV.16, driver with diamond eye, flower and chevrons. CM A2027; *CVA* Cyprus I, pl. 6.1.

IV.18 Klavdhia, amphoroid krater, confronted chariots with groom between (genitals indicated), chariot right, two adults lifting child. BM C342; *CVA* British Museum I, pl. 8.12; V. Karageorghis, *AJA* 62 (1958) 385, pl. 99.5, 6.

IV.19 Unknown provenance, amphoroid krater, single team right, flowers over reins and below bellies, palms left and right, quirks under tails, circles inside wheel, dotted circles, chevrons; driver has good arms and thumbs. Driver and passenger in spotted robes, box outlined in spots, white paint for harness and on wheel, simpler ornaments on reverse. CM A1645; E. Gjerstad, *Studies on Prehistoric Cyprus* (1926) 216, no. 1; *CVA* Cyprus I, pl. 7; Karageorghis, *MycArt*, 12 f., pl. II.2; *Civilization of Prehistoric Cyprus* (1976) no. 128; F. Vandenabeele, *RDAC* 1977, pl. 21.1; Vandenabeele, Olivier, *Idéogrammes*, 1118, fig. 80.

IV.20 Unknown provenance, fragmentary amphoroid krater, one team left, one right, rich white harness in ladder pattern, curlicues; in front of one team, tall undulating rock pillar with double border, filled with horizontal bars and dashes; flowers, chevrons, and quirks in the field. Larnaka District Museum, CM 1958/V-20/3; *CVA* Cyprus I, pl. 8.5-6.

IV.21 Enkomi, amphoroid krater, team on each side, right; quirks over reins, palms and flowers in field, flowers and chevrons under bellies and handles. Driver and passenger in spotted robes, box outlined in spots, U-pattern, single and antithetic, trains of dashes, chevrons, circles in wheel, rein-rings clear. T. 3 no. 163 (Swedish excavations), Medelhavsmuseet, Stockholm; Sjöqvist, *Problems*, fig. 19, no. 2; *SCE* I, pl. 121.1; Benson, *HBM*, pl. IX.8.

IV.22 Enkomi, amphoroid krater, team left, chevrons above, striped pole brace. T. II no. 3578 (French excavations). Coche de la Ferté, *Essai*, pl. I.2.

IV.23 Maroni, amphoroid krater fragment, forepart of team, large oval on yoke, chevrons and flowers. BM C363; H. W. Catling, *BSA* 60 (1965) pl. 60.8.

IV.24 Pyla-Verghi, amphoroid krater, very worn; tall palms in field, team right, dashes, quirks, chevrons. Driver and passenger in spotted robes, box outlined in spots. T. 1 no. 2; Larnaka District Museum; P. Dikaios, *Enkomi* (1969-71) pl. 235.2.

IV.25 Alalakh, krater fragments, team right, chevrons above and below reins and under tails, striped pole brace, spotted robes. L. Woolley, *Alalakh* (1955) pl. 128 a, ATP/46/307; *AntJ* 30 (1950) 16, pl. 8 a.

IV.26 Kition, amphoroid krater, team right, reins high above line of quirks to white neckstrap with yoke-saddle or tassels, flowers, quirks, and chevrons in field, double spiral "rock" under belly; white for harness, spotted robes and box. V. Karageorghis, *BCH* 84 (1960) 518 f., figs. 13-14.

IV.27 Klavdhia, amphoroid krater, high-rumped maladroit horses, left; flowers and profuse groups of chevrons. BM C343; *CVA* British Museum I, pl. 10.11.

IV.28 Moutti tou Marathou, Valia forest, Gastria (Famagusta district), amphoroid krater, team on each side, right, with pale or split legs deep through framing band, quirks below reins and under belly, tall shorthand flowers and whorl shell in field, reins directly from driver's chest, armless passenger, both in spotted robes, flattened heads through upper framing band. Collection A. Georghiades, Nicosia; V. Karageorghis, *BCH* 101 (1977) 732f., fig. 54.

IV.28.1 Maroni, krater fragment, team right, chevrons over reins, flowers behind, spotted robes and box; human eyes are large ovals tilted on end. BM C360; *BMCatV*, 71.

IV.29 Enkomi, krater fragment, team right, chevrons and dashes under bellies and tails, quirks (and flower?) behind, spotted robes and box, oval eye; horses have split legs. Firm good drawing. BM C346; *ExcCyp*, 39, fig. 67.838; *CVA* British Museum I, pl. 11.7. See Chapter IV, note 8.

IV.30 Enkomi, amphoroid krater fragments, team left, quirks above and below reins, ogival "rock" under belly, large flowers in front of horses and behind chariot; figures in chariot, spotted robes and chariot box. T. 3/I (Swedish excavations), Medelhavsmuseet, Stockholm; V. Karageorghis, *OpAth* 3 (1960) 143, pl. 6.1-2.

IV.31 Enkomi, amphoroid krater fragments, large palm-flowers in front of team. Brussels, Musée du Cinquantenaire A1247; *CVA* Belgique 3, pl. 3.18, 21.

BULLS

IV.32 Enkomi, amphoroid krater, bulls and cows in a meadow with attendants. T. 10.23 (Dikaios); P. Dikaios, *Enkomi* (1969-71) pls. 203 f., 224; A. H. S. Megaw, *JHS* 71 (1951) 259, fig. 1; P. Dikaios, *Guide to the Cyprus Museum* [3] (1961) pl. 37.3; Karageorghis, *MycArt*, 13, pl. 3.1-2; *Civilization of Prehistoric Cyprus* (1976) nos. 119-120; *Cyprus B.C.* (1979) 39, no. 89; Buchholz, Karageorghis, *Altägäis*, no. 1620.

IV.33 Unknown provenance, amphoroid krater fragment, dappled bull, head lowered to a sharp flower. CM 1958/VI-20/7; *CVA* Cyprus I, pl. 5.3; V. Karageorghis, *BCH* 83 (1959) 338 f., fig. 3.

IV.34 Enkomi, upper part of an amphoroid krater; side A, two antithetic bulls with dapples and spots, flowers, chevrons, seashells; side B, two facing bulls, fighting(?). T. 94, 1896; CM A2022 a, d, e; *CVA* Cyprus I, pl. 4.1-3.

IV.35 Enkomi, fragment of krater, bull charging right in field of U-pattern, net design over back, frontal and profile view combined, various fillings. BM C367; H. W. Catling, *BSA* 60 (1965) pl. 59.5.

IV.36 Maroni, shoulder fragment of amphoroid krater, confronted bulls or bull and cow touching muzzles, chevrons and dashes. BM C405? (does not correspond to description), *BMCatV,* 83, or 1898.12-1.278.

IV.37 Enkomi, fragment of open krater, two black bulls galloping right, one after the other, white seashells on their hides, striped loops. T. 12, 1896; BM C369, *BMCatV,* 73 (described as Cretan goats).

BIRDS

IV.38 Maroni, amphoroid krater, black and white water birds facing over nest with fledgings. BM C332; *CVA* British Museum I, pl. 9.12; Furumark, *MP,* FM 34.3 (LH III A:2); S. Benton, *JHS* 81 (1961) 50, pl. 4.1; R. Higgins, *Minoan and Mycenaean Art* (1967) fig. 136; Benson, *HBM,* pl. 24.2.

IV.39 Klavdhia, amphoroid krater, vertically ornamental birds and "nest" (rock). BM C373; *CVA* British Museum I, pl. 8.4.

IV.40 Enkomi, amphoroid krater, frieze of plump birds right, filled with vertical stripes and horizontal dashes. T. 10 no. 200 (Dikaios); P. Dikaios, *Enkomi* (1969-71) pls. 203, 223.

IV.41 Enkomi, fragmentary amphoroid krater, frieze of birds right, in drier style, set off by handsome belt of checkerboard pattern, filling of chevrons and dashes; the "extra" raised wing becomes a plume or crest. Chevron-flower dividers. CM 1958/I-10/1 plus BM C374 and BM C681; V. Karageorghis, *AJA* 64 (1960) 278 f., pl. 79.1-3; H. W. Catling, *BSA* 60 (1965) pl. 59.6.

IV.42 Arpera, fragment of krater, birds(?) with chevron dividers. CS 338; V. Karageorghis, *AJA* 64 (1960) pl. 79, fig. 4.

IV.43 Enkomi, amphoroid krater, frieze of birds right, crosshatched bodies, "ogival chest," wave pattern beneath. T. 3/259 (Swedish excavations), Medelhavsmuseet, Stockholm; *SCE* I, pl. 77; V. Karageorghis, *OpAth* 3 (1960) 142 f., pls. 5.1-2, 4.

IV.44 Maroni, amphoroid krater fragment, by the painter of IV.43, crosshatched bird right with "plume" wing. BM C375; V. Karageorghis, *OpAth* 3 (1960) pl. 5.3; H. W. Catling, *BSA* 60 (1965) pl. 61.1.

IV.45 Enkomi, amphoroid krater, striped birds right, loose chevron fillers. T. 3/260 (Swedish excavations), Medelhavsmuseet, Stockholm; *SCE* I, pl. 121.5.

OCTOPODS

IV.46 Unknown provenance, Hubbard amphoroid krater, facing "octopus" with tentacles, chevron filler on crown. CM 1962/V-31/1; *CVA* Cyprus I, pl. 2; *BCH* 87 (1963) 330, fig. 8; Karageorghis, *Treasures,* 14, pl. 15; *Civilization of Prehistoric Cyprus* (1976) no. 124; *Greek Museums: The Cyprus Museum* (1975) no. 29.

IV.47 Kourion, fragments of a similar krater. CM A2025 c, e, i; *CVA* Cyprus I, pl. 3.6.

MIDDLE III

CHARIOTS

IV.48 Kourion, amphoroid krater, chariot left, rocks, whorl shells and lozenges; six holes pierced through foot. BM C338; *ExcCyp,* 73, fig. 126; *CVA* British Museum I, pl. 7.6; *BMCatV,* fig. 109.

IV.48.1 Ialysos, amphoroid krater (see XII.3).

IV.49 Tel Dan, amphoroid krater, chariot left among flowers. A. Biran, *Israel Exploration Journal* 20 (1970) 92 ff.; V. Karageorghis, *Qadmoniot* 4 (1970) 11 f.

IV.50 Ugarit, amphoroid krater, chariot with three figures, four men on ground. C. F. A. Schaeffer, *Annales Archéologiques de Syrie* 11 (1961) 191 f., figs. 8-9. Drawing, Mme R. Kuss.

IV.51 Enkomi, amphoroid krater, chariot with three figures, two silhouetted figures on ground facing it with outstretched arms; flowers. T. 3/277 (Swedish excavations), Medelhavsmuseet, Stockholm; V. Karageorghis, *OpAth* 3 (1960) 136 f., pl. I.

IV.52 Enkomi, fragment, team right with robed figure standing before it, white overpaint. BM C349; H. W. Catling, *BSA* 60 (1965) pl. 59.2.

IV.53 Maroni, amphoroid krater fragment (belongs with next?), heads of three people in chariot right, curly hair. Fine drawing, rich flowers, overpaint. BM C336.

IV.54 Maroni, amphoroid krater fragment (which may belong with last), flowers over team, spotted box, pole brace with reserved zigzag. BM C362; H. W. Catling, *BSA* 60 (1965) pl. 60.7.

IV.55 Cyprus, amphoroid krater, chariot right, and attendants; flowers, quirks, dotted circles. Musée du Sèvres; *CVA* France 15, pl. 13.1, 2, 4, 5.

IV.56 Hala Sultan Tekké, fragmentary krater, chariot on each side, attendant facing team with sword or stick, carriage dog(?) following, windblown flags on pole brace. T. 2 no. 215; V. Karageorghis, *Hala Sultan Tekké* I (1976), pl. 74.

IV.57 Enkomi(?), fragmentary amphoroid krater, chariot left, driver in spotted robe, reserved pole brace, flowers and U-pattern. CM A2041; *CVA* Cyprus I, pl. 6.3; Vandenabeele, Olivier, *Idéogrammes,* 119, fig. 81.

IV.58 Enkomi, fragmentary amphoroid krater, driver and passenger in spotted robes, seashells under reins. T. 3/IIIa (Swedish excavations), Medelhavsmuseet, Stockholm; V. Karageorghis, *OpAth* 3 (1960), pl. 7.1-2.

IV.59 Maroni, fragmentary amphoroid krater, chariot right, two men in spotted robes, quirks over and under reins, ogival rock under belly. BM C355; *CVA* British Museum I, pl. 11.8, 10.

IV.60 Enkomi, fragmentary amphoroid krater, spotted box and passenger, chevrons. BM C350; *CVA* British Museum I, pl. 11.5.

IV.61 Maroni, two fragments of a krater, team right, quirks above and below reins, ogival rock under belly, trefoil markings on box, flowers and chevrons; horse collar picked out in white. BM C354; *CVA* British Museum I, pl. 11.3, 6.

IV.62 Enkomi, amphoroid krater, helmeted(?) driver and passenger; driver with sword(?); helmeted footman facing chariot. T. 3 no. 261 (Swedish excavations), Medelhavsmuseet,

Stockholm; Sjöqvist, *Problems*, fig. 19, no. 3; *SCE* I, pl. 77.2;
C. F. A. Schaeffer, *BSA* 37 (1936-37) 221, fig. 11.

IV.63 Maroni, fragment of krater (same vase as next?),
team left, two men in spotted robes; by painter of Tel Dan
krater (IV.49)? BM C359; H. W. Catling, *BSA* 60 (1965) pl.
60.4.

IV.64 Maroni, fragment of krater, team left, smudged
faces of driver and passenger, curly hair, dashes above reins.
BM C358; *BMCatV*, 71.

IV.65 Maroni, two fragments of krater, team left,
flowers, prong-nosed passenger. BM C361; H. W. Catling, *BSA*
60 (1965) pl. 60.5-6.

IV.66 Enkomi, fragments of krater (joins IV.67), team
left, N- and U-pattern. BM C347; *ExcCyp*, 39, fig. 67.842;
CVA British Museum I, pl. 11.1; H. W. Catling, *BSA* 60 (1965)
pl. 59.1.

IV.67 Enkomi, fragment of krater, neck of horse, dashes
and zigzags. BM C351.

IV.68 Kourion, two fragments of krater, split-legged
team, striped genitals, reserved inner hind leg, tassel from pole
brace, ogival rock. BM C353; H. W. Catling, *BSA* 60 (1965) pl.
61.3.

IV.69 Klavdhia, lower part of amphoroid krater, team
right, tall flowers, ovals; yoke-saddle and white harness, ribbons ending in arrows. BM C364; H. W. Catling, *BSA* 60
(1965) pl. 61.6.

IV.70 Kition, Area I, fragment of krater, team right with
mane plumes, partridges(?) over reins. Unpublished.

IV.71 Ain Shems, fragments of krater, eager (robed?)
driver, reins growing from fingers, quirks. Stubbings, *MycLevant*, 65, fig. 21.

IV.72 Ain Shems, fragment of krater, legs of groom
right, whorl shell and dotted circles, wheel rim(?). Stubbings,
MycLevant, 65, fig. 21.

IV.73 Amman, fragments of amphoroid krater, driver
alone right, body a spotted triangle, quirks and flowers, flaring
reins, chariot wheels filled with spots. No. 6261; V. Hankey,
BSA 62 (1967) 139f., figs. 10-11, pl. 33.

IV.74 Tell el-Ajjul, fragment of krater from the "Gov-
ernor's Tomb," chariot right, tall flowers, striped pole brace detached from box; near or by the Tel Dan painter. Stubbings,
MycLevant, 86, fig. 33.

IV.75 Alalakh, fragment of krater, team right, dash fillers. L. Woolley, *Alalakh* (1955) pl. 128 g, ATP/37/287.

IV.76 Alalakh, fragment of krater, legs, tail, part of
wheel. L. Woolley, *Alalakh* (1955) pl. 129, ATP/38/209 C.

IV.77 Ugarit, fragment of krater, team left, tall figures in
box, hair as dark mass on passenger's face, tassels on pole
brace, flower in field, quirks, flaring reins; Schaeffer, *Ugaritica*
II, fig. 94.

HORSE
IV.78 Sarepta (Sarafend), pilgrim flask, single horse in
field of flowers. D. Baramki, *Berytus* 12 (1956-58) 129 f., pl.
15, no. 26; J. L. Benson, *AJA* 72 (1968) 207 f., pl. 68, figs.
21-22; V. Hankey, *BSA* 62 (1967) 121.

Cyprus and the East: Ripe Pictorial

RIPE I

CHARIOTS
V.1 Cyprus, amphoroid krater, chariot left, spotted robes
and box, tall flowers and trefoil filler. Rochester Memorial Art
Gallery 51.204. V. Karageorghis, *The Memorial Art Gallery of
the University of Rochester, Gallery Notes* 17, no. 5 (1952);
BCH 93 (1969) 162 f., figs. 1, 6-9. By the painter of IX.1.1
(Painter 30); from the collection of Frederick Morgan, acquired
in Cairo (1901-1903), photographed long ago with V.76, 80,
128; V. 76, at least, is from the British Museum Excavations of
1896 at Enkomi.

V.2 Nicosia, amphoroid krater, chariot left, standing
woman, flowers. Metropolitan Museum, old CP 1405, new
74.51.966. Furtwängler-Loeschcke, *MV*, 29, fig. 17 (reversed);
D. Fimmen, *Die Kretisch-mykenische Kultur* (1924) 97, fig. 82
(reversed); Furumark, *MP*, FM 1.10, 1.17 (III B) (reversed); S.
Immerwahr, *AJA* 49 (1945) 545, figs. 11, 12; 549 f.; *Archaeology* 13 (1960) 9, fig. 9; G. M. A. Richter, *Handbook of the
Greek Collection²* (1953) pl. 4 g; S. Iakovides, *AJA* 70 (1966)
46; Vandenabeele, Olivier, *Idéogrammes*, 102, fig. 65.

V.3 Ugarit, bell krater fragment, "goddess" with spiral
breasts. Schaeffer, *Ugaritica* II, fig. 124, 4.

V.4 Cyprus, amphoroid krater, chariot right, driver with
raised hands, pendent chains in tracery, preceded by footman
with staff. Rochester Memorial Art Gallery 51.203. V. Karageorghis, *The Memorial Art Gallery of the University of Rochester, Gallery Notes* 17, no. 5 (1952) front page; *BCH* 93 (1969)
162 f., figs. 1-5.

V.5 Enkomi, amphoroid krater, dappled chariot right,
shrunken driver and passenger, groom wearing tunic, in front
with staff. T. 68; CM A1646; V. Karageorghis, O. Masson,
Rev Arch 47 (1956) 20 f.; *CVA* Cyprus I, pl. 8.1-4; V.
Karageorghis, *Civilization of Prehistoric Cyprus* (1976) no. 127.

V.6 Cyprus, amphoroid krater, exceptionally long team
right, triangles from reins, quirks above and below team, palm
by handle. Bonn, Akademisches Kunstmuseum no. 777; *SCE* IV
I C, 316, v; L. Åström, *OpAth* 4 (1963) 125 f., pl. 1; *CVA*
Bonn 2, pl. 32; *Antiken aus dem Akademisches Kunstmuseum,
Bonn* (1969) no. 102, pl. 64.

V.7 Enkomi, amphoroid krater, "triple"-boxed chariot
right, antithetic spiral under belly, two grooms in front with
staffs. T.51, BM C352; *ExcCyp*, 49, fig. 75.981; *BMCatV*, 69,
fig. 116; *CVA* British Museum I, pl. 11.13; E. Mercklin, *Rennwagen in Griechenland* I (1909) 21, no. 51; C. F. A. Schaeffer,
BSA 37 (1936-37) 229, fig. 28; J. L. Benson, *AJA* 65 (1961) 344,
no. 2, pl. 109, fig. 41; *HBM*, pl. VIII.8; H. W. Catling, *BSA* 60
(1965) pl. 59.3.

V.8 Ugarit, amphoroid krater, chariot right with three
figures (one on pole); on one side, groom with staff in front,
on the other, bird on ground with "quirk chain" to the earth.
Louvre A0 20376; C. F. A. Schaeffer, *BSA* 37 (1936-37) 212 f.,
figs. 1-3; *Ugaritica* II, pl. 35, figs. 89-90.3-4; V. Karageorghis,
AJA 62 (1958) pl. 101, fig. 10; S. Benton, *JHS* 81 (1961) 48; J.

L. Benson, *AJA* 65 (1961) pl. 109, figs. 45-46; P. Demargne, *The Birth of Greek Art* (1964) 257, fig. 355. Benson, in *AJA* 65, 344, attributes V.7, 8, and 34 to the Bamboula Painter. (See Painter 12 in Chapter XIV.)

V.9 Enkomi, amphoroid krater fragments, flat-headed prong-nosed passenger, palm, flowers; neat drawing. Brussels, Musée Cinquantenaire, A 1253; *CVA* Belgique 3, pl. 3. 11, by exchange with the British Museum (BM Excavation, 1896). V.30, with a boxer (or groom?) (pl. 3.17) may belong to the same vase, as well as with V.29, in which case there were boxers on the reverse.

V.10 Enkomi, fragmentary amphoroid krater, two persons in chariot right, arcaded pole, groom with curled fingers ready to control or fondle team. T.3/276, Stockholm; V. Karageorghis, *OpAth* 3 (1960) 140, pl. 3.

V.11 Enkomi, worn, fragmentary amphoroid krater, driver and passenger right in pointed helmets(?), arcaded pole, antithetic spiral under belly; two grooms walking in front. T.3/272, Stockholm; V. Karageorghis, *OpAth* 3 (1960) 139, pl. 2.

V.12 Tell Kazel, Syria, fragment, arcaded drops from reins, latticed lozenges over horses' backs. V. Hankey, *BSA* 62 (1967) 116, fig. 3.

V.13 Enkomi, amphoroid krater, team right slanted upward, arcaded reins, two grooms with staffs in front, one behind touching the chariot box and turning away. T.3.258; *SCE* I, pl. 120.1; Sjöqvist, *Problems*, fig. 20.2; C. F. A. Schaeffer, *BSA* 37 (1936-37) 231, fig. 32; *Enkomi-Alasia* I, 362, fig. 111.

V.14 Cyprus, amphoroid krater, long team right, scale-patterned chariot, arcaded reins; in front, a pair of belt-wrestlers in action. Museum of Fine Arts, Boston, 01.8044. J. Doell, *Sammlung Cesnola* (1873) pl. XVII.8, 9; Furtwängler-Loeschcke, *MV*, 27, figs. 14-15; A. Fairbanks, *Catalogue of Greek and Etruscan Vases in the Museum of Fine Arts, Boston* (1928) pl. X.143; E. Vermeule, *CJ* 53 (1958) 102-103, fig. 8; G. H. Chase and C. C. Vermeule, *Greek, Etruscan and Roman Art* (1963) fig. 13; P. Bocci, "Cipro," *Enciclopedia dell'Arte Antica* II, 641, fig. 870; F. C. Hibben, *Prehistoric Man in Europe* (1958) 233f.; A. D. Lacy, *Greek Pottery in The Bronze Age* (1967) 212-213, fig. 85b.

An unpublished amphoroid krater from Enkomi has belt-wrestling soldiers in chain mail.

V.15 Hala Sultan Tekké, fragments of amphoroid krater, chariot right, groom leading. T.2, no. 214; *HST* I, pls. LVI, LXXIV.

V.16 Stephania, amphoroid krater, chariot, groom right, groom with "Naue II" sword. Sydney, Australia. From a looted tomb (no. 2); unpublished. See J. B. Hennessy, *Stephania* (1964) 2.

V.17 Cyprus? (bought in Egypt, as were V.1, 4), amphoroid krater, chariot right with three dark figures (reserved contours), groom wearing sword behind, horseback rider in front. Allard Pierson Stichting Museum no. 1856 (Collection Scheurleer); *CVA* Pays Bas 1, pl. 3.7; V. Karageorghis, *BABesch* 33 (1958) 38 f., figs. 1-3; J. Wiesner, *Fahren und Reiten*, in *Archaeologia Homerica* F (1968) 114, fig. 20 a; Benson, *HBM*, 137, n. 29; J. Crouwel, *BABesch* 47 (1972) 24 f., figs. 14-20. A graffito on top of each handle.

V.18 Enkomi, amphoroid krater, chariot with two pom-pous, bent figures right, pursued by a giant fish. Long waving pendants from the reins, double-spoked wheels, flying yoke ring; spirals under the horses' bellies, marked genitals. T.11.33. *SCE* I, pl. 121.6; Sjöqvist, *Problems*, fig. 20.1; C. F. A. Schaeffer, *BSA* 37 (1936-37) 222, fig. 13; Furumark, *MP*, FM 1.18; Vermeule, *GBA*, 205, pl. XXXII, B; S. Marinatos, *EphArch* 1964, 2, fig. 1; T. B. L. Webster, *From Mycenae to Homer* (1958) 48, 127, 204, fig. 14; S. Hood, *The Arts in Prehistoric Greece* (1978) fig. 21 A.

V.19 Aptera, Suda Bay, Crete, bell krater, chariot right with four (side A) and three (B) persons, armed groom in front and two behind (A), three behind (B). Chania Museum 812; H. Drerup in F. Matz, *Forschungen auf Kreta* (1942) 82-88, pls. 3.2, 65.4-6; Vermeule, *GBA*, 206, pl. XXXII D.

V.20 Ugarit, fragmentary amphoroid krater, three armless persons in long double chariot box, driver in spotted robe, two passengers in dark robes with reserved contours. Reins rise in high arc from driver's chest, front of chariot box is on team's rump and tail; arcaded pole. Ugarit 9064; Schaeffer, *Ugaritica* II, figs. 62.24, 90.1.

V.21 Minet el-Beida (Tomb 4), amphoroid krater, chariot right, attendant soothing team, bird beneath handle. Louvre AO 11724; C. F. A. Schaeffer, *BSA* 37 (1936-37) 225, fig. 16; *Ugaritica* II, figs. 57.29, 124.8, 10. (Now nearly complete.)

V.22 Klavdhia, bell krater, driver and passenger sunk in separate parts of chariot box, checkered robes. BM C398; *CVA* British Museum I, pl. 7.8; C. F. A. Schaeffer, *BSA* 37 (1936-37) 229, fig. 27; Furumark, *MP*, FM 1.19; Vandenabeele, Olivier, *Idéogrammes*, 135, fig. 92.

V.23 Aradippo, amphoroid krater, chariot with two or three boxes, flat-headed grooms before and behind. Louvre AM 625; E. Pottier, *BCH* 31 (1907) 231, figs. 8-9; Furumark, *MP*, FM 1.20 ac; V. Karageorghis, *Syria* 34 (1957) 87f., figs. 7-9; Vandenabeele, Olivier, *Idéogrammes*, 133f., fig. 90 a-b.

V.24 Tell el-Muqdâm, Egypt, amphoroid krater, chariot right, high arched front box, low oval wing, flat-headed driver, passenger in flat cap with ribbon behind; with faience fragments bearing cartouches of Ramesses II, Merneptah. Swiss private collection.

SCRAPS

V.25.1 Kourion, krater fragment, yoke-saddle and four reins. B 1070; J. L. Benson, *AJA* 65 (1961) pl. 29, fig. 8; *Bamboula at Kourion* (1972) pl. 30.

V.25.2 Kourion, krater fragment, parts of three men with angular heads, probably behind chariot rail. B 1071; J. L. Benson, *AJA* 65 (1961) pl. 29, fig. 14; *Bamboula at Kourion* (1972) pl. 30.

V.25.3 Byblos, krater fragment, charioteer's(?) head right, flat hair swirling up to peak in front, spotted robe. 1958; Stubbings, *MycLevant*, 76, fig. 27.

V.25.4 Byblos, krater fragment (part of preceding?), head right with flat hair sharpened in front. 1861; Stubbings, *MycLevant*, 76, fig. 27.

V.25.5 Gezer, krater fragment, man with round skull, beaked profile, open mouth right. R. A. S. Macalister, *Gezer* III (1912) pl. 151.5; Stubbings, *MycLevant*, 84, fig. 30; H. G. Buchholz, *AA* 1974, 419, fig. 69 c.

V.25.6 Gezer, krater fragment, head of man in flat cap with long, pronged nose. R. A. S. Macalister, *Gezer* III (1912) pl. 151.23; Stubbings, *MycLevant*, 84, fig. 30; H.-G. Buchholz, *AA* 1974, 419, fig. 69 d.

V.25.7 Gezer, two krater fragments, split hind legs of horse, seashells and stacked chevrons in field; rump, spotted pole with hanging triangles, arcades above. R. A. S. Macalister, *Gezer* III (1912) pl. 151.3, 8; Stubbings, *MycLevant*, 84, fig. 30; H.-G. Buchholz, *AA* 1974, 419, fig. 69 a–b.

V.25.8 Tell Abu Hawam, thirteen krater fragments, including: 308, spiral under team's belly (f), joined team head (s); 307, spiral reins and fillers (c, d), spotted box and wheels (k), spotted robes of driver and passenger (g); and three sharp-nosed mini-headed outlined passengers, close to the Tiryns painter of XI.14, 15 (u). R. Hamilton, *QDAP* 4 (1935) pl. XXI; Stubbings, *MycLevant*, fig. 29.

V.25.9 Ashdod, krater fragment, small spotted square box above large (six-spoked?) wheel, two small flat feet(?) in air behind box. T. Dothan, *Israel Exploration Journal* 13 (1963) 340; *Archaeology* 16 (1963) 61; *Archaeology* 20 (1967) 181. Palestinian Late Bronze II.

V.25.10 Alalakh, amphoroid krater fragment, team right, joined heads, groups of slashes in field (may be Middle period). ATP/37/287; L. Woolley, *Alalakh* (1955) pl. CXXVIII g.

V.25.11 Enkomi, fragment of amphoroid krater, charioteer and passenger right, wearing spotted collars and robes; double contour lines, loop arms and arrow hands to four reins, neat spirals over reins. 1987/1; P. Dikaios, *Enkomi* (1969–71) II, color frontispiece, and III a, pls. 61.24, 87.24 (Room 142, Floor X, may be Middle).

V.25.12 Enkomi, bell krater fragment, three small schematic passengers in chariot right, heads obliterated by upper framing band, dual box filled with slashes. *CVA* Reading, pl. 1.19 and fig. 2.

V.25.13 Enkomi, bell krater fragment, heads and shoulders of two men slanted back, lightly spotted robes. *CVA* Reading, pl. 1.20. For contemporary chariot fragments from Troy see XIII.19-21 (Asia Minor).

HORSES AND RIDERS

V.26 Minet el-Beida, fragments of bell krater. T. VI. Schaeffer, *Ugaritica* II, figs. 61 B, C, 94 E; *Ugaritica* I, 103, fig. 96 E; *Syria* 14 (1933) 105; Furumark, *MP*, FM 2.5; J. Wiesner, *Fahren und Reiten*, in *Archaeologia Homerica* F (1968) 117, fig. 21 a, b.

GRIFFINS AND SPHINXES

V.27 Enkomi, bell krater, griffins confronted across stylized palm in horns of consecration; griffin on right pulling two-man chariot; confronted sphinxes. T.48, BM C397; *BMCatV*, 80, fig. 135 a and b; *CVA* British Museum I, pl. 7.1; F. Poulsen, *JdI* 26 (1911) 245, figs. 29–30; L. B. Holland, *AJA* 33 (1929) 184, fig. 5; C. F. A. Schaeffer, *BSA* 37 (1936-37) 228, fig. 25; S. Immerwahr, *Archaeology* 13 (1960) 12 f., fig. 15. Cf. E. Vermeule, *JHS* 85 (1965) 139; R. Higgins, *Minoan and Mycenaean Art*, fig. 134; A. M. Bisi, *Oriens Antiquus* 1 (1962) pl. LIV.5; N. Yalouris, *Papers of the XI International Congress of Classical Archaeology* (1979) pl. 46 c.

V.28 Enkomi, amphoroid krater. Side A, sphinxes, palms, dog. T. 45, BM C333. See V.28, side B.

ARCHERS

V.28 Side B, archers and boxers(?). T. 45, BM C333; *CVA* British Museum I, pl. 11.18; H. T. Bossert, *Altkreta*[3] (1937) 265, fig. 482; Furumark, *MP*, FM 1.26; Benson, *HBM*, pl. 27.6.

BOXERS

V.29 Enkomi, amphoroid krater fragment, long-legged boxers sparring across flower, interlocked U's in field. T. 93, BM C334; *ExcCyp*, 9, fig. 15; F. Poulsen, *JdI* 26 (1911) 220, fig. 5; H. Catling, *BSA* 60 (1965) pl. 58.1. (See V.9, V.30.)

V.30 Enkomi, fragment of amphoroid krater, long-legged boxer(?) lunging right in field of flowers and chevrons; interlocked U's in field. Brussels A 1249, *CVA* Belgique 3, pl. 3.17, by exchange with the British Museum (BM Excavation, 1896). May be part of V.9 as well as V.29.

V.31 Maroni, fragmentary amphoroid krater (from shoulder to foot), pairs of facing boxers, one arm up, one down, divided by laddered "palm" fronds. T. 15 (1897), BM C335; H. Catling, *BSA* 60 (1965) pl. 60.1.

V.32 Amphoroid krater, confronted boxers divided by sketchy birds. G. G. Pierides Collection no. 35; *CVA* Cyprus II, pls. 2-3; V. Karageorghis, *Syria* 34 (1957) 89, figs. 10–11, p. 90, fig. 12.

V.33 Kition, fragments of deep bowl, boxers with raised fists; 14/2418, Area II; V. Karageorghis, *BCH* 95 (1971) 385, fig. 94; *Kition*, fig. 33.

V.34 Kourion, fragment of kylix. B 1056; J. L. Benson, *AJA* 65 (1961) pl. 29, fig. 6; *Bamboula at Kourion*, pl. 30. Benson named the Bamboula Painter from this fragment and associated V.7 and 8 with him.

V.35 Kourion, fragment of a kylix. B 1057; J. L. Benson, *AJA* 65 (1961) pl. 29, fig. 13.

OTHER HUMAN FIGURES

V.36 Ugarit, rhyton with spearmen. C. F. A. Schaeffer, *AAS* 13 (1963) fig. 29; J.-C. Courtois, *Ugaritica* VI (1969) 117, fig. 16; H.-G. Buchholz, *AA* 1974, 403, fig. 59.

V.36.1 Ugarit, rhyton fragment, standing man. Schaeffer, *Ugaritica* II, fig. 91.8.

V.37 Ugarit, fragmentary bowl, frieze of men right, stemmed-lozenge dividers. C. F. A. Schaeffer, *AAS* 13 (1963) 127, fig. 18.

V.38 Enkomi, amphoroid krater, officers and men on shipboard. T.3/262, Stockholm; *SCE* I, pl. 121.3-4; Sjöqvist, *Problems*, fig. 20.3; F. Stubbings, *BSA* 46 (1951) 175, fig. 3; V. Karageorghis, *AJA* 62 (1958) 387, pl. 101, fig. 12; *OpAth* 3 (1960) 146, pl. X; P. Dikaios, *Enkomi*, 925, n. 789; Vermeule, *GBA*, pl. XXXII, A; H. Catling, *AA* 1970, 447, fig. 10; D. Gray, *Seewesen*, in *Archaeologia Homerica* G (1974) 46, fig. 10.

V.39 Enkomi, fragmentary amphoroid krater, man picking fruit from tree. T.3/278; V. Karageorghis, *OpAth* 3 (1960) 141 f., pl. IV; *AJA* 62 (1958) 386, pl. 100.

BULLS

V.40 Enkomi, amphoroid krater, large and small bulls in meadow filled with birds; dotted white circles as body ornament. T.18, S.6; *SCE* I, pl. 120.2; Sjöqvist, *Problems*, fig. 21.1;

Vermeule, *GBA*, pl. XXXII, C; P. Kahane in N. Robertson et al., *The Archaeology of Cyprus* (1975) 164, fig. 5; S. Hood, *The Arts in Prehistoric Greece* (1978) fig. 21 B.

V.41 Cyprus, amphoroid krater, bulls facing across flower, rosettes and flowers in field, birds under handles, dipinto sign on base. CM A1647; S. Casson, *Ancient Cyprus* (1937) pl. V.2; Stubbings, *MycLevant*, pl. XI.2; *CVA* Cyprus I, pl. 5.1-2; J. L. Benson, *AJA* 65 (1961) pl. 103, fig. 15; V. Karageorghis, *Kupriakai Spoudai* (1961) pl. 6 a; *MycArt*, pl. 7.3; *Treasures*, pl. XVI; *Civilization of Prehistoric Cyprus* (1976) no. 126; Buchholz, Karageorghis, *Altägäis*, no. 1624; *Archaeologia Viva: Cyprus* (1969) 130, fig. XLIV.

V.42 Klavdhia, amphoroid krater, bull, bird, and fish. BM C365; *CVA* British Museum I, pl. 7.12, Furumark, *MP*, FM 3.5.

V.43 Enkomi, bell krater, bull facing out, fanged fish. T.91 (British excavations), BM C403; *ExcCyp*, 42, fig. 70; F. Poulsen, *JdI* 26 (1911) 241, fig. 25; *BMCatV*, 82, fig. 139; *CVA* British Museum I, pl. 10.3; H. R. Hall, *Aegean Archaeology* (1915) 106, fig. 35; Evans, *Palace of Minos* I (1921) 513, fig. 370 B; H. T. Bossert, *Altkreta*³ (1937) 264, fig. 477; Furumark, *MP*, FM 3.4; P. Demargne, *The Birth of Greek Art* (1964) fig. 345.

V.44 Enkomi, bell krater, charging bull with cattle egret on neck. BM C416; *ExcCyp*, 48, fig. 74; *BMCatV*, 86, fig. 147; H. R. Hall, *Civilization of Greece in the Bronze Age* (1928) 213, fig. 276; *CVA* British Museum I, pl. 10.7; A. Lane, *Greek Pottery* (1948) pl. 26; V. Karageorghis, *AJA* 60 (1956) 144 f., pl. 56, figs. 3-4; *MycArt*, pl. 6.3; S. Immerwahr, *Archaeology* 13 (1960) 10, fig. 11; S. Benton, *JHS* 81 (1961) pl. 1.1-2; J. L. Benson, *AJA* 65 (1961) 340 f.; A. D. Lacy, *Greek Pottery in the Bronze Age* (1967) fig. 84 a; R. Higgins, *Minoan and Mycenaean Art* (1967) fig. 135; G. Hafner, *Geschichte der griechischen Kunst* (1961) fig. 47; P. Warren, *The Aegean Civilizations* (1975) 133; B. Cook, *Greek and Roman Art in the British Museum* (1976) 30, fig. 20; N. K. Sandars, *The Sea Peoples* (1978) fig. 43.

V.45 Kition district(?), bell krater, bull running right, bent front legs; bird with "light bulb" tail feeding right. G. G. Pierides Collection no. 42; *CVA* Cyprus II, pl. 5.1-3; Karageorghis, *MycArt*, pl. 6.2; Buchholz, Karageorghis, *Altägäis*, no. 1626.

V.46 Klavdhia, bell krater, bull in three patterned sections, bird cleaning horns (A) and resting (B), filled lozenges in field. BM C402; *CVA* British Museum I, pl. 10.4; Furumark, *MP*, FM 3.7; F. Stubbings, *BSA* 46 (1951) pl. 18 a; S. Immerwahr, *AJA* 60 (1956) 138, pl. 52, figs. 4-5; J. L. Benson, *AJA* 65 (1961) pl. 103, fig. 14; S. Benton, *JHS* 81 (1961) pl. 1.5-6.

V.47 Enkomi, bell krater, bull right, filled with dotted circles, stemmed lozenge in front. T.89, BM C404; *ExcCyp*, 49, fig. 76; E. Pottier, *BCH* 31 (1907) 241, no. 4; *BMCatV*, 83, fig. 140; *CVA* British Museum I, pl. 6.14.

BULLS AND HUMAN FIGURES

V.48 Kition(?), bell krater, bull and toreador (A), cow and calf right (B). G. G. Pierides Collection no. 234. V. Karageorghis, *AJA* 60 (1956) 145 f., pls. 56-57, figs. 5a-5b, 6a-6b; *CVA* Cyprus II, pl. 4; *MycArt*, pl. 6.1; J. L. Benson, *AJA* 65 (1961) pl. 103, fig. 12; Buchholz, Karageorghis, *Altägäis*, no. 1625.

V.49 Fragmentary bell krater by the painter of V.48, bulls right. CM A2026b. *CVA* Cyprus I, fig. 2, pl. 4.4; V. Karageorghis, *AJA* 60 (1956) pl. 57, figs. 7a (reversed), 7b.

V.50 Enkomi, bell krater, two bulls each side with long curled horns; man fallen under leader's nose, lozenges in field. T.18 S.46 (Swedish excavations). Sjöqvist, *Problems*, fig. 21.2; V. Karageorghis, *Medelhavsmuseet Bulletin* (forthcoming).

V.51 Pyla-Verghi, bell krater, long bull with Π marks, human figure holding tail. T.1 no. 44. Larnaka District Museum. P. Dikaios, *Enkomi* (1969-71) pl. 234.3.

V.52 Arpera, bell krater, bull facing out, four chains of ornament across belly, two palm trees behind, lozenges in field. Louvre AM 678 (formerly Boysset Collection); E. Pottier, *BCH* 31 (1907) 229, fig. 5; *Recueil E. Pottier* (1937) 171, fig. 7; cf. Louvre AM 679, ibid., no. 3, from Aradippo.

STAGS

V.53 Enkomi, bell krater, three embroidered stags right (A), two stags (B). BM C408; *BMCatV*, 83, fig. 141; Stubbings, *MycLevant*, pl. IX.8; Furumark, *MP*, FM 5.3; S. Immerwahr, *AJA* 60 (1956) 141, pl. 55, fig. 16; Karageorghis, *MycArt*, pl. 9.1.

V.54 Enkomi, bell krater, three stags right, heads turned back, three birds under their bellies. BM C409; *CVA* British Museum I, pl. 9.10; Furumark, *MP*, FM 5.2; W. Heurtley, *QDAP* 5 (1936) 97, fig. 6.2; H. T. Bossert, *Altkreta*³ (1937) 264, fig. 475; F. Stubbings, *BSA* 46 (1951) pl. 19 e; S. Immerwahr, *AJA* 60 (1956) 141, pl. 54, figs. 13-14; J. L. Benson, *AJA* 65 (1961) 344 f., pl. 108, fig. 37; A. J. B. Wace, F. Stubbings, *A Companion to Homer* (1962) 354, fig. 19; P. Demargne, *The Birth of Greek Art* (1964) fig. 347.

V.55 Enkomi, bell krater, three stags with "bubble" horns right, rosettes in field. T. 82 (1896), CM A1546. Stubbings, *MycLevant*, pl. X.1; *BSA* 46 (1951) pl. 19 f; *CVA* Cyprus I, pl. 10.1-3; Karageorghis, *MycArt*, pl. 9.4; Buchholz, Karageorghis, *Altägäis*, no. 1627; H.-G. Buchholz, G. Jöhrens, I. Maull, *Jagd und Fischfang*, in *Archaeologia Homerica* J (1973) 49, fig. 9.

V.56 Ugarit, fragment (of bell krater?), stag(?), belly filled with vertical wavy lines; diagonals on haunch, dark legs. T. IV; Schaeffer, *Ugaritica* II, fig. 77.

V.57 Psilatos, fragment, sharp striped hoof in field of flowers and lozenges; Ashmolean Museum 1953.339; H. Catling, *BSA* 60 (1965) pl. 61.5.

GOATS

V.58 Hala Sultan Tekké, bell krater, two dark goats prancing right, looking back at fanged fish. Loose double trefoils in field. BM C410; *CVA* British Museum I, pl. 9.1; *HST* 1, pls. XXXIII-XXXIV.

V.59 Bell krater, Louvre AM 2663; C. F. A. Schaeffer, *Missions en Chypre* (1936) pl. 35.5, fig. 37, bottom. Note also a fragment from Ugarit with a long-horned bearded goat, Schaeffer, *Ugaritica* II, fig. 62, no. 18 (1937, "bicolor").

HUNTS

V.60 Aradippo, bell krater, hunter, hounds, deer, boar(?), and goat. Louvre AM 675. E. Pottier, *BCH* 31 (1907) 234, figs. 13-15; *Recueil E. Pottier* (1937) 176 f., figs. 15-17; Furumark, *MP*, FM 5.4; W. Heurtley, *QDAP* 5 (1936) 104, fig. 10.6; Å. Åkerström, *OpAth* 1 (1953) 22, fig. 8; Stubbings,

MycLevant, 38, fig. 7; H. Erlenmeyer, *AntK* 4 (1961) pl. 1.14; H.-G. Buchholz, V. Karageorghis, *AAA* 3 (1970) 389, fig. 3; H.-G. Buchholz, G. Jöhrens, I. Maull, *Jagd und Fischfang*, in *Archaeologia Homerica* J (1973) fig. 8 b.

BIRDS

V.61 Enkomi, bell krater, two long embroidered birds right, tailed lozenge under wing. BM C411. *ExcCyp*, 48, fig. 73; *CVA* British Museum I, pl. 9.3; *BMCatV*, 84, fig. 143; W. Heurtley, *QDAP* 5 (1936) 97, fig. 6.1; Stubbings, *MycLevant*, pl. IX.7.

V.62 Klavdhia, fragmentary bell krater, three dark-necked "swans" right, filled with dashes for feathers, strokes in field, syllabic dipinto on base. BM C412, *CVA* British Museum I, pl. 10.10. (Restored.)

V.63 Enkomi, fragment of amphoroid krater, birds feeding, facing over flower or berry plant; triangular "wing," lozenge behind neck, scalloped interior contours. CM 1958/1-10/6; *CVA* Cyprus I, pl. 9.7.

V.64 Enkomi, fragmentary bell krater, birds right with heads turned back, filled with vertical stripes bordered by loops. T.7/IX; V. Karageorghis, *OpAth* 3 (1960) 152, pl. 13.

V.65 Ugarit, fragment of bell krater, large bird like V.61, filled with ovals and stripes. Schaeffer, *Ugaritica* II, fig. 94 c.

V.66 Enkomi, jug. T. 7/4748 (Schaeffer). Unpublished.

V.67 Enkomi, bell krater, four darkly outlined birds hovering in air. T. 18, S.47; *SCE* I, pl. 118.4.

V.68 Enkomi, jug, frieze of grazing birds filled with vertical wavy lines, T. 91, BM C583; *CVA* British Museum I, pl. 6.3; F. Stubbings, *BSA* 46 (1951) pl. 19 d; S. Immerwahr, *AJA* 60 (1956) pl. 55.15; S. Benton, *JHS* 81 (1961) pl. 2.1; J. L. Benson, *AJA* 65 (1961) pl. 104.18.

V.69 Hala Sultan Tekké, three-handled jar, sketchy "plant birds" of two fringed "leaves" with heads, by the painter of V.38; two incised signs on the handles. BM C434 (98.12-1.223); *CVA* British Museum I, pl. 8.8; F. Stubbings, *BSA* 46 (1951) 176, fig. 4; *HST* I, pl. IX.

V.70 Minet el-Beida, fragment of bowl, bird with raised striped wing and "plume" from shoulder, flower. T. 78; Schaeffer, *Ugaritica* II, fig. 108 B.

V.71 Cyprus, jug, on shoulder, frieze of birds right, filled with rows of simple dashes; hooked bills; bird near handle has round feet like wheels. CM A1559; *CVA* Cyprus I, pl. 9.4-5.

V.72 Unknown provenance, amphoroid krater, curious birds with "feet" on back and extra front legs; multiple fillers in field. Fitzwilliam Museum, Cambridge, GR.132A-1908; *CVA* Cambridge 2, pl. 6.8 a-b.

V.72.1 Cyprus(?) or Rhodes(?), two-handled globular flask, late in series; under pendent triangles filled with semicircles and dots, large dark bird on each side, raised fringed wing, rounded tail filled with semicircles, feeding on rippling weed; late thirteenth-century reminiscence of Early style? Louvre AM 833.

RIPE II

BULLS

V.73 Klavdhia, bell krater, hunted bull in collapsed flying gallop, huntsman and hounds. By the painter of V.74 and the Tiryns krater, IX.21. BM C399; *CVA* British Museum I, pl.

6.16; H. T. Bossert, Altkreta³ (1937) 264, fig. 478; Furumark, *MP*, FM 3.14; V. Karageorghis, *Syria* 34 (1957) 84 f., figs. 4-6; E. Vermeule, *CJ* 53 (1958) 102, fig. 7; P. Demargne, *The Birth of Greek Art* (1964) fig. 348; Slenczka, *Tiryns* VII, 11.2; part, H.-G. Buchholz, G. Jöhrens, I. Maull, *Jagd und Fischfang*, in *Archaeologia Homerica* J (1973) 111, fig. 39. (Restored: upper part of huntsman, right-hand dog; foot wrongly restored.)

V.74 Kition(?), jug, bull right on shoulder, filled with white crosses, filled lozenges in field, sunburst rosettes below. G. G. Pierides Collection no. 34. V. Karageorghis, *Syria* 34 (1957) 82 f., figs. 1-3; *MycArt*, pl. 8.1; J. L. Benson, *AJA* 65 (1961) 341, pl. 103, fig. 16; V. Karageorghis, *Nouveaux Documents*, pl. XVIII.1; *CVA* Cyprus II, pl. 6.1-3; Buchholz, Karageorghis, *Altägäis*, no. 1631; Slenczka, *Tiryns* VII, pl. 10.2.

V.74.1 Tell Sukas, krater fragment, bull with dewlap collar, crosses on hide. F. Schachermeyr, *AA* 1962, 378, fig. 90.

V.75 Enkomi, fragment of jug shoulder, three spotted bull protomes right, with slightly ruffled outlines, horns curving up. T. 12 (1896), BM C686; *BMCatV*, 130.

V.76 Enkomi, bell krater, striped bull and bird, bull and palm. CM T.17.16. *CVA* Cyprus I, pl. 11.4-6; V. Karageorghis, *BCH* 93 (1969) 163, fig. 1.

V.77 Enkomi, fragment of bell krater, weak striped bull right. Brussels A 1258; *CVA* Belgique 3, pl. 3.9, by exchange with the British Museum (BM excavations, 1896).

V.78 Enkomi, fragment of jug(?), bull with spotted haunch and scalloped belly. P. Dikaios, *Enkomi* (1969-71) pl. 90 (upper right).

V.79 Tell Abu Hawam, fragment, bull. R. Hamilton, *QDAP* 4 (1935) pl. XX.o.

V.80 Cyprus, bell krater, bull and bull protome, by Protome Painter A. CM 1943/II-20/1; E. Gjerstad, *Studies on Prehistoric Cyprus* (1926) 213, no. 1; S. Immerwahr, *AJA* 60 (1956) pl. 53, figs. 6-7; V. Karageorghis, *CVA* Cyprus I, pl. 11.1-3; *BCH* 93 (1969) 163, fig. 1; in Schaeffer, *Alasia* I, 124 f., figs. 1-2; *Archaeologia Viva: Cyprus* (1969) 129, fig. XLII.

V.81 Enkomi, fragment of jug, scalloped bull protomes right, filled lozenge. T. 12, inv. 1053; P. Dikaios, *Enkomi* (1969-71) pl. 214, no. 2.

V.82 Hala Sultan Tekké, jug with pinched lip, bull protomes with bubble-triangle borders, lozenges, long horns overlapping horns of next. BM C575 (98.12-1.211); *BMCatV*, fig. 198; *CVA* British Museum I, pl. 4.14; Stubbings, *MycLevant*, pl. XIII.10; S. Immerwahr, *AJA* 60 (1956) pl. 54.10-11; J. L. Benson, *AJA* 65 (1961) pls. 101.3, 102.7; Karageorghis, *MycArt*, pl. 8.2; *HST* I, pl. V; in Schaeffer, *Alasia* I, 123 f.; Slenczka, *Tiryns* VII, pl. 46.3.

V.82.1 Athienou, jug shoulder fragment, bulls with bubble triangles on inner contour lines, locking horns, right one weakly striped. T. Dothan, A. Ben-Tor, *Excavations at Athienou 1971-1972* (The Israel Museum, Jerusalem, cat. no. 116, 1974).

V.83 Hala Sultan Tekké, jug, similar to the last; bulls with guilloche borders, crosshatched lozenges. BM C576; *CVA* British Museum I, pl. 4.18; Stubbings, *MycLevant*, pl. XIII.9; S. Immerwahr, *AJA* 60 (1956) pl. 54.12; J. L. Benson, *AJA* 65 (1961) pl. 102.10; H. T. Bossert, *Altsyrien* (1951) fig. 217.18; V. Karageorghis, in Schaeffer, *Alasia* I, 123 f.; *HST* I, pl. XII; Slenczka, *Tiryns* VII, pl. 46.2

V.84 Klavdhia, shallow bowl, one wishbone handle, bulls with cross-stitched haunches and forequarters, standing tail to tail, joined by rippling lines. T. A. 19, BM C623; *BMCatV*, 120, pl. III; F. Stubbings, *BSA* 46 (1951) pl. 18 b; S. Immerwahr, *AJA* 60 (1956) pl. 53.8; J. L. Benson, *AJA* 65 (1961) pl. 102.11; Karageorghis, *MycArt*, pl. 8.3, and in Schaeffer, *Alasia* I, 126, fig. 3.

V.85 Enkomi, jug, round lip, facing bull protomes with bubble-triangle borders, crosshatched lozenges, as on V.82. T. 7.4780; V. Karageorghis, in Schaeffer, *Alasia* I, 128, figs. 5, 6.

V.86 Enkomi, fragmentary bell krater, bull (and cow?) facing over calf, rippled stripe filling. Dikaios 4545; *BCH* 1959, 350, fig. 15 *bis*; J. L. Benson, *AJA* 65 (1961) 338 f., pl. 102.8; P. Dikaios, *Enkomi* (1969-71) pl. 109.1; V. Karageorghis, in Schaeffer, *Alasia* I, 127, fig. 4.

V.87 Kition, stemmed kylix, bull right, lowered head, cross-stitched fore- and hindquarters, scallop-bordered belly. T. 9.66; V. Karageorghis, in Schaeffer, *Alasia* I, 131, fig. 7; *Kition* I, *The Tombs*, pls. L, XCIII, CXLI; *Kition*, fig. 15.

V.88 Enkomi, jug with pinched lip, two facing outlined bull protomes with bird between. T. 88, BM C577; *ExcCyp*, 34, fig. 62; F. Stubbings, *BSA* 46 (1951) pl. 18 c; S. Immerwahr, *AJA* 60 (1956), pl. 52.3; S. Benton, *JHS* 81 (1961) pl. 4.4.

V.89 Klavdhia, stirrup jar, two confronted bull protomes with scalloped borders, dot-rosettes, parted by Cypriote lozenge chain, dipinto palm(?) under foot. T. 19 (1899), BM C514; S. Immerwahr, *AJA* 60 (1956) pl. 52.1-2; F. Stubbings, *BSA* 46 (1951) pl. 18 d; J. L. Benson, *AJA* 65 (1961) pl. 101.1.

V.90 Enkomi, bell krater; A: four bull protomes right, scalloped borders, long horns curving upward, parted by dot- or petal-rosettes; B: two similar bull protomes right, parted by vertical panel filled with scale pattern, dot-rosettes in left field, petal-rosettes in right. Louvre AO 18591.

V.91 Klavdhia, shallow bowl, four bull protomes right, dotted borders and Π filling, separated by dot-rosettes. T. A. 14, BM C672; *BMCatV*, 128; *CVA* British Museum I, pl. 5.13; V. Karageorghis, *BSA* 52 (1957) pl. 8 b; *MycArt*, pl. 11.4.

V.92 Minet el-Beida, bowl, bull protomes right, dotted borders, circle filling. T. VI(?); Schaeffer, *Ugaritica* II, figs. 59.34, 61.

V.93 Pyla-Verghi, fragmentary bowl, four bull protomes right, dotted borders, separated by dot-rosettes. T. 1.71. P. Dikaios, *Enkomi* II (1971) pl. 299.4-5.

V.94 Kition, fragmentary bowl, bull protomes right, dotted borders, Π filling. T. 9/75; V. Karageorghis, *Kition* I, *The Tombs*, 50, pls. LXI, CXLVIII.

V.95 Kition, fragmentary bowl, bull protomes right, dotted borders, circle filling, separated by dot-rosettes. T. 4 and T. 5/196; V. Karageorghis, *Kition* I, *The Tombs*, 31, pls. XXXV, CXXXII; *Kition*, fig. 6.

V.96 Kition, jug, bull right, arrow and T filling, genitals. T. 4 and T. 5/109; V. Karageorghis, *Kition* I, *The Tombs*, pl. XXI.

V.97 Cyprus(?), Sikes chalice, bull protomes right, dotted borders, circle filling, separated by dot-rosettes; fine bands and stripes below. V. Karageorghis, *BSA* 52 (1957) pl. 8 a; *Nouveaux Documents*, pl. 19.5; J. L. Benson, *AJA* 65 (1961) pl. 102.9; Buchholz, Karageorghis, *Altägäis*, no. 1635.

V.98 Ugarit, fragment, bull right, fore- and hindquarters with Π filling. Schaeffer, *Ugaritica* II, fig. 91.2.

V.99 Enkomi, jug, two bulls right, stars on neck, dot-rosettes and crossed ladders on hindquarters, T. 18, S. 74,

Stockholm; *SCE* I, 557, pl. 90, third row from top, right.

V.100 Enkomi, jug, bull right, filled with arrows, circles on hindquarters. T. 18, S. 5, Stockholm; *SCE* I, 554, pl. 90, third row from top, left.

V.100.1 Hala Sultan Tekké (1898), fragment, weakly outlined small bull left, with pointed nose, raked-back horns, slumping legs. BM C692; *BMCatV*, 131; *HST* I, pl. XXXV e.

V.101 Haghia Paraskevi, Nicosia, bell krater, ornamented bulls right, "accordion" bellies. Staatliche Museen, Berlin, no. 8103; Furumark, *MP*, FM 3.10; V. Karageorghis, *BCH* 86 (1962) 11 f.; *MycArt*, pl. 13.2; N. Kontoleon, *EphArch* 1969, pl. 43 a.

BULLS' HEADS

V.102 Enkomi, fragmentary stirrup jar, facing bull's head framed by symmetrical horns curved down to ground line, interior network of scales and stripes for ruffled hair; voluted palmette flowers from spotted triangle in spout quadrants. T. 74 (1896); BM C697; *ExcCyp*, 53; *BMCatV*, fig. 260.

V.103 Aradippo, bell krater, facing bulls' heads or skulls hung on chains, with central checkerboard panel. Louvre AM 677; E. Pottier, *BCH* 31 (1907) 230, fig. 7; Furumark, *MP*, FM 4.2; V. Karageorghis, *BCH* 86 (1962) 14, figs. 3-4.

STAGS

V.104 Ugarit, fragmentary bell krater, frieze of stags right, dark quarters, light bellies with arrow and T fillers, connected by chain cables. Schaeffer, *Ugaritica* II, fig. 94 B; Stubbings, *MycLevant*, 72, fig. 23.

V.105 Minet el-Beida, fragmentary rhyton, stag (not horse?) with little one skipping behind. MB 1931; Schaeffer, *Ugaritica* II, fig. 91.5, 16.

V.106 Enkomi, fragmentary bell krater, stags with arrow-filled hides, right, vertical wavy line dividers, rosette of petals and concentric circles. CM A2023; *CVA* Cyprus I, pl. 10.6; Karageorghis, *MycArt*, pl. 9.2, 3.

GOATS

V.107 Kition region (?), shallow bowl, opposed dark goats on interior connected at hooves. G. G. Pierides Collection no. 44; *CVA* Cyprus II, pl. 10.1-2; Karageorghis, *MycArt*, pl. 11.2; Buchholz, Karageorghis, *Altägäis*, no. 1640.

V.108 Enkomi, bell krater, dark goats rearing against central hatched checkerboard panel bordered with loops. T. 18, S.43; *SCE* I, pl. 90, top right; Schaeffer, *Enkomi-Alasia*, fig. 98.

V.109 Enkomi, bell krater, like V.108 but with extra stripe around lower body. T. 18, S.44; *SCE* I, pl. 118.6, pl. 90, top left; Schaeffer, *Enkomi-Alasia*, figs. 99.4, 100.11.

V.110 Minet el-Beida, two fragmentary rhyta: A, goats pawing thin vertical stripe filled with zigzag; B, dark goats with pale faces, back to back, eating leaves. Schaeffer, *Ugaritica* II, fig. 91.10.

V.111 Minet el-Beida, fragmentary bell krater, dark goat in panel, in arrow-filled field, head seen from top, turned over back; two round eyes, long outlined bottle nose, round ears; influenced by ivory or gem carving? Schaeffer, *Ugaritica* II, figs. 95.29, 124.5. (Local or Syrian?).

V.112 Enkomi, fragmentary amphoroid krater, frieze of goats and kids(?) on shoulder. BM C370; *ExcCyp*, 39, fig. 67; *BMCatV*, 73, fig. 119; *CVA* British Museum I, pl. 11.9; F.

Stubbings, *BSA* 46 (1951) pl. 18 f; cf. BM C389 (VI.8), and the skipping goat on a fragment of an amphoroid krater from Byblos, no. 1474, Stubbings, *MycLevant*, 76, fig. 27.

HUNTS

V.113 Unknown provenance, fragments of bell krater, hunter wearing scale-corselet(?); deer(?) and hound(?); diving fish. CM A2024 a, b, e. *CVA* Cyprus I, pl. 12.4–5; V. Karageorghis, *BCH* 83 (1959) 201, fig. 3; V. Karageorghis, E. Masson, *AA* 1975, 220 f., fig. 20.

LIONS

V.114 Shemishin, amphoroid krater, two pairs of confronted lions with heads turned back, on one side separated by horned lily, on the other by petal rosettes; elongated bodies filled with circles; petal rosettes and chains of circles in field. CM A1648. S. Casson, *Ancient Cyprus* (1937) pl. III.1; *CVA* Cyprus I, pl. 10.4–5; Stubbings, *MycLevant*, pl. XI.1; Buchholz, Karageorghis, *Altägäis*, no. 1630; Karageorghis, *MycArt*, pl. 7.2; *Archaeologia Viva: Cyprus* (1969) 129, fig. XLI; N. K. Sandars, *The Sea Peoples* (1978) 138, fig. 95. See also the hunt krater from Ugarit, XIII.27, and the Pastoral lions, VI.22, 24.

BIRDS

V.115 Klavdhia, bell krater. BM C400; *BMCatV*, 81, fig. 137; *CVA* British Museum I, pl. 9.8; W. Heurtley, *QDAP* 5 (1936) 97, fig. 6.4; Furumark, *MP*, FM 7.19; S. Benton, *JHS* 81 (1961) pl. 4.2.

V.116 Cyprus, bowl, on inside, six birds with oval spotted bodies and long tubular necks; raised wing a single line; dot-rosette in field. Lowie Museum of Anthropology, University of California, Berkeley, LMAUC no. 8.294a; Karageorghis, *MycArt*, 20, pl. 11.1.

V.117 Hala Sultan Tekké, bowl, three striped footless birds circling interior, raised wings; lozenge in field. T. 2, no. 197. V. Karageorghis, *AAA* 1 (1968) 57, fig. 1; *BCH* 93 (1969) 529, fig. 166; *MycArt*, pl. 12.1; *RDAC* 1968, pl. III.5; *HST* I, pls. LVII, LXXVII.

V.117.1 Enkomi, bowl fragment, crude striped bird and lozenge in interior. Brussels A.1254; *CVA* Belgique 3, pl. 3.13.

V.118 Hala Sultan Tekké, bowl fragment, footless, wingless, spotted birds right. BM C690 (98.12-31.12); *BMCatV*, 131, fig. 257; V. Karageorghis, *AA* 1967, 163, fig. 1; *HST* I, pl. XXXV.c, d.

V.119 Kition (1963), bowl, seven bracket-winged swallows circling. T. 4 and T. 5/132; V. Karageorghis, *BCH* 88 (1964) 347, fig. 80; *AA* 1967, 166, fig. 5; *Cyprus* (1968) pl. 73 right; *MycArt*, pl. XII.2; *Kition* I, *The Tombs*, pls. XXXI, CXXII; *Kition*, pl. II, left; Buchholz, Karageorghis, *Altägäis*, no. 1643.

V.120 Ugarit, bowl, schematic outlined "swallows" with round heads, bracket wings, triangle tails. T. VI (1932) no. 41; Schaeffer, *Ugaritica* II, fig. 61 B; V. Karageorghis, *AA* 1967, 164, fig. 2.

V.121 Unknown provenance, bowl, schematic dark "swallows" with bracket wings, triangle tails. Bonn, Akademisches Kunstmuseum inv. no. 780; V. Karageorghis, *AA* 1967, 166, fig. 4; *Antiken aus dem Akademischen Kunstmuseum, Bonn* (1969) no. 104, pl. 65.

V.122 Ugarit, bowl, schematic dark "swallows" with strongly curved bracket wings, long beaks, no tails. Collection C. Schaeffer; V. Karageorghis, *AA* 1967, 164, fig. 3, 166.

V.123 Enkomi (1937), bowl, group of seven darting swallows, six dark, one with striped wings; full bracket wings, split tails. Collection C. Schaeffer; V. Karageorghis, *AA* 1967, 168, fig. 6.

V. 124 Bowl, eleven spotted bird protomes left. G. G. Pierides Collection, no. 55. *CVA* Cyprus II, pl. 10.4–5; Karageorghis, *MycArt*, pl. 11.3; Buchholz, Karageorghis, *Altägäis*, no. 1642.

V.125 Cyprus, conical rhyton, five "flamingos" with bodies backward. CM A1936; *CVA* Cyprus I, pl. 9.6; Karageorghis, *MycArt*, pl. 15.2.

FISH

V.126 Hala Sultan Tekké, fragment of shallow bowl, bird in "galoshes" and fish right, crosshatched block. BM C689 (98.12-1.210). *BMCatV*, 131, fig. 256; *HST* I, pl. IV.

V.127 Enkomi, bell krater, open-bodied fish in panels separated by checkerboard with elaborate striped and looped border. T. 18, S.45; *SCE* I, pl. 90, upper row, second from left.

V.128 Cyprus, bell krater, eight fish on each side, two large ones having each swallowed two small ones, who show through the outlines. CM A1543 (formerly Karemphybikes Collection); *CVA* Cyprus I, pl. 12.1–3; Stubbings, *MycLevant*, pl. X.2; S. Marinatos, *Praktika tēs Akademias tōn Athenōn* 41 (1966) pl. 4.1; V. Karageorghis, *BCH* 93 (1969) 163, fig. 1; H.-G. Buchholz, G. Jöhrens, I. Maull, *Jagd und Fischfang*, in *Archaeologia Homerica* J (1973) pl. V b.

V.129 Cyprus, fragmentary bell krater, three fish, one with vertebrae exposed. CM 1958/I-10/5; S. Marinatos, *Praktika tēs Akademias tōn Athenōn* 41 (1966) pl. 4.2.

V.130 Cyprus, one-handled jug, eight dark, fanged fish on shoulder, diving; groups of bands below. G. G. Pierides Collection, no. 38; *CVA* Cyprus II, pl. 8.1–4; Karageorghis, *MycArt*, pl. 10.2; Buchholz, Karageorghis, *Altägäis*, no. 1628.

V.131 Ugarit, conical rhyton, five dark fish upright on their tails, curved fins, striped snouts; a flower and concentric circles in field. Schaeffer, *Ugaritica* II, fig. 94, bottom.

V.132 Enkomi, fragmentary conical rhyton, fish standing on tail, as on V.131, ruffled fins in staggered pairs, central body reserved in stripe, white paint for minor lateral stripes. T. 12, BM C606; *BMCatV*, 117.

V.133 Ugarit, shallow bowl, two opposed dark fishes with tails attached to central circle (cf. V.107), open mouths, tongues. Louvre AO 18641; Schaeffer, *Ugaritica* II, fig. 126.9.

V.134 Klavdhia, shallow bowl, three dark fish circling inside, ruffled running-loop fins, open mouths with sharp striped teeth. BM C671; *BMCatV*, 128, fig. 245.

V.135 Hala Sultan Tekké, fragmentary shallow bowl, five dark fish with saw beaks right, one feeding at central circles; trefoils and lozenges in field. BM C676 (98.12–1.229); *HST* I, pl. XX e, f.

V.136 Enkomi, shallow bowl, three fish with round stupid heads, bodies formed of running loop contours. BM C614; *ExcCyp*, 36, fig. 64; *BMCatV*, 119, fig. 218.

V.137 Cyprus, shallow bowl, three striped "sea slugs" (cf. bird type of V.117.1) in compartments divided by vertical ladder.

Lowie Museum of Anthropology, University of California, Berkeley, 8-294b.

V.138 Kition, shallow bowl, three spotted and one "vertebrae" fish left; outer band of hatched lozenges. T. 9.90; V. Karageorghis, *BCH* 88 (1964) 349, fig. 84; *MycArt*, pl. 10.1; *Cyprus* (1968) pl. 73 left; *Kition*, pl. II right; *Kition I, The Tombs*, pls. LXXIII, CLIX; *Civilization of Prehistoric Cyprus* (1976) no. 138; Buchholz, Karageorghis, *Altägäis*, no. 1641; S. Marinatos, *Praktika tēs Akademias tōn Athenōn* 41 (1966) pl. 4.3; *Archaeologia Viva: Cyprus* (1969) 111, fig. XXV.

V.139 Kition, fragmentary shallow bowl; inside, parts of two dark fish right, sharp short fins; thin vertical divider filled with zigzag. T. 9, lower burial, no. 115A and B; V. Karageorghis, *Kition I, The Tombs*, pls. LXII, CXLVIII.

V.140 Enkomi, fragmentary pyxis, on shoulder, outlined spotted fish swimming toward rows of dotted arcs like an undersea grotto. T. 12, BM C687, *BMCatV*, 130, fig. 254.

V.141 Kouklia/Palaipaphos, shallow bowl, single dolphin-like fish right, dark back, pale spotted underbelly, sharp reserved fins. T. 1, no. 25; courtesy F. G. Maier.

V.142 Kition, shallow bowl, sketchy outlined fish, right. T. 4 and T. 5/151A; V. Karageorghis, *Kition I, The Tombs*, pl. CXXXII.

Cyprus and the East: Pastoral

EARLY PASTORAL

BULLS AND GOATS

VI.1 Enkomi, bell krater, goat and tree, bull. T. 19 no. 66, Cyprus Museum; *SCE* I, pl. 118; S. Casson, *Ancient Cyprus* (1937) pl. III.2; Sjöqvist, *Problems*, fig. 21.3; V. Karageorghis, *Kypriakai Spoudai* 25 (1961) 13, pl. 66; *Nouveaux Documents*, 234 ff., pl. XXIII.1–2.

VI.2 Kouklia, fragmentary upper part of bell krater, bull and tree. Kouklia Museum; *Nouveaux Documents*, 236, pl. XXIII.5.

VI.3 Kition, fragmentary bell krater, bull and tree. Cyprus Museum; *Nouveaux Documents*, 236 f., pl. XXIII.6; stratified to end of Late Cypriote II.

VI.4 Kouklia, fragmentary bell krater, lion and bull. T. 3.35; Kouklia Museum; F. G. Maier, *RDAC* 1969, pl. IV.2; *AA* 1969, 400 f., fig. 21.

VI.5 Ugarit, bell krater, bull and bush. Musée des Antiquités Nationales, St. Germain-en-Laye, inv. 76721; Schaeffer, *Ugaritica* II, figs. 60.22, 23 and 124.7, 12; *Nouveaux Documents*, 237 f., pl. XXIII.3–4.

VI.6 Ugarit, fragment of a bell krater, goat right. Schaeffer, *Ugaritica* II, figs. 91.11 and 61.

VI.7 Enkomi, bell krater, lion chasing goats. T. 18, S.50 (Swedish excavations), Medelhavsmuseet, Stockholm; Sjöqvist, *Problems*, fig. 21.4; *SCE* I, pl. 119.7; *Nouveaux Documents*, 238 f.

VI.8 Maroni, amphoroid krater, four goats feeding on trees. BM C389; F. Stubbings, *BSA* 46 (1951) 174, pl. 18f.; *Nouveaux Documents*, 239, pl. XXIII.7.

VI.9 Kazaphani, amphoroid krater, grazing goats and bushes. T. 2, Cyprus Museum, CS 1829; *BCH* 96 (1972) 101 f., fig. 11a–b.

MIDDLE PASTORAL

BULLS, SPHINXES

VI.10 Kouklia, jug, two bulls and three birds. T. 1.33, Kouklia Museum; F. G. Maier, *RDAC* 1967, pl. VII.3; *Archaeologia Viva* 2, no. 3 (1969) 123, fig. 115; *Archäologie und Geschichte. Ausgrabungen in Alt-Paphos* (1973) fig. 11.

VI.11 Klavdhia, bell krater, bull and bush. BM C421; *CVA* British Museum I, pl. 10.9; F. Stubbings, *BSA* 46 (1951) pl. 18e; S. Immerwahr, *Archaeology* 13 (1960) 11, fig. 12; *Nouveaux Documents*, 239, pl. XXIV.6.

VI.12 Larnaka District, fragments of bell krater, bull and bush. CM 1958/IV-20/9; *Nouveaux Documents*, 240, pl. XXIV.1; *CVA* Cyprus I, 15 f., pl. 14.5.

VI.13 Pyla-Verghi, bell krater, bull and bush. T. 1.47, Cyprus Museum; P. Dikaios, *Enkomi* (1969-71) pl. 233.1.

V.14 Pyla-Verghi, bell krater, bull and bush. T. 1.45, Cyprus Museum; P. Dikaios, *Enkomi* (1969-71) pl. 233.3.

VI.15 Aradippo, bell krater, bull and bush. Louvre AM 679; *Recueil Edmond Pottier* (1937) 171, fig. 8.

VI.16 Enkomi, bell krater, bulls, two male sphinxes, and tree. BM C417; *ExcCyp*, 49, fig. 76, no. 1260; *BMCatV*, 86, fig. 148; *CVA* British Museum I, pl. 10.1; H. T. Bossert, *Altkreta*³ (1937) 264, fig. 476; Stubbings, *MycLevant*, 37 f., pl. IX.4 and 6.

VI.17 Minet el-Beida, fragmentary krater, bull, confronted sphinxes. Musée des Antiquités Nationales, St. Germain-en-Laye; Schaeffer, *Ugaritica* II, figs. 59.46, 60.18; *Nouveaux Documents*, 241 f., pl. XXIV.4–5.

VI.18 Enkomi, fragmentary bell krater, sphinx. CM 1958/II-17/5; *Nouveaux Documents*, 242, pl. XXIV.3; *CVA* Cyprus I, 14, pl. 13.4.

VI.19 Kyrenia, bell krater, bull and bush. Cyprus Museum, CS 1746; *BCH* 94 (1970) 206 f., figs. 21–22.

VI.20 Enkomi, bell krater, bull and bush. T. 19.24 (Swedish Excavations), Cyprus Museum; *SCE* I, pl. XCI, third row from top, fourth from left; *Nouveaux Documents*, 242 f., fig. 53, pl. XXIV.7.

VI.21 Cyprus, fragmentary bell krater, bull and bush. CM 1959/II-26/1; *Nouveaux Documents*, 244, pl. XXIV.2; *CVA* Cyprus I, 15, pl. 14.3.

VI.22 Angastina, bell krater, two lions. T. 1.193, Cyprus Museum; K. Nicolaou, *RDAC* 1972, 84, fig. 4, pl. 15.4; H.-G. Buchholz, *AA* 1974, 383, fig. 44. The tomb also contained a bell krater with a bull and spiral on one side, two goats and a tree on the other, not included in this catalogue. (T. 1.9, K. Nicolaou, *RDAC* 1972, 84, fig. 4.)

VI.23 Byblos, bell krater, long bull. M. Dunand, *Fouilles de Byblos* I (1937) pl. 157.1534.

VI.24 Maroni, fragmentary bell krater, heraldic lions. BM C405; *BMCatV*, 83; *CVA* British Museum I, pl. 11.11; *Nouveaux Documents*, 244, pl. XXV.2.

GOATS

VI.25 Hala Sultan Tekké, fragmentary bell krater, goat. CM 1934/I-28/1; *Nouveaux Documents*, 245, pl. XXV.8.

VI.26 Enkomi, fragmentary bell krater, goats and tree. CM A2020g; *Nouveaux Documents*, 245, pl. XXV.3; *CVA* Cyprus I, 15, pl. 14.4.

VI.27 Kalopsidha or Alambra, fragment of bell krater, goat. Medelhavsmuseet, Stockholm; *Nouveaux Documents*, 245, pl. XXV.7.

VI.28 Enkomi, fragments of bell kraters, goats. CM A2020 and A2021a; *Nouveaux Documents*, 245, pl. XXV.4; *CVA* Cyprus, I, 16, pl. 15.1. See also VI.36 (reverse).

BIRDS

VI.29 Enkomi, fragmentary bell krater, birds with spread wings. BM 1938/11-20/1; *Nouveaux Documents*, 246, pl. XXV.6.

VI.30 Enkomi, fragmentary bell krater, birds. BM 1938/11-20/3; J. L. Benson, *AJA* 65 (1961) 342, pl. 106, fig. 26.

VI.31 Enkomi, bell krater, birds. BM C423; J. L. Benson, *AJA* 65 (1961) 342, pl. 106, fig. 28; *CVA* British Museum I, pl. 8.3.

VI.32 Enkomi, bell krater, birds. CM A1760; J. L. Benson, *AJA* 65 (1961) 342, pl. 105, figs. 24-25; pl. 106, fig. 31; *Nouveaux Documents*, pl. XXVI.1; *CVA* Cyprus I, 14, pl. 13.5-7.

VI.33 Enkomi, bell krater, birds. BM C422; J. L. Benson, *AJA* 65 (1961) 342, pl. 106, fig. 29; *CVA* British Museum I, pl. 8.1.

VI.34 Enkomi, fragmentary bell krater, birds with spread wings. Musée du Cinquantenaire, Brussels, A1251; J. L. Benson, *AJA* 65 (1961) 342; *Nouveaux Documents*, pl. XXV.5.

VI.35 Cyprus, bell krater, birds left. G. G. Pierides Collection, Nicosia, no. 36; *Nouveaux Documents*, 246 f., pl. XXVI.2-3; *CVA* Cyprus II, 4, pl. 7.1-4; J. L. Benson, *AJA* 65 (1961) pl. 105, fig. 23.

VI.36 Enkomi, fragmentary bell krater (reverse of VI.28), birds and tree. CM A2020 and A2021a; *Nouveaux Documents*, pl. XXVI.4.

VI.37 Enkomi, bell krater, birds. Medelhavsmuseet, Stockholm, T. 13.114; *Nouveaux Documents*, 247, pl. XXVI.6-7.

VI.38 Kouklia, fragmentary bell krater, bird. Kouklia Museum, T. E III, 36 A; F. G. Maier, *RDAC* 1969, 40, pl. III.6; *AA* 1969, 399, fig. 19.

VI.39 Enkomi, fragmentary three-handled jar, birds. Medelhavsmuseet, Stockholm, T. 7.VI; *Nouveaux Documents*, 247, pl. XXVI.5; V. Karageorghis, *OpAth* 3 (1960) 151, pl. 13.6.

VI.40 Maroni, fragmentary bell krater, confronted birds. Manchester University Museum; *Nouveaux Documents*, 247, fig. 55.2.

VI.41 Enkomi, fragmentary bell krater. Cyprus Survey, Nicosia; *Nouveaux Documents*, 248, fig. 55.3.

LATE PASTORAL

BULLS

VI.42 Enkomi, fragmentary bell krater, bull and bush. Medelhavsmuseet, Stockholm, T. 7.IX; V. Karageorghis, *OpAth* 3 (1960) 152, pl. XIII.IX.

VI.43 Enkomi, bell krater, bull, goat. BM C420; *CVA* British Museum I, pl. 7.9; F. Stubbings, *BSA* 46 (1951) pl. 19c; *Nouveaux Documents*, 249, pl. XXVII.1-2.

VI.44 Enkomi, bell krater, bull sniffing leafy tree right. CM A1759; *Nouveaux Documents*, 249, fig. 54.

VI.45 Enkomi, bell krater, confronted bulls. BM C418; F. Stubbings, *BSA* 46 (1951) pl. 19 a; *Nouveaux Documents*, 249 f., pl. XXVII.4.

VI.46 Enkomi, fragmentary jug(?), bulls' heads. P. Dikaios, *Enkomi* (1969-71) pls. 307.188, 312.

VI.47 Uncertain provenance, bell krater, bull and tree. CM A1758; *Nouveaux Documents*, 250, pl. XXVII.5-6; *CVA* Cyprus I, 15, pl. 14.1-2; E. Gjerstad, *Studies on Prehistoric Cyprus* (1926) 222.

VI.48 Enkomi, bell krater, bull and fodder(?). BM C419; *CVA* British Museum I, pl. 7.3; F. Stubbings, *BSA* 46 (1951) pl. 196; *Nouveaux Documents*, 249, pl. XXVII.3.

VI.49 Enkomi, fragmentary bell krater, bull and tree. BM C427; *Nouveaux Documents*, 250, pl. XXVIII.1.

VI.50 Enkomi, fragmentary bell krater, bulls fighting. BM C425; *ExcCyp*, 34, fig. 62, no. 1235; *BMCatV*, 88, fig. 153.

GOATS

VI.51 Enkomi, bell krater, goats. Cyprus Museum, Dikaios T. 1; P. Dikaios, *Enkomi* (1969-71) 335, no. 12, pls. 192.15, 311.367.

MISCELLANEOUS

VI.52 Morphou-Gnaftia, fragmentary amphoroid(?) krater, chariot right. Cyprus Museum, CS 5103; *Nouveaux Documents*, 250, pl. XXVIII.2; H. W. Catling, *AJA* 72 (1968) 48, pl. 21, fig. 2.

VI.53 Enkomi, fragmentary bell krater, trees. Medelhavsmuseet, Stockholm, T. 3.VIII; *Nouveaux Documents*, 254; V. Karageorghis, *OpAth* 3 (1960) 147, pl. X.VIII.

VI.54 Enkomi, bell krater, trees. Medelhavsmuseet, Stockholm, no. 355 a; *Nouveaux Documents*, 252, pl. XXVIII.7.

VI.55 Pyla-Verghi, bell krater, trees. Larnaka District Museum, Dikaios T. 1.48; P. Dikaios, *Enkomi* (1969-71) pl. 233.4 (48).

VI.56 Enkomi, fragmentary bell krater, trees. Medelhavsmuseet, Stockholm; *Nouveaux Documents*, 254; V. Karageorghis, *OpAth* 3 (1960) 147, pl. X.IX.

VI.57 Hala Sultan Tekké, fragmentary bell krater. BM A390; *Nouveaux Documents*, 254, pl. XXVIII.3.

VI.58 Nicosia, fragmentary bell krater, leaves. CM 1958/IV-7/2; *Nouveaux Documents*, 254, fig. 55.4.

LATE HELLADIC III C:1

VI.59 Hala Sultan Tekké, fragment of krater, warrior in short embroidered tunic, in violent motion. *BCH* 97 (1973) 659, fig. 90.

VI.60 Sinda, fragmentary krater, horse leaping over rock. A. Furumark, *OpAth* 6 (1965) 108, fig. 6.

VI.61 Sinda, spouted jar with side handle, birds with triple outline and interior spots, in spiral design. A. Furumark, *OpAth* 6 (1965) 108, fig. 8.

VI.62 Open krater, vertical confronted fish sharing a

weed; spirals and trumpets. Cesnola Collection, Metropolitan Museum of Art 435; J. L. Myres, *Handbook of the Cesnola Collection of Antiquities from Cyprus* (1914) no. 435; G. M. A. Richter, *Handbook of the Greek Collection*² (1953) pl. 4 e; 74.51.429 (CP 227).

The Greek Mainland: Early Pictorial

FORERUNNERS AND IMPORTS

VII.A Akrotiri, Thera, soldiers thrusting and resting. S. Marinatos, *Praktika* 1968, pl. 114 a; *Thera* II (1969) 44, fig. 30.

VII.B Akrotiri, Thera, head of griffin right. 1968.51.

VII.C Aigina, helmeted(?) sailor on ship or fish. G. Welter, *Aigina* (1938) 19, fig. 22; Vermeule, *GBA*, 76, fig. 13; Buchholz, Karageorghis, *Altägäis*, no. 869.

VII.D Iolkos, ship(s) right, polychrome. D. Theochares, *Ergon* 1956, 46; *Archaeology* 11 (1958) 15; Vermeule, *GBA*, 259, fig. 43 a; W. Taylour, *The Mycenaeans* (1964) 163; J. Morrison, R. Williams, *Greek Oared Ships* (1968) 9, pl. 1 a. Drawing, D. Theochares.

VII.E Argos, fish around an octopus tentacle. P. Courbin, *BCH* 80 (1956) 375, fig. 25; cf. J. D. Buck, *Hesperia* 33 (1968) 278, and fish and double axe on a cup from Aigina, S. Hiller, *Alt-Ägina* IV: *Mykenische Keramik* (1975) no. 14, pl. I.14.

VII.F Mycenae, ewer with back-tilted spout, birds flying right. Nauplion Museum 13 477, Grave *Nu*-165; G. Mylonas, *AAA* 2 (1969) 210, fig. 1; *Taphikos Kuklos B* (1973) pl. 143 a–b.

VII.G Mycenae, spouted jug, round bird walking right. Athens NM 8699, Grave *Gamma*-31; G. Mylonas, *AAA* 3 (1970) 89–90, figs. 1–2; *Taphikos Kuklos B* (1973) pl. 45 b.

VII.H Argos, three-handled jar, ducks courting in foliage. Athens NM 5650, W. Vollgraff, *BCH* 28 (1904) 377f., figs. 3-5 (Deiras T. VI.12); Evans, *Palace of Minos* IV, 332 f.; O. Montelius, *GP* II, 201, fig. 709; Staïs, *MycColl*², 142; G. Rodenwalt, *Tiryns* II (1912) 20; R. Dussaud, *Civilisations*, fig. 126; H. T. Bossert, *Altkreta* (1923) 191, fig. 261; A. Persson, *Arsberättelse* 1924-25, 88, pl. XXXIX, fig. 1; W. Heurtley, *QDAP* 5 (1936) 98, fig. 7.1; Furumark, *MP*, FM 7.1, pp. 195, 197, 405; *OpArch* 6 (1950) 261; J. Deshayes, *BCH* 77 (1953) 73f., pls. XXI.3, XXII.1, 2; Popham, *DestrKnossos*, 83; S. Hood, *The Arts in Prehistoric Greece* (1978) fig. 19 A.

VII.I Mycenae, lidded pyxis, birds flying in foliage and rocks. Athens NM 2257; Chr. Tsountas, *EphArch* 1888, 138 (T. 7); Staïs, *MycColl*², 109; Popham, *DestrKnossos*, 77.

VII.J Varkiza, basket-shaped vase, four tunny diving. Athens NM 8556; M. Theocharis, *Antiquity* 1960, 266 f., fig. 1, pl. 35 a; E. Vermeule, *AJA* 67 (1963) 198; *GBA*, 143, fig. 27; M. Popham, *AJA* 68 (1964) 350; M. Benzi, *Ceramica Micenea in Attica* (1975) pl. V.101.

VII.K Thebes, fragment of a large vase or larnax, purse net with twisted rope at mouth, lure and spinners, five live fish. T. Spyropoulos, *Deltion* 24 (1969) Chron. B'1, 183, pl. 193 a; *JHS ArcRep* 1970-71, 14-15, fig. 27; *BCH* 95 (1971) 925, fig. 275; J. Sakellarakis, *AAA* 7 (1974) 390, fig. 30.

EARLY

HUMAN FIGURE

VII.1 Aigina, human figure in spotted robe right (from a chariot krater?), striped billowing rock(?) left. H. Walter, *Deltion* 25 (1970) Chron. B'1, 137, pl. 106 b.

QUADRUPED?

VII.2 Mycenae, alabastron, humped animals. A. Wace, *Chamber Tombs at Mycenae* (1932) 112 (T. 532, no.1) pl. LIII; F. Zeuner, *A History of Domesticated Animals* (1963) fig. 13.14.

BULLS

VII.3 Mycenae, fragment of krater or larnax, dappled bull right. Athens NM 1298 lot.

VII.4 Mycenae, krater fragment, bull under suspended striped rock. Athens NM 1280 lot, "Acropolis."

BIRDS

VII.5 Thebes, one-handled jug with cutaway neck, dark birds flying toward lily. Thebes 482; A. Keramopoullos, *Deltion* 3 (1917) 156, fig. 117 (Kolonaki T. 14.30); Furumark, *MP*, FM 7.33 (LH III A:1). Keramopoullos fig. 123 may be parts of birds.

VII.6 Attica(?), spouted ewer. Louvre CA 2958.

FISH

VII.7 Athens, Agora, spouted ewer, octopus and fish. Agora P 21246; H. Thompson, *Hesperia* 21 (1952) pl. 26 a; *Archaeology* 4 (1951) 225; E. Townsend, *Hesperia* 24 (1955) 211, pl. 73.17; S. Immerwahr, *The Athenian Agora* XIII (1971) 133, VII.17, pl. 39.

VII.8 Mycenae, three krater fragments, fish pursuing right. Athens NM 1298 lot, 3685.4 and .24, 3686 b 4; Furtwängler, Loeschcke, *MV*, pl. XXXIX.401 a, b (without the third sherd).

VII.9 Pylos (Englianos), fragment of strap-handled krater, fish diving. Frame 36 under Hall 65; C. W. Blegen, *Pylos* I (1966) 288; C. W. Blegen, M. Rawson, W. Taylour, W. Donovan, *Pylos* III (1973) pl. 139. We are indebted to the late Professor Blegen and Miss Rawson for permission to photograph this and the next.

VII.10 Pylos (Englianos), fragment of jug or stirrup jar, dark fish with open beak. EBS '62, section W 21; C. W. Blegen et al., *Pylos* III (1973) pl. 152.

VII.11 Argive Heraion, alabastron, three fish swimming right. C. Waldstein, *The Argive Heraeum* II (1905) 94, no. 11 (Tholos T. 1), fig. 28; Furumark, *MP*, FM 20.1 (LH III A:1). Because the labels for the vases from the tholos were lost in transportation, it is not clear which of the three layers produced this vase; if Early, it underscores the difficulty of dating pictorial material by style.

VII.12   Argive Heraion, bowl, spotted fish inside. C. Waldstein, *The Argive Heraeum* II (1905) 80, fig. 12.

The Greek Mainland: Middle Pictorial

CHARIOTS

VIII.1   Berbati, amphoroid krater fragment, chariot right, two passengers, long-stemmed flowers in field. Åkerström, "MykKrukVerk," 35, fig. 5.

VIII.2   Berbati, amphoroid krater fragment, chariot, two armless passengers. Å. Åkerström, *I° Congresso di Micenologia* (Rome, 1968) I, 48 f., pl. 2 no. 2.

VIII.3   Berbati, amphoroid krater fragment, chariot. Å. Åkerström, *I° Congresso di Micenologia* (Rome 1968) I, 48 f., pl. 2 no. 3.

VIII.4   Nauplion, Palamidi, krater fragment, chariot. Furtwängler-Loeschcke, *MV*, 45, pl. XV.97; J. Kastorchis, *Athenaion* 7 (1878) 183, and 8 (1879) 517; H. Lolling, *AthMitt* 5 (1880) 143. For the complete chariot krater from Nauplion, see IX. 1.1.

VIII.5   Mycenae, fragment of amphoroid krater, acropolis, House of the Idols (W. Taylour); charioteer in spotted robe going left, vertical scales over reins. By Painter 9? Nauplion Museum 14 685; J. Crouwel, *BSA* 67 (1972) 99, fig. 1, pl. 30 a.

VIII.5.1   Mycenae, larnax, chariot going right, flowers in field. E. French, *BSA* 56 (1961) 88, fig. 1, pl. 14; cf. E. Vermeule, *JHS* 85 (1965) 140.

HUMAN FIGURES

VIII.6   Melathria, cutaway jug, hovering warrior. Sparta Museum 5533; K. Demacopoulou, *BSA* 66 (1971) 95, pl. 12; *EphArch* 1977; *AAA* 1 (1968) 41; F. Schachermeyr, *Die ägäische Frühzeit* 2 (1976) 136, pl. 36 ("a goddess").

VIII.7   Ayios Stephanos, krater fragment, man left, wearing baldric(?). HS 112, W. D. Taylour, *BSA* 67 (1972) 259, fig. 34, pl. 50 b.

VIII.8   Mycenae, miniature hydria with upright handle at rear, two loop handles at sides, the "Circus Pot"; three human figures, goose, goat, bird, tree, wheels. A. Wace, *Chamber Tombs at Mycenae* (1932) 28–30, pls. 18–19.5, Kalkani T. 521 no. 5; Furumark, *MP*, 459, 465, early LH III A:2; M. P. Nilsson, *The Minoan-Mycenaean Religion*[2] (1950) 419, n. 83; S. Marinatos, *EphArch* 1964, 8, 9, fig. 7; *Praktika tes Akademias ton Athenon* 41 (1966) pl. 6; S. Dow, *AJA* 75 (1971) 199; F. Stubbings, *BSA* 42 (1947) 56; *Wandlungen* (1975) 16, pl. 2 b; Vermeule, *GBA*, 313, fig. 50 c, f.

VIII.9   Zygouries, deep bowl fragment, goat-bird.

C. W. Blegen, *Zygouries* (1928) 139, fig. 131, no. 10.

VIII.10   Aigina, one-handled jug, goat and goat-bird. Aigina Museum 2097; S. Hiller, *Alt-Ägina* IV: *Mykenische Keramik* (1975) 40, 41, fig. 2, no. 259, pl. 29.

VIII.11   Menelaion, krater fragments, human figures. R. M. Dawkins, *BSA* 16 (1909-10) 8, fig. 3 bottom (upside down?).

BULLS

VIII.12   Mycenae, krater fragments, bulls and flowers. Athens NM 3600-5, 1272, 1298/30 (Schliemann?); Furtwängler-Loeschcke, *MV*, pl. XLI.423; Furumark, *MP*, FM 3.2, LH III A:2; H. T. Bossert, *Altkreta* (1923) 193, fig. 264.

VIII.13   Mycenae, krater rim fragment, facing bull's head. Athens NM 5424; the bowl has remnants of large circles inside.

BIRDS

VIII.14   Mycenae, krater, frieze of birds, by the painter of IV.6 (BM C372) from Enkomi. I. Papademetriou, *Praktika* 1950, 220, fig. 23; V. Karageorghis, *AJA* 64 (1960) 280; J. L. Benson, *AJA* 65 (1961) 342.

VIII.15   Koukounara (Pylos), krater, birds and fish. S. Marinatos, *Ergon* 1963, 87, fig. 89; *Praktika* 1963, 119 f., pl. 93 a; *EphArch* 1964, 7 f., fig. 5; *Praktika tēs Akademias tōn Athenōn* 36 (1961) 56, and 41 (1966) 1 f., pl. 5

VIII.16   Koukounara (Pylos), krater, two "swans" each side. S. Marinatos, *Ergon* 1963, 87, figs. 90, 91 (upside down); *Praktika* 1963, pl. 93 b, c.

VIII.17   Koukounara (Pylos), ewer, three birds in frieze on shoulder, leader containing "eggs." S. Marinatos, *Ergon* 1960, 147, fig. 159 right; *Ergon* 1963, 86, fig. 88; *EphArch* 1964, 10, fig. 8; *Praktika tēs Akademias tōn Athenōn* 41 (1966) pl. 5; Vermeule, *GBA*, 313, fig. 50a.

VIII.18   Mycenae, fragment (ovoid rhyton?), bird head and neck, dot-rosette, raised nipple. Athens NM 3674.4 (1298/30).

VIII.19   Mycenae, top of rhyton, bottle or jug(?), two long-necked birds rising toward spout. Athens NM 3051.

VIII.20   Mycenae, krater fragment, crosshatched bird, partridge type, raising both wings in flight, open beak. E. Wace, *BSA* 49 (1954) 274, pl. 48 a.4; the general context is early Amarna Age, in the Cyclopean Terrace Building.

VIII.21   Mycenae, open krater fragment, thick-bordered bird filled with U-pattern and laddered contours, right. Athens NM 1212-5.

VIII.22   Mycenae, krater fragment, crosshatched bird belly; may belong with last. Athens NM (1212-5).

VIII.23   Mycenae, krater fragment, bird left, solid neck, crosshatched breast, U-patterned body. Athens NM 1275.

VIII.24   Mycenae, krater fragment, dark long-legged bird left in flight; raised nipple in field with dot-and-circle filler. Athens NM 1308(-4).

VIII.25   Asine, fragmentary amphora(?), crested hoopoe right, dot "seeds." P. Ålin, *OpAth* 8 (1968) 99 f., figs. 4.18 and 20, 7c.

VIII.26   Athens, krater fragment, bulbous crosshatched bird body right. Graef-Langlotz, *VA*, 5, pl. 2.36.

VIII.27 Delphi, fragmentary open krater, frieze of "toucans" right. L. Lerat, *BCH* 59 (1935) 355, pl. XXIII.

VIII.28 Eleusis, small jug fragment, bird (ostrich or bustard type) by handle, in frieze(?), filled with fanned-out teardrops like feathers. Unpublished? Another fragment of crosshatched bird, G. Mylonas, *AJA* 40 (1936) 423, fig. 10, lower left.

VIII.29 Thebes, krater fragment, dark bird's head right, striped wing of one in front; in style very like VIII.30-31. N. Pharaklas, *Deltion* 23 (1968) Chron. B'1, pl. 161 top.

BIRDS, HUMAN FIGURES, AND SPHINXES

VIII.30 Mycenae, fragmentary stirrup jar, human figures or sphinxes and birds. Athens NM 2654.

VIII.31 Mycenae, pair of low stirrup jars (one published) with sphinxes, birds, and papyrus plants. I. Papademetriou, Ph. Petsas, *Praktika* 1951, 196, fig. 6; "Corridor C 2, found with over one hundred terracotta figurines of human beings and animals."

[**VIII.32** Munich, three-handled jar, forged painting of long-nosed sphinxes wearing plumed caps and five-strand necklaces, wings filled with scale-net pattern. Munich, Antikensammlung 6079; before the forgery was removed, R. Hackl, *JdI* 22 (1907) 78, 101, 141, pl. 2; after removal, J. Sieveking, R. Hackl, *Die königliche Vasensammlung zu München* (1912) pl. 4 no. 27. The sphinx scene later published by A. Dessenne, *Le Sphinx* (1957) I, 150, no. 325, pl. XVIII; Buchholz, Karageorghis, *Altägäis*, no. 966; J. Boardman, *RDAC* 1976, 153.]

ALTAR AND DOUBLE AXE

VIII.33 Athens, fragmentary open krater with altar, horns of consecration and double axe. Agora P 21564; S. Immerwahr, *Archaeology* 13 (1960) 8, fig. 7; *The Athenian Agora* XIII (1971) 248, no. 425, pl. 60; cf. *Archaeology* 4 (1951) 225; *Hesperia* 24 (1955) 203.

HELMETS

VIII.34 Nichoria, fragmentary kylix, frieze of abstract ornaments converted to helmets. NP 14, LH III A; W. McDonald, *Hesperia* 41 (1972) 259, pl. 50 c; drawing by D. Bingham. Cf. the later stirrup jar from Delphi, P. Perdrizet, *Fouilles de Delphes* V (1908) fig. 32, or the shoulder of the trick vase from Kea, IX.16. A new helmet kylix from Knossos is published by M. Popham, *BSA* 73 (1978) 180, fig. 1 a.

The Greek Mainland: Ripe Pictorial

CHARIOTS AND HORSES

IX.1 Corinth, amphoroid krater, chariot and groom. S. Weinberg, *Hesperia* 18 (1949) 154 f., pls. 23-24, from a pit behind the Julian Basilica; S. Immerwahr, *Archaeology* 13 (1960) 9, fig. 8; Vandenabeele, Olivier, *Idéogrammes*, 131 f., fig. 89 a-b.

IX.1.1 Nauplion, amphoroid krater, team left toward palm trees, spirals framing reins, spotted box and robes. By the painter of V.1.A. Deïlaki, *Deltion* 28 (1973) Chron. B'1, 90-93, pl. 90 st; *BCH* 102 (1978) 669, fig. 68; *JHS ArcRep* (1978-79) 18, fig. 22.

IX.2 Mycenae, amphoroid krater, chariots, groom. A. J. B. Wace, *BSA* 48 (1953) 6, pl. 1 b, in a III B context; W. Taylour, *BSA* 50 (1955) 226, no. 36; H. Wace and C. Williams, *Mycenae Guide* (1963) pl. 11; C. M. Bowra, *Horizon* III.3 (1961) 81; S. Marinatos, M. Hirmer, *Crete and Mycenae* (1960) pl. 234; M. Davidson, L. Cottrell, et al., *Horizon Book of Lost Worlds* (1962) 278; H. Catling, *AJA* 72 (1968) pl. 22.12; drawing by C. Williams.

IX.3 Kopreza, open krater fragment, chariot, groom. Athens NM 3472, exhibited as though from Nauplion; V. Staïs, *EphArch* 1895, 213, pl. 10.12; O. Montelius, *GP*, pl. 112, fig. 5; M. Benzi, *Ceramica Micenea in Attica* (1975) pl. XIX.283. Staïs, p. 259, remarks that the fragment is from a vase of the same technique as the next.

IX.4 Kopreza, open krater fragment. V. Staïs, *EphArch* 1895, pl. 10.13, not found in the Athens National Museum. O. Montelius, *GP*, pl. 112, fig. 6; M. Benzi, *Ceramica Micenea in Attica* (1975) pl. XIX.282; Furumark, *MP*, FM 1.40; it could be III C, though the context does not support this.

IX.5 Mycenae, krater fragments, running horse. A. J. B. Wace, *BSA* 51 (1956) 118-119, fig. 6, pl. 26; drawing by P. de Jong. S. Immerwahr, *Archaeology* 13 (1960) 8, fig. 6; H. Wace and C. Williams, from "The House of Lead," *Mycenae Guide* (1963) 8. Both E. French and J. Crouwel have doubted the Bronze Age character of the sherds.

IX.6 Tiryns, fragment, horse. Athens NM 1514; H. Schliemann, *Tiryns* (1885) pl. XIX a.

IX.7 Mycenae, krater fragment, galloping horse(s). Collection of the American School of Classical Studies, 1950.

IX.8 Mycenae, krater fragments, (chariot), horses and groom. Athens NM 1272 a, b, and a third unnumbered fragment; Furtwängler-Loeschcke, *MV*, pl. XLI.429 a, b; Furumark, *MP*, 243, FM 2.7.

IX.9 Mycenae, krater fragment, horse hooves bunched high for a jump. Athens NM 3051.

IX.10 Mycenae, krater fragment, four hooves and a tail(?). Athens NM 3631.

HUMAN FIGURES

IX.11 Argive Heraion, jar fragment; naked dancer(?). C. Waldstein, *The Argive Heraeum* II (1905) pl. LV.47.

IX.11.1 Tiryns, open krater fragment, man on campstool. Nauplion Museum 15 37; Slenczka, *Tiryns* VII, 25, no. 39, fig. 6, pl. 8.1 d.

IX.12 Kopreza, open krater, figures clasping hands. Athens NM 9863; V. Staïs, *EphArch* 1895, pl. 10.9, 9 a; Montelius, *GP* I, pl. 112 a, b; Furumark, *MP*, 443, 447 ("boxers"), FS 7:2, FM 1 g (LH III A:2 e), FM 14.6 (LH III A:2); V. Karageorghis, *BCH* 83 (1959) 204; R. Lorandou-Papantoniou, *EphArch* 1974, 85 f., pls. 29-31. M. Benzi, *Ceramica Micenea in Attica* (1975) pl. XI.215, XII.215.

IX.13 Alyke (Voula), jug, lady. J. Papademetriou, *Ergon* 1954, 10, fig. 8; *Praktika* 1954, 78 f., figs. 5-6; M. Benzi, *Ceramica Micenea in Attica* (1975) pl. IV.99. From T. 3, the jug was accompanied by five terracotta figurines (four psi type, one enthroned) and twenty-five other fine late LH III B-C vases.

IX.14 Athens, Acropolis, fragment, robed figure. Montelius, *GP* I, fig. 501, with a hoard of late bronzes.

IX.14.1 Nauplion, fragmentary krater, scale pattern and kithara player; A. Dragona, *EphArch* 1977, 86 f.; *BCH* 103 (1979) 560, fig. 83; *JHS ArcRep* 1979-80, 30, fig. 53.

IX.15 Tiryns, rhyton, robed figures and trees. Nauplion Museum 13 202; N. Verdelis, *EphArch* 1956, Par. 6, fig. 12; Slenczka, *Tiryns* VII, no. 87, pl. 7.

IX.16 Kea, trick vase, robed figures and bull. Kea 2071; J. L. Caskey, *Hesperia* 33 (1964) 332, pl. 62 a; S. Immerwahr, *Hesperia* 46 (1977) 32 f., pl. 18; Buchholz, Karageorghis, *Altägäis*, no. 994.

BOXERS

IX.17 Mycenae, krater(?) fragment, boxers. Athens NM 1272; Furtwängler-Loeschcke, *MV*, pl. XLI.426. The style is not unlike that of Munich 47, from Rhodes (cf. IV.16, XII.4), possibly Middle rather than Ripe.

IX.18 Mycenae, fragment, boxers. Mycenae 60-327; W. Taylour in J. Chadwick et al., *The Mycenae Tablets* III (1963) 44, fig. 91; Citadel House, Room 4, with tablets.

BULL JUMPER

IX.18.1 Mycenae, rhyton(?) fragment, bull jumper. Athens NM 2675; Tsountas, 1886; M. Mayer, *JdI* 7 (1892) 72; W. Reichel, *Homerische Waffen*² (1901) 109, fig. 49; Lorimer, *HM*, pl. XVI.3; Furumark, *MP*, FM 1 *ad* (without hat); J. Younger, *AJA* 80 (1976) pl. 20, fig. 22.

BULLS

IX.19 Berbati, bell krater with wishbone handles, confronted bulls and "calf." Nauplion Museum 11 628; Buchholz, Karageorghis, *Altägäis*, no. 1024.

IX.20 Tiryns Epichosis, krater fragment, bull and cattle egret. Nauplion Museum 13 211; N. Verdelis, *EphArch* 1956, Par. 7, fig. 14; Slenczka, *Tiryns* VII, no. 78 A, pl. 13.1.

IX.21 Tiryns, krater fragments, bull, lozenges. Nauplion Museum 14 234. German Archaeological Institute photo 583, tracing by S. Chapman. W. Rudolph, in *Tiryns* V (1971) 91,

no. 2, pl. 42; Slenczka, *Tiryns* VII, no. 6, pl. 10.1 a, b, c; cf. no. 151, pl. 10.1 f, no. 165, pl. 11.3 a. By the painter of V.73 and 74.

IX.22 Tiryns Epichosis, krater fragments, bull, lozenges, dotted circles. Nauplion Museum 13 207. Slenczka, *Tiryns* VII, no. 84, pl. 21.2.

IX.23 Tiryns, jug neck, bulls. Nauplion Museum 14 268; Slenczka, *Tiryns* VII, no. 41, pl. 22.1-2; p. 27, fig. 7.

IX.24 Tiryns Epichosis, krater fragment, bull with weak knees. N. Verdelis, water channels; Nauplion Museum 14 304; Slenczka, *Tiryns* VII, no. 77, pl. 5.2 q.

IX.25 Tiryns, fragmentary one-handled jug, bull and protomes. Nauplion Museum 14 366; Slenczka, *Tiryns* VII, no. 149, pl. 12.1-3, p. 65, fig. 18; drawing from Slenczka.

IX.25.1 Tiryns, fragments of a shallow bowl, bull protomes, white on dark. Nauplion Museum 14 363; Slenczka, *Tiryns* VII, no. 146, pl. 18.1; p. 63, fig. 17.

IX.26 Argos, one-handled jug, weak cross-filled bull right on shoulder. J. Deshayes, *Argos, Les Fouilles de la Deiras* (1966) 164, T. XXVI, DV 108, pls. XXII.1, LXXVI.1-2; *BCH* 80 (1956) 364, fig. 5. The relation to V.47 (BM C404) proposed by J. Benson, *AJA* 65 (1961) 341, seems tenuous; Slenczka, *Tiryns* VII, pl. 44.3.

IX.27 Argos, one-handled jug, facing bull's head. J. Deshayes, *Argos, Les Fouilles de la Deiras* (1966) 165, T. XXIII, DV 149, pl. LXIII.3-4.

IX.28 Berbati, bell-krater fragment, bulls and bird. Å. Åkerström, "*MykKrukVerk*," 44, fig. 11; *I° Congresso di Micenologia* (1968) I, 48 f., pl. 2.1; S. Immerwahr, *Archaeology* 13 (1960) 10, fig. 10; J. L. Benson, *AJA* 65 (1961) pl. 104.19; Benson, *HBM*, pl. 24.C 14.

IX.29 Dendra, sherd, horse or bull hooves. G. Walberg, *OpAth* 7 (1967) 172, fig. 2.23; Benson, *HBM*, pl. 10.6.

IX.30 Mycenae, bell krater fragment, bull right, filled with circles, loops, dashes. Athens NM 1272 (-7, -26); Furtwängler-Loeschcke, *MV*, pl. XLI.424; Furumark, *MP*, FM 3.6 (LH III B).

IX.30.1 Mycenae, krater rim fragment, dappled bull with long vertical eye fringed with spots, reserved streamer in horn, filled lozenges in field, close to IX.21. *BCH* 98 (1974) 608, fig. 79; cf. Slenczka, *Tiryns* VII, no. 150, pl. 11.3 b; no. 203, pl.14.2 e; no. 212, pl. 20.1 h.

IX.31 Mycenae, krater fragments, bull and bird. Athens NM 1298/30 and 1275 lots; cf. Slenczka, *Tiryns* VII, no. 62, pl. 15.1 d, e, f, g.

IX.32 Mycenae, krater fragment, bird from a bull scene. Athens NM 1309 (-5, -33); H. Schliemann, *Mycenae and Tiryns* (1880) pl. VIII.33; German Archaeological Institute photo Myk. 216. By the painter of BM C409(?), but cf. J. L. Benson, *AJA* 65 (1961) 344.

IX.33 Mycenae, krater fragment, front of bull, wavy lines. Athens NM 3621.4 (1275/28).

IX.34 Mycenae, krater fragment, haunch of bull, N-pattern and wavy lines. Athens NM 1298.6.

IX.35 Mycenae, krater fragment, haunch of bull, rippled filling. Athens NM 1275 (2250).

IX.36 Mycenae, krater rim fragment, head of bull, close to Protome Painter A. Athens NM 1298/30 (3-20).

IX.37 Mycenae, krater rim fragment, fighting bulls. Athens NM 1275 (-5).

IX.38 Mycenae, bell krater fragment, bull's head goring the handle. Athens NM 1298/30; H. Schliemann, *Mycenae and Tiryns* (1880) pl. X.44.

IX.39 Mycenae, bell krater fragment, fighting bulls. Athens NM 1309; H. Schliemann, *Mycenae and Tiryns* (1880) pl. XI.48; Furumark, *MP*, FM 3.13, LH III B.

IX.40 Mycenae, bell krater rim fragment, bull's brow and horn. Athens NM 1298/30.

IX.41 Mycenae, bell krater rim fragment, bull's horn. Athens NM, no number (4).

IX.42 Mycenae, krater fragment, three legs of a bull. Athens NM 3632.2 (1298).

IX.43 Mycenae, jug fragment, bull or goat protome. Athens NM 3618.3 (1298/30). For the muzzle, cf. V.45.

IX.44 Argive Heraion, bowl fragment, bull protomes. C. Waldstein, *Argive Heraeum* (1905) II, 91, fig. 19; Furumark, *MP*, FM 3.18, LH III B.

IX.45 Nauplion (Pronoia), three-handled jar, cow and calf. Nauplion Museum 38 87 (1892); V. Staïs, *EphArch* 1895, 261, pl. 11.4 a; Chr. Tsountas and J. Manatt, *The Mycenaean Age* (1897) fig. 137; Montelius, *GP* II, pl. 127, 10.

IX.46 Athens, fragment of closed vessel, bull, dapples. Agora AP 2753.

IX.47 Attica(?), krater, bulls. Munich, Antikensammlung, formerly von Schoen; K. Schefold, *Meisterwerke Griechischer Kunst* (1960) no. 29.

STAGS

IX.48 Tiryns, krater fragment, deer and fawn. Nauplion Museum 14 270; German Archaeological Institute photo 550, west stairs, north edge; now Slenczka, *Tiryns* VII, no. 43, pl. 35.1 a. Cf. his no. 33 A, 167, 168, pl. 35.1 g.

IX.49 Mycenae, krater fragments, skipping deer. Athens NM 3254.5 (1275), 3254 (3625b). With this pair of sherds should be associated IX.50 and 51.

IX.50 Mycenae, krater fragment, Great Poros Wall, deer's chest and legs, wavy lines, striped legs, by the same painter as IX.49. A. J. B. Wace, *BSA* 50 (1955) 225 (W. Taylour) no. 21, pl. 44 h.

IX.51 Mycenae, krater fragment, dark-headed stag with bottle-nose following arrow-filled haunch. Athens NM 310x (1275/28).

IX.52 Mycenae, krater fragment, legs. Athens NM 3629.4.

IX.53 Mycenae, krater fragment, chest and forelegs. Athens NM 3690.4 (1298/30).

IX.54 Tiryns, krater fragment, sharp stag hooves. Schliemann's excavations. H. Schliemann, *Tiryns* (1885) fig. 154.

IX.55 Tiryns, krater fragment, head with elaborate branched antlers. Nauplion 14 353. N. Verdelis, Tiryns water channels; now Slenczka, *Tiryns* VII, no. 135, pl. 35.1 c.

IX.56 Tiryns, krater fragment, neat angular striped hind legs, right. German Archaeological Institute photo 583, west wall over stairs.

IX.57 Tiryns, krater fragment, striped hind legs, spotted haunch, tail and genitals in transverse dashes. Nauplion Museum 14 384; now Slenczka, *Tiryns* VII, no. 167, pl. 352 c.

IX.58 Tiryns, krater rim fragment, head of stag left, back-swept horn, rippled neck. Nauplion Museum 14 239; German Archaeological Institute photo 582, west stairs, south edge. Now Slenczka, *Tiryns* VII, no. 11A, pl. 35.1 b.

IX.59 Tiryns, krater fragment, hind legs right. German Archaeological Institute photo 583, west wall above stairs.

IX.60 Mycenae, krater fragment, stag with turned-back head, three-pronged antlers, square eye. Athens NM (no. unknown); J. F. Daniel photograph in S. Immerwahr, *AJA* 60 (1956) pl. 55, fig. 17, upper left, prewar Case 57 e. Type of V.54 (BM C409).

IX.61 Mycenae, krater rim fragment, stag's head, three-pronged antlers, round eye. Athens NM (no. unknown); S. Immerwahr, *AJA* 60, pl. 55, fig. 17, prewar Case 57 f.

IX.62 Mycenae, krater fragment, head with low horizontal antlers, three vertical spurs, ladder pattern undulating over antlers. Athens NM basement, no number.

IX.63 Mycenae, krater fragment, arrow-filled haunch, dark body, weak striped legs. Athens NM 4090(?) (1290/30), (.4), German Archaeological Institute photo box 175, Myk. 255 (P. 5667).

IX.64 Mycenae, krater fragment, galloping spotted animal left. Athens NM 3245.

IX.65 Mycenae, krater fragment, striped animal pacing left, dark legs, small scale. Athens NM 1298/30.

GOATS

IX.66 Mycenae, krater rim fragment, horned head, dark goat to right. Athens NM 3634.4.

IX.67 Mycenae, two krater wall fragments, foreparts of two dark goats right. A: head, chest, forelegs, and half the body; B: legs and body between horns and haunch. Athens NM 1294; Furtwängler-Loeschcke, *MV*, pl. XL.416 a, b. A is H. Schliemann, *Mycenae and Tiryns* (1880) pl. IX.35 and pl. XI.52. B is pl. X.46 without the leg fragment.

IX.68 Mycenae, krater fragment, striped hind legs to the right. Athens NM 3629.4.

IX.69 Mycenae, krater fragment, dark chest and striped forelegs prancing right, body modeled with streaky paint. Athens NM 3626.4 (1298/4).

IX.70 Mycenae, krater fragment, chest, body, and forelegs prancing right, body streaked, legs striped. Athens NM 3626.5 (1298/5).

IX.71 Mycenae, krater with hunted(?) goats. Athens NM 2677.

IX.72 Mycenae, krater fragment, wounded goat(?). Athens NM 3244.

IX.73 Mycenae, bowl or cup fragment, goat eating at tree. Athens NM 4032.4 (1303 lot); Furtwängler-Loeschcke, *MV*, pl. XXXIX.412; Furumark, *MP*, FM 6.8.

IX.74 Mycenae, cup fragment, goats eating tree. Athens NM 1303 lot (-220, -7, .24); Furtwängler-Loeschcke, *MV*, pl. XXXIX.413; Furumark, *MP*, FM 6.7.

IX.75 Prosymna, ewer, three goats. C. W. Blegen, *Prosymna* (1937) 118, T.35, no. 536, figs. 271, 702.

IX.76.1 Tiryns, open krater fragment, checkerboard panel, goat pawing it to left; head and body reserved, scalloped dark contour on chest, inset wheel pattern. Nauplion Museum

14 400; Slenczka, *Tiryns* VII, no. 183, pl. 39.1 c. It is hard to follow Slenczka's interpretation of the goat as a bird-headed ship with a ram.

IX.76.2 Tiryns, open krater fragment, legs of running goat(?) right. Slenczka, *Tiryns* VII, no. 207, pl. 20.1 c.

IX.76.3 Tiryns, open vessel fragment, dark leaping animal, goat or hunting dog, right. Slenczka, *Tiryns* VII, no. 210, pl. 20.1 f.

IX.77 Nauplion, tower of St. Irene, T. B, basket-shaped vase with vertical loop handles from rim, dappled goat leaping right in landscape of striped rocks above and below, "olive bush" and date palm(?). A. Deïlaki, *Deltion* 28 (1973) Chron. B'1, 91, pl. 90 a; *BCH* 102 (1978) 669, fig. 67.

OTHER ANIMALS

IX.78 Mycenae, bowl, "Minotaur" or goat eating at a tree. C. Tzavella, *EphArch* 1960 (1965) 136, fig. 1; N. Verdelis, *Ergon* 1962, 104, fig. 124 (upside down), from T. D at Palaiomandri, 1.5 km. west of the acropolis of Mycenae, apparently in an LH III B context. Opinions by Caskey, Karouzou, and Verdelis at the end of Tzavella's article.

IX.79 Mycenae, krater fragment, dog right, head turned back. Athens NM 1272 ("26"); Furtwängler-Loeschcke, *MV*, pl. XLI.428; German Archaeological Institute photo Myk. 243, P. 4655.

IX.80 Argos, krater fragment, dog or boar. J. Deshayes, *Argos, Les Fouilles de La Deiras* (1966) pl. XXX.2.

IX.81 Mycenae, krater fragment, shaggy dog or lion. Athens NM 3612.5 (1298/30).

IX.82 Mycenae, krater fragments, lion, bulls. Athens NM 2581. Cf. lion and griffin faience fragment from Mycenae, *BSA* 51 (1956) pl. 21 b.

IX.83 Mycenae, top of three-handled jar, dung beetle with ball of dung. E. French, *BSA* 61 (1966) 223, pl. 48 a.

IX.84 Mycenae, jar fragment, "bird on four wheels." A. J. B. Wace, *BSA* 25 (1921-23) 22, fig. 6 b, Lion Gate Stratum II, "a curious animal"; Furumark, *MP*, 256, "a mole."

IX.85 A sherd found much earlier at Mycenae, presumably by Schliemann, may be part of the same vase. Legs and "wheels" not fully preserved, but body filling and beak similar. Athens NM 1275 lot (-5).

IX.86 Delphi, krater fragment, "four-footed bird." L. Lerat, *BCH* 59 (1935) 356, fig. 14; cf. pl. 21.

IX.87 Makrysia (Olympia), krater fragments, goat-birds. N. Gialouris, *Praktika* 1954, 297, fig. 12; Buchholz, Karageorghis, *Altägäis*, 910 a, b.

IX.88 Mycenae, fragment, crab or cult ship. Athens NM2899. Chr. Tsountas and J. Manatt, *The Mycenaean Age* (1897) 333, fig. 158; C. Laviosa, *Annuario* 47-48 (1969–70) 21, fig. 15.

BIRDS

IX.89 Attica, rhyton, birds, grass, flowers. Berlin, Altes Mus. Inv. 31105; F. Stubbings, *BSA* 42 (1947) 55, pl. 18.5.

IX.90 Athens, Acropolis, fragment, "bustard," heavy contour, slapdash spot filling, stunted wings; three drops of food

or blood(?). Graef-Langlotz, *VA*, pl. 7.221 (Prov. 208); Montelius, *GP* I, pl. 107.4; identification by S. Benton.

IX.91 Athens, Acropolis, krater fragment, tails of two spotted birds (bull krater?). Graef-Langlotz, *VA*, 22, no. 232 (Prov. 207).

IX.92 Spata, krater fragment, round dark bird, recurved head, curled beak. Athens NM 2213; V. Staïs, *EphArch* 1895, 210; G. Perrot, C. Chipiez, *Histoire de l'Art dans l'Antiquité* VI.2 (1894) 402, fig. 485; Furtwängler-Loeschcke, *MV*, pl. XVII.116; Montelius, *GP* I, pl. 111.3; Furumark, *MP*, FM 7.21 (reversed).

IX.92.1 Spata, fragment (of a three-handled jar?), two spotted birds with heavy contours, right, in handle zone. Athens NM 2213a; M. Benzi, *Ceramica Micenea in Attica* (1975) pl. VII.162.

IX.93 Argive Heraion, krater(?) fragment, oval bird with ripple filling. C. Waldstein, *The Argive Heraeum* II (1905) pl. LV.43.

IX.94 Argive Heraion, bowl fragments, frieze of birds, ladder-barred contours, crosshatched necks and wings. C. Waldstein, *The Argive Heraeum* II (1905) pl. LV.44 a–d; see also no. 45 a.

IX.95 Argive Heraion, Prosymna, spouted cup, four dark ladder-winged birds in circle inside. E. Protonotariou-Deïlaki, *EphArch* 1960 (1965) 123 f., 132-133, pl. 5, no. 21; she thought of them as swimming ducks.

IX.96 Argos, two-handled globular flask, frieze of nine birds. J. Deshayes, *Argos, Fouilles de la Deiras* (1966) 58, T. XXI, DV 64, pls. XXII.3, LXII.1-2; *BCH* 80 (1956) Chronique, 362, fig. 2; G. Hafner, *Geschichte der Griechischen Kunst* (1961) 51, fig. 48.

IX.97 Mycenae, two-handled jug with strainer spout, round bird, striped neck, rippled filling with reserved contours, feet forward, four bars for claws. N. Verdelis, in J. Chadwick et al., *The Mycenae Tablets* III (1963) 21, fig. 21; West House, in a pile of "luxury" vessels near the tablets, burned before the end of LH III B.

IX.98 Mycenae, krater, symmetrical pair of birds each side; striped necks, long bills, one rippled tail. Athens NM 3635 (1275 lot, 1280, 1303); Furtwängler-Loeschcke, *MV*, pl. XXXIX.404. Similar background fillers (rare in the Argolid) on IX.36, bull krater, perhaps by the same artist. A bird with analogous fillers at Tiryns: Slenczka, *Tiryns* VII, no. 233, pl. 26.2 b.

IX.99 Mycenae, krater fragment, bird filled with ripples, neck bent under body; cf. V.54. A. J. B. Wace, *BSA* 25 (1921-23) 25, fig. 7 g, Lion Gate Stratum V.

IX.100 Mycenae, neck fragment, round bird, head bent close to breast; rippled fillers; cf. V.54, and Slenczka, *Tiryns* VII, pl. 17.1. Athens NM 1309; H. Schliemann, *Mycenae and Tiryns* (1880) pl. VIII.33; S. Immerwahr, *AJA* 60 (1956) 141; J. L. Benson, *AJA* 65 (1961) 344, his Painter of the Shield-Bearers, no. 6.

IX.101 Mycenae, two krater fragments, round crosshatched bird, dark neck, fan tail, crooked legs; animal rump. Athens NM 1303 (397), (3-42.4); Furtwängler-Loeschcke, *MV*, pl. XXXIX.397.

IX.102 Mycenae, krater fragment, round striped bird flapping pointed wings; bull's horns and foreleg; separate ground line. Athens NM 1303 (398), (-1.4250); Furtwängler-Loeschcke, *MV*, pl. XXXIX.398.

IX.103 Mycenae, krater fragment, bird, thick outlines, filled with rows of spots, pointed tail; cf. IX.109.1.

IX.104 Mycenae, krater fragment, bird left, raised head, spots; bull rump, spotted(?). Athens NM 1275 lot, also German Archaeological Institute photo box 180, Myk. 233.

IX.105 Mycenae, shallow bowl, round bird (from a frieze), striped, ladder wings, long legs, cropped tail. Athens NM 2684.

IX.106 Mycenae, krater rim fragment, frieze of birds right, scale filling. Athens NM, no number, labeled Akro. (Mycenae Akropolis).

IX.107 Tiryns, krater rim fragment, bird left in "breeze." Nauplion Museum 14 401; German Archaeological Institute photo Tiryns 561; Slenczka, Tiryns VII, no. 1, pl. 24.2 a.

IX.108 Tiryns, shallow bowl fragments, (four) birds in circle, left. Nauplion Museum 14 362; Slenczka, Tiryns VII, no. 145, pl. 27.1 a–b, fig. 16.

IX.109 Tiryns, krater fragment, spotted marsh birds right, cranes or herons, spots around contour and down center, striped legs. Athens NM AXΛ.150.

IX.109.1 Tiryns, fragment, marsh bird on bull. H. Schliemann, Tiryns (1885) fig. 150. Lost?

IX.109.2 Tiryns, marsh bird, similar to IX.109, with dark legs. H. Schliemann, Tiryns (1885) fig. 149; many others from the old excavations; cf. Slenczka, Tiryns VII, pl. 31.

IX.110 Tiryns, two krater fragments, frieze of "flamingos," wavy line filling. H. Schliemann, Tiryns (1885) pl. XXIII b (color). Lost?

IX.111 Tiryns, krater fragments, "flamingos," wavy-line girdle, dot-rosettes. Nauplion Museum 14 245; German Archaeological Institute photo Tiryns 547; Slenczka, Tiryns VII, no. 17, pl. 24.2 b.

IX.111.1 Tiryns, krater fragment, bird and bull? Beak crosses rectangular, rippled area; oval area spotted. Cf. the III C birds from Kition, Palaipaphos, and Tarsus; now Slenczka, Tiryns VII, no. 160, pl. 24.1 d.

IX.112 Achaia, Teichos Dymaion, fragmentary krater, frieze of flamingos right. E. Mastrokostas, Deltion 18 (1963) Chron. B, 111 f., pl. 155.

IX.113 Phylakopi, Melos, fragment, neck and body(?) of a thick bird(?) in dark silhouette with rippled filling ornament in added white. Collection of the British School at Athens.

IX.114 Phylakopi, Melos, fragment, body and curled toes of wispy bird flying left, body filled with concentric arcs. Collection of the British School at Athens.

FISH

IX.115 Spata, stirrup jar, frieze of fish right. Athens NM 2209; B. Haussoullier, BCH 2 (1878) pl. 19.2; cf. A. Milchhöfer, AthMitt 2 (1877) 82 f., 261 f.; Furtwängler-Loeschcke, MV, pl. XVII.111; Montelius, GP I, pl. 111.9.

IX.116 Delphi, fragment, feeding fish. L. Lerat, BCH 59 (1935) 353, fig. 12.8. Cf. also 359, fig. 15.1-2, for other possible fish.

IX.117 Amyklai, fragment of rounded closed vessel, three fish rising. R. M. Dawkins, BSA 16 (1909-1910) 9, fig. 4.

IX.118 Argive Heraion, fragment, two oblique fish. C. Waldstein, The Argive Heraeum II (1905) 78, no. 1, pl. LI.17.

For another possible fish, see pl. LV.41.

IX.119 Mycenae, krater fragment, round fish. Athens NM 2648. The type is rather like Furumark, MP, FM 20.5, III B.

IX.120 Achaia (Klauss-Koukoura), one-handled bowl, three fish inside. Patras Museum no. 266; N. Kyparissis, Praktika 1937, 87 f., no. 70, figs. 6-7; E. Vermeule, AJA 64 (1960) 11, no. 40, pl. 4, fig. 28.

IX.121 Tiryns, shoulder fragment (of a jug?), bull facing left (head preserved) to large snouted fish right. Nauplion Museum 14 327; Slenczka, Tiryns VII, no. 106, pl. 39.1 a.

IX.122 European art market, one-handled jug, eellike fish. Münzen und Medaillen, Basel, Auktion 18, Kunstwerke der Antike (1958) 19, no. 75.

IX.123 Berlin, private collection, one-handled cup with a frieze of rising thin fish, slightly angled right, collared necks, wavy-line filling. "Antiken aus Berliner Privatbesitz," Antikenmuseum Berlin (exhibition, December 1975–February 1976) no. 193. Another fish sherd listed under no. 196.

IX.124 Scoglia del Tonno, kylix, fish. F. Biancofiore, Civilta Micenea nell' Italia Meridionale (1967) pl. XII.145.

The Greek Mainland: Transitional

CHARIOTS AND HORSES

X.1 Tiryns, fragmentary krater, chariot, soldiers, dogs. Athens NM 1511; H. Schliemann, Tiryns (1885) 353, fig. 152, pl. XIV; V. Staïs, MycColl², 195; K. Müller, Tiryns III (1930) 210 f.; Montelius, GP II, 248, fig. 816; W. Helbig, Das Homerische Epos (1884) 196, fig. 51; H. T. Bossert, Altkreta (1923) 195, fig. 267; Altkreta³ (1937) 74, fig. 136; H. R. Hall, The Civilization of Greece in the Bronze Age (1928) 262, fig. 339; M. Mackeprang, AJA 42 (1938) 543, 558; Lorimer, HM, 149, fig. 9; Furumark, MP, 447 f., FM 1.27, 2.6, 8.4, 39.21 (III B; the others in this group are labeled III C, FM 1.36-37); OpAth 1 (1953) 62 f., fig. 9; Å. Åkerström, OpAth 1, 10 f., figs. 1-2; S. Charitonides, EphArch 1953-54, II, 101 f., fig. 2; J. L. Benson, AJA 65 (1961) 344 f. (associated with V.54, BM C409), pl. 107, fig. 32; S. Marinatos, Kleidung, Haar-und Barttracht, in Archaeologia Homerica A (1967) 31, fig. 6. The new fragments, passenger and driver from each side, foot soldier and team from the reverse, are Slenczka, Tiryns VII, 46 f., nos. 100, 101 A–B, and 102 A–D, all pl.1 (Nauplion Museum 14 321, 14 322, 14 323). Slenczka thinks of two separate vases. See also X.42; J. Crouwel, BSA 71 (1976) pl. 8 a, c, d.

X.2 Mycenae, two sets of krater fragments, chariot, team, driver, passenger, dog, and groom to right, all liberally enriched with white. G. Mylonas, Praktika 1970, 122, pl. 168; Ergon 1970, 98, fig. 102; BCH 95 (1971) 869, fig. 136; Ergon 1971, 135, fig. 164; BCH 96 (1972) 643, fig. 135.

X.3 Mycenae, krater fragment, chariot, driver, passenger,

and team right, white ripples on reins, arcades, and team. Nauplion Museum 54 75; A. Wace, *BSA* 24 (1919–21) 207, pl. 14 d; S. Charitonides, *EphArch* 1953–54, II, 103, fig. 3.

X.4 Mycenae, krater fragments, chariot, "prince" and attendant with sunshade; rump and tail of team outlined in white, "M" arcades. J. Chadwick et al., *The Mycenae Tablets* III (1963) 39, fig. 78; J. Crouwel, *BSA* 68 (1973) 331, fig. 19, pl. 59 c; *BSA* 71 (1976) pl. 8 b.

X.5 Mycenae, krater fragment, helmeted person with raised hand, white ripples. Athens NM 2681; Å. Åkerström, *OpAth* 1 (1953) 13, fig. 3.1.

X.6 Mycenae, krater fragment, "bustle man" with spear, white stripes and spots. Athens NM 1212 (2683?); Furtwängler-Loeschcke, *MV*, 66, fig. 35; Å. Åkerström, *OpAth* 1 (1953) 14.

X.7 Mycenae, krater fragment, "bustle man" (from a chariot krater?). London, BM A1077.3, presented by the Hellenic government, 1923; *BMCatV* I.i.205 f., fig. 288.

X.8 Mycenae, krater rim fragment, man making commanding gesture; no white. Nauplion Museum 15 37; S. Charitonides, *EphArch* 1953-54, II, 101, fig. 1; see his n. 1 for the problem of provenance, Mycenae or Tiryns; J. L. Benson, *AJA* 65 (1961) 344, pl. 107, fig. 33.

X.9-15 The seven krater fragments from Schliemann's Tiryns excavations seem to have these relations: Athens NM 1507, body and legs of horse (11); Athens NM 1508, mane and plumes of horse (12); Athens NM 1509, three large joining sherds of a chariot scene (9); Athens NM 1510, charioteer (9); Athens NM 1511, krater, name piece by painter of Tiryns Shield Bearers (1); Athens NM 1512, parts of two charioteers (10); Athens NM 1514, legs and tail of horse, part of chariot (13); Athens NM 1654, rump of horse, front of chariot (15). 1507, 1509, 1510, and 1512 belong to the same vase but do not join; 1508 may belong to this vase too. 1514 may also be part of the front or back of 1509, into which 1510 is now inserted. 1654 is unglazed inside, unlike the others, which are glazed. It is possible that all these fragments, except 1654, should reduce to a single krater.

X.9 Tiryns, three krater fragments, chariot, passenger, driver, groom, team. Athens NM 1509, 1510; H. Schliemann, *Tiryns* (1885) pls. XV a, XVII b; Furumark, *MP*, FM 1.36-37 (III C:1); FM 2.8 (restored drawing with NM 1514); J. L. Benson, *AJA* 65 (1961) 346.

X.10 Tiryns, krater rim fragment, "bald" passenger, armed footman. Athens NM 1512; H. Schliemann, *Tiryns* (1885) pl. XV c.

X.11 Tiryns, wall fragment from lower down on X.10; body and legs of horse, right; pointed knees, left leg striped, right spotted. Athens NM 1507; H. Schliemann, *Tiryns* (1885) pl. XXI a.

X.12 Tiryns, krater rim fragment, neck, mane plumes, and ear of horse. Athens NM 1508; H. Schliemann, *Tiryns* (1885) pl. XXI b.

X.13 Tiryns, krater wall fragment, hind legs and tail of horse, curved fore-rail of chariot. Athens NM 1514; Furumark, *MP*, FM 2.8 (pastiche).

X.14 Tiryns, krater fragment, charioteer's feet kicking. Nauplion Museum.

X.15 Tiryns, krater fragment, solid-bodied chariot, rump of horse, diagonal white ripples. (The driver appears as a tubular figure through the side of the box, apparently only because he was painted first and the chariot washed in dark glaze over him.) Athens NM 1654; H. Schliemann, *Tiryns* (1885) pl. XXII e.

X.16 Tiryns, krater fragment, dark team right, outlined in white, white cheek straps for bridle. Nauplion Museum 14 243; German Archaeological Institute photo Tiryns 580; Slenczka, *Tiryns* VII, no. 15, pl. 5.1 d. Cf. XI.21.

X.17 Tiryns, krater fragment, team head right, spotted neck, dark muzzle, dotted eyes. Nauplion Museum 14 273; German Archaeological Institute photo 550; Slenczka, *Tiryns* VII, no. 47, pl. 5.1 b.

X.18 Tiryns, krater rim fragment, outlined tall-necked soldier right with spear in drawn-back right arm(?), dot-rosette in field. Nauplion Museum 14 387; Slenczka, *Tiryns* VII, no. 170, pl. 1.1 c.

X.19 Tiryns, krater rim fragment, outlined soldier's head left, bulging back of skull. Nauplion Museum 14 388; Slenczka, *Tiryns* VII, no. 171, pl. 1.1 d.

X.19.1 See Addenda.

X.20 Mycenae, two krater fragments, horse and flower. Athens NM 1303 lot; Furtwängler-Loeschcke, *MV*, pl. XXXIX.405 and 407.

X.21 Mycenae, krater fragment, hind legs of horse right. *BSA* 64 (1969) pl. 62 a 3. Normally the reserved strip highlighting the back edge of one hind leg does not occur until toward the end of thirteenth century, but it should be noted that the excavators would date it to III B:1.

X.22 Mycenae, two bowl fragments, walking horses. London, British Museum, BM A1077.1-2.

X.23 Mycenae, fragment of krater (or collared jar?); haunch of horse with highlights in slanting frame of bordered zigzags and loops. Athens NM 1308-3, with fragment NM 2654; see also X.52.

X.24 Mycenae, krater rim fragment, horse in bridle, groom, right. American School of Classical Studies, 1950, north road, Schliemann's dump.

X.25 Mycenae, Acropolis, bowl or krater fragment, pony left on leading reins. Athens NM 4024 (4924?).

X.26 Mycenae, Great Poros Wall, krater fragment, horse head right. W. Taylour, *BSA* 50 (1955) 230, no. 78, pl. 44 g, thought to be possibly III C.

X.27 Mycenae, krater fragment, horse or donkey nibbling flower. Athens NM 1303 lot; Furtwängler-Loeschcke, *MV*, pl. XXXIX.403.

X.28 Athens Acropolis, bowl or small krater fragment, pony in reins right. Athens NM (not found); Graef-Langlotz, *VA* I, pl. 7.233; Montelius, *GP* I, pl. 107.10. Graef notes traces of what might be the mane of a second horse at the lower right edge of the sherd, though the relation of the bodies would be difficult; it might be a "hedgehog" helmet.

SOLDIERS

X.29 Mycenae, krater fragment, soldier with helmet and shield. Athens NM 2379; Chr. Tsountas, *EphArch* 1888, 161, fig. 14, T. 15 (with the fish fragment X.83); G. Perrot, C. Chipiez, *Histoire de l'Art dans l'Antiquité* (1894) VI.2, 814, fig. 382; N. Yalouris, *AthMitt* 75 (1960) Beil. 26.1.

X.30 Mycenae, bowl fragment, man left, with ration bag(?), crosshatched panel. Athens NM 1272 lot (-7); Furtwängler-Loeschcke, *MV,* pl. XLI.425; Furumark, *MP,* FM 1.35 (III C:1).

X.31 Mycenae, krater or bowl fragment, fallen soldier(?) in fur(?) helmet. Athens NM 1294 lot; H. Schliemann, *Mycenae and Tiryns* (1880) 69, no. 82; Furtwängler-Loeschcke, *MV,* pl. XL.422; Lorimer, *HM,* pl. XVI.4.

X.32 Dendra, Midea, open vase fragment, man's head right, crosshatched cap or helmet, round eye, lips applied outside the contour. G. Walberg, *OpAth* 7 (1967) 162, no. 5, pl. 1.5, still LH III B.

X.33 Tiryns, bowl rim fragment, man's head right, long pointed nose, tilted N for lips, slanted-arc eyes without pupil, loops at back of head like "feather" crown. Nauplion Museum 14 231; German Archaeological Institute photo 580, west stairs, north edge; Slenczka, *Tiryns* VII, no. 3, pl. 8.2 d.

X.34 Tiryns, krater fragment, man's head right, long nose, parted lips, slanted eye, ruffled back of head like Indian bonnet (cf. X.31). Nauplion Museum 14 319; Slenczka, *Tiryns* VII, no. 90, pl. 8.2 e.

X.35 Tiryns, krater fragment, chest, neck, and arms of spearman (or groom) right, spotted tunic, bent right arm, neck filled with vertical ripples. Nauplion Museum 14 248; German Archaeological Institute photo 580; Slenczka, *Tiryns* VII, no. 20, pl. 8.2 b.

BATTLE SCENES

X.36 Amyklai, krater fragment, three men in battle, solid silhouette. W. von Massow, *AthMitt* 52 (1927) 46, fig. 26; context, Beil. VI.

X.37 Tiryns, krater fragment, three men in battle, solid silhouette, reserved round eye. Nauplion Museum 24 46.

X.38 Phylakopi, krater fragment, spear thrower right. C. Edgar, *Phylakopi in Melos* (1904) pl. XXXII.16.

X.39 Phylakopi, krater fragment, legs of man walking left, ship's prow(?). C. Edgar, *Phylakopi in Melos* (1904) pl. XXXII.17. A small Phylakopi fragment preserves the foot of a man in dark silhouette walking right, in the collection of the British School of Archaeology at Athens.

X.40 Naxos, Aplomata, krater fragment, dark legs with very curved thighs, knobby knees, right; hand with splayed fingers(?) behind thigh; N. Kontoleon, *BCH* 96 (1972) 769, fig. 412 (horse?).

X.41 Athens, krater fragment, two hands on long arms or, possibly, bird legs and claws. North Slope, AP 3001.

X.41.1 Athens, krater fragment, single hand with five splayed fingers; from the wheel marks it seems to be pointing downward. Cf. North Slope AP 2908 (V B); O. Broneer, *Hesperia* 8 (1939) fig. 78 o.

SPHINX

X.42 Mycenae, flat-bottomed, straight-sided pyxis with vertical loop handles; sphinx, bird, and chevron trees, liberal white paint. G. Mylonas, *Ergon* 1975, 94, fig. 89; *BCH* 100 (1976) 608, fig. 39.

STAGS

X.43 Mycenae, krater fragment, stag's head, white spots. Athens NM 2678; Å. Åkerström, *OpAth* 1 (1953) 23, fig. 9:2; J. L. Benson, *AJA* 65 (1961) pl. 107, fig. 35.

X.44 Tiryns, krater fragment, stag's head left, parted lips, rippled antlers. Athens NM 1631; H. Schliemann, *Tiryns* (1885) pl. XX c; Furumark, *MP,* FM 5.1, III B.

X.45 Tiryns, krater fragment, frieze of stags right, haunch of leader, most of follower; bars hang from antlers, bars, chevrons, and solid filling. German Archaeological Institute photos 580, 582, 583; west stairs, north edge west wall, and Spätmykenisches Loch; Slenczka, *Tiryns* VII, no. 12, pl. 34.1.

X.46 Tiryns, krater fragment, torso and haunch of stag right; belly and area between hind legs spotted, haunch and leg dark, pendent genitals. German Archaeological Institute photo 550.

X.47 Mycenae, bowl fragment, small stag right, spotted and barred. Athens NM, no number but "89," Acropolis.

X.48 Mycenae, krater fragment, stag left in checkerboard-panel frame. G. Mylonas, *Ergon* 1968, 8, fig. 6, north edge of Acropolis, Room 3; *BCH* 94 (1970) 966, fig. 163.

X.49 Mycenae, bowl fragment, eye and neck of animal, zigzag inside contour; excellent fabric, confused drawing. Athens NM 1293/30.

X.50 Argolid (Tiryns?), krater fragment, frieze of stags right, blocks of vertical ripples on body, upright branched antlers. Slenczka, *Tiryns* VII, no. 244, pl. 36.1 a.

X.51 Amarynthos, Euboia, small krater fragment, dark chest and striped forelegs of stag right, dark rosette with double reserved contours. L. Sackett, V. Hankey, R. Howell, T. Jacobsen, M. Popham, *BSA* 61 (1966) 103, pl. 16 b.

GOATS

X.52 Mycenae, krater fragment, hind legs of goat (eating at tree?) in zigzag and loop frame. Athens NM 2654; Benson, *HBM,* pl. IV.2-3.

X.53 Mycenae, bell krater fragment, highlighted goat left, diamond eye. Athens NM 1303 lot; H. Schliemann, *Mycenae and Tiryns* (1880) pl. VIII, 31; Furtwängler-Loeschcke, *MV,* pl. XXXIX.409.

X.54 Mycenae, fragment, unicorn animal right, vertically twisted horn. Athens NM 3678.7 (1269); Furtwängler-Loeschcke, *MV,* pl. XXIII.169.

X.55 Mycenae, krater rim fragment (flanged), goat right under zigzag-filled curved bar (cf. X.23, 52); solid muzzle, reserved neck with "ingrown hairs," horns swept back, ears forward. Athens NM 3617.4.

X.56 Mycenae, krater rim fragment (rolled), goat right, reserved face with "ingrown hairs," solid neck, long swept-back horn. Athens NM 3633.4 (1298 lot).

X.57 Mycenae, krater fragment, dark goat right, horns back in deep curve, alert loop ears. G. Mylonas, *Praktika* 1970, pl. 169.

X.58 Mycenae, bowl fragment, goat with pricked ear, drooping whiskers, chevron pattern on muzzle. G. Mylonas, *Praktika* 1970, pl. 169.

X.58.1 Tiryns, puzzling krater rim fragment, goat or stag(?) with horn of double spiral curls, loop ear, parti-colored muzzle? German Archaeological Institute photo Tiryns 580, Spätmykenisches Loch.

X.58.2 Tanagra, krater fragment, odd squared-off dark animal with reserved dotted squares set in at eye and chest, short curled three-barred tail waving over stern; published as a horse, not in the normal equine tradition. T. Spyropoulos, *Ergon* 1976, 13, fig. 10.

BIRDS

X.59 Tiryns, three krater fragments, geese filled with triangles, solid necks, barred tails, right. Athens NM 1622; H. Schliemann, *Tiryns* (1885) pl. XX d; Slenczka, *Tiryns* VII, no. 213, pl. 32.1.

X.60 Tiryns, bird filled with vertical stripes and wavy lines. Collection of the British School of Archaeology at Athens.

X.61 Tiryns, krater fragment, bird left, filled with irregular spots, jagged inner contour, barred legs through the ground line. W. Rudolph, *Tiryns* V (1971) 92, no. 5, fig. 3; Slenczka, *Tiryns* VII, no. 154, pl. 31.2 i.

X.62 Tiryns, fourteen krater fragments, dark "quail" outlined in spots, hissing. N. Verdelis, Tiryns water channels; Slenczka, *Tiryns* VII, nos. 127–130, pl. 33; distributed among three separate kraters(?).

X.63 Tiryns, krater fragment, "flamingo" right under handle, dark body, striped head, hooked bill. Oxford, Ashmolean Museum 1966.586; *Sir John and Lady Beazley Gifts* (1967) no. 45, pl. III.

X.64 Mycenae, stirrup jar shoulder, two flying birds, open loop bodies, dotted "spine." A. Wace, *BSA* 25 (1921–23) 72, pl. XIV c; *Mycenae*, fig. 84 r; Furumark, *MP*, FM 7.39, III C:1.

X.65 Mycenae, krater or deep bowl fragment, light-bodied water bird with wavy lines, spotted neck, right, panel of vertical stripes, loop border. Athens NM 1275 lot.

X.66 Mycenae, krater fragment, dark bird left, barred neck, tilted tail, curved thin feet, panel bordered by triple arcs. Athens NM 2688.

X.67 Mycenae, bowl fragment, crosshatched bird, long legs, curled bill; panel bordered by loops.

X.68 Mycenae, bowl fragment, dark "duck" left, "teeth" in bill. Athens NM 1303.4; Furtwängler-Loeschcke, *MV*, pl. XXXIX.400.

X.69 Mycenae, group of small bowl fragments, bird heads with hooked bills, dotted eyes, one body filled with concentric loops, under row of zigzags. Athens NM 1275 lot, nos. 5, 7, and 3.

X.70 Mycenae, krater fragment, twisted rope handle and lattice of white paint below, bird right with hooked bill. Athens NM 1275.28.

X.71 Mycenae, Citadel House, duck's head as protome(?) on hatched triangle. H. Wace, C. Williams, *Mycenae Guide* (1963) 34.

X.72 Mycenae, krater fragment, two birds left, one filled with wavy lines, one with spirals. Athens NM 3670.6 (1275).

X.73 Mycenae, bowl fragment scraps, two dark tails and feet, one body striped, one filled with scales. Athens NM 1292, 3383, 1298, 3653.

X.74 Mycenae, krater fragments, dark birds in compartments, arched zigzag frame, triangle-filled circles. Athens NM 1303; Furtwängler-Loeschcke, *MV*, pl. XXXIX.399 a–b.

X.75 Mycenae, bowl fragment, dark bird, spread wings, white dotted collar, slashes on wings, curled claws. G. Mylonas, *Praktika* 1970, pl. 169.

X.76 Dendra, fragment, bird left at ground line, body of spiral curves. G. Walberg, *OpAth* 7 (1967) 163, no. 17, pl. I.

X.77 Athens, Acropolis, bowl fragment, checkerboard panel bordered with dark filled loops, round bird with long flamingo neck left, filled with horizontal wavy lines. Graef-Langlotz, *VA* I, no. 229, pl. 7 (two lower framing bands lost since publication).

X.78 Athens, Acropolis, bowl fragment, panel of zigzags in verticals, bird right filled with wavy lines, fringed tail and wing. Graef-Langlotz, *VA* I, no. 230, pl. 7. Cf. BM A706.

X.79 Athens, Acropolis, bowl fragment, panel of verticals enclosing loops, bird right, crosshatched triangular tail. Graef-Langlotz, *VA* I, no. 231.

X.80 Athens, Acropolis Fountain, fragment of closed shape, dark ducks right. O. Broneer, *Hesperia* 8 (1939) 397, fig. 78 p.

X.81 Athens, North Slope, krater fragment, two dark birds, open loop bodies, right. Agora AP 1072; O. Broneer, *Hesperia* 8 (1939) 360, fig. 37 j. Fig. 37 f and h preserve feet and bodies of two more birds.

X.82 Unknown provenance, intact krater with strap handles, three birds right, variously filled. Münzen und Medaillen, Basel, Auktion 10 (1951) no. 390, pl. 18; K. Schefold, *Meisterwerke Griechischer Kunst* (1960) no. 28.

FISH

X.83 Mycenae, fragment of small rounded vase (found with soldier, X.29); fish right, scalloped contours, interior wavy lines. Athens NM 2380; Chr. Tsountas, *EphArch* 1888, 161; N. Yalouris, *AthMitt* 75 (1960) Beil. 26.2 (upside down).

X.84 Mycenae, deep bowl fragment, neat outlined fish right, pointed mouth, five stripes on shoulder, wavy line on body, sharp dorsal and ventral fins. Athens NM 2654.

X.85 Mycenae, banded bowl rim, two fish right in pursuit; striped and oblique filling. H. Wace, C. Williams, *Mycenae Guide* (1963) 34.

X.86 Mycenae, jar shoulder fragment, vertical panel with zigzag, zigzag arc in field, one fish right filled with fine zigzags and slanted dashes like vertebra, chasing two fish with long fringed tails. Subsidiary S-pattern, arc-filled triangle. Athens NM 3051.

X.87 Mycenae, fragment from upper body of stirrup jar(?), fish filled with wavy lines and patches of stripes, right toward vertical panel with loop border. Athens NM 1303 lot; Furtwängler-Loeschcke, *MV*, pl. XXXIX.402; Furumark, *MP*, FM 20.12, III C:1.

X.88 Mycenae, krater rim fragment, heavy outlined fish filled with parallel dashes, rising to rim, scale-patterned ground. Athens NM (illegible) (.4, .30); part of 1298 lot?

X.89 Mycenae, bowl rim fragment, loop border, simple

fish right, filled with zigzag. Athens NM 1298 lot (.338 or .358).

X.90 Mycenae, bowl rim fragment, two striped fish close to top, one with three dorsal fins. Athens NM 1298 lot (.30).

X.91 Mycenae, deep bowl fragment, crosshatched fish with forked tail right. Athens NM 3692.

X.92 Mycenae, closed vessel fragment, fish body and tail with white spots. E. Wace, *BSA* 49 (1954) pl. 48 c 4.

X.93 Mycenae, two sherds with simple striped fish. Athens NM 3693.4, 3694.

X.94. Mycenae, sherd, striped fish. Athens NM 3686.

X.95 Mycenae, bowl rim fragment, humped fish obliquely striped upside down at rim, rock semicircles and "seaweed." Athens NM 3687 (.4) (1294); Furtwängler-Loeschcke, *MV,* pl. XL.415.

X.96 Argos, fanged dark dolphin with curled snout left, reserved contours, swimming toward vertical panel bordered in loops. Leiden 1905/1.64; W. Vollgraff, *BCH* 30 (1906) 43, fig. 71, "un fragment d'un vase archaïque," from dump after excavation; Furumark, *MP,* FM 20.11 (III C:1); J. Crouwel, *BABesch* 47 (1972) 14, fig. 1.

X.97 Athens, Acropolis Fountain, paneled krater fragment, fantailed fish, in metope with zigzag verticals, long lower fin like bird's wing. Agora AP 2658 (IX B); O. Broneer, *Hesperia* 8 (1939) 360, fig. 37g (posed swimming right to left).

X.98 Athens, Acropolis Fountain, krater fragment, fish right, wavy-line filling. Agora AP 2661 (V); O. Broneer, *Hesperia* 8 (1939) 360, fig. 37 c.

X.99 Athens, Acropolis Fountain, lekane (-kalathos) fragments, white on black, fish right, wavy-line filling. Agora AP 2779 (VII B); O. Broneer, *Hesperia* 8 (1939) 373, fig. 54 s, t, u, v. There would have been three fish swimming in a circle inside.

X.100 Athens, Agora, lekane (-kalathos), three fish, or two fish and a bird, right, crude wavy line filling. Agora P 21200; H. Thompson, *Hesperia* 21 (1952), pl. 26 a; E. Townsend, *Hesperia* 24 (1955) 214, pl. 75, no. 24; S. Immerwahr, *Agora XIII: The Neolithic and Bronze Ages,* 188, VII-24, pl. 40, no. 24.

X.101 Salamis, concave cup, fish, diagonal striped filling. Koulouri, 1964; *BCH* 92 (1968) 773, fig. 2 left.

X.102 Salamis(?), krater, three thick fish right. *Hesperia Art Bulletin* I (spring 1957) no. 28; reference courtesy of the late J. R. Stewart; *CVA* Kassel I, pl. I.1-2 (T.705); *AA* 1972, 3, fig. 4; H.-G. Buchholz, G. Jöhrens, I. Maull, *Jagd und Fischfang,* in *Archaeologia Homerica* J (1973) pl. IV b.

X.103 Tanagra, ring vase with arched basket handle and spout, dark fish left on top of ring, light fish right below them, two dark fish on handle. T.15; T. Spyropoulos, *Praktika* 1969, pl. 11 B. For ring vase with whorl shells, *BCH* 102 (1978) 700, fig. 128.

X.104 Tiryns, krater handle fragment, dark fish with light rippled fantail obliquely upward from handle. Nauplion Museum 14 267; German Archaeological Institute photo 546; Slenczka, *Tiryns* VII, no. 40, pl. 37.1 a.

X.105 Tiryns, fragment of closed vase, two dark fish with reserved contours right, open mouth, stripe fins, splayed tail. N. Verdelis, *Deltion* 18 (1963) pl. 88 c; south water channel. Nauplion Museum 14 355; Slenczka, *Tiryns* VII, no. 137, pl. 37.1 b.

X.106 Tiryns, cup fragment, two dark fish with reserved contours obliquely right, open mouth, barred "beard," stripe fins, splayed tail. Nauplion Museum 14 356; Slenczka, *Tiryns* VII, no. 138, pl. 37.1 c.

X.107 Tiryns, foot of stirrup jar, dark fish with reserved contours right along the base line (a III C octopus stirrup jar?), neat groups of three stripes for fins. Nauplion Museum 14 302; German Archaeological Institute photo 546; Slenczka, *Tiryns* VII, no. 76, pl. 37.1 d.

X.108 Tiryns, krater fragment, massive-headed dark fish feeding right along base line, trefoil rosette as "seaweed." Nauplion Museum 14 301; German Archaeological Institute photo 546; Slenczka, *Tiryns* VII, no. 75, pl. 37.1 e.

X.109 Tiryns, bowl rim fragment, light outlined fish right, single wavy line down center. Nauplion Museum 14 300; German Archaeological Institute photo 546; Slenczka, *Tiryns* VII, no. 74, pl. 37.2 a.

X.110 Tiryns, krater fragment, simple outlined fish obliquely upward right, two wavy line fillers. Nauplion Museum 14 258; German Archaeological Institute photo 567; Slenczka, *Tiryns* VII, no. 30, pl. 37.2 c.

X.111 Tiryns, krater fragment, two fine light fish one above the other in school, above base line; central horizontal ripple, stripe fins, fringed fantails. Nauplion Museum 14 370; Slenczka, *Tiryns* VII, no. 153, pl. 37.2 e; cf. *Tiryns* V (1971) 92, no. 5, fig. 3.

X.112 Tiryns, open vase fragment, two fine fish right in narrow frieze inside vase, open mouth, small eye, barred gill arc, delicate multiple horizontal ripples, fins hooking backward, under curved arc filled with neat zigzag. Nauplion Museum 14 399; Slenczka, *Tiryns* VII, no. 182, pl. 37.2 d.

X.113 Tiryns, open vase fragment, perhaps lekane (-kalathos), simple fish right, white-on-black technique, two interior ripples framing straight "spine," blunt nose, stripe fins. Nauplion Museum 14 354; Slenczka, *Tiryns* VII, no. 136, pl. 37.2 b.

X.114 Tiryns(?), Argolid, krater fragment, handsome fish right, chevron vertebrae, open mouth, rectangular gill area with centered eye, barred contour lines. Slenczka, *Tiryns* VII, no. 252, pl. 38.1 a.

X.115 Tiryns(?), Argolid, inside center of shallow bowl or cup, dark fish with large open mouth and teeth, circling after a diving crosshatched fish with reserved contours and dark fins. Slenczka, *Tiryns* VII, no. 252, pl. 38.1 b.

X.116 Tiryns, fragmentary strap-handled krater, large dolphin type right, massive head, reserved undulating stripe with interior streamers along body, dark streamers (seaweed) in field, stripes for grass on bottom. P. Gercke, U. Naumann, *AAA* 7 (1974) 23, fig. 15.

X.117 Monemvasia, stirrup jar, lower body filled with large fish right, dark head, reserved eye, ripples along body; P. Demakopoulos, *Deltion,* 1968 a, pl. 76.1.

The Greek Mainland: Late Pictorial

CHARIOTS AND HORSES

XI.1 Mycenae, two krater fragments, two shield-bearing soldiers on each, in light open chariot with high rail, non-charioteer armed with spear. **A:** Athens NM 3596 (1272 lot); Furtwängler-Loeschcke, *MV*, pl. XLI.427; Montelius, *GP* II, pl. 135.6; Furumark *MP*, FM 1.34, III C:1; Lorimer, *HM*, 316, pl. II. 3. **B:** the sherd from Schliemann's dump, Nauplion Museum 83 57; A. J. B. Wace, *Mycenae* (1949) pl. 71 c; H. Wace, C. Williams, *Mycenae Guide* (1963) 31; A. Snodgrass, *Early Greek Armour and Weapons* (1964) pl. 20. Both: H. Catling, *AJA* 72 (1968) pl. 23.19; Benson, *HBM*, pl. XII.2, 4; M. A. Littauer, *AJA* 76 (1972) 146, ill. 2; N. K. Sandars, *The Sea Peoples* (1978) 188 f., fig. 123.

XI.2 Mycenae, two krater fragments; on each, chariot, driver, and rear legs of horse right. Athens NM 1141; Furtwängler-Loeschcke, *MV*, pl. XXXVIII.390–391; H. Catling, *AJA* 72 (1968) pl. 23.20.

XI.3 Mycenae, krater fragment, driver or groom left in tunic and greaves, backing a horse into a chariot? Athens NM 2580; Chr. Tsountas, *EphArch* 1891, 26, pl. 3.2 (from house remains northwest of the Lion Gate); Staïs, *MycColl²*, 135, from the entrance to a tholos tomb; W. Reichel, *Homerische Waffen²* (1901) fig. 30; Lorimer, *HM*, pl. 12.2; *JHS* 49 (1929) 155, fig. 4; for the armament see Tsountas' discussion; N. Verdelis, *AthMitt* 82 (1967) Beil. 33.2; Buchholz, Karageorghis, *Altägäis*, no. 1000; P. Åström, *The Cuirass Tomb and Other Finds at Dendra*, SIMA IV.I (1977) pl. XXXII .2.

XI.4 Mycenae, krater rim fragment, driver right with horses' reins. G. Mylonas, *Praktika* 1970, pl. 169 top.

XI.5 Mycenae, krater rim fragment, driver right with goad(?). G. Mylonas, *Praktika* 1970, pl. 169 center.

XI.6 Mycenae, bowl rim fragment, poorly drawn, driver in high-railed open chariot right; another follows. Fine fabric. Athens NM 1294.25; Furtwängler-Loeschcke, *MV*, pl. XL.420; Furumark, *MP*, 334, FM 1.39, III C:1 (the head is not cut off as in this drawing, but overlaps the upper frame); FM 39.22 (restored), III C:1.

XI.7 Mycenae, krater fragment, polychrome, soldier backing horse (left) into chariot (right). Athens NM 4691; Staïs, *MycColl²*, 135 (with XI.3, same provenance although the numbers are far apart); G. Rodenwaldt, *Der Fries des Megarons von Mykenai* (1921) 24, fig. 14; Lorimer, *HM*, pl. XII.1; Furumark, *MP*, FM 2.9 (III C:1); J. L. Benson, *AJA* 65 (1961) pl. 108, fig. 39; N. Verdelis, *AthMitt* 82 (1967) Beil. 33.1; Buchholz, Karageorghis, *Altägäis*, no. 1001; P. Åström, *The Cuirass Tomb and Other Finds at Dendra*, SIMA IV.1 (1977) pl. XXXII.1.

XI.8 Mycenae, krater rim fragment, diamond-eyed helmeted soldier with staff, leading horse right. Athens NM 1141; H. Schliemann, *Mycenae and Tiryns* (1880) pl. X.47; Furtwängler-Loeschcke, *MV*, pl. XXXVIII.395; Montelius, *GP* II, pl. 135.5; Furumark, *MP*, FM 1.31 (III C:1).

XI.9 Mycenae, krater fragment, dispirited horse filled with concentric arcs, left. Athens NM 1141 lot; Furtwängler-Loeschcke, *MV*, pl. XXXVIII.389; Montelius, *GP* II, pl. 135.12.

XI.10 Mycenae, krater fragment, chariot horse left with hook-spiral reins, dark rump, crosshatched belly, chevron flower under belly. Athens NM 1141 lot; Furtwängler-Loeschcke, *MV*, pl. XXXVIII.392; Montelius, *GP* II, pl. 135.15.

XI.11 Mycenae, bowl fragment, thin tube-bodied horse (or stag?) right, dark legs, body filled with arcs, zigzag tail with herringbone hairs. Athens NM 1303 lot; Furtwängler-Loeschcke, *MV*, pl. XXXIX.406.

XI.12 Mycenae, bowl fragment, facing horse's head. Athens NM 1294 lot; Furtwängler-Loeschcke, *MV*, pl. XL.421.

XI.13 Mycenae, collared jar, three dark horses right, two dark and four light birds. W. Taylour, *JHS ArcRep* 1964-65, 11, fig. 12; *BCH* 89 (1965) 716, fig. 19; J. L. Benson, *AJA* 72 (1968) 207, pl. 67, fig. 10; *HBM*, pl. VII.2; G. Kopcke, in *The Dark Ages in Greece* (1977) 47, no. 25.

XI.14 Tiryns, fragment of large open krater; on one side, team, chariot box and wheel, four passengers, groom in front; on the other side, chariot wheel, rail, and part of horse. Nauplion Museum 13 208; N. Verdelis, *EphArch* 1956, Par. 6, fig. 10; Slenczka, *Tiryns* VII, no. 86, pl. 3.2, pl. 4.

XI.15 Tiryns, fragmentary krater, two chariots right, front chariot omitted and passengers installed on back of team. Nauplion Museum 13 214; N. Verdelis, *EphArch* 1956, Par. 6, fig. 11; E. Slenczka, *Tiryns* VII, no. 85, pl. 3.1; the author considers it a view of three horseback riders abreast.

XI.15.1 Nauplion Museum 14 315, *Tiryns* VII, no. 97, pl. 2.2 c.

XI.15.2 Groom with splayed hand behind large chariot wheel, square axle-box. Nauplion Museum 14 340; Slenczka, *Tiryns* VII, no. 119, pl. 6.2 d.

XI.16 Tiryns, fragmentary krater, two or three open chariots right, each with driver and shield-bearing spearman. Nauplion Museum 14 336; part, N. Verdelis, *Deltion* 18 (1963) Chron., B'1, pl. 85 b ("III B-C"); more sherds added in *AthMitt* 82 (1967) pl. 1, Beil. 34.3; M. A. Littauer, *AJA* 76 (1972) 146, ill. 1. There are more joins since then, especially the mane from the north water channel joined on the second team from the south channel; feet on the chariot straps of the leading vehicle, parts of two men in tunics with bent knees behind the chariot rail, from between the channels. X.16.1 may also belong. Incomplete pictures, Benson, *HBM*, pl. X.5; Buchholz, Karageorghis, *Altägäis*, no. 997; G. Kopcke, in *The Dark Ages in Greece* (1977) 46, no. 24; P. Åström, *The Cuirass Tomb and Other Finds at Dendra*, SIMA IV.1 (1977) pl. XXXII.8. The fullest version is in Slenczka, *Tiryns* VII, no. 115 A, B, C, 53, fig. 15, pl. 2.1, pl. 2.2 a, b, and Beil. 1. (Beil. 1 includes the head of a man in a hat, placed over the last chariot, which we understood to belong with the horse fragments of XI.16.1, perhaps wrongly.)

XI.16.1 Tiryns, two or three krater fragments, horse right, with fine mane plumes, dark body, belly panel filled with ripples; top of mane, neck, chest, and belly preserved. The soldier in a bonnet agrees in fabric and color; if the horse is from the reverse of XI.16, the soldier could go on either side; Slenczka decided to keep the fragments distinct. Nauplion Museum 14 337, Slenczka, *Tiryns* VII, head, no. 115 B, pl. 2.2 a; horse, no. 116 A, B, pl. 5.2 c, f; head, P. Åström, *The*

Cuirass Tomb and Other Finds at Dendra, SIMA IV.1 (1977) pl. XXXII.6.

XI.17 Tiryns, two fragments of paneled krater, drivers immediately right of panel, no passenger, reins high. Nauplion Museum 14 372; Slenczka, *Tiryns* VII, no. 155, p. 69, fig. 19, pl. 9.1 a, b.

XI.18 Tiryns(?), krater fragment, parts of two warriors in open-railed chariot, wearing tunic and greaves, one warrior with two spears. Heidelberg Inv. 27/12; *CVA* Heidelberg 3, pl. 92, no. 22; E. Jastrow, *AA* 1927, 250; F. Schachermeyr, *Anthropos* 46 (1951) 727, n. 25; G. Becatti, *Studi Luisa Banti* (1965) 45, pl. 13; N. Verdelis, *AthMitt* 82 (1967) Beil. 34.1; H. Catling, *AJA* 72 (1968) pl. 23.21; P. Åström, *The Cuirass Tomb and Other Finds at Dendra, SIMA* IV.1 (1977) pl. XXXII.7.

XI.19 Tiryns, bowl fragment, two chariots racing(?) right. Athens NM (unknown); H. Schliemann, *Tiryns* (1885) fig. 155; Furumark, *MP*, FM 1.38 (III C:1). See Addenda.

XI.20 Tiryns, fragment of collared jar, team and three soldiers right (crying?). German Archaeological Institute photo Tiryns 550.

XI.21 Tiryns, krater fragment, team right, dark neck, pale face, harness. Nauplion Museum 14 265, German Archaeological Institute photo Tiryns 550, west stairs, north edge; Slenczka, *Tiryns* VII, no. 37, pl. 5.1 f.

XI.22 Tiryns, small krater fragment, team right with outlined weak face, round eye, dark neck; in front, facing back and gesturing with right arm up, small soldier holding round shield by hand-grip. H. Schliemann, *Tiryns* (1885) fig. 153.

XI.23 Tiryns, krater fragment, nose, chest, and striped forelegs of horse (or stag?) right, body edged with scale pattern. H. Schliemann, *Tiryns* (1885) fig. 151.

XI.24 Tiryns, krater fragment, team right, heads separated by vertical line between eyes, so it seems "facing," outlined mane plumes, dark scallops edging neck so pale face continues down in vertical ripple. Nauplion Museum 14 379; Slenczka, *Tiryns* VII, no. 162, pl. 5.1 c. A comparable piece is no. 161, which keeps the traditional pendants from the pole brace but opens up the face in a dark body.

XI.25 Tiryns, krater fragments. A: team right, dark body, reserved bulbous "octopus" face filled with transverse slashes. German Archaeological Institute photo Tiryns 580, upper right; B: team right, dark body, reserved bulbous face, pendent ripples from pole brace, ibid.; C: tunic and legs/greaves of soldier, reserved contours on skirt of tunic? German Archaeological Institute photo Tiryns 550, right center; D: bird with belt and arcs, under the handle; all now Nauplion Museum 14 244; Slenczka, *Tiryns* VII, no. 16, pl. 6.1.

XI.26 Tiryns, krater fragment, open chariot with curved rail right, dark driver, arms bent up at elbow. Nauplion Museum 14 305; Slenczka, *Tiryns* VII, no. 80, pl. 6.2 b.

XI.27 Tiryns, krater fragment, driver in spotted robe right, in closed-panel chariot ornamented with arc or scale. The fragment may be earlier and is in the Ripe tradition of men in robes and the old-style chariot. Nauplion Museum 14 307; Slenczka, *Tiryns* VII, no. 81, pl. 6.2 c.

XI.28 Tiryns, fragment of krater, two soldiers in chariot(?) moving left, wearing new hip-length tunics with interior scalloped borders and fringed hem, "hedgehog" helmets, carrying new small round shields, with two light spears.

Driver(?) at left raises both arms (to lost reins?). *JHS ArcRep* 1977-78, 27, fig. 48. See Addenda.

XI.29 Tiryns, krater fragment, disjointed horse's neck right, striped, strokes for mane, fringed eye in front of neck. German Archaeological Institute photo Tiryns 583.

XI.30 Tiryns, larnax fragment, rear legs of tall spotted horse, attached to chariot by drooping strap; wheel rim. Nauplion Museum 14 338; N. Verdelis, *Deltion* 18 (1963) Chron. B'1, pl. 85 a; Slenczka, *Tiryns* VII, no. 117, pl. 5.2 h.

XI.31 Tiryns, larnax or pinax fragment, driver right, round helmet or cap, long hair behind, curls on brow, striped neck, reserved chest with nipples, arc-filled arm, zigzag-filled tubular body. Nauplion Museum 14 341; N. Verdelis, *AthMitt* 82 (1967) 28, no. 18, pl. 2.3, Beil. 34.2; E. Vermeule, *A Land Called Crete* (1968) fig. 38; Buchholz, Karageorghis, *Altägäis*, no. 996; Slenczka, *Tiryns* VII, no. 120, pl. 8.2 h; P. Åström, *The Cuirass Tomb and Other Finds at Dendra, SIMA* IV.1 (1977) pl. XXXII.3. The other Tiryns fragments that may once have formed part of chariot compositions are:

31.1 Weak outlined horse's head right, heavy contour under jaw, but no head surface where the eye hangs; three reins hang from lips. Traces of groom-soldier leading. German Archaeological Institute photo Tiryns 550.

31.2 Outlined horse's head left, tracery of curves before face with reverse curves beyond; ears pricked up. German Archaeological Institute photo Tiryns 550.

31.3 Striped bird(?) perched on dark horse rump, reins and traces. German Archaeological Institute photo Tiryns 580.

31.4 Dark hand holding reserved circular object with two striped vertical slots; a yoke or railing? German Archaeological Institute photo Tiryns 580; Slenczka, *Tiryns* VII, no. 9, pl. 8.2 c.

31.5 Two disjointed four-spoked wheels near ground line, evidently not just ornament. German Archaeological Institute photo Tiryns 550; Slenczka, *Tiryns* VII, no. 51, pl. 38.2 e.

XI.32 Athens, Acropolis, krater rim fragment, outlined driver right, high long arm, two reins. Graef-Langlotz, *VA* I, 223.

XI.33 Athens, Acropolis, krater rim fragment, charioteer clasping both hands to head; stripe to right from body, reins tied around waist? Graef-Langlotz, *VA* I, pl. 7.220; Montelius, *GP* I, pl. 107.6.

XI.34 Athens, Acropolis, krater rim fragment. Chariot rail(?), triangle with curved top, straight bar under it, projecting line left toward bottom of line, double loop at lower left. Graef-Langlotz, *VA* I, no. 224.

XI.35 Athens, Acropolis, bowl rim fragment, gesturing dark figure with splayed hand left. Graef-Langlotz, *VA* I, no. 225.

XI.36 Athens, Acropolis, Fountain, paneled krater fragments, rear of horse left. Agora AP 2668, 2670 a; O. Broneer, *Hesperia* 8 (1939) 361, fig. 38; another fragment has what may be seen as either the legs of a running man or the claws of a bird.

XI.37 Leukandi, krater rim and wall fragment, charioteer right, driver with four thongs from calf to chariot floor, arrow hands, two reins, diagonal strap from driver's waist to dark horse's rump. M. Popham, *BSA* 61 (1966) 103, fig. 25, pl. 16 a; H. Catling, *AJA* 72 (1968) 41, pl. 21, fig. 1; M. A. Littauer, *AJA* 76 (1972) 157, ill. 10; N. K. Sandars, *The Sea Peoples* (1978) fig. 123.

XI.38 Leukandi, krater fragment, dark horse rump and tail left, leaping soldier higher left, wearing tunic and greaves, upward diagonal to his waist with barb(?) pointing toward him. M. Popham, L. Sackett, *Excavations at Lefkandi, Euboea* (1968) 20, fig. 40.

XI.39 Leukandi, krater fragment, black and white soldier-groom right, raised arms, black team with white stripes behind him. M. Popham, L. Sackett, *Excavations at Lefkandi, Euboea* (1968) 20, fig. 41.

XI.40 Perati, stirrup jar, horse left with "axe" over back, "arrow" from mane. Perati T. 92, no. 715; S. Iakovides, *Ergon* 1959, 10, fig. 6; *Perati, To Nekrotapheion* (1970) A:204, B:151, fig. 24, pl. 60; *BCH* 84 (1960) 661, fig. 1; F. Schachermeyr, *AA* 1962, 230; Benson, *HBM*, 23–24, pl. III.2.

XI.41 Salamis, krater with vertical strap handle, chariot and driver right, hunting down a deer(?). E. Mastrokostas, press report, *Ethnous* (A. Paradeisis) 10 August 1959.

SOLDIERS

XI.42 Mycenae, krater with twisted handles and bull(?) protomes; side A, woman and six soldiers right; side B, five soldiers set to throw spears, right. Athens NM 1426; H. Schliemann, *Mycenae* (1880) 132, fig. 213; Furtwängler-Loeschcke, *MV*, pls. XLII–XLIII; P. Arndt, *Studien zur Vasenkunde* (1887) 4; O. Rayet, M. Collignon, *Histoire de la céramique grecque* (1888) 18, fig. 16; F. Dümmler, *AthMitt* 13 (1888) 291; A. Dumont, J. Chaplain, *Céramiques de la Grèce propre* (1888–1890) 58; Chr. Tsountas, *EphArch* 1891, 26, n. 4; *EphArch* 1896, 1 f.; K. Schuchhardt, *Schliemann's Excavations* (1891) 280, figs. 284–285; P. Girard, *La Peinture antique* (1892) 127 f., fig. 71; G. Perrot, C. Chipiez, *Histoire de l'Art* VI (1894) 937; E. Pottier, *RevArch* 28 (1896) 19; Chr. Tsountas, J. Manatt, *The Mycenaean Age* (1897) 190, pl. 18; W. Reichel, *Homerische Waffen*[2] (1901) 46, figs. 24, 37; G. Nicole, *Supplement au catalogue des vases peints du Musée National d'Athènes* (1911) no. 309; H. Brunn, *Zur Griechischen Kunstgeschichte* (1905) 44, fig. 48; W. Klein, *Geschichte der griechischen Kunst* (1904) I, 29; E. Pottier, *BCH* 31 (1907) 247; D. Mackenzie, *BSA* 13 (1906-07) 433; Staïs, *MycColl*[2], 106-107, no. 1426; M. G. Zimmerman, *Kunstgeschichte des Altertums* (1914) 18, fig. 14; H. T. Bossert, *Altkreta* (1921) figs. 198-199; (1923) 193 f., figs. 265-266; (1937) 72 f., figs. 133-135; G. Glotz, *The Aegean Civilization* (1925) 72, fig. 9; H. R. Hall, *The Civilization of Greece in the Bronze Age* (1928) 262, fig. 338; J. Charbonneaux, *L'Art Égéen* (1929) pl. LXIV; L. B. Holland, *AJA* 33 (1929) 201, fig. 11; W. Schuchhardt, *Kunst der Griechen* (1940) fig. 28; P. Ducati, *L'Arte Classica* (1944) 82, fig. 95; A. Wace, *Mycenae* (1949) pl. 82 a-b; Lorimer, *HM*, 146, 200, pl. III:1 a-b; A. Furumark, *MP*, FM 1.28-29; 425, 437, 448, 452; F. Matz, *Die Ägäis* (1954) pl. 39.1; B. Schweitzer, *RömMitt* 62 (1955) 82, pl. 36.1; G. Becatti, *Studi in Onore di Luisa Banti* (1956) 33 f., pls. 11-13; T. B. L. Webster, *From Mycenae to Homer* (1958) pl. 7; D. Gray, *BICS* 6 (1959) 49, pl. V; S. Marinatos, M. Hirmer, *Crete and Mycenae* (1960) pls. 232-233; N. Yalouris, *AthMitt* 75 (1960) Beil. 24; F. Schachermeyr, *Griechische Geschichte* (1960) pl. 11 a; A. Wace, F. Stubbings, *A Companion to Homer* (1962) 502, 508,

pl. 29; F. Matz, *Kreta, Mykene, Troia* (1962) pl. 109; M. Davidson, L. Cottrell et al., *The Horizon Book of Lost Worlds* (1962) 291; H. Müller-Karpe, *Germania* 40 (1962) 258, fig. 1; J. Wiesner, *Bilder zur abendländischen Kunst* (1963) fig. 352 b; V. Desborough, *The Last Mycenaeans and Their Successors* (1964) 63; P. Demargne, *The Birth of Greek Art* (1964) figs. 331, 336; A. Snodgrass, *Early Greek Armour and Weapons* (1964) 57 f.; *Arms and Armour of the Greeks* (1967) 30, pls. 10–11; W. Taylour, *The Mycenaeans* (1964) pl. 7; E. Vermeule, *Greece in the Bronze Age* (1964) 208 f., pl. XXXIII b; W. H. Hale, *The Horizon Book of Greece* (1965) 46; N. Oakeshott, *JHS* 86 (1966) pl. 5; N. Verdelis, *AthMitt* 82 (1967) 23, 34, Beil. 32.1; P. Mingazzini, *Annuario* 45-46 (1967-68) 327 f., figs. 1, 5; S. Marinatos, *Kleidung, Haar-und Barttracht*, in *Archaeologia Homerica* B (1967) pl. III d; R. Higgins, *Minoan and Mycenaean Art* (1967) fig. 143; A. Lacy, *Greek Pottery in the Bronze Age* (1967) fig. 94 c; W. Schuchhardt, *Festschrift U. Jantzen* (1969) 153; Benson, *HBM*, pls. 18.4, 36.2; *IEE*, 285; J.-C. Stobart, R. Hopper, *The Glory That Was Greece* (1971) fig. 37 b; J. Borchhardt, *Homerische Helme* (1972) 37 f., pls. 12.3, 16.3, 18.2; A. Sakellariou, G. Papathanasopoulos, *Prehistoric Collections, The National Museum, Athens* (1970) 44, pl. 166; Buchholz, Karageorghis, *Altägäis*, no. 1025; N. K. Sandars, *The Sea Peoples* (1978) figs. 91, 119, 123-125; and many others.

XI.43 Mycenae, limestone stele covered with stucco and painted; three tiers: A, homage scene(?), B, five soldiers right with raised spears; C, stag, three does, and hedgehog right. Athens NM 3256; Chr. Tsountas, *EphArch* 1896, 1 f., pls. 1-2; *EphArch* 1888, 127; Rodenwaldt, *Tiryns* II, 186; F. Studniczka, *Griechische Kunst an Kriegergräbern* (1915) pl. 1.2; H. T. Bossert, *Altkreta*[3] (1937) 33, fig. 45; P. Ducati, *L'Arte Classica* (1944) 83, fig. 96; Lorimer, *HM*, pl. II.2; Furumark, *MP*, 240, 256, 449, 453; G. Becatti, *Studi in Onore di Luisa Banti* (1956) pl. 13 a; A. Wace, F. Stubbings, *A Companion to Homer* (1962) pl. 29 b; H.-G. Buchholz, *BJV* 5 (1965) 71, pl. 13.5; Vermeule, *GBA*, fig. 47; N. Verdelis, *AthMitt* 82 (1967) 24, Beil. 32.2; G. Hafner, *Art of Crete, Mycenae and Greece* (1968) 55; M. Andronikos, *Totenkult in Archaeologia Homerica* W (1968) 117, fig. 9; Buchholz, Karageorghis, *Altägäis*, no. 1071; F. Stubbings, *Prehistoric Greece* (1973) 37, fig. 36.

XI.44 Mycenae, krater fragment, soldier in check-skirted tunic, right, with spear and ration bag(?). Athens NM 1141 lot; Furtwängler-Loeschcke, *MV*, pl. XXXVIII.394; Furumark, *MP*, FM 1.33 (III C:1); N. Verdelis, *AthMitt* 82 (1967) 24, Beil. 33.5; P. Åström, *The Cuirass Tomb and Other Finds at Dendra*, *SIMA* IV.1 (1977) pl. XXXII.5.

XI.45 Mycenae, krater fragment, two soldiers in "hedgehog" helmets, right. Collection F. Wiegand; E. Pernice, *RömMitt* 59 (1944 [1948]) 185; H.-G. Buchholz, *BJV* 5 (1965) 80, fig. 10; J. Borchhardt, *Homerische Helme* (1972) pl. 18.1.

XI.46 Mycenae, krater fragment, soldier in "hedgehog" helmet (with horns fore and aft) right. Athens NM 2674; W. Reichel, *Homerische Waffen*[2] (1901) 107, fig. 44; M. Mayer, *JdI* 7 (1892) 195, fig. 5; Furumark, *MP*, FM 1.32 (III C:1); E. Pernice, *RömMitt* 59 (1944) 189, fig. 4; Lorimer, *HM*, 230, fig. 26; J. Borchhardt, *Homerische Helme* (1972) pl. 18.4.

XI.47 Mycenae (Charvati), krater fragment, two heads, one in "hedgehog" helmet, one in hat, right. Athens NM, not found; Furtwängler-Loeschcke, *MV*, fig. 37; Furumark, *MP*, FM 1.30, III C:1; Slenczka, *Tiryns* VII, pl. 9.4.

XI.48 Mycenae, krater fragment, top of conical helmet with striped, triangular cup-socket, plume with dots down back, single plume in front. Athens NM 1212 lot.

XI.49 Tiryns, rhyton or stirrup jar(?) fragment, soldier leaping high in full armor, short sword in right hand. N. Verdelis, *AthMitt* 82 (1967) 28, no. 17, pl. 2.1, Beil. 33.3; Slenczka, *Tiryns* VII, no. 121, pl. 8.1 a; P. Åström, *The Cuirass Tomb and Other Finds at Dendra*, SIMA IV.1 (1977) pl. XXXII.4.

XI.50 Tiryns, krater fragment, three checkerboard and three reserved panels; dark figure (thigh to foot) skipping or dancing left at top, dark shape lower left. Nauplion Museum 14 271; Slenczka, *Tiryns* VII, no. 44, fig. 8, pl. 9.1 c; cf. H. Bulle, *Orchomenos* I (1907) 72 f., pl. 28.

XI.51 Tiryns, krater fragment, soldier in "hedgehog" helmet with spear, left. Courtesy the late N. Verdelis, 1965; Nauplion Museum 14 344; Slenczka, *Tiryns* VII, no. 123, pl. 8.2 h.

XI.52 Tiryns(?), small krater fragment, soldier or charioteer in "hedgehog" helmet with reserved contours and long bristle spikes, arm right with spread fingers, two lines on rising diagonal, reins or javelins. Slenczka, *Tiryns* VII, no. 185, pl. 9.2 b.

XI.53 Tiryns, krater fragment, four dark legs and pale feet right, greaves with reserved ankle-ties(?); shoes pointed down like XI.49. The small scale might suggest two registers. Nauplion Museum 14 272; German Archaeological Institute photo Tiryns 550; Slenczka, *Tiryns* VII, no. 46, fig. 9, pl. 8.2 f.

XI.54 Tiryns, water channels, closed vessel fragment, striped neck of soldier in dark tunic, right arm raised behind head, holding sword with round outlined pommel(?). Courtesy the late N. Verdelis, 1965; Nauplion Museum 14 343; Slenczka, *Tiryns* VII, no. 122, pl. 8.1 b.

XI.55 Tiryns(?), krater fragment, small dark man running right, in panel with dark filled arcs against inner border. Slenczka, *Tiryns* VII, no. 187, pl. 9.2 d.

XI.55.1 Tiryns, krater fragment, dark leaf-bladed spear on shaft, helmet(?). German Archaeological Institute photo Tiryns 550. See also Athens Acropolis, krater fragment, two leaf-bladed spears(?), Graef-Langlotz, *VA* I, pl. 2.56.

XI.56 Amarynthos, krater fragment, man (driver) right with three long ripples of hair floating behind, followed by (man in) "hedgehog" helmet. L. Sackett, V. Hankey, R. Howell, T. Jacobsen, M. Popham, *BSA* 61 (1966) 33 f., 64, no. 62, 103, fig. 28, no. 66, pl. 16 b right.

XI.57 Iolkos, krater; side A, rim fragment, two soldiers in "hedgehog" helmets marching right with spears; side B, man in metal(?) corselet gesturing left. D. Theochares, *Ergon* 1960, 60, fig. 73 a; *Praktika* 1960, 58, fig. 4; G. Daux, *BCH* 85 (1961) 769, fig. 29; F. Schachermeyr, *AA* 1962, 298, fig. 59; H. Buchholz, *BJV* 5 (1965) 80, fig. 9; J. Borchhardt, *Homerische Helme* (1972) 41, fig. 5, pl. 18.3.

XI.58 Iolkos, krater fragment, archer right. D. Theochares, *Ergon* 1960, 60, fig. 73; *Praktika* 1960, 59, fig. 5.

XI.59 Leukandi, krater handle fragment, soldier in checkered kilt with sword, right, toward handle; beyond handle, legs and tail of horse; bull's head modeled on handle with hourglass pattern on tubular muzzle, pellet eyes, punched nostrils, open mouth. LK/66/P319; M. Popham, *JHS ArcRep* 1966-67, 13, fig. 18; M. Popham, L. Sackett, *Excavations at Lefkandi, Euboea* (1968) 20, figs. 38–39; M. Popham, E. Millburn, *BSA* 66 (1971) 340, pl. 57.3.

XI.60 Leukandi, krater rim fragment, capped bearded head right. LK/65/P 122, courtesy M. R. Popham.

XI.61 Leukandi, krater fragment, helmeted warrior left with javelins and shield. LK/65/P 40; M. Popham, L. Sackett, *Excavations at Lefkandi, Euboea* (1968) 20, fig. 43.

XI.62 Leukandi, krater fragment, helmeted warrior right. M. Popham, L. Sackett, *Excavations at Lefkandi, Euboea* (1968) 20, fig. 44.

XI.63 Naxos, krater fragment, soldier's dark legs (reserved contours) right. N. Kontoleon, *Ergon* 1966 (1965) 118–119, fig. 149; *Praktika* 1965, 173, pl. 215B, from the region of the circular hearth by the sacrificial pit.

XI.64 Unknown provenance, krater or bowl rim fragment, helmeted head right. E. Bielefeld, *Wissenschaftliche Zeitschrift der Martin Luther Universität, Halle Wittenburg* 2 (1952-53) 89, no. 37, pl. 4.3; inv. 116.

XI.64.1 Krater rim fragment, two outlined heads right. Tübingen 1467; C. Watzinger, *Griechische Vasen in Tübingen* (1924) no. 6; Slenczka, *Tiryns* VII, 144, pl. 45.1.

OTHER HUMAN FIGURES

XI.65 Leukandi, krater fragment, priest(?) with mother and baby sphinx. LK/65/P 188; M. Popham, L. Sackett, *Excavations at Lefkandi, Euboea* (1968) 19, fig. 37; M. Popham, E. Millburn, *BSA* 66 (1971) pl. 53.6.

XI.66 Leukandi, krater fragment, large and small legs left, two-handled bowl. M. Popham, L. Sackett, *Excavations at Lefkandi, Euboea* (1968) 20, fig. 42.

XI.67 Naxos, hydria, line or ring of dancing men. N. Zapheiropoulos, *Praktika* 1960, pl. 277 c left; *Deltion* 1960, 250, pl. 219.

XI.68 Perati, stirrup jar, man tilted through shoulder bands left. Perati no. 615, T. 75; S. Iakovides, *Ergon* 1958, fig. 29; *Praktika* 1958, pl. 23 d; *Perati* A (1969) 90; B (1970) 151, fig. 24.53, pl. 28 c; Buchholz, Karageorghis, *Altägäis*, no. 995.

XI.69 Tiryns, collared jar(?) fragment, lyre with three strings, player right, sharp five-fingered hand, obscure head. Nauplion Museum 14 376; Slenczka, *Tiryns* VII, no. 159, pl. 9.1 d.

HUNTING SCENES

XI.70 Mycenae, three krater fragments, two huntsmen, two deer, four dogs right. M. Mayer, *JdI* 7 (1892) 195, fig. 5; W. Reichel, *Homerische Waffen²* (1901) fig. 50; Lorimer, *HM*, 230, fig. 25; Å. Åkerström, *OpAth* 1 (1953) 18 f., figs. 5–6; cf. H. Buchholz, V. Karageorghis, *AAA* 3 (1970) 391.

XI.71 Mycenae, two krater fragments, three deer, one dog right. Athens NM 2682, 2687, Tsountas' House; Å. Åkerström, *OpAth* 1 (1953) 21, fig. 7.2, 3.

XI.72 Mycenae, krater rim fragment, fawn (not hare?) and dog left. Athens NM 1303 lot; Furtwängler-Loeschcke, *MV*, pl. XXXIX.411; Montelius, *GP* II, pl. 135.17. A piece of the rim, detached, is in a tray in the basement.

XI.73 Mycenae, krater rim fragment, dog left. Athens NM 1303 lot (3640.3); Furtwängler-Loeschcke, *MV*, pl. XXXIX.410.

XI.74 Mycenae bowl fragment; inside, white-on-black, dog over doe; outside, buff tail and leg. Athens NM 1294; Furtwängler-Loeschcke, *MV*, pl. XL.417; Furumark, *MP*, 449, no. 14; Å. Åkerström, *OpAth* 1 (1953) fig. 7.1.

XI.75 Mycenae, small krater fragment, deer right. Athens NM 1290 lot (300?3).

XI.76 Mycenae, krater fragment, stag running right. Athens NM 1303 lot, Furtwängler-Loeschcke, *MV*, pl. XXXIX.408 (German Archaeological Institute photo Mykenae 254, P.5666). Variations in firing made the legs pale red, the neck and back dark, the spots darkest.

XI.77.1 Mycenae, krater fragment, stag with groups of stripes, bottle nose, triple concentric eye, body pierced by *aiganeé*. Athens NM 2654, Mycenae Acropolis; H. Buchholz, V. Karageorghis, *AAA* 3 (1970) 386; L. J. D. Richardson, *AAA* 4 (1971) 262; Buchholz, Karageorghis, *Altägäis*, no. 998.

XI.77.2 Mycenae, region south of Tsountas' House, III B–C levels, amphora shoulder fragment; stag right, striped neck, groups of wavy lines on body, haunch strewn with light arcs, loops on antlers; dark *aiganeé*, open leaf-shaped point, hook on shaft, pierces mid-back from above. G. Mylonas, *Ergon* 1973, 77, fig. 69; *BCH* 98 (1974) 608, fig. 79.

XI.78 Tiryns, krater fragments, bitten doe and dog right. N. Verdelis, water channels; Nauplion Museum 14 356; Slenczka, *Tiryns* VII, no. 139, pl. 34.2.

XI.79 Leukandi, fragments from both sides of a krater, dog/lions and "deer" right. LK/65/P 181; *JHS ArcRep* 1966, 11, fig. 19; M. Popham, L. Sackett, *Deltion* 21 (1966) 233, pl. 230 e; *Excavations at Lefkandi, Euboea* (1968) 21, fig. 46; *BSA* 66 (1971) pl. 54.6.

XI.80 Pylos, krater one-third preserved, hunter and three dog/lions left, stag and two dog/lions right. T. K-2, CM 1999; C. W. Blegen, *AJA* 63 (1959) 127, pl. 25.18. The fragments and restoration were studied courtesy of Professor Blegen and P. de Jong, 1965. C. W. Blegen, M. Rawson, W. Taylour, W. Donovan, *The Palace of Nestor at Pylos* III (1973) 229, pl. 289, a–e; H.-G. Buchholz, G. Jöhrens, I. Maull, *Jagd und Fischfang* in *Archaeologia Homerica* J (1973) 47, fig. 8 a.

XI.81 Duck-askos, dog and deer(?) right. Patras Museum (no number or provenance); E. Vermeule, *AJA* 64 (1960) 11, no. 44, pl. 4, fig. 30; pl. 6 k.

GOATS

XI.82 Salamis(?), krater with vertical strap handles; side A, three goats right; side B, goat and paneled ornaments. Boston Museum of Fine Arts 59.710; C. Vermeule, *CJ* 59 (1964) 193, figs. 1, 2; G. Chase, C. Vermeule, *Greek, Etruscan and Roman Art* (1963) fig. 14; *FastiA* XV (1960) nos. 208, 210; cf. *CVA* Frankfurt I, pl. 3; H. Hoffmann, *AJA* 70 (1966) 77; M. Benzi, *Ceramica Micenea in Attica* (1975) 51, n.1, 162.

XI.83 Perati, stirrup jar, ibex and flock of birds, palm tree and bushes. S. Iakovides, Perati T. 124, no. 8, P.892; *Perati, To Nekrotapheion* B (1970) 181, fig. 65, pl. 129, drawing, S. Iakovides; H.-G. Buchholz, G. Jöhrens, I. Maull, *Jagd und Fischfang* in *Archaeologia Homerica* J (1973) 5, fig. 1.

XI.84 Leukandi, krater, one-third preserved, heraldic wild goats and paneled leaves. LK/66/P 163; M. Popham, E. Millburn, *BSA* 66 (1971) pl. 54.1, III C phase 2; *Deltion* B (1967) pl. 175.

XI.85 Leukandi, krater fragment, goats copulating(?). LK/65/P 39, courtesy of M. Popham. Drawing, F. Wolsky.

XI.85.1 Tiryns, fragmentary rhyton in form of bull(?); on right hind leg are painted two goats erect at tree. Dark body and tail, forelegs and genitals reserved, inner face of hind leg spotted. *BCH* 102 (1978) 667, fig. 62. The rhyton form has an analogue in the Amyklai cow, Chr. Tsountas, *EphArch* 1892, pl. 3.

OTHER ANIMALS

XI.86 Mycenae, seven krater fragments, added white paint, panel dividers, arcs, caterpillars. Athens NM 1294 lot; Furtwängler-Loeschcke, MV, pl. XL.418 a, b; Furumark, *MP*, FM 8.12 (III C:1).

XI.87 Asine, deep bowl fragment, dark hedgehogs in panel right. T. I, no. 6; 0. Frödin, A. Persson, *Asine*, fig. 267; H.-G. Buchholz, *BJV* 5 (1965) 78, fig. 7; Furumark, *MP*, FM 8.6 (III C:1).

XI.88 Mycenae, bowl with tilted loop handle, hedgehog right under handle; Athens NM 1294 lot, Furtwängler-Loeschcke, *MV*, pl. XL.414 b (rim should be finished); Furumark, *MP*, FM 8.7 (III C:1); H.-G. Buchholz, *BJV* (1965) 71, fig. 4 f.

XI.89 Tiryns, bowl fragment, two hedgehogs strolling right. Nauplion Museum 14 358; Slenczka, *Tiryns* VII, no. 141, pl. 39.1 b.

XI.90 Mycenae, deep bowl, snake with white slashes and contours, right. Athens NM 2775; Staïs, *MycColl²*, 124; P. Kavvadias, *Proïstoriki Archaiologia* (1909) 334; Furumark, *MP*, FM 8.8 (III C:1); cf. O. Broneer, *Hesperia* 2 (1933) 369, fig. 42 b.

XI.91 Leukandi, three-handled pyxis, two griffins and young in nest, sphinx, deer, and fawn. LK/64/P 4; M. Popham, L. Sackett, *JHS ArcRep* 1964-65, 19, fig. 22; *Excavations at Lefkandi, Euboea* (1968) 18, fig. 35; *BSA* 66 (1971) pl. 54.2; *Archaeology* 25 (1972) 15; R. Higgins, *Minoan and Mycenaean Art* (1967) fig. 144.

SHIPS

XI.92 Pylos, Tragana tholos, pyxis, ship. K. Kourouniotes, *EphArch* 1914, 108-110, figs. 13-15; Furumark, *MP*, FM 40.2 (III C:1); Evans, *Palace of Minos* II (1928) 246, fig. 143; S. Marinatos, *BCH* 57 (1933) pl. XIII.17; W. Heurtley, *QDAP* 5 (1936) 92, fig. 2.11; G. Kirk, *BSA* 44 (1949) 118; L. Casson, *The Ancient Mariners* (1959) pl. 3 b; Vermeule, *GBA*, fig. 43 b; J. Morrison, R. Williams, *Greek Oared Ships* (1968) 9, pl. 1 b; C. Laviosa, *Annuario* 47-48 (1969-70) 23, fig. 21; D. Gray, *Seewesen*, in *Archaeologia Homerica* G (1974) fig. 15 b; I. Sakellarakis, *EphArch* 1971, 210, fig. 9; N. K. Sandars, *The Sea Peoples* (1978) fig. 121; new fragments, *BCH* 102 (1978) 678.

XI.93 Eleusis, bowl fragment, ship. A. Skias, *EphArch* 1898, 71, fig. 11; J. Morrison, R. Williams, *Greek Oared Ships* (1968) 10.

XI.94 Asine, stirrup jar, ship. O. Frödin, A. Persson, *Asine*, House G, p. 301, fig. 207.2, LH III C context; G. Kirk, *BSA* 44 (1949) 117, fig. 5; Furumark, *MP*, FM 40.3 (III C:1); L. Casson, *The Ancient Mariners* (1959) pl. 3 c; Vermeule, *GBA*, fig. 43 d; J. Morrison, R. Williams, *Greek Oared Ships* (1968) 10, pl. 1 c; C. Laviosa, *Annuario* 47-48 (1969-70) 24, fig. 23; D. Gray, *Seewesen*, in *Archaeologia Homerica* G (1974) fig. 15 d; N. K. Sandars, *The Sea Peoples* (1978) fig. 121.

XI.95 Skyros, stirrup jar, octopus on front, long bird-headed ship on rear. H. Hansen, discoverer; German Archaeological Institute photo Sporades 31-33 (E. Czako); Vermeule, *GBA*, fig. 43 f; H. Hencken, *Tarquinia* II (1968) fig. 486; J. Morrison, R. Williams, *Greek Oared Ships* (1968) 11 (curiously not considered as a warship); C. Laviosa, *Annuario* 47-48 (1969-70) 25, fig. 24; D. Gray, *Seewesen* in *Archaeologia Homerica* G (1974) fig. 15 c; N. K. Sandars, *The Sea Peoples* (1978) fig. 85.

XI.96 Phylakopi, three bowl fragments, two ships on exterior. C. Edgar, *Excavations at Phylakopi in Melos* (1904) pl. XXXII.11 A–C; S. Marinatos, *BCH* 57 (1933) pl. XIII.16; Furumark, *MP*, 454, n. 1; G. Kirk, *BSA* 44 (1949) 116; J. Morrison, R. Williams, *Greek Oared Ships* (1968) 10; C. Laviosa, *Annuario* 47-48 (1969-70) 23, fig. 20.

XI.97 Phylakopi, two bowl fragments, ship with crooked hull, oars both sides of keel line, looped thick stay. C. Edgar, *Excavations at Phylakopi in Melos* (1904) pl. XXXII.12.

BIRDS

XI.98 Korakou, bowl, panels fringed with scale pattern, bird filled with concentric arcs in each. Corinth Museum; C. W. Blegen, *Korakou* (1921) 62, fig. 86; Furumark, *MP*, FM 7.50 (III C:1); W. Heurtley, *QDAP* 5 (1936) 92, fig. 2.6.

XI.99 Korakou, bowl fragment, dark rosette, reserved contours, pecked by birds. Corinth Museum; M. Mackeprang, *AJA* 42 (1938) pl. 25.3; J. L. Benson, *JNES* 20 (1961) pl. VI.1; *AJA* 65 (1961) 342.

XI.100 Mycenae, bowl fragment, two birds one above other, pecking rosettes, ladder-striped raised wing. Athens NM 1275 lot (.3).

XI.101 Mycenae, three bowl fragments, birds with raised wings pecking rosette, close-set pendent scale triangles. Athens NM 1275 lot (.4).

XI.102 Mycenae, bowl fragment, bird with fine arc fillers, rosette, scale triangle. Athens NM 2685; J. L. Benson, *JNES* 20 (1961) pl. VI.2; *AJA* 65 (1961) pl. 104, fig. 20.

XI.103 Mycenae, bowl fragment, crude bird flying up to peck scale-berries. Athens NM 1141; Furtwängler-Loeschcke, *MV*, pl. XXXVIII.383; Furumark, *MP*, FM 7.49 (III C:1).

XI.104 Mycenae, bowl fragment, broad bird with thick fringed arc-filled wing right brushing pendent triangles. Athens NM 1275 lot (marked .3 like XI.100, but not the same bowl).

XI.105, 106, 107 Mycenae, fragments of three bowls, one with two birds, right; arc fillers, scale triangles. 107 is poor. Athens NM 1275 lot.

XI.108 Mycenae (Charvati), three cup fragments, two antithetic birds feeding at tree, three pairs of curved branches and trunk of vertical circles. Athens NM, no number, in blue box; the left-hand fragment is Furtwängler-Loeschcke, *MV*, 67, fig. 36.

XI.109 Mycenae, bowl fragment, bird feeding from left at tree, thin fringed raised wing. Athens NM 1275 lot.

XI.110 Mycenae, east basement of Granary, nearly complete deep bowl, three "flying swans" right, upper border of triangular scale pattern, bands below. Nauplion Museum 25 63; A. Wace, *BSA* 25 (1921-23) pl. VII b; *Mycenae*, fig. 82 c; Furumark, *MP*, FM 7.51 (III C:1); J. L. Benson, *AJA* 65 (1961) pl. 105, fig. 22; V. Desborough, *The Last Mycenaeans and Their Successors* (1964) pl. IV c.

XI.111 Mycenae, bowl rim fragment, concave profile, compressed frieze, cramped bird crouching right, filled with spots and arcs, pendent scale triangles. Athens NM 1275 lot; H. Schliemann, *Mycenae* (1880) pl. X.43.

XI.112 Mycenae, bowl fragment; inside, two birds walking right, striped necks, arcs in bodies; outside, lumpy bird, very good pendent scale triangles. Athens NM 1309; H. Schliemann, *Mycenae* (1880) pl. X.42; cf. XI.127 (Tiryns?).

XI.113 Mycenae, bowl, low frieze, parts of three footless arc-filled birds flying right, scale triangles. Athens NM 1768; H. Schliemann, *Mycenae* (1880) pl. X.40 (and 45?). In the group of bird bowls from Schliemann's excavations, the numbers are confused; *Mycenae*, pl. X.40 seems the same as pl. X.45, drawn twice from different angles.

XI.114 Mycenae, three bowl fragments, probably Schliemann, arc-filled birds; running loop border on two. Athens NM 1275 lot; one labeled *Muken*. 4040.3.

XI.115 Mycenae, stirrup jar, shoulder covered with rows of zigzag and scale-triangle peaks pointing up toward staff; below, frieze of birds right, preserved only as head and bill, raised wing filled with zigzag. Neat drawing. Athens NM 1275 lot, .6. The rosette on a tree trunk, illustrated in Furtwängler-Loeschcke, *MV*, pl. XXXVI.376, is allied.

XI.116 Mycenae, stirrup jar, east basement of Granary, narrow belly frieze of birds and arc "rocks." A. Wace, *BSA* 25 (1921-23) pl. X g; *Mycenae* (1949) pl. 75 a; W. Heurtley, *QDAP* 5 (1936) 92, fig. 2. A; Furumark, *MP*, FM 7.52 (III C:1); F. Matz, *Kreta, Mykene, Troja* (1956) pl. 112, top left; Benson, *HBM*, pl. XIX.4.

XI.117 Mycenae, tall stirrup jar with raised disc, friezes of triangles, filled arcs, rosettes, birds. Furtwängler-Loeschcke, *MV*, pl. XXXVIII.393; Montelius, *GP* II, pl. 132.11; Furumark, *MP*, FM 7.48 (III C:1); J. L. Benson, *AJA* 65 (1961) 342, no. 7; V. Desborough, *The Last Mycenaeans and Their Successors* (1964) pl. 4 b.

XI.118 Mycenae, burned bichrome stirrup jar, scale peaks on shoulder, frieze of birds on upper body. Athens NM, number not visible; for type of bird, cf. Furumark, *MP*, FM 7.47 (= XI.42).

XI.119 Mycenae, four-handled jar (Schliemann, Granary), octopus on each side, dark rosettes on shoulder, birds in arcades with scale triangles, protome birds in tree-spiral under handles. Athens NM 1126; Furtwängler-Loeschcke, *MV*, pl. XXXVII.380; H. R. Hall, *The Civilization of Greece In The Bronze Age* (1928) 237, fig. 315; Montelius, *GP* II, pl. 132.9; A. Wace, *BSA* 25 (1921-23) 46, pl. IX b; M. Mackeprang, *AJA* 42 (1938) pl. 25.5; J. L. Benson, *AJA* 65 (1961) 342, no. 6; V. Desborough, *The Last Mycenaeans and Their Successors* (1964) pl. 4 a.

XI.120 Mycenae, krater fragment, bird protomes mounted on stacked chevrons, right, between arcades. Furtwängler-Loeschcke, *MV*, pl. XXXV.361; Montelius, *GP* II, pl. 133.18.

XI.121 Mycenae, krater fragment, white bird protomes on chevrons, left, on dark ground, Furtwängler-Loeschcke, *MV*, pl. XXXV.360. White-on-dark designs of this period are most frequent in Mycenae and Athens; cf. G. Mylonas, *Praktika* 1970, pl. 168 a.

XI.122 Mycenae, krater fragment, facing bird protomes over elaborate arcade, on filled triangle bodies. Furtwängler-Loeschcke, *MV*, pl. XXXVI.363.

XI.123 Mycenae, krater fragment, bird with spiral body bordered inside with running loops, round head, eye, curved bill made of spiral end. Athens NM 1294; Furtwängler-Loeschcke, *MV*, pl. XL.419.

XI.124 Mycenae, krater fragment, spiral flaring left into trumpet tube ornamented with stripes and semicircles, bird pecking at it right, lightly drawn, streamer wing, bands of zigzag, neck neatly striped. Athens NM 3051.

XI.125 Mycenae, krater fragment, bird filled with arcs; fish. Athens NM 1141; H. Schliemann, *Mycenae* (1880) pl. XI.50 (upside down); Furtwängler-Loeschcke, *MV*, pl. XXXVIII.384.

XI.126 Tiryns, krater fragment, double-ended bird with tubular spotted body, long necks, upswept bills, holding three sets of stacked concentric arcs on its back. Nauplion Museum 19 88; Slenczka, *Tiryns* VII, no. 45, pl. 39.1 e, classified as a bird-headed ship.

XI.127 Tiryns(?), bowl fragment, frieze of arc-filled, stripe-necked birds right, under pendent scale triangles. Slenczka, *Tiryns* VII, no. 223, pl. 32.2 d. Cf. XI.112.

XI.128 Tiryns, bowl fragment, frieze of birds right, raised wing, filled with dotted concentric arcs, separated by dotted circles. Nauplion Museum 14 390; Slenczka, *Tiryns* VII, no. 173, pl. 25.1 a.

XI.129 Tiryns, stirrup jar(?) fragment, crude bird right, raised wing with zigzag and stripes, striped neck, irregular dark body filling. Nauplion Museum 14 349; Slenczka, *Tiryns* VII, no. 131, pl. 25.1 b.

XI.130, 131 Tiryns, krater fragments, two birds in startled angled poses with feet stuck out, white contour inside dark oval bodies, white spot filling. Nauplion Museum 14 299 and 14 394; Slenczka, *Tiryns* VII, nos. 73 and 177, pl. 25.2 a, b.

XI.132 Tiryns, krater fragment, dark bird with light border right. Nauplion Museum 14 397; Slenczka, *Tiryns* VII, no. 180, pl. 25.2 h.

XI.133 Tiryns, krater fragment, dark bird flying right with hooked talons curled before him, fringes on body contour, striped wings framing the body above and below; lively. German Archaeological Institute photo Tiryns 549 A; Slenczka, *Tiryns* VII, no. 38, pl. 27.1 i.

XI.134 Tiryns(?), stirrup jar shoulder fragment, bird right with four separated quadrants of concentric arcs, striped wing, fringed dark fantail. Slenczka, *Tiryns* VII, no. 220, pl. 32.2 a.

XI.135 Tiryns, bowl fragment, painted white on dark, bird quarreling(?) left, open beak and high raised wing as though flailing at opponent, striped neck and wing. W. Voigtländer, *AAA* 4 (1971) 400, fig. 3 c.

XI.136 Patras-Lopesi, four-handled jar, fringed semicircles converted to birds. Patras Museum 7; E. Vermeule, *AJA* 64 (1960) 5, no. 2, pl. 1, fig. 2; cf. no. 3, and *BCH* 101 (1977) 570, fig. 123.

XI.137 Asine, House G, deep bowl, bird filled with arcs

pecking tassel. A. Furumark, *OpArc* 3 (1944) 209, fig. 3, no. 20.

XI.138 Dendra-Midea, bird protome with fringed neck emerging from spiral. G. Walberg, *OpAth* 7 (1967) 163, no. 17, pl. I.

XI.139 Athens, Acropolis, Fountain, deep bowl fragments, chevron mounted by bird's head on line of running spiral. Agora AP 2715 (VII A); O. Broneer, *Hesperia* 8 (1939) 368, fig. 45 a.

XI.140 Athens, Acropolis, two fragments, one with two birds right, bodies loosely filled with loops and chevrons, one with tail(?). Graef-Langlotz, *VA*, 18, no. 188, pl. 5.188; 22, no. 231.

XI.141 Leukandi, deep bowl fragments, mother and baby bird charging left at panel bordered by loops; arc and stripe filling. LK/65/P 176; M. Popham, E. Millburn, *BSA* 66 (1971) pl. 54.4; *Archaeology* 25 (1972) 15.

XI.142 Leukandi, paneled bowl fragments, dark birds raise light-bordered wings at each other aggressively across thin panel with dark bordered semicircles. LK/66/P 71; M. Popham, E. Millburn, *BSA* 66 (1971) pl. 54.5.

XI.143 Leukandi, kalathos, bird with raised wings, striped, zigzag neck, dark body. LK/66/P 76; M. Popham, E. Millburn, *BSA* 66 (1971) pl. 54.3.

XI.144 Naxos, krater fragment, vertical panel-divider with row of crosshatched lozenges, spraying arc-filled plant stems either side, bird with raised wing toward panel, fringed arc at breast, barred tail. N. Kontoleon, *Praktika* 1950, 278, fig. 11; cf. 1960, pl. 219.

XI.145 Perati, stirrup jar, octopus, birds, fish; one bird swooping down. S. Iakovides, *Perati* B (1970) no. 261, 149, fig. 23; 184, fig. 70; V. Desborough, *The Last Mycenaeans and Their Successors* (1964) pl. 6 d.

XI.146 Perati, stirrup jar, bird on shoulder, filled with dark arcs with light borders, among scale triangles. S. Iakovides, *Perati* B (1970) no. 750, 149, fig. 23; 175, fig. 62.

XI.147 Perati, stirrup jar, birds chasing right on shoulder, open oval bodies, one filled with ripples, one with dark bordered oval; open beaks, raised wings. S. Iakovides, *Perati* B (1970) no. 127, 149, fig. 23; 171, fig. 55.

XI.148 Perati, stirrup jar, two sketchy birds with double outlines, oval bodies, one rippled, one solid, facing across chevron tree, set centrally among three fish swimming right, filled triangles. S. Iakovides, *Perati* B (1970) no. 229, 149, fig. 23; 175, fig. 62.

XI.149 Perati, stirrup jar, two birds as decorative punctuation between octopods, dark-filled oval bodies, streamer wings, striped necks, fantails. S. Iakovides, *Perati* B (1970) no. 569, 149, fig. 23; 187, fig. 73.

XI.150 Perati, stirrup jar, family of three straggly birds, "mother" with light filling of inverted triangles, others dark. S. Iakovides, *Perati* B (1970) no. 779, 149, fig. 23; 171, fig. 55.

XI.151 Perati, octopus stirrup jar, bird protomes with fringed or dotted heads on chevron designs from octopus tentacles. S. Iakovides, *Perati* B (1970) no. 152, 127, fig. 14.39; 182, fig. 66.

XI.152 Perati, krater fragment, two birds in frieze left, raised laddered wing, striped neck; crest? S. Iakovides, *Perati* C (1971) pl. 114 b.

Rhodes and the Dodekanese

RHODES

EARLY

XII.1 Rhodes, Ialysos, three-handled jar, birds and flowers. T. XIX.6; A. Maiuri, *Annuario* 6-7 (1923-24) 129f., figs. 50, 52; *CVA* Rodi (Italia) 2, pl. 5.2-3; Vermeule, *GBA*, fig. 26 e; Furumark, *MP*, FM 7 i (reversed), LM III A.

XII.2 Ialysos, one-handled cup, upper frieze with birds and altar or horns of consecration, lower with diving fish. BM A 846; *BMCatV* I.i, 149 f., fig. 201, pl. XIII; G. Perrot, C. Chipiez, *Histoire de l'Art* VI (1894) 920, fig. 474; W. Ridgeway, *Early Age of Greece* (1901) I, 16, fig. 13; Baumeister, *Denkmäler*, 1941, fig. 2063; Furtwängler-Loeschcke, *MV*, pl. X.63; W. Heurtley, *QDAP* 5 (1936) 95, fig. 4.5; Furumark, *MP*, FM 7.2 (III A:2 early), FM 20.3 (III A:2); presented by John Ruskin.

MIDDLE

XII.3 (= IV.48.1) Ialysos, chariot krater, two men in chariot, three robed figures on ground. T. LX.2; A. Maiuri, *Annuario* 6-7 (1923-24) 233 f., figs. 149-150; *CVA* Rodi (Italia) 2, pl. 4.4-5; W. Heurtley, *QDAP* 5 (1936) 98, fig. 7.9; H. Bossert, *Altkreta*³ (1937) fig. 458; Stubbings, *MycLevant*, 12; J. Wiesner, *Olympos* (1960) 245.

XII.4 Rhodes (Ialysos?), chariot krater, team galloping through flowers. Munich 47 (now 6028); J. Sieveking, R. Hackl, *Die Königliche Vasensammlung* (1912) I, 6, fig. 7; Furumark, *MP*, FM 39.12 (III A:2 late).

XII.5 Rhodes, chariot krater, passenger in box, driver on pole. Louvre A-277-285.

XII.6 Rhodes, Ialysos, chariot krater, single driver, flowers. T. XXVII.4; A. Maiuri, *Annuario* 6-7 (1923-24) 151 f., figs. 74-75; Furumark, *MP*, 334; Stubbings, *MycLevant*, 12.

XII.7 Rhodes(?), amphoroid krater, bull, cow, and papyrus. Louvre C.A. 1584; R. Dussaud, *Les Civilisations Préhelléniques* (1914) 242, fig. 174; J. Charbonneaux, *L'Art égéen* (1929) pl. LXIII.3; Furumark, *MP*, 440; S. Charitonides, *Deltion* 16 (1960) 84, pl. 91.

XII.8 Rhodes, amphoroid krater fragment, bull and papyrus. Rhodes Museum 471 (Skiathites Collection, no provenance); S. Charitonides, *Deltion* 16 (1960) 84, fig. 1, pl. 91 a.

XII.9 Rhodes, three-handled jar, bull right in flowers and grass, each side. Louvre Inv. S 615 bis.

XII.10 Rhodes, Ialysos, one-handled jar, two goats on shoulder, flower and whorl shell. T. LIX.4; A. Maiuri, *Annuario* 6-7 (1923-24) 227, fig. 144 (captions reversed).

XII.11 Rhodes(?), kylix, antithetic goats rearing up on papyrus tree. BM A719, *BMCatV*, pl. IX; Evans, *Palace of Minos* IV, 370, fig. 309 e; 374, fig. 312 a.

XII.12 Rhodes, Ialysos, oinochoe, two birds on shoulder, necks in open loops, with palm tree, palm patterns, and rocks, double-U fillers. T. LIX.5; A. Maiuri, *Annuario* 6-7 (1923-24) 227, fig. 144 (captions reversed); Furumark, *MP*, FM 7.24-25 (III A:2).

XII.13 Rhodes, Ialysos, kylix, two birds in frieze right, extra "wing" behind neck, plumes with chevron ends. One flower spreads horizontally in field. T. VII.6; A. Maiuri, *Annuario* 6-7 (1923-24) 110 f., figs. 30-31; *CVA* Rodi (Italia) 2, pl. 6.2; W. Heurtley, *QDAP* 5 (1936) 95, fig. 4.3; Furumark, *MP*, FM 7.22, III A:2.

XII.14 Rhodes, kylix, two birds in frieze right, each side. Heidelberg Inv. M 21; *CVA* Heidelberg 3, pl. 99.1.

XII.15 Rhodes, Vatoi, kylix, two dark birds right, millsail wing; spirals in field. Copenhagen NM 7570, *CVA* Copenhagen 2, pl. 53.8; Furumark, *MP*, FM 7.9 (reversed) (III A:2 late).

XII.16 Rhodes, Zukalades, beaked jug, bird protome on loop, papyrus blossoms, chevron-flowers, slashes. L. Laurenzi, *Memorie dell' Istituto F.E.R.T. di Rodi* 2 (1938) 49, pl. XL. 1,2.

RIPE

XII.17 Rhodes, Kalavarda, conical rhyton, three boars or men in boar costumes, dancing, holding rattle(?) and high-handled kylix, birds flying up between them. L. Laurenzi, *Memorie dell' Istituto F.E.R.T. di Rodi* 2 (1938) 49-51, pls. XLI-XLII; P. Demargne, *REG* 58 (1945) 248, fig. 1; 61 (1948) 45; C. Picard, *RevArch* 28 (1947) 66; *FastiA* 2 (1947) no. 618; K. Majewski, *ArcWroc* 3 (1949) 409; *Archeologia* 3 (1949) 411; G. Germain, *Genèse de l'Odyssée* (1954) 148.

XII.18 Rhodes, pilgrim flask, robed (armless) women or goddesses facing out under handles on each narrow side. Rhodes Museum BE 1223 (29), formerly Akavi Collection or 1943 confiscation; H. Catling, *AA* 1970, 26, fig. 4.

TRANSITIONAL AND LATE

XII.19 Rhodes, Ialysos, stirrup jar, octopus with birds nesting in tentacles, fish swimming between, scorpion. T. LXX-III.1; G. Jacopi, *Annuario* 13-14 (1930-31) 292, fig. 36, pl. 21.

XII.20 Rhodes, Ialysos, stirrup jar, spirals, fish diving, birds with dot-outlined heads rising. T. XXXII.1; A. Maiuri, *Annuario* 6-7 (1923-24) 178, fig. 103.

XII.20.1 Rhodes, Ialysos, pyxis, crosshatched lozenges with bird protomes, dot-rosettes, running loops. T. XVII.51; A. Maiuri, *Annuario* 6-7 (1923-24) 124, fig. 43 (2740).

THE OTHER ISLANDS

XII.21 Amorgos(?), kylix, stag protomes facing frontal bull's head. MFA, Boston 01.8042, Pierce Fund (E. P. Warren); G. Chase, C. Vermeule, *Greek, Etruscan, and Roman Art* (1963) fig. 12 b.

XII.22 Kalymnos, Pothia, lekane-kalathos, birds pecking nests(?), fish leaping. BM A1016; *BMCatV*, 104, pl. XV; W. R. Paton, *JHS* 8 (1887) pl. lxxxiii; *CVA* British Museum 5, pl. 9.8 a-b; Furumark, *MP*, 635, no. 291:9, FM 7.40, FM 20.9 (III C:1); J. L. Benson, *AJA* 72 (1968) 204, pl. 66, fig. 9, pl. 67, fig. 14.

XII.23 Kalymnos, near Pothia, octopus stirrup jar with birds, goats, hedgehogs, eggs, crabs, scorpion. BM A1015; *BMCatV*, 192f., fig. 276; *CVA* British Museum 5, pl. 9.7 a-b; F. Houssay, *RevArch* 26³ (1895) 1; 30 (1897) 81; E. Pottier, *RevArch* 28³ (1896) 24; H. Walters, *JHS* 17 (1897) 75, fig. 13; W. Heurtley, *QDAP* 5 (1936) 94; Furumark, *MP*, 613, no. 176:1, FM 6.9, FM 8.6, 10, 11; *OpArc* 3 (1944) 223, fig. 8 c; V.

R. Desborough, *The Last Mycenaeans and Their Successors* (1964) 161, 272; H.-G. Buchholz, *BJV* 5 (1965) 78, fig. 8; J. H. Crouwel, *BABesch* 47 (1972) 19, figs. 7-8; P. P. Kahane in N. Robertson et al., *The Archaeology of Cyprus* (1975) 166, fig. 6.

XII.24 Kalymnos, near Pothia, collared jar with four handles, two pairs of goats facing palm tree. BM A1022, *BMCatV*, 196, fig. 280, pl. XVI; *CVA* British Museum 5, pl. 8.27; H. R. Hall, *The Civilization of Greece in the Bronze Age* (1928) 263, fig. 340; W. Heurtley, *QDAP* 5 (1936) 95, fig. 4.10; H. Bossert, *Altkreta*³ (1937) fig. 456; Furumark, *MP*, FM 6.9-10 (III C:1); cf. J. L. Benson, *AJA* 72 (1968) 203.

XII.25 Karpathos, near Pigadia, half double basket-handled vase, birds facing checkerboard "chalice(?)," flowers. S. Charitonides, *Deltion* 17 (1961-62 [1963]) 68, no. 97, pl. 26 a, b, d, i.

XII.26 Karpathos, near Pigadia, three-handled jar, papyrus, argonauts, bird, two fish. S. Charitonides, *Deltion* 17 (1961-62 [1963]) 43, no. 21, figs. 4, 5, 5a, pl. 17 a, c, e.

XII.27 Karpathos, near Pigadia, ewer with dark facing bull's head. S. Charitonides, *Deltion* 17 (1961-62 [1963]) 45, no. 22, fig. 6, pl. 16 a, c.

XII.28 Karpathos, near Pigadia, open krater with vertical strap handles, rattle or sistrum(?), wheel, pilgrim flask, two high-handled kylikes. S. Charitonides, *Deltion* 17 (1961-62 [1963]) 61f., no. 82, figs. 12, 13, pl. 25 e.

XII.29 Kos, Seragio, krater fragment with low beveled rim, two warriors right in tongued and tufted helmets; shield(?). L. Morricone, *Annuario* 50-51 (1972-73) 360, fig. 357 a; N. K. Sandars, *The Sea Peoples* (1978) fig. 92.

XII.30 Kos, Seragio, krater wall fragment, three soldiers right in helmets with tall Y-forks or feathers. L. Morricone, *Annuario* 50-51 (1972-73) 360, fig. 357 b; N. K. Sandars, *The Sea Peoples* (1978) fig. 92.

XII.31 Kos, Seragio, amphoroid(?) krater rim fragment, soldier right in feathered headdress, long rippling arm(?) high in front, vertical sword(?). L. Morricone, *Annuario* 50-51 (1972-73) 359, fig. 356.

XII.32 Kos, Seragio, krater wall fragment, mustachioed soldier right in striped crested helmet; unidentified object behind him. L. Morricone, *Annuario* 50-51 (1972-73) 360, fig. 357 c; N. K. Sandars, *The Sea Peoples* (1978) fig. 92.

XII.33 Kos, Seragio, lower wall fragment of krater, cross-section of lower deck of ship with two rowers in turbans. L. Morricone, *Annuario* 50-51 (1972-73) 360, fig. 358; Benson, *HBM*, pl. 39.1; N. K. Sandars, *The Sea Peoples* (1978) fig. 92.

XII.34 Kos, Langadha, stirrup jar, three goats circling right on shoulder. Inv. 44 (chance find); L. Morricone, *Annuario* 43-44 (1965-66) 292, figs. 100, 339. Cf. Langadha T. 39, no. 153.

XII.35 Kos, Seragio, open krater with vertical strap handles, three goats right, last two bearded, two birds on backs, one under belly; flower spray, guilloche stalk. Inv. 1190; L. Morricone, *Bollettino d'Arte* 35 (1950) 319, fig. 91; *Annuario* 50-51 (1972-73) 188, fig. 73, pl. IV (col.); related fragments, 361-363, figs. 359-361.

XII.36 Kos, Seragio, fragment, animal with hairy outlines and long barrel body right, both hind legs off ground. Cf. the arc-filled quadruped and diving fish, L. Morricone, *Annuario* 50-51 (1972-73) 369, fig. 367.

XII.37 Kos, Seragio, krater fragment, head of horned goat-bird (or wild goat) right. L. Morricone, *Annuario* 50-51 (1972-73) 362, fig. 360 c.

XII.38 Kos, Seragio, krater fragment, fine fish right, from a frieze, triangular fins, dark and light triangular body filling. Cf. L. Morricone, *Annuario* 50-51 (1972-73) 367, fig. 365 for various types.

XII.39 Kos, Langadha, octopus stirrup jar with birds and fish. T. 39, no. 152; L. Morricone, *Bollettino d'Arte* 35 (1950) 324, fig. 99; *Annuario* 43-44 (1965-66) 188-193, figs. 196-197; V. Desborough, *The Last Mycenaeans and Their Successors* (1964) frontispiece and 271; Furumark, *OpArc* 3 (1944) 201, 224; S. Stucchi, *Quaderni di Archeologia della Libia* 5 (1946) 4.

XII.40 Kos, Langadha, stirrup jar with palm, bird, and fish. Inv. 269 (chance find); L. Morricone, *Bollettino d'Arte* 35 (1950) fig. 100; *Annuario* 43-44 (1965-66) 289 f., figs. 335 a-e; cf. Langadha, T. 44, no. 167, fig. 217.

XII.41 Kos, Langadha, lekane, sea horse. T. 14, no. 45; L. Morricone, *Annuario* 43-44 (1965-66) 118 f., figs. 100-101.

XII.42 Dodekanese, unknown provenance, collared jar with horses and fish. Toronto, ROM 920.68.52; J. L. Benson, *AJA* 72 (1968) 203; *HBM*, pl. III.4.

Asia Minor and the Near East

ASIA MINOR

XIII.1 Ankhiale, Cilicia, fragments of deep bowl (T. Burton-Brown). Evans, *The Palace of Minos* IV, 534, fig. 485 ("MM III Mino-Cilician"); W. Heurtley, *QDAP* 5 (1936) fig. 10.15; Furumark, *MP*, 459, 464; J.-C. Courtois, *The Mycenaeans in the Eastern Mediterranean* (1973) 147.

XIII.2 Miletos, krater fragment, charioteer or boxer. C. Weickert, *Bericht über den VI Internationalen Kongress für Archäologie* (1939) pl. 24.

XIII.3 Miletos, dish fragment, quadruped, sea animals? P. Hommel, *IstMitt* 9-10 (1959-60) 52, pl. 48.2-3.

XIII.4 Miletos, krater fragment, bird. P. Hommel, *IstMitt* 9-10 (1959-60) 51, pl. 48.1.

XIII.5 Miletos, krater fragment, bird's head and "pillar." C. Weickert, *IstMitt* 9-10 (1959-60) 65, pl. 72.1.

XIII.6 Miletos, krater fragment, parts of three oared ships. C. Weickert, *IstMitt* 9-10 (1959-60) 65, pl. 72.2.

XIII.7 Miletos, tripod-beaker, birds and fish. W. Schiering, *IstMitt* 9-10 (1959-60) 24, 30, pls. 16-17; J. M. Cook, *Greeks in Ionia and the East* (1963) 19, fig. 1; Vermeule, *GBA*, 315; R. Higgins, *Minoan and Mycenaean Art* (1967) fig. 137; Buchholz, Karageorghis, *Altägäis*, no. 1036.

XIII.8 Pitane (Çandarlı), octopus stirrup jar with birds and animals. Istanbul 2276; G. Perrot, C. Chipiez, *Histoire de l'Art* VI (1894) 931, figs. 489-491; F. Houssay, *RevArc* 26 (1895) 1; *RevArc* 30 (1897) 81; E. Pottier, *RevArc* 28 (1896) 26; Furumark, *MP*, FM 6.10 (III C:1); H. T. Bossert, *Altkreta*³ (1937) 256, fig. 454; *Alt-Anatolien* (1942) pl. 3.7; K. Bittel,

Istanbuler Forschungen 17 (1950) 21, pl. 5; V. Desborough, *The Last Mycenaeans and Their Successors* (1964) 161, 228, 271; H.-G. Buchholz, *BJV* 5 (1965) fig. 4 g, pl. 14.1-2, 15.2; J. H. Crouwel, *BABesch* 47 (1972) 22, fig. 12; Buchholz, Karageorghis, *Altägäis*, no. 1032; part, H.-G. Buchholz, G. Jöhrens, I. Maull, *Jagd und Fischfang*, in *Archaeologia Homerica* J (1973) pl. 1 E. Photos, Crawford Greenewalt.

XIII.9 Tarsus, krater(?) fragment, back and haunch of bull filled with V's, dots. H. Goldman, *Tarsus* II (1956) sherd 1329, fig. 335. Cf. 1328.

XIII.10 Tarsus, deep bowl fragment (black interior), humped duck with circle head, turned-up bill, spotted belted body, three wavy lines on top of back. H. Goldman, *Tarsus* II (1956) sherd 1324, fig. 335.

XIII.11 Tarsus, deep bowl fragment, head and beginning of body of spotted humped duck. H. Goldman, *Tarsus* II (1956) sherd 1323, fig. 335.

XIII.12 Tarsus, krater(?) fragment, two flying birds with raised wings and necks bent down. H. Goldman, *Tarsus* II (1956) sherd 1325, fig. 335.

XIII.13 Tarsus, local krater(?) fragment, simple outlined bird, right, wing disconnnected, flowing from back of neck. H. Goldman, *Tarsus* II (1956) sherd 1326, fig. 335.

XIII.14 Tarsus, local(?) one-handled jug, frieze of long-necked birds. H. Goldman, *Tarsus* II (1956) sherd 1348, fig. 337. Cf. *BASOR* 1939, no. 76.2.

XIII.15 Tarsus, jar fragment, rippled diving fish. H. Goldman, *Tarsus* II (1956) sherd 1330, fig. 335.

XIII.16 Tarsus, panel with fork-tailed fish, backbone shown(?). H. Goldman, *Tarsus* II (1956) sherd 1331, fig. 335.

XIII.17 Tarsus, bowl rim, neat spotted fish. H. Goldman, *Tarsus* II (1956) sherd 1332, fig. 335.

XIII.18 Tarsus, spiral bird and zigzag fish. H. Goldman, *Tarsus* II (1956) sherd 1333, fig. 335.

XIII.19 Troy, krater fragment, driver in spotted robe right, four reins, seashell filler. C. W. Blegen et al., *Troy* III (1953) fig. 412, no. 16.

XIII.20 Troy, krater fragment, team right, added white paint. C. W. Blegen et al., *Troy* III (1953) fig. 412, no. 6 a; S. Immerwahr, *AJA* 60 (1956) 456; A. J. B. Wace, F. Stubbings, *A Companion to Homer* (1962) 378, fig. 24 C.

XIII.21 Troy, krater fragment, neck and reins of team, white rosettes and ladder pattern. C. W. Blegen et al., *Troy* III (1953) fig. 412, no. 6.

XIII.22 Troy, fragment, outlined goat. C. W. Blegen et al., *Troy* III (1953) fig. 419, no. 26 (cf. fig. 444, no. 12).

XIII.23 Troy, kylix or bowl rim fragment, two birds right, added white. H. Schmidt, *Heinrich Schliemann's Sammlung Trojanischer Altertümer* (1902) 165, no. 3405; cf. H. Schliemann, *Troja* (1875) fig. 173.

XIII.24 Troy, bowl fragment, four striped fish. C. W. Blegen et al., *Troy* III (1953) fig. 417, no. 10.

XIII.25 Unknown provenance, Istanbul, Archaeological Museum, one-handled jug, two delicate birds with spiral breasts. Unpublished.

THE NEAR EAST

XIII.26 Megiddo, jar, birds in branches and spirals. T. T 1101 A, upper level, Palestine Archaeological Museum. V.

Hankey, *BSA* 62 (1967) 126, pl. 28 b; P. Guy, *Megiddo Tombs* (1938) 160, pls. 8.1, 87.2.

XIII.27 Ugarit, topographical point 4460, house of Patiluwa, fragmentary krater, lions hunting stags. RS 64; J.-C. Courtois, *The Mycenaeans in the Eastern Mediterranean* (1973) 141 f., figs. 2, 3, pl. XXI.5.

XIII.28 Ugarit, topographical point 4522, Rm. 219, S. Palace, fragmentary open krater; side A, soldier between horses, four fish, goat, tailed lozenges; side B, soldier between horses, four fish, lozenges. RS 27.319; C. Schaeffer, *Annuaire du Collège de France* 1965; *Ugaritica* V, 765-766, pls. 3-7; *Archiv für Orientforschung* 21 (1966) 133, fig. 17; J.-C. Courtois, *Archeologia* 20 (1968) 19; *The Mycenaeans in the Eastern Mediterranean* (1973) 149 f., figs. 8-9, pl. XXI.4; H.-G. Buchholz, *AA* 1974, 402, fig. 57 a, b; N. K. Sandars, *The Sea Peoples* (1978) fig. 104.

XIII.29 Ugarit, topographical point 4070, house with medico-magical tablets, fragmentary krater, warrior left holding fish by tail at horned altar. RS 25.501; Schaeffer, *Ugaritica* V, pl. 3, bottom; J.-C. Courtois, *The Mycenaeans in the Eastern Mediterranean* (1973) 156 f., fig. 10.

XIII.30 Ugarit, fragmentary closed vessel, quadruped-spiral. RS 60 (2809); J.-C. Courtois, *The Mycenaeans in the Eastern Mediterranean* (1973) 161 f., pl. XXI.2.

ADDENDA

III.6, note 23: concerning whips, see also P. Kalligas, *AAA* 9 (1976) 61f.

X.19.1 A surprisingly traditional war scene appears on a Tiryns krater fragment with sponge print inside, stratified in a LH III:B 2 working phase of the lower town under a crushed lead cauldron (*JHS ArcRep* 1979-80, 29, fig. 51). Two handsome soldiers, left, are high enough in the picture to be in a chariot. The first wears a boars'-tusk helmet and carries a rectangular tower shield covered in blotched hide, and a spear with a knob on the upper shaft, like a scepter; the second has a spotted figure-eight shield. Both men wear spade beards, which are unusual with boars'-tusk helmets when those have a cheekpiece, as on the series of ivory heads. They match the bearded unhelmeted heads of metal inlays at Mycenae and Pylos and the beards worn with differently shaped helmets by Late soldiers (XI.7, 42, 80). The alternating shield forms recall the old iconography of the Shaft Grave lion hunt dagger, and the vivacious, detailed drawing seems connected to certain late III B frescoes like the Mycenae fragment with the helmeted divinity cradling an infant griffin (*BCH* 96 [1972] 643, fig. 134).

XI.28 The new fragments (*JHS ArcRep* 1979-80, 29, fig. 50) give the soldiers dark tied greaves and pale boots with pointed curled toes (suggesting that XI.53 is related, possibly from the other side; cf. XI.49); they balance heel and toe on the platform of the open car. The breastwork rises steeply before them, filled with zigzag like the team's lower legs; the hindquarters are scalloped in loops to match the tunics, with dark inserts, and the tails end in a spear-shaped plume as on earlier bulls (IX.21, 28). The chariot platform thickens at the rear, suggesting the traditional "spur," and the spokes broaden at the felloe as in fresco pictures. The big dark rosette with pale contours under the horses recalls the Amarynthos stag sherd (X.51). The contrast of light and dark is striking, the whole scene elegant and elaborate.

XI.43 M. Andronikos, *Deltion* 17 (1961-62) A, 162, pl. 84 c, d.

XI.77.1 F. Schachermeyr, *Ägäische Frühzeit* (1976) 104, fig. 21.

XI.19.1 The theme of the chariot race is confirmed by a fascinating if fragmentary amphoroid krater from Tiryns, where the race is likely to be in a funerary context (K. Kilian, *AthMitt* 95 [1980] 21 f.). Although the chariot race at funeral games may be as early as the stelai over the tumuli in Grave Circle A at Mycenae (G. Mylonas, *AJA* 52 [1948] 77), the theme has not been securely identified before in painting. Its long afterlife in painting, fresco, and on relief plaques as well as other media is a sign of the importance and popularity of the chariot race theme in the arts of Greece, Asia Minor, and Etruria; it is especially important to find a Mycenaean model for the tradition. Mycenaean art now offers illustrations of all the major modes of classical mourning.

One side of the vase preserves parts of two racing teams angled high to the left, front hooves off the ground, the apparently single, unarmed driver leaning forward in an urgent pose, with whip and rein in the left hand and a second (paired?) rein in the right. The chariot box is a simple flattened rectangle, shaped like that of a traditional chariot but open so the driver's legs show; the team's head is reserved, perhaps with a diamond eye, and the front hooves are pale. The teams rush toward a panel-closing bar of running loops. Beyond the handle, facing left toward a second race, a softly curved goddess sits on a high-backed throne, holding an archaic-looking stemmed kylix with ring handles; her feet kick up (no footstool is drawn). A krater is set on a ringstand by the throne. The drivers in the second race may wear armor. The connection of the scene to older versions of a woman watching chariots (III.12, V.2., 3) or of the enthroned goddess (III.29, XI.43) is as clear as the sequel in the Hubbard and Ormidhia vases (V. Karageorghis, J. Des Gagniers, *La Céramique Chypriote de Style Figuré* [1974] 7) or the Geometric series of chariots in cult and funerary contexts (J. Wiesner, *Archaeologia Homerica* F [1968] 65 f., 73).

ILLUSTRATIONS

III.A

III.B

III.1

III.1

III.1

III.1

III.2

III.2

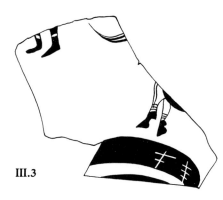

III.3

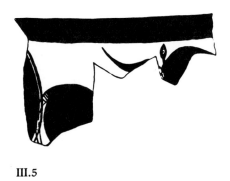

III.5

III.6

III.6

III.7

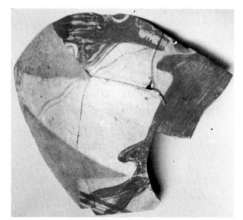

III.9

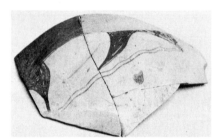

III.9

III.9

III.10

III.11

III.12

III.12

III.12

III.13

III.13

III.13

III.13

III.13

III.14

III.15

III.16

III.16

III.17

III.18

III.18

III.18

III.19

III.20

III.20

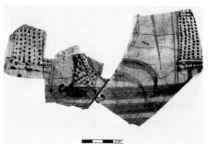

III.20

III.21

III.22

III.23

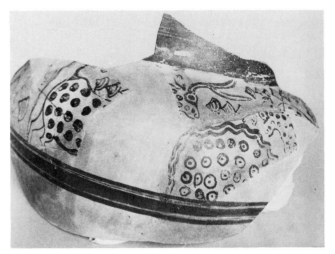

III.24

III.25

III.26

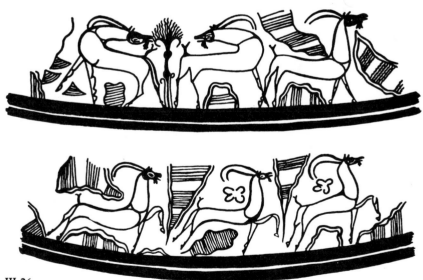

III.26

III.29

III.29

III.29

III.29

III.30

III.31

IV.1

IV.2

IV.3

IV.4

IV.4

IV.4

IV.5

IV.6

IV.7

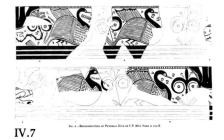

IV.7

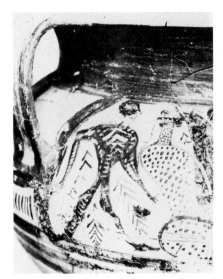

IV.12

IV.12

IV.13

IV.13

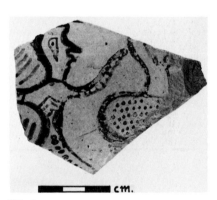

IV.14

IV.15

IV.15

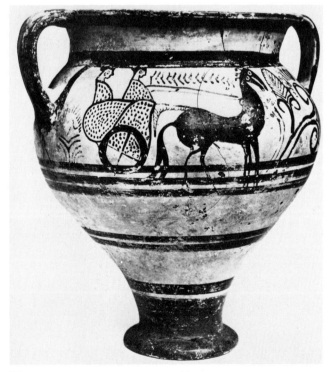

IV.16

IV.16

IV.17

IV.18

IV.18

IV.19

IV.18

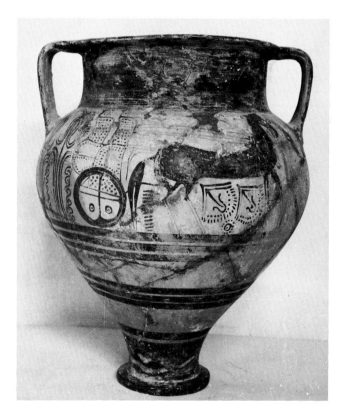

IV.19

IV.20

IV.21

IV.20

IV.23

IV.25

IV.26

IV.27

IV.29

IV.30

IV.28

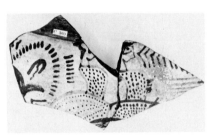

IV.28.1

IV.32

IV.32

IV.32

IV.33

IV.34

IV.35

IV.36

IV.37

IV.38

IV.38

IV.38

IV.39

IV.40

IV.41

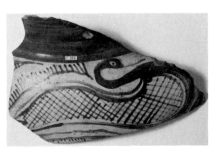

IV.44

IV.45

IV.46

IV.48

IV.49

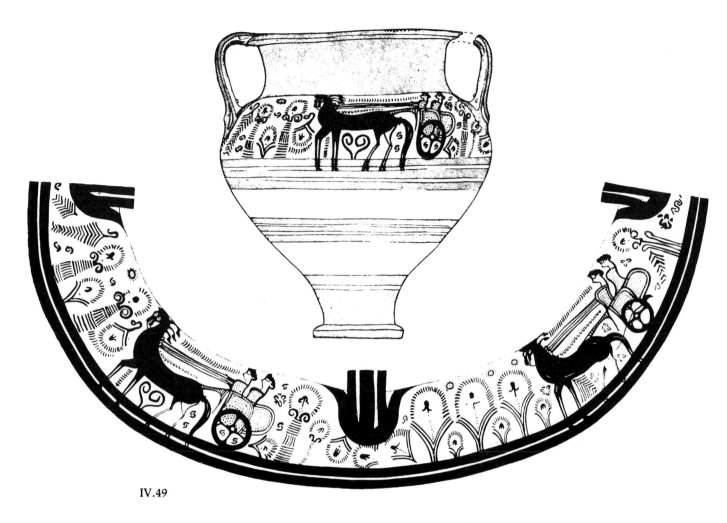

IV.49

IV.50

IV.51

IV.52

IV.53

IV.54

IV.55

IV.55

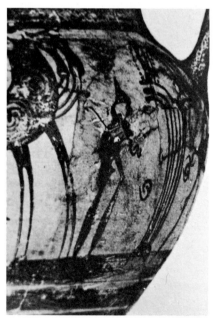

IV.55

IV.55

IV.58

IV.56

IV.59

IV.60

IV.61

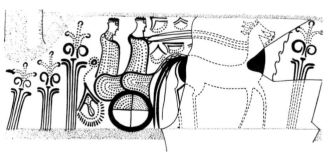

IV.62

IV.62

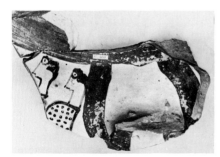

IV.63

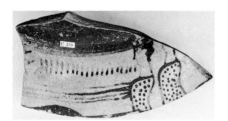

IV.64

IV.65

IV.65

IV.66

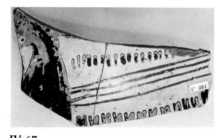

IV.67

IV.69

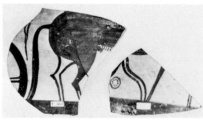

IV.68

IV.70

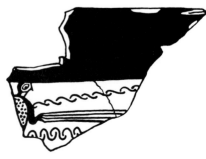

IV.71

IV.72

IV.74

IV.73

IV.77

IV.78

V.1

V.1

V.2

V.2

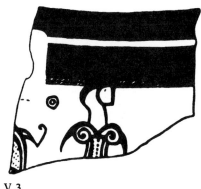

V.3

V.4

V.4

V.5

V.5

V.6

V.6

V.7

V.8

V.8

V.8

V.8

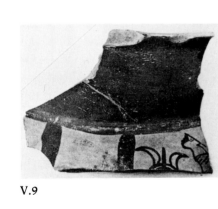

V.9

V.10

V.11

V.13

V.14

V.14

V.14

V.16

V.14

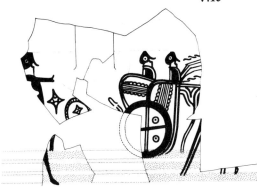

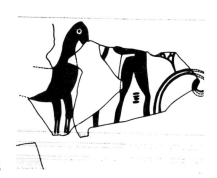

V.15

V.17

V.17

V.17

V.17

V.18

V.18

V.19

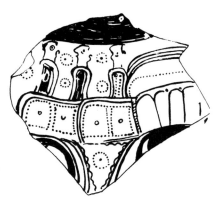

V.20

V.19

V.21

V.22

V.23

V.23

V.23

V.24

V.24

V.25.2

V.24

V.25.3

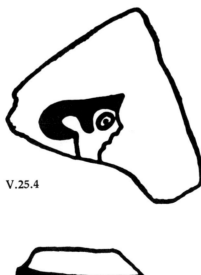

V.25.4

V.25.5

V.25.6

V.25.8u

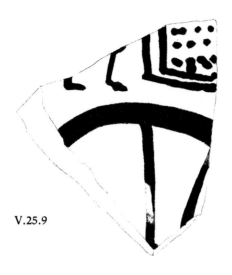

V.25.9

V.26

V.26

V.26

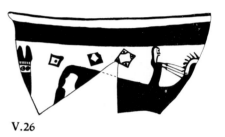

V.26

V.27

V.28

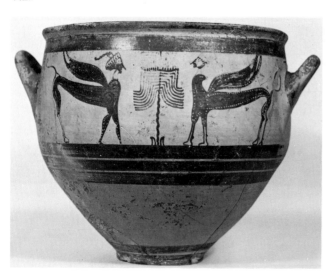

V.27

V.28 Side A

V.29

V.30

V.28 Side B

V.31

V.32

V.36

V.32

V.33

V.34

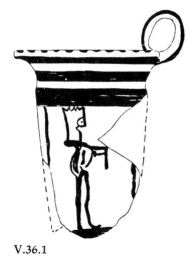

V.36.1

V.37

V.38

V.40

V.39

V.41

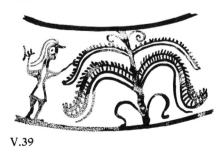

V.39

V.41

V.42

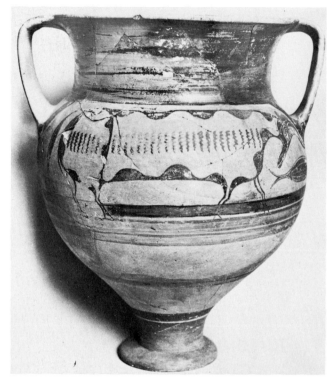

V.42

V.43

V.43

V.44

V.44

V.45

V.46

V.46

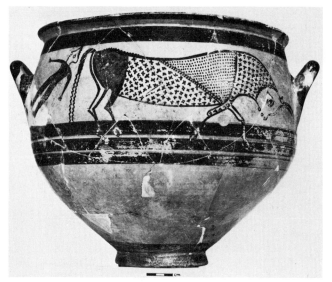

V.48

V.48

V.48

V.49

V.50

V.50

V.51

V.51

V.52

V.52

V.53

V.53

V.54

V.55

V.55

V.55

V.58

V.58

V.58

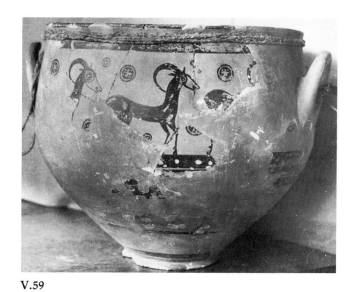

V.59

V.60

V.60

V.60

V.61

V.62

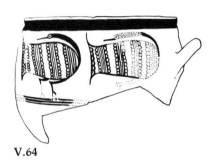

V.64

V.67

V.68

V.69

V.69

V.71

V.72

V.72.1

V.72.1

V.73

V.73

V.74

V.74

V.74.1

V.76

V.80

V.81

V.82.1

V.82

V.83

V.84

V.85

V.85

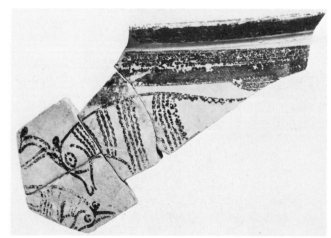

V.86

V.87

V.88

V.88

V.90

V.89

V.90

V.91

V.93

V.96

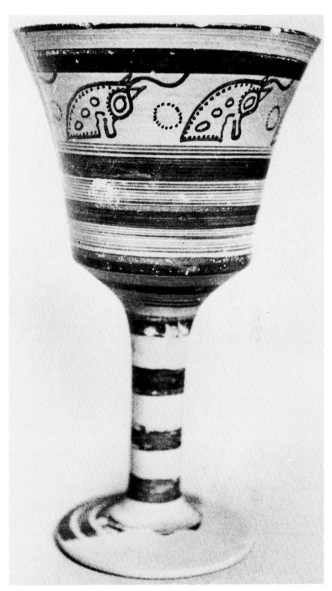

V.97

V.99

V.99

V.100

V.101

V.100.1

V.101

V.102

V.103

V.103

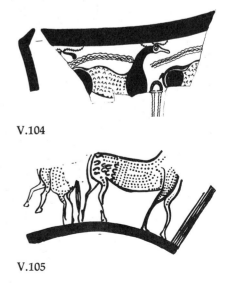

V.104

V.105

V.106

V.109

V.110 A

V.110 B

V.107

V.111

V.114

V.113

V.114

V.114

V.115

V.115

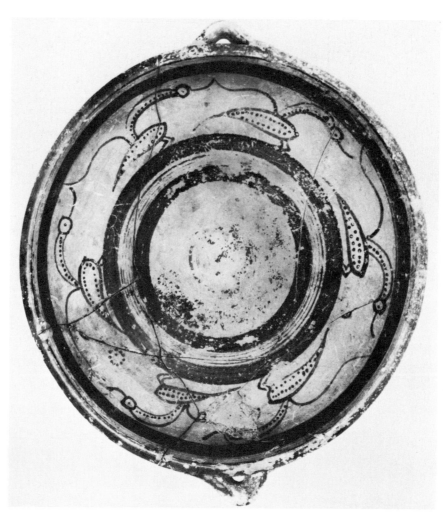

V.116

V.117.1

V.117

V.118

V.119

V.120

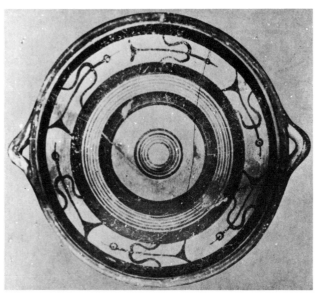

V.121

V.122

V.123

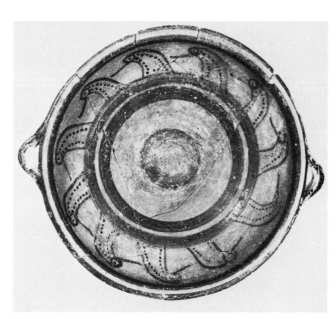

V.124

V.125

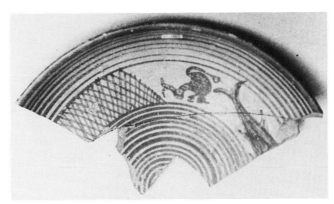

V.126

V.127

V.128

V.128

V.129

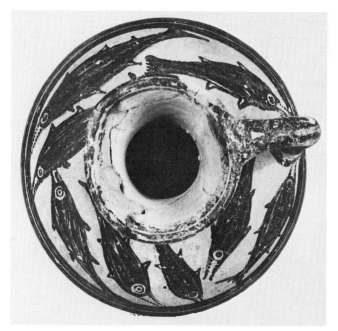

V.130

V.130

V.131

V.132

V.133

V.134

V.137

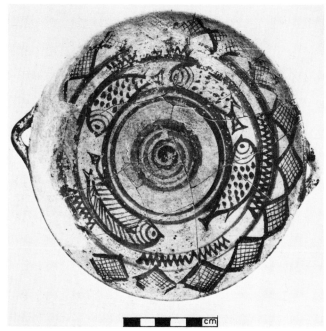

V.138

V.140

V.141

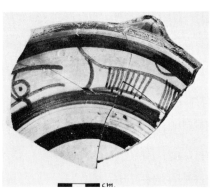

V.142

VI.1

VI.2

VI.4

VI.3

VI.5

VI.8

VI.9

VI.9

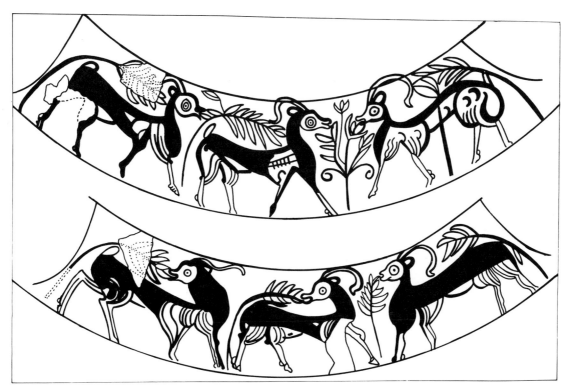

VI.9

VI.10

VI.10

VI.11

VI.12

VI.13

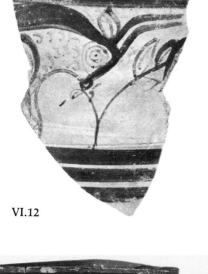

VI.14

V.15

VI.16

VI.17

VI.17

VI.19

VI.19

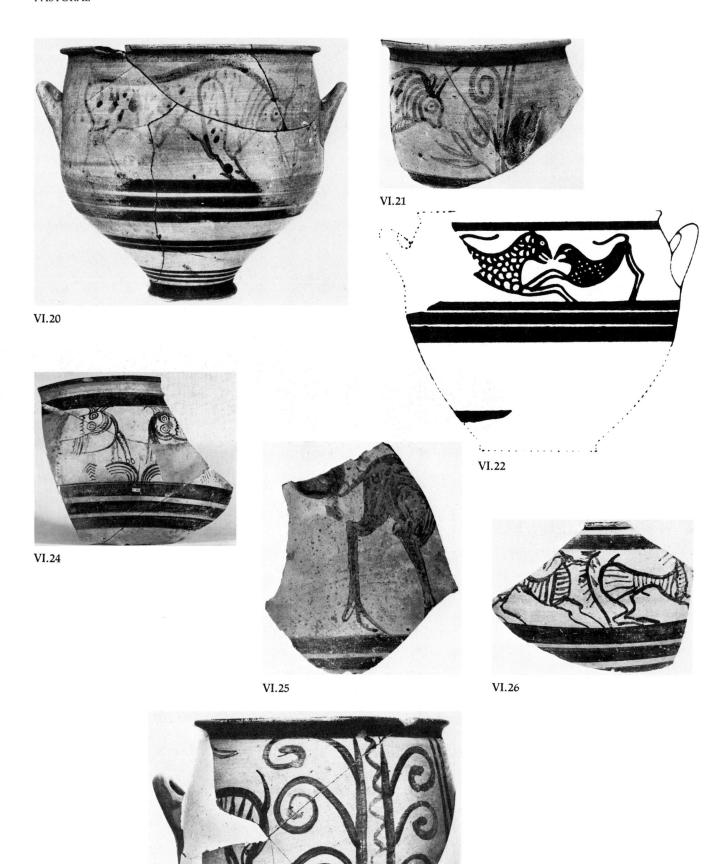

VI.20

VI.21

VI.22

VI.24

VI.25

VI.26

VI.28

VI.29

VI.32

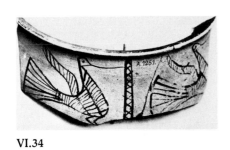

VI.34

VI.35

VI.36

VI.37

VI.37

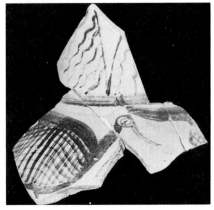

VI.38

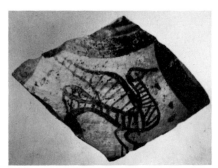

VI.39

VI.43

VI.43

VI.45

VI.47

VI.48

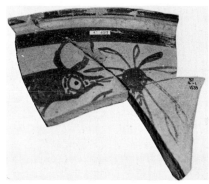

VI.49

VI.50

VI.51

VI.52

VI.55

VI.59

VI.60

VI.61

VI.62

VII.A

VII.A

VII.B

VII.C

VII.D

VII.E

VII.F

VII.G

VII.H

VII.H

VII.H

VII.H

VII.I

VII.J

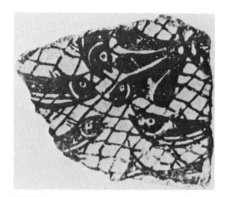

VII.K

VII.1

VII.2

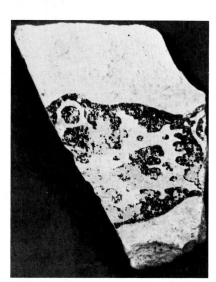

VII.3

VII.4

VII.5

VII.6

VII.6

VII.7

VII.9

VII.10

VII.8

VII.11

VII.12

VIII.1

VIII.2

VIII.3

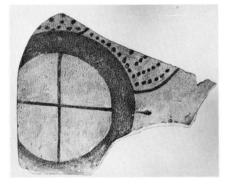

VIII.4

VIII.5

VIII.5.1

VIII.5.1

VIII.6

VIII.6

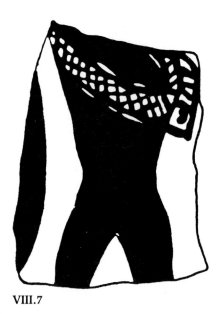

VIII.7

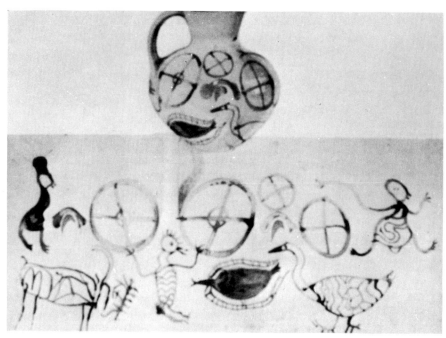

VIII.8

VIII.8

VIII.9

VIII.10

VIII.11

VIII.12

VIII.13

VIII.14

VIII.15

VIII.14

VIII.15

VIII.16

VIII.16

VIII.17

VIII.17

VIII.18

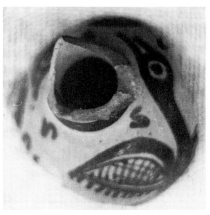

VIII.19

VIII.20

VIII.21

VIII.24

VIII.25

VIII.27

VIII.29

VIII.30

VII.31

VIII.31

[VIII.32 Before]

[VIII.32 After]

VIII.33

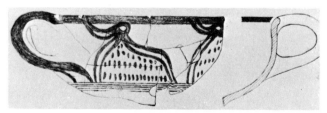

VIII.34

IX.1

IX.1.1

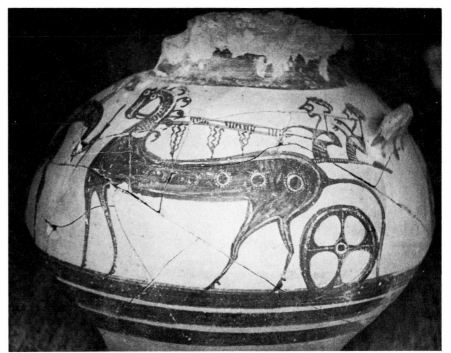

IX.1

IX.2

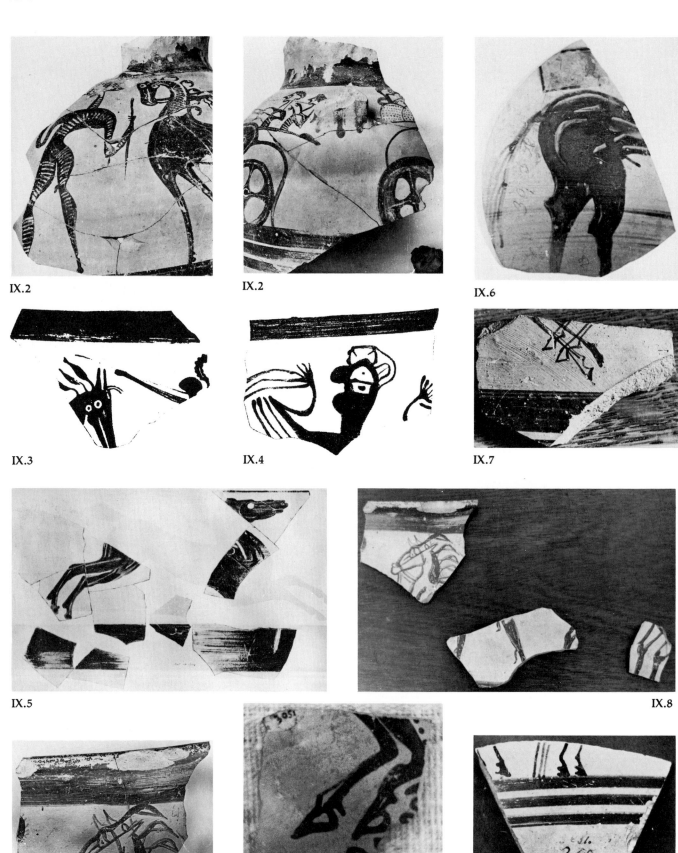

IX.2

IX.2

IX.6

IX.3

IX.4

IX.7

IX.5

IX.8

IX.8

IX.9

IX.10

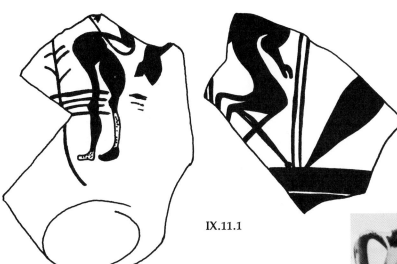

IX.11.1

IX.11

IX.12

IX.12

IX.13

IX.12

IX.13

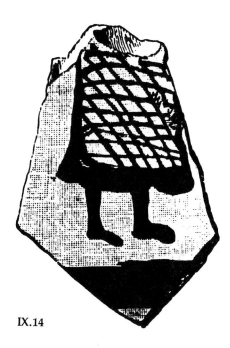

IX.14

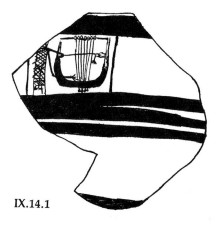

IX.14.1

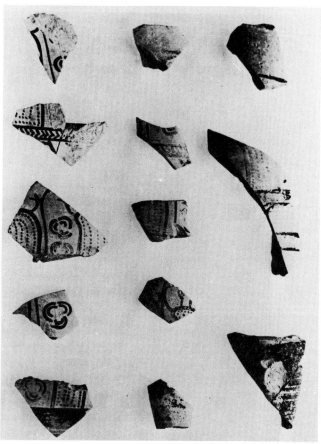

IX.15

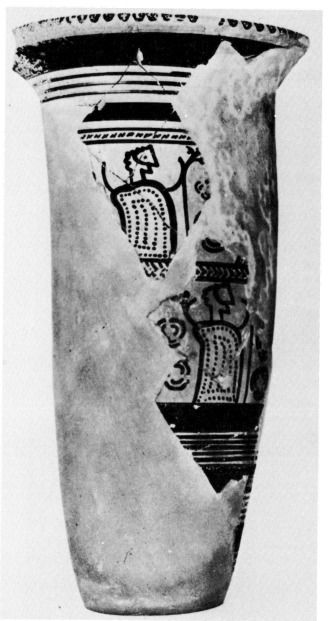

IX.15

IX.16

IX.16

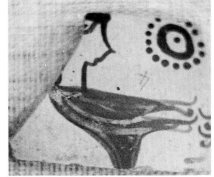

IX.17

IX.18

IX.18.1

IX.19

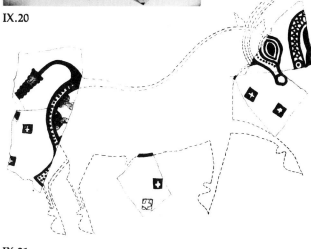

IX.20

IX.21

IX.22

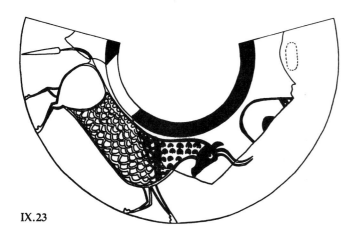

IX.23

IX.24

IX.24

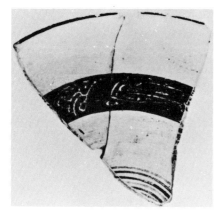

IX.25.1

IX.26

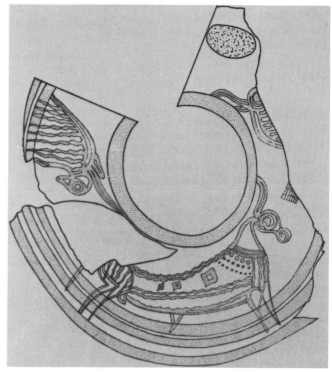

IX.25

IX.27

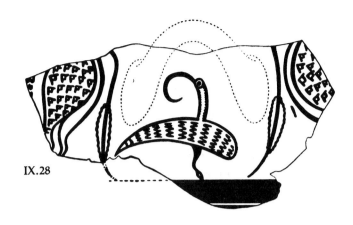

IX.28

IX.30

IX.30.1

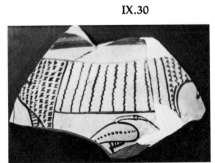

IX.31

IX.33

IX.34

IX.35

IX.36

IX.37

IX.38

IX.39

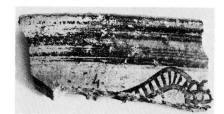

IX.41

IX.40

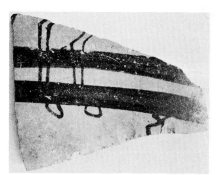

IX.42

IX.43

IX.44

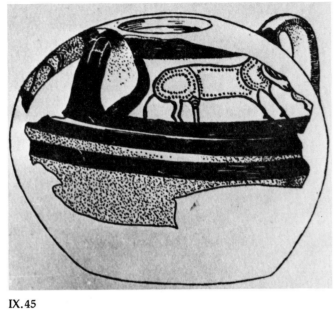

IX.45

IX.47

IX.48

IX.49

IX.51

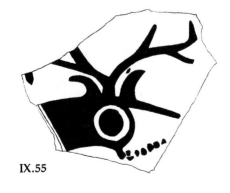

IX.55

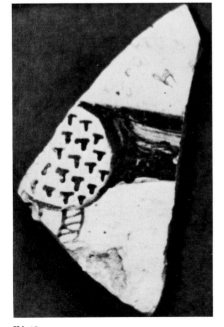

IX.63

IX.53

IX.64

IX.66

IX.67B

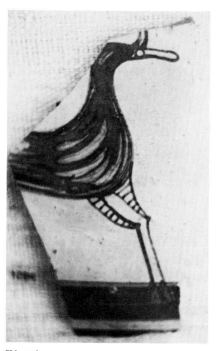

IX.67A

IX.68　　　　　IX.69　　　　　IX.70

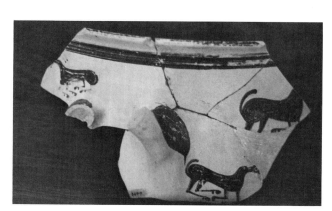

IX.71

IX.72

IX.73

IX.74

IX.76.1

IX.75

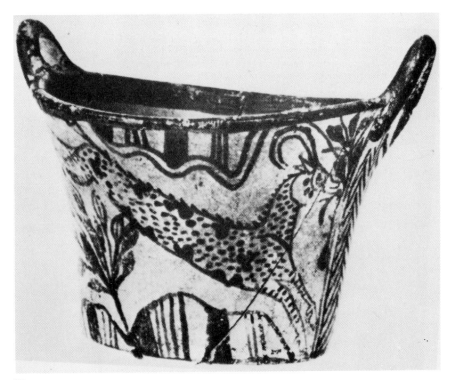

IX.77

IX.78

IX.79

IX.80

IX.81

IX.82

IX.82

IX.83

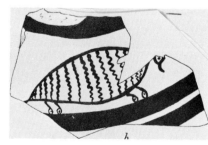

IX.84

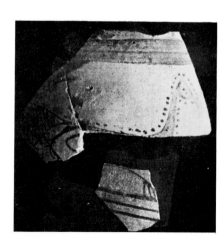

IX.86

IX.87

IX.88

IX.90

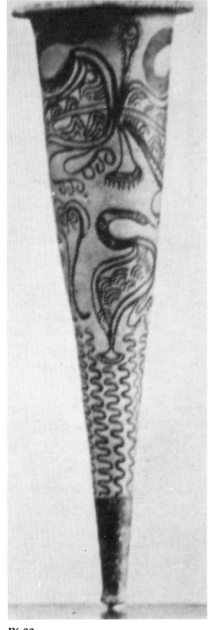

IX.89

IX.92

IX.95

IX.96

IX.97

IX.98

IX.99

IX.100

IX.101

IX.102

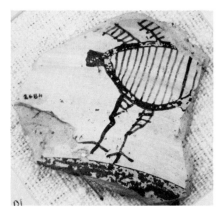

IX.105

IX.106

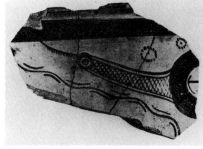

IX.107

IX.108

IX.109

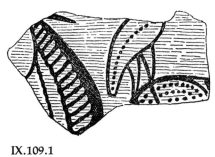

IX.109.1

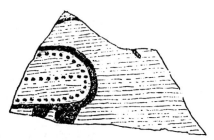

IX.109.2

IX.110

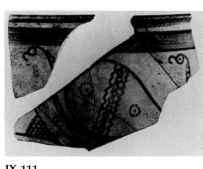

IX.111

IX.111.1

IX.112

IX.115

IX.116

IX.117

IX.119

IX.120

IX.121

IX.122

IX.123

X.1

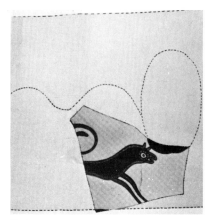

X.1

X.1

X.1

X.1

X.1

X.1

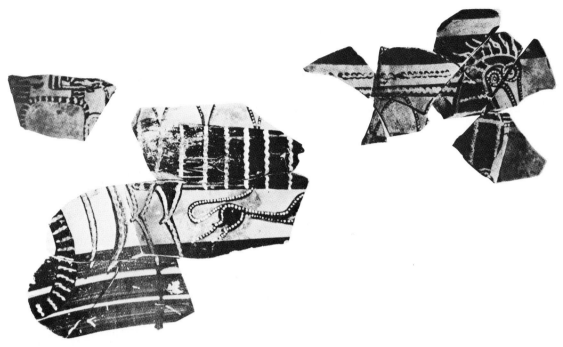

X.2

X.4

X.3

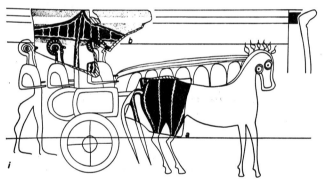

X.5

X.6

X.7

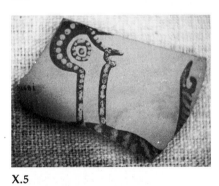

X.8

X.9

X.9

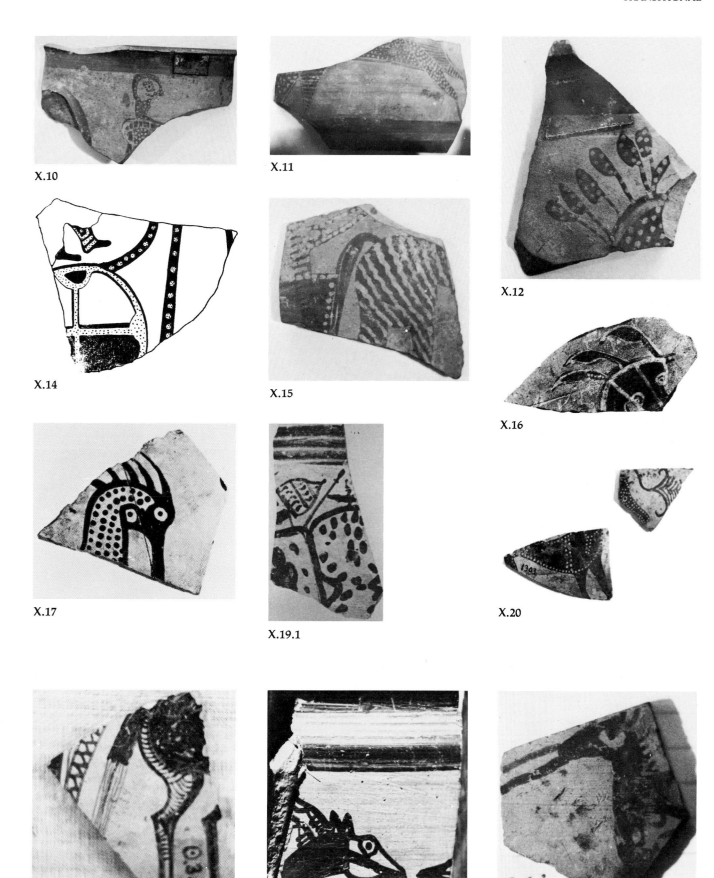

X.10

X.11

X.12

X.14

X.15

X.16

X.17

X.19.1

X.20

X.23

X.24

X.25

X.27

X.28

X.29

X.30

X.31

X.33

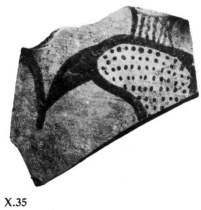

X.34

X.35

X.36

X.37

X.37

X.38

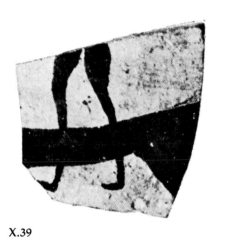

X.39

X.40

X.41

X.41.1

X.42

X.43

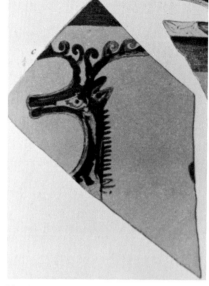

X.44

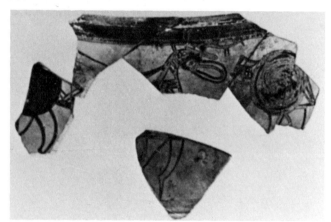

X.45

X.48

X.46

X.47

X.49

X.50

X.51

X.52

X.53

X.54

X.55

X.56

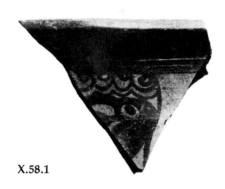

X.58.1

X.59

X.59

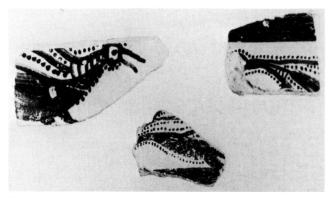

X.62

X.62

X.63

X.65

X.66

X.67

X.68

X.69

X.70

X.71

X.72

X.74

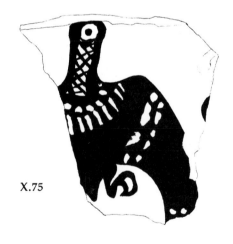

X.75

X.76

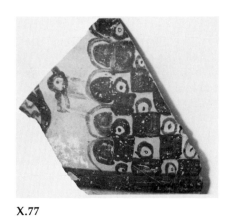

X.77

X.78

X.79

X.80

X.82

X.81

X.83

X.84

X.85

X.86

X.87

X.88

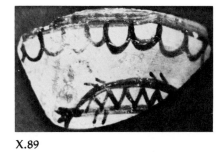

X.89

X.95

X.96

X.97

X.98

X.99

X.100

X.102

X.102

X.103

X.104

X.105

X.106

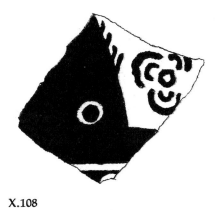

X.108

X.111

X.113

X.114

X.115

X.116

X.117

XI.1A

XI.1B

XI.2

XI.2

XI.3

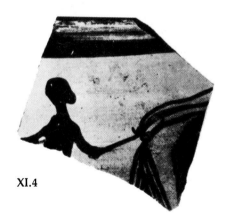

XI.4

XI.5

XI.6

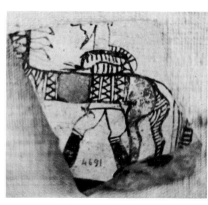

XI.7

XI.8

XI.9

XI.10

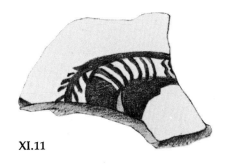

XI.11

XI.12

XI.13

XI.14

XI.14

XI.15

XI.15.1

XI.16

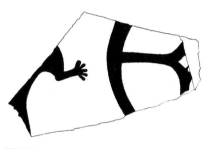

XI.15.2

XI.16.1

XI.17

XI.17

XI.18

XI.19

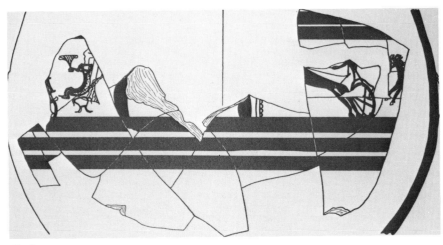

XI.19.1

XI.20

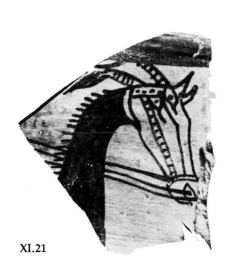

XI.21

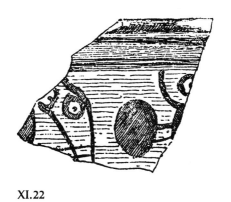

XI.22

XI.24

XI.25

XI.25

XI.25

XI.26

XI.27

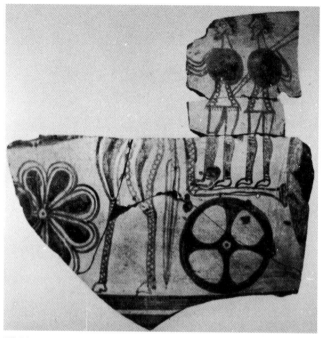

XI.28

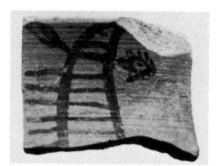

XI.29

XI.31

XI.31.2

XI.30

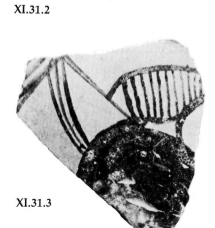

XI.31.3

XI.31.4

XI.31.5

XI.32

XI.33

XI.34

XI.35

XI.36

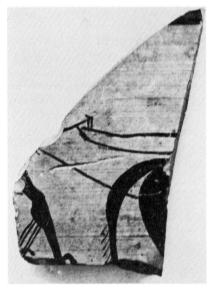

XI.37

XI.38

XI.39

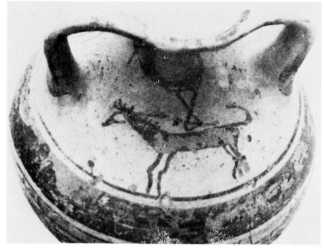

XI.40

XI.41

XI.42

XI.42

XI.42

XI.42

XI.42

XI.42

XI.42

XI.43

XI.43

XI.43

XI.44

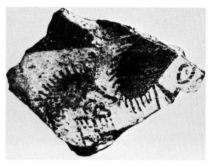

XI.45

XI.45

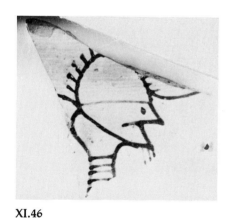

XI.46

XI.47

XI.48

XI.49

XI.50

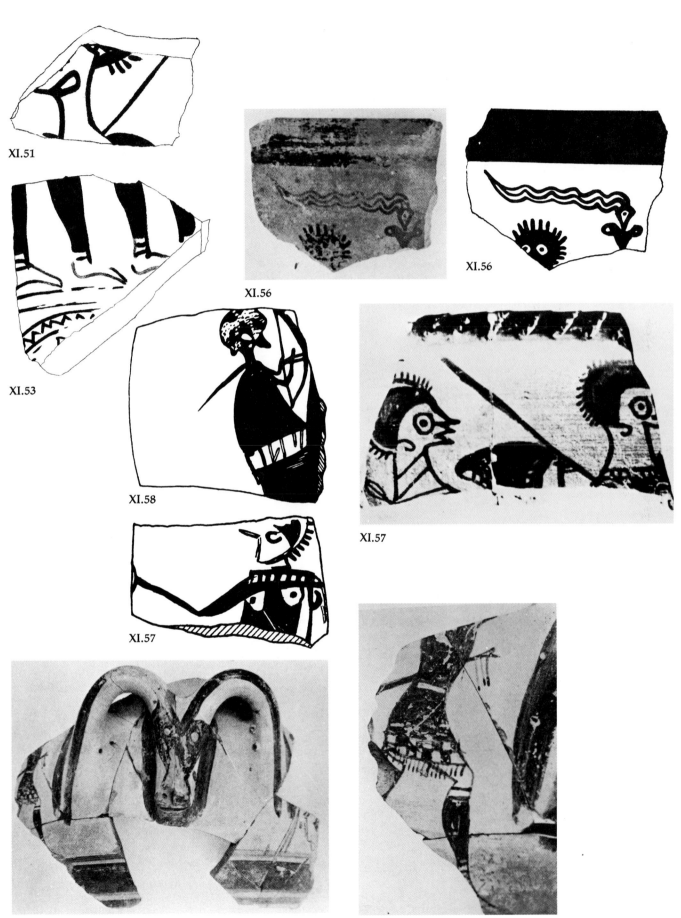

XI.51

XI.56

XI.56

XI.53

XI.58

XI.57

XI.57

XI.59

XI.59

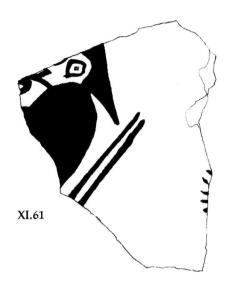

XI.61

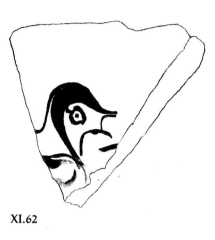

XI.62

XI.63

XI.64

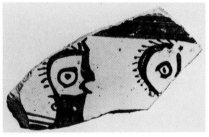

XI.64.1

XI.65

XI.67

XI.66

XI.68

XI.69

XI.70

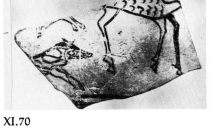

XI.70

XI.70

XI.70

XI.71

XI.71

XI.72

XI.73

XI.74

XI.75

XI.76

XI.77.1

XI.78

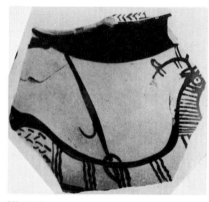

XI.77.2

XI.80

XI.80

XI.79

XI.82

XI.83

XI.84

XI.85

XI.85.1

XI.86

XI.86

XI.87

XI.88

XI.89

XI.90

XI.91

XI.91

XI.92

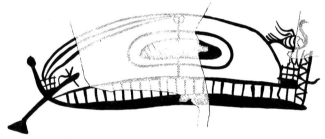

XI.92

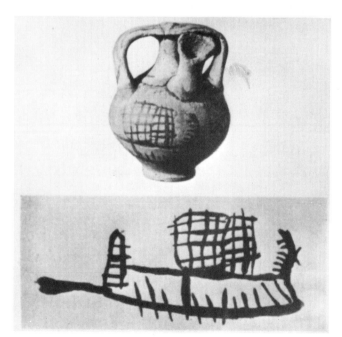

XI.94

XI.95

XI.96

XI.98

XI.99

XI.100

XI.101

XI.102

XI.103

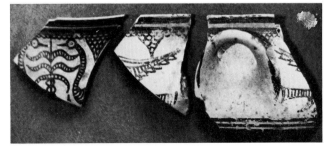

XI.108

XI.112

XI.112

XI.110

XI.116

XI.117

XI.118

XI.119

XI.120

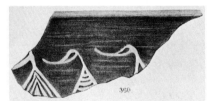

XI.121

XI.123

XI.124

XI.125

XI.126

XI.127

XI.133

XI.136

XI.136

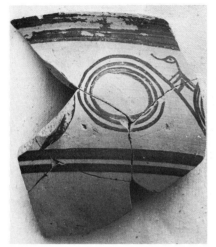

XI.139

XI.141

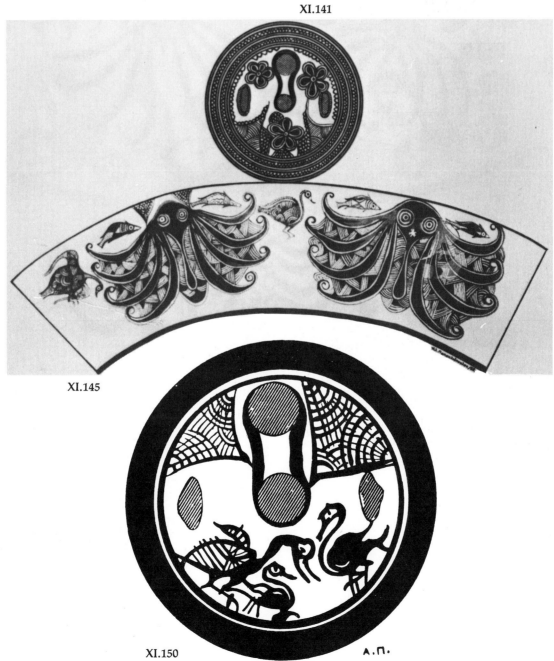

XI.145

XI.150

Λ.Π.

XII.1

XII.2

XII.3

XII.3

XII.4

XII.5

XII.6

XII.6

XII.6

XII.7

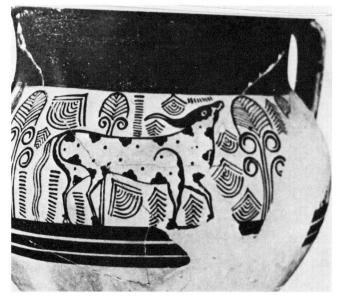

XII.7

XII.8

XII.9

XII.10

XII.11

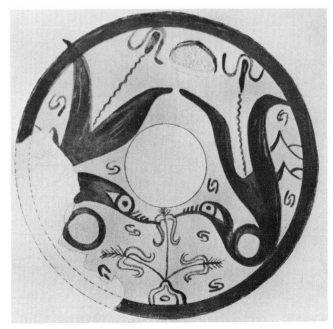

XII.12

XII.13

XII.15

XII.16

XII.17

XII.17

XII.18

XII.18

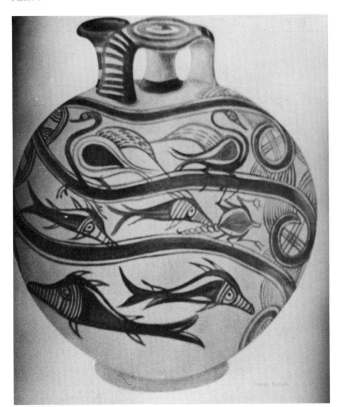

XII.19

XII.20

XII.20.1

XII.21

XII.21

XII.22

XII.23

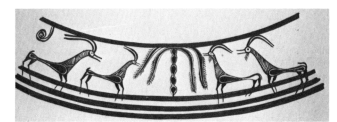

XII.24

XII.23

XII.25

XII.26

XII.27

XII.27

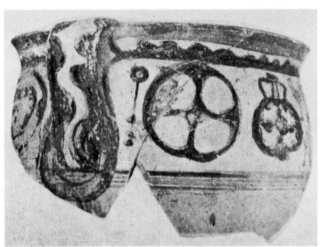

XII.28

XII.29

XII.30

XII.31

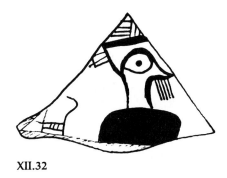

XII.32

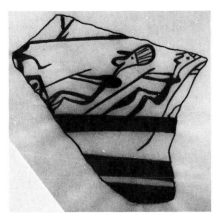

XII.33

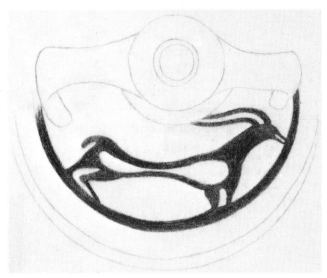

XII.34

XII.35

XII.35

XII.35

XII.37

XII.39

XII.40

XII.41

XII.41

XII.42

XII.42

XIII.1

XIII.2

XIII.4

XIII.5

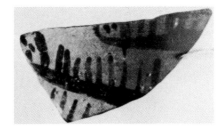

XIII.6

XIII.7

XIII.7

XIII.8

XIII.8

XIII.8

XIII.8

XIII.10

XIII.11

XIII.12

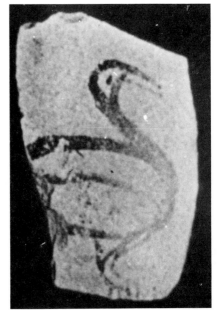

XIII.13

XIII.15

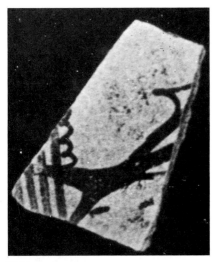

XIII.16

XIII.17

XIII.18

XIII.19

XIII.20

XIII.22

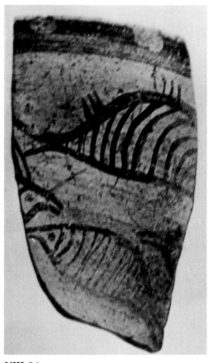

XIII.24

XIII.25

XIII.26

XIII.27

XIII.27

XIII.28

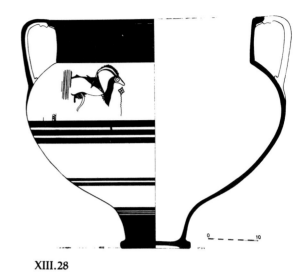

XIII.28

XIII.28

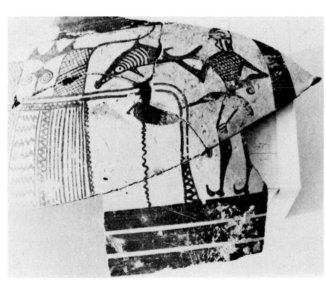

XIII.29

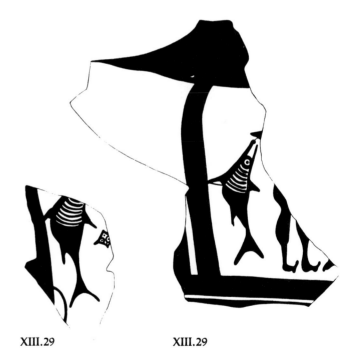

XIII.29

XIII.29

XIII.30

Index of Museums and Collections

Arranged alphabetically by city

MUSEUM NUMBER	CATALOGUE NUMBER	SITE	SHAPE	SUBJECT
AIGINA				
2097	VIII.10	Aigina	jug	goat-bird
AMMAN				
6261	IV.73	Amman	amphoroid krater	chariot
AMSTERDAM, ALLARD PIERSON STICHTING				
1856	V.17	Cyprus?	amphoroid krater	chariot, rider
ATHENS, ACROPOLIS (*see* ATHENS, NATIONAL MUSEUM)				
ATHENS, AGORA				
AP 1072	X.81	Acropolis	krater	bird
AP 2658	X.97	Acropolis	krater	fish
AP 2661	X.98	Acropolis	krater	fish
AP 2668	XI.36	Acropolis	krater	horse
AP 2715	XI.139	Acropolis	bowl	bird protome
AP 2753	IX.46	Acropolis	closed	bull
AP 2779	X.99	Acropolis	lekane	fish
AP 2908	X.41.1	Acropolis	krater	hand
AP 3001	X.41	Acropolis	krater	hand
—	X.80	Acropolis	closed	bird
P 21200	X.100	Agora	lekane	fish
P 21246	VII.7	Agora	ewer	fish, octopus
P 21564	VIII.33	Agora	krater	altar
ATHENS, AMERICAN SCHOOL OF CLASSICAL STUDIES				
—	IX.7	Mycenae	krater	horse
—	X.24	Mycenae	krater	horse

MUSEUM NUMBER	CATALOGUE NUMBER	SITE	SHAPE	SUBJECT

ATHENS, BRITISH SCHOOL OF ARCHAEOLOGY

—	IX.113	Phylakopi	fragment	bird
—	IX.114	Phylakopi	fragment	bird
—	(X.39)	Phylakopi	krater	man
—	X.60	Tiryns	fragment	bird

ATHENS, NATIONAL MUSEUM

Many pieces, especially fragments, have an original "lot number" and a later individual number; some numbers represent several phases of cataloguing. Within the groups with a single lot number, the index runs in sequence according to the catalogue of this book.

—1.4250 (=1303, =398)	IX.102	Mycenae	krater	bird
397 (=1303)	IX.101	Mycenae	krater	bird
398 (=1303)	IX.102	Mycenae	krater	bird
1126	XI.119	Mycenae	four-handled jar	bird
1141	XI.2	Mycenae	krater	chariot
	XI.8	Mycenae	krater	soldier, horse
	XI.9	Mycenae	krater	horse
	XI.10	Mycenae	krater	horse
	XI.44	Mycenae	krater	soldier
	XI.103	Mycenae	bowl	bird
	XI.125	Mycenae	krater	bird, fish
1212 (—5)	VIII.21	Mycenae	krater	bird
(—5)	VIII.22	Mycenae	krater	bird
(=2683?)	X.6	Mycenae	krater	soldier
	XI.48	Mycenae	krater	helmet?
1269 (=3678.7)	X.54	Mycenae	krater?	"unicorn"
1272 (=3600—5, 1298/30)	VIII.12	Mycenae	krater	bull
a, b	IX.8	Mycenae	krater	soldier, horse
	IX.17	Mycenae	krater	boxer
(—7, —26)	IX.30	Mycenae	krater	bull
("26")	IX.79	Mycenae	krater	dog
(—7)	X.30	Mycenae	bowl	soldier, bag
(=3596)	XI.1	Mycenae	krater	chariot
1275	VIII.23	Mycenae	krater	bird
(=1298130)	IX.31	Mycenae	krater	bull, bird
(=2250)	IX.35	Mycenae	krater	bull
(—5)	IX.37	Mycenae	krater	bull
(—5)	IX.85	Mycenae	jar?	bird
(=1280, =1303, =.3635)	IX.98	Mycenae	krater	bird
	IX.104	Mycenae	krater	bird
	X.65	Mycenae	krater/bowl	bird
5, 7, 3	X.69	Mycenae	bowl	bird
.28	X.70	Mycenae	krater	bird
(=3254.5, 3254, 3625 b)	IX.49	Mycenae	krater	deer
(=3670.6)	X.72	Mycenae	krater	bird
(.3)	XI.100	Mycenae	bowl	bird
(.4)	XI.101	Mycenae	bowl	bird
	XI.104	Mycenae	bowl	bird
	XI.105	Mycenae	bowl	bird

MUSEUM NUMBER	CATALOGUE NUMBER	SITE	SHAPE	SUBJECT
	XI.106	Mycenae	bowl	bird
	XI.107	Mycenae	bowl	bird
	XI.109	Mycenae	bowl	bird
	XI.111	Mycenae	bowl	bird
(=4040.3)	XI.114	Mycenae	bowl	bird
.6	XI.115	Mycenae	stirrup jar	bird
1275/28 (=3621.4)	IX.33	Mycenae	krater	bull
(=310−)	IX.51	Mycenae	krater	deer
1280	VII.4	Mycenae "Acropolis"	krater	bull
(=1275, 1303, 3635)	IX.98	Mycenae	krater	bird
1290 (=300?3)	XI.75	Mycenae	krater	deer
1290/30 (.4) (=4090?)	IX.63	Mycenae	krater	deer
1292 (1298, 3383, 3653)	X.73	Mycenae	bowl	bird
1293/30	X.49	Mycenae	bowl	stag
1294	IX.67	Mycenae	krater	goat
	X.31	Mycenae	krater/bowl	soldier
(=3687, .4)	X.95	Mycenae	bowl	fish
.25	XI.6	Mycenae	bowl	chariot
	XI.12	Mycenae	bowl	horse
	XI.74	Mycenae	bowl	deer, dog
	XI.86	Mycenae	krater	caterpillar
	XI.88	Mycenae	bowl	hedgehog
	XI.123	Mycenae	krater	bird
1298	VII.3	Mycenae	larnax	bull
	VII.8	Mycenae	krater	fish
.6	IX.34	Mycenae	krater	bull
(=3632.2)	IX.42	Mycenae	krater	bull
(.4?)	X.88	Mycenae	krater	fish
(=3633.4)	X.56	Mycenae	krater	goat
(1292, 3383, 3653)	X.73	Mycenae	bowl	bird
(.30)	X.88	Mycenae	krater	fish
(.338 or .358)	X.89	Mycenae	bowl	fish
(.30)	X.90	Mycenae	bowl	fish
1298/4 (=3626.4)	IX.69	Mycenae	krater	goat/deer
1298/5 (=3626.5)	IX.70	Mycenae	krater	goat/deer
1298/30 (=3600−5, 1272)	VIII.12	Mycenae	krater	bull
(=3674.4)	VIII.18	Mycenae	rhyton?	bird
(1275)	IX.31	Mycenae	krater	bull, bird
(3-20)	IX.36	Mycenae	krater	bull
	IX.38	Mycenae	krater	bull
	XI.40	Mycenae	krater	bull
(=3618.3)	IX.43	Mycenae	jug	bull/goat
(=3690.4)	IX.53	Mycenae	krater	stag
	IX.65	Mycenae	krater	animal
(=3612.5)	IX.81	Mycenae	krater	dog/lion
1303 (=4032.4)	IX.73	Mycenae	bowl/cup	goat
(−220. −7, .24)	IX.74	Mycenae	cup	goat
(=3635, 1275, 1280)	IX.98	Mycenae	krater	bird

MUSEUM NUMBER	CATALOGUE NUMBER	SITE	SHAPE	SUBJECT
(397, 3__42.4)	IX.101	Mycenae	krater	bird
(398, −1.4250)	IX.102	Mycenae	krater	bird
	X.20	Mycenae	krater	horse
	X.27	Mycenae	krater	horse/donkey
	X.53	Mycenae	krater	goat
.4	X.68	Mycenae	bowl	bird
	X.74	Mycenae	krater	bird
	X.87	Mycenae	stirrup jar?	fish
	XI.11	Mycenae	bowl	horse/stag
	XI.72	Mycenae	krater	dog, deer
(=3640.3)	XI.73	Mycenae	krater	dog
(=4032.4)	IX.73	Mycenae	bowl/cup	goat
	XI.76	Mycenae	krater	stag
1308.(−4)	VIII.24	Mycenae	krater	bird
.(−3, +2654)	X.23	Mycenae	krater	horse
1309 (−5, −33)	IX.32	Mycenae	krater	bird
	IX.39	Mycenae	krater	bull
	IX.100	Mycenae	fragment	bird
	XI.112	Mycenae	bowl	bird
1426	XI.42	Mycenae	krater	soldiers
1507	X.11	Tiryns	krater	horse
1508	X.12	Tiryns	krater	horse
1509, 1510	X.9	Tiryns	krater	chariot
1511	X.1	Tiryns	krater	chariot
1512	X.10	Tiryns	krater	horse
1514	IX.6	Tiryns	krater	horse
	X.13	Tiryns	krater	horse
1622	X.59	Tiryns	krater	bird
1631	X.44	Tiryns	krater	stag
1654	X.15	Tiryns	krater	horse
1768	XI.113	Mycenae	bowl	bird
2209	IX.115	Spata	stirrup jar	fish
2213	IX.92	Spata	krater	bird
2213 a	IX.92.1	Spata	three-handled jar?	bird
2250 (=1275)	IX.35	Mycenae	krater	bull
2257	VII.I	Mycenae	pyxis	bird
2379	X.29	Mycenae	krater	soldier
2380	X.83	Mycenae	closed	fish
2580	XI.3	Mycenae	krater	soldier, horse
2581	IX.82	Mycenae	krater	lion, bull
2648	IX.119	Mycenae	krater	fish
2654	VIII.30	Mycenae	stirrup jar	sphinx, bird
(+1308−3)	X.23	Mycenae	krater	horse
	X.52	Mycenae	krater	goat
	X.84	Mycenae	bowl	fish
	XI.77.1	Mycenae	krater	stag
2674	XI.46	Mycenae	krater	soldier
2675	IX.18.1	Mycenae	rhyton?	bull jumper

MUSEUM NUMBER	CATALOGUE NUMBER	SITE	SHAPE	SUBJECT
2677	IX.71	Mycenae	krater	goat
2678	X.43	Mycenae	krater	stag
2681	X.5	Mycenae	krater	soldier
2682 (+2687)	XI.71	Mycenae	krater	hunt
2683 (1212)	X.6	Mycenae	krater	soldier
2684	IX.105	Mycenae	bowl	bird
2685	XI.102	Mycenae	bowl	bird
2687 (+2682)	XI.71	Mycenae	krater	hunt
2688	X.66	Mycenae	krater	bird
2775	XI.90	Mycenae	bowl	snake
2899	IX.88	Mycenae	fragment	crab/ship
300?3 (=1290)	XI.75	Mycenae	krater	deer
3051	VIII.19	Mycenae	rhyton?	bird
	IX.9	Mycenae	krater	horse
	X.86	Mycenae	jar	fish
	XI.124	Mycenae	krater	bird
310__ (=1275/28)	IX.51	Mycenae	krater	deer
3244	IX.72	Mycenae	krater	goat
3245	IX.64	Mycenae	krater	animal
3254, 3254.5, 3625 b (=1275)	IX.49	Mycenae	krater	deer
3256	XI.43	Mycenae	stele	soldiers, deer, hedgehog
3383 (1292, 1298, 3653)	X.73	Mycenae	bowl	bird
3472	IX.3	Kopreza	krater	chariot
3596 (1272) (see Nauplion 83 57)	XI.1	Mycenae	krater	chariot
3600-5 (1272, 1298/30)	VIII.12	Mycenae	krater	bull
3612.5 (1298/30)	IX.81	Mycenae	krater	dog/lion
3617.4	X.55	Mycenae	krater	goat
3618.3 (1298/30)	IX.43	Mycenae	jug	bull/goat protome
3621.4 (1275/28	IX.33	Mycenae	krater	bull
3625 (3254, 3254 b, 1275)	IX.49	Mycenae	krater	deer
3626.4 (1298/4)	XI.69	Mycenae	krater	goat/deer
3626.5 (1298/5)	IX.70	Mycenae	krater	goat/deer
3629.4	IX.52	Mycenae	krater	deer
	IX.68	Mycenae	krater	goat/deer
3631	IX.10	Mycenae	krater	horse
3632.2 (1298)	IX.42	Mycenae	krater	bull
3633.4 (1298)	X.56	Mycenae	krater	goat
3634.4	IX.66	Mycenae	krater	goat
3635 (1275, 1280, 1303)	IX.98	Mycenae	krater	bird
3640.3 (1303)	XI.73	Mycenae	krater	dog
3653 (1292, 1298, =3383)	X.73	Mycenae	bowl	bird
3670.6 (1275)	X.72	Mycenae	krater	bird
3674.4 (1298/30)	VIII.18	Mycenae	rhyton?	bird
3678.7 (1269)	X.54	Mycenae	fragment	"unicorn"
3686	X.94	Mycenae	fragment	fish
3687 (.4), (1294)	X.95	Mycenae	bowl	fish

MUSEUM NUMBER	CATALOGUE NUMBER	SITE	SHAPE	SUBJECT
3690.4 (1298/30)	IX.53	Mycenae	krater	deer
3692	X.91	Mycenae	bowl	fish
3693.4	X.93	Mycenae	fragment	fish
3694	X.93	Mycenae	fragment	fish
4024 (4924?)	X.25	Mycenae	krater/bowl	horse
4032.4 (1303)	IX.73	Mycenae	bowl/cup	goat
4040.3 (1275)	XI.114	Mycenae	bowl	bird
4090? (.4, 1290/30)	IX.63	Mycenae	krater	deer
4691	XI.7	Mycenae	krater	soldier, horse
4924? see 4024				
5424	VIII.13	Mycenae	krater	bull's head
5650	VII.H	Argos	three-handled jar	bird
8556	VII.J	Varkiza	basket vase	fish
8699	VII.G	Mycenae	jug	bird
9863	IX.12	Kopreza	krater	"dancers"
Nos. incomplete or unknown				
(4)	IX.41	Mycenae	krater	bull
	IX.60	Mycenae	krater	stag
	IX.61	Mycenae	krater	stag
	IX.62	Mycenae	krater	stag
"Acropolis"	IX.106	Mycenae	krater	bird
.150	IX.109	Tiryns	krater	bird
"Acropolis," 89	X.47	Mycenae	bowl	stag
(.4, .30; 1298?)	X.88	Mycenae	krater	fish
	XI.19	Tiryns	bowl	chariot
	XI.108	Mycenae	cup	bird
	XI.118	Mycenae	stirrup jar	bird
Not found				
(Athens, Acropolis 233)	X.28	Athens	krater/bowl	horse
	XI.47	Mycenae	krater	soldiers

ATHENS, NATIONAL MUSEUM: ACROPOLIS COLLECTION (*Graef-Langlotz numbers*)

36	VIII.26	Acropolis	krater	bird
188	XI.140	Acropolis	fragment	bird
220	XI.33	Acropolis	krater	driver
221	IX.90	Acropolis	fragment	bird
223	XI.32	Acropolis	krater	driver
224	XI.34	Acropolis	krater	chariot
225	XI.35	Acropolis	bowl	man
229	X.77	Acropolis	bowl	bird
230	X.78	Acropolis	bowl	bird
231	X.79	Acropolis	bowl	bird
232	IX.91	Acropolis	krater	bird
233 (not found)	X.28	Acropolis	krater/bowl	horse
	IX.14	Acropolis	krater	robed man

MUSEUM NUMBER	CATALOGUE NUMBER	SITE	SHAPE	SUBJECT
BERKELEY, LOWIE MUSEUM OF ANTHROPOLOGY				
8.924 a	V.116	Cyprus	bowl	bird
8.924 b	V.137	Cyprus	bowl	sea slug
BERLIN, STAATLICHE MUSEEN, ANTIKENABTEILUNG				
8103	V.101	Nicosia	bell krater	bull
31105	IX.89	Attica?	rhyton	bird
See also	IX.123			
BONN, AKADEMISCHES KUNSTMUSEUM				
777	V.6	Cyprus	amphoroid krater	chariot
780	V.121	—	bowl	bird
BOSTON, MUSEUM OF FINE ARTS				
01.8042	XII.21	Amorgos?	kylix	stag, bull
01.8044	V.14	Nicosia?	amphoroid krater	chariot, belt wrestler
59.710	XI.82	Salamis?	krater	goat
BRUSSELS, MUSÉE DU CINQUANTENAIRE				
A 1247	IV.31	Enkomi	amphoroid krater	chariot
A 1249	V.30	Enkomi	amphoroid krater	boxer?
A 1251	VI.34	Enkomi	bell krater	bird
A 1253	V.9	Enkomi	amphoroid krater	chariot
A 1254	V.117.1	Enkomi	bowl	bird
A 1257	IV.8	Enkomi	amphoroid krater	bird?
A 1258	V.77	Enkomi	bell krater	bull
CAMBRIDGE, FITZWILLIAM MUSEUM				
GR.132 A -1908	V.72	—	amphoroid krater	bird
CHANIA MUSEUM				
812	V.19	Aptera, Suda Bay	bell krater	chariot, vases
COPENHAGEN, NATIONAL MUSEUM				
7570	XII.15	Vatoi, Rhodes	kylix	bird
CORINTH MUSEUM				
—	IX.1	Corinth	amphoroid krater	chariot
—	XI.98	Korakou	bowl	bird
—	XI.99	Korakou	bowl	bird
CYPRUS, ARCHAEOLOGICAL SURVEY SHERD COLLECTION				
CS 338	IV.42	Arpera	krater	bird
CS 1746	VI.19	Kyrenia	krater	bull
CS 1829	VI.9	Kazaphani	krater	goat
CS 5103	VI.52	Morphou	krater	chariot
—	VI.41	Enkomi	krater	bird

MUSEUM NUMBER	CATALOGUE NUMBER	SITE	SHAPE	SUBJECT
A 2041	IV.57	Enkomi?	amphoroid krater	chariot
T.17/16	V.76	Enkomi	bell krater	bull, bird
1934/I-28/1	VI.25	Hala Sultan Tekké	bell krater	goat
1943/II-20/1	V.80	—	bell krater	bull protome
1952/IV-12/1	III.13	Pyla-Verghi	krater	chariot
1958/I-10/1 +BM C 374, 681	IV.41	Enkomi	amphoroid krater	bird
1958/I-10/5	V.129	—	bell krater	fish
1958/I-10/6	V.63	Enkomi	amphoroid krater	bird
1958/II-17/5	VI.18	Enkomi	bell krater	sphinx
1958/IV-7/2	VI.58	Nicosia	bell krater	leaf
1958/IV-20/9	VI.12	Larnaka	bell krater	bull
1958/V-20/3	IV.20	—	amphoroid krater	chariot
1958/VI-20/1	III.20	Enkomi?	krater	men, animal?
1958/VI-20/7	IV.33	—	amphoroid krater	bull
1959/II-26/1	VI.21	—	bell krater	bull
1962/V-31/1	IV.46	—	amphoroid krater	octopus
1965/VIII-17/3	IV.14	Enkomi	krater	man
1971/?XII-6/1 (=BM C 391)	III.12	Kourion	krater	women, chariot
HALLE WITTENBURG				
116	XI.64	—	krater/bowl	soldier
HEIDELBERG, UNIVERSITÄT				
27/12	XI.18	Tiryns	krater	chariot
M 21	XII.14	Rhodes	kylix	bird
ISTANBUL, ARCHAEOLOGICAL MUSEUM				
2276	XIII.8	Pitane	stirrup jar	octopus, animal, bird
—	XIII.25	—	jug	bird
JERUSALEM, ISRAEL ARCHAEOLOGICAL MUSEUM				
—	XIII.26	Megiddo	krater/jar	bird
KASSEL				
T.705	X.102	Salamis?	krater	fish
LEIDEN				
1905/1.64	X.96	Argos	krater	fish
LONDON, BRITISH MUSEUM				
A 390	VI.57	Hala Sultan Tekké	bell krater	leaves (Cycladic?)
A 719	XII.11	Rhodes?	kylix	goat
A 846	XII.2	Ialysos	cup	bird, altar, fish
A 1015	XII.23	Kalymnos	stirrup jar	octopus, goat, crab, scorpion, hedgehog, bird
A 1016	XII.22	Kalymnos	lekane	bird, fish

MUSEUM NUMBER	CATALOGUE NUMBER	SITE	SHAPE	SUBJECT
A 1022	XII.24	Kalymnos	collared jar	goat
A 1077.1-2	X.22	Mycenae	krater	horse
A 1077.3	X.7	Mycenae	krater	soldier
C 332	IV.38	Maroni	amphoroid krater	bird, nest
C 333	V.28	Enkomi	amphoroid krater	sphinx, boxer, archer
C 334	V.29	Enkomi	amphoroid krater	boxer
C 335	V.31	Maroni	amphoroid krater	boxer
C 336 (cf. C 362)	IV.53	Maroni	amphoroid krater	chariot
C 337	III.30	Maroni	amphoroid krater	fisherman
C 338	IV.48	Kourion	amphoroid krater	chariot
C 339	III.21	Enkomi	amphoroid krater	chariot, sunshade
C 340	IV.12	Enkomi	amphoroid krater	chariot
C 341	IV.16	Enkomi	amphoroid krater	chariot
C 342	IV.18	Klavdhia	amphoroid krater	chariot
C 343	IV.27	Klavdhia	amphoroid krater	chariot
C 344 (+348)	III.17	Enkomi	amphoroid krater	chariot
C 345	IV.13	Enkomi	amphoroid krater	chariot
C 346	IV.29	Enkomi	amphoroid krater	chariot
C 347 (=351?)	IV.66	Enkomi	amphoroid krater	chariot
C 348 (+344)	III.17	Enkomi	amphoroid krater	chariot
C 349	IV.52	Enkomi	amphoroid krater	chariot
C 350	IV.60	Enkomi	amphoroid krater	chariot
C 351 (=347?)	IV.67	Enkomi	amphoroid krater	chariot
C 352	V.7	Enkomi	amphoroid krater	chariot
C 353	IV.68	Kourion	krater	chariot
C 354	IV.61	Maroni	amphoroid krater	chariot
C 355	IV.59	Maroni	amphoroid krater	chariot
C 356 (=355?)		Maroni	amphoroid krater	chariot
C 357	–	Maroni	krater	chariot
C 358	IV.64	Maroni	krater	chariot
C 359	IV.63	Maroni	amphoroid krater	chariot
C 360	IV.28.1	Maroni	amphoroid krater	chariot
C 361	IV.65	Maroni	krater	chariot
C 362	IV.54	Maroni	amphoroid krater	chariot
C 363	IV.23	Maroni	amphoroid krater	chariot
C 364	IV.69	Klavdhia	amphoroid krater	chariot
C 365	V.42	Klavdhia	amphoroid krater	bull, bird, fish
C 366	III.24	Enkomi	amphoroid krater	bull
C 367	IV.35	Enkomi	amphoroid krater	bull
C 368	III.26	Maroni	amphoroid krater	goat
C 369	IV.37	Enkomi	amphoroid krater	bull
C 370	V.112	Enkomi	amphoroid krater	goat
C 371 (=370?)		Enkomi	amphoroid krater	animal
C 372	IV.6	Enkomi	amphoroid krater	bird
C 373	IV.39	Klavdhia	amphoroid krater	bird, nest
C 374 (+681 +1958/I-10/1)	IV.41	Enkomi	amphoroid krater	bird

MUSEUM NUMBER	CATALOGUE NUMBER	SITE	SHAPE	SUBJECT
C 375	IV.44	Maroni	amphoroid krater	bird
C 377	III.7	Enkomi	amphoroid krater	octopus
C 378	III.9	Maroni	amphoroid krater	fish
C 389	VI.8	Maroni	amphoroid krater	goat
C 391 (= CM 1971/XII-6/1)	III.10	Kourion	krater	chariot, women
C 397	V.27	Enkomi	bell krater	griffin
C 398	V.22	Klavdhia	bell krater	chariot
C 399	V.73	Klavdhia	bell krater	bell, hunter, dog
C 400	V.115	Klavdhia	bell krater	bird
C 401	III.23	Enkomi	krater	bull's head, axe
C 402	V.46	Klavdhia	bell krater	bull, bird
C 403	V.43	Enkomi	bell krater	bull, fish
C 404	V.47	Enkomi	bell krater	bull
C 405	VI.24	Maroni	bell krater	bull
C 406	III.25	Enkomi	krater	bull
C 407	–	Enkomi	krater	animal
C 408	V.53	Enkomi	bell krater	stag
C 409	V.54	Enkomi	bell krater	stag
C 410	V.58	Hala Sultan Tekké	bell krater	goat
C 411	V.61	Enkomi	bell krater	bird
C 412	V.62	Klavdhia	bell krater	bird
C 416	V.44	Enkomi	bell krater	bull, bird
C 417	VI.16	Enkomi	bell krater	sphinx, bull
C 418	VI.45	Enkomi	bell krater	bull
C 419	VI.48	Enkomi	bell krater	bull
C 420	VI.43	Enkomi	bell krater	bull, goat
C 421	VI.11	Klavdhia	bell krater	bull
C 422	VI.33	Enkomi	bell krater	bird
C 423	VI.31	Enkomi	bell krater	bird
C 425	VI.50	Enkomi	bell krater	bull
C 426	–	Maroni	bell krater	goat?
C 427	VI.49	Enkomi	bell krater	bull
C 434	V.69	Hala Sultan Tekké	three-handled jar	bird
C 461	–	Enkomi	three-handled jar	goat
C 514	V.89	Klavdhia	stirrup jar	bull
C 575	V.82	Hala Sultan Tekké	jug	bull protome
C 576	V.83	Hala Sultan Tekké	jug	bull
C 577	V.88	Enkomi	jug	bull protome, bird
C 583	V.68	Enkomi	jug	bird
C 606	V.132	Enkomi	rhyton	fish
C 614	V.136	Enkomi	bowl	fish
C 623	V.84	Klavdhia	bowl	bull
C 671	V.134	Klavdhia	bowl	fish
C 672	V.91	Klavdhia	bowl	bull protome
C 676	V.135	Hala Sultan Tekké	bowl	fish
C 679	–	Hala Sultan Tekké	trick vase?	goat?

MUSEUM NUMBER	CATALOGUE NUMBER	SITE	SHAPE	SUBJECT
C 681 (+374 +CM 1958/I-10/1)	IV.41	Enkomi	amphoroid krater	bird
C 686	V.75	Enkomi	jug	bull protome
C 687	V.140	Enkomi	pyxis	fish
C 689	V.126	Hala Sultan Tekké	bowl	fish
C 690	V.118	Hala Sultan Tekké	bowl	bird
C 692	V.100.1	Hala Sultan Tekké	fragment	bull
C 697	V.102	Enkomi	stirrup jar	bull's head
1898/XII-1/278	IV.36	Maroni	amphoroid krater	bull
1911/IV-28/1	IV.1	Enkomi or Psematismeno	amphoroid krater	chariot
1938/II-20/1	VI.29	Enkomi	bell krater	bird
1938/II-20/3	VI.30	Enkomi	bell krater	bird
1938/II-20/4	III.27		krater	bird
Sikes Collection (loan)	V.97	Cyprus?	chalice	bull protome

MANCHESTER, UNIVERSITY MUSEUM

BM 1938/11-20/4	III.27	—	krater	bird
—	VI.40	Maroni	bell krater	bird

MUNICH, ANTIKENSAMMLUNG

6079	[VIII.32]	Mycenae	three-handled jar	[sphinx]
—	IX.47	Attica?	krater	bull
6028 (47)	XII.4	Ialysos	krater	chariot

NAUPLION MUSEUM

The museum in Nauplion serves as repository for most excavations in the Argolid, but in general we have only the numbers for Tiryns pieces, not those from Argos, Berbati, Mycenae, or Nauplion itself. Pieces without museum numbers in Athens or Nauplion are listed in the Site Index.

11 628	IX.19	Berbati	bell krater	bull, bird
13 202	IX.15	Tiryns	rhyton	robed men
13 207	IX.22	Tiryns	krater	bull
13 208	XI.14	Tiryns	krater	chariot
13 211	IX.20	Tiryns	krater	bull, bird
13 214	XI.15	Tiryns	krater	chariot
13 477	VII F	Mycenae	ewer	bird
14 231	X.33	Tiryns	bowl	soldier
14 234	IX.21	Tiryns	krater	bull
14 239	IX.58	Tiryns	krater	stag
14 243	X.16	Tiryns	krater	chariot
14 244	XI.25	Tiryns	krater	chariot
14 245	IX.111	Tiryns	krater	bird
14 248	X.35	Tiryns	krater	soldier
14 258	X.110	Tiryns	krater	fish
14 265	XI.21	Tiryns	krater	chariot
14 267	X.104	Tiryns	krater	fish
14 268	IX.23	Tiryns	jug	bull
14 270	IX.48	Tiryns	krater	deer, fawn

MUSEUM NUMBER	CATALOGUE NUMBER	SITE	SHAPE	SUBJECT
14 271	XI.50	Tiryns	krater	dancer?
14 272	XI.53 (see XI.28)	Tiryns	krater	charioteers?
14 273	X.17	Tiryns	krater	chariot
14 299	XI.130	Tiryns	krater	bird
14 300	X.109	Tiryns	bowl	fish
14 301	X.108	Tiryns	krater	fish
14 302	X.107	Tiryns	stirrup jar	fish
14 304	IX.24	Tiryns	krater	bull
14 305	XI.26	Tiryns	krater	chariot
14 307	XI.27	Tiryns	krater	chariot
14 315	XI.15.1	Tiryns	krater	chariot
14 319	X.34	Tiryns	krater	soldier
14 327	IX.121	Tiryns	jug?	fish
14 336	XI.16	Tiryns	krater	chariot
14 337	XI.16.1	Tiryns	krater	chariot
14 338	XI.30	Tiryns	larnax	chariot
14 340	XI.15.2	Tiryns	krater	chariot
14 341	XI.31	Tiryns	larnax?	soldier
14 343	XI.54	Tiryns	closed vessel	soldier
14 344	XI.51	Tiryns	krater	soldier
14 349	XI.129	Tiryns	stirrup jar	bird
14 353	IX.55	Tiryns	krater	stag
14 354	X.113	Tiryns	lekane?	fish
14 355	X.105	Tiryns	closed vessel	fish
14 356 A	X.106	Tiryns	cup	fish
14 356 B	XI.78	Tiryns	krater	deer, dog
14 358	XI.89	Tiryns	bowl	hedgehog
14 362	IX.108	Tiryns	bowl	bird
14 363	IX.25.1	Tiryns	bowl	bull protome
14 366	IX.25	Tiryns	bowl	bull protome
14 370	X.111	Tiryns	krater	fish
14 372	XI.17	Tiryns	krater	chariot
14 376	XI.69	Tiryns	collared jar	lyre player
14 379	XI.24	Tiryns	krater	chariot
14 384	IX.57	Tiryns	krater	stag
14 387	X.18	Tiryns	krater	soldier
14 388	X.19	Tiryns	krater	soldier
14 390	XI.128	Tiryns	bowl	bird
14 394	XI.131	Tiryns	krater	bird
14 397	XI.132	Tiryns	krater	bird
14 399	X.112	Tiryns	krater	fish
14 400	IX.76.1	Tiryns	krater	goat
14 401	IX.107	Tiryns	krater	bird
15 37 lot	IX.11.1	Tiryns	krater	seated man
15 37 lot	X.8	Mycenae?	krater	man
19 88	XI.126	Tiryns	krater	double bird
24 46	X.37	Tiryns	krater	battle
25 63	XI.110	Mycenae	bowl	bird

MUSEUM NUMBER	CATALOGUE NUMBER	SITE	SHAPE	SUBJECT
38 87	IX.45	Nauplion	three-handled jar	bull
54 75	X.3	Mycenae	krater	chariot
—	X.14	Tiryns	krater	chariot
83 57 (*see* Athens 3596)	XI.1	Mycenae	krater	chariot

NEW YORK, METROPOLITAN MUSEUM

74.51.429 (=CP.435)	VI.62	Cyprus	krater	fish
74.51.5850 (=CP.3815)	IV.7	Cyprus	amphoroid krater	bird
74.51.964 (=CP.1403)	III.16	Maroni	amphoroid krater	chariot
74.51.996 (=CP.1405)	V.2	Nicosia	amphoroid krater	chariot, woman

OXFORD, ASHMOLEAN MUSEUM

1948.448	IV.11	Alalakh	fragments	bird
1948.465	III.8	Alalakh	krater	octopus
1953.335	IV.9	Arpera	krater	bird
1953.339	V.57	Psilatos	fragment	hoof
1966.586	X.63	Tiryns	krater	bird

PALESTINE ARCHAEOLOGICAL MUSEUM, *see* JERUSALEM

PARIS, COLLECTION C. F. A. SCHAEFFER

—	V.122	Ugarit	bowl	bird
—	V.123	Enkomi	bowl	bird

PARIS, MUSÉE DES ANTIQUITÉS NATIONALES, SAINT-GERMAIN-EN-LAYE

76721	VI.5	Ugarit	bell krater	bull
—	VI.17	Minet el Beida	krater	bull, sphinx

PARIS, MUSÉE DU LOUVRE

A-277-285	XII.5	Rhodes	amphoroid krater	chariot
AM 625	V.23	Aradippo	amphoroid krater	chariot
AM 675	V.60	Aradippo	bell krater	hunt
AM 676	III.29	Aradippo	krater	soldiers, goddess
AM 677	V.103	Aradippo	bell krater	bull's head
AM 678	V.52	Arpera	bell krater	bull
AM 679	VI.15	Aradippo	bell krater	bull
AM 833	V.72.1	Cyprus? Rhodes?	flask	bird
AM 2663	V.59	—	bell krater	goat
AO 11724	V.21	Minet el Beida	amphoroid krater	chariot, bird
AO 18591	V.90	Enkomi	bell krater	bull protome
AO 18641	V.133	Ugarit	bowl	fish
AO 20376	V.8	Ugarit	amphoroid krater	chariot
AO 22293	III.18	—	krater	chariot
CA 1584	XII.7	Rhodes?	amphoroid krater	bull
CA 2958	VII.6	Attica?	ewer	bird
Inv. S 615	XII.9	Rhodes	three-handled jar	bull
—	III.A	Qatna	amphoroid krater	guilloche
—	III.19	Ugarit	krater	soldiers

MUSEUM NUMBER	CATALOGUE NUMBER	SITE	SHAPE	SUBJECT
—	IV.4	Enkomi	amphoroid krater	bull
PATRAS MUSEUM				
7	XI.136	Lopesi	four-handled jar	bird
266	IX.120	Klauss	bowl	fish
—	XI.81	—	duck	hunt
READING, UNIVERSITY MUSEUM				
—	V.25.12	Enkomi	bell krater	chariot
—	V.25.13	Enkomi	bell krater	chariot
RHODES MUSEUM				
471	XII.8	Rhodes	amphoroid krater	bull
BE 1223 (29)	XII.18	Rhodes	pilgrim flask	woman
See also XII.1–XII.20.1				
ROCHESTER, MEMORIAL ART GALLERY				
51.203	V.4	Cyprus	amphoroid krater	chariot
51.204	V.1	Cyprus	amphoroid krater	chariot
SÈVRES, MUSÉE NATIONAL				
—	IV.55	Cyprus	amphoroid krater	chariot
SPARTA MUSEUM				
5533	VIII.6	Melathria	jug	soldier
STOCKHOLM, MEDELHAVSMUSEET				
—	III.3	Enkomi	krater	bullring
—	III.4	Enkomi	krater	bull
—	III.5	Enkomi	krater	bull
—	IV.3	Enkomi	amphoroid krater	chariot
—	IV.21	Enkomi	amphoroid krater	chariot
—	IV.30	Enkomi	amphoroid krater	chariot
—	IV.43	Enkomi	amphoroid krater	bird
—	IV.45	Enkomi	amphoroid krater	bird
—	IV.51	Enkomi	amphoroid krater	chariot
—	IV.58	Enkomi	amphoroid krater	chariot
—	IV.62	Enkomi	amphoroid krater	chariot
—	V.10	Enkomi	amphoroid krater	chariot
—	V.13	Enkomi	amphoroid krater	chariot
—	V.38	Enkomi	amphoroid krater	ship
—	V.39	Enkomi	amphoroid krater	man, tree
—	V.40	Enkomi	amphoroid krater	bull, bird
—	V.50	Enkomi	bell krater	bull
—	V.64	Enkomi	bell krater	bird
—	V.99	Enkomi	jug	bull
—	V.100	Enkomi	jug	bull
—	VI.7	Enkomi	bell krater	lion, goat

MUSEUM NUMBER	CATALOGUE NUMBER	SITE	SHAPE	SUBJECT
—	VI.27	Kalopsidha or Alambra	bell krater	goat
—	VI.37	Enkomi	bell krater	bird
—	VI.39	Enkomi	three-handled jar	bird
—	VI.42	Enkomi	bell krater	bull
—	VI.53	Enkomi	bell krater	bush
355 a	VI.54	Enkomi	bell krater	tree
—	VI.56	Enkomi	bell krater	tree

SYDNEY, NICHOLSON MUSEUM

—	V.16	Stephania	amphoroid krater	chariot

SWITZERLAND, PRIVATE COLLECTION

—	V.24	Tell el-Muqdâm	amphoroid krater	chariot
—	IX.122	—	jug	fish

TORONTO, ROYAL ONTARIO MUSEUM

920.68.52	XII.42	—	collared jar	horse, fish

TÜBINGEN, UNIVERSITÄT

1467	XI.64.1	—	krater/bowl	soldier

Site Index

CAT. NO.	SHAPE	SUBJECT

Greek Mainland

ACHAIA

CAT. NO.	SHAPE	SUBJECT
IX.112	krater	bird
IX.120	bowl	fish
XI.81	duck askos	hunt
XI.136	four-handled jar	bird

AIGINA

CAT. NO.	SHAPE	SUBJECT
VII.C	jar	sailor, fish/ship?
VII.1	krater	charioteer
VIII.10	jug	goat-bird

ALYKE (VOULA)

CAT. NO.	SHAPE	SUBJECT
IX.13	jug	woman

AMARYNTHOS

CAT. NO.	SHAPE	SUBJECT
X.51	krater	stag
XI.56	krater	charioteer, soldier

AMYKLAI

CAT. NO.	SHAPE	SUBJECT
IX.117	closed	fish
X.36	krater	battle

ARGIVE HERAION

CAT. NO.	SHAPE	SUBJECT
VII.11	alabastron	fish
VII.12	bowl	fish
IX.11	jar	dancer?
IX.44	bowl	bull protome
IX.93	krater?	bird
IX.94	bowl	bird

CAT. NO.	SHAPE	SUBJECT
IX.118	fragment	fish

ARGOS

CAT. NO.	SHAPE	SUBJECT
VII.E	krater	octopus, fish
VII.H	three-handled jar	bird
IX.26	jug	bull
IX.27	jug	bull's head
IX.80	krater	boar/dog
IX.96	flask	bird
X.96	krater	fish

ASINE

CAT. NO.	SHAPE	SUBJECT
VIII.25	amphora?	bird
XI.87	bowl	hedgehog
XI.94	stirrup jar	ship
XI.137	bowl	bird

ATHENS AND ATTICA (*see also* ALYKE, ELEUSIS, KOPREZA, PERATI, SALAMIS, SPATA)

CAT. NO.	SHAPE	SUBJECT
VII.6	ewer	bird
VII.7	ewer	octopus, fish
VIII.26	krater	bird
VIII.33	krater	altar
IX.14	krater	robed man
IX.46	closed	bull
IX.47?	krater	bull
IX.89	rhyton	bird
IX.90	fragment	bird
X.28	krater	horse
X.41	krater	hand

CAT. NO.	SHAPE	SUBJECT
X.41.1	krater	hand
X.77	bowl	bird
X.78	bowl	bird
X.79	bowl	bird
X.80	closed	bird
X.81	krater	bird
X.97	krater	fish
X.98	krater	fish
X.99	lekane	fish
X.100	lekane	fish, bird
XI.32	krater	charioteer
XI.33	krater	charioteer
XI.34	krater	chariot?
XI.35	bowl	man
XI.36	krater	horse
See XI.55.1	krater	spear
XI.139	bowl	bird protome
XI.140	fragments	bird

AYIOS STEPHANOS

CAT. NO.	SHAPE	SUBJECT
VIII.7 (HS 112)	krater	man

BERBATI

CAT. NO.	SHAPE	SUBJECT
VIII.1	amphoroid krater	chariot
VIII.2	amphoroid krater	chariot
VIII.3	amphoroid krater	chariot
IX.19	bell krater	bull
IX.28	bell krater	bull, bird

CORINTH

CAT. NO.	SHAPE	SUBJECT
IX.1	amphoroid krater	chariot

DELPHI

CAT. NO.	SHAPE	SUBJECT
VIII.27	krater	bird
IX.86	krater	bird
IX.116	krater?	fish

DENDRA

CAT. NO.	SHAPE	SUBJECT
IX.29	fragment	hooves
X.32	krater?	soldier
X.76	fragment	bird
XI.138	fragment	bird protome

ELEUSIS

CAT. NO.	SHAPE	SUBJECT
VIII.28	jug	bird
XI.93	bowl	ship

IOLKOS

CAT. NO.	SHAPE	SUBJECT
VII.D	krater?	ship
XI.57	krater	soldier
XI.58	krater	archer

KOPREZA

CAT. NO.	SHAPE	SUBJECT
IX.3	krater	chariot
IX.4	krater	chariot
IX.12	krater	"dancer"

KORAKOU

CAT. NO.	SHAPE	SUBJECT
XI.98	bowl	bird
XI.99	bowl	bird

KOUKOUNARA

CAT. NO.	SHAPE	SUBJECT
VIII.15	krater	bird, fish
VIII.16	krater	bird
VIII.17	ewer	bird

LEUKANDI

CAT. NO.	SHAPE	SUBJECT
XI.37	krater	chariot
XI.38	krater	soldier, horse
XI.39	krater	soldier
XI.59	krater	soldier
XI.60	krater	soldier
XI.61	krater	soldier
XI.62	krater	soldier
XI.65	krater	priest, sphinx
XI.66	krater	men, vases
XI.79	krater	dog, deer
XI.84	krater	goat
XI.85	krater	goat
XI.91	pyxis	griffin, sphinx, deer
XI.141	bowl	bird
XI.142	bowl	bird
XI.143	kalathos	bird

MAKRYSIA

CAT. NO.	SHAPE	SUBJECT
IX.87	krater	goat-bird

MELATHRIA

CAT. NO.	SHAPE	SUBJECT
VIII.6	cutaway jug	soldier

MENELAION

CAT. NO.	SHAPE	SUBJECT
VIII.11	krater	men

MONEMVASIA

CAT. NO.	SHAPE	SUBJECT
X.117	stirrup jar	fish

MYCENAE

CAT. NO.	SHAPE	SUBJECT
VII.F	ewer	bird
VII.G	jug	bird
VII.I	pyxis	bird
VII.2	alabastron	animals
VII.3	larnax/krater	bull
VII.4	krater	bull

CAT. NO.	SHAPE	SUBJECT
VII.8	krater	fish
VIII.5	amphoroid krater	charioteer
VIII.5.1	larnax	chariot, octopus ✓
VIII.8	miniature hydria	"circus"
VIII.12	krater	bull
VIII.13	krater	bull's head
VIII.14	krater	bird
VIII.18	rhyton?	bird
VIII.19	rhyton/jug?	bird
VIII.20	krater	bird
VIII.21	krater	bird
VIII.22	krater	bird
VIII.23	krater	bird
VIII.24	krater	bird
VIII.30	stirrup jar	human figure/ sphinx, bird
VIII.31 (2)	stirrup jars	sphinx, bird
IX.2	amphoroid krater	chariot
IX.5	krater	horse
IX.7	krater	horses
IX.8	krater	soldier, horse
IX.9	krater	horse
IX.10	krater	horse?
IX.17	krater?	boxers
IX.18	krater?	boxers
IX.18.1	rhyton?	bulljumper
IX.30	bell krater	bull
IX.30.1	krater	bull
IX.31	krater	bull, bird
IX.32	krater	(bull), bird
IX.33	krater	bull
IX.34	krater	bull
IX.35	krater	bull
IX.36	krater	bull
IX.37	krater	bull
IX.38	bell krater	bull
IX.39	bell krater	bull
IX.40	bell krater	bull
IX.41	bell krater	bull
IX.42	krater	bull
IX.43	jug	bull/goat protome
IX.49	krater	deer
IX.50	krater	deer
IX.51	krater	stag
IX.52	krater	deer
IX.53	krater	deer
IX.60	krater	stag
IX.61	krater	stag

CAT. NO.	SHAPE	SUBJECT
IX.62	krater	stag
IX.63	krater	deer
IX.64	krater	deer?
IX.65	krater	deer?
IX.66	krater	goat
IX.67	krater	goat
IX.68	krater	deer/goat
IX.69	krater	deer/goat
IX.70	krater	deer/goat
IX.71	krater	goat
IX.72	krater	goat?
IX.73	bowl/cup	goat
IX.74	cup	goat
IX.78	bowl	goat/"Minotaur"
IX.79	krater	dog
IX.81	krater	dog/lion
IX.82	krater	lion, bull
IX.83	three-handled jar	dung beetle
IX.84	jar	bird
IX.85	jar	bird
IX.88	fragment	crab/ship
IX.97	spouted jug	bird
IX.98	krater	bird
IX.99	krater	bird
IX.100	fragment	bird
IX.101	krater	bird
IX.102	krater	bird
IX.103	krater	bird
IX.104	krater	bird
IX.105	bowl	bird
IX.106	krater	bird
IX.119	krater	fish
X.2	krater	chariot
X.3	krater	chariot
X.4	krater	chariot, sunshade
X.5	krater	soldier
X.6	krater	soldier
X.7	krater	soldier
X.8	krater	soldier
X.20	krater	horse
X.21	krater	horse
X.22	bowls	horse
X.23	krater/jar	horse
X.24	krater	horse
X.25	krater/bowl	horse
X.26	krater	horse
X.27	krater	horse/donkey

413

CAT. NO.	SHAPE	SUBJECT
X.29	krater	soldier
X.30	bowl	soldier, bag
X.31	krater/bowl	soldier
X.42	pyxis	sphinx, bird
X.43	krater	stag
X.47	bowl	stag
X.48	krater	stag
X.49	bowl	animal
X.52	krater	goat
X.53	bell krater	goat
X.54	fragment	"unicorn"
X.55	krater	goat
X.56	krater	goat
X.57	krater	goat
X.58	bowl	goat
X.64	stirrup jar	bird
X.65	krater/bowl	bird
X.66	krater	bird
X.67	bowl	bird
X.68	bowl	bird
X.69	bowls	bird
X.70	krater	bird
X.71	fragment	bird protome
X.72	krater	bird
X.73	bowl	bird
X.74	krater	bird
X.75	bowl	bird
X.83	round vase	fish
X.84	bowl	fish
X.85	bowl	fish
X.86	jar	fish
X.87	stirrup jar?	fish
X.88	krater	fish
X.89	bowl	fish
X.90	bowl	fish
X.91	bowl	fish
X.92	closed	fish
X.93	fragments	fish
X.94	fragment	fish
X.95	bowl	fish
XI.1	krater	chariot
XI.2	krater	chariot
XI.3	krater	soldier, horse
XI.4	krater	chariot
XI.5	krater	charioteer
XI.6	bowl	chariot

CAT. NO.	SHAPE	SUBJECT
XI.7	krater	soldier, horse
XI.8	krater	soldier, horse
XI.9	krater	horse
XI.10	krater	horse
XI.11	bowl	horse
XI.12	bowl	horse
XI.13	collared jar	horse, bird
XI.42	krater	soldier, woman, bird
XI.43	stele	soldier, deer, hedgehog
XI.44	krater	soldier
XI.45	krater	soldier
XI.46	krater	soldier
XI.47	krater	soldier
XI.48	krater	helmet?
XI.70	krater	hunt
XI.71	krater	dog, deer
XI.72	krater	dog, fawn/hare
XI.73	krater	dog
XI.74	krater	dog, deer
XI.75	krater	deer
XI.76	krater	stag
XI.77.1	krater	stag
XI.77.2	amphora	stag
XI.86	krater	caterpillar
XI.88	bowl	hedgehog
XI.90	bowl	snake
XI.100	bowl	bird
XI.101	bowl	bird
XI.102	bowl	bird
XI.103	bowl	bird
XI.104	bowl	bird
XI.105	bowl	bird
XI.106	bowl	bird
XI.107	bowl	bird
XI.108	cup	bird
XI.109	bowl	bird
XI.110	bowl	bird
XI.111	bowl	bird
XI.112	bowl	bird
XI.113	bowl	bird
XI.114	bowls	bird
XI.115	stirrup jar	bird
XI.116	stirrup jar	bird
XI.117	stirrup jar	bird
XI.118	stirrup jar	bird
XI.119	four-handled jar	bird, bird protome

CAT. NO.	SHAPE	SUBJECT
XI.120	krater	bird protome
XI.121	krater	bird protome
XI.122	krater	bird protome
XI.123	krater	bird
XI.124	krater	bird
XI.125	krater	bird, fish

NAUPLION

CAT. NO.	SHAPE	SUBJECT
VIII.4	krater	chariot
IX.1.1	amphoroid krater	chariot
IX.14.1	krater	lyre player
IX.45	three-handled jar	bull
IX.77	kalathos	goat

NICHORIA

CAT. NO.	SHAPE	SUBJECT
VIII.34	kylix	helmet

PATRAS, see ACHAIA

PERATI

CAT. NO.	SHAPE	SUBJECT
XI.40	stirrup jar	horse
XI.68	stirrup jar	man
XI.83	stirrup jar	goat, bird
XI.145	stirrup jar	bird, fish
XI.146	stirrup jar	bird
XI.147	stirrup jar	bird
XI.148	stirrup jar	bird
XI.149	stirrup jar	bird
XI.150	stirrup jar	bird
XI.151	stirrup jar	bird protome
XI.152	krater	bird

PROSYMNA

CAT. NO.	SHAPE	SUBJECT
IX.75	ewer	goat
IX.95	cup	bird

PYLOS (see also TRAGANA)

CAT. NO.	SHAPE	SUBJECT
VII.9	krater	fish
VII.10	jug/stirrup jar	fish
XI.80	krater	hunt

SALAMIS

CAT. NO.	SHAPE	SUBJECT
X.101	cup	fish
XI.41	krater	chariot, hunt

The following, sold in Europe, may come from SALAMIS

CAT. NO.	SHAPE	SUBJECT
IX.47	krater	bull
X.82	krater	bird
X.102	krater	fish
XI.82	krater	goat

SPATA

CAT. NO.	SHAPE	SUBJECT
IX.92	krater	bird

CAT. NO.	SHAPE	SUBJECT
IX.92.1	three-handled jar?	bird
IX.115	stirrup jar	fish

TANAGRA

CAT. NO.	SHAPE	SUBJECT
X.58.2	krater	goat?
X.102	ring vase	fish

THEBES

CAT. NO.	SHAPE	SUBJECT
VII.K	larnax/jar	fish, net
VII.5	one-handled jug	bird
VIII.29	krater/stirrup jar	bird

TIRYNS

CAT. NO.	SHAPE	SUBJECT
IX.6	fragment	horse
IX.11.1	krater	seated man
IX.15	rhyton	robed men
IX.20	krater	bull, bird
IX.21	krater	bull
IX.22	krater	bull
IX.23	jug	bull
IX.24	krater	bull
IX.25	jug	bull, bull protome
IX.25.1	bowl	bull protome
IX.48	krater	deer, fawn
IX.54	krater	deer
IX.55	krater	stag
IX.56	krater	deer
IX.57	krater	deer
IX.58	krater	stag
IX.59	krater	deer
IX.76.1	krater	goat
IX.76.2	krater	goat?
IX.76.3	krater?	goat/dog
IX.107	krater	bird
IX.108	bowl	bird
IX.109	krater	bird
IX.109.1	krater	bull, bird
IX.109.2	krater	bird
IX.110	krater	bird
IX.111	krater	bird
IX.111.1	krater	bird, bull?
IX.121	jug?	bull, fish
X.1	krater	chariot, soldier, dog
X.9	krater	chariot
X.10	krater	soldier
X.11	krater	horse
X.12	krater	horse
X.13	krater	horse

415

CAT. NO.	SHAPE	SUBJECT
X.14	krater	charioteer
X.15	krater	chariot
X.16	krater	chariot
X.17	krater	chariot
X.18	krater	soldier
X.19	krater	soldier
X.33	bowl	soldier?
X.34	krater	soldier?
X.35	krater	soldier
X.37	krater	battle
X.44	krater	stag
X.45	krater	stag
X.46	krater	deer
X.58.1	krater	stag/goat
X.59	krater	bird
X.60	krater?	bird
X.61	krater	bird
X.62	krater	bird
X.63	krater	bird
X.104	krater	fish
X.105	closed	fish
X.106	cup	fish
X.107	stirrup jar	fish
X.108	krater	fish
X.109	bowl	fish
X.110	krater	fish
X.111	krater	fish
X.112	krater/bowl	fish
X.113	lekane?	fish
?X.114	krater	fish
?X.115	krater	fish
X.116	krater	fish
XI.14	krater	chariot
XI.15	krater	chariot
XI.15.1	krater	chariot
XI.15.2	krater	groom
XI.16	krater	chariot
XI.16.1	krater	horse, soldier
XI.17	krater	charioteer
XI.18	krater	chariot
XI.19	bowl	chariot
XI.20	collared jar	chariot, soldier
XI.21	krater	chariot
XI.22	krater	chariot, soldier
XI.23	krater	horse/deer
XI.24	krater	chariot
XI.25	krater	chariot
XI.26	krater	chariot

CAT. NO.	SHAPE	SUBJECT
XI.27	krater	chariot
XI.28	krater	chariot
XI.29	krater	horse
XI.30	larnax	horse
XI.31	larnax/pinax	charioteer?
XI.31.1	krater	horse
XI.31.2	fragment	horse
XI.31.3	fragment	horse, bird?
XI.31.4	fragment	hand, object
XI.31.5	fragment	wheels?
XI.50	krater	soldier/dancer
XI.51	krater	soldier
XI.52	krater	soldier
XI.53	krater	chariot/soldier
XI.54	closed	soldier
XI.55	krater	man
XI.55.1	krater	spear
XI.69	collared jar?	lyre player
XI.78	krater	dog, deer
XI.85.1	rhyton	goat
XI.89	bowl	hedgehog
XI.126	krater	bird
XI.127	bowl	bird
XI.128	bowl	bird
XI.129	stirrup jar?	bird
XI.130	krater	bird
XI.131	krater	bird
XI.132	krater	bird
XI.133	krater	bird
XI.134	stirrup jar?	bird
XI.135	bowl	bird

TRAGANA

XI.92	pyxis	ship

ZYGOURIES

VIII.9	bowl	goat-bird

Greek Islands

AMORGOS?

XII.21	kylix	stag protome, bull

KALYMNOS

XII.22	lekane	bird, fish
XII.23	stirrup jar	octopus, animal, bird, fish
XII.24	collared jar	goat

KARPATHOS

XII.25	double vase	bird, vase

CAT. NO.	SHAPE	SUBJECT
XII.26	three-handled jar	bird, fish
XII.27	ewer	bull's head
XII.28	krater	vases

KEA

CAT. NO.	SHAPE	SUBJECT
IX.16	trick vase	robed men, bull

KOS

CAT. NO.	SHAPE	SUBJECT
XII.29	krater	soldier
XII.30	krater	soldier
XII.31	krater	soldier
XII.32	krater	soldier
XII.33	krater	ship
XII.34	stirrup jar	goat
XII.35	krater	goat
XII.36	fragment	animal
XII.37	krater	goat-bird/goat
XII.38	krater	fish
XII.39	stirrup jar	octopus, bird, fish
XII.40	stirrup jar	bird, fish
XII.41	lekane	sea horse

MELOS, PHYLAKOPI

CAT. NO.	SHAPE	SUBJECT
IX.113	fragment	bird
IX.114	fragment	bird
X.38	krater	soldier
X.39	krater	man, ship?
XI.96	bowl	ship
XI.97	bowl	ship

NAXOS

CAT. NO.	SHAPE	SUBJECT
X.40	krater	legs
XI.63	krater	legs
XI.67	hydria	dancers
XI.144	krater	bird

RHODES, IALYSOS

CAT. NO.	SHAPE	SUBJECT
XII.1	three-handled jar	bird
XII.2	cup	bird, altar, fish
XII.3	krater	chariot
XII.4?	krater	chariot
XII.5	krater	chariot
XII.6	krater	chariot
XII.7	krater	bull
XII.8	krater	bull
XII.10	jar	goat
XII.12	oinochoe	bird
XII.13	kylix	bird

RHODES, KALAVARDA

CAT. NO.	SHAPE	SUBJECT
XII.17	rhyton	boar/dancer

RHODES, VATOI

CAT. NO.	SHAPE	SUBJECT
XII.15	kylix	bird

RHODES, ZUKALADES

CAT. NO.	SHAPE	SUBJECT
XII.16	beaked jug	bird protome

RHODES, UNKNOWN

CAT. NO.	SHAPE	SUBJECT
XII.9	three-handled jar	bull
XII.11	kylix	goat
XII.14	kylix	bird
XII.18	pilgrim flask	woman

SKYROS

CAT. NO.	SHAPE	SUBJECT
XI.95	stirrup jar	octopus, ship

THERA, AKROTIRI

CAT. NO.	SHAPE	SUBJECT
VII.A	fragment	soldier
VII.B	fragment	griffin

Distribution of Pictorial vases at Cypriote sites

Angastina: Pastoral, 1
Aradippo: Early, 1; Ripe, 3; Pastoral, 1
Arpera: Middle, 2; Ripe, 1
Athienou: Ripe, 1
Dhekelia: Early, 1
Enkomi: Early, 14: Middle, 32; Ripe, 52; Pastoral, 28
Hala Sultan Tekké: Early, 1; Middle, 1; Ripe, 12; Pastoral, 2; Late, 1
Kalopsidha?: Pastoral, 1
Kazaphani: Pastoral, 1
Kition: Early?, 1; Middle, 2; Ripe, 9; Pastoral, 2
Klavdhia: Middle, 4; Ripe, 10; Pastoral, 1
Kouklia-Palaipaphos: Early?, 1; Ripe, 1; Pastoral, 4
Kourion: Early, 1; Middle, 4; Ripe, 4
Kyrenia: Pastoral, 1
Maroni: Early, 4; Middle, 12; Ripe, 1; Pastoral, 3
Morphou: Late, 1
Moutti tou Marathou: Middle, 1
Nicosia-Haghia Paraskevi: Ripe, 3; Pastoral, 1
Psematismeno?: Middle, 1
Psilatos: Ripe, 1
Pyla-Verghi: Early, 2; Middle, 1; Ripe, 3; Pastoral, 3
Shemishin: Ripe, 1
Sinda: Late, 2
Stephania: Ripe, 1